Youth and Empire

YOUTH and EMPIRE

Trans-Colonial Childhoods in British and French Asia

David M. Pomfret

Stanford University Press
Stanford, California

Stanford University Press
Stanford, California
©2016 by the Board of Trustees of the Leland Stanford Junior University

All rights reserved.

No part of this printing may be reproduced or transmitted in any form or by any means, electronic or mechanical, including photocopying and recording, or in any information storage or retrieval system without the prior written permission of Stanford University Press.

Printed in the United States of America on acid-free, archival-quality paper

Library of Congress Cataloging-in-Publication Data

Pomfret, David M., author.
  Youth and empire : trans-colonial childhoods in British and French Asia / David M. Pomfret.
      pages cm.
  Includes bibliographical references and index.
  ISBN 978-0-8047-9517-3 (cloth : alk. paper)
  1. Children—Southeast Asia—Social conditions—19th century.
2. Children—Southeast Asia—Social conditions—20th century. 3. Children—Great Britain—Colonies—Social conditions. 4. Children—France—Colonies—Social conditions. 5. Great Britain—Colonies—Asia—Social conditions. 6. France—Colonies—Asia—Social conditions   I. Title.
HQ792.A785P66   2015
305.230959'09034—dc23   2015010583

ISBN 978-0-8047-9686-6 (electronic)

Typeset at Stanford University Press in 10/12.5 Minion

For my mother and father

Contents

List of Illustrations viii
Acknowledgments ix
List of Abbreviations xii

1. Introduction: Childhood and the Reordering of Empire 1
2. Tropical Childhoods: Health, Hygiene and Nature 22
3. Cultural Contagions: Children in the Colonial Home 54
4. Magic Islands: Children on Display in Colonialisms' Cultures 81
5. Trouble in Fairyland: Cultures of Childhood in Interwar Asia 115
6. Intimate Heights: Children, Nature and Colonial Urban Planning 147
7. Sick Traffic: 'Child Slavery' and Imperial Networks 178
8. Class Reactions: Education and Colonial 'Comings of Age' 209
9. Raising Eurasia: Childhood, Youth and the Mixed-Race Question 243
10. Conclusion 277

Notes 289
Bibliography 357
Index 381

Illustrations

1.1. Map of East and Southeast Asia 16
2.1. Children at Saigon's Botanical Gardens, 1920s 51
3.1. "Slave Girls Carrying Children," Hong Kong, c. 1900 60
4.1. "Great Britain and Ireland and Her Colonies Where M.C.L. Is Actively at Work," 1906 92
4.2. Jules Gervais-Courtellemont, "Quatre naïfs du poste de Hien-Luong," 1901 98
4.3. Honoré Daumier, "La République," 1848 99
4.4. Clémentine-Hélène Dufau, "Gouvernement Général de l'Indo-Chine, exposition de Hanoï," 1902 101
4.5. Paul Tournon, "La France Protectrice," 1902 102
4.6. The Ministering Children's League Bazaar, 1916 108
4.7. The Ministering Children's League Bazaar, 1916 108
4.8. "Twinkle, twinkle, little star," Lillian Newton as a Fairy, 1899 111
5.1. "Le jeune Empereur Duy-Than et son entourage," c. 1907 119
5.2. Emperor Duy Tân on display 119
5.3. "Le départ pour le Tonkin," c. 1890 122
5.4. "Oh! La la, les vilaines figures . . . qui vive!" c. 1890 122
5.5. "Enfoncé le pavillon noir," c. 1890 123
5.6. "An Incident from the Queen of Hearts," Ministering Children's League Penang Branch, 1928 128
5.7. "Proud Mothers with Their Prize-Winning Babies," 1928 135
5.8. Fun o' the Fair, Lee Gardens, Hong Kong, 1938 137
5.9. Marie-Antoinette Boullard-Devé, Untitled portrait of a child, 1927 140
5.10. Marie-Antoinette Boullard-Devé, "Annam," 1926 140
6.1. "At the Peak," 1874 159
7.1. "Ah Moy, A Child Slave of Hong Kong," 1930 192
9.1. "The Retort Courteous," 1867 249

Acknowledgments

In the years it has taken to produce this book I have been fortunate to draw upon the support and expertise of many people. Librarians and archivists in different countries kindly facilitated research. In Vietnam I would like to thank staff who helped me at Vietnam National Archives Centre 2, Ho Chi Minh City; Vietnam National Archives Centre 1, Hanoi; Vietnam National Archives Centre 4, Dalat; and at the library of the Ho Chi Minh History Museum. In the United Kingdom I should like to thank the staff at Rhodes House, the National Archives, Surrey History Centre, the Wellcome Library, Cambridge University Library, the School of Oriental and African Studies Library, the National Maritime Museum and HSBC Archives. In Hong Kong I thank the University of Hong Kong Library and special collections department and the Hong Kong Public Record Office. In Singapore, I am grateful to the staff of the National Archives and National University of Singapore Library. In France, my thanks go to staff at the Archives Diplomatiques (Nantes and La Courneuve), Association pour l'Autobiographie et le Patrimoine Autobiographique (Amberieu-en-Bugey), Archives Nationales d'Outre-mer, Missions Étrangères de Paris, Musée Social, Crédit Agricole, Service Historique de la Défense, Bibliothèque Centrale du Muséum National d'Histoire Naturelle, Bibliothèque de Documentation Internationale and the Bibliothèque Nationale. In Switzerland I should like to thank staff at the League of Nations Archive. And in the United States my thanks go to staff at the libraries of Cornell University, the University of California, Berkeley and Princeton University.

I am also grateful to the many individuals, institutions and publishers who have granted permission for me to reproduce materials in this book. Timothy Whitworth kindly allowed the reuse of extracts from Phoebe Whitworth, *View from the Peak: An Autobiography* (Cambridge: T. G. Whitworth, 2001); Pelanduk Publications gave permission to reuse parts of *From Poor Migrant to Millionaire (Chan Wing, 1873–1947)* (Kuala Lumpur: Malaysian Branch of the Royal Asiatic Society, 1997), as did Éditions La Bruyère for Françoise Autret, *Pousse de bambou* (Paris: Éditions La Bruyère, 1999). Pierre Fave generously allowed me to reuse sections of Marguerite Fave, "Souvenirs d'Extrême-Orient." Marie-Antoinette le Chanjour permitted me to cite her unpublished memoir, "Et Souffla le Vent." Alain Boullard kindly gave permission to use images of work by his great aunt, Marie-Antoinette Boullard Devé. Earlier versions of parts of Chapters 7 and 9 appeared in "'Child Slavery' in French and British Far-Eastern Colonies, 1880–1945," *Past and Present* 201, no. 1 (November 2008): 175–213; and "'Raising Eurasia': Age, Gender and Race in Hong Kong and Indochina," *Comparative Studies in Society and History* 51, no. 2 (April 2009): 314–43, respectively. Material from Chapter 6 appeared as "Beyond Risk of Contagion: Childhood, Hill Stations and the Planning of British and French Colonial Cities," in *Imperial Contagions: Medicine and Cultures of Planning in Asia, 1880–1949*, ed. Robert Peckham and David M. Pomfret (Hong Kong: Hong Kong University Press, 2013), 81–104. I thank the journals and the presses for giving their permission to republish sections of these essays in revised form in this volume.

Youth and Empire was made possible with generous support from the Hong Kong Research Grants Council General Research Fund (project reference: HKU 748413) and the University Grants Committee's Teaching Excellence Award. The Louis Cha Fund, Hsu Long-sing Fund and Outstanding Young Researcher fund of The University of Hong Kong also provided support. These sources allowed me to travel to archives and research centres and to write up the book manuscript. I should also like to thank the Doris Zimmern Charitable Foundation for awarding me the Doris-Zimmern HKU-Cambridge Hughes Hall Fellowship, and the researchers and staff at Hughes Hall and the Faculty of Asian and Middle Eastern Studies at Cambridge University, especially Hans van de Ven and Susan Daruvala, for providing such a warm welcome and a wonderful environment in which to research and write.

Many colleagues and friends provided help in the realisation of this project. Helen Meller at Nottingham University has been a source of profound inspiration from the very beginning. Christine Boyer at Princeton University and Paul-André Rosenthal at the École des Hautes Etudes en Sciences Sociales, Paris, generously gave their time and advice. I have been fortunate to count upon the support of colleagues at The University of Hong Kong, including Frank Dikötter, Robert Peckham, Peter Cunich, Charles Schencking, Xu Guoqi, John Carroll, Bert Becker, Priscilla Roberts, Maureen Sabine, Elizabeth Sinn and Marie-Paule Ha. Greg Thomas generously shared his expertise on art historical approaches to childhood. The Centre for Humanities and Medicine at The University of Hong Kong provided a wonderful forum for discussion. Great thanks are due to Lydia Murdoch, Sander Gilman and Colin Heywood, who read the book manuscript and provided valuable comments and advice. Many others helped in a variety of ways, and I should very much like to thank Akira Iriye, Nick Hewitt, Leslie Paris, Mona Gleason, Jialin Christina Wu, Rachel Leow, Mark R. Frost, Nara Milanic, Rick Jobs,

John Gillis, Bengt Sandin, Bill Ashcroft, Sarada Balagopalan, Karen Vallgårda and Laurence Monnais. I am also extremely grateful to Eric Brandt, Executive Editor at Stanford University Press. This book benefitted enormously from the input of anonymous reviewers, and I would like to take this opportunity to thank all of them for their valuable comments on the original manuscript.

Finally, I should like to thank my wife and children for their love, support and willingness to tolerate my having spent so much time away from home, searching in distant archives for traces of others' childhoods. And I would like to dedicate this book to my parents, Colin and Brenda, whose love and support profoundly shaped the way I grew up and prompted me to reflect more deeply upon the significance of childhood.

Abbreviations

ANOM	Archives Nationales d'Outre-mer, Aix-en-Provence
APA	Association pour l'Autobiographie et le Patrimoine Autobiographique
BLO	Bodleian Library, Oxford
CADN	Centre des Archives Diplomatiques de Nantes
CUL	Cambridge University Library
GGI	Gouvernement Général de l'Indochine
Goucoch	Gouvernement de la Cochinchine
LNA	League of Nations Archive, Geneva
MCL	Ministering Children's League
MEP	Missions Étrangères de Paris
MHN	Mairie de Hanoi
MSFLF	Musée Social, Paris, Fonds Legrand-Falco
PRO	Public Record Office
RHL	Rhodes House Library, Oxford
RSA	Résident Supérieur d'Annam
RST	Résident Supérieur de Tonkin
SHC	Surrey History Centre
VNNA1	Vietnam National Archives Centre 1, Hanoi
VNNA2	Vietnam National Archives Centre 2, Ho Chi Minh City
VNNA4	Vietnam National Archives Centre 4, Dalat
WL	Wellcome Library, London

Youth and Empire

CHAPTER 1

Introduction: Childhood and the Reordering of Empire

In 1905 Helena May, the wife of a British colonial administrator, reflected upon the long journey back to England from Hong Kong with the words, "We had quite a nice voyage home, in spite of the 24 children!"[1] As May's comment suggests, empire set not only adults on the move but children too. Scholars interested in the movement of children and their families in empire have often discussed this in relation to zones of white settlement and metropolitan emigration schemes.[2] Compared with those travelling to white settler colonies, the number of European children moving out to Hong Kong and other possessions in East and Southeast Asia remained few. Adults defined their presence in such places as, ideally, fleeting. This has led scholars to neglect such children in imperial and colonial history. But this study argues that the activities, mobilities and identities of children in parts of the world where white settlement was considered neither possible nor desirable were central to the fashioning of empire and global modernity. Youth, defined here as both a cultural category and a social group, constituted a principal point around which the relationship of empire was reconstructed in modern times.

Empires were sustained by a fundamental mobility of people, commodities, capital and information and by novel technologies of global communication.[3] And as these technologies reduced travel times in the late nineteenth century, greater numbers of European women and children moved between metropoles and colonies. With this, the management of the domestic environment became entwined with new forms of social ordering. The presence of young people reshaped cultures of colonialism. Children's mobility transformed the bases of colonial domination. *Youth and Empire* examines how childhood and youth were produced and lived in empire for what this can tell us about the reordering of colonial space, aesthetics of colonial modernity, practices of racial reproduction and fantasies of control in the imperial imagination. It does so by focusing upon the East and Southeast Asian centres of Europe's two largest imperial powers, Britain and France, and the networks that connected them.

The scope of this book extends to colonial centres in Asia defined as 'Tropical' in order to show how childhood was crucial to definitions of race and thus European authority. Notions of age-related vulnerability drew childhood to the centre of a long-running battle over the viability and longevity of the European presence in these parts of the world. The period discussed is bracketed by important events: from the 1880s, when children and families moved out to East and Southeast Asian centres in larger numbers, to the onset of the Second World War, when Japanese military expansion curtailed European imperial power. During this period childhood emerged at the heart of claims for a new, morally informed governance built around the home. While the coercive technologies of gunboat and garrison were never entirely superseded, they were complemented by assertions of superiority in the field of culture focusing upon children, the family and new domestic norms.

Women and children had begun to move from metropolitan Britain to Asia in greater numbers after the East India Company lost the power to restrict immigration in 1833. Their presence grew much more rapidly after the Suez Canal opened in 1869, reducing travel times and increasing levels of safety and comfort on board oceangoing vessels. As passenger lists lengthened, European children formed an increasingly noticeable part of the societies developing in important East and Southeast Asian colonial centres. While children made up only a small proportion of the total populations of these centres (and the accuracy of these figures must remain in doubt), census data suggests they made up a substantial proportion of 'European' colonial communities. In Hong Kong, the number of children rose fivefold from 1893 to 1908. In Singapore some 499 of the 2,302 Europeans and Americans enumerated as 'residents' were under age fifteen by 1891.[4] In 1883 the 230 children recorded as living in Saigon constituted 25 percent of the European population, while a census taken in February 1905 in Hanoi revealed that 470, or approximately 20 percent of the 2,665 French civilians were children.[5] The young remained well represented as a proportion of the foreign societies in these centres up to the Second World War. In 1929, a census snapshot revealed 2,833 European children under age fifteen living in Saigon (with slightly more boys than girls), or 21 percent of the European population, compared with 1,744 in Hanoi (where girls predominated), or 38 percent.[6] There were 2,160 women and 1,183 children in Singapore in 1931, and 2,557 women and 1,814 children in Hong Kong in the same year. Often children outnumbered civilian women in British and French Empire centres in Asia.[7]

Indeed, 'European' children often constituted a larger proportion of their ethnic-racial grouping than did those defined as indigenous to Asia. This was especially noticeable in societies with 'frontier' characteristics, such as Singapore and Hong Kong, where for much of the period male migrant labour predominated and women were relatively few. In Singapore, for example, children formed a larger proportion of the European population (at 22%) in 1891 than they did among the Chinese (10%) and 'Tamils and other Indians' (13%), and they were only slightly smaller as a proportion of 'Malays and other natives of the archipelago' (26%).[8] In Hong Kong approximately 23 percent of the 'British Resident Civil Population' of 3,761 were under age fifteen in 1911, but only around 15 percent of the Chinese population were in the same range. In British colonies children remained well represented as a proportion of the European population well into the interwar era.[9] While native children often made up much larger proportions of those living in Vietnamese-dominated centres under French rule, such as Saigon and Hanoi, young people also constituted around 30 percent of the total European population of the colony Cochinchina (present-day southern Vietnam) and the protectorate of Tonkin (now northern Vietnam) from 1922 to 1937.[10]

The significance of young people in empire extended far beyond the mere sociological fact of their presence. The arrival of greater numbers of children in Asia triggered a reordering of empire that made childhood a focal point of projections of imperial authority. Across empires foreign communities debated not only whether children should be accommodated in the tropics, but how they might help to define the boundaries of elite identity. At points of intense interethnic contact dominated by fast-paced commercial activity, childhood and youth served claims for a moral shift, and for 'progress,' as this was contested and redefined. The arrival of children in larger numbers sparked engagements with middle-class norms of childrearing and the need for their wider dissemination. And these in turn sustained essentialist ideals of childhood and race in places where racial-national identity was constantly threatened with effacement.

Across empires ideals of childhood held out the tantalising promise of tying together societies composed of 'settlers' and 'expatriates' proclaiming diverse ethnic affiliations. Recent histories have begun to revise older views of French and British 'communities' in East and Southeast Asia as mere accomplices of imperial expansion, revealing these groupings of settlers, businessmen, officials and religious workers instead as fractured and fissiparous. Robert Bickers, Christian Henriot, Eric Jennings, J. P. Daughton and others have revealed that they were rarely committed to any overarching programme or imperial aim.[11] In the face of such diversity, those determined to assert the nation on the 'frontier' rallied behind more aloof genres of colonialism. As they built claims for racial difference upon evidence of the impossibility of white settlement, childhood became a key resource through which racial difference could be defined. Consequently, the question of how to raise children in nonsettlement colonies linked the 'low pragmatism' of colonialism, as Bickers and Henriot have termed it, with high politics.[12]

This helps to explain why contemporaries were so fascinated by children on the move, as the quote above suggests. Helena May adopted a mock-exasperated tone to document the presence of children at sea, but she and women like her emerged as celebrants-in-chief of children in nonsettlement colonies as they embodied new elite norms. In places such as Hong Kong and Singapore, which lacked the grandeur of the imperial cities of the British Raj, childhood and youth became especially important—in different guises—as referents of cultural authority and markers of 'civilisation.' And as Japanese military expansion became a menacing norm during the interwar years, debates over rival 'civilisations' pushed children, and the ability to protect them under the British and French flags, powerfully to the fore.

In colonial contexts childhood functioned as a central interpretive device, a measure of the highest societal and national values. And it could serve by extension as an index not only of 'civility' but also of 'incivility.' For the British, the example of the massacre of women and in particular children during the Siege of Cawnpore (modern Kanpur) in 1857 served to monumentalise Indian barbarity and immaturity and to summon a sense of white racial solidarity, and maturity. For the French, too, children and childhood would prove to be central to the iconography of empire, to imperial rhetoric and to the cultural disparagement that supported claims to rule. To be sure, British and French engagements with the question of youth and empire diverged along the fault lines of quite different intellectual traditions, views of nature and imperial ideals, but across empires childhood and youth became surrogates for culture, and central themes in the justificatory rhetoric of the so-called civilising mission.

As childrearing became more closely tied up with European claims for cultural and political authority, the bodies of children, circulating between metropoles and colonies, defined colonial rhythms of social mobility and made abstractions such as imperialism and empire real. The significance of childhood and youth extended from domestic interiors to the highest levels of the colonial state where they sustained European efforts to segregate space, make populations legible, symbolise empires and define practices such as hygiene. Childhood and youth served as 'screens' onto which cultural authority, prestige and ideas about the future of imperialisms could be projected into the wider realms of colonial culture, well beyond the 'intimate' domain of the home.

HISTORIES OF CHILDREN AS HISTORIES OF EMPIRE

Whilst travelling in Asia in the early 1920s the press baron Lord Northcliffe remarked upon the sight of "little English children, wearing great pith helmets, in the care of Chinese amahs (nurses), playing under the trees."[13] For all that groups of adults sought to segregate their own children, the empire centres studied here were places where indigenous, immigrant and foreign cultures mixed. European children's tendency to forge contacts across lines of ethnicity and to engage in hybrid relations, not only with domestic servants but also with indigenous children, was a consequence of growing up in places where national culture and its institutions were often weak. While for some, children remained emblems of disassociation and dichotomy—the key to ensuring interaction did not check inequality—for others, precisely because children's social agency (their will to act in the world) was considered distinct from that of adults it could embody possibilities for new and 'hybrid' interactions between diasporic communities. Colonial cultures of childhood were often profoundly mixed and disruptive of claims for racial homogeneity. Turning our attention to categories of age and how they were produced and lived in empire allows us to disrupt the conventional picture of 'stable' groups in colonial societies, and to highlight dynamism and mobility instead. Far from signalling a 'closing up' of European society—as scholars have often suggested—this book argues that the growing presence of children opened European communities up to new and unsettling influences.[14]

Since the 1960s a copious literature has exposed the shifting constructedness of 'childhood' and 'youth.'[15] An important starting point for such discussions was Philippe Ariès's seminal work, *Centuries of Childhood*, and much subsequent scholarship picked up on his general argument that youth was culturally constructed and performed. Studies traced shifting interpretations of childhood from the Enlightenment period in Europe. As older, Augustinian assumptions of childhood as constituting a site of 'original sin' began to be hemmed back, so too were Calvinist injunctions for the use of corporal punishment to discipline children. The Swiss-born naturalised French philosopher Jean-Jacques Rousseau, whose work was fashionable in elite circles in the second half of the eighteenth century, promoted childhood as a site of 'innocence.' During the nineteenth century European elites reimagined childhood as predegenerate and degenerate, malleable and essential, while challenging children's economic value.[16] Family size declined across the century as Europe industrialised. The extension of public secular education and the reduction of child labour gradually made children a charge upon, rather than benefit to, household economies. The protection of vulnerable children, through labour reform, education reform and the abolition of slavery, emerged as a cause upon which key liberal victories were won. Consequently, the category of 'the child' came to define modernness and, as Ann Pellegrini has observed, it underwrote many of European modernity's pivotal moral claims.[17]

This study follows such work in that it does not rely upon an a priori, sociological definition of 'youth' or 'childhood' or a legalistic/biological one affixing a determined age. Instead what counts as childhood or youth here is what contemporary actors understood these categories to mean. In the nineteenth and early twentieth centuries distinctions between childhood, adolescence and youth as discrete phases became clearer. However, slippage also often occurred. Commentators often drew children within a larger category of 'youth,' or referred to those who were almost adults as 'children.' The youth of the title is therefore drawn in quite deliberately broad terms to include younger and older children (the latter sometimes referred to as 'adolescents').

As recent scholarship has emphasised, age categories were always enmeshed with other variables—gender, class, ethnicity, sexuality and race—in the reproduction of hierarchies of power.[18] However, while acknowledging that age always acts in concert with other variables in structuring power relations and that age categories are unstable, scholars have argued that youthful subjectivities do share certain cross-cultural continuities. As anthropologists have pointed out, notwithstanding considerable cultural variance the differences understood to mark children and childhood out from adults and adulthood in Europe can also be found in other cultures. Such differences include, for example, a close association of childhood with societal reproduction, links to time, becoming and ephemerality.[19] Children's experiences of childhood in empire were qualitatively different from those of adults on account of their age. A critical question addressed here is how categories of age could sometimes become so important that they might at times obscure other social differences—such as those of race, class, and gender—while never existing entirely independently of them. As this book shows, age categories could function as a focal point of trans-ethnic connections as well as dislocations. They delimited difference but could also sometimes function to disavow it.

'Colonial childhoods' were coproductions between adults and children. Within specific spaces of empire the categories of childhood and youth were abstracted and materialised, and built around normative concepts, social institutions and subjective identities; but individual children negotiated and contributed to this process. The experience of mobility, of living and travelling *across* empires, defined colonial childhoods. As children moved within the networks connecting the major centres that developed under British and French governance in Asia, they gave expression to new cultures of movement. They forged interethnic connections on sea lanes and liners, wrote back home and participated in a variety of other fluid, trans-colonial practices. They contextualised experiences in relation to different European and Asian settings and accessed new knowledge and social interactions, which sometimes connected them to discrete national identities but which also led them to explore new subjectivities beyond national affiliations. In doing so, children found ways to speak back to assumptions of their own vulnerability, upon which segregation, difference and ultimately colonial authority were coming to depend. Consequently, as we shall see, in colonial homes and in public spaces young people never merely maintained empires' social and racial hierarchies; they also destabilised them.

This book focuses upon imperial projects as global processes with which young people engaged on their own terms. To foreground such engagements it examines young people in empire in their own right instead of addressing them as embedded within or appendictory to larger social units such as the family. In this book, being young is not simply emphasised as a preparatory stage to being adult and nor are youthful desires interpreted as necessarily being coterminous with those of adults.[20] Instead young people are identified as agents in the construction of colonial societies who developed their own ways of understanding and engaging with one another. Youth is therefore seen less as a straightforward trajectory—a becoming adult—and more as a distinct practice and a way of imagining community capable of linking distant but connected spaces.[21] The young have left few traces in the historical record. However, as Nara Milanic has argued, the question of how empire was constitutive of a sense of their own youthful subjectivities deserves attention.[22] An in-depth analysis of children's personal experiences of growing up under colonialism falls beyond the focus of this study. However, I have attempted throughout to nuance adults' debates and representations of childhood by using materials offering insights into children's lives, such as diaries, personal letters and memoirs. Sensitivity to the dialogic nature of this relationship and to children's voices can help us to shed light upon the difference that children made to histories of empire.

Another key argument made in this book is that European children's presence within and across empires, often in didactic modes, drew different, racialised models of childhood into contrastive relation. The more intensively state and nonstate actors projected protective, civilising claims onto European children 'out East,' the more they highlighted the supposed inadequacies of Asian children and childrearing practices. However, because colonial governance was couched in terms of a 'civilising mission,' the resulting disparities left authorities vulnerable. In the twentieth century international agencies and Asian reformers exploited the gulf between ideal and real childhoods to critique colonialisms as neglectful or insufficiently benevolent. Across the period European and Asian elites grew increasingly concerned with the implications of understanding childhood as a state of *difference*. As an idea and a set of cultural practices, childhood became a key battleground in Asian reformers' struggles to become modern. Modernisers exposed crosscutting strands of moral incommensurability *and* moral universalism running through representations of children in colonial contexts; and between protective ideals and social realities. Meanwhile youthful adherents of anticolonial nationalist movements contested imperial governments' tutelary claims over children as a source of legitimacy. These struggles exposed the peril of building justifications of liberal governmentalities around appeals to the unstable subjectivities of youth.

A new typology of 'other' children, dangerous and endangered, threw the limits of European responsibility for child subjects into question. The plight of Vietnamese, Chinese and other children trafficked into 'slavery' in British- and French-governed centres became a global cause célèbre and a test case for empire. The clamour around 'native education' from the turn of the century drove French and British officials to address the question of how to manage the problematic figure of the socially mobile young scholar. The problem of the abandoned 'Eurasian' child also demanded urgent attention, especially as indigenous anticolonial nationalism took shape against the backdrop of the looming Japanese threat. The essentially comparative debates carried on in relation to such children provoked initially reluctant colonial governments into surprisingly far-reaching commitments because European claims to civility and the future of empire itself were at stake. Examining the histories of these engagements, this book argues that children and youth, far from being a marginal and ephemeral presence in colonial places, were key constituents in the modern history of empire.

Historians, anthropologists and sociologists influenced by gender studies have contributed to a recent 'turn' in the historiography of empire highlighting the significance of the home, family and childrearing and the significance attributed by contemporaries to categories of age.[23] Recent analyses of the colonial 'intimate'—particularly domestic practices, childrearing and sexuality—have flagged the importance of childhood to the fashioning of subjectivities and the racial membership of colonial communities.[24] Ann Stoler's insightful works on the French and Dutch empires, for example, have highlighted the significance of sentiment and sexuality, the family and domesticity to the fashioning of racial identity. As she puts it, "how children acquired thoughts and feelings was a key to colonial strategies that looked more to consent than coercive control."[25]

Elizabeth Buettner has focused upon Britons in the Indian subcontinent, addressing the question of how race and age connected with imperial identity. She asserts the importance of networks connecting British children with 'home' to their acquisition of an imperial identity. She also examines the significance of family practices, including childrearing, to the reproduction of imperial rule by discussing medical and climatic anxieties surrounding children and adolescents, concerns about British children's contacts with Indian servants, and education.[26] By taking the focus to the level of children, such work is suggestive of how we can shed new light upon hegemonic practices while unsettling the claims for comprehensiveness of older histories focusing upon state-level political and economic change.

This book seeks to build upon the insights that these works have provided into the fluidity and instability of class, gender and racial formation projects, and the significance of intimacy to the working out of "colonial regimes of truth."[27] It acknowledges the key argument of Stoler and others about the importance of sexuality to colonial governance.[28] However, this book also proceeds from the viewpoint that governance was not *always* about sex, or gender. Colonial 'frictions' were shot through with other important, subjective trajectories, notably those of age. Indeed, the feminist-inspired turn in the historiography of empire has provided a tantalising glimpse of the significance of age to empire. But precisely because these works primarily focused upon gender, the dimension of age has yet to be as fully explored. There have been many analyses of European women in colonial contexts, but very few of children and childhood.[29] Earlier studies have, then, highlighted the potential for further work linking the presence of young people in empire with continental and global projects of empire building.[30]

Britain and France, which possessed the two largest empires in the period under discussion, offer a valuable focus for discussion. In both metropoles, across the nineteenth century, modern ideals and experiences of youth developed in direct or indirect relation to nation and empire. Though sociocultural categories of age emerged in dialogic fashion and were broadly comparable across cultures, ideals of childhood varied from one national culture to the next, and within the cities and neighbourhoods of an urbanising Europe.[31] Empire building was central to Britain's earlier and more intensive and extensive experience of industrial urbanism, but it also directly informed thinking about youth. Britain had reached the point of urban-rural equipoise in 1850. France would take another century to do the same. As European society secularised, the British middle classes invested childhood with new, romantic, class-coded moral meanings. As John Gillis and others have shown, childhood was recast in domestic mode, as a noneconomic, 'sacralised' stage of life, and a time of innocence before the 'fall.'[32] While the ideally happy middle-class British child was recast within this domestic frame, elites reread working-class children as racially 'other' using terminology imported from empire.[33] From midcentury Social Darwinist ideas of progress or regression as the outcome of competition between nations or races gained ground in educated circles. This drew into sharper focus the threat posed by working-class youth to the nation. The term 'degeneracy' functioned as a shorthand to refer to a variety of pathologies acting upon urban populations. Understood both as environmentally induced and inheritable, this condition helped to make the living conditions of working-class youth a critical issue in the eyes of those with aspirations to revive imperial Britain.

By the late nineteenth century the British Empire, an assemblage of territories acquired through conquest, treaty and exchange, had passed its zenith and appeared to be heading toward eclipse. Britain had recovered from the loss of the American colonies, the Indian Rebellion of 1857 and the Jamaican Uprising of 1865 to fashion the largest empire in the world, but in the face of the challenges posed by the United States, Japan, a renascent France and a dynamic Germany, late-century British imperialism displayed a broadly conservative dynamic. New territorial acquisitions in this phase of hegemonic maturity came mainly to protect existing trade routes or prize possessions such as India. In the period of 'new imperialism' a stark contrast opened up between styles of governance in settlement colonies pursuing trajectories toward self-government and those considered part of the empire of 'possessions.'

In the early twentieth century the rise of anticolonial nationalism added a new edge to predictions of impending crisis. Nevertheless, an overall philosophy of empire remained lacking. Instead British imperialists often continued to justify their cause with reference to notions of evolution as a clash or conflict between incommensurable entities. Amid anxieties over fragmentation, middle-class reformers learned to interpret metropole and empire as different fronts in the same 'civilising' battle. At home the fate of the nation appeared to rest upon reaching and reforming working-class youth—a sizeable part of the human matériel available to the nation. In the early twentieth century the poor performance of the British armies in the Boer War and the abject condition of youthful recruits offered alarming evidence of the interlinked fates of youth and empire. Reformers identified the exposure of children to modernising political and social rationalities as crucial to warding off imperial decline. They meanwhile recast colonies as metaphorical 'laboratories' where new methods, or those introduced to reform young metropolitans, could be tested upon young *indigènes*.

In France the reconstruction of empire also coincided with state-led efforts to prepare young nationals for citizenship and modern living. The need to protect the young in order that they could in turn protect the nation became an important topic in public debate earlier here than Britain owing to the more immediate sense of threat to the nation's borders. From the fashioning of a public primary school system in 1833 to liberal-inspired legislation of 1841 creating an eight-hour working day for children aged eight to twelve (twelve hours for those aged twelve to sixteen) the history of state-level engagement with children proceeded against this backdrop of continental rivalry. After the defeat against Prussia in 1870–71 and the loss of Alsace and Lorraine the new republican government made children the cornerstone of efforts to reconstruct the nation. The governance of children came to be closely linked to the legitimacy of the state. A republican labour law of 1874 reinforced the noneconomic status of some children. Jules Ferry's education reforms of 1881–82 created a free, compulsory, secular education for children aged six to thirteen and enhanced legal curbs upon abusive labour conditions. Republicans sought to consolidate power by using schools as vehicles to inculcate their political ideals and secular values in children. Education reforms aimed to free the young from clerical influence, upon which the defeat against Prussia was blamed. In political iconography the revolution had often been embodied as a vigorous though vulnerable infant, exposed like the nation to threats from within and without. Republicans revived such imagery, depicting children as representatives of the new 'civilisation' that they hoped might awaken France from religious backwardness. A more active ideal of the child as citizen than seen in Britain emerged, though it was also a more contested one. The multitude of threats facing the nation, inside and out, including evidence of demographic weakness, ensured that childhood came to be seen more as a time to be survived than celebrated in France, and as a period of transition to adult duties (or beliefs) rather than an extended phase of idealised innocence.[34]

Crucially, this French republican concept of civilisation was intended for export. From the 1880s the diverse colonial lobby overcame ambivalence toward empire by casting imperial expansion in moral, civilising terms as a 'duty' of spreading universal liberation abroad. For Ferry and others, imperial reconstruction was certainly important to reasserting national status and prestige. Devastating defeats in the eighteenth century and in the Napoleonic Wars had reduced the French Empire to a few Caribbean holdings, Indian *comptoirs*, and the prison colony of Guyana. In 1871 the new French Republic took charge of the 'old colonies' of the first empire and those of the second: Algeria, Senegal and West Africa, Tahiti and New Caledonia, Cochinchina and Cambodia. But when the French parliament voted to reconstruct the French Empire in the 1880s, the motive force for this fragile consensus was a fusion of republican and colonial visions of empire as a collective project imbued with humanitarian and liberatory values. In this view, colonial subjects would become 'childlike' wards of a tutelary metropole ushering them toward a theoretically egalitarian end point. On this basis the French government had by 1914 assembled the second largest empire in the world.[35]

In Britain and France, empire, like youth, often served as a biological metaphor—the renewal of a living organism or the virile (national) body. Fears of imperial eclipse and evidence that Europe was 'ageing'—especially when read against the 'youthful' vigour of Asian populations—haunted both colonial cultures. Critics touted empire as a solution to the damaging effects of low birth rates and other degenerative 'pathologies.' Desires to read empire in such terms were stronger in France, where low birth rates and other degenerative 'pathologies' pushed the spectre of national decline onto the public agenda somewhat earlier than in Britain. But the concept of childhood lurked within the justificatory promises of both imperialisms in the modern era.

Embedded in various policies carried out in both British and French colonial contexts was the paternal claim that colonial overlordship might transform indigenous peoples into self-disciplining subjects. French thinking about empire remained marked by struggles between competing strands of thought: revolutionary and secular, religious and aristocratic, assimilationist and associative. But colonial administrators serving republican metropolitan governments invested in comparative claims for French 'tutelage' as more benevolent and emancipatory than that of the British.[36] In practice these claims encountered numerous setbacks on both sides. However, as Satadru Sen has shown in the case of the reformatory in British India, even the ostensible 'failure' of reformist tactics was in a sense productive, for it could be used to validate arguments for the innate incapacity of the individual *indigène*, and his unfitness for self-government. Failure could be used to legitimate the rejection of nationalists' claims for self-rule and the deferral of the colonial 'coming of age.'[37]

Paternal arguments for empire were more sternly tested in the early twentieth century as advocates of empire embraced a more active view of their social role. Critics grounded comparative interpretations of imperialism in evidence of how colonials treated *their* children, 'native' and nonnative alike. Consequently, in the postwar context childhood's universalist dimensions came to serve powerful critiques of claims for empire as progress, social elevation or 'civilisation'. Urban-based Vietnamese, Chinese, Malay and other elites in British and French Asia identified children as integral to nation building and to the very project of becoming modern. Childhood came to be seen less as a subject of sentimental reflection and much more as a battleground for rival visions of the future.

NEW VARIANTS: TRANS-COLONIAL APPROACHES TO CHILDHOOD

This is a study of Europe in Asia and not primarily a study of Chinese, Vietnamese, Malay or other local ethnic-racial children and childhoods, but it does not theorise a unidirectional domination originating in Europe and simply acting upon the Asian 'other.' Instead it considers colonial childhoods as interacting, relational and mutually constitutive. This is a history that focuses not upon a diffusionist paradigm—the spread of ideas and people from Europe to Asia—but more on reciprocal relations and how those ideas travelled. In the commercial and administrative centres that burgeoned in Asia under British and French rule the serial nature of interethnic interconnections ensured childhoods were never simply projections of their metropolitan equivalents. They were, rather, a set of new variants engaged in a dialogue with metropolitan models but shaped by local pressures, conflicts and desires.

Europeans shared knowledge across empires, and stakeholders in empire centres produced 'childhood' in the aggregate. But such false unities broke down in practice along lines of gender, race and age. 'On the ground,' colonial childhoods took on a variety of durations, forms and meanings. The relationship between 'Western' and 'local' childhoods in colonial culture, in a period marked by European overseas expansion and entrenchment, needs to be understood in pluralistic and dialectical terms. European conceptualisations of childhood emerged from a dialogue with childhoods in East and Southeast Asia, and orientalist versions thereof. And India, Malaya, Vietnam and the China coast, as much as metropolitan France and England, were sites upon which modern childhoods were produced.[38] The value of resituating the development of 'modern European ideas' of childhood in a trans-colonial and imperial framework is that we can then see that these ideas were in fact only partly 'European.'

Showing how ideas about childhood went mobile and changed over time reveals how important they were to ways of thinking about, representing and contesting empire. Rather than locating some common overarching 'imperial discourse of childhood' acting on the global stage, the goal here is to tease out local differences and to explore how and for what purpose contemporaries—Asian and European—participated in the construction of social categories of age. Interethnic contact triggered quite different trajectories within European empires.[39] As we shall see, it was precisely because childhood was flexible enough to work as a signifier of elite norms, racial authority *and* as a potential bridge permitting cross-cultural collaboration that it became so important to the cultures of colonialism that flourished at points of intense interethnic contact.

Until recently, historians have tended to write histories of empire within well-established national paradigms. However, in a recent 'turn' in imperial history, scholars have begun to argue for multicentric approaches that look to the importance of connections built beyond Europe. To be sure, the study of empires remains fundamentally about relationships between centres and peripheries, but this recent scholarship has challenged older assumptions of the metropole as 'centre' and the colony as 'periphery.' Catherine Hall has argued that metropole and colony were mutually constitutive, while Ann Stoler and Frederick Cooper have examined them as part of a "single analytic field."[40] Scholars have sought to break with the metropole-colony binary by studying multiple colonies within a single domain or empire and by turning their attention to the networks connecting them.[41] Some have theorised 'trans-national' or diasporic networks strung between empire centres as a "web." Tony Ballantyne, for example, has called for a reimagining of empires as "bundles of relationships" rather than as fixed and bounded entities.[42] By devoting attention to imperial networks scholars have revealed these as vehicles for creating, moving and subverting European colonialisms.

Those who have called for a shift in focus beyond the singular nation-state have drawn upon 'trans-national' approaches, which have come into academic vogue lately. Interpretations of what is meant by 'trans-national' vary, but generally this involves a focusing upon units smaller or larger than nations and extending across national borders. Scholars have grasped the potential of this perspective to critique the binarisms of colonial discourse, to expose heterogeneity and to uncover the intricate processes and negotiations through which empires were fabricated.[43] This perspective allows nations to be seen as fragile, constructed, ephemeral and imagined.[44] Recent studies drawing upon this approach have examined, for example, how Indian Ocean connections sprang up alongside, or bypassed, the hegemonies of the British Empire, while others have examined the mobile processes—particularly the movement of goods and labour—drawing regulatory responses from authorities resulting in colonial border formation.[45] The term 'trans-national' sounds somewhat anachronistic when applied to colonial contexts in periods when national liberation remained a distant dream. And recent research has also challenged its idealistic overtones, placing greater emphasis upon 'frictions,' frustrations and violence instead.[46] Scholars have adopted the term 'trans-colonial' to refer to approaches linking multiple sites or centres, and connecting the global and national with an essentially porous 'local.'[47]

The trans-colonial perspective is interesting and valuable precisely as it presupposes an alternative (but complementary) spatial framework to that of the nation or even British or French Empire 'worlds,' and one emphasising slippage, transfer and the *weakness* of national cultures. Thus far, however, even those who have adopted multisited approaches that redefine the 'periphery' *as centre* have tended to confine their studies to single empires. Revealing and important though multisited studies have been, the question remains as to whether single-empire studies can fully account for the reciprocity that defines their subject, especially at points where imperialisms overlap.[48] After all, "cultural traffic," to adopt Tony Ballantyne's phrase, flowed serially across empires as well as within them. By moving beyond studies of unitary, nationally defined 'empire worlds' to embrace multicentred, pan-imperial studies, we can engage more directly with this important facet.

The need for such an approach becomes more evident when we consider places where multiple imperialisms overlapped. By the late nineteenth century, Asia had become such a place. From the Indian Ocean to the China coast the French and British imperial presence overlapped with that of the Dutch in Southeast Asia, with the Qing Empire further north (until 1911), with Germany as it emerged as a direct rival of Anglo-French commercial interests after the acquisition of Kiachow in 1898, and with the United States after Spain ceded the Philippines in the same year. Japan's victory over China in 1895, its participation in the alliance suppressing the Boxer Uprising in 1900, and its defeat of Russia in 1905 stimulated shared fears over its further, aggressive expansion. Certainly, great-power rivalry between Britain and France played an important role in driving imperial acquisitions. The French invasion of Saigon prompted the British to secure the Kowloon peninsula in 1860 on a ninety-nine-year lease. The creation of the Union Indochinoise in 1887 influenced the British decision to create the 'Federated Malay States' on 1 July 1896, and to secure the lease of Wei-hai-wei and the New Territories in Hong Kong on a ninety-nine-year lease, both in 1898. Traditional accounts of empire, written as stories of nations, have often emphasised rivalry. However, multisited studies can provide new insights by bringing into focus flux, the agency of nonstate actors and ways in which empire was often essentially a collaborative venture on the ground.

In order to shed light upon the global impact and significance of youthful mobility in the British and French Empires this study looks beyond conventional national or imperial frameworks and focuses upon networked inter-Asian and interimperial interactions. It deliberately exceeds the boundaries of a single specific 'nation,' 'empire,' 'region' or 'territory.' It does so from the conviction that such an approach might better reflect the linkages of these centres as points of intense impact into wider trans-colonial and global relations. To move beyond these analytical confines I apply a multisited approach that focuses upon Europe's two largest empires and the way youth and childhood, both in terms of ideas, ideologies and identities and as an embodied presence, moved between them.

Few have attempted comparisons between empires. A notable recent exception is Julian Go's *Patterns of Empire*. This usefully models the benefits of the comparative approach, which historians have appreciated for its ability to allow true points of commonality or specificity between different cases to be more easily discerned. Comparison can shed light upon structures, patterns and evolving discourses. It can highlight what was exceptional or equivalent.[49] Applied to the global history of empires it can illuminate the duality of nation and empire, and disparities between local effects and imperial purpose. However, as critics have pointed out, the danger that lurks in comparative work is that the overarching patterns identified simply reinforce or reassert the nation, in all its 'natural' and preeminent distinctiveness, as the central actor in the story. Go acknowledges this criticism, insisting that "colonial policies were not shaped by national character, values or styles but by the very spaces and scenes they aimed to manipulate and manage."[50] While 'big comparison' makes it difficult to do justice to local pressures and dynamics, he like others who have adopted a comparative approach to study empire, notably Philippa Levine, argue that "empire is in the details."[51] Adopting a multisited, comparative approach can help to avoid underestimating the multidimensionality and contingency of the cases discussed. Such an approach offers a picture of empires and communities as multiple, overlapping and diverse. It enables us to link multiple centres into wider global movements without jettisoning the detail that is so important to fine-grained empirical approaches dealing with questions of race, gender and other subjectivities.

Youth and Empire seeks to build upon this insight by bringing trans-colonial perspectives and the comparative method into complementary relation. Though the trans-national perspective emerged from critiques of the comparative method, the two approaches are by no means mutually exclusive, as Heinz-Gerhard Haupt and Jürgen Kocka have argued.[52] In places where imperialisms overlapped, in an era of rising nationalism, it is difficult to say much about 'empire' without taking into account its different national varieties. However, an empirically grounded comparison can allow us to critique certain established narratives or unspoken assumptions about imperialisms. As Nancy Leys Stepan has shown in her discussion of 'Tropical' nature, notions of empire had very different meanings in different national colonial spaces.[53] But these meanings developed in conversations that cut across borders. A multicentred approach can help to show how certain 'strategies' worked 'on the ground' at different times and places within and between empires.[54] This approach is used here to enable us to see how youth *travelled* as an idea and social group, and how it changed and was changed in the process. This approach resonates strongly with that of 'connective comparison' modelled by contributors to the important 'Modern Girl around the World' pro-

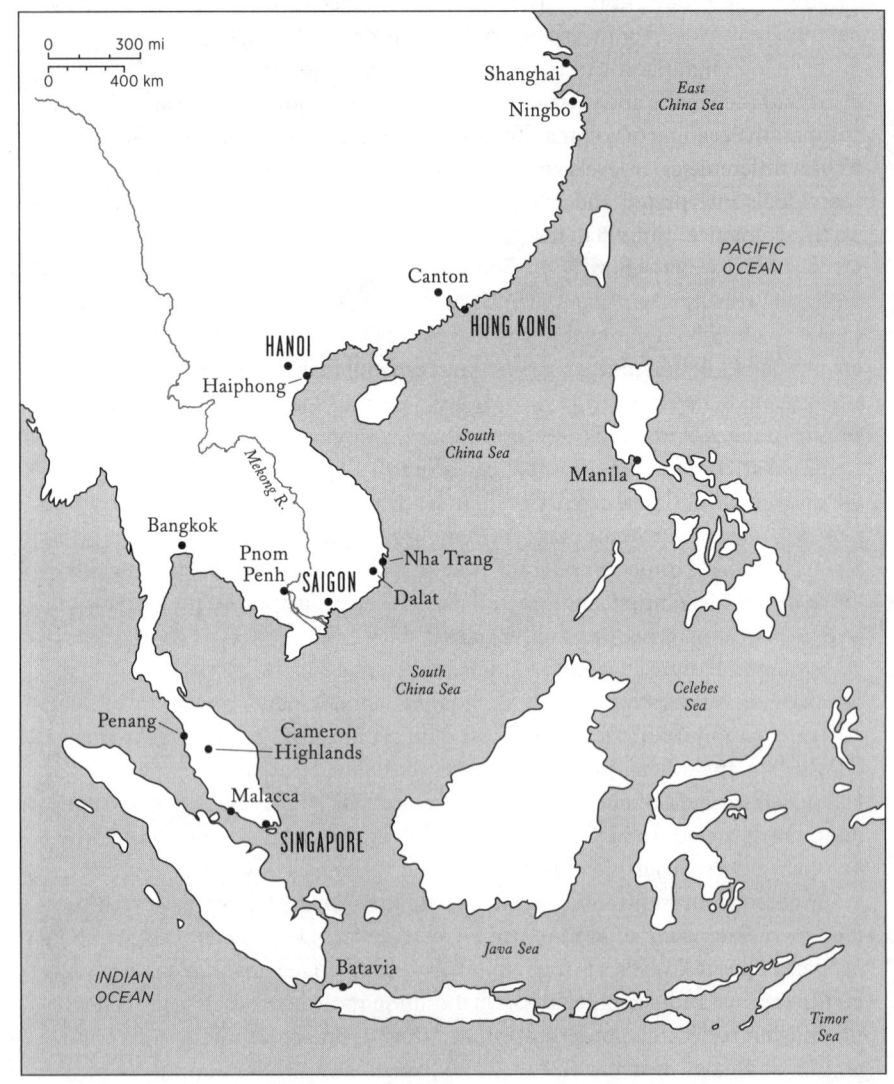

FIG. 1.1. Map of East and Southeast Asia. *Source*: Author.

ject in that it promises to take us beyond and between imperialisms without losing sight of microhistorical detail and specific, local processes.[55]

In order to throw light upon the global impact and significance of youth in empire this book focuses upon connective processes, movement across political units and situated entanglements in specific centres across Asia. It examines childhood and youth as the product of a series of encounters within and between Hong Kong, Hanoi, Singapore and Saigon, which were all important colonial centres of the French and British Empires in the period under discussion. A close, comparative reading of colonial centres through a multisited approach enables us to link different scalar levels while keeping in the foreground the ways in which individuals interpreted and manipulated ideas and rooted them in social and political practice. But what did these four places have in common that allows them to be usefully compared?

Clearly, they present us with different demographic profiles and models of colonial rule, but their interconnectedness nevertheless made these centres representative cases of the more general phenomenon of empire. Though they were not geographically proximate, the centres discussed in this book had long been points of conjuncture connected by external trade. Their histories had been shaped by Chinese and Southeast Asian networks, as well as by newer European and Indian Ocean networks. Small craft had plied intermediary trade routes between the China coast, Cochinchina, Siam, Singapore, Sumatra and Java long before European ambitions to monopolise trade with China had an impact. Europe's presence enhanced preexisting connections and linked Asian networks, through British and French Empire networks, to the rest of the world.[56]

The general aim of accessing the China trade, rather than any detailed plan for imperial domination, had driven successive territorial acquisitions by British and French empire-builders in Asia. In 1819 Thomas Stamford Raffles, an East India Company official based in Sumatra, advised the governor-general in India to secure the island of Singapore for the East India Company in order to protect trade between India and China via the Straits of Malacca. The island's location on the east–west Straits of Malacca trade route allowed it to develop into a crucial entrepôt between India and China. The British secured the cession of Singapore from the Temengong of Johore in 1819, extended sovereignty over the island in 1824 and relocated the seat of government here from Penang in 1832. Two years earlier the East India Company had lost its monopoly over Asian trade and with this Singapore became a mere presidency of India, until in 1867 it became a Crown Colony as part of the Straits Settlements (which also included Penang, Dinding and Malacca).[57]

A free port, Singapore grew rapidly after the opening of the Suez Canal as a centre for the import of Western manufactured goods and for the export and processing of raw materials and plantation crops. Tin, copra, tapioca, rice, rubber and other goods moved through Singapore from the Malay Peninsula where expanding British power had by 1896 brought about the creation of the Federated Malay States (FMS), which included Perak, Selangor, Negeri Sembilan and Pahang. The FMS had a resident general based in Kuala Lumpur who reported to the governor in Singapore, the seat of the Legislative Council of the Straits Settlements. The rapid growth of trade saw Singapore emerge by the late nineteenth century as a regional economic hub.

In 1841 Singapore had served as the base for operations in the First Opium War (1839–42) with China, which delivered Hong Kong into British hands. On Tuesday, 26 January 1841, the hoisting of the British flag at the foot of Taipingshan formally marked the taking of Hong Kong Island. Hong Kong's creation as a Crown Colony on 5 April 1843 followed from the Treaty of Nanking of 1842 ratifying its cession 'in perpetuity' to Britain from China. Hong Kong gradually rose to prominence to become an important trading and mercantile centre by the late nineteenth century.

Joint French and British action in China in the Second Opium War in 1856–60 provided the backdrop for the formal expansion of French colonial power in Asia. An important spark for the invasion of Saigon in 1858–59 was the Nguyễn emperor's antagonism of Christian missionaries. This led to the taking of Cochinchina (formed from the three eastern provinces of Cochinchina, taken from the Vietnamese court in 1862, and the western provinces, taken in 1867) as a colony. However, it remained unclear until the late nineteenth century as to whether French power would endure in Asia. The rise of a powerful, new unified German neighbour saw the colonial lobby's influence grow in France, and following the seizure of Hanoi in 1882 empire-builders advanced projects to tap the commercial and mineral potential of the Chinese provinces of Yunnan, Guangxi and Guangdong via the Red River. Five years later came the establishment of a so-called Indochinese Union. This comprised the formal colony of Cochinchina, the protectorates of Tonkin in the north and Annam (part of central Vietnam today), and Cambodia, Laos and Guangzhouwan (the latter secured on a ninety-nine-year lease in 1899).

Technology was crucial to the web of connections linking these centres. Regular steamship services connected India, Britain and China from the 1840s. In 1846, P&O commenced its service between Singapore and Calcutta, with fortnightly services from Europe in 1855. Following the opening of the Suez Canal, in the wake of what Chris Bayly has termed the 'great acceleration,' these centres emerged as important sites in the history of the transmission of ideas, ideologies and identities between Europe and Asia. The canal reduced the length of the journey from Europe to Asia from three months to less than thirty days. The use of the Malacca Straits as the main route to the East dramatically increased trade.[58] From Saigon it was 935 miles to Hong Kong, 677 miles to Singapore and 712 miles to Hanoi along the coastal route. Though Saigon was a river port (like Hải Phòng) situated slightly off the main steamship route from Singapore to China and Japan, regular steamship services linked it to other centres.[59] Hanoi was also linked via Hải Phòng and overland routes to Canton (present-day Guangzhou) and other centres.

Imperial expansion in Asia also speeded up flows of information between these centres. Telecommunications technologies accelerated preexisting trade-based connections and facilitated the establishment of financial services, notably insurance and banking.[60] Saigon emerged primarily as a centre for the sale and onward shipment of rubber and more especially rice to Singapore, Bangkok, Hong Kong and Batavia.[61] Hong Kong, the main market for rice from Tonkin and Cochinchina, emerged as South China's foremost port and remained deeply connected to Singapore, while the latter functioned to export the tin and agricultural output of the Malay Peninsula and linked up trade between India and China. The intensity of economic activity varied, but the economic activity of the British centres outstripped even Saigon, the most dynamic of French centres, for much of the period.[62] Singapore had by 1903 become the seventh seaport of the world, but Saigon, situated 80 kilometres from the coast, still ranked only sixth among French-run ports.

These myriad connections also ensured that the economic, social and cultural histories of these centres were profoundly interlinked. As they were driven through familiar stopping points, contemporaries theorised the connectedness of these places for themselves, as sites upon routes linking Europe to Asia, and discussed their distinctive, but interlinked nature.[63] The sheer volatility of human and other forms of traffic prompted frequent reflections upon these centres as 'crucibles of modernity' and 'sites of acceleration.' In the Straits Settlements, for example, the textile merchant J. M. Allinson observed that

> A 'centre' may, I think, be well described as the 'nucleus around which or into which things are collected.' We need go no further than our own tight little Island to find a most excellent illustration of a trade centre. In Singapore we collect things, and these things are manipulated and prepared for distribution all over the world.[64]

These centres became foci for branches of the heavily capitalised trade and financial firms and trans-shipment points for the China trade; places where the 'great acceleration' took concrete form.[65]

Another common feature of these sites was that they all experienced rapid population growth and as 'large cities' they formed nodal points in imperial systems and were notable for the increasing ethnic-racial diversity of their populations.[66] They therefore became spaces where travel and "intercultural connections" were not the exception but the norm.[67] In each place, Chinese immigration was an important driver of growth, but mobility was pan-Asian. After the Chinese government abolished restrictions on emigration in 1893, Singapore grew from 67,752 people in 1871 to 425,912 in 1921, and its population became strikingly plural in the process. In 'British Malaya' (the FMS, Straits Settlements and unfederated Malay

States), Chinese, mostly Hokkiens and Teochews, lived alongside a significant Tamil, Indian and Malay population. By 1931 the Chinese population reached 1,709,392 (compared with 1,644,173 Malays, 624,009 Indians and 317,848 'others'), and the colonial government imposed restrictions on Chinese immigration. In Hong Kong, the flow of migrants remained unrestricted across the period and here too a diverse range of Asian migrants resided. These included Indians, 'Lascar seamen,' Parsi merchants and Portuguese alongside the majority Southern Chinese. In-migration transformed what had been an island with a few thousand inhabitants into a large international trading city with a population of 301,967 by 1906, and 1,028,619 by 1938. The growth of Saigon was also breathtaking. Among its inhabitants were 'Malabars,' Chinese, Pondicherry Indians and others as well as the majority Vietnamese. The population here surged from 14,000 in 1882 (with 150,000 in nearby Cholon) to 126,000 by 1930.[68] The city of Hanoi also became more ethnically diverse as it grew rapidly from 50,000 inhabitants in 1880, to 127,880 by 1931, and 200,000 by 1940.[69]

The growth and diversity of these centres served to highlight the status of their 'European' residents as equivocal, fragile and in constant need of being shored up. While 'whiteness' was often defined in terms of a hierarchy of national identities, the term 'European' was often used to refer to whites in general. Even so, this group only ever constituted a very small proportion of the total population. As statisticians observed, 'British Asia' was the part of the empire where the white presence was the smallest as a proportion of the total population.[70] In Singapore, Europeans "barely left an impression upon the eye," and in 1921 the 6,231 enumerated constituted less than 2 percent of the total population.[71] In Hong Kong, the picture was similar.[72] In the French-governed cities of what would later become Vietnam, European populations were approximately the same size of those under British rule, though the total number of inhabitants residing in Hanoi and Saigon was significantly less than in Hong Kong and Singapore.[73]

However miniscule the sociological reality of the foreign presence vis-à-vis other resident groups and however much their contribution may have been overplayed in older literature on empire, the projection of European power defined these places as 'colonial.'[74] Indeed, these sites were also comparable as sites of colonial authority and military power as well as waterborne trade. With privileged access to information, access to credit and backed up by political and military power, Europeans were becoming a dominant trading group. Models of governance varied in form but were starkly exclusionary and segregationist.[75]

Far from being the 'indirect rule' with which the British Empire was often associated, governance in the British Crown Colonies of Hong Kong and the Straits Settlements was intentionally direct. Both formed part of an imperial system with a constitutional structure that confined merchant power, closed off wider representation and concentrated power in nonelective executive and legislative councils and a governor (who was monitored by the Colonial Office and parliament).[76] This system was intended to avoid the pitfalls of 'older' colonialisms, in particular those of British India where large Anglo-Indian and poor white populations had come to be condemned as a problem, and centres such as Shanghai, where municipal government endowed 'settlers' with a powerful voice.[77]

Saigon and Hanoi functioned as the principal sites of governance within a 'French Indochina.' By the late nineteenth century Indochina had come to embody French claims to be a Southeast Asian (and thus global) imperial power. Officially at least, French colonial policy was defined from the 1880s in terms of 'assimilation.' Ostensibly this policy aimed to achieve the incorporation of the colony and its subjects within 'Frenchness.' This involved projects ranging from the introduction of metropolitan opera and architecture, legal and penal codes and education, to the creation of mixed representative institutions such as the Colonial Council. Around the turn of the century colonial theorists undermined this model and won official endorsement for an 'associationist' policy instead. This emphasised respect for the customs and mores of 'natives' but was often understood to require the imposition of greater distance between coloniser and colonised and the deferral of the need to deliver equality to an unspecified future time.

Though the general perception may have been that, as one scholar puts it, "the empire that mattered was the countries of settlement," by the early twentieth century it was in the so-called tropics—in places such as Hong Kong, Singapore, Hanoi and Saigon—that contemporaries believed the fate of imperial nations would be decided.[78] As John Darwin has noted elsewhere, by the early twentieth century it was Asia that proved to be "the ultimate test of Europe's capacity to construct a stable and co-operative colonial order."[79] And as the strategic, economic and cultural value and significance of these centres grew on the global stage, the implications of children's presence there also became more profound. Debates over childhood informed debates over the possibility that the French and British presence in Asia might endure, especially as nationalist, Communist and other anticolonial factions more directly threatened European rule. While youth and its cognates provide a lens through which to read different colonial cultures, scholars have only recently begun to examine how trans-colonial mobility impacted upon more marginal groups in empire, including children. Conversely, the importance of children's trans-nationality to empire is only now being brought to light. As this book aims to show, far from being irrelevant or inconsequential, the presence (and absence) of children in empire had a profound impact upon the histories of colonies, metropolitan societies and empires in the modern era.

CHAPTER 2

Tropical Childhoods: Health, Hygiene and Nature

In 1884, the military officer, travel writer and historian Major Henry Knollys was strolling through Hong Kong's Botanical Gardens when a disturbing sight stopped him dead in his tracks. In the distance Knollys observed what he described as the "pallid, washed-out offspring of English residents" as they crept, "listlessly, joylessly by the side of their amas." The spectacle of this group shuffling quietly along moved him to draw a contrast with the "healthy shouting, romping [and] dirt-pie-making" of the metropolitan child, "without which," Knollys added, "childhood seems so unnatural." The striking vigour so evident at home was markedly absent in Hong Kong where, he predicted, children transferred would "inevitably droop and pine, and drift into weakly health." They would never recover from the damage suffered. Worse, they were likely to pass on these traits to their own children, permanently affecting the quality of the race. This led Knollys to warn 'British mothers,' sternly, "do not bring out your children, whatever their age, to Hong Kong except under dire necessity."[1]

In this reading of the stigmata of degeneracy from the bodies of white children in Hong Kong, Henry Knollys drew upon a cultural shorthand that was by then quite comprehensible to his readers. Around half a century before the major wrote, scientists had begun to redefine 'the Tropics' in terms of the degenerative impact of this specific geographical space upon white bodies. From the 1830s experts had reappraised race in empire as they lost confidence in older assumptions that 'seasoning' or acclimatisation might recalibrate white bodies. Previously this process had been considered capable of allowing Europeans to endure lengthy periods of residence, and even settlement. But by midcentury, Europe had rediscovered the tropics as a space of death and disease. Experts on climate correlated the extreme fertility and 'supercapacity' of tropical zones with the lower competency of its human populations while attributing supposedly superior racial aptitudes to those from temperate zones.[2]

This chapter argues that children proved crucial to the ways in which a stark sense of environmental difference—articulated through 'tropicality'—became entwined with a sense of sociocultural difference.[3] In the tropics children's bodies evidenced an environmentally induced degeneracy that could be inherited. This strengthened claims that the 'country born' would not survive beyond a third generation. By the 1880s, literature using children to evidence tropical degeneracy was reaching new audiences, beyond scientific journals. Knollys's travel writing formed part of this corpus. But the shrillness of his warning also reflected a paradoxical fact. At a time when assumptions of endangerment had achieved the status of an orthodoxy, European children were living in and moving to the *zones torrides* in larger numbers than ever before.[4]

After the opening of the Suez Canal in 1869 reduced travel times between Europe and Asia, more Europeans brought families 'out East' with them. The number of young people under age fifteen described as 'British and other Europeans' who were resident in Hong Kong surged from 1,378 in 1891 to 2,053 by 1906.[5] In Singapore this trend surprised some contemporaries. In 1890 the engineer Maurice Cameron, attending a birthday party organised for the five-year-old daughter of the lawyer John Burkinshaw, confessed, "I had no idea there were so many children in the place to assemble"; the number of Europeans under age fifteen had reached 755 by 1911.[6] In 1897, 405 of the 2,487 civil inhabitants of Saigon recorded as 'European' were children, almost double the number in 1883.[7] Meanwhile, in Hanoi at the turn of the century, Grace Corneau observed approvingly, "the number of European children who live in Tonkin is growing day by day" and the novelist Eugène Jung wrote of them as "the future of a colony."[8] By 1905 one publisher of travel guides covering the 'Far East,' Claudius Madrolle (himself a former colonial functionary), recorded 470 children among Hanoi's European population along with 1,350 men and 545 women.[9]

European children were not only increasing in number but also at this time emerging as the focal point of a new middle-class morality and ideals of domesticity. In this chapter I argue that while views of nature differed across national cultures, from the 1880s the presence of European children in East and Southeast Asian centres sustained demands for a more morally informed colonial governance built around the home. Both British and French elites hoped children would provide a moral leaven for male-dominated centres where social heterogeneity and ethnic intermixing threatened ideals of racial and cultural 'authenticity' and white prestige. From the late nineteenth century these elites therefore introduced a range of prescriptive interventions to address the problems posed, as they saw it, by the presence of emigrants from lower- or middle-class backgrounds in the tropics. For British writers the example of significant numbers of 'poor whites' in India offered a cautionary tale. For French elite commentators, especially those governing on behalf of a supposedly egalitarian republic, prescriptive interventions over class and the required types of child emigrant were the subject of ongoing debate.

An additional complication was that while children, for some, could exemplify ideals of race in places where racial-national identity was constantly threatened, for others recreating the home was impossible and even irresponsible in East and Southeast Asia on account of the assumed dangers of the climate and environment. Families facing this predicament in Hanoi, Saigon, Hong Kong and Singapore turned to a growing body of literature produced by medical professionals for advice. In the second part of this chapter I examine the variations between new norms of child management as they emerged from quite different national and local projects and debates over how children should be raised. These helped to create different colonial childhoods, developing along quite distinct trajectories. In British colonial contexts, as developmental-evolutionist thinking gained ground the fragile white child sustained claims to racial (and maternal) authority and hierarchy understood as fixed in nature and biology, though in different ways from Hong Kong to Singapore. By contrast, in French centres, where transformist thinking remained more influential, ideals of robust settler children jarred alongside elite administrators' preferences for newer, 'associative' visions of colonial childhood.

SACRIFICE OF THE INNOCENTS: THE BRITISH CHILD IN THE TROPICS

Children were thrust early into the long-running British debate over 'white settlement.' In the first half of the nineteenth century works such as those by James Johnson and James Annesley on the topography and climate of India had argued that human races, like exotic plants, could not be transferred, but by midcentury, studies building on these early works focused more explicitly upon white children's vulnerability to tropical living.[10] For Joseph Ewart of the Bengal Medical Service, degeneracy was more evident in children than in any other group.[11] For Sir William Moore, a former surgeon general of the Government of Bombay, children in India "grow up weak and weedy, deficient in energy and lacking in strength" with a "marked disposition to relaxation" and "idleness."[12] This research drew a direct line between tropical space and physical and mental enfeeblement.

An important influence upon such findings was the state-led shift in Indian policy around midcentury. During the Indian Uprising of 1857, sepoy forces had laid siege to Lucknow and Cawnpore (modern Kanpur). Amid the violence there and during the siege of Lucknow numerous children perished. In the aftermath the staggering scale of public mourning for the British children killed served the interests of those keen to assert Indian barbarity. However, it also exposed the sense of risk surrounding the involvement of children in imperial projects. As Lydia Murdoch has shown, these events recast children in empire as children in harm's way, as lives threatened and liable to be prematurely extinguished.[13] This powerful public sentiment linked up with a wholesale reassessment of colonialism that would impact heavily upon cultures of colonialism emerging in Ceylon, Singapore, Hong Kong and other eastern possessions.

Following the uprising a British parliamentary select committee reappraised conditions in India. The committee endorsed a new vision of state-run colonialism as more distant and aloof. Authorities perceived entanglement—for which they held settlers primarily responsible—as blurring the lines of racial identity and eroding authority. This shift heralded a quite different political vision of the colonial future and one that clashed with the interests of planters in India, many of whom had raised children there. It was in the teeth of settler resistance to this new line that medical authorities in the pay of the state marshalled arguments based upon evidence of children's health behind attempts to prove the impossibility of white settlement. These medical and administrative interventions had the effect of producing European children in colonial India as the ultimate symbol of white racial endangerment and of the degenerative impact of the tropics. Young people's vulnerability made them exemplars of national cultures whose exotic bodies served as a site of 'essential' civilisational difference. Children's presence came to validate claims for the tropics as endangering whites, but also, by extension, assumptions that geographical dislocation offered proof of a civilisational superiority that was fixed in the environment.[14]

Why did children offer such a powerful focus for anxieties over the mutability of authority in empire? In part this was because middle-class Britons were already accustomed to reading working-class children in the metropole as ciphers of an environmentally induced 'degeneration.' From midcentury, reformers read social divisions in rapidly urbanising Britain in environmentalist terms. As class conflict sharpened in the 1880s, urban explorers interpreted child residents of working-class areas of London and other large cities through the distorted lens of tropicality. Far from the countryside, and the supposed wellsprings of national identity, the urban young appeared in such writings as racially 'other' ('street arabs,' 'guttersnipes'). Urban explorers compared parts of the East End of London with 'Darkest Africa.' While the terminology used to describe this process in metropolitan contexts had partly come 'home' from empire, it was readily available for re-export. Indeed, as British sovereign power in Asia expanded, empire tout court was redefined along a similar racialised binary. A white empire of 'settlement' stood in contradistinction to a tropical empire of 'possessions.' This fault line mirrored the contemporaneous division of childhood in Britain into 'true' and 'other' variants.[15]

The notional distinction between 'true' childhood—voiced by Knollys in Hong Kong—and that which was *not* childhood in the true sense of the word emerged in the wake of liberal reformers' efforts to advance child protection through state intervention. In the mid-nineteenth century, metropolitan child labour reformers established the economically worthless, domestic childhood as a middle-class ideal. This ideal was driven into sharper relief after 1870 as evangelical-inspired activists and school attendance officers laboured to achieve its extension across class lines. In Britain, Enlightenment thinking had advanced assumptions of the supposedly essential malleability of children and their special receptiveness to environmental influences. Reformers therefore focused not only upon longer-term solutions to address the moral and physical problems of the labouring poor, such as urban renewal, but also on the retrieval and reform of children from working-class milieux.

By the 1880s, the social purity movement (based around the Church of England Purity Society founded in 1882) boosted efforts to reach and reform children by defining public morality in Britain as an area for legislative intervention. Crucial to this was the victory of women reformers and churchmen in the battle over the Contagious Diseases Acts. The three acts, introduced in 1864, 1866 and 1869, were intended to prevent venereal disease among military personnel stationed in the British Isles in a period when a series of imperial crises, in India, the Crimea and Jamaica, were increasing demands upon military forces. The acts were eventually repealed in 1886 after a public outcry over the powers they conferred to police to arrest, incarcerate and subject to medical examination any woman suspected of being a prostitute. And the fact that women's bodies became a subject of national debate inspired greater attention to the defilement of children, too, most notably in the case of W. T. Stead's exposé of child prostitution, "The Maiden Tribute of Modern Babylon," in the *Pall Mall Gazette*, which scandalised middle-class society in 1885.

It did not take long for the impact of this social movement to ripple out to empire, where the Contagious Diseases Acts had originated. The first was implemented in 1857 in Hong Kong, while a second, passed in 1867, had provided police there with additional powers.[16] The success of the metropolitan reformers' campaign tactics soon led them to extend their critique to the colonies. And as demands for the repeal of the acts extended to empire, so too did other aspects of the purity movement. The 1880s emerged as a period of reflection upon sin at home and abroad. Stead's *Pall Mall Gazette* published an article in which 'Public Servant' asked, "Is Empire Consistent with Morality?" (He answered the question with a resounding "No!")[17] For a growing number of critics the male-dominated society of empire 'commissioned sin,' and in light of this elite commentators argued for imperial reform through the introduction of domestic values, that is, through the presence of wives, families and children.

Sir John Pope Hennessy, the reform-minded governor of Hong Kong, was keenly aware of such criticisms. During his governorship (1877–82) the Crown Colony had repeatedly come under fire from both metropolitan campaigners and its own liberal-minded chief justice for its lax moral standards. Hennessy himself initiated an inquiry into aspects of Hong Kong's Contagious Diseases Ordinance but failed to convince the Colonial Office to repeal it. Struggling to defend the colonial record amid condemnation of the acts (which remained on the statute) and evidence of 'child slavery' (discussed in Chapter 8), he turned to census data to argue, "The tropical Colony where European children flourish cannot be very unhealthy."[18] Drawing a veil over disastrous sanitary conditions, brothel slavery and other problems, Hennessy connected 'progress' with the proliferating presence of European children 'Out East.'

The governor was not alone in identifying the presence of the European child as a barometer of imperial-moral health. As the medical and social costs of male profligacy to British imperialism came under attack, other residents of British-governed territories in Asia joined this chorus. Alicia Little, a travel writer, anti-footbinding campaigner and sometime resident of Shanghai, attacked the old bachelor-dominated 'mess system,' claiming that "the greatest change of all" was "the superseding of the old hong life by family life. Shanghai is full, happily, now of ladies and children and they have broken up the junior messes."[19] In Singapore, Dr. David Galloway, a Scottish medical doctor who had arrived in the Straits in 1895, celebrated children as corroborating the ideal of the dutiful wife as mother.[20] In Hong Kong the chaplain to the resident British armed forces, the Reverend E. J. Hardy, explained in a lecture of 1903 how "wife and children are a kind of discipline" in the tropics. For these commentators, children's presence in empire was suggestive of a sexually disciplined colonial masculinity. The family with children, in their view, might provide a far more authentic foundation for social order built around the home than could bachelorhood in the messes and chummeries.[21] Trans-colonially, 'true children' emerged as a corrective to empire's 'spoilt children.'[22]

Though these critics imagined the child in the home in opposition to the bachelor in his 'chummery,' both in fact remained linked poles in an emerging colonial social order. Empires continued to depend heavily upon the migrant labour of young, mobile, unmarried men. Indeed, recruitment procedures, training schemes and marriage policies developed in the 1880s undergirded expatriate 'bachelorhood' as a social norm. Professional gatekeepers overseeing postings to and within Asia quite deliberately conceived of policies delaying family formation and curtailing settlement, for example by linking promotion to age. Such restrictions ensured that the child emerged as an awkward, partly celebrated and partly derided presence in empire. But it also became a key focus of respectable desires. For many, 'the child' was to be a moral bulwark, a potential balm for the pathologies of brutishness and sexual indiscipline, a diminutive guardian of the man. Good governance in empire would radiate from the smallest of social units.

In this vein, in 1889 James Cantlie, by then one of Hong Kong's foremost medical doctors, declared before a meeting of the Hong Kong Literary Society, "A home means in its essential sense a place wherein children can be reared."[23] Having arrived in Hong Kong two years earlier with his wife and baby son, Cantlie was himself engaged with the challenge of realising the colonial home. Whilst in the metropole, he had authored *Degeneration amongst Londoners* (1885) and played a leading role in 'Tropicalising' readings of the labouring poor in London's slums.[24] In Hong Kong, this prominent though controversial supporter of the domestication of metropolitan male working-class culture underlined the essentially degenerative impact of the tropical environment upon children's health. Nevertheless he clung, like Hennessy, to the notion of the child as barometer of the moral health of a community being redefined in terms of 'exile.'

The commentaries of Cantlie and others drew their power from metropolitan notions of mother and child as a powerful moral unit. These had deep historical roots, being tangled up in Britain with Puritan traditions of the family and marriage. From the 1840s, evangelical writers, congregational ministers, temperance and moral reformers and physicians invoked ideals of the family as an affective relationship, and the home as a sacred and intimate space, separated from the outside world of work, competition, the market and politics. Adultery and commercial sex embodied in the figure of the prostitute or 'public woman' contravened the spiritual essence of reproductive sexual union in the home. Through the close links it developed with the reform of labour practices, philanthropy and evangelicalism, childhood for some educated observers came to represent an essentially ethical space, a space of innocence and one ideally to be protected.[25] As James Cantlie was at pains to emphasise, in the tropics it was children and not their mothers who assumed the mantle of supreme referents of the 'home,' and by extension European civilisational superiority.

In Hong Kong such concerns resonated with special force among those who were long-time residents on the China coast. In this part of the world, where empires abutted and overlapped, imperial competition had dragged the family (or its absence) early into issues of authority. Before frustration with the Canton system (1757–1842) triggered the annexationist war that would deliver Hong Kong into British hands, the Qianlong court had forbidden Europeans to bring their wives and children onto Chinese-administered territory, or to establish homes there.[26] After the system was overturned by force, connections between family and authority lingered. So too did a sense of grievance, sharpened by ongoing Chinese assertions of British cultural inferiority and vulgarity. This critique came to focus in particular upon the opium trade, but also upon other practices deemed to be immoral.

Western missionaries worked up a counter-critique of Chinese culture as uncivilised, by foregrounding family practices. Jesuits had prepared the ground for this critique long before by informing the world of female infanticide. While decivilising attacks on Chinese culture often emphasised polygamy, they turned more particularly upon infanticide, footbinding and bond service—practices impacting upon children. Protestant and Catholic interpretations of the extent and nature of such practices converged toward the end of the nineteenth century.[27] And as the presence of European children on Chinese soil grew, colonials reread childhood through a familiar, though even more heavily racialised binary. On one side stood the prescriptive, sacralised ideal of childhood within the European colonial home, and on the other its stereotypically brutalised, inverse mirror image. With this, by the late nineteenth century children were emerging as key referents of racial and moral authority in empire.

But if this is the case, it is also well worth noting that James Cantlie's intention had been to present childrearing in the tropics not only as a solution but as a problem for Europeans. In many respects, children's assumed vulnerability threatened to undermine the very elite aspirations for a morally informed, 'civilised' and *durable* genre of colonial rule that they were being called upon to embody. Heat, for example (a subject on which Cantlie wrote extensively), was understood as an endemic threat to the child. In Anglophone scientific culture tropical heat was found to accelerate physical rhythms. The environment both stimulated and arrested mental development *early*, ending childhood prematurely. The specific problem with allowing children to grow up in tropical environments was that heat triggered an earlier transition to adolescence. Experts such as Cantlie linked heat to the earlier onset of puberty, the definitive signifier of sexual maturity. After Darwin, those who studied the human sciences understood children's growth as a lateral movement along an axis. From an evolutionist perspective this process was in effect a recapitulation of the moral and cultural aetiology of the race. The American psychologist G. Stanley Hall would later famously theorise such thinking in his two-volume work, *Adolescence*, of 1904.[28] In the evolutionist perspective, physical and cultural underdevelopment were connected. If European children came of age in tropical colonies the problem was that they would never fully recapitulate. And environmentally acquired defects would become fixed flaws in their constitution. This precocious but unfinished maturation process would leave youth, irrespective of class, racially and culturally marooned at an earlier stage of civilisational development than their metropolitan peers.[29]

Indeed, precocious maturation could be used to explain what was holding 'Far Eastern' races back in the evolutionary scheme of things. Their environment had left many stranded at an earlier racial-cultural stage of development, akin to that of the European child. For some, this environmentally induced condition even helped to explain the adult Asian's 'juvenile' physical appearance. James Cantlie described Chinese in Hong Kong as having a

> flattened bridge of the nose, a flat forehead and shallow eye socket. It is this form of face the adult Chinese retain, and thus associated with the want of pain about the face give a youthful appearance to the end of their days.[30]

European children, as others noted, with their "flat noses, forward-opening nostrils, wide-set eyes, large mouths and undeveloped frontal sinuses" conversely "resembled primitive peoples."[31]

Experts agreed that only the stark environmental shift of the return 'home' could prevent tropically induced degeneracy from resulting in permanent damage to the European child. To be on the safe side it was essential that the return home be organised well before the end of innocence and the onset of sexual maturity (and 'impurity'). Therefore puberty did not define the upper boundaries of childhood in the tropics as it did in the metropole. This threshold was set, somewhat arbitrarily, around age six or seven instead. This was an orthodoxy that took some time to cohere, but it did so trans-colonially in the second half of the nineteenth century.

In the 1860s, Sir James Emerson Tennant, who studied children in Ceylon, argued that British youth could remain in the tropics "till eight or ten years of age" and could enjoy a "charmed life" almost anywhere in the British Empire until the onset of adolescence brought "the attenuation of the frame and the apparent absence of strength in proportion to development."[32] In the 1870s the naval surgeon Alexander Rattray studied a sample of forty-eight naval cadets, age fourteen and a half to seventeen years, during a voyage at sea and linked their diminished strength and health to the dangers of tropical heat. He found that the children grew too rapidly and lost weight as they reached the tropics.[33] These findings travelled across imperial spaces through the networks linking India to the China coast. A little later in Hong Kong, James Cantlie would explain how the action of heat slowed breathing, increased perspiration and lessened tendencies toward physical exertion, impeding children's growth.

In light of these findings British medical experts studying children in empire inverted the older logic of 'seasoning' and invented a new calculus of endurance. In the early nineteenth century it had often been assumed that European bodies took seven or so years to acclimatise to tropical living, whereafter they were fitted for extended residence. But by the late nineteenth century, the length of time formerly judged necessary to become acclimated was redefined as the ideal upper threshold in terms of age for child life 'out East.' While early childhood remained, statistically speaking, the life phase associated with the highest risk of tropical mortality, experts boldly asserted that children could survive it almost undamaged.[34] By contrast, late childhood and in particular 'adolescence' came to be seen as the most dangerous age. As this knowledge travelled, medical experts in turn-of-the-century Singapore such as Dr. David Galloway could inform readers of the *Straits Chinese Magazine* that "after 6 or 7 years, deterioration, mental, moral and physical is the rule" among children.[35] However, the *Straits Times* reassured parents that tropical Singapore was "an ideal place for European children up to the ages of six and seven."[36]

Environmentalist interpretations of childhood were not applied irrespective of sex in British colonial culture but instead were deeply gendered. A common view, influenced by Darwin's *The Descent of Man* (1871), was that men were more fully evolved than women. Since boys were expected to become 'carriers' of civilisation, the risk of damage from keeping them with their families in such centres was seen as disproportionately greater. So while David Galloway for example considered keeping a boy in the tropics beyond age five "the height of folly," he believed girls could remain in Singapore "much longer than boys without prejudice to their health."[37] Galloway explained this discrepancy in some detail. Girls in Singapore, he advised, experienced "one great developmental epoch" from eleven to fourteen, but boys experienced two. Because boys suffered one earlier 'crisis' (when they supposedly grew faster than girls from age five to ten), this meant their growth was more profoundly disrupted in hot climates, and from a younger age.[38]

This mythos had practical consequences for the ways in which European elites sought to manage children's presence in colonial contexts. Because gender mores held that the adolescent male body posed a greater danger to its possessor (and the imperial nation) in tropical space than did the female adolescent body, the failure of boys to return home before or during adolescence more powerfully connoted becoming physically and culturally déclassé. Failing to make the transition early was a serious matter, especially among those who were more keenly aware of the growing importance of children's roles to achieving social status. One mother in Hong Kong, facing circumstances where "any chance of a public school life" for her son in the metropole was "out of the question," admitted this was "a great disappointment to him—and to me."[39]

Since girls, from an evolutionist perspective, were considered 'civilisational retards,' elite interdictions against their prolonged presence in tropical colonies were somewhat weaker than for sons. Elite education consisted of 'finishing,' a set of practices allowing girls to conduct themselves in society. This was important since middle-class convention held that daughters would marry earlier than sons. Finishing in the colonies was a far from ideal scenario. But as status-conscious elites carved out spaces where the moral order of things could be 'naturally' illustrated, the risks of tropical residence appeared somewhat less immediate for them. Though writers and administrators interpreted Singapore, Hong Kong and other centres as places where modernity and tradition clashed, ultimately they were regarded as civilisationally behindhand compared with the metropole. The ability to segregate colonial space, as we shall see in Chapter 6, was imagined to counteract degeneration by creating relatively salubrious enclaves wherein the presence of children, usually girls, could be prolonged. Consequently, notions of them as 'spaces of childhood' extended beyond literary flights of the imagination and informed attitudes to childrearing on the ground. So, for example, Helena May, the wife of a high-ranking colonial administrator in Hong Kong, took her daughter

Phoebe back to Britain with a view to placing her in boarding school. However, before long her resolve weakened and she returned to Hong Kong with Phoebe in October 1908.[40] Meanwhile Aileen Hastings, one of Phoebe's sister Stella's friends, was only sent back to England at age fifteen to be educated at Eastbourne (and later Paris).[41] Subsequent visits to Britain and Canada impressed upon Phoebe May how 'young for their age' life in Hong Kong had made her and her sisters in comparison with other girls of the same age.[42]

If the age of return could in practice be somewhat elastic even for elites and especially for girls, most parents seem to have striven to observe the orthodoxy of return for their children if they could afford it. Not all could, of course. Lillian Newton, growing up in the small and heterogeneous expatriate community in turn-of-the-century Singapore, reflected upon how unusual her status was as one of the few children to stay on. The death of her father, a former assistant municipal engineer (1877 to 1896), from cholera in Bombay had left Newton's family in straitened circumstances and prevented her from accessing metropolitan education, unlike the majority of her friends. She sensed the impact this failed transition had upon her (and her family's) status. For by then, among those who counted as 'society,' sending children home to be educated had become de rigueur. Official and nonofficial spokespersons boasted that this suggested the tone of the 'community' was improving. The *Straits Times* observed that in Singapore, in 1914, "little charges generally the children are, for a big boy or girl is seldom seen."[43] In Hong Kong the picture was similar. Census officials celebrated distributions of age, remarking that "after age 7 the number of children declines, the reason being all who can afford it send their children home for education at that age."[44] Contemporaries interpreted wider recognition of this upper limit to colonial childhood and the orthodoxy of breaking the empire family apart as evidencing 'progress' toward higher sexual and social standards than were apparent in other parts of empire.

However, for those who experienced it, this rupturing of the family was often shockingly abrupt. Among young Europeans the prevailing sense was of being torn from a privileged existence. As one former Hong Kong resident recalled: "It didn't seem to be the thing to stay at school here . . . I didn't see my parents for three years. I spent holidays with my grandparents. You just accept it. It was the normal thing to do."[45] Families, once separated, poured emotional longing into literary practices, writing to one another across the vast open spaces of empire in personal correspondence. But some also pushed nostalgia into public view, for example in published work. For the engineer C.M.M. Smith the chief stimulus to writing *The British in China and Far Eastern Trade* "was the desire to record some facts which I want my three boys, now at school in England, to appreciate. For they spent with me many happy hours of their young lives in China."[46]

Childhood was becoming essential, then, to establishing a divide, both within the colonial 'self' and between self and 'other.' It was a division that in turn evidenced the supposed moral-sacrificial role of white women and children in the tropics. Secular practices of childrearing were in the process mapped onto earlier missionary narratives of martyrdom, and stakeholders invoked the anguish of separation publicly as a referent of social 'tone.' In Singapore, for example, in 1914, mothers who gathered in the Botanical Gardens to watch their children play had "aching hearts for the older ones at home, who must grow up away from them, and again the little ones must follow."[47] Policing the upper boundary of colonial childhood allowed elite families, especially married (or widowed) women, to elevate the symbolic significance of childhood, and by extension their own emotional sacrifices. This perspective soon became so powerful that it reciprocally influenced and gave meaning to colonial policy. And as we shall see in the next chapter, it made children into active shapers of a trans-colonial culture expressed in terms not only of vulnerability but also of stoicism.

"ALIVE AND KICKING": TROPICAL CHILDHOODS IN FRENCH INDOCHINA

In 1901, the anthropologist and health expert Paul d'Enjoy outlined ambitious plans for the French child in Indochina. In a handbook written for newly arrived *colons*, d'Enjoy dismissed the arguments of sceptics, reassured parents that their child would remain "alive and kicking" in the tropics and declared, "we will make of him a being full of energy." D'Enjoy even went so far as to suggest that through this process the "little colonial" in French Indochina might become a paragon: "an example for his brothers in Europe."[48] This vision of the vigorous child on the colonial landscape differed markedly from that of degenerate displacement conjured by Henry Knollys and other Anglophone writers around the same time.

How could such strikingly different visions of childhood in the tropics coexist? After all, these centres were profoundly connected. Regimes of knowledge flowed between and mingled within them and French experts had drawn for some time upon their British counterparts' research into colonial conditions. Since the 1860s, military medical men had conveyed new discoveries relating to the white settlement question across international networks linking colonial and metropolitan contexts. Moreover, as Eric Jennings has shown in several recent works, French geographers, doctors and hygienists, like their British counterparts, frequently contended that white settlement was impossible in the tropics.[49] As the imperial ambitions of the French state expanded, Francophone experts elaborated upon earlier Anglophone studies of the *zones torrides*. For example, the medical geographer Arthur Bordier and the Swiss-French doctor H.-C. Lombard examined tropical disease.[50] Other medical men such as Joseph Onéisme Orgeas, studying Guyana, and Alfred Jousset, broadly agreed with the Anglophone consensus that acclimatisation initiated racial degeneration.[51]

And by the 1880s in France, as in Britain, pejorative depictions of tropical environments were reaching wider audiences. The controversy surrounding the republican government's 'Tonkin Expedition,' for example, helped these to penetrate popular consciousness. During the subsequent war against Chinese forces supporting the Vietnamese Emperor Tự Đức, the French retreat from Lạng Sơn in March 1885 sparked fears of defeat and culminated in a political crisis in France that swept Jules Ferry from the premiership. As the French newspaper press reported extensively upon parliamentary debates, it drew the full ghastliness of the tropics, evidenced in high mortality and morbidity rates among colonial troops, before the eyes of a shocked public.

However, the very stridency of the work of experts such as Auguste Danguy des Déserts and Léon Villedary, who condemned the degenerative impact of the tropics, needs to be understood as part of a context in which other voices were just as plaintively arguing for emigration and protesting that a modernised variant of 'seasoning' might work.[52] These disagreements reveal much about the quite different attitudes to tropical nature that shaped ideals of childhood in France and its colonies. And this clash emerged from the midst of a fulminating debate over degeneration and social decline in France informed by theories of 'organic economy.'

According to such theories, imbalance between an organism and its environment resulted in dysfunction. 'Pathologies,' such as alcoholism, low fertility and suicide, were symptoms of disequilibrium. This condition was described as 'degeneration' and it was considered to disproportionately affect those living in large cities. Commentators' concern over the implications of degeneration intensified as French birth rates dipped below death rates.[53] As in England, degeneration provided a language through which those who felt their (or the nation's) interests to be threatened could articulate fears. It was generally believed that the nature of urban lifestyles, rather than just the environment, was a key cause of 'overstimulation' or 'nervous exhaustion' (some adopted the term 'neurasthenia,' coined by the American neurologist George Miller Beard, to identify this condition). Fears about the propensity of French youth to be 'overstimulated' in schools caused a panic in the 1880s.[54] Symptoms of internal degeneration took on an especially threatening aspect in the shadow of a rising (and demographically prolific) Germany across the border. For this reason, while British scientists cast children's bodies as sites of racial degeneration in empire, some sections of the Francophone scientific community fundamentally disagreed with such a view.

Members of the influential and ideologically diverse French colonial lobby (or Union Coloniale Française) found the prospect of settlement in 'new France' tantalising. As Marie-Paule Ha has shown, lobbyists threw their weight behind a fin de siècle campaign promoting women's emigration to the colonies, organised by the Société Française D'Émigration des Femmes.[55] While others supported emigration partly as a solution to fin de siècle problems of depopulation and a 'blocked' metropolitan marriage market, the colonial lobbyist Joseph Chailley-Bert identified it as a means of ensuring that the French colonial presence in Asia would not only persist but take on a higher social tone. In the propaganda whipped up around this campaign supporters advocated the careful selection of women capable of 'improving' colonial societies which were considered at this time in France to comprise felons, frauds and *fruits secs*. But the presence of these women was also a means to an end: the production of a new generation of children capable of upholding and performing Frenchness authentically in a way that critics argued mixed-race children born of unions between male colonials and native women were not.

In discussions of feminine emigration the vexed question of the child in the tropics was never far away. As Germany revised its citizenship law to encourage emigration to the colonies, leading political figures in France waxed lyrical about the productive potential of white child settlers on Vietnamese agricultural concessions. This fantasy drew together some unlikely bedfellows. The Jesuit Jean-Baptiste Piolet, a man outraged by the creeping secularisation of France, identified the tropics as a source of national reinvigoration, an unspoilt *pays agrariens* where children would work in scenes redolent of an imagined French past.[56] Meanwhile, the left-leaning republican deputy, Jules Siegfried, addressing a festival organised by the Union Amicale des Enfants de la Seine in 1905, was also an enthusiast for Indochina's climate, which he believed was "better than our own" and which "delicate young people, as those in our society often are, would find beneficial."[57] Joseph Chailley-Bert celebrated the news that while thirteen European babies had been born in Tonkin in 1887 the figure reached sixty-two in 1894. He saw this as proof of the capacity of colonies to reinvigorate the fertility of settlers and of the metropolitan-run 'feminine emigration society' to produce families "rooted in the soil."[58] Travel writers and photographers visited Indochina with a view to confirming French children's capacity to survive and flourish in alien nature. Among them the photographer and populariser of empire Jules Gervais-Courtellemont, for example, advertised Indochina as a boon for youth otherwise destined "to vegetate and wither in some province of France."[59]

What helped to lend credence to these provocative visions of tropical childhood was the enduring intellectual influence of transformist theories of adaptation in France. Geoffroy Saint-Hilaire and Jean-Baptiste de Monnet Chevalier de Lamarck had elaborated these theories in the late eighteenth and early nineteenth centuries. From the neo-Lamarckian perspective tropical lands were not qualitatively different from temperate zones. Transformists argued that all organisms everywhere lived in harmony with the natural environment. In the tropics greater humidity, heat and light produced regimes of reproduction that left beasts outsized and herbs looking like trees. However, since nature was in this view a continuum, contact with new conditions of life would stimulate a process of adaptation capable of materially altering the organism, fitting it for survival.

The French imperial revival of 1830 brought new state sponsorship and greater respectability for scholarly studies of 'acclimatisation.' State funding poured into research informed by this intellectual tradition in the hope that this would allow the more efficient exploitation of natural resources newly drawn under French control. However, because the French rebuilt their empire piecemeal until the 1880s, geographers and scientists—unlike their British counterparts—tended to map disease at one remove. Exploratory scientific expeditions to Southeast Asia brought back samples, but it was metropolitan scientific communities who by and large defined tropical nature. And they did so without direct experience of 'problems' equivalent to those posed by the Indian Uprising, or the management of a large resident population of 'poor whites,' as in the British Raj. In Paris, institutions such as the Société Zoologique d'Acclimatation in Paris, a stronghold of neo-Lamarckian research, kept the tradition of transformist thinking alive. It was precisely the institutional strength of this intellectual tradition that helped to attenuate the impact of Darwinism in France and its empire, as Michael Osborne has argued.[60]

In the mid- to late nineteenth century those doctors and biologists who challenged cosmopolitan interpretations of humankind, such as Paul Broca, Charles Naudin and André Sanson, attacked the neo-Lamarckian position. By this time germ theory and the new science of tropical laboratory medicine (drawing upon the Cuverian tradition) were undermining transformism in the metropole. However, when the colonial lobby in France finally secured an unambiguous commitment to empire from the republican government in the 1880s the exponents of transformist adaptation and their institutions received a boost. Intellectually their outlook dovetailed with that of republican social theorists of imperial governance. Transformism could be interpreted democratically since the environment was assumed to act upon, and transform, *all* organisms. Thus, theories of acclimatisation articulated well with 'solidarism,' which Léon Bourgeois had by the late nineteenth century shaped into the official social philosophy of the French Third Republic, and which was informed by the work of the biologist Alfred Fouillé. Theorists of French imperialism such as Jules Harmand drew upon the concept of 'association' elaborated by the biologist Edmond Perrier. Harmand appealed to notions of 'scientific imperialism' as the development of harmonious relations between coloniser and colonised in seeking to justify empire building. These intellectual connections led the acclimatisation lobby to identify the republican reconstruction of empire as a vital means of reasserting their diminished authority.[61]

Saigon and Hanoi both emerged as centres for experiments informed by transformist thinking owing to the support of high-ranking government officials. These officials also lent support to resettling French families in empire. The interest of Charles-Marie le Myre de Vilers, the first civil governor to be appointed in Cochinchina, in 1879, saw him later become president of a new section of the

Société Zoologique d'Acclimatation dealing with colonisation. During his governorship he also championed the right of administrators to raise their children, on the grounds that this would enhance economic efficiency and reduce the frequency of their returns on leave. Soon after taking up the post of resident general of Annam and Tonkin in 1886, Paul Bert, an enthusiastic colonialist and man of the left, picked up on de Vilers's line. He invited

> all civil servants who come to Indochina [to] bring their family with them; those who come as bachelors, I would like to assist them in marrying, I would like to be witness to their marriage and I would volunteer in advance to be the godfather of their children.[62]

Bert's sudden death from dysentery later the same year presumably did little to reassure those who remained sceptical about the possibility of white settlement. Nevertheless his proposal raised the question within Indochina of whether French children were capable of 'staying on' without degenerating, and if so, how this could be achieved.[63]

To many the perils of tropical living appeared legion, but as French power shifted northward through the 'pacification' of Tonkin, official interest in childrearing persisted. Admiral Pierre Benoît de la Grandière (governor of Cochinchina, 1863–68) was said to have been the first high-ranking colonial to bring his wife and (seven) children to Saigon, late in 1865, an act emulated by some officers and entrepreneurs.[64] However, the Grandière family left Saigon in 1868, and detailed information on the lives of 'settlers' is difficult to find. One individual celebrated by contemporaries for his efforts to raise a family was General Edmond Bichot. The general, who was married to Cécile Michelet, a cousin of Hubert Lyautey, raised two daughters and a son in Indochina. All three children seem to have moved with their father to the new French protectorate of Tonkin (where he became commander in chief of French forces in March 1889). There the general's daughters eventually married, and his son, after following a military career, set up a concession raising buffaloes.

Bichot's renown owed much to the fact that the conditions for such 'domesticating' projects did not initially appear promising in the northern outpost of Hanoi. Following its invasion by French forces in 1873, Hanoi became the site of a small French concession, established in 1875, before it was eventually seized outright in 1882. The 6 June 1884 Patenôtre treaty, negotiated by the French with the Vietnamese monarchy, recognised French control. The terms defined Tonkin as a 'protectorate,' but Hanoi was classified as 'colonial land.' An imperial decree of 1 October 1888 formally bestowed the city upon the French. A decade later, when Paul Doumer took up the governorship of Indochina in 1897 at the age of thirty-nine, Hanoi began to emerge from Saigon's shadow as a centre of French imperial power.

Doumer was in touch with the metropolitan currents of thought that would soon bring the official endorsement of an 'associationist' colonial policy. Saigon, with its larger cohort of Francophone commercial elites, with its deputy in the French National Assembly in Paris, municipal council and opera, retained stronger links to an earlier 'assimilationist' phase of empire building. For some, it still stood for the possibility that through institutional and cultural contact Vietnamese might become 'French.' Vietnamese had participated within the burgeoning infrastructure of the colonial state here, notably the Colonial Council from 1880 and the municipal council, and some had become naturalised French citizens. Some also sent their children to metropolitan France for education, or to French schools in Cochinchina. However, as assimilationist ideas fell out of favour in official circles, Hanoi came to be imagined as a site upon which a shift away from this earlier genre of French colonialism could be pursued.

As governor from 1897 to 1902, Paul Doumer drew Indochina closer to Paris, subsumed Saigon's influence within the union and oversaw Hanoi's transformation into an imperial capital. He promoted Hanoi at Saigon's expense, making it the host centre for the reorganised Indochinese Civil Service and capital of the union.[65] From 1898, when the lands of the union became financially interdependent, Cochinchina continued to provide 40 percent of the general budget but observed the political influence of its spokesmen in Paris weaken. Doumer intended that the new Hanoi would more unambiguously embody French prestige than cramped, commercially oriented and heterogeneous Saigon. The government therefore organised the supply of water, sanitation and electrification of the French quarter, extended streets in the dense cluster of native-domestic streets near the 'Petit Lac,' built a vast new governor's residence and constructed or extended other outsized administrative buildings from which the protectorate and municipality were administered. Broad boulevards cut through the city centre in a metropolitan style intended to reflect this imperial 'politics of grandeur.'[66] While Saigon remained the most economically dynamic centre in the Vietnamese peninsula, planning transformed Hanoi into an imperial capital. It took on an expansive, ceremonious character quite different from the southern centre.[67]

Doumer's ambition was to project French power and interests from Hanoi much further afield (notably into the Chinese Empire). For these plans to succeed Doumer was convinced that effecting Hanoi's physical transformation was not sufficient. France also required colonials of a higher calibre—men less overly entangled with the tropical milieu, capable of upholding a more aloof genre of colonialism. The governor was convinced that 'progress' depended upon "the quality of the new *colons* who have come to set up here ... more than their quantity" and determined that it was necessary to raise the quality of those who came out to empire to staff the ranks of the administration.[68] In the north as in Cochinchina, Cambodia and other *pays*, the administration was staffed largely by discharged, former naval soldiers of relatively low social rank who had joined the Tonkin expedition. Some had taken Vietnamese or Eurasian wives. Many remained bachelors.

In 1901, Doumer issued a circular to Residents Superior declaring it "essential" that administrators' private conduct and their integrity and impartiality be beyond criticism.[69] Those involved in open liaisons with Vietnamese women were informed to break them off immediately in the hope that the magistracy and civil service might become bastions of morality and 'good conduct.'

Like many of his contemporaries Doumer speculated that the presence of women and children was critical to producing a different kind of *colonial*—and fitter, more refined, loyal and efficient cadres. Evidently, the presence of Eurasian, or *métis(se)*, children, discussed in depth in Chapter 9, threatened aspirations for the realisation of a 'French Indochina.' What was required was to populate the tropics not with settler children, but with expatriates who were more unambiguously French. And at the turn of the century the new Hanoi emerged as a key site from which visions of a more authentically French child in the tropics could be projected.

As the new Hanoi took shape its promise in this regard was underlined by the fact that the governor was in residence for eight months of the year and could therefore play an influential role in shaping the capital's burgeoning social scene. The European population was still small but socially mobile. Two-thirds of the six hundred enumerated, according to one waspish observer, could claim by virtue of education or social position to be members of 'society.'[70] Advocates of 'French Hanoi' such as the journalist Jean Star (aka Jules Clément Lubanski) enthused over the prospect that the domestic *foyer* might underpin the prestige of a new urban-based colonial elite. Improved contracts presented to new recruits to the Indochinese Civil Service therefore underpinned the practice of bringing out young wives from home. As the sex ratio began to change, the administrator Louis Salaün insisted that in Hanoi "life is more stable" than in Saigon because "the proportion of young men who are not married, in relation to the families, is fewer."[71] Because the cost of living was also generally lower in Tonkin than in Cochinchina (salary differences for Vietnamese diverged by up to 75 percent between north and south), more servants could be hired to support the elite home. In 1902, as Hanoi prepared for its *exposition*, Jean Star declared it a place where "sir, madame, baby and *congaï*" formed a "symbolic and authentic colonial foursome."[72] His interposition of the child *between* the European *madame* and the Vietnamese *congaï* reflected emerging desires to realise a new colonial order based upon white conjugality. The contours of a didactic childhood distinguishing subject peoples from rulers began to take shape.[73] Medical experts supported this line. Dr. Charles Grall, the colonial medical inspector, in whose arms Paul Bert died in 1886, argued that while childrearing was a problem in sweltering Saigon, in contrastingly cooler Hanoi, "the European family may live and develop almost normally."[74]

Self-proclaimed experts began to make claims about child life that resonated with those espoused in elite British colonial cultures. Grace Corneau, an advocate of female emigration, writing of Tonkin struck a familiar note as she advised: "to the age of about eight years [children] grow superbly, without ever having to fear the terrible illnesses of the throat or of the chest, that claim so many victims in France; but later, they weaken and have need, in order to grow, of a harsher and less debilitating climate."[75] From the 1880s French medical experts working in Indochina, like their British counterparts, underlined the correlation between tropical living and precocious sexual maturity. Dr. A. T. Mondière, in Saigon, warned that puberty arrived "earlier in Cochinchina than in our temperate climates."[76] Hanoi's colonial elite applied gendered assumptions to the management of the family in the tropics. Paul Doumer, whose own humble origins made him keenly aware of the importance of upholding prestige, managed his household in accordance with such elite norms. He brought with him to Hanoi his daughters Hélène (age sixteen) and Lucile (age four) but left behind in France his five sons (Fernand, age seventeen, Marcel, age ten, René, age nine, André, age seven and Armand, age six) so as not to interrupt their studies.[77]

But there was little consensus on colonial childhood. Calls to realise new, elite prescriptions around family life reflected a society that was becoming, if anything, more divided. The elevation of administrators, with their various perks, stirred resentment within other sections of colonial society. Bilious commentary spilled into the pages of Hanoi-based newspapers. With the future of the French colonial presence in question a slanging match erupted in the colonial newspaper press over the relative merits of Eurasian or 'truly French' children as auxiliaries of empire. For one writer, white conjugality alone could produce "children who . . . will make comprehensible to the conquered race the superiority of our civilisation."[78] This cast the earlier exploits of empire generations, who had married or cohabited with Vietnamese women, in a quite different light. Heroic pioneers became sexually incontinent vestiges of a disorderly past. 'Old colonials' had indiscriminately committed both male and female offspring to Indochina.

Administrators' dreams of the colony as an expression of French prestige and economic potential jarred with visions of settlement, or 'pretty pink babies' on agricultural settlements. But many colonials did not draw salaries from state coffers and were unable or unwilling to pursue status as defined by a self-professed elite. Some realised that they could exploit anxieties over destitute white children to secure resources, notably free passages or minor administrative positions, from the colonial state. But as domestic visions of childhood became more important to the performance of an embourgeoisified Frenchness in empire, the future of the 'settler child' was generally thrown into doubt. The uncertain rhythms and evident risks of colonial living recast children who might be termed 'creoles' as an ambiguous and provocative presence. In 1903, not long after Paul d'Enjoy emerged as an advocate of the "alive and kicking" colonial child, Gustave Reynaud, a former chief doctor of the Corps de Santé des Colonies and a teacher at the Institut Colonial in Marseille, published a hygiene manual advising agricultural entrepreneurs to leave their children in Europe.[79] Two years on, the collapse of rice markets threw many French-run agricultural concessions in Tonkin back on their resources, and reinforced this line. A little later, Charles Grall would assert that childrearing was possible "only on the condition that [the family] had sufficient resources to secure genuine comfort. They must have true *aisance*."[80] The normative child in the colonial home had begun to take on a marked class coding.

As 'child settlers' came into view as a problem for the state, social transformations in Hanoi triggered a critical engagement in Saigon with the problem of marginal children. One response came from the satirist 'E. Postal' who wrote in the journal *Satires Coloniales*, "we [in Cochinchina] have succeeded in 'moralising' Indochina; like M. Doumer, but better." He added, "Family life has been created, slack habits have been improved, greater self respect has been brought about by force."[81] But while sarcastically applauding Doumer and his counterparts in the south for 'moralising' Indochina, Postal and others like him raised the provocative question of how far the colonial state was willing to go in the full colony of Cochinchina to defend its moral-racial authority by addressing the presence of the 'other' children who failed to live up to elite norms. He posed this question in series of satirical sketches depicting the misadventures of five French orphans, Poisvert, Paudeballe, Lécorché, Labombe and Poilaumain, ostensibly sent by a fictional metropolitan 'Société de protection de l'enfance abandonné ou coupable' to "moralise" Cochinchina. In Postal's tale, immediately after their arrival in Saigon the youth declare themselves impressed by the 'macaques' (racist slang for Vietnamese women) but they also quickly realise that in French Indochina "you've got to put on fancy airs." So they repair to the 'Café de la Musique.' Once there they succeed only in emptying the place of patrons in minutes through a combination of their foul language and general offensiveness.[82] Postal's youthful folk-devils exemplified the ways in which children were an unstable presence, and a focal point in trans-colonial struggles over the future of French imperialism. Far from reflecting broad consensus or heralding the construction of a homogeneous 'community,' visions of the impoverished and unpredictable non-elite European children were suggestive of the way in which colonial society was fracturing along mutually antagonistic lines.

HYGIENIC MODERNITY: DEFINING CHILDHOOD IN ADVICE LITERATURE

As we have seen, officials and elites in different colonial contexts came to define children as symbols of a shift toward hegemonic rule. This shift informed new prescriptive literatures emerging in response to the problem of maintaining children in the tropics. The writers of these texts defined the rules and rituals of 'hygiene' and childrearing, and their work provided a channel through which new norms and expectations were disseminated to families. Within British and French Empire centres in the late nineteenth century, families became more keenly aware of the expectations surrounding their children and how they should be raised. They could turn to this literature for clues as to how to offset 'Tropical' degeneration and to raise their children in accordance with modern methods. Or so, at least, these experts hoped. Whether or not families put these hygienic edicts into practice is a question explored further in Chapter 3.

Scholars have noted that hygiene rules tended to be broadly similar when it came to childrearing in the tropics. Informed by the long British experience of life in India, guides covered accommodation, diet (which was to be light, simple and nonstimulating), washing, exercise and clothing (which was not to leave chest, neck and arms exposed). Particular emphasis was placed upon prophylactics—notably the prevention of children's direct exposure to the rays of the sun. This was to be achieved mainly through the wearing of pith helmets (topees). Colonial childhoods may have been emphatically gendered, as construct and experience, as we have seen, but their principal sartorial referent was the genderless topee.

Sometimes experts disagreed over the exact prophylactic methods that were to be employed to preserve child life. For example, some advised that in addition to protective headgear children should also wear flannel belts when playing outdoors, but others counselled against this.[83] For the most part, however, hygiene literature reveals strong trans-colonial similarities. This is unsurprising given that its authors were generally retrofitting codes devised to protect colonial troops for use by children. Instructions on the design of colonial homes to protect youthful bodies drew directly upon designs for barracks, for example. Advice on dress resonated with older codes intended to sustain colonial troops.[84] In this respect children in the tropics stood at the intersection of home and barracks, as the very embodiment of contradictory coercive and protective impulses within empire.

But while British and French hygiene guides may have offered quite similar suggestions on child management in the colonial home, this literature also varied in important ways. It emerged from strikingly disparate intellectual traditions and was informed by different views of 'Tropical' nature. What resulted were different visions of youth in empire. Although turn-of-the-century French authors of hygiene literature such as Paul d'Enjoy could insist that the colonial child might actually be an improvement upon his metropolitan equivalent, no similar sentiment emerged in British writing on the subject. Careful attention to these codes can reveal important variations that further illuminate our understanding of trans-colonial convergence and divergence around questions of childrearing and racial reproduction in the tropics.

Let us start by discussing Anglophone child management literature. This was rather slim, lacking in detail and somewhat amateurish in style. Often written by women for women, it was doled out not only in manuals or guides but also in dribs and drabs in the newspaper columns of the colonial press. The authors of this literature often eschewed fine detail in preference for broad-brush counsel. A certain reticence marked the interventions of these self-proclaimed 'authorities.' This was not surprising at a time when authority was coming to rest upon claims for the colonial home as a 'naturally' moral space, on account of the essentially virtuous presence of women and children.

Still, what lurked within such manuals was the assumption that the child in the tropics could fall sick at any time. The new human sciences had made clear that varieties of humankind existed in a hierarchy set in geographical relation to one another. It was therefore natural that medicine should also explain illness in terms of place. When Henry Knollys made Hong Kong's Botanical Gardens the scene of his warning to British mothers, he drew upon prevailing British understandings of such spaces not as 'laboratories' for the engineering of new organisms through acclimatisation, but as didactic, pseudo-museums, exhibiting fixed species likely to be 'broken' by transfer.[85] The reticence of Anglophone writings on hygiene reflected the assumption that nowhere in the tropics could children be saved from degeneracy through tinkering with hygienic codes.

British writers associated certain variants of childhood with purity, and adolescence with impurity. But because statistically at least in tropical spaces the years of purity were the most dangerous, European children embodied wider threats of pollution. They represented 'matter out of place,' in constant need of 'purifying,' liable to 'fall' at any moment. And because this was true anywhere in the tropics, children's vulnerability helped to link together and define Britain's empire of possessions. The value of hygienic management lay not in salvation but in drawing moral distinctions; in distinguishing European childrearing from other, supposedly inferior, variants. In this period in metropolitan Britain, child health was coming to be seen not only as a sign of parental competence but also increasingly as a barometer of the vigour of the nation. However, in colonial centres hygiene codes at best offered a temporary absolution of sins; a kind of secular communion in the face of death. They implied recognition of a set of medical and moral imperatives necessary to uphold middle-class status. Their observance connoted membership of an elite defined by its unwillingness to set down roots.

Though this literature appeared flat and expansive it varied on the ground. In Singapore, for example, residents of this 'younger' and more ethnically plural Crown Colony took longer than their counterparts in Hong Kong to elaborate a racially bounded vision of childhood. A growing, and increasingly diverse group of European expatriates defined a sense of community through more elaborate definitions of 'true' childhood. To this the wearing of topees assumed crucial importance. But as rapid growth stimulated increasingly fine-grained social stratifications, 'inferior variants' of childhood defined through aspects of children's play and behaviour that had hitherto been overlooked also emerged as the subject of expert criticism. In 1884 one Singapore resident complained in the *Straits Times* that at Pearl's Hill

> I was perfectly astonished at seeing groups of European children playing and wandering in the heat of a tropical sun. Some were poorly clad, bareheaded and shoeless. Dear Mr. Editor it is a deplorable thing to see these children, of European parents, roaming the streets in the manner I have just described.[86]

A few years later Dr. David Galloway weighed into this debate with the following criticism:

> I dare say you have all seen, in your wanderings about the town, children belonging to European parents in the humbler walks of life who were permitted to run about in or out of doors at all hours of the day without any head covering, until their hair was bleached a lint-white.[87]

As both interventions suggest, children's physical appearance (in this case the pigmentation of their hair) was becoming an index of a racially defined community's moral standards. A social cohort that claimed to speak for Singapore's Europeans was becoming increasingly self-aware vis-à-vis 'other Europeans'—both 'poor whites' and elites of other colonial societies in Asia.[88] For those living in the Straits these social contrasts were becoming more important around the turn of the century, and especially after 1903, when the onset of opening programmes brought a dramatic influx of planters into British Malaya, via Singapore, especially from Ceylon and South India. Among these so-called creepers were low-ranking administrators, demobilised soldiers and indigents, as well as fortune seekers from the worlds of shipping and commerce. As the rubber trade burgeoned and the planter class grew dramatically, the result was a shift in political power and a social transformation. A large settler community developed, circulating within and between Singapore and the Malay Peninsula, raising European or mixed-race children on the land.[89]

In the face of these transformations, elites in Singapore, the seat of political power, looked to European children to affirm the colony's health. The latter's mere presence was no longer sufficient. What was required was their performance of childhood to acceptable standards. These standards were defined comparatively. In 1899 Dr. Galloway had expressed his disappointment that it was "a matter of common remark that the children of Singapore are paler and pastier than of any of the neighbouring colonies."[90] However, by 1914 Singapore's elite drew upon sightings of healthy-looking children as proof of progress. As one observer, R.S., noted:

> In olden days white-faced Indian children were known at once by their woe-begone little sad faces; but in Singapore just now a healthier little set would be hard to find whether down in the town in the Cathedral compound or up in the Botanical Gardens. Certainly, the children in the spring who arrive here from North China on their way

to England after the bracing winter there boast of more rosy cheeks, and the little ones who have lately landed here from Europe are naturally very pink and plump; but even so our Eastern infants might yet take a prize at a baby show.[91]

Three key points emerge from R.S.'s report on "Children in Singapore." First, as a key port of call, the city offered the observer an unrivalled vantage point from which to judge Singapore's 'own' youth in relation to the 'other' children of empire. Second, what defined these children was their status as participants in a culture of trans-colonial circularity, within Asia and between metropole and colonies. Children's mobility evidenced European families' willingness to break up the colonial family and to respect the normative upper threshold of childhood in the tropics. Third, the relative good health of the children and their transition from 'Indian children' of yore to a well-dressed, topee-wearing 'Singapore set' evidenced this centre's transformation from an Indian dependency to a Crown Colony as part of the Straits Settlements. Those who lived on the margins of respectable society at this time and were unable to go home for schooling, such as Lillian Newton, felt this consensus crystallise around them. Newton confessed to running about in the garden confines of her mother's boardinghouse "barefoot like a Malay." However, performing childhood in public required the observation of different rules. Only a few years after Galloway's complaint, she admitted, "no child dared to run outside during the day without everyone shouting at you to 'Put your topee on.'"[92]

As Anglophone commentators and medical professionals focused a critical eye upon children's public appearances, what helped to undergird their generally less prescriptive approach to childrearing practices *inside* the home was the early development of an infrastructure supporting early child life. In British colonies this was facilitated by weaker cultural resistance among British women to the bottle feeding of infants. New bottle designs and India-rubber teats had become available in Europe from the 1850s. In colonial centres mothers continued to adopt feeding practices drawn from their own ethnic backgrounds, and from Asian practices too. Though, according to Christine Doran, sweetened condensed milk and other infant food preparations were being imported to the Straits Settlements from the British Isles from the 1870s, some resorted to feeding infants with buffalo milk from small, mostly Bengali-run dairies.[93] Speculation that adulteration was causing illness among children prompted the colonial state to more stringently regulate the production and sale of milk.[94] Frozen milk from Australia became available from Singapore Cold Storage by 1910 and supplies of pure, fresh and unadulterated milk were produced locally by the late 1920s.

In Hong Kong, where the sense of an external threat across overland borders was greater and the urge to showcase 'civility' through the family was stronger, private initiatives supporting early child life attracted earlier and more intensive investment. From 1856 the veterinary surgeon John Kennedy had begun such a project, and by 1883 small dairies already existed in the colony. However, the medical doctor Patrick Manson remarked upon the difficulty of finding clean bottled milk soon after he arrived in Hong Kong with his wife, three sons and daughter. During his six-year stay Manson cofounded a public company, Dairy Farm, in Pokfulam, with the specific aim of supplying inexpensive milk (which he described as "the staff of life") to European children.[95] By 1892 production levels were sufficient to warrant the construction of a central depot. These innovations enabled the Reverend E. J. Hardy to boast in 1903 that "sealed bottles of very good milk can be bought" for children in Hong Kong.[96] This situation arose earlier in Hong Kong due to the concentration of medical expertise and technology, but also as an accompaniment to assertions of European cultural primacy drawn upon the moral leverage of the family.

In both Hong Kong and Singapore these endeavours addressed certain challenges involved in raising young children and underpinned the assumption that mothers' principal task was to manage the return home in *later* childhood. However, by the interwar era enhanced sanitation and reduced mortality gave rise to views of colonial centres, from Saigon to Hong Kong, as increasingly healthy places for children. Even so, demands that children observe established hygiene rules influenced by climatology did not simply fade away. In the 1920s English-language guides such as *The Home and Health in India and Tropical Colonies*, authored by the medical doctor Kate Platt, continued to insist, "Topees must always be worn."[97] In the elite neighbourhood of the Peak in Hong Kong the author Bella Woolf (whose husband was Thomas Southorn, the colonial secretary) described how, even in 1930, "European children with topees over their flaxed hair play about by the barracks on scooters and little tricycles."[98] Long after adults had given them up, children continued to wear topees. Indeed, in the face of sustained attacks upon climatological interpretations of racial endangerment and the declining exoticism of the tropics, children's vulnerability and their capacity to embody it appears to have increased in value between the wars.[99] Assumptions about children's vulnerability allowed them to embody racial differences that could no longer be as easily reflected in the environment and which adult European bodies could no longer as easily perform.

In French Indochina, anxieties over racial dissipation led French hygienists to devise a noticeably tighter and more thorough set of regulatory schemes than their British counterparts. The tone of hygiene manuals published in Paris, Hanoi and Saigon was less amateurish than Anglophone equivalents. Quantitatively more guides were also published and experts were more sharply critical of mothers' failure to observe their prescriptions. Francophone experts had little compunction about invading the family home. Georges Treille signalled this intent as early as 1899, advising, "the first place to start in the programme of colonisation is obviously . . . the home."[100] While British advice guides made broad-brush suggestions on the supervision of native nursemaids, French guides were much more exacting and specific. They attempted to more carefully regulate the innermost aspects of children's lives. Small children were to be carried in prams, not on arms or hips, for example, while the litany of bad habits they might pick up in the company of 'boys' and *congaïes*, and their consequences, were quite explicitly spelt out for readers.[101]

Experts saw their role in terms of structuring behaviour not only within the domestic interior but also in public. In his manual *Hygiène colonial appliquée* Dr. Charles Grall described how, whilst out on an evening walk in the 'furnace' of Saigon, he had encountered a family with young girls who were carrying umbrellas and dressed in fashionable headgear imported from Europe (rather than distinctly unfashionable but hygienic topees). Grall thundered, "From 8am to evening" it must be "the topee and hygienic hairstyle for the mother, for the children and for the husband, it is essential to repeat this unceasingly."[102] The timbre of this criticism perhaps reflected the frustration that hygienists' advice was falling on deaf ears. But it may also have reflected stronger underlying anxieties about the difficulty of disentangling French children from the tropical milieu. The weaker association of the upper threshold of colonial childhood with a definitive return home did little to attenuate these anxieties.

In Saigon and Hanoi, as in France, cultural preferences for the use of wet nurses remained stronger than in British centres. This ensured that the issue of infant feeding emerged as a source of tension between hygienists and mothers from the earliest days of the child's life to the extent it did not in British centres. Nowhere else in Europe was wet nursing conducted on a similar scale to France. From the 1870s French doctors had attacked wet nursing, which they blamed for high infant mortality. Théophile Roussel, the deputy of Lozère, introduced a bill to extend the regulation of this industry across France, on 23 December 1874.[103] Though in France the trend toward more general adoption of condensed milk and other feeding formulae was by now becoming more apparent, many experts and mothers continued to distrust the bottle.

The same was true in the colonies where alternatives to breast feeding were not as easily sourced. As the number of families in Hanoi and Saigon grew, the inexpensive labour of indigenous women and the need of many French women to work to support their families created strong demand for native wet nurses. In turn-of-the-century Hanoi, Jean Star celebrated the emergence of two separate categories of female labour moving into the middle-class homes in the *quartiers blanches*: the *congaï-bonne* and *congaï-nourrice*, as a sign of upward social mobility. Doctors admitted that the employment of native *nourrices* was generally seen as a marker of higher status. As Charles Grall put it, "the European woman in Tonkin belongs to a social milieux where breastfeeding is becoming the exception."[104] Yet wet nursing was also controversial as it involved intimate flows of maternal milk between native nursemaids and French infants. The very practices associated with the desired social elevation of French families in the tropics simultaneously threatened racial reproduction. In the face of this conundrum, Grall resorted to rather meekly calling for French mothers to breast-feed, arguing that tropical heat made milk flow more easily and that dispensing with native wet nurses would ensure that "health, vigour, moral and intellectual energy are more completely transferred" to the baby.[105] His intervention, while rather equivocal, is suggestive of the way that while English hygiene literature often simply affirmed middle-class mores, French writers on tropical living actively sought to reshape them.

Ongoing anxieties over the health of the French child in the tropics and responses to them need to be read against the backdrop of low fertility and high (and often rising) infant mortality rates in France. This led doctors to worry much more than their Anglophone counterparts about the dangers of *going* out to empire, and somewhat less about *staying* there. Doctors saw the period from birth to around five or six years, so-called *première enfance* (statistically the most dangerous phase of life), as the key to national regeneration. These convictions inspired the emergence of the politically powerful, broadly based *puériculture* (childraising) movement for the protection of children in 1895, as William H. Schneider has shown.[106] Anxieties centring upon this particular stage of life informed late-nineteenth-century assumptions that childbirth in the tropics equated to a 'death sentence' for mother and child. When the British travel writer Isabella Bird visited French Indochina en route from Hong Kong to Singapore, she found it noteworthy that officers, missionaries and traders believed that "most of the children born of white parents die shortly after birth."[107] As the *puériculture* movement in metropolitan France flexed its political muscles in the first decade of the twentieth century, concern over the lack of medical infrastructures capable of defending child health in the colonies shaped the contours of the French colonial childhood.

In French Indochina, European women had long depended upon private practices for obstetric services, as state-funded infrastructures developed slowly. The same was true in other East and Southeast Asian contexts. From 1901, for example, the Hongkong Nursing Institution provided subscribers, including the five ladies on its management committee, with access to the services of trained nurses.[108] When the colonial government oversaw a public subscription to fund the construction of a hospital to serve women and children of "all ranks and classes" in 1897, J. M. Atkinson, the principal civil medical officer, complained, "it is principally for European women and children that greater accommodation is required."[109] The Matilda Hospital opened in January 1907, for the treatment of Europeans only. Similarly, in turn-of-the-century Singapore, David Galloway admitted that when it came to obstetric provision, "we have entirely overlooked the crying needs of the children of the dominant race."[110]

In Indochina convictions about the 'impossibility' of supporting early child life and the lack of clarity around how they should be addressed served to slow the pace of regulatory intervention by the colonial state in this field. The construction of the Lanessan Hospital began in Hanoi in 1891 but a *pavillon* for women was only installed much later, in 1898. In 1900 Grace Corneau complained that Hanoi had only one midwife, and she had only arrived recently.[111] A maternity ward opened in Saigon only in 1902, but even ten years later, Jean Ajalbert could still sarcastically remark, "Europeans, whatever their rank, are so blessed with medical care that one Governor General brought his own midwife" to Hanoi.[112] Outside major centres, for the very *colons* whom some had imagined raising 'pretty pink babies' the situation was even worse. The agricultural entrepreneur Marius Borel described how he had attended the birth of his first child equipped only with a copy of *Le livre des jeunes mères*, published by the Librairie Agricole de la Maison Rustique.[113] After 1905, the state-funded Assistance Médicale Indigène began to expand the provision of health care services for Vietnamese women and children, but Charles Grall continued to insist that European women who fell pregnant in Saigon faced the stark choice of return to the metropole or death, and that "the European child was all but condemned to death in advance."[114] Not until February 1914 did the colonial state legislate to extend hygiene inspections to the production and sale of milk in Tonkin.[115]

Here a striking contrast emerged. Compared with 'Anglo-Saxon' experts, French doctors considered *seconde enfance* (the period of life after roughly five years of age) to be an age at which risks of hereditary degeneracy were relatively less. An example was Dr. Gustave Reynaud. As Reynaud knew well from existing research, those under age fifteen were statistically at greatest risk of death (and they would remain so into the interwar years). But from the turn of the century Reynaud had grown interested in British research on children in Bengal showing that mortality dropped steeply among children *after* age five. He used this evidence to argue that while young children should not be brought out to the *zones torrides* (and in particular Indochina) the danger was substantially less after age five.

In the early twentieth century the colonials who shuttled between metropole and colonies were in touch with debates over degeneracy and depopulation, and some wondered whether Reynaud's proposed age threshold for taking children out to the colonies should even be pushed higher. In this vein, in 1910, the head of the education service in Annam, Edmond Nordemann, warned students studying in the Section Indochinoise of the École Coloniale in Paris:

> If the household, upon its departure for Indochina, includes one or more young children, it is preferable to allow them to grow up in France until they are six or seven years old; the tropical climate is quite inclement for these young saplings born in our temperate regions.[116]

The upshot of this was that at roughly the same age that British counterparts (especially boys) were preparing to return home from the tropics, French children—at least in the hygienists' ideal—were reaching an age where they were deemed ready to go out.[117]

French medical doctors by the late nineteenth century tended toward racial-fixist positions. And because the precise cause of diseases yielding high infant mortality remained unclear, even in the metropole, many of them rejected tropical settlement altogether and condemned hygiene manuals. They understood the metropolitan state's expertise to be crucial to remedying deficiencies in maternal care.[118] However, its underdevelopment in the colonies prompted those hygienists who still clung to the possibility of preserving child life 'Out East' to define rituals of care in minute detail and to produce far more detailed 'catechisms' than did their Anglophone counterparts. Hygiene in the French tropics appears in these manuals less as an expression of moral exegesis with a clear end point—the environmental shift of the return 'Home'—and more as a *catéchism*, an age-related rite of passage, perhaps even a step on the road toward salvation in 'New France.'

It is also significant that French hygienists often wrote not for mothers (as did Henry Knollys, Kate Platt and other Anglophone writers) but rather for male household heads.[119] And in such writings, the child subject raised in empire was often gendered masculine. Indeed, childrearing sometimes appeared more as a project involving men making men, on the frontier. In republican France, the performance of manliness did not revolve to quite the same extent around the observance of elite codes as it did in Britain's more rigidly class-based society. In France women had traditionally taken greater responsibility for policing class, notably through childrearing. But in a colonial culture where masculine virility and unpretentiousness were cherished, and officials often paid only lip service to republican ideals of egalitarianism, childrearing was never simply conceded to women. Indeed, at a time when more women were populating French Empire centres it is striking how hygienists addressed themselves to fathers, and insisted that they take responsibility for this task.[120]

Hygienists enjoined male heads of households to emulate 'rational' experts, to become in effect 'citizen-scientists,' assuring the lives of their offspring. While the British home in empire, however hygienic, had to be broken, from their perspective the French home could potentially become a miniature laboratory, the proving ground of a 'new France.' These attitudes had profound consequences for the ways children experienced tropical living. Thérèse de Hargues recalled how as a child living in a semidetached villa on rue Rousseau in Saigon during the 1930s, her father, an employee of the Cartographic Service, and not her mother, oversaw daily hygiene inspections. If her fingernails, or those of her siblings, were found to be bitten or dirty, the consequences for the children could be severe.[121]

Sustaining such practices was the provocative notion that hygiene in the home could potentially deliver 'small acclimatisation.' Advocates of this transformist position held that since nature was a continuum, its variants in Asia like those in

FIG. 2.1. Children at Saigon's Botanical Gardens, 1920s. *Source*: Author's collection. Asia. *Source*: Author.

Europe might be actively managed into maturity. By the late nineteenth century, French doctors considered links between plant and animal life to be risible. But colonial hygienists continued to assert that children were more likely candidates for hygienic adaptation on account of their greater malleability. Experts in Indochina remained fascinated with assumed links between the sapling and the child.[122] In 1911 no less a figure than Alexandre Kermorgant, inspector general of the Service de Santé in the Colonies, a member of the Academy of Medicine and a hygienist specialising in health stations, could claim:

> We can compare, and with good reason, the European who goes to live in the Tropics, with a plant transported out of its land of origin. We know what kind of care must be taken to allow it to grow in a new soil; we also know that the young and vigorous shrub will endure transplantation better than a tree that is already old.[123]

Medical doctors in France might scoff at plant-animal metaphors, but those invested in colonial projects were tantalised by the notion that in Asia improvements in the environment might be passed on to the next generation in improved genetic traits.

The return 'home' was only part of this regime, for those who could afford it, and even in late childhood not necessarily its conclusion. The persistence of older thinking about climate weakened acceptance of managing children's definitive return as the foremost duty of mothers, even among the elite. As the writer Henriette Célarié noted, even in the late 1930s many in Saigon remained convinced that "once you are acclimated, that's it. You can stay ten years, twenty years."[124] And when the 'section colonial' of the Comité National de l'Enfance prepared to report on children in the colonies before an international conference in Rome, Passa, the general inspector of the Colonial Health Service, insisted (on the basis of reports from Hanoi) that the European child "can develop favourably almost anywhere, if he is the subject of a rational and well supervised hygiene."[125] The French child stood, unsteadily, at the confluence of dissenting theories and fears for racial dissipation, between the old colonial order and the new.

CONCLUSION

Children featured prominently in the long-running debates over the viability and the longevity of the European presence in East and Southeast Asia. In defining colonial childhoods, experts and officials engaged with quite different interpretations of 'Tropical' nature. They also drew upon different medicoscientific definitions of risk and negotiated diverse and conflicting sets of priorities. Consequently, there were many different 'maps' or 'pictures' of childhood in the tropics. However, among them the colonial trope of the endangered child proved powerful and persistent.

In the late imperial era these beliefs informed desires to fashion new communities in empire defined in terms of race and class, and to assert European cultural superiority vis-à-vis colonial subjects through middle-class domestic norms. Children's vulnerability could function to support claims to authority and a racial hierarchy understood as fixed in nature and biology. The European child in the tropics became essential to the realisation of new genres of morally informed colonial governance built around the home. Colonial childhoods also proved fundamental to elite-led efforts for the embourgeoisification of European colonial societies. As this ideal cohered, it helped to produce the alarming prospect of the déclassé settler child. Consequently, children embodied a volatile combination of dangers and desires. This led experts in fields such as colonial hygiene, medical geography and cultural anthropology to elaborate a raft of practices to maintain child life.

British doctors and hygienists in Hong Kong and Singapore dwelt primarily on tropicality as a threat to population quality to be resolved by an early return to the metropole. Assumptions about gender in empire and the imperative of return led them to concede somewhat greater authority to mothers over their own children. By contrast, in Hanoi and Saigon some experts identified the management of childhood in the tropics as fundamental to aspirations that empire might form part of a project of national regeneration. Hence, at a time when in the metropole French men increasingly conceded responsibility for their children to an emerging partnership between women and the interventionist republican state, in colonial contexts where the state was weaker and culture was more male-dominated and masculinist, experts and fathers reasserted paternal responsibility for colonial childhood.

Though experts shared knowledge across empires, local pressures ensured that colonial childhoods developed quite different meanings and parameters on the ground. British and French experts were often at odds about the nature of the dangers to European children present in the colonial environment, and therefore also about the age at which European children were most at risk. However, childhood flexibly absorbed many of the contradictions of racial thinking in the late imperial era. In none of the contexts discussed did the emergence of the orderly middle-class home as a marker of cultural authority mean that children experienced colonial living merely as vulnerable, ornamental symbols of status. As we have seen, many children failed in practice to perform childhood in accordance with these new norms set down by hygienists and others. Moreover, in spite of prevailing views, children in these centres never only saw themselves as being 'at risk.' They were also 'risk takers.' And they often ascribed quite different social meanings to these risk-taking behaviours than did adults, as the next chapter reveals.

CHAPTER 3

Cultural Contagions: Children in the Colonial Home

In the late imperial era childrearing came to be identified as exemplary of moral order and good governance came to be more closely linked to domestic values. The home emerged as a site of colonial power, and in the process children took on a social and cultural significance that far outstripped their numerical presence in the tropics. As adults recast children as exemplars of supposedly homogeneous national cultures, their actions within the home—their encounters with native servants, nursemaids, and others—began to attract interest at the highest levels of colonial society. As we have seen, hygienists, some of whom viewed children as 'perfected degenerates' and others as 'acclimated auxiliaries,' became deeply concerned with childrearing practices. And yet these experts were only too well aware that they lacked influence over the shape and structure that colonial childhoods ultimately took within the home. In practice, as this chapter argues, childhood in colonial contexts was profoundly porous, mixed and disruptive of the very claims for racial homogeneity that it was called upon to impart.

Children experienced colonial childhoods in homes that were thoroughly interpenetrated by local and global forces. Young Europeans, who were by definition unstable and partially formed, could not be shielded from the pressures effacing national cultures. Indeed, precisely because adults considered youth to be a more malleable condition, and children's social agency to be qualitatively different from that of their own, it could function as a site of 'hybrid' interactions *between* diasporic communities. Youth in empire was in practice produced dialogically, and on the move. The presence of children did not necessarily lead to a 'closing up' of European society, but could instead expose European communities to new and potentially disruptive influences.

This chapter asks how parents and children produced colonial childhoods by looking to interactions within the home with Asian children and domestic servants, and to children's experiences of disease and ill health. By getting sick, forging 'unsuitable' affiliations and accessing inadmissible knowledge in and around the profoundly trans-cultural space of the home, children bridged between the intimate and the wider realms of colonialisms' cultures. In the process, they sometimes affirmed but also often challenged discourses of imperialism and the boundaries of what it meant to be European.

Evidence for children's agency is highly fragmentary and heavily mediated in the historical record. Yet diaries, letters and reminiscences reveal something of how British and French child residents of empire centres imposed their own meanings upon childhood. Children participated in a conversation with adults that shaped expectations of, and ways of inhabiting, colonial childhoods. They were never merely passive recipients of notions of 'place' and 'race,' not even in the home. Their voices 'spoke back' to homogenising, adult-shaped historical and cultural discourses of childhood, the nation and their own position in empire. They challenged tropes of vulnerability, forged contacts across lines of ethnicity and engaged in 'hybrid' relations with indigenous children and servants. In colonial homes and surrounding spaces, young people never simply upheld the social and racial hierarchies of empire; as we shall see, they also undermined them.

"MORE A MOTHER THAN A SERVANT": AGE AND INTIMACY, AYAHS AND AMAHS

In his portrait of tropical Hong Kong of 1885, Major Henry Knollys quite deliberately foregrounded the connection between the degenerate European child and the native 'ama.'[1] This colonial couple had become a recognisable feature on the landscape, not only in Hong Kong but in other empire centres too as the number of European women and child residents surged in the decades bracketing the turn of the century. The arrival of children brought new and quantitatively greater demands for particular categories of domestic staff. In the late nineteenth century, alongside cooks, houseboys and cleaners, demand for 'baby amahs' rose accordingly.

The recruitment of domestic servants in general and amahs in particular underpinned European families' claims upon elite status.[2] And yet the resulting proximity of European children and Asian women created tensions, as Knollys's account suggests. For the relationships that children forged with domestic servants occasioned interethnic intimacy. This proximity was on the face of it suggestive of a rupture in the supposed moral-biological order of mother and child. For this reason British writers tended to link the amah-child relationship to the wider dangers occasioned by children's impecunious transfer, and to their exposure to dangerous flows or contagions—cultural and pathogenic—cutting across racial boundaries. To many the child-amah couplet offered a stark provocation: the end product of a strategy authenticating elite status might be an inauthentic or 'unnatural' childhood.

In both Singapore and Hong Kong around the turn of the century, some of the wealthier members of European society addressed this conundrum by seeking to recruit nurses, guardians and governesses from Europe to care for their children. These they brought with them or paid to have brought out from Europe. In Hong Kong, for example, the colonial administrator Henry May hired a German governess for his children, Fraulein Fremgen, an authoritative figure who inspired fear according to his daughter, Phoebe.[3] As wealthier residents in Singapore also strove from the late nineteenth century to define a more moral colonialism, one commentator wrote enthusiastically of "the many English nurses who are here now."[4] Those working in the burgeoning financial and administrative sectors recruited female nursemaids to serve their families. Among them was the French consul Comte Raphael de Bondy. He had arrived in 1902, taking up residence in Orchard Road and hiring a European domestic to care for his three sons and daughter. In the eyes of contemporaries the presence of these domestics no doubt helped to undergird the shift traced in the previous chapter from 'white-faced Indian children' to a rosy-cheeked 'Singapore set.'

Yet the expense and increasing difficulty of securing female domestic labour from Europe restricted this practice to only a tiny minority. Later in the period those wealthy enough to be able to afford such a mark of distinction represented a very small section of the elite (and usually the financial elite at that).[5] Much earlier, European women who were engaged in setting up homes began to source domestic servants from local labour markets instead. Indeed, a key consequence of the arrival of greater numbers of children in colonial Asia was a reordering and 'feminisation' of the labour supplying colonial homes. In 1879, Isabella Bird had estimated that of 15,368 domestic servants in Singapore only 844 were women, though most of them presumably served non-European homes. According to census data, by 1891 some 635 Chinese women were in the employ of Europeans in Hong Kong.[6] However, by the 1920s the ratio of male to female labour had shifted markedly and an increasing number of Asian women served European mistresses.[7] These they referred to in Singapore, using terminology imported from India, as 'memsahibs.' In the rapidly growing and remarkably plural society of Singapore women could choose to draw upon the labour of Chinese *amahs*, Malay *ayahs* or others to serve in their homes. In the early twentieth century the labour of Chinese women remained somewhat rarer in the market and more expensive than that of their Malay counterparts. However, by the 1920s a general preference for the former among European mistresses had begun to become more evident.[8]

In the memoirs and autobiographies of those who spent their childhoods in Hong Kong, Singapore and other Asian centres, depictions of these women are often strikingly affectionate. Because mistresses in Hong Kong and Singapore relied upon domestics to eschew drudgery, this brought amahs and very small children together. Edwin Ride, born in 1931 to an academic father, described his mother as "a somewhat distant figure," but referred to Ah Sin, the amah, as "more a mother and friend to us than a servant.... As small children we had everything done for us by Ah Sin."[9] In Singapore the cheaper Malay ayahs often did not 'live in' with families. However, female Chinese servants working as baby amahs looked after children all day and slept in the same quarters, often alongside younger children. Dione May, daughter of the Hong Kong administrator Henry May, for example, slept in the nursery alongside the domestic Ah Soo (or 'Sooey'). Close bonds often arose as a consequence of physical proximity.[10]

Biological mothers usually saw their proper role as being to concern themselves with the surveillance of the entire household. This was a notion reinforced by advice guides. Certainly mothers were expected to regulate the (potentially intimate) relationships that developed between their own children and servants. But scaling back their duties in relation to young children allowed women to free up time to ensure the return of older children to the metropole or, in the case of girls who remained, to oversee the performance of femininity to an acceptable standard in public. Domestic servants were thus essential to the implementation of elite ideals of childhood and girlhood, as well as elite status more generally, in public and private.

However, as the moral unit of the mother and child in the home emerged as a core justification of racial authority, critics disparaged European mothers' overreliance upon amahs. This, they believed, was productive of children 'spoilt' through overindulgence, a lack of discipline, by the transmission of bad language and by inappropriate feeding.[11] 'Veronica,' the pseudonymous male author of the satirical book *The Islanders of Hong Kong*, depicted a motley of fictional colonial characters, including a stereotypically neglected 'child.' The inclusion of this character presented an opportunity for the author to make an unfavourable contrast between British and Chinese attitudes to children. Provocatively, Veronica commiserated with 'the child' and his tendency

> to see all around you other children who have not been unfortunate like yourself, who are the valued treasures of their parents, while you are left to the tender mercies of your amah, and feel sure in your heart that you are of less consequence than the least item in your mother's collection of curios.[12]

This invective appeared at a time when Hong Kong elites, as we shall see in the next chapter, were staking out racial authority in public around the figure of the white child.

Feeding practices were another favourite focus for critical commentary, but so too were linguistic exchanges between amah and child. Those who encountered children in public observed that daily contact with amahs had created cross-cultural channels for intimate dialogue. Such connections endured between the wars. So, having departed Singapore in January 1923, the businessman and travel writer Allister Macmillan remarked on how, in Hong Kong, "the little ones soon learn to prattle Chinese."[13] According to Edwin Ride, his amah, Ah Sin, "spoke a sort of pidgin English, but generally we conversed in Cantonese."[14] Meanwhile, in Singapore, Malay was used as a lingua franca and instead of 'pidgin' English, ayahs would often teach children to speak Malay.[15] As Geoffrey Barnes later recalled, "Mother said that at this time I used Malay almost as much as English ... since so much of my time was spent with Amah and our servants, and it was common for European children to have a fairly fluent range of 'bazaar Malay.'"[16]

As children developed facility in pidgin, Cantonese or Malay, the home became a shared space of trans-cultural connection and multilingual competence. Such domestic dialogues raised an alarming prospect. Home life might generate linguistic distance between parents and their biological offspring, drawing young Europeans into unlikely alliances with Chinese and Malay women. Since both children and servants were involved in the process of negotiating European adult authority, the intensity of child-amah relations and children's reliance upon Asian women for intimate assistance was suggestive of the potential for colonial authority to flip in the very place where it was supposedly most secure. One commentator in Singapore reflected this tension by commenting that when British youth "becomes very ironic about the poor Malay of its parents it will be agreed [this] is a strong argument against the *ayah*."[17]

Age proved crucial to resolving the conundrum presented by sentimental amah/ayah-child bonds. Originally, the term *amah*, thought to derive from the Portuguese *ama*, was an Anglo-Indian term meaning 'wet nurse.' But as we saw in the previous chapter, by the mid-nineteenth century cultural anxieties among British women over bottle feeding had weakened. The development of commercial and medical infrastructures supporting early child life, along with the wider availability of animal milk for infant feeding, meant demand for labour in Hong Kong and Singapore tended not to be skewed toward younger women.[18] In Singapore both ayahs and amahs were distinguished by their relative maturity. On the ayah in general one observer in Singapore suggested, "If she were a European peasant woman one would put her nearer sixty than fifty but in view of the tender age of her youngest born she is probably something like fifteen years less," for "the torrid sun of the tropics hustles them too speedily from childhood into maidenhood, thence from womanhood and premature old age."[19] By the turn of the century in Singapore the "Old Ayah," and by the 1920s "old amah," had become easily recognisable figures on the colonial landscape. Female servants were defined principally—for Mrs. E. F. Howell, author of a collection of pen-pictures of Singapore life, and other self-proclaimed authorities—by their age.[20]

In Hong Kong, age was also reflected in the naming of Chinese women recruited to serve in colonial homes. 'Baby amahs' were referred to as *ma cheh* or *amah cheh* in Cantonese, which literally meant 'older sister.' The migrant labourers who moved to Hong Kong and Singapore usually originated in the Canton Delta where, as Janice Stockard has shown, the demands of the sericulture industry augmented the value of female labour, resulting in delayed-transfer marriage and marriage-resistance practices, notably sworn spinsterhood.[21] With demand for silk in long-term decline from the early twentieth century and with political upheaval cutting off access to northern Chinese markets, more women moved into domestic service in colonial centres. This movement speeded up with the onset of the Great Depression in the late 1920s. By then most amahs who arrived in Hong Kong and Singapore were in their thirties and theirs was an identity construed around seniority, which in turn connoted status. Across the period baby amahs were better paid than most other members of the domestic retinue (usually second only to the cook). European homes generally paid higher wages than others, and the women's role was given added professional authority through a distinctive black and white dress, which by the interwar years European employers came to expect them to wear.[22]

As a result, in British colonial homes the servant-child relationship often tended to be defined by a wide age gap. The contrast across the period with Chinese homes, where children were employed as domestic servants (*mui tsai* if girls and, less commonly, *hsi minh* if boys), was striking.[23] To some less wealthy Chinese families, the unwaged work of child bond servants might represent the only affordable form of domestic labour. But even elite families might purchase several *mui tsai* and appoint each of them to specific offspring. Similar practices persisted in Singapore.[24] However, in both places the taking of children as bond servants attracted growing criticism within European communities. From the 1870s, critics associated such labour with illegal secret societies, and 'slavery' and the practice eventually formed the focus in the interwar years of a long-running abolitionist campaign, discussed in Chapter 7.

Importantly, these older, unmarried women who served European homes embodied both maturity *and* immaturity. As *cheah*, or older 'sisters,' amahs were also often spinsters. Many of these mobile women were members of a sisterhood who had done up their hair, wore distinctive dress and had taken vows not to marry. They therefore tended not to bring their own children into the colonial home or its vicinity. While on one hand these vows endowed them with seniority, economic opportunity and mobility, on the other their position as *childless* women denied them maternal authority in European eyes. Their status was somewhat closer to the infantilised 'old maid' of Europe. As a presence defined both as infantile and aged, these women's tutelage could be assumed to be naturally inferior or deficient in comparison with that of their mistress. The gulf in age between amah and child also set limits to intimacy and to some extent stymied cultural transfer between servants and served.

To be sure, such checks constantly broke down. For instance, European children overcame incomprehension by learning Asian languages or pidgin English. Some taught their amahs European languages too. Though common languages

FIG. 3.1. "Slave Girls Carrying Children," Hong Kong, c. 1900. *Source*: Author's collection.

emerged, Europeans checked amahs' authority by denigrating these as essentially 'childish.' From the mid-nineteenth century, Canton pidgin English was frequently derided by European observers as a "gross caricature of the language of the nursery" and a "barbarous and childish *patois*."[25] By construing pidgin, which by the turn of the century had all but disappeared from commercial domains, as an essentially childish tongue used in the home, commentators accommodated it within British elite assumptions about childhood as a separate 'world,' distinct from that of adults.

Viewed in this way, British children's use of pidgin, Malay, Chinese and other common tongues picked up from amahs and other servants, seemed relatively benign. Clemence Baar, a turn-of-the-century resident of the elite Peak neighbourhood in Hong Kong, regaled her friends with tales of her two-year-old son Jimmy's emergent facility in pidgin ("he constantly asks to 'go chair top side!'").[26] On board the SS *Nyanza* travelling from Hong Kong to Singapore on 28 November 1921, the British newspaper baron Lord Northcliffe took great amusement in attempting to speak Chinese to small British children: "Some of the tiny ones speak nothing but Chinese, having been brought up by Chinese servants. I say to them, 'Chin-chin' (How are you?) and 'Chow' (food), the only Chinese I know."[27]

The 'infantilisation' of the female amah was built upon prior strategies developed in European households to extend mastery over male servants. This had already been articulated in many ways, but most notably perhaps through a trans-colonial discourse constructing men as 'boys.'[28] As Asian men moved out of domestic employment in the early twentieth century, European women recruited Chinese and Malay women to secure their elite status. Their construction of mature women as childlike temporarily resolved the threat posed by adult Asian women to their own authority within the intimacy of the home.[29] As childlike adults, amahs could only ever be interlopers in the realm of European babies. But they could continue to stand as icons of cultural irrelevance and the subservience of an infantilised and effeminate dominated culture. Tellingly, in a satirical sketch written for a Hong Kong audience, 'Veronica' addressed the European child with the words, "Your *amah* will be as unfit to govern you as a Chinaman would be to govern this Colony."[30]

Desires to infantilise Asian populations through association with European cultures of childhood also informed adults' approaches to their children's dressing up and play. Parents had few qualms over dressing up their children *à la Chinoise* in Hong Kong and Singapore. European children also dressed up in Malay clothing in the Straits for photographs, trips home or just for fun.[31] As Blake Bromley, the son of a colonial schoolmaster, who with his brother Harvey lived across the strait from Singapore, recalled, "I had a Malay sarong and Fez and Harvey had a Chinese outfit in which we attended children's parties and we both have formal photographs of these costumes taken at that time."[32] Earlier, adults visiting the photographic shops clustering in busy urban centres had posed in similar costumes. But by the early twentieth century such practices had largely devolved to children, whose play with Oriental markers was less threatening and set up a contrast that could even serve to underline their own claims upon whiteness.[33]

While shared assumptions about early childhood helped to defuse the threat posed by intimate flows of native language, shared views of adolescence or late childhood offered no similar reassurance. In British colonial culture what was referred to as 'late childhood' or 'adolescence' was, as we saw in the previous chapter, identified as a time of great danger. Well beyond medical literatures, contemporaries discussed the implications of this dangerous age for the management of servants in the colonial home. 'Free Lance,' the editor of a column in a Singapore newspaper, voiced a common view when he insisted that only small children could be entrusted to Chinese amahs. While he admitted, "Their devotion to our children often takes a form disastrous to discipline," still "it would be difficult to think of our babies deprived of this erring affection."[34] However, as the child approached adolescence, the dangers of trans-ethnic contact could no longer be safely managed. 'R.S.' in Singapore in 1914 warned, "For elder children they are the greatest mistake, as often their code of morality allows of no limit to conversations which, though carried on in Chinese, the children easily learn to follow."[35]

In this regard, the child-servant relationship mirrored the child-environment relationship discussed in Chapter 2. Since Asian servants were often regarded as 'outgrowths' of this environment, this is hardly surprising. Both relationships locked children into a trajectory leading inevitably to degeneracy and the end of innocence. But both were also ultimately productive of British elite colonial culture. They affirmed middle-class women's elite status and underpinned the orthodoxy of sending children 'Home.' This allowed colonial homes to remain primarily spaces of childhood. The adolescent in the colonial home by contrast embodied the alarming prospect that intimate relations set down across lines of class and race might persist into adulthood. Lord Northcliffe, visiting Singapore, summed this problem up quite succinctly, and its solution, when he noted: "The European children here seem happy. I saw them playing today guarded by their Chinese or Malay amahs of whom they are very fond. These nurses spoil them, however, and they have to be ordered home when they are seven years of age."[36]

OF BOYS AND BÉCONS: CHILDREN AND THE COLONIAL HOME IN HANOI AND SAIGON

In French-governed centres such as Saigon and Hanoi quite different practices of child management emerged. As we saw in the previous chapter, French experts' attitudes to tropical nature and concerns over natality led them to articulate sharper anxieties over *early* childhood in the colonies. By the early 1880s this made the question of assigning native nursemaids to look after children a subject for anxious debate. In theory British middle-class women's claims to moral primacy allowed them opportunities to carve out a natural authority over their offspring and the home. In practice these assumptions created a space within which remarkably close interethnic relationships could flourish between European children and Asian servants. These relationships did not go uncriticised, but as Lord Northcliffe's quote above suggests, elites assumed that since the child's link with the tropics would soon be unfastened, lasting damage might be avoided.

While this expectation may have somewhat attenuated the criticism of British women, French mothers were, by contrast, confronted with a variety of divergent demands. Some expected them to fashion colonials-in-waiting while somehow preventing racial-cultural dissipation. Others considered their principal duty as being to oversee return. Some complained women were failing to heed their responsibilities in the home. Yet others suggested these responsibilities were properly the remit of men, notably fathers. In the face of these contradictory claims women struggled to impose their own authority over domestic space. What made this task still more difficult was the fact that both French and Vietnamese men contested women's authority in the home.

Within French-governed Cochinchina fathers, doctors, hygienists and the servant retinue (the so-called *boyerie*) presented rival claims for authority in domestic space on a daily basis.[37] Within centres burgeoning under French rule, sex ratios were markedly more 'normal' and stable across the period than those in the British-governed centres studied here. Because of this, supplies of female labour were more readily available. Hence, Vietnamese male labourers who had carved out positions of authority within colonial homes fought longer and harder to defend them. In the first few decades of the French presence in Cochinchina male servants of the 'boyocracy' lived out in the Saigon suburbs, but by the late nineteenth century some had given expression to domestic authority and growing economic power by taking up the practice of 'living in.' In Cochinchina 'boys' reinforced their status within the internal hierarchies of the colonial home by adopting a uniform (much earlier than amahs did in British centres). They wore white, like the Europeans they served, along with bright silk belts. And by the end of the century this group were also sufficiently self-confident to fend off French efforts at regulation.[38]

In the early twentieth century in the migrant-dominated societies of Hong Kong and Singapore, the rising cost of male labour brought the introduction of cheaper female labour into the home. But in Saigon and Hanoi this process was slower. When Lord Northcliffe travelled around Asia in the early 1920s he was surprised to see so many European children on ocean liners in the care of 'annamite men.'[39] The tenacity of such men in clinging on to service (and selling their labour in this market even further afield) was illustrated during the protest strike of 1922 when the Astor House was known to be the only hotel in Hong Kong that could continue to function normally, on account of the fact that it employed "Annamite boys who are disinterested in the strike."[40]

While Vietnamese men continued to defend their authority in the colonial home, the recruitment of native domestics in Vietnam was far from uncomplicated. Given the heterogeneous social status of the French families resident in Cochinchina and Tonkin, some secured servants by adopting the kinds of cost-saving practices used in Vietnamese and Chinese homes, including the employment of children. In British-governed migrant societies, gender imbalances limited the number of women available for domestic labour. And yet in British homes the perceived need to raise barriers to cross-cultural intimacy and the emerging critique of Chinese practices of taking domestic bond servants limited demand for child servants. By contrast the use of child labour was common in French households in Indochina (and in French homes in British colonies too, where this practice would soon attract controversy, as we shall see in Chapter 7).

One reason for this was that children's labour was cheaply and readily available in Saigon and Hanoi; or at least more so than in emigrant societies with skewed sex ratios such as Singapore and Hong Kong where young female servants remained in high demand. Also, fewer cultural barriers seem to have existed to the employment of children as domestic servants in French homes. In the late nineteenth century many of those who employed children had stayed on in Vietnam after the northern expedition to Tonkin. These former military men occupied low-level positions within the colonial state, and when they started families they economised by recruiting children to work in their homes. For wives attempting to organise domestic staff, labouring children may have represented less of a threat to their authority than did Vietnamese *boys* or *bonnes* (the latter being equivalent to the amah), both of whom were regarded with degrees of suspicion. While male domestics were gradually coming to be seen as expensive and insufficiently docile, replacing them with the adult female domestic labourer (or *congaï*) also had its drawbacks. Respectable European colonial society was gradually coming to associate Vietnamese women's employment in male-led households with impropriety, even further down the social spectrum. So in 1896 when P. Dupla, a teacher at the Collège Chasseloup-Laubat in Saigon, presented readers with the argument that the educated, French-speaking *congaï* would allow French households to be run more economically, he felt compelled to address the issue of immorality (allaying concerns by explaining that this 'solution' had worked well in Tahiti!).[41]

So prevalent was the practice of taking female child servants that French employers used a loan word, *bécon* (literally meaning 'small child,' but used here with shades of the term 'apprentice'), to classify this emerging group.[42] The *bécon*, a young domestic servant usually aged between ten and fourteen, remained a recognisable member of the retinue of servants in colonial households right up to the end of the period. By this time, some wealthier European households employed not only Vietnamese but also Chinese women as dry nurses (as they were understood to be "in general cleaner").[43] But the practice of hiring young Vietnamese girls appears to have cut across social strata. The *bécon*'s position in society was not easy to read. With her teeth unlacquered, this child occupied a liminal position within both the household and Hanoi society. Hers was a position created by the demands of the French family and in particular by the presence of European children. Even in the 1930s the orientalist writer Christiane Fournier felt it necessary to decipher her appearance for readers. She is

> a girl in a white turban, with smiling eyes, silk trousers. She is thirteen. She is not a little girl. She is not a young woman. She is an annamite *bécon*, plaything of the European babe.[44]

Owing to their age, these girls' labour was cheap and they often also performed a variety of menial tasks in French homes. In 1882 Arthur Delteil observed in Saigon: "In a household with children we often need a female domestic. Quite good ones can be found at the *Sainte-Enfance* . . . I heard that the service of these domestics was not bad. They make do with them for the lack of anything better."[45] But an additional benefit of recruiting Vietnamese and Eurasian girls 'placed out' by the Holy Childhood Society into French homes was that they possessed useful skills. They left the Society's care knowing how to sew, work and use French.

Linguistic competence enhanced these girls' value in colonial economies where the performance of cultural Frenchness was crucial to gaining access to resources. With the notable exception of those staffing administrative cadres, funds permitting frequent contact with the metropole were not necessarily available. While some administrators and merchants might be able to afford to bring out a French teacher or governor for their children, many others could not.[46] So, for example, as Germaine and Marie-Louise Borel, daughters of a well-known agricultural entrepreneur in Hanoi, were "beginning to grow up," the family "took a young Eurasian raised by the Sisters to amuse the children and to teach them to read."[47] In Hanoi into the late 1930s, parents continued to hire girls, including fresh graduates from the École Normale des jeunes filles, for this purpose.[48]

These children may not have presented a direct threat to the male-dominated 'boyocracy,' but the latter nevertheless seems to have felt the need to assert its authority over these girls in the home. As the journalist Jean Star noted, they were often the focal point of male servants' physical and verbal violence. He described how, by the turn of the century, the *bécon* had become "the cabin girl on the domestic ship; the punchbag, the drudge. The hardest working and the lowest paid."[49] The *bécon*'s low status was partly a function of her youth. This permitted her to take up a position within the colonial home, but it was one marked by vulnerability, ambiguity and transience. Male aggression also appears to have connected with anxieties surrounding the sexual threat these girls were imagined to pose in French households, especially as they neared adolescence.

Writing of Cochinchina in 1882, Arthur Delteil had explained with reference to the girls of the Saint-Enfance, "unfortunately when they are pretty, they often turn bad, as often happens in France for girls of the same category."[50] Hiring youthful servants ostensibly handed French women greater control of the household, but it also involved a trade-off exposing European youth and adult males to young Vietnamese or Eurasian girls whose presence could be conceived of as a sexual threat. Jean Star articulated the sexual charge surrounding labouring girls in the colonial home as they 'came of age.' Though the *bécon* may have been hitherto "kind, intelligent, bright, capable of loyalty,

> she transforms brusquely with puberty: with the age of loving and 'the age of lying,' as the quaint annamite adage suggests, disappear the agreeable qualities of childhood. It

is necessary then to dismiss her, as she is at an age when she can stand on her own two feet, and make her own way.[51]

As administrative elites shifted toward the formal proscription of taking *congaïs* (the term derived from the Vietnamese for 'little girl'), the *bécon*, on the brink of sexual maturity, became a conflict-ridden presence on the margins of the colonial family. Nevertheless, the practice of taking children and girls or young women into employment persisted. The tensions surrounding Vietnamese girl servants in the home found frequent expression in colonial literature. In the novel *Femmes d'outre-mer* by Charlotte Rouyer, for example, the author included an exchange between a young man in Saigon and his young French wife over precisely this issue:

> He: Why don't you take, to help you, a congaie as a chamberwoman? One of these good little women of sixteen or seventeen years old?
> She (without laughing): Yes, young and pretty.[52]

The presence of the *bécon* was also important in illustrating the more general tendency for parents to tolerate or even encourage cross-cultural entanglements between their own children and the Vietnamese and Eurasian girls serving in French homes. Thérèse de Hargues, the daughter of an employee of the Cartographic Service in Saigon, later described how she and her siblings found themselves able to develop close relations not only with their *bonne* but also with the cook's daughters, whom they grew up alongside in their home in Saigon. In her account de Hargues hints at the profundity of this exchange, remarking, "If we taught them a few western things they taught us much about the orient."[53]

Here as in other autobiographical accounts written by (often elderly) adults, childhood sometimes seems to appear as an experience defined by a rather rosy picture of interracial relations within the colonial home. Françoise Autret, the daughter of a pharmacist at the Institut Pasteur who lived in Hanoi from 1938, wrote of the domestic retinue in similar terms. She described

> the Boys who were always smiling for us and whose children and younger brothers were our companions in games. At our house, in Hanoi, Ngoh was truly a brother. He helped our Boy in the house and in the kitchen, but he always found the time to teach me all sorts of games. I could not conceive of life without him.[54]

This recollection is typical of the spate of similar retrospective reflections on childhoods in colonial contexts that have recently been published in that it appears to unreflexively expose colonial norms through the use of loaded terminology such as 'Boy.' Historians seeking to make reference to these memoirs and autobiographies must take considerable care for, as Rosalia Baena has recently argued, such accounts may seek to reinscribe or even justify imperialist or stereotypically orientalist views of empire. In its veneration of individual child-servants and the children of servants, this kind of literature may also service a politics of apology driven by an awareness of postwar discourses. Indeed, Baena suggests that some authors may even seek to exploit assumptions about their own childhood innocence and naïveté in order to challenge postcolonial readings of their own complicity with the discredited 'colonial project.' In effect writers of colonial autobiography appear to be attempting to 'set the record straight' by extrapolating on the basis of their experience of their own idyllic colonial childhoods.[55]

And yet these kinds of materials do offer the historian potentially profound insights into the colonial history of childhood. Though they certainly privilege the adult voice, memoirs offer deep and often carefully considered reflections on childhood selves. Even retrospective writings on childhood in empire, if used prudently, and if challenged, can be valuable. As Elizabeth Buettner has suggested, it is possible that through a 'connected reading' of common themes and strategies such sources may support revisionist perspectives reasserting the cultural agency of children. They can provide new insights into how social realities varied across empires.[56] Indeed, they may in particular allow us to gain new insights into the profoundly complex, mixed nature of colonial society and identity and thereby challenge narratives imposing homogeneous identities in places where these were transient at best.

The frequent patterns and similar references these accounts contain are suggestive of tendencies for personal ties to develop along lines of age, and across lines of race. Hierarchies obvious in other social contexts do appear to have broken down at times within colonial homes. The detailed and affectionate descriptions of social interactions with servants suggest that relations between children and servants may not necessarily have been dominated only by a casual, depersonalising racism. Indeed, with their emphasis upon fondness and reliance these accounts provide glimpses beyond the orientalist codings typically found in much colonial writing.

Some adults did attempt to reflect retrospectively upon the authenticity of the emotion that they were recalling as they sought to define these intimate interethnic links. Writing in this vein, Jacqueline Erbar, whose father was an army officer and who lived in Hanoi, recalled that at age ten in 1925,

> we thought that we were loved by... the congaies who served us... I will never forget the tears of Thi Ba—her letter received in France, written by a [professional] writer, and above all the outpourings of Thin, the cook, ... crying, holding his arms aloft, he cried and we felt despair.[57]

Looking back across the colonial divide, and given the flagrant racism of colonial Hanoi, the writer felt compelled to interrogate her own emotional memory and to question whether what she had experienced as love could really have been sincerely felt. In spite of this confusion she seems, in the end, to suggest not only that her feelings were sincere, but also that they were mutual.

This case helpfully demonstrates how age could serve as a pretext for the more flexible accommodation of behaviours otherwise considered transgressive or infra dig. In fact, so far could rules be bent that at times children's behaviour could present a significant challenge to adult domestics. Vietnamese women servants' livelihoods depended upon monitoring boundaries and managing children's conduct. As a surrogate authority over white children, these women faced up to the dual challenge of negotiating and enforcing racial boundaries, notably between French children and their own offspring (who might also be in residence within the boundaries of the home). This was a difficult and delicate enough task in the home, for French women were under pressure to stringently regulate such contact. One guide warned, "Be careful too that your residence is not transformed into a *caravansérail*, since your minions will soon introduce their wives, children, parents and friends if you do not put a stop to it."[58]

Transgressions that occurred beyond the home, in public places, in cities declared 'French,' perhaps posed even more of a challenge to domestics whose authority was circumscribed. European and Vietnamese children appear to have recognised this, as one account by Marie-Antoinette le Chanjour, whose father was a director of telegraphic services, suggests. Dining out on Sunday *en famille* (a custom among the French in Hanoi), she recalled:

> It was party time for us. We invited, to the horror of nanny, her children, there were four of them. They brought their food, and we supplemented it with our own, which they enjoyed. Then we played hide and seek ... Nounou [the nanny] was beside herself.[59]

This insight is intriguing given that in Hanoi, with its large administrative complex, hopes persisted that 'society' might be more directly influenced by the aristocratic model of the elite imperial administrator than in cramped, commercially oriented Saigon. In Hanoi the French initially lived clustered in the centre of the city around the Petit Lac, and in the decades that followed they spread out residentially into the three large boulevards to the south of the lake. In descriptions of her childhood in Hanoi from age eleven in 1937, Marie-Antoinette le Chanjour insisted that the atmosphere of the imperial capital for a child was quite stultifying, or akin to living in an 'ivory tower.'

Saigon, by contrast, was a place considered to afford more "direct contact between European populations and the indigenous mass."[60] Certainly, colonial town planning also imposed European patterns on Saigon, and residential patterns here were also dominated by segregation. On the grounds of the old Vauban-style citadel, razed in 1859, between Catinat Street and around the Botanical Gardens, an exclusive white residential quarter developed. Around the turn of the century this area—known as the Plateau—expanded, and in 1906–7, as new streets were laid out, indigenous accommodations were cleared on the pretext of sanitary improvement. Nevertheless, here, as one observer remarked, in contrast to Hanoi, "commerce trumps administration and money circulates easily; spirits are freer and [residents] could not care less about gossip."[61] Opportunities for impromptu contact in street space also existed for French children living in Saigon in the 1930s. Bernadette Jay played on her bicycle on the boulevard de la Somme and other streets around her home in the late 1930s, under the surveillance of her *congaï*. The bicycle provided far greater opportunity for movement than the auto-skiff she had received the previous year that "could neither be ridden on the cobblestones, nor the paved pathways."[62] Evidently she had tried both.

French children living in Indochina learned from adult society that there existed a spectrum of civility, distinguishing one neighbour, and neighbourhood, from another, but also defining the urban-rural divide. Many memoirs describe the sense of how controls over trans-ethnic contact loosened outside large urban centres. When Marie-Antoinette le Chanjour moved to Kiến An, between Hanoi and Hải Phòng, she and her siblings came into much more frequent contact with Vietnamese youth of their own age. Aside from occasional lessons with a Vietnamese tutor, and 'Mr. Do,' her piano teacher, the rest of the children's time was spent playing. Chanjour recalled:

> The children of the nine operators who worked with my father came to play with my brother, my sister and me. So until the age of 10 I had no contact with European children.

Marie-Antoinette le Chanjour participated in the festivities of the village in Kiến An, including the moon festival, and she even 'clandestinely' attended Vietnamese festivals for the dead.[63]

By contrast, in Hanoi, French children were more likely to be spectators than participants in such rituals, as in the case of Bernadette Jay, the young daughter of the railway engineer Antoine Jay, who was fascinated by the Vietnamese *fête des enfants* (an event akin to the Chinese Mid-Autumn Festival). As children grew older, parents rearranged their lives so they could access schools in large urban centres. As girls neared adolescence, parents also undertook a careful recalibration of their manners in order that they would be ready to move in 'society' and access the marriage market. So, for example, le Chanjour's parents moved back to Hanoi in the late 1930s so that their daughter might join the 'sixth' form at school (at age eleven). Her mother prepared her for her introduction into 'society' with reference to Blanche Soyer's *Usages du monde* (1891).[64]

Even in supposedly more orderly, mannered and 'imperial' Hanoi, however, Anglophone visitors were often struck by European children's public interactions with Vietnamese children. These appeared to be governed by somewhat different rules and expectations from those they claimed to have witnessed in British colonies (though as we have seen, the latter were far from uniform). The American travel writer Harry Franck, visiting Hanoi in the mid-1920s, expressed surprise at the opportunities for mixing across racial lines beyond the home in organised commercial entertainments for children. During a Guignol puppet show performance he observed, "There are not only French children with their amas in the front seats, and half-breed ones already posing as French, as they will through life, but purely native children as well." It was a scene lacking "any outward evidence of that racial dissonance emphasised in our own or British colonies."[65] Franck added:

> French boys are deferential and even obedient to half-breeds, even to well dressed natives, such as an American or English boy brought up in a colony would scorn to glance at. Native and Eurasian boys of Indo-China act toward white boys as if they quite expected to be accepted as their equals, though that attitude does not exactly hold among adults.[66]

While Franck may have had his own reasons for emphasising this contrast, the interactions he described, if they were accurate, were governed not by some overarching imperial logic but by the position of individuals and families within social networks on the ground. In French colonial settings, as we saw in the last chapter, the orthodoxy of the return home remained more heavily contested. Foreign residents of these centres often identified empire as *opportunity*, not only for themselves but also for their offspring. Among those described as *colons*, desires to contest administrators' claims to embodied elite norms persisted. Even among those recruited to the administrative cadres between the wars, markedly higher rates of pay and the *supplément colonial* offered inducements not to break families, but to make more insistent demands for the creation of authentically French milieux in Indochina. The sense of linguistic exchange as opportunity among a group keen to cling onto the privileges of colonial living may help to explain why injunctions against contact between domestic staff, such as the *bécon* and other youthful Vietnamese, and European children, remained intermittent and comparatively weak.

This is not to say that these aspirations eliminated anxieties surrounding interethnic contact altogether; far from it. The language of boys, coolies and *bécons* continued to be identified as having a deleterious effect upon the supposedly chaste ears of French children in the home. The administrator's daughter and novelist Christiane Fournier articulated this concern in her novel *Bébé colonial*. In this cautionary tale the main protagonist, the eponymous 'Bébé colonial,' befriends a young son of the cook (*bep*) and visits him in the *boyerie*, where he observes the 'correct' way to spit.[67] As Fournier's work suggests, misgivings over contact in and around the home certainly did not disappear.[68] Nevertheless, as the language surrounding the *bécon* indicates, while intimate unions between French men and Vietnamese women became a matter for secrecy in middle-class circles, colonials continued to identify childhood (though not adolescence) as a life stage with its own 'agreeable' qualities. This was a time of life when intimacy between children could still potentially flourish across the racial divide.

As we saw in the last chapter, in British-governed centres families' engagements with trans-colonial knowledge often led them to attempt to draw boundaries in social space in the name of their children. In turn-of-the-century Hong Kong, the rapidly burgeoning presence of women and children led ruling elites to advance demands for the racial segregation of entire neighbourhoods, notably the Peak Hill District Reservation (as we shall see in Chapter 6). Within this segregated space, adults expected their children to perform 'true' and happy childhoods. However, this performance was interpreted not as a wilful act but more as a natural illustration of the moral order of things. Helena May, whose husband was a senior colonial administrator in the Hong Kong government, accounted for her family's move to the Peak to the governor, Sir Matthew Nathan, in exactly these terms:

> I moved up here as soon as the house was painted and we are so glad we did so—this is a delicious place isn't it, so cool and lovely, and the garden is looking magnificent now with all the hydrangias in full bloom. The children love this place and they are very happy.[69]

That the stark reality of the colonial underpinnings of privilege apparently eluded May's young children in this setting should not surprise us. Though colonial homes were profoundly porous places, in British colonial culture children were quite intentionally to be kept 'innocent.'

Whilst Helena May's daughter Phoebe and her sisters participated fully in a sense of privileged abstraction, elite culture opened up new spaces and opportunities through which girls could assert mastery over their environment. The later writings of Dione Clementi, the twelve-year-old daughter of Sir Cecil Clementi (governor of Hong Kong 1925–30) and a resident of Hong Kong's Peak neighbourhood, are suggestive of this sense of elite privilege, and of adults' expectations of the kind of childhood children were to perform. But they also reflect a potentially disruptive sense of mobility and entitlement. As the governor's daughter wrote in a letter to Nathan:

> I like Hong Kong now as much as Ceylon. We have lovely bathing picnics here. It was a pity you came when Daddy was so busy and I was ill. Otherwise we might have gone and had nice picnics in the New Territory.[70]

Clementi's determination to picnic where she pleased is suggestive of a sense of agency, of an individual able to offer comparative insights into colonial living and to project her own desires onto the landscape, far beyond her home. It is also suggestive of her apparent belief that such a performance of young female selfhood was socially acceptable.

In other accounts a much stronger sense of colonial conditions as threatening—of a safe 'inside' and dangerous 'outside'—emerges. This sense often encouraged even privileged children to interpret adventures beyond the 'cordon sanitaire' of the Peak in terms of danger, and to define social interactions, with adults and children alike, in quite similar terms. In a period when European administrators and medical experts denigrated Chinese as outgrowths of a pathologised alien nature, and racially incapable of adopting modern hygienic codes, European children learned to read the bodies of Chinese children in congruent ways. Letters, as technologies of the self, formed boundaries within which children imagined enclosure. In autobiographical writing too there is a strong sense of drawing upon this tactic as a means of self-affirmation. For example, Phoebe May described a visit to the New Territories in the early 1900s in the following terms:

> As we passed through Chinese villages the children would come out and stare at us. They were so dirty that I did not like looking at them. Often they had sores on their faces, and running eyes.[71]

Though the May children longed to buy cakes and sweetmeats sold by Chinese street vendors when visiting downtown areas, they were unable to do so as parents or chaperones declared these goods unsafe to eat. French children who visited Hong Kong voiced their experiences in similar terms. Marguerite Fave, who travelled with her children to the British Crown Colony from French Indochina in the late 1930s, described how "we had the very strong impression of being in danger ... we remembered that we were told to be careful. ... It is not rare for Europeans to go missing."[72]

European children living in Hong Kong appear to have internalised this segregationist logic and to have deployed it in the context of play. Around the time the Mays were in residence on the Peak, one Eurasian family also lived there—that of the wealthy entrepreneur Sir Robert Ho Tung. Jean Gittins, Ho Tung's daughter (born 1908) later recalled that when she and her siblings played hopscotch or other games with European children on the Peak, "on occasion and without any apparent reason, the others might suddenly refuse to play with us because we were Chinese, or they might tell us that we should not be living on the Peak."[73] Gittins's recollection speaks powerfully to the bitter experience of growing up in a context defined by racial cant. Read against the grain, however, it is also suggestive of the tendency for white children to *inconsistently* apply racially segregationist rules, even on the Peak—the supposed epitome of antiassimilationist racial administration. Gittins's comment reveals the extent to which slippage could and did occur in and through play, in and around elite colonial homes.[74] With the recruitment of Chinese women in childcare roles, colonial homes remained spaces where parental discipline was inherently intermittent. Daily 'exposure' to non-European variants of childhood stood in flat and constant contravention of the fantasy of a neat divide.

Around the same time as European and Eurasian children were playing together on the Peak in Hong Kong, spaces within and around the colonial home also afforded children in Singapore opportunities for ungoverned interethnic interactions. Here, as pressure on land was somewhat less intense, European homes often featured gardens. These sometimes contained servants' quarters, either on a separate level of the same building or (more commonly in the Straits) within compounds. If the house was a space subdivided to reflect the psychological interior, the garden—an enclosed space embodying the domestication of nature, but also a link between the home and the world beyond—was another crucial referent of modernness.[75] However, in Singapore, as in Hanoi, the presence of servants, cooks, gardeners and chauffeurs (who were often married and in some cases were allocated outhouses or rooms in separate outbuildings) increased the likelihood that children might come into contact with servants' children. For some children the colonial home and compound became spaces of disorderly and trans-ethnic engagements, which young people themselves recognised as having a transgressive charge.

Lillian Newton lived in Tanglin in 1901. This was an elite neighbourhood, and to maintain this address her mother had to work full time. The desire to uphold social status thus had the unintended consequence of affording her daughter time and space, which she used to experiment with a variety of illicit behaviours within the garden compound. Lillian Newton sneaked into servants quarters, smoked cigarettes, observed Malay infant feeding methods and copied servant practices such as chewing sireh leaves with betel nut and lime. At a moment when European society in Singapore was more forcefully drawing boundaries around itself, Newton articulated the emerging sense of her own marginal status, both as a child and as a child who could not—unlike absent friends—fulfil the remit of 'true childhood,' that is, by not being present at all.[76]

Newton stood between two worlds, neither of which she fully understood. One was the increasingly exclusionary world of the boarding institution, where young male bachelors in residence scoffed at the infra dig behaviours of her and her mother (such as their attendance at philanthropic 'banana meetings,' as the boarders put it). The other was her school and the garden compound, sites of interethnic experiment and discovery. Newton was well aware of the sense of boundary crossing that accompanied her actions in the garden compound. Again, one is struck by the extent to which girls were apparently capable of and interested in asserting mastery over this space. Though youthful femininity was constructed in biological and cultural opposition to 'boyhood,' girls reveled in the study of nature and seized opportunities to experiment with socially unacceptable behaviors. And boys often described similar acts themselves.

Much later, in Malacca, Geoffrey Barnes recalled how on Sunday evenings when his parents had gone to church,

> the Tamil gardener and some of his friends would sometimes play wild games of 'kickball' with us in the garden. Ken and I loved these games, the more so perhaps because we suspected they would have been disapproved of if our parents had known.[77]

Others, like Blake Bromley, whose father was a schoolteacher living in Johor Bahru, just across the strait from Singapore, reflected, "there seemed to be few of the curbs that we would have experienced in England."[78]

In autobiographical accounts of childhood, as scholars have noted, the sun often shone and life was good. Such nostalgic reflections upon colonial living need to be treated with special care. Nevertheless, these depictions of life in the tropics are valuable in that they suggest ways in which adult attitudes toward childhood were shifting. By the 1930s, for example, parents do appear to have become more sceptical about claims for the tropical environment as having an inevitably degenerative impact upon their children. Later in the period, models of colonial childhood structured upon Victorian interiority began to look quite outdated, unhealthy even. As the modernist mantra of 'space, light and air' challenged the orthodoxy of protective enclosure, this logic exposed European children more to the outside environment. But older models could not easily be jettisoned because they were so tightly bound up with performances of racial identity and authority. Consequently, as tensions revived around the question of 'white settlement,' performing childhood in its vulnerable-domestic mode became still more crucial to elite efforts to defend established boundaries between European and Asian populations.

DELICATE DENIALS: CHILDHOOD EXPERIENCES OF DISEASE IN THE TROPICS

While opportunities for interethnic play could be minimised or sometimes supervised in domestic space, disease, with all of its racialised connotations of illness, often eluded control. As the dynamic, trans-colonial field of laboratory-based science generated new findings in the late nineteenth century, sickness emerged as a powerful point in common, connecting children across racial lines. Insights gleaned within the racialised space of the laboratory drove desires for new prophylactic methods capable of preventing disease transmission. Symptoms of disease, classified vaguely as 'fevers,' had long been seen as products of specific, climatologically defined spaces. The discovery of new disease aetiologies stimulated the rethinking of Asian populations, who were condemned as unable to live up to European hygienic standards and came to be seen as 'reservoirs' of disease.[79] And yet earlier understandings of endangerment based upon medical geography and climatology were not completely eclipsed. Indeed, the ongoing overlap and confusion between the two heightened the sense of childhood as crucial to the clear definition of racial boundaries.

In Hong Kong, Singapore and other contexts, childhood had come to be closely linked to moral reform. In effect, the colonial childhood rested upon theories of disease conflating physical and moral health and dirtiness. These produced the Chinese child as distinct, as the quote from Phoebe May above illustrates. With purity under threat, from outside and inside, ideal childhood required displacement beyond the impure. Prophylactic measures intended to control microbes, pathogens and disease vectors focused upon the invasive agency of the Asian (and Eurasian) child. The resulting interventions underpinned assumptions that 'public' health was secured in domestic spaces. But paradoxically, as this view of childhood was elaborated trans-colonially, it produced efforts toward the hygienic regulation of the home in British contexts that were notably less didactic than in Saigon and Hanoi.

Understandings of indigenous peoples' deficient sanitary practices, defined as racial-cultural in origin, left some European children uneasy about their role as sickly exemplars of European vulnerability.[80] Autobiographies and reminiscences of childhood suggest that both boys and girls fashioned a response highlighting the sickness of the *indigène* and used this to challenge assumptions of their own status as normatively sick. Encounters with disease left its sufferers marked by a 'double degeneracy.' Inasmuch as disease was understood as a process of physical and moral degeneration, European children's insistence that indigenous children and not they themselves were contagious agents was a quite deliberate strategy. While their own vulnerability undergirded racial authority, those expected to embody these ideals rejected the professional 'medicalisation' of their bodies.

A related strategy involved reading sickness back into the plain. In 1904, Phoebe May, the nine-year-old daughter of acting governor Henry May, fell ill with pneumonia. She later recalled being

> ill so long that my hair had to be cut off. I felt quite a different child when I got up. Unfortunately I was now classified as delicate and had to rest a lot and take Parish's Food through a glass tube. I was teased about this and nicknamed 'Little Weaky' much to my disgust.[81]

The practice of cutting off hair (and usually burning it) followed the diagnosis of disease and symbolised approaching death.[82] May's disgust is interesting, for it shows how girls resisted the ascriptions of weakness that figured their childhoods so prominently in empire. Instead of corroborating such claims, in practice they filled correspondence with accounts of survival and of lucky escapes from the clutches of death. Instead of dignifying disease they diminished it. To do so they used their own vocabulary—referring to 'goes' of 'fever,' or 'feeling poor thingish'—not that of the doctors. Their desires to downplay illness transformed the term 'sickly' into an insult. This sensibility connected girls on the Peak to others in humbler settings. Lillian Newton, for example, who caught malaria in 1915 and remained ill for three years, recorded her recovery as personal triumph. When in July 1920 Hong Kong's English-language newspaper *The China Mail* added a 'Children's Corner' column edited by 'Peter Pan,' the editor remarked upon how often children of both sexes wrote to him with tales of having defied illness. Such an observation is perhaps unsurprising given the extent to which otherness had been pathologised and symbolised through images of disease in the Western colonial imaginary.[83]

By diminishing the threat of disease in the home and fashioning accounts of danger and violence beyond it, children forged links between the domestic realm and that of nature and adventure. While downplaying their vulnerability to disease, children *over*emphasised the dangers of their environment by way of underlining their own nonchalance and bravado in the face of suffering. Girls as well as boys adopted the language of fairy stories to conjure a sense of mastery over colonial space. Their writings were in this way linked with more general literary forms of collective imagination. Journals and diaries reflected more than individual selves. They were spaces in which children publicly projected achievement, inventiveness and expressions of other potentially disruptive selves. When prepared for an adult audience, the ways in which children wrote were often suggestive of not only individual pathology but a self-conscious desire to meet what they thought were adults' expectations of how childhood should be performed. Thus Dione Clementi wrote:

> We had a small typhoon here last Sunday, . . . It wasn't very strong but it came so suddenly that quite a lot of junks were sunk and many people drowned. It is much more exciting living in Hong Kong than in Ceylon; where you never have typhoons. Besides, there are the pirates . . . If we had looked out of one of Mountain Lodge's windows at the right moment, we might have seen the pirate launch.[84]

Through such reflections children entered into a dialogue with adult colonials. They asserted claims to be coparticipants in a shared culture of stoicism and thus to equal membership of the elect. Others emphasised physical trials, notably the hot climate (Edwin Ride later recalled his early childhood in Hong Kong in the 1930s as a "listless daze"), to similar effect.[85] By doing so, children imagined themselves, and sought to present themselves, as part of a unified self.

In Hanoi and Saigon misgivings about children's place in the colonial home combined with stronger desires to project medical expertise into it. But these misgivings also clashed in some quarters with hopes of a radical, productive 'creolisation' through contact with Asian cultures. As we have seen, expectations of 'French colonial childhood' ranged between extremes of instant death and regenerative fecundity. The exact boundaries of the ideal childhood inside and outside the home remained correspondingly obscure. In Saigon and particularly Hanoi, the French child was not quite the carefree 'sprite' of the British hill station, or even the Singapore garden compound. A stronger sense of antipathy toward constraints placed upon youthful agency and toward parents' efforts to curtail girls' freedom of action in particular emerges from many retrospective reflections. Suzanne Prou, a soldier's daughter who spent her childhood in Tonkin in the 1920s, described quite deliberately discarding her *casque* and evading the required afternoon siesta in order to surreptitiously explore the garden compound while her parents slept. She recalled how, when the siesta was over,

I submitted to the constraints imposed upon children, without resentment: for those who ordered me about, who imposed their adult will upon me, did not know that I was queen of a marvellous kingdom and that I possessed land in the form of this garden that they . . . never dreamt of exploring, which they saw as nothing more than a feature on the horizon.[86]

The 'modernness' of the French child continued to be refracted through its relationship with a more open-ended, scientifically informed process, and the constraints this imposed. Doubts remained as to whether French children could even live up to expectations of performing exemplary childhood, though that could not be consensually defined.

The private lives of British children were also ideally set in secluded homes and gardens, but the weight of adults' expectations made squaring private with public dimensions of the French child's social identity more of a challenge. The sense of a more extended commitment, the lack of a similar commitment to the colonial 'best before' date and the sense of the metropole more as a regular rather than as a definitive panacea may explain why French children's encounters with illness in Indochina tended to be defined by a quite different, and noticeably less stoic, vernacular. By way of illustration, Marguerite Fave's son, Pierre, declared one day after a journey from Saigon to Nha Trang, "Mother . . . I want to die! When I don't have a stomachache I have a headache. When I don't have a headache I have a sore throat or ear. Yes, I believe that I would be better off dead!"[87] Notions of youth spent in the tropics as an unrecognised and underappreciated sacrifice surfaced repeatedly in colonial literature into the late 1930s. Christiane Fournier, who had grown up in Hanoi, portrayed the colonial doctor as an effete, ineffectual and unfeeling presence before the inert form of the sick child.[88] In one scene from her novel the author described the "dance of the little colonial children, whose bodies are a little cadaverous, their faces a little haggard, in spite of the cold lash of the Tonkin winter."[89] Far from being robust these children were inveterate sufferers of a "colonial anaemia which France itself could not cure."[90]

Colonial childhoods were inevitably ephemeral. The horizons of return loomed large, even for those forced to remain. The latter stared into the gulf between unrealised ideals of the future and the ticking clock of the colonial present. As they did, children articulated the sense that going 'Home' entailed being torn from a privileged existence, or possession. Children usually (but not always) had little say in their eventual aetiologies. Those not permitted to remain entered into a lively dialogue with adults upon the issue of departure. This experience appears in much writing as an emotional caesura. Though ethnic-national affiliations, departure points and destinations may have been quite different, children leaving colonial Asia often wrote about their experience in strikingly similar terms.

In 1905 Helena May boarded a ship destined for England accompanied by her children. She was looking forward to the trip, for her daughter Phoebe had finally reached an age at which May felt she would be able to more fully appreciate the joys of 'Home.' However, the children soon made their ambivalence about this move quite clear. May was horrified to note that "whenever we passed a ship bound for Hong Kong my children said how they wished they could go back in it."[91] Once in the metropole the May children wrote to Sir Matthew Nathan insisting, "We like being in England very much, but it is not nearly so nice as Hong Kong."[92] The experience of the return home revealed that colonial living had led these children, like many others, to project their affinities in the 'wrong' direction. Writing of the experience many years later, Phoebe Whitworth (née May) recalled: "When I was six we went home to England on a year's leave. . . . This was my first visit to England since I was a baby and I found it very disappointing."[93] Such feelings of disappointment upon return were quite common. Elite children often experienced the return 'Home' as an inversion of the expectation that greater age would bring more and not less power, autonomy and authority.

The same was true for French children residing in Hong Kong. Marguerite Marty, a young relative of the French shipping magnate A R. Marty (whose company had offices in Hong Kong and Hải Phòng), wrote from her boarding school in Bezons, near Paris, "I regret [sic] very much Hong-Kong."[94] 'My Indochina,' 'my Singapore' and 'my Hong Kong' crop up regularly in correspondence and reminiscences alike. These remembered places were often idyllic spaces. The return home was by contrast traumatic. This sensibility dominates autobiographical writing on empire in French and English. But it also pervaded contemporary commentary, to the alarm of many a parent.[95]

Expressions of regret strongly reflected the sense that these children had made colonial space 'their own,' through taking risks, exploring opportunities for self-assertion and in some cases by building alliances across racial lines. Through such counter-narratives children contested adults' claims for their vulnerability and being fundamentally *out of place*. Such writings fit within a set of accounts and practices resisting return, emphasising rootedness and a deep sense of connection with the land in early childhood. However, children were also sensitive to adults' perceptions of the degenerative, decivilising impact of colonial living. Adults' desires to reassert middle-class credentials lurk in accounts of childhood experiences, especially those of 'displacement' from colonial space. The journey home, the ocean liner, became a context in which difficult lessons were learned and children were prepared for more convincing performances of civility. And they sought to negotiate these adult anxieties by laying claim to membership, in spite of their age, to the ideal colonial 'self.'

Very often children read genres of colonial literature in which boys and not girls emerged as adventurers-in-chief. However, in colonial space, as we have seen, gender norms permitted girls the right to reside for longer. For this reason, many surviving reflections on colonial childhood feature the voices of girls and women.

Staying on longer, being older, they often possessed greater capacity for mature reflection than did boys. Very often it was girls who were the ones recasting vulnerability in terms of mastery. They dramatised self-control and stoicism as enabling control not of domestic space, but of wider realms beyond. In all of these places, the contours of a 'colonial girlhood' seem to have begun to emerge around desires to contest the special burden of fragility that girls were expected to embody. The sense in British colonial cultures that boys were *more* unequivocally endangered helped to reinforce this. For as risk-taking agents some girls reconceptualised their lives using different scripts of girlhood, and experimented by enacting the supposedly masculine traits of the scientist and adventurer. In 1914, during her own (temporary) return 'Home' to an England she did not know (and which she found cold and confining), Lillian Newton wondered, "Was it Home to me?" And in this melancholy frame of mind she drew strength from the contrasting ignorance she observed among metropolitan youth on matters she, the 'jungle fowl,' considered herself an authority, such as her ability to name a wide variety of species of tropical plants and animals.[96]

CONCLUSION

Scholars have identified a late-nineteenth-century shift in European colonial society toward introspection drawn around the child, family and simulacra of 'Home.' However, as we have seen in all of these centres, children's lives were interpenetrated on a day-to-day basis by local and global forces. European children lived out colonial childhoods at the interstices of scientific orthodoxies, elite norms and local milieux, between a sense of privilege and precariousness. However, children were never only 'at risk.' They were also 'risk takers.' In colonial homes young people ascribed their own meanings to life stages and spaces. They defined their sense of being young in relation to situated entanglements with indigenous children, nursemaids, schoolmates, servants and others. In consequence, the presence of children was one that, paradoxically, opened communities up to new and different influences. These ranged across a spectrum from the delicate forging of contacts across lines of ethnicity to full-blown hybridity, and children navigated their position in accordance with their social circumstances and degree of confinement. Establishing new worlds of interiority—within carefully established boundaries of house and home—required the resolution of a variety of other challenges relating to contact with colonial space. Because the solutions applied could not prevent porosity, colonial cultures of childhood were, in practice, to use Shirley Geok-lin Lim's turn of phrase, "mixed, discontinuous, disruptive," and rarely "assimilable to constructions of homogeneous cultural identities."[97]

In elite sections of British colonial communities a generally clearer consensus surrounded childhood, one exemplified by the orthodoxy of early departure. This had two consequences. First, it created leeway for children to challenge tropes of vulnerability and to experiment with transgressive behaviours, and second, it presented them with a somewhat more coherent set of adult assumptions against which they defined their own emerging sense of subjectivity. In French centres, by contrast, the upper limit of childhood was never as unambiguously affirmed or as stringently policed. Rival interpretations of the imperial future engendered disjunctive visions of colonial childhood. French children thus spoke back to a more multivalent and less consensual culture, making it more difficult to discern clear patterns in their response.

However, in practice, in all of these centres childhood failed to emerge as a site of consensus, not least owing to the actions of children themselves. Adults nonetheless remained tantalised by the iconic power of childhood in empire. For this category held out the promise of tying together fractured and fissiparous trans-colonial communities of empire. This is why, before the First World War, adults made remarkable investments in the projection of visions of it beyond the colonial home and into public space, through a remarkable set of new child-centric rituals. And it is to these that we shall turn our attention in the next chapter.

CHAPTER 4

Magic Islands: Children on Display in Colonialisms' Cultures

As we have seen, across empires during the late nineteenth century children were becoming integral to the refashioning of cultures of colonialism and to the investment of the European presence in the tropics with higher purpose. New elite-generated visions and practices of colonial childhood emerged from the late nineteenth century within the carefully established boundaries of homes and gardens. However, the production of childhood did not stop at the confines of the colonial home; it also played out in full public view. From the late nineteenth century childhood was projected forcefully out into public places of British and French colonial centres in Asia. There it connected with projects launched from within the colonial state.[1] This chapter reveals how the urban public sphere emerged as a crucial site upon which elite ideals of childhood were acted out and children projected connotations of cultural authority and prestige beyond the 'intimate' domain of the home. It shows how exemplary childhoods went mobile and children took centre stage in colonial space, in a set of new rituals, representations and invented traditions serving a variety of interests.

One of these interests was the fashioning of a more coherent sense of 'community' around the nation. Those living in colonial centres did not automatically regard themselves as a national community with some common political destiny. Rather, such perceptions had to be carefully cultivated. Children provided a focus around which desires for unity and for the nation could be expressed in places where these were perpetually under threat. As active participants in performances of ideal childhoods they inscribed and sustained the connective tissues linking communities across empires. In British Empire centres, such as Singapore and Hong Kong, as we shall see, foreign residents latched onto new traditions developing from Christmas rituals and fairy tales to fashion a sense of common purpose through a shared, public culture of childhood. In French centres, such as Hanoi and Saigon, conflict over key questions such as settlement and what empire was for in the midst of the shift toward a purportedly 'associative' genre of colonialism influenced public presentations of childhood. Provocative visions of French settler children jostled alongside new official visions of Vietnamese childhood. Across empires, these rituals metamorphosed, at times facilitating the brokering of partnerships across ethnic-racial lines, at others serving exclusionary, didactic aims. The public roles that children assumed as embodiments and symbols of authority became all the more important in a period marked by intensifying imperial rivalry and a growing sense of British and French vulnerability.

CHRISTMAS IN THE TROPICS: CHARLES BUCKLEY AND THE 'SINGAPORE TREAT'

In 1864 Charles Burton Buckley, the twenty-year-old son of the Reverend John Wall Buckley of St. Mary's Church in Paddington, London, arrived in Singapore. One of the many things Buckley found surprising as he settled into his new environs was that in this part of the British Empire children enjoyed no organised Christmas 'Treat.' In England by this time the Christmas holiday was identified as *the* national holiday, and it had developed from a celebration of *a* child into a celebration of childhood. The close associations forged between childhood and the nation through this holiday emerged from an experience of urban industrialism that reconfigured attitudes to age in Britain.[2]

Christmas emerged as a break in the rhythms of industrial capitalism, as a kind of 'time out of time' during which men retreated from public into the home to celebrate the higher values embodied by the child.[3] From the mid-nineteenth century, middle-class ideology separated childhood from adulthood and recast it as proof of the divine as families limited fertility and reforms moved children out of the workplace and into schools. While childhood became less economically valuable, it was sacralised, becoming, as Viviana Zelizer puts it, "emotionally priceless."[4] With this, images of children gained new iconic power. These appeared in a variety of new rituals and invented traditions, and in particular celebrations of the Yule.

In January 1861 F. R. Kendall, an agent for the Peninsular and Oriental Steam Navigation Company resident in Singapore observed, "No one here seems to take an interest in Christmas somehow. . . . There is nothing to remind one of the season at all."[5] When Charles Buckley organised his first Christmas gathering a few years later it drew only twenty participants, mostly from his small Sunday school class at St. Andrew's Church. However, the celebration soon began to attract wider interest. Buckley's philanthropic gesture resonated among members of the small merchant-dominated community as it gave greater public prominence to a certain idea of British leadership and civil values at a moment when Singapore's elite was seeking to draw closer to London. Singapore had long been an Indian dependency, but by the mid-1860s its merchants were petitioning London for separate Crown Colony status. Before the onset of formal colonial rule in 1867 the shared ambition to break free of rule by the East India Company sustained the early development of collaborative interethnic relations between European elites, Chinese merchants (*towkay*) and English-speaking 'Straits Chinese.' In Singapore, permanent communities of Chinese (mainly of Hokkien descent) predated formal British rule, as did the 'Peranakan,' Malay-speaking ancestors of early migrants from Penang and Malacca. Though they had resided in port cities of Asia for centuries and married into Malay communities, this group retained aspects of Chinese identity. However, many Chinese emigrants who settled also became part of an Anglophone community and took on key roles in the growing administrative and commercial life of the city. For example, Chinese merchants emerged as members of government boards and voluntary institutions and as justices of the peace. The Singapore Chamber of Commerce, the only formal organisation of the early colonial period, created in February 1837 to communicate with the London government, was open to all.[6]

The marshalling of 'Christmas children' in public offered a means of fashioning a sense of empire as collaborative venture, or shared purpose, reordered in accordance with middle-class Christian principles in the face of fragmentation. It competed for attention with a remarkable range of other rituals and processions, from military marches accompanying the changing of barracks to Hindu, Malay and Chinese festivals. However, amid this ferment Buckley's celebration exemplified ideals of Anglican charity, as well as authority, instrumental civilisation, discipline and duty. It also marked the celebrants as distinct from other organisers of Christian social provision (a field dominated by Portuguese and French missionary associations). And it chimed with desires to claim authority through culture at a time when Christmas was emerging as a valuable set-piece celebration of the nation across the British Empire.

'Buckley's Treat,' as it came to be known, was far from being the only Christmas event for children in Singapore, but it soon achieved a remarkable level of public prominence. Buckley gradually scaled up this 'civic' ritual until it became one of the largest events in Singapore's social calendar; and it remained so for decades. Usually staged on the evening of Boxing Day, in the Town Hall or other principal public buildings, by the end of the century it drew audiences of more than a thousand and lavish praise from the newspaper press. Ultimately, three generations of Singapore residents would come to know or participate in the event. And by the last quarter of the century Buckley had become a well-known figure, as much for his organisation of the Treat as for his editorship of the *Singapore Free Press* or for his claims to be the 'historian of Singapore.'

From its early years the Treat featured theatrical performances. These were based loosely around Jacob and Wilhelm Grimm's fairy tales and were performed by children.[7] However, in 1887 Buckley dispensed with German fairy stories and instead spent months writing and producing his own original 'fairy plays.' As Walter Makepeace later observed, Buckley "always succeeded in producing something which had not been seen before, and always pointing up some patriotic sentiment or illustrating some point in the history of Singapore or the Empire's best men."[8] The first such production was an event entitled "The Talisman of the Enchanted Island." When the curtains rose at the Town Hall in 1887, the audience marvelled at the performance of a cast of more than seventy children. This included a climactic final scene featuring three small child-fairies winched up and 'flying' above the stage, their costumes illuminated by electric lights rigged up to cables run from the offices of the Telegraph Company. An awestruck crowd looked on as scores of children chorused from the stage:

> And this our tale of Sailor and Princess,
> In depths of time, shall bring it sweet success;
> Until our Isle, Enchanted then no more,
> Will to the world be known as Singapore;
> A Magic Island still, its Magic then,
> The energy and work of Englishmen.[9]

In Buckley's spectaculars Singapore often appeared as a magic island or 'fairyland.' And by fashioning Singapore into an 'Enchanted Isle'—a place and time out of time—his work appeared distinct from other celebrations of the Yule in British Asia. Elsewhere, residents often complained of the melancholy results of the entanglement of Yuletide tradition with a pathologised 'Tropical' nature. In India, for example, a little earlier, Emily Eden, sister of Governor General Lord Auckland, complained of the *Indianness* of Christmas, while the *Times of India* found it a depressing reminder of exile.[10] Buckley, by contrast, looked to children to lift audiences beyond such melancholy reflection.

The child participants who performed in Buckley's Treat were a strikingly mixed group. Both audience and performers were composed mainly of English-speaking children attending schools notable for their ethnic plurality. Many were Straits Chinese and Eurasian. By the turn of the century, by way of illustration, of the 2,078 boys attending English-language boys' schools in Singapore, 429 (or 20%) were 'European and Eurasian,' 81 were Malay, 1,432 were Chinese and 136 were Indian. In the girls' schools there were 402 (86%) Europeans and Eurasians, 1 Malay, 50 (11%) Chinese and 16 Indians and 'others.'[11] While Buckley's romantic vision of cultural leadership by children tapped ideals of the family and the sacral resonance of childhood in British middle-class culture, it also projected these across ethnic lines.

The Treat powerfully and prominently associated Singapore with a timeless, placeless fairy lore of childhood in both subject matter and 'special effects' while also showcasing new technologies such as electrification. News of the event spread, and it fit within an emerging culture of interport rivalry linking merchant communities from India to Singapore, to Hong Kong and Shanghai, articulated through claims to host the superior Christmas.[12] By the 1880s, as more European children and families were moving out to and passing through Singapore, they carried knowledge of the Treat with them through empire networks running out to other centres in Southeast Asia and along the China coast. The Treat was only one of many Christmas events for children run by associations and schools across the British Empire, but its scale raised awareness among mobile Europeans in Asia of the potential of public displays of Christmas children in the fairy play mode. In the following decades the event informed the elaboration of colonial norms of childhood in public that were essentially connective, comparative and trans-colonial, as the case of Hong Kong illustrates.

WILD PROCEEDINGS: HONG KONG'S 'FAIRYLAND' AND THE MINISTERING CHILDREN'S LEAGUE

Two years after Buckley's first performance of the "Enchanted Island," the aristocratic Anglo-Irish travel writer, Lewis Strange Wingfield departed Singapore for Hong Kong. On the evening approach into Victoria Harbour he was so moved by the sight of the mass of tiny lights that pocked the island that he described the Crown Colony as "the nearest thing to the wildly unorthodox proceedings of fairyland."[13] Many of the lights Wingfield observed emanated from European-style villa residences recently constructed on the upper reaches of Victoria Peak. On 30 May 1888 a funicular tramline had opened, allowing passengers to move easily from the town to the 'Peak' above. A new elite neighbourhood was emerging in the heights. From here, in the following decade, elite British residents would project new rituals of childhood so pervasive that the colony itself would come to be referred to as 'fairyland.'

While Buckley's "Enchanted Island" was wowing Singapore society, Christmas celebrations in Hong Kong still turned upon humdrum rounds of toasts in homes, churches and mess rooms.[14] But as the elite neighbourhood on the Peak developed, Christmas celebrations centred increasingly upon European child residents. The number of children jumped sixfold in Hong Kong in a decade, and the number of residents under age fifteen on the Peak nearly doubled from 1891 to 1897, from 49 to 87.[15] William Goodwin, attorney general of Hong Kong and a Victoria Peak resident, noted "a great many juvenile parties" around the Yule, which he had been known to attend dressed as Father Christmas.[16] In 1904 the Hong Kong government secured the Hill District reservation as a racial enclave, ostensibly to defend 'vulnerable' European women and children. Around the same time, new child-centric rituals, centring upon dramatised productions of 'fairyland,' emerged.[17] These attracted such support from both official and unofficial interest groups in Hong Kong's European society that they broke beyond the confines of seasonal celebrations and spread throughout the colony's social calendar.

A key figure in the creation and dissemination of this 'fairyland' was Sir Matthew Nathan, the governor of Hong Kong. Nathan's reputation as an engineer and administrator paved the way for him to take up the governorship in summer 1904, but he soon came to be known as a leading promoter of what contemporaries termed the 'aesthetic of childhood.' Nathan announced his intent soon after his arrival by hosting a party attended by ninety children at Mountain Lodge, the governor's summer residence, late in August 1904.[18] In the years that followed, he personally arranged gatherings, attended birthday celebrations and showered gifts upon the children of the so-called Hill District Reservation.[19] Youthful participants in this burgeoning scene, such as the daughters of Henry May, referred to Sir Matthew as their 'fairy godfather.'[20] When Nathan announced his departure from the colony in 1907, the entrepreneur Sir Ellis Kadoorie declared, "Not only we who have known him but our children also will always remember him with affectionate regard."[21]

Fairy plays organised and run by families living on the Peak were particularly important to this celebration of childhood. On 27 December 1904, just a few months after the passage of the Peak Reservation ordinance, J. M. Barrie's *Peter Pan* had opened in London before a capacity audience, and the famous line, "Do you believe in fairies?" had resounded through the stalls. Sir Matthew Nathan was so fond of young Peak residents' performances of Lewis Carroll's *Alice through the Looking Glass* and *Alice's Adventures in Wonderland* that he insisted on addressing the children of his senior officials by the names of the books' principal characters.[22] By publicly foregrounding childhood in the fairy play format, what Nathan and others did in Hong Kong, as Buckley had in Singapore, was to pick up on missionaries' earlier and ongoing incitements to childhood as an embodiment of racial, domestic and religious purity while at the same time producing newer, idealised visions of the child. They looked not to the Bible but instead to this new national literary and theatrical canon, adapting the works of Charles Kingsley, Lewis Carroll and J. M. Barrie in particular to their needs.[23]

Fairy tales had come to prominence rather later in Britain than in France and Germany, in the first half of the nineteenth century. Such stories offered new vantage points from which to question the 'progress' delivered by rational utilitarianism and the seemingly irresistible advance of the market.[24] By the 1880s, as literacy among children expanded in the wake of state education reform and commercial innovations such as 'children's pages' in provincial newspapers, Socialist educators began to integrate fairy tales into school curricula. These educators drew upon the ideas of German pedagogues such as Friedrich Fröbel, a student of Johann Heinrich Pestalozzi who had emphasised teaching through play. These theorists emphasised childhood as separate, natural and a context for the romantic imagination.[25] In empire this new child-centric aesthetic provided a focal point around which cultural authority and a sense of colonial prestige or noblesse could be publicly built.

Fairyland's architects directed their affective energies toward sympathy with the child, in effect a preformed self. They thereby highlighted the superior values of self-sacrifice that the veneration of childhood supposedly connoted.[26] As one resident of Hong Kong's elite Peak neighbourhood, Eleanor Hastings, explained to Sir Matthew Nathan, "I do not think that there is in this world a happier quality to possess—for children's love at least is unfeigned and without *arrière pensée* of any kind."[27] Hastings's view is also suggestive of how Nathan's energy connected with wider aspirations among Hong Kong's fragmented European 'community' to produce the moral power of childhood for public consumption. Child-fairies were assumed to elevate their beholders above what foreign residents disparaged as the grubby individualism, mechanism and institutional rationalism of the colonial port city. But those charmed were many of the same individuals profiting from the unfettered and rapacious flow of capital in the 'Chinese city' below. Appreciation of this aesthetic served as a salve. It allowed for self-congratulation, mutual recognition and community building around claims for the common guardianship of 'civility.' It provided a rare, shared source of values connecting individuals who could often agree on little else.[28]

In Britain modern thinking about childhood had transformed middle-class homes, producing new domestic spaces aligned with consumption, such as the nursery. But in empire, fairyland was projected out beyond such disciplining domestic spaces. Significantly, from there it also looped back into the intimate domain of children's play. So, for example, the daughters of Helena May, whose husband Francis Henry May was a senior officer in the colonial administration, dubbed a small cave that they discovered on the Peak 'the fairy dell' and used it to store treasures that they found whilst out on walks.[29]

By 1909 the cultural motif of 'fairyland' had become so prevalent that Amos P. Wilder, the US consul, invited guests at a banquet to toast Hong Kong with the words, "Little children have clapped their hands with glee at the fairy land."[30] Fairyland—where every child was an island separate from the adult world and from its own adult self—had broken free of the confines of the older paternalistic Christmas treats. It had come to stand, mimetically, for the island colony writ large, within its imperial archipelago.[31] It proved particularly valuable in Hong Kong for several reasons. First, 'British Hong Kong' had not been secured by treaty, like Singapore, but annexed through war. As British sovereign territory in China it was an anomaly, and in the eyes of some an affront. Whatever liberal idealism may have existed among early settlers rubbed along uneasily with the more overtly carceral and didactic dimensions of British rule. Conflict with China, instability across the border and repeated population influxes engendered a sense of insecurity among Europeans that translated into close controls over the Chinese population.[32] The social character of British colonialism in consequence became more exclusive, earlier, here than in Singapore. And in Hong Kong the central infrastructure of courts, military base and barracks emerged early as a highly visible spatial cluster manifesting British power, at a time when visitors to Singapore could still remark on the relative lack of any similar 'public' architecture.

While a more confrontational style also marked colonial administration in Hong Kong, so too did a more intense interethnic rivalry. For example, Chinese 'secret societies' were banned in Hong Kong only four years after the founding of the colony, but much later, in 1890, in Singapore. A European-dominated General Chamber of Commerce was founded in Singapore in 1861, but no Chinese chamber of commerce existed in Hong Kong until 1896. Chinese secured representation on the Straits Settlements governing body in 1869. By contrast, the first Chinese unofficial representatives, Ng Choy and Wong Shing, joined Hong Kong's Legislative Council only in the 1880s.

This experience of being governed, coupled with the fact that the return home was comparatively easy, inclined Chinese in Hong Kong to display less loyalty toward colonial officialdom than in Singapore, where generations of residents had by the late nineteenth century developed an affinity with the place. However, by the late nineteenth century the prevalence of coercive forms of governance led elites, notably Governor John Pope Hennessy, to openly question their strategic value. Those keen to forge grounds for an enduring partnership with rising Chinese elites in Hong Kong looked to new methods. It was essential that the ruling elite assert the moral dimensions of power if they were to validate claims for the Crown Colony as a supposed showcase of British civility *in China*. In European eyes, the public production of childhood offered another means of countering criticisms of imperial power as morally indefensible. By the late nineteenth century such criticisms had grown more strident, emanating not only from Chinese but also from British metropolitan sources, following recent exposés of the 'coolie trade,' the opium trade and child labour. After reform began in China from 1898 (by 1906 the Government of China was issuing edicts for the suppression of opium consumption and production), the existence of opium dens in Hong Kong left the British colonial government vulnerable to allegations of a reactionary and uncivilised overlordship. This was an ongoing problem at the start of a new century in which it was becoming clear that the success or failure of British imperialism would depend less on military power and more upon cultural hegemony.

"NO DAY WITHOUT A DEED TO CROWN IT": THE MINISTERING CHILDREN'S LEAGUE

Sir Matthew Nathan played the Buckley role as 'Friend of the Children' with aplomb in Hong Kong, but fairyland's true foot soldiers were a new generation of colonial women. 'Fairyland' in the tropics could hardly have achieved such wide cultural influence without institutional underpinnings linking it into wider empire networks. Imbued with an evangelical sense of duty, philanthropically minded women drew upon empire-wide networks and put their own children centre stage as they pushed fairyland beyond its heartlands on Victoria Peak. A key institution here was the Ministering Children's League, and it was to have a profound and long-lasting impact upon colonial society and culture in the empire centres of East and Southeast Asia. An important figure in its history in Asia was Helena May.

The daughter of Lieutenant General Digby Barker, British commanding officer in China and Hong Kong (1890–95), Helena May, was a longtime resident of Hong Kong. She had met and married her husband, Henry May (a former cadet), in the colony in August 1891. Summering in England in 1901, Helena May had attended the annual meeting of the Ministering Children's League (MCL) at the invitation of Mrs. Harrington Balfour of the Finsbury and Camberley branch. The league's creator was Mary Jane Brabazon, the Countess of Meath. Lady Meath established the league on 10 January 1885, and her motives for doing so were much in line with wider concerns among the educated metropolitan women of her generation to address the linked dilemmas of growing secularisation, crushing poverty and a politically dangerous class divide.

Far from confining themselves to domestic interiors, educated women were at this time taking an increasingly prominent role in public.[33] In British elite culture new notions of childhood, sentimentalised and sacralised, were an accompaniment to the domestic ideal of womanhood. The stark contrast between this elite norm and the 'waifs and strays,' 'hooligans' or 'street arabs' who could not live up to it galvanised a flurry of action intended to improve the condition of poor children. Evangelical reformers increasingly saw their own children as adjuncts in a battle to reverse the secularisation of society, and to raise its moral tone. The initiatives of middle-class organisers such as the Boys' Clubs and Institute movement that had emerged in London in the 1870s and the Boys' Brigade (1883) reflected the desire to tap the energies of children and to address the yawning class divide. Some feared that if evangelical zeal did not infect the younger generation of 'smart little children,' momentum would be lost.

Decades before, Maria Louisa Charlesworth, the daughter of an evangelical clergyman, had authored *Ministering Children: A Tale Dedicated to Childhood* (1854). This didactic text was intended to train children in developing kindly feelings toward the poor. The book sold 170,000 copies and remained in print for decades. Charlesworth retired to Surrey, the home of the Countess of Meath, and the book inspired Meath to start up a league of the same name. Meath ran the league from her own home in London and its chief aim was to elicit sympathy among elite children for those less fortunate than themselves. Unsectarian but evangelical and philanthropic, the league quickly burgeoned. By 1893 it was already a vast international organisation with forty thousand members in Britain, the United States and Canada, Australia, South Africa and New Zealand when it began to spread rapidly within British communities in Asia, initially in India, then in Japan and along the China coast.[34]

Impressed by what she had seen of the league in England, Helena May established a branch on her return to Hong Kong in 1903. After a few months, membership in three districts, the Peak, Victoria and Kowloon, stood at 71 adults and 113 children. While this was only a small percentage of the European child population of the colony, the league quickly acquired powerful friends. Governor Nathan was a keen supporter, rarely missing a meeting.[35] And the league capitalised on these links to raise charity donations through sales of work and fairy plays.[36] Expatriate women in particular grasped the value of the league, not least to legitimate their own growing presence within colonial society.

As the number of women arriving in the 'East' increased, this inspired optimistic predictions of moral uplift (discussed in Chapter 2)—and also bitter condemnations of their presence as unproductive. Critics of colonial women larded their attacks with reference to the 'spoilt children of empire.' The Countess of Meath herself, during a tour of Asia in 1909, complained, "Loving deeds and loving words are not as frequently done and heard amongst Europeans" and that "children are often lamentably selfish in the Far East."[37] At the same time, Meath advanced the league with its global infrastructure (which by now included a magazine) as a resource which British women in Asia might use to rebut precisely such criticisms. Evidence of children's good deeds, particularly in the form of fundraising performances in fairy plays, undercut male claims that women's movement in colonial space was disruptive, or productive only of indolence. In Hong Kong, a centre crisscrossed by missionary networks where female missionaries were an influential presence, May and others like her felt considerable pressure to ensure that their own children corroborated expectations that women might function as a moralising presence in empire. Child participants were certainly impressed by the seriousness of this endeavour. Helena May's daughter, Phoebe, later wrote:

> "No day without a deed to crown it" was the motto of this society ... I was racked by fears and doubts every evening. Had I done a good deed or not? Eventually I kept a note book in which every day I entered the honest admission of my failures and successes. The stark words Yes and No in long columns filled the pages of the little brown book.[38]

Fairyland proved valuable as a means of publicly celebrating the moral-sacrificial nature of women and children's contribution to the nation in the tropics. Fairies were, in the end, fallen angels, and as such closer to the dead. In ritual, dressed up as fairies, children performed crossings between the real and spirit worlds. Elite framings of childhood in this timeless fairy mode reflected adherence to the orthodox elite view of colonial childhood as a kind of limbo—before the essential return 'Home.' Performances reminded audiences of links between tropical nature and mortality, and also of mothers' spirit of self-sacrifice, their willingness to suffer the departure of their children for the greater good.

These rituals encouraged a shared focus upon human interiority. They reflected a sense of exile *and* anchored the racialised self. Performances of folktales, popularised in new literary forms as fairy tales, helped to assuage fears over children's acculturation in the colonies. Rather than simply securing obedience through material payoffs (an ongoing problem with Christmas), children's acting out of folk and fairy tales was considered a kind of training in national culture. Folklore had emerged as a subject of academic study from the mid-nineteenth century, and both folklorists and some of those working in the emerging field of anthropology, such as Edward Burnet Tylor, claimed that folktales revealed the cultural and racial origins of peoples.[39] Within the British Empire developmentalist theories of evolution posited that each individual, in growing up, recapitulated the premodern stages of the history of his own race. Folk or fairy tales helped to link children directly into this mythic past and could therefore serve as an important part of children's socialisation. Public celebrations of 'true' children in Hong Kong corroborated ideals of racial distance, authority and sexual discipline.[40]

Hence, while elite childhood served as a site for nostalgia it was more important as a forward-looking assertion of imperial power and racial virility. Parties provided opportunities for the stage-managed denial of vulnerability. 'Fairies' at children's parties in Hong Kong therefore indulged in physical jerks: "The little guests were provided with all seasonable forms of amusement," wrote one observer, "such as tennis, aunt sallies, races, croquet and a toboggan slide, the latter being extremely popular and providing a great amount of amusement."[41] Fairy plays also presented children in public eviscerated (albeit temporarily) from the influence of their amahs, the source of much male criticism of colonial women, as we saw in the last chapter. In this mode, colonial childhood served the desires of women who refused to be defined in colonial space in terms of reproductive needs and disorders alone. They re-presented themselves as something more than merely 'incorporated wives,' memsahibs or neurasthenics, while the league's incarnation of the child as a pure vision of "kind and helpful service" superseded the 'good child' disciplined once annually at Christmas.[42]

These visions met with a stirring response, as the remarkable sums collected from the plays and sales of work reveal. This support prompted European women to push fairyland free of the confines of the Christmas holiday. The league and knowledge of it *moved*. Crucially, the infrastructure of the Ministering Children's League enabled organisers to project a normative ideal of childhood across Asia through global networks. Volunteers promoted their work to a global audience through the league magazine. The fashioning of exemplary public performances of childhood was an essentially trans-colonial and comparative process. In London by the first decade of the new century the 'Hong Kong example' was being held up as evidence of the league's potential global reach. At Empire Day fêtes in Britain league representatives of the Crown Colony appeared alongside those

FIG. 4.1. "Great Britain and Ireland and Her Colonies Where M.C.L. Is Actively at Work," 1906. ('Hong Kong' is represented on the back row, second from left.) *Source*: *Ministering Children's League Magazine* (July 1906): 54, Ministering Children's League Collection, Surrey History Centre, 7919/7/16. Reproduced by kind permission of Surrey History Centre, Copyright of Surrey History Centre.

of the dominions. The 'Hong Kong example' may even have influenced Meath's decision to embark upon a tour of Asia herself, in 1909. New branches emerged soon after her visits to Shanghai, Singapore and Penang.

The work was also productive of rivalry between expatriate British communities in Asia. After the first funds donated to the league's charitable works arrived, Lady Meath rewarded Helena May by acknowledging Hong Kong in metropolitan celebrations of the league. However, after Shanghai's branch started up she used the magazine to make provocative references to work being done in 'China proper.'[43] Meath admitted that "the success which had attended the working of the 'MCL' in Hong Kong rendered it a comparatively easy task to persuade workers in Singapore that our Society was worthy of support."[44] League activities thus produced new standards, expectations and norms by which the public performances of colonial childhood were to be judged. In the process they raised the question as to which children could be called upon to embody it.

While admitting the usefulness of the league to 'English-speaking folks,' Lady Meath confessed herself to be "still more eager to start the League amongst those who were natives of the East."[45] Like her husband, Lord Meath, she envisaged the British Empire as the future site of a moral-evangelical revolution capable of reaching (and converting to Christianity) one fifth of the world's population. When starting up the league in Shanghai, she pleaded for the admission of "those who belong to the land."[46] Metropolitan organisers emphasised the universal dimensions of childhood as a focus for "love for all humanity, and a sympathy with all things living."[47]

However, such imperial visions did not always sit easily with colonial priorities along the China coast. In Shanghai organisers quickly declared it "rather difficult to work this league amongst the Chinese."[48] Meanwhile, in Hong Kong, league organisers defined an exemplary childhood that cut across class but not race lines. Performances featured exclusively European casts. Given the relative lack of children, this encouraged the accommodation of lower-status European families within league structures. From the outset the league ran branches in Victoria and Kowloon where lower-status Europeans resided. Later on, branches opened for the children of dockworkers, soldiers and the police. Because the power from which childhood derived its force in this vision was romantic and collective, in fairyland gender distinctions were actually played down. Children of both sexes were expected to tap into natural wisdom and spiritual authority.[49] While the MCL admitted both boys and girls, the dominant gender mores discussed in Chapter 2 ensured that girl residents were more numerous among league members and that boys, who were younger, were not called upon to model distinctively masculine traits.

While soldiers' and dockworkers' children of both sexes might be 'fairies,' organisers redrew the familiar socially dichotomous model of childhood along racial lines to exclude Chinese.[50] In empire, recognition of fairyland relied as much upon pejorative depictions of Chinese childhoods as 'other' as it did British middle-class ideals of the norm for its coherence. In contemporary accounts of port city life, Chinese children rarely played but often worked, owing to a supposedly innate tendency to act 'like little adults.' Travel writers mocked the solemnity of children participating in Chinese festivals in public, which they read as evidencing a racialised precocity absent from the 'true life' of childhood.[51] In such writings even Anglophone Chinese students, whose nonworking status meant they lacked economic value, were framed not as 'emotionally priceless' but as aberrant, for they studied *too* hard and expressly for pecuniary gain. Meanwhile, younger Chinese children appeared in colonial writing as commercial objects such as 'dolls' or other material objects. Lacking in spirit or agency, they were curiosities embedded in the commercial landscape. Such visions contrasted with the transcendent spiritedness of the European fairy child.[52] The denial of 'true' childhood to Chinese children underpinned depictions of Chinese society as fixed and unchanging.

So dominant had this tendency to read childhood through a racial lens become that by the early twentieth century the voyeuristic act of seeing beauty across the 'colour line' elicited a powerful frisson. In February 1906, Frederick Noel of St. Paul's College wrote to Sir Matthew Nathan to inform him:

> Dear Sir Matthew, you said the other day you would like to see some Chinese children! W. Fung is going to bring his (I hope) 4 eldest grandchildren to tea here on Monday [19] at 4 o'clock; they will be in their best garments, and look delicious. If you cared to come in for a minute between 4 and 5 I should be very glad to show you a rather pretty quaint sight (which doesn't include Fung himself!).[53]

Nathan kept the appointment, but such appreciative readings of children who were not European required absolute discretion. In a place where race-bound interpretations of childhood had become fundamental to the colonial order of things, and new rituals bridged between official and nonofficial worlds, they appeared iconoclastic. This is exactly why such readings formed such a bold warp thread in the work of the Scots engineer James Dalziel, a rare critic of segregation and the arbitrariness of racial divisions under colonialism.[54]

UNE INDOCHINE FÉERIQUE: PUTTING CHILDHOOD ON DISPLAY IN FRENCH COLONIAL CENTRES

In August 1887, the same year in which C. B. Buckley was electrifying audiences in Singapore with his "Talisman of the Enchanted Island," the mayor of Saigon, Roch Carabelli, was drawing up plans to make children the focal point of another spectacular display. The mayor had been delighted to receive the news that Louis Levy, aka 'Achard,' had agreed to take up the directorship of the Saigon opera house. Looking forward to his arrival, Carabelli made arrangements for a spectacular new season. Concerned that the problem of staffing the opera chorus within the available budget should not thwart desires to create a truly edifying and ennobling spectacle, he envisioned a magnificent multiethnic display integrating schoolgirls: Vietnamese, Eurasian and French.

This was no idle dream. The mayor took steps to contact the principal of the École Municipale des Filles to request the participation of schoolgirls in a production of Hervé's *La Roussotte* in the coming winter season. But to his evident surprise this proposal created a firestorm. When the director of education, Joseph Rul, learned of the plan, he was mortified. The director wrote to the school principal, remarking that the mayor "should have known better" than to have even made such a request.[55] The resulting clash between the colonial state and the municipality left Carabelli's dream in tatters.

This outcome seems curious given that opera, which had begun in Saigon as early as 1864, shortly after the annexation of Cochinchina, had long been identified as a key ritual-cultural means of conveying authority and shared 'French' values. The opera troupe represented a direct cultural link to France, and in particular Paris. It also offered potentially consensual grounds for elite-led community building (not unlike the Christmas Treats and fairy plays proliferating across the British Empire). The French in Saigon certainly needed little convincing of the value of the dramatic arts to colonial governance.[56]

Carabelli's problem was that he had proposed the integration of schoolgirls into the Saigon opera at a time when the transition from military to civilian rule was bringing officials face to face with demands that colonialism be reinvented along moral, middle-class (not martial) lines. After the first civil governor, Charles-Marie Le Myre de Vilers, took up his duties in 1879, tensions increased around rival claims for the moral guardianship of young people in Cochinchina. The end of the era of rule by admirals heralded a transition to a style of governance that was supposed to better reflect republican values. Proposals for the reform of education threatened vested interests. These pressures soon permeated the lower reaches of the colonial state. By 1882 the municipal council had ceded control over the École de Garçons. However, it fought harder to retain control over the girls' school as this was considered the more important institution.[57] Under increasing scrutiny, the council's alleged mismanagement of the École de Filles would soon lead to a full-blown scandal featuring rumours of soldiers frequenting the girls in residence, and the discovery that the teenage son of the principal, Madame Dussutour, was residing in the school building.[58]

Putting children on display in public, especially girls, even in such a quintessentially 'French' context, presented significant risks. Tensions swirled around the issue of girls' involvement in public spectacle because it remained unclear as to whether those growing up in Saigon could actually achieve normative middle-class respectability. In the colonial arena it was unclear what that even meant. The public presentation of girls in the opera even on a small scale aroused anxieties over acculturation rather than assuaging them. As moral guardians expressed outrage over the porosity of boundaries separating vulnerable childhood *from* public space (as the case of Dussutour's son and the soldiers would soon illustrate), Carabelli's proposal foundered. It did not help that he intended that the girls should take part in a work by Hervé, known for his lowbrow *comédie-opérettes*. The state-sponsored induction of girls into such a production as viable subjects, visual objects, for a consuming male gaze in public and across race, invited controversy. Placing girls at the centre of modern colonial spectacle raised provocative questions about the commodification of femininity and the relationship of sexuality to public performance in empire. Moreover, such a move would hardly be likely to play well with the new Vietnamese elite emerging around Cochinchina's rice trade but still anxious about entrusting their daughters to the alternative pedagogies of the colonial state.

Carabelli's proposal and the response it received were also significant for the light they shed upon a wider and increasingly bitter battle over whom or what Indochina was actually for. In the metropole republicans and Catholics had by now drawn battle lines penetrating the home. For each, the family offered a model around which society might be reorganised, and children figured prominently in their competing visions of the nation. For republicans children were model democratic citizens-in-training, as the antislavery campaigner Victor Schœlcher had famously suggested.[59] For Catholics the family was a space for the socialising of children and countering secularism. In a context of growing religious strife in France the influential work of the late mining engineer and conservative sociologist Frédéric Le Play informed a rising tide of right-wing criticism blaming the decline of patriarchy upon an effeminising, egalitarian republic.[60] As J. P. Daughton has shown, these debates also played out at one remove in colonial space. And here, in centres where patriarchal ideologies remained deeply ingrained, the colonial government's willingness to entertain notions of children as partners or auxiliaries of the state raised fears over a direct threat to Catholic authority.[61]

The secular-clerical divide over the moral-social role of the family was further complicated in Saigon by Hanoi's emerging challenge to Cochinchina's political influence. A year before he made his ill-fated proposal, Carabelli had published a pamphlet urging the creation of an Indochinese Union with Saigon as its capital.[62] However, a year later, in October 1887, the creation of the union brought the creation of the post of lieutenant governor of Cochinchina as subordinate to the authority of a governor general based in Hanoi. In the same year, the retired marine pharmacist Arthur Delteil published a book explaining his "fear that Cochinchina will remain a *colonie de passage* like India."[63] For many if not most French residents of Indochina, theories of 'assimilation' or 'association' had little day-to-day significance, but Saigon's potential political eclipse by Hanoi sparked concerns over the reproduction of the French family as a seat of civilised values. As we saw in Chapter 2, domestic norms and the family became thoroughly tangled with the defence of the southern mercantile elite's established interests. Ultimately, this left administrators wary of laying claim to 'colonial childhood' as a unity for public consumption. Such an intervention might actually undermine the family, even as that institution was being called upon to mediate between children's identities in public and private.

FRENCH CHILDREN AS THE FUTURE OF LA PLUS GRANDE FRANCE

It was not only in Cochinchina that children's public presence in colonial society emerged as a focus for rivalry. Extraordinary depictions of French children also emerged from Hanoi as it was expanded and rebuilt in the late nineteenth century. These framed childhood not in terms of a decontextualised 'fairyland' but as a situated entanglement with 'Tropical' nature. To be sure, French writers and commentators were, like the British, fascinated by the literary power of childhood to represent strange lands. Novelists from Balzac to Daudet had presented childhood as "another world."[64] In France the seventeenth-century literary institutionalisation of fairy tales by writers such as Charles Perrault, Marie-Cathérine D'Aulnoy and Jeanne-Marie Le Prince de Beaumont gave expression to an emerging aristocratic sensibility. Those who wrote of their experiences in Indochina drew upon these well-established literary associations. The flamboyant writer and playwright Jean Richepin, for example, celebrating the visit to Indochina of the Duc de Montpensier (the younger brother of the pretender to the throne), referred to a "fairylike Indochina [*Indochine féerique*]."[65] However, it is significant that Richepin also cast fairyland as the creation of "the little ones, the humble, the anonymous, the blue collared boys, the children of the people, the sons of gentle France."[66] He posited French children not as exiles from paradise, like their British counterparts, but instead as *creole* settlers in a 'new France.'

The photographer Jules Gervais-Courtellemont was thinking along very similar lines. In 1898 he and his wife, Hélène Lallemand, planned to visit Indochina. By this time Gervais-Courtellemont was well known in France as an editor, author and journalist. Based in Algiers, he was particularly well known for his work in photogravure, which he used to illustrate his writings. He set out for Indochina to capture images of the French presence in Asia, to arouse public interest and pride in the empire and to salvage the reputation of the new 'protectorate' of Tonkin, which was still often associated with sickness, death and disease in the metropolitan imaginary.

Travelling in Hiền Lương, to the west of the soon-to-be imperial capital of Hanoi, Gervais encountered a sentryman for the *garde indigène* and managed to convince him to allow his wife and four children—all residents of the garrison—to be photographed. The resulting image, which Gervais published in a collection of images of Indochina, reveals the four children seated on the grass, amid the tropical verdure. At first glance their pose appears to lack much of the rigid convention of turn-of-the-century middle-class family portraiture. Instead, its disjunctive, confrontational mode brings to mind the contemporary medical portraiture of disease. This may have been intentional, since Gervais's purpose was to confront and refute arguments for degeneracy and to underline the fecund promise of *la plus grande France*. In the accompanying text he wrote enthusiastically of "pretty pink babies" proliferating on French concessions. The rosiness of these tots set up a contrast with the more familiar sickly yellows and greys of medical literature and colonial writing. Usefully for Gervais's purpose, all four of the sentryman's children had been born in Tonkin. They were therefore "natives of the post of Hien-Luong." And the photographer accompanied the image with a description of the children as

> four dear little colonials, wearing topees, sitting on the grass at the feet of their mother. Alive and well, the living refutation of detractors of the Tonkinese climate.[67]

FIG. 4.2. Jules Gervais-Courtellemont, "Quatre naïfs du poste de Hien-Luong," 1901. *Source*: Jules Gervais-Courtellemont, *Empire Colonial de la France: L'Indochine. Cochinchine, Cambodge, Laos, Annam, Tonkin* (Paris: Librairie de Paris Firmin-Didot, 1901), 183.

The children appeared essentially as emanations of tropical nature, even as their white attire and hygienic topees marked them out as distinct from it.

What made this image especially provocative was Gervais-Courtellemont's ironic reference to the visual framing of mother and child. For his edgy renderings of French children in 'new France' drew explicitly upon the visual grammar of Honoré Daumier's older, iconic state painting, *The Republic* (1848). From revolutionary times, visions of children connoting the vigorous but vulnerable infant republic had pervaded French political symbolism. But unlike Daumier's babies, who were male and focused intently upon their mother, Gervais's colonial children were all girls. Their mother was a much more marginal figure than in Daumier's work. She was a passive onlooker, seated not amid the tropical verdure like her children but on a bench a few feet to one side. This imposition of distance, and the fact that the girls gazed out into the surrounding countryside from a space lacking enclosure or private interiority, underlined the their potential as self-determining individuals whose imperial trajectories were unconfined.

FIG. 4.3. Honoré Daumier, "La République," 1848. *Source*: Copyright of RMN/Imaginechina. Reprinted with permission.

While the internal hierarchy of the image is obvious, it suggests not intimacy between mother and children but detachment. What harmony there is on display is that between the girls and 'their' *pays colonial*. Casually arrayed, their legs splayed, these youthful figures are apparently unconcerned with the technological process of photography, and they resist the orthodox postures of bourgeois portraiture—appropriately, perhaps, since they were purportedly *naïfs*. Their somewhat bedraggled appearance is also suggestive of self-sacrifice rather than the leisurely freedoms of home and garden. But what Gervais-Courtellemont intended his audiences to glimpse here, growing in the mists of the jungle, was a provocative vision of the colony as a bucolic wellspring of national vigour, a *pays agrarien* not dissimilar to ideals of an imagined French past. It was not long before this portrayal of colonial childhood was publicly contested.

'DOCILE WARDS': VIETNAMESE CHILDREN AT
THE HANOI EXPOSITION, 1902–1903

Around the turn of the century new public portrayals of children emerged in particular from the imperial capital of Hanoi. In these, unlike Gervais-Courtellemont's photography, Vietnamese and not French youth took centre stage. Though children remained a deeply contentious presence in French Empire centres, the colonial administration sponsored attempts to locate a visual language through which to depict 'colonial' childhoods in public.

The backdrop for this development was the sweeping modernisation campaign that was transforming Hanoi under the governorship of Paul Doumer. This culminated in a grandiose exhibition, from November 1902 to January 1903. Though Paul Beau (who took up the governorship in October 1902) oversaw the opening of the exposition, Doumer was its architect. The latter's ambitions in devising this event extended well beyond assembling the agricultural, industrial and craft products of Indochina. He intended it to be a celebration of 'Hanoi Modern' and an announcement to the world of the city's new status as an imperial capital. The organising team was well aware of the importance Doumer invested in this task, and the value of visual art in achieving this aim. The inspector general of museums, Roger Marx, worked with the Beaux-Arts commissioner Taglio to superintend art in gallery space purpose-built for the event. And Doumer commissioned Paul Vivien, a member of the Société Coloniale des Beaux-Arts, to secure through competition artworks that could exemplify the lofty ideals for which the new Hanoi supposedly stood.

To tempt artists in France to enter the Hanoi competition, the Ministry of Colonies offered travel bursaries and promised that the winning paintings would be prominently displayed in the new, purpose-built Palais Central and in the Gallery of Fine Arts constructed alongside it. Many of those who submitted work were affiliated with the Société des Peintres Orientalistes Français founded by the art historian and *conservateur* of the Musée du Luxembourg, Léonce Bénédite, in 1893. Bénédite had started the society after the *exposition universelle* of 1889 to raise awareness in France of the growing importance of the empire in Asia. And by the time the society completed its tenth show in 1902, it included among those on display more than forty paintings of Indochina.[68]

In such work, and that which metropolitan artists submitted to the competition, the dominant republican political symbolism of childhood is very clear to see. The bond between mother and child, referred to above in relation to Daumier, was by the 1880s central to a revival of republican iconography and political rhetoric. In painting, coinage and public sculpture the natural and nurturing woman, embodied in the form of 'Liberty' or 'Marianne,' offered a unifying focus for men learning to love the republican nation. Children functioned in political allegory

Children on Display in Colonialisms' Cultures 101

FIG. 4.4. Clémentine-Hélène Dufau, "Gouvernement Général de l'Indo-Chine, exposition de Hanoï," 1902. *Source*: Paul Bourgeois et G. Roger Sandoz, *Rapport général—exposition d'Hanoï 1902–3* (Paris: Comité Français des Expositions à l'étranger, n.d., c. 1904), 225.

as emblems of the vigorous infant republic.[69] Similar representations permeated the French Empire, proliferating on the surfaces of French colonialism's material culture in the years before the First World War.[70] And as the lavish exhibition opened in Hanoi on 16 November 1902, it centred upon images of native children.

As it turned out, some five hundred paintings featured in the Hanoi Exposition, prompting the writer Alfred Cunningham to describe it as "the finest collection of paintings ever seen in the Far East."[71] But depictions of the nurtured native child featured strongly in poster art and official publications at the Hanoi Exposition. Paul Tournon's work, for example, depicted a young Vietnamese girl seated at the feet of a robust, armoured, Marianne-style figure, symbolising France. Clémentine-Hélène Dufau's contribution represented a Khmer mother watching over a naked child gathering knowledge.[72]

These images suggest that as Doumer drew Hanoi closer to Paris politically, the governor also reached for childhood as an allegory of the modern, moral, scientifically based authority of the colonial state. While connoting the newness and vulnerability of the republican project, these portrayals of docile, nurtured *Indochinese* children also need to be read as part of an official counterpoint, if

FIG. 4.5. Paul Tournon, "La France Protectrice," 1902. *Source*: Paul Bourgeois et G. Roger Sandoz, *Rapport général—exposition d'Hanoï 1902–3* (Paris: Comité Français des Expositions à l'étranger, n.d., c. 1904), 221.

not riposte, to subversive celebrations of the French 'creole' child.[73] It is perhaps significant that by the time the exposition opened Jules Gervais-Courtellemont was far away, recording images of Tibet and China, on the orders of Paul Doumer.

In some of the paintings selected by exposition organisers 'children of Indochina' appeared as wards of an idealised French mother figure, but in others, notably Dufau's work, 'mother France' was absent. This may have reflected the ongoing struggle in France and its empire to square imperial authority with a revolutionary philosophical tradition, from the 'assimilationist' approach of Paul Bert to the more aloof 'association' of Jules Harmand. Casting the colonised as a child sidestepped the oxymoron of an aristocratic republican rule and neatly encapsulated the shift away from assimilation toward an associative line.

Well beyond Hanoi, racialisation and infantilisation formed linked strategies of French imperial domination. The metaphor of childhood proved so useful in undergirding imperial ambitions because, for at least a century, efforts to understand racial difference and the development of man had been forged upon similar conceptual ground. As the modern view of childhood as nonrational emerged, philosophers linked it to notions of 'savagery.'[74] Child and 'savage' thus became mutually interdependent concepts. Even as scientific explanations of physical difference challenged moral considerations in accounting for differential levels of 'progress,' these links persisted. In Francophone circles racial theory remained somewhat more fluid and pluralistic than in the English-speaking world, where scientific racism was more prevalent.[75] In France notions of race tended to hinge more upon social hierarchies of difference. Because of this the identity of the child could more easily embody the transitional possibilities residing within race.[76] Visions of colonised people as children, while 'naturally' justifying dominance over subject peoples, could "articulate the porosity of this taxonomy."[77]

In the late nineteenth century metropole, childhood emerged as a key target for state-led reform, and in the colonies—supposedly laboratories for social experiments—some emphasised Vietnamese children's importance to civilising projects. While certain experts argued that French children could be improved through acclimatisation, others caught glimpses of the contemporary French youth in studies of the Vietnamese child. The army doctor Albert Challan de Belval reported in 1886 that the "young, [Vietnamese] seems intelligent, impudent, almost the *gamin* of Paris."[78] A variety of commentators, from the ethnographers Bouinais and Paulus to the former administrator Raoul Postel and the writer Louis Peytral, hinted that if this source could be tapped before the child fell from a vital minority into an acculturated, degenerate maturity, societal progress might follow.[79] In contrast to much writing in English on the subject, native childhood often appeared in Francophone literature as a reservoir of common humanity.

Children were especially important to such visions of republican-led progress in parts of empire where 'natural man' proved more difficult to locate. The ancient civilisation of Vietnam, like that of the Empire of China to which it formerly paid tribute, did not easily fit within views of the world contrasting European 'culture-bearers' with primitive 'child peoples.' Indeed, a key argument of imperialists seeking credits for the Tonkin expedition had been that this was "a colony of relatively advanced civilisation" whose people could be "partners in the work of civilisation and progress."[80] After the conquest, demands for the loyalty of Vietnamese associates to a 'French Indochina' clashed repeatedly with the remnants of a sophisticated precolonial infrastructure. This was somewhat less evident in the 'younger' city of Saigon, where the mandarinate had fled and local institutions had been replaced with French equivalents. But in the 'thousand-year-old city' of Hanoi, and in Tonkin, even after a lengthy process of 'pacification,' conflict rumbled on.

In these circumstances childhood became a deeply contested field for the expression of imperial rivalry across borders. French authorities dreamed of penetrating China but worried about Tonkin's dense land and sea connections with the politically turbulent provinces of the Chinese Empire. In 1900 the struggle between European colonialisms and the Chinese Empire triggered an explosion of antiforeign attacks, dubbed the Boxer Uprising. Amid the resulting violence Chinese-made 'victory pictures' proliferated.[81] Disseminated from workshops in Shanghai and Suzhou, these included engravings representing the European imperial scourge. The engravings featured serialised imagery. Alongside the stereotypical 'drunken British soldier' and 'sleeping German soldier' appeared a French sailor, "cutting long lockets [of hair] from his head to give to the Chinese children holding his hand."[82] In these pictures Chinese engravers appear to have been responding to French colonialism's distinctively affective, sentimental claims upon Asian children, which they re-presented as a form of neo-paedophilic exploitation.

It was against the backdrop of a China grappling with the failure to eradicate foreign incursions—including the presence of French armies as part of the anti-Boxer alliance—that the Hanoi Exposition put the pliant, malleable Indochinese child subject on display. The very complexity and sophistication of Vietnamese (and Chinese) society made it more important to the *administration* that children lacking clothes (as well as private property, hierarchy, sexual taboos and religion) be pictured. Dufau's Khmer child, like the French children in earlier republican imagery, was naked. And as Hanoi was transformed into a modern French city at the turn of the century, French writers celebrated the nakedness of Vietnamese children. They saw these youngsters as vestiges of a pure, robust and egalitarian nature being driven back by the extension of Western sanitary practices into suburban zones (the so-called *chasse à paillottes*). Louis Peytral observed in 1897:

> As in all the milieux where poverty resides, nippers swarm in foul slums as yet untouched by civilisation. Naked as worms, no matter what time of day, they scamper from their shanties, clamber upon roofs and into trees and, visibly happy in this liberty of action that is the true life of childhood, spend the best days of their lives wallowing in putrid ponds, [running] pell mell with swine, their friends and brothers.[83]

In these accounts, children appeared naked or dirty, or both. Caked in the rime of regenerative barbarism, they plunged into streams, rolled in mud, and played with animals.[84] Hardy and free, they were unencumbered by civilisation and "happy all the same, because of their freedom."[85]

The naked child, connoting backwardness, fit well with theories of 'association.' For association did not necessarily entail the denial of possibilities for civilisational advance, but projected the colonial coming of age far into the future. The organising committee of the Hanoi Exposition saw this kind of child as a reassuring sign of the backwardness justifying public representations of a benevolent Mother France. Portrayals of Asian peoples as 'children' of the same mother allowed the rigidities of race to be attenuated. These supple, fluid understandings of childhood as a vulnerable period of life remained interwoven with ideas of Western racial superiority. As a trans-colonial gesture, the use of children to represent colonised peoples also functioned to provide visitors and residents with a means of mediating the shock of strange and unpredictable encounters they experienced at the exposition. Visual imagery resonated with the infantilising linguistic shorthand that newcomers were encouraged to adopt (the English term *boy*, for male servants, but also *congaï*, for women, a corruption of the Vietnamese term for 'young girl').

It is significant also that here real children, once again, could not be presented in public. The only trace of them at the exposition of 1902–3 was their schoolwork, which featured among the displays as it had in the first Hanoi Exposition of March–April 1887.[86] That it was unthinkable that real children should be called upon to perform at a time when 'live' colonial subjects regularly appeared in dioramas of metropolitan expositions is suggestive of how unstable and potentially subversive visions of colonial childhood had become in turn-of-the-century Tonkin. However, as we shall see in the next chapter, within a few years authorities in Hanoi would gamble upon precisely such a strategy, with quite disastrous consequences.

IMPERIAL FAIRYLANDS:
COLONIAL CHILDHOODS IN BRITISH ASIA

Within two years of Lady Meath's visit to Asia in 1909, contrary to expectations, the racial exclusivity of fairyland in Hong Kong dissolved. The catalyst for this shift was the arrival in this British Crown Colony of the renowned journalist Flora Shaw. As an influential and well-connected political journalist, Shaw was widely known as the first female colonial editor of *The Times* (a position she took up in 1891) and as an eminent authority on empire.[87] After marrying the colonial administrator Sir Fredrick Lugard she resigned her post and gave up her career at the height of her influence. In July 1907 Shaw accompanied Lugard as he took up the governorship of Hong Kong. Seeking new outlets for her energies, Shaw took over the presidency of the Ministering Children's League from Helena May, who departed Hong Kong for Fiji on 21 January 1911, where her husband was to take up the governorship. Shaw quickly saw the potential of the league, with some changes, to the achievement of imperial ambitions.

Unlike May, whose connection with the colony dated back to the early 1890s, Flora Shaw arrived in Hong Kong with little expectation that she would stay for very long. Her views of the league and its role and meaning within the British Empire were much closer to those of Lady Meath. She saw the league in imperial terms as an organisation with the potential to raise Europeans and other peoples alike to their greatest (though ultimately different) potential. This conviction prompted Shaw, in one of her first acts as president, to change the league's membership policy to permit the admission of Chinese girls. In March 1911 she declared:

> It seems to me particularly suitable that Chinese children who must want to be good and unselfish and to help to make the world better just as English children do should join with English in a league of kindness here.... If there are any Chinese mothers who would like their children to join we shall be very happy to have their names.[88]

If this was a controversial step it was not an entirely unheralded one. Reform-minded British women along the China coast had long interpreted their contribution to empire in terms not only of showcasing their own children as exemplars of an ideal childhood, but also of 'rescuing' Chinese children (and girls in particular) from the supposed depredations of their own culture. In the preceding years the MCL magazine had quite explicitly and repeatedly printed gendered imagery of the mute, passive Chinese child, her feet unbound, as an appropriate recipient of alms.[89] However, Shaw's initiative needs to be seen also as part of a strategic response to the 'provocation' of a highly dynamic elite Chinese culture of philanthropy in Hong Kong.

From the late nineteenth century a growing range of voluntary institutions served the interests of Chinese in Hong Kong, the Tung Wah 'Chinese Hospital' being the largest. Within these institutions the dynamism of an increasingly confident Chinese elite, composed of merchants—self-made men, not scholars—inspired unease among Europeans. Colonial officials saw these institutions, and particularly the Tung Wah hospital committee, as attenuating their own authority, and responded by diluting their influence.[90] Nevertheless, Chinese philanthropic dynamism continued to expose the shortcomings of foreign rule characterised by segregationist measures and an overlordship that managed to appear both coercive and neglectful at the same time. As China shifted toward reform that would culminate in revolution, it became clear that the future of the Crown Colony of Hong Kong depended upon finding new strategies for the better integration of Chinese and European elites. But this was not Shanghai. There was no powerful municipal council to provide expatriates or 'settlers' with influence. And there was far less freedom to manoeuvre, politically. Consequently, European-led voluntary work became an altogether more important channel through which new efforts to broker agreement between Chinese and British elites could proceed in a manner acceptable to officialdom. Flora Shaw quickly grasped the potential of the league to provide new ground for collaborative action.

Her confidence was quickly rewarded. With the colour bar lifted, from April 1911 Chinese girls flocked to join the MCL. By 1913 Hong Kong's MCL had 750 child members, many of whom were girls attending the elite, Church Missionary Society-sponsored schools, St. Stephen's Girls' College and Diocesan Girls' School. Channelling Chinese and European charitable efforts through the same organisation made the league larger than branches in other densely populated centres of the British Empire. This joint effort also dislodged vast sums in charitable donations enabling the league to win new levels of authority and prestige on a global scale into the interwar era.[91] On her return to Hong Kong from Fiji, Helena May reclaimed the presidency from the departing Shaw, with the arch observation, "I find the Ministering Children's League has increased in numbers."[92] But she did not reverse the membership policy. Whilst in Fiji she too had become convinced of the league's value in reaching and reforming 'dark mothers' and their children.

Crucial to the league's success among Chinese was the fact that it was an essentially conservative, elite institution. It catered for girls (and very small European boys). Its leadership stressed the impossibility of struggle against 'Nature,' and saw empire as a space for their expression. As one 'Elizabeth' later wrote in the league magazine, "it is the essential differences, and not the likenesses, between the sexes which make it imperative that we scure [*sic*] the right to do our duties as citizens, and see that those duties are the ones for which Nature designed and fitted us."[93] This conservative ethos checked the more radical aspects of a programme that was at the same time in effect producing *girlhood* as a space of comparative, interethnic engagement.

Even so, the decision to induct Chinese children into fairyland and into public roles within the official vernacular of childhood stunned onlookers. Charlotte Ehrlicher, a superintendant nurse from New York City, gazed upon a double line of children presenting bunches of flowers upon Fredrick Lugard's departure in 1912, and noted, "Everybody was surprised to find them so beautiful."[94] Because league organisers remained wary of interethnic engagement, they continued to formally order activities along an internal divide. Chinese and European children joined separate branches. And when Chinese and European children were brought together at Government House, as in the League Bazaars held in 1915 and 1916, organisers divided the grounds into different sections with some stalls run by the Chinese members and others by Europeans. The 'European' sections featured children's work stalls, a Christmas tree and a 'cave,' where European children dressed as fairies sold books; while in the 'Chinese' section girls ran a tea stall and distributed 'Lucky Bags.'

However, on these occasions the movement of participants and guests around

FIG. 4.6. The Ministering Children's League Bazaar, 11 November 1916.
Source: Public Record Office Hong Kong 08-19C-317. Reprinted with permission.

FIG. 4.7. The Ministering Children's League Bazaar, 11 November 1916.
Source: Public Record Office Hong Kong 08-19C-318. Reprinted with permission.

the grounds of Government House obscured the intended formal divide between 'true children' and the rest.[95] While adult organisers set down internal boundaries, juvenile participants riotously breached them. As images of the events reveal, they offered opportunities for children to mix socially across ethnic lines. Small numbers of male Chinese elites had been invited to functions at Government House from the time of John Pope Hennessy (governor 1877–83), but league work now propelled much larger numbers of their children, thrillingly, into new social engagements in the same spaces.

No doubt part of the reason why league activities proved attractive to Chinese girls was that they held out intriguing new possibilities for social action. Fairyland cast Chinese girls in the role of miniature philanthropists. Here philanthropy emerged as a new realm for the expression of youthful female agency and the uplift of not only Chinese children but also British children in the metropole. Through proceeds from the sales of work the girls supported—among other things—cots for British children in the Ministering Children's League Homes at Ottershaw, Sussex. An orphan named Lily Peacock slept in the 'Hong Kong cot' at the MCL home beneath a coverlet made by the Chinese girls of the Belilios School branch of the league. The girls made this not under the guidance of their teacher but on their own initiative, in their own homes.[96] After receiving the gift, Lady Meath sent a note of personal thanks to the girls, read aloud to them by Helena May.[97]

These efforts conferred a sense of power, and their effects seem to have exerted an attraction over former members into adulthood. In 1924, E. Middleton-Smith, the principal of St. Stephen's School, observed how "some of the girls of this school have been members of the Ministering Children's League for 16 years now."[98] Individuals found opportunities for public recognition of their efforts, as in the case of one girl, Kwan Un Chan, a student at St. Stephen's Girls' College, who collected $500 in funds for various causes and organised a Christmas treat for poor children in the school playground and a Christmas party for child bond servants and amahs.[99] Girls clearly found these new possibilities for social action intriguing. Benevolent gestures toward working-class British children exposed the fragility of supposedly fixed notions of racial hierarchy and underlined the emerging status of participants in an elite culture brokered across the racial divide.

However, the expansion of 'fairyland' proved to be a fraught process for the organisers. Theatrical productions were often profoundly edgy since fairy plays tipped power in the direction of child performers. They involved the invocation of spirits beyond control, and fairyland on the colonial frontier invoked the threat of sex even as it rejected it. The very term 'fairy' was at the time coming to be associated in English with 'deviant' male sexual identity. Chinese league members were usually older than their European equivalents and some saw this age gap as underlining European 'innocence' vis-à-vis a more libidinous (and precocious) indigenous agency. The concern surrounding fairy theatricals related not simply to worries about racial identity but also to fears over engaging girls in practices that might be perceived as potentially corrupting.

This was often because children grasped the rare opportunities fairyland afforded for independent, pseudo-autonomous and sometimes borderline rebellious, public self-expression. While the league remained an essentially didactic structure predicated upon a deeply conservative vision of femininity, European girls described the sense that it opened up 'new worlds' of possibility. For Phoebe May,

> At about this time we began acting in children's plays, which opened up a new world to us all. Daddy coached us and organized everything, while Mummy set the tailor to work making the clothes. We acted scenes from Alice Through the Looking Glass and a fairy play.... even Iris and Dione [her younger sisters] took part. When Sir Matthew Nathan asked us to act at a children's party at Government House, I felt I was in heaven.[100]

The consequences of extending these potentially transformative collective endeavours to Chinese participants remained worryingly unclear.

This concern led even ostensible supporters of the extension of Western fairy lore across racial boundaries, such as Middleton-Smith, to urge its confinement to literary explorations.[101] But by the interwar era enthusiasm for these new modes of theatrical expression could not easily be contained. It spilled quickly over into elite Chinese schools, via the league. At the League Bazaar held at Government House in 1921, only European children were permitted to perform as 'fairies.' But at the Diocesan Girls' School annual prize ceremony just a few months later the colonial secretary's wife, Lady Severn, observed a children's operetta ("The Enchanted Forest") featuring a distinctly mixed cast.[102] These events created a new arena for the public articulation of youthful female subjectivities, forming part of what Helen Siu has referred to as the "underlying structure of opportunity" that young elite females experienced in coastal south China.[103]

THE LIMITS OF HYBRIDITY: SINGAPORE CHILDREN AND THE END OF BUCKLEY'S TREAT

While visual vocabularies of ideal childhoods, for so long grounded in segregated, racialised conventions, had begun to transcend race in Hong Kong, in Singapore momentum was shifting in the opposite direction. Buckley's Treat had functioned for three generations to foreground values knitting together English-speaking European, Straits Chinese and Eurasian communities. The vision of 'colonial childhood' on display had been far less overtly, racially essentialist than that emanating from the early league work in Hong Kong. Charles Buckley had made Singapore plays intentionally hybrid. Participants and audience were conspicuously *local*.[104] One comical sketch in 1900 met with particular success, "as the juveniles were able to appreciate the local Malay of the rikisha puller."[105] The 1909 performance featured choruses in Malay. As Edwin A. Brown, a member of

FIG. 4.8. "Twinkle, twinkle, little star," Lillian Newton as a Fairy, 1899. *Source*: Cambridge University Library, Royal Commonwealth Society Collection, Lillian Newton photograph collection on Singapore GBR/0115/Y303113/55. Reprinted with permission.

the St. Andrew's Cathedral choir of which Buckley was choirmaster, explained, "No man was better loved by the local-born."[106]

The tendency in Singapore, where external pressure and official interest was weaker, was for children to push boundaries further. Performing in the Singapore Treat, Lillian Newton recalled, "I danced a cake walk one year, it was very modern and Mr. Buckley was a bit put out!"[107] The racial connotations of the hybridised 'cakewalk' were presumably not lost upon Buckley, whom Walter Makepeace recalled raging at the children as he struggled to impose order in rehearsals. In spite of this, the bacchanalian dimensions of the Treat created new spaces for children's agency in public and the tone of these events continued to differ markedly from those in Hong Kong. So, for example, the coronation of King Edward VII in August 1902 featured much "banging of drums, blowing of trumpets" and "'touts' in all sorts of weird costumes bawling out the merits of their respective shows," as well as pantomime donkeys, 'headless men' and an overweight American consul in drag. Meanwhile, seated on a raised platform at the very centre of the festival ground, Buckley barked instructions at 'his children' through a megaphone.[108]

By this time the sheer mobility of moralising visions of childhood across East and Southeast Asia had left Buckley's Treat and similar events looking increasingly anachronistic. Singapore had grown rapidly. Colonial rule had moved onto a firmer administrative footing. The government had made headway in the long struggle to impose control over immigration, labour markets and policing.[109] As European elites focused more intensively upon their children as representatives of a more racially homogeneous 'Singapore set,' they brought into question Buckley's vision. However, child participants in public celebrations were still routinely described as 'Christmas party children' or "Mr. Buckley's Children."[110] And Buckley's dominance continued to present obvious difficulties for those expatriate European women interested in claiming guardianship of middle-class mores and espousing a more moral colonialism in public, as their counterparts had done in Hong Kong and Shanghai. The Ministering Children's League, run by the Reverend H. C. Izard and his wife out of St. Andrew's Cathedral, remained a noticeably more fragile growth in Singapore. Buckley's involvement in it, while nominal, proved somewhat awkward.[111]

In consequence, by the turn of the century the place of the bacchanalian Treat and the mixed vision of childhood it presented were no longer assured. In 1904 the colonial government knocked down the old town hall before the new Victoria Memorial Hall had been completed, effectively 'evicting' Buckley's entertainment.[112] Its creator was on the defensive. Responding furiously to criticism over the moral tone of the Treat, he declared no performer would be named in official programmes (for "no one wants them to be thought actors").[113] The year 1906 found him protesting that 'his' celebration was "entirely a private party," and though "some persons seem to regard it as a public entertainment," in fact "it never was, or was intended to be."[114]

Buckley's Treat was never the only festive show in town. It formed part of a wider set of events run by a variety of associations. But it was the largest ritual associated with children in Singapore and the organiser's template was mapped onto other vast public rituals, such as the coronation celebrations. As officials ducked growing criticism from Chinese elites over desperate urban conditions, Buckley's gesture and the charity it connoted managed to look both manifestly inadequate in the eyes of those demanding serious reform and dangerously egalitarian to parsimonious officials.[115] Its interethnic flavour did little to assuage growing concerns that Singapore's separate 'communities' might overcome segregation and confront the colonial government.

As this vision of childhood slipped from favour, the Treat's originator took a return visit to England in May 1912 and suddenly and unexpectedly died. A large charity collection was organised in his name. Hundreds attended the unveiling of a commemorative portrait. Singapore's newspapers lavished affectionate praise upon Buckley's memory. And the Yuletide celebrations went on under the auspices of the missions and other associations; but no one could be found to carry on the Treat.

CONCLUSION

In the late nineteenth century, as the boundaries around white prestige and racial distance receded, British and French colonial governments recognised that the limits of overtly coercive power had been reached. Elites struggling to reconcile regimes of 'exchange' and uncontrolled flows with desires for stability asserted claims to rule in new cultural forms, and assigned to children the duty of embodying colonial power, representing nations, empires and imagined communities. The urban public sphere emerged as a crucial site in which children appeared, bridging between the intimate domain of the home and the wider realms of colonial culture, tying domestic and public worlds together.

In the French centres discussed here, childhood lay at the heart of divisive ongoing battles over the meaning of empire, colonialism and nation. So explosive did issues around colonial childhood remain that efforts in Saigon to induct real children into new rituals in public failed utterly. When more coherent visions of imperial childhood surfaced, as in the Hanoi Exposition, they reflected tendencies toward somewhat more pragmatic ideological conceptualisations of childhood, and the sense of childhood's importance to moral, liberal claims for a republican imperialism. They also offered a riposte to alternative nonstate-sponsored visions of the children under French tutelage.

While John Darwin has argued that compared to India the scope 'for an empire of the imagination' in China was more restricted, I have attempted to show, to the contrary, that within British-ruled centres in Asia childhood served as a focal point of the European colonial imaginary.[116] Didactic public rituals of childhood anchored the racialised adult self and offered forward-looking assertions of imperial power. But these engagements involved far more than merely the working up of 'long distance nationalism.'[117] In Singapore they involved the extension of sentimentalised readings of childhood to colonial subjects. Even in Hong Kong an aristocratic view of empire ultimately allowed 'other' children access to a new child-centric philanthropic culture fashioned by women. Childhood functioned as the grounds upon which neat divisions between Chinese and European elites were breached, nuancing scholars' claims that each was locked into its "own exclusive social world."[118]

Children in public emerged as a focal point for new visions of empire. But far from merely undergirding European claims for moral authority and civility, these productions, as we shall see, ultimately inspired and sustained powerful new challenges to colonial rule. Childhood was constantly in the process of being reshaped across the period, not only in the metropole but within and between empire centres. As the next chapter shows, during and after the First World War nationalist anticolonial protests and demands for imperial reform exposed the incompatible strands of incommensurability and universalism that ran through colonial childhoods. Elites struggled in response to reinvent rituals and representations of youth and to underwrite imperialisms' faltering moral claims.

CHAPTER 5

Trouble in Fairyland: Cultures of Childhood in Interwar Asia

During the Great War British and French officials celebrated the elimination of the German colonial presence from Asia. But as the conflict dragged on they found themselves making concession after concession to secure military and financial support from colonial subjects. This support helped the British and French Empires to survive the conflict of 1914–18. But it came at a cost. While the war undermined the claims of Europe to represent progress and civility, the failure of British and French colonial governments to deliver on concessions promised in wartime further damaged their authority. Though some predicted that after the armistice it would be 'business as usual' in colonial Asia, changed circumstances on the ground quickly revealed such confidence to be misplaced.

Nationalists clamoured for self-rule in India and in East and Southeast Asia; tensions boiled over into open confrontation. In Hong Kong, China's failure to secure the restitution of Shandong at the Paris Peace Conference of 1919 infuriated Chinese youth and revealed new depths of nationalist feeling. In Singapore, where a garrison had revolted in 1915, Straits Chinese youth inspired by the student-led, anti-imperialist May Fourth Movement protested violently on the streets. In Indochina, students repeatedly staged walkouts and strikes in protest at the government's failure to make good on Governor Albert Sarraut's postwar vow to deliver a truly 'associative' overlordship leading to Vietnamese independence. Meanwhile, the consolidation of the Bolshevik hold on power in Russia after 1917 presented the world with an alternative model of societal organisation opposed to that of liberal capitalism. The presence of Soviet advisors in Canton stoked fears of a spreading Bolshevik threat. Japanese gains and the recrudescence of Germany from the mid-1920s heightened British and French anxieties over imperial defence.

Young people's prominence in the public disturbances of the postwar era posed a special problem for colonial elites. They had made children and childhood symbolically central to justifications of liberal imperialism. But in the early twentieth century the young generation appeared to be leading anticolonial protest. Reform-minded Asian elites grasped for the symbolism of childhood as they pursued nation-building agendas. Moreover, newly created international organisations, in particular the League of Nations in Geneva (founded in January 1920), championed universal ideals of childhood as a basis upon which to rebuild the postwar order. Drawing at times upon the moral leverage of such new international agencies, Asian reformers highlighted disparities between Western and non-Western childhoods and critiqued prewar narratives of empire as paternal and benevolent. These criticisms exposed the peril of building justifications of liberal governmentalities around appeals to unstable categories of youth.

However, colonial elites did not simply jettison public rituals and representations of childhood as a means of justifying colonial rule. Instead they reinvigorated them. In a period marked by claims for empire as a form of 'trusteeship' it appeared more essential than ever that colonial regimes showcase the 'best of French and British civilisation.' As the rhetoric of new beginnings faded, claims to represent childhood remained crucial to the struggle to defend a more obviously imperilled 'old' order. This chapter shows how colonial elites reshaped rituals and representations of childhood in response to multiple threats. And it argues that as governments continued to employ childhood to gain legitimacy, youth came to play a major role in the development of anticolonial nationalisms in Asia.

THE CHILD ENTHRONED, AND DETHRONED: EMPEROR DUY TÂN ON DISPLAY

Nothing more clearly revealed the perils of political appeals to the symbolism of childhood in Vietnam than the curious case of Emperor Duy Tân. The emperor, whose birth name was Nguyễn Phúc Vĩnh San, was handpicked by the French to replace his father, Thành Thái, after the latter was deposed on the grounds of insanity. He became the eleventh emperor of the ruling Nguyễn dynasty when he acceded to the throne in 1907. And the new emperor began his reign at the tender age of seven years old.

The selection of a child as emperor was not a new tactic. Thành Thái himself had reigned from age ten in 1889. French intervention in imperial succession policy was not new either. Paul Bert had arranged the enthronement of twenty-one-year-old Đồng Khánh on 14 September 1885. But the case of Duy Tân is worthy of discussion here for several reasons. First, it reveals how colonial governments projected the imagery of indigenous childhood worldwide to publicly negate precolonial forms of knowledge and imperial authority. Second, it reveals how efforts to exploit this imagery backfired, endangering French interests. And third, it shows how youth could act to transform the outcome of the colonial contest.

In the years before Duy Tân came to the throne, the conditions that led French officials to arrange his accession took shape. At the turn of the century, cross-border links with Canton, ironically facilitated by French modernisation projects, enabled young reform-minded individuals to tap into new ideas about modernisation in the restive territories of northern Vietnam. The Qing emperor's abortive 'Hundred Days Reform' of China from 1898 provided inspiration. These reforms resonated with special force among young intellectuals in northern Vietnam because here Chinese cultural influence remained evident in Vietnamese traditions, institutions and beliefs. The ongoing battle for reform in China continued to inspire young antiforeign and reform-minded elements in Vietnam who were convinced that the limits of traditional sociopolitical organisation had been reached.

The French eyed movements for imperial reform nervously because dynastic loyalism and cross-border connections had long served as a rallying point for anticolonial protest in the north. A month after the Treaty of Tientsin (9 June 1885) put an end to the two-year Franco-Chinese war and severed Vietnam's links with China, the young emperor Hàm Nghi rallied opponents of French rule around the 'Cần Vương' (Save the King) movement. This grew into a large-scale insurgency until French troops finally regained control of the restive provinces and the emperor was captured and deported in 1888. But after this, around the turn of the century and especially after Japan's victory over Russia in 1905, a wave of 'modernisation' movements with noble patronage continued to spread across Vietnam. Prince Cường Để's newly formed 'Đông Du' (Eastward Travel) movement, for example, argued for military intervention by Japan to free Vietnam from French rule.[1] Like Hàm Nghi before him, Duy Tân's father, Emperor Thành Thái, linked up with protest movements. It was Thành Thái's decision to flee Huế on 30 July 1905 to join the Đông Du movement that ultimately led to his deposition by the French (following his capture on 30 August 1907). Phan Chu Trinh, who had travelled to Japan as part of the Đông Du movement returned, to establish a 'Free School' in Hanoi from where he preached a reformist critique of the monarchy. The colonial government moved to close the school in 1908, the same year in which its former pupils emerged as prime suspects in the dramatic attempt to poison the Hanoi garrison.

These disturbances revealed the potential of the monarchy and the court in Annam to function as a symbol of reformist nationalism in Vietnam.[2] But French officials were reluctant to eliminate the emperor and his court altogether because the monarch's presence was critical to claims that colonialism had liberated a downtrodden people from an alien court in Huế.[3] Still, with new threats spreading through overland and maritime networks, it seemed imperative that French officials find new ways of weakening links between monarch, mandarinate and people. Paul Doumer had begun efforts to attenuate monarchical power by reorganising the mandarinate and developing a separate Indochinese Civil Service in Hanoi. In 1906, with similar aims in mind, Governor Paul Beau revamped educational policy, creating a 'Council for the Improvement of Native Education' and introducing French into the national triennial examinations. This had the effect of eroding the connections between Chinese and Vietnamese culture grounded in an extensive system of vernacular education. At this point, Thành Thái's capture and removal from power in 1907 provided an opportunity to further disempower the monarchy.

With the issue of succession requiring resolution, *résident supérieur* of Annam Ernest Fernand Lévecque sought Beau's approval for Prince Vĩnh San's investiture as emperor. From the outset Lévecque intended that the body of a child, defined by its lack of independent manhood, would convey an effeminised, emasculated vision of the monarchy. The figurative 'cutting down to size' of the Nguyễn monarch in Huế transformed courtly rituals of power into scenes bordering upon farce. The emperor *as a child* cut a forlorn and preposterous figure. Observers recorded how, arriving for the investiture ceremony, Duy Tân was "lost in the stiff folds of his royal robes," while the gem-studded gold brocade he wore was clearly "too heavy for the child's shoulders."[4] The stage-managed juxtaposition of the child emperor beside the towering figure of Paul Beau presented a visual slight to elite cultural nationalism. Prince Vĩnh San embodied the ideas of the colonial subject as docile ward and evidenced French claims that degenerate Chinese rule had left Vietnam too weak to stand on its own.

While child emperors in Vietnam were nothing new, the level of interest and exposure that officials ensured this one in particular received on the global stage certainly was. Details of the investiture were reported in newspapers around the world. For example, the *Syracuse Herald* described "the gorgeous coronation of a baby ruler of the Orient."[5] Duy Tân also became the popular subject of picture-postcard images disseminated for global consumption. In them he appeared as an exotic relic, a curiosity lost in time but rediscovered, cloistered within the archaic inner sanctum of the imperial palace. The sight of the emperor in his ill-fitting garb provoked much comment, and a question of particular interest was whether, as a child, and therefore an 'innocent,' he could or should be rescued from the decrepitude of his own culture.

The playwright Eugène Brieux thought that he should. Brieux was so fascinated by the image of Duy Tân that he travelled to Huế to meet him in person. Writing of this encounter, he like many other commentators sympathised with the emperor as a child denied a 'true' childhood. For Brieux, Vĩnh San appeared as a legitimate target for romantic rescue from the stifling artifice of his public persona, 'Duy Tân.' "Ah! The poor child!" he wrote:

> His palace has the air of an ethnographic museum where they preserve, its every need fulfilled, the last and precious specimen of an extinct species.... [The emperor] has an intelligent face, which reveals, on close inspection, more boredom than solemnity. He is visibly frightened of making a faux pas, his little hands pull at a silk handkerchief, betraying his nerves. And listening to the words of 'his majesty,' which

FIG. 5.1. "Le jeune Empereur Duy-Than et son entourage," n.d., c. 1907. *Source*: Author's collection.

FIG. 5.2. Emperor Duy Tân on display. *Source*: Pierre Dieulfils, *L'Indochine pittoresque et monumentale* (Hanoi: P. Dieulfils, 1905).

he often quietly repeats, I see this little nose in the air, and this small brow, and I want to say to him: 'It's alright. You have answered correctly. Now go and play.' ... Before speaking, there is a long silence while he racks his memory and if it wasn't so sad one would laugh to observe the effort he makes to appear interested in the answers translated for him.[6]

In these ways, the production of Duy Tân for global consumption affirmed French colonial claims and undermined the authority of the Asian patriarch—whether monarch, mandarin, or father.

What played beneath the surface of much writing on this subject was the emperor's embodiment of an unstable binary—he was both docile, malleable, innocent and (like his father) potentially a brutal 'Asiatic' tyrant. Reports evoked themes of sumptuous excess and the potential lurking within the child's uncivilised body for an overcivilised monarch to wield power brutally and excessively upon a whim. This was precisely the kind of behaviour for which Thành Thái had become notorious. In France the tyrant-father remained a resonant revolutionary theme. In Indochina, through the careful stage management of one child in particular a government acting in the name of the republic (self-proclaimed heir to a parricide revolution, and nemesis of the French paterfamilias) recapitulated its attack on mature authority.

The court in Huế was only too well aware of French intentions. The mandarinate had bestowed the name 'Duy Tân,' meaning 'modernisation,' at the inauguration on 5 September 1907 to associate the emperor with the Meiji restoration in Japan and progressive movements in Vietnam, in the hope this might counter impressions of the monarchy as effeminate and irrelevant. The court also insisted that Duy Tân (born in Huế on 3 August 1900) was eight years old, in accordance with the Chinese calendar, rather than seven, as the French claimed, perhaps to add (a little) to his stature. It also oversaw his early marriage at age fifteen.[7] In the years that followed, the emperor's court steadfastly declined to acknowledge Duy Tân's youthfulness, and even the emperor's young companions were reluctant to do so. Whilst summering at Cửa Tùng beach not far from Huế in 1914, Hồ Thị Hạnh, the nine-year-old daughter of the Vietnamese high official Hồ Đắc Trung, described a conversation with the emperor in which the latter candidly expressed his frustrations about a tutor. The emperor's friend responded evasively with the words, "We are still young ... and do not dare discuss the business of grown ups." When Duy Tân insisted he was not a grown-up either, his friend told him, "Your situation and your soul are so elevated that we dare not speak our minds with you!" The emperor's protests ("But I am your age!") were in vain.[8]

French efforts to denigrate the Vietnamese emperor fit within a broader trans-colonial tradition that involved the portrayal of colonised peoples as innately dependent and childlike.[9] In Indochina ideals of docile wards reflected wider anxieties that Vietnamese children were not passive innocents but agents with suspect (or divided) loyalties. In a climate of growing tension, exacerbated by the poisoning of the Hanoi garrison in 1908, French writers often criticised children's involvement in public rituals with Chinese roots. Earlier in Hanoi, for example, Jean Star had derided child participants in the Mid-Autumn Festival, an adaptation of a ritual with Chinese origins, as "little blackamoors, serious as Popes!"[10] In Cholon, Saigon's Chinatown, George Dürrwell, president of the Société des Études Indochinoises and a longtime resident of Cochinchina, observed overly serious "little wax dolls."[11] But this criticism was inconsistent. As the case of Eugène Brieux illustrates, French observers often also sympathised with native children.

Indeed, while assumptions about the contrary dispositions of Europeans and Asian peoples mapped closely to a rational, nonrational dichotomy, an unresolved problem within republican imperialism was that coloniser and colonised were *both* reflected back in the image of the child. This metaphorical connection had its roots set deep in the revolutionary era, but was resuscitated in political iconography after 1870 and also in adult-organised movements of youth. During the early years of the Third Republic, nationalists offended by the loss of Alsace and Lorraine revived the revolutionary ideal of children as a reserve army through military preparation societies. And from 1882 *battalions scolaires* (organising government-authorised gymnastic and military exercises) marched under the *tricolore* through the streets of large French cities. So while childhood in France was often considered a vulnerable period of life in which children's essential difference legitimated protective intervention and nurturance, it was also seen as a time of struggle for survival when the child was supposed to face internal and external threats on its own. A long-standing militaristic strand, exemplified by the *battalions*, lurked within visions of childhood in modern France.

Even as childhood became much more heavily commodified in Paris and other large centres during the Belle Époque, the child-soldier trope continued to resurface in new literatures and in the imagery adorning consumer goods and advertisements, some of which celebrated the reconstruction of the French Empire. In one series of chromolithograph artworks produced by the Paris printer H. Laas and E. Pécaud, and used to advertise chocolate, shoes and other commercial goods, French colonial troops appeared as children embarking upon the Tonkin Expedition. These cute caricatures reflected associations with national glory in scenes from battles that Jules Ferry and his fellow colonial lobbyists had described as an investment in the future of "our children."[12]

However, when even militarised colonial masculinity could be seen as childlike, this suggested that infantilised colonial subjects might not even need to 'come of age' in order to recognise themselves as equals and break the imperial bond. In his influential book *De la colonisation chez les peuples modernes*, Paul Leroy-Beaulieu had warned that subject peoples "will become one day adults and that, inevitably,

FIG. 5.3. "Le départ pour le Tonkin," chromolithograph, Chocolat Poulain, printed by H. Laas and E.-Pécaud, n.d., c.1890. *Source*: Author's collection.

FIG. 5.4. "Oh! La la, les vilaines figures... qui vive!" chromolithograph, Chocolat Poulain, printed by H. Laas and E.-Pécaud, n.d., c. 1890. *Source*: Author's collection.

FIG. 5.5. "Enfoncé le pavillon noir," chromolithograph, Chocolat Poulain, printed by H. Laas and E.-Pécaud, n.d., c. 1890. *Source*: Author's collection.

they will claim more and more, and eventually absolute, independence."[13] Worse still, as the colonial theorist Jules Harmand pointed out, by assuming paternal rights within a 'filial imperialism,' the egalitarian republic was compelled to play the role of the *bon tyran*. And if the innocuous Duy Tân could potentially metamorphose at any moment from innocent child into Asian tyrant, then why could not the childlike coloniser just as easily slip from his 'civilising' role into the punitive mode of the despot under the heat of the tropical sun? From this point of view the irrational 'native' colonial child emerged as a *zerrspiel*, or distorting mirror, reflecting back, horrifyingly, the image of the coloniser himself in the monstrous guise of the senescent child.[14]

Officials had in fact elevated the child emperor Duy Tân to the throne at a moment when colonialism appeared to be slipping onto a more 'despotic' trajectory. Paul Doumer's 'new Hanoi' and other large public works projects required the use of *corvée* labour. Workers "died like flies" and deserters were executed.[15]

Paul Beau's tax reforms created starvation conditions in the Tonkin countryside. Violence permeated colonial society from the highest level of state right down to the intimate interior of the home. This had not gone unnoticed in France where writers such as Claude Farrère, whose novel *Les Civilisés* (1906) won the Goncourt Prize, were busy attacking colonial culture. New arrivals in Vietnam also picked up on this critical line. The travel writer and explorer Isabelle Massieu, for example, was one of an increasing number of recent arrivals to Indochina who worried at the banality of violence in the colonial home. Massieu had arrived in Saigon on 6 October 1896, and her travels in Indochina left her convinced that *colons* had grown far too accustomed to treating servants brutally—in effect adopting the punitive mode of the Asian despot within domestic space. This was exemplified in their treatment of the infantilised *boy*. She noted:

> We often strike in anger, in any old way, and the boy revolts. In reality one must treat the Annamite as an inferior or rather retain with regard to him the attitude and the rank of a man vis-à-vis a child. Our vivacity and our anger troubles this pusillanimous being. In Annam, as in China, getting carried away is a sign of weakness which surprises and inspires contempt.[16]

Massieu perhaps hoped that by exposing this problem she might augment French women's authority in the home, and by extension in empire. Certainly, she argued that in the home *colons* were insufficiently 'mature' to manage the childlike Vietnamese, for they were too much like children themselves. *Colons*' anger appeared in the eyes of domestics as 'immaturity.' With each casual blow the day drew closer when Leroy-Beaulieu's prediction would come true.[17]

As a lone female traveller, Massieu was something of a rarity, but in voicing her concerns over colonial violence she was not. Such views became more prevalent after 1900, and especially as shock waves reverberated from Hanoi after the poisoning of the garrison in 1908. Myriam Harry, writing three years later, described the *colon* as a combination of tyrant and pathetic infant, who "speaks of '*partir pour France*' (he intentionally omits the article) as a child would say '*aller chez maman*.'"[18] Stung by this rising tide of criticism and struggling in the face of internal and external problems, French administrators sought to elaborate a more 'moral,' 'associationist' basis for French colonialism in Indochina. After Beau, Governor Antony Klobukowsky set the tone with emphasis upon respect for Vietnamese traditions and beliefs. In April 1909 the Chamber of Deputies in Paris heard calls for greater sensitivity to cultures of the colonised. However, this reappraisal was still getting under way when the First World War began. And two years after that, in 1916, Duy Tân himself exposed the threat that European authority over the colonised 'boy' might invert, as he emerged as the leader of an intended revolt.[19]

YOUTHFUL IMPULSES AND TREACHEROUS ACTS: DUY TÂN'S 'BETRAYAL'

Shortly after the French declaration of war in 1914, the colonial administration in Indochina arranged for posters to be plastered (in French and Quốc ngữ) around the public places of Saigon and Hanoi. These made heavy play of the imperial bond as a form of kinship. For instance, one declared, "France loves the Annamites like its favourite children."[20] Another demanded

> proof of your deep affection to the great nation which has made you its loved sons. You see very well that it treats you like its children and that it has no doubt as to your loyalty. To this absolute trust you will respond with a filial trust.[21]

A year later, as realisation dawned of the need to fight a long, drawn-out campaign on French soil, metropolitan authorities fashioned the empire into an emblem of unity, loyalty and goodwill. What the demands of war actually translated into in Indochina was the forcible draft of troops and workers from villages, which in turn galvanised anticolonial protest.[22] Riots broke out on 28 September 1915 in Lao Bảo (Quảng Trị province). The Việt Nam Quang Phục Hội (League for the Restoration of Vietnam), an anti-French group formed in 1912 and led by Prince Cường Để and the pioneer nationalist Phan Bội Châu, sought to instigate unrest with German support. In 1916, after the Battle of Verdun, thirteen provinces in Cochinchina went into open revolt, and on 16 February peasant protesters attacked a prison in Saigon, seeking to liberate the incarcerated mystic Phan Xích Long. Rebellions from 3–4 May in the provinces of Quảng Nam, Quảng Ngãi and Thừa Thiên followed 'messianic' revolts planned by a Cholon-based group called 'Tù Mắt.'

In the same month, protesters entered Huế in support of a plan to mobilise disgruntled trainee soldiers who were preparing to embark for France. Among the instigators of this plot was Trần Cao Vân, a mandarin who had served six years in jail for his role in planning a tax protest. He had used his connections as a scholar to approach Emperor Duy Tân through the Quang Phục Hội network, and to ask him to help foment a wider uprising. The emperor's willingness to act emerged in the wake of the Government General's scrapping of the triennial examinations in Tonkin in 1915. This act in effect removed the last remaining link between the individual Vietnamese child and monarch in the *pays*. Trần Cao Vân was able to convince the emperor, who had also become resentful through his long experience of serving as an exemplar of irrelevance and servility, that immediate action was imperative. Duy Tân agreed to issue a royal order calling for general revolt.

Unfortunately for the young emperor, the French were already aware of these plans. Lacking the element of surprise, the attempted revolt was soon crushed. In a curious echo of Hàm Nghi's earlier fate the young emperor was captured in the mountains near Huế. Fourteen rebel leaders were executed and acting *résident supérieur* of Annam Henri Le Marchant de Trigon demanded the death sentence for the emperor too. However, members of the Cơ mật Viện (a council of ministers chaired by the *résident supérieur*), in particular Hồ Đắc Trung, minister of public education, pleaded for clemency on the grounds that Duy Tân was still a minor.[23] The emperor's preceptor, Eberhardt, and his medical doctor, Gaide, also demanded leniency on the grounds that the monarch had acted "on the impulse of youth."[24]

Instead of being executed, Duy Tân was sent into exile in La Réunion together with his father, Thành Thái, with whom he was accused of colluding. Governor General Roume selected the thirty-two-year-old Prince Nguyễn Phúc Bửu Đảo to become Duy Tân's successor as Emperor Khải Định. And with this, the disastrous experiment with child rulers came to an end. But memories of Duy Tân's youthful revolt lingered on. When Khải Định died in 1925, his twelve-year-old son, Nguyễn Phúc Vĩnh Thụy, was next in line to the throne. However, the colonial government refused to allow Khải Định's son, Emperor 'Bảo Đại,' to rule. Instead the French despatched him to the metropole, placing a regent on the throne in his place until the boy came of age in 1932.

TROUBLE IN FAIRYLAND: CULTURES OF CHILDHOOD IN BRITISH ASIA

In the same year that the French experiment with a child emperor was heading for disaster, Chinese children were flocking into the gardens of Government House, Hong Kong. On the morning of Saturday, 30 October 1915, the gardens of the governor's residence had been draped with festive bunting and partitioned into enclosures where organisers were adorning stalls with an array of toys and fancy articles, ices and sweets. A bran tub stood resplendent upon the lawn alongside a Christmas tree. Children dressed as fairies played around a 'fairy cave.' Nearby stood a 'Fan Oi stall' and others run by Chinese and Eurasian children from St. Stephen's Girls' College and the Diocesan Girls' School. This was the Ministering Children's League's (MCL) Bazaar, and in its wartime iterations, framed against an inclusive public and philanthropic concept of fairyland, it provided a rare template for sociable, interethnic collaboration.[25]

In the preceding years, as we saw in Chapter 4, the MCL had flourished across Asia, and especially along the China coast. From the 1890s the rise of the league here had counterbalanced its slow decline in the metropole. In Britain the society, with its Victorian emphasis upon self-help, elevating the deserving poor and showcasing domestic values, looked increasingly antiquated in the face of newer uniformed youth movements. In Eastern centres, and especially in Hong Kong and Shanghai, the strength of the MCL still allowed organisers in England to make claims to "represent the youth of the empire."[26] However, it was not long before 'fairyland' in British Asia also appeared to be coming apart at the seams.

In the early 1920s, in centre after centre organisers struggled to start league branches up again or closed them down definitively. In Singapore the Ministering Children's League shrank back within the confines of St. Andrew's Cathedral before finally closing in the autumn of 1923, with "no hope of revival."[27] In Penang, the branch closed in 1922 but reopened in 1924, though by the early 1930s its membership had slipped to just thirty children. This mirrored a general decline in the organisation's global membership to four hundred branches and 24,000 members and associates by 1924.

The decline of the league revealed much about the changing role of youth in empire and for some it reflected urges toward more active models epitomised by the Scouts and Guides, emphasising strength, vigour and adventure in the great outdoors. Under the leadership of Lieutenant-General Robert Baden-Powell, the Boy Scout movement had gathered momentum after the Brownsea Island camp of 1907. Promising to build 'character' and fashion an imperial mind-set among British youth, the movement quickly spread across gender lines. While Boy Scouts modelled the manly mastery of undomesticated space from 1910, the Girl Guide movement encouraged girls to embody a a modernised domesticity. Baden-Powell's import to Britain from its empire was reexported to the world. The first Scout troops in France, the 'Éclaireurs Unionistes,' started in 1911; an Association des Éclaireurs de France was formed in 1912, and a Catholic Association (the Scouts de France) was established in 1920. By 1922, the first world census of the Boy Scout Association counted over one million members.

However, in tropical colonies where colonial childhood functioned as a place marker of white vulnerability and authority, the presence of adolescents was defined in terms of civilisational failure, and these uniformed movements targeting this cohort grew slowly. Scouts and Guides in British Malaya and Hong Kong garnered little enthusiasm in elite circles, started relatively 'late' (in 1908 and 1910 respectively) and remained numerically unimpressive before the Great War. It was not until the late 1920s, when political unrest stimulated greater official interest in uniformed organisations as a potential tool for resisting communism, disciplining youthful colonial subjects and channelling the rising tide of indigenous nationalism, that the number enrolled grew more rapidly.[28] In other parts of empire, notably colonies of white settlement such as Australia, the visibility of these movements and the 'modern' models of boyhood and girlhood they put on display led many to complain that the Ministering Children's League had become little more than a 'training society' for the Girl Guides or the Boy Scouts. However, in South, East and Southeast Asia organisers accounted for the decline of the league in Asia in terms not only of a sense of failing, in a comparative sense, to compete with more thrusting, often militaristic models of youth but of an inability to meet other standards of childhood elaborated in other colonial centres, notably those of the MCL along the China coast.

FIG. 5.6. "An Incident from the Queen of Hearts," Ministering Children's League Penang Branch, 22 September 1928. *Source*: Ministering Children's League Collection, Surrey History Centre, 7919/6/30. Reproduced by kind permission of Surrey History Centre, Copyright of Surrey History Centre.

In those places memberships were still large enough to allow league work to remain segregated along racial lines (though these lines broke down on social occasions). But in Southeast Asia, dwindling numbers made racial heterogeneity more apparent, especially in public performances. Here, as we saw in the previous chapter, even before the war organisers had begun to doubt the value of more 'cosmopolitan' visions of colonial childhood. This was a matter of growing concern as expatriates living in other Asian centres of the British Empire fretted over how to shore up their attenuated racial authority. In a period when nationalists were winning concessions, the sense of a looming imperial 'end game' had spread within foreign communities in India. The influx of a wealthy indigenous middle class made hill stations more racially heterogeneous, prompting organisers to complain, "It does not seem possible ... to have work parties or meetings."[29] Organisers also seem to have linked the value of their work to their ability to put racially homogeneous childhoods on display. In Penang, league president Grace Keppel Garnier wrote wistfully in correspondence with London, "It is splendid to read about the Hong Kong branch and Shanghai, they keep very strong."[30] She advised correspondents that in her branch of the league "all classes and all colours work very happily together," but added, revealingly, "Don't insert this last remark in a Magazine I think."[31] Soon after, the Penang branch closed down.

As Keppel Garnier's observation suggests, while many of the other league branches failed to adapt to interwar conditions the 'model branches' of Shanghai and Hong Kong bucked the global trend. Between the wars they achieved unparalleled positions of strength and significance in terms of both membership and funding. By 1927, with a membership of more than one thousand, Hong Kong's league had grown to roughly twice the size of the second-largest centre outside the metropole, Melbourne, and it dwarfed the local Scout movement (which had only reached six hundred members by 1931). During the 1930s, membership would consistently remain over one thousand for children alone.[32]

Elite Chinese interest in the league, as evidenced quite publicly in the multiethnic bazaars, ensured that even as the overall number of European child residents fell the organisation retained a critical mass of participants, and that it projected a remarkable cultural vitality and visibility. The league's importance in the immediate postwar era was reflected in the decision of the governor's wife, Lady Stubbs, the new president, to draw "all organised women's charities" in Hong Kong under its aegis.[33] Following this, league events increased still further in size, with some two thousand adults and five hundred children attending the bazaar held in 1921 at Government House.[34]

European elites continued to invest in the league and its fairylike vision of childhood, in part because in the early 1920s the changing political balance in China left British colonialism more intensely imperilled. As power structures in China fragmented in the immediate postwar era, British political and commercial interests also weakened. When industrial unrest hit the Crown Colony in 1922, the governor, Reginald Edward Stubbs, claimed this was a Communist insurgency instigated by Soviet advisors in south China. Then another massacre, this time perpetrated by Shanghai Municipal Police on 30 May 1925, triggered the anti-imperialist 'May 30th Movement,' and a strike-boycott followed in Hong Kong, lasting from June 1925 to October 1926.

These turbulent conditions made the mutual appreciation of childhood—as a public focal point for Anglo-Chinese collaboration—look more important than ever.[35] The value of the league lay in its ability to project British cultural leadership even, or rather *especially*, at a time when the social character of European colonialism was changing. This portrayal of childhood served to underpin a sense of the stable symbolic contrasts upon which claims to rule depended, and an older colonial order of things. So while the league formed part of a dynamic associative life on the China coast in Hong Kong, such associations represented much more than simply British "cultural alienation from the omnipresent Chinese."[36]

In the eyes of Hong Kong's wealthy Chinese merchants, whose daughters attended elite schools and joined the league, childhood had long been connected with philanthropy, reform and nation building. From the 1880s an elite Chinese-run charitable institution, the Po Leung Kuk, assisted women and children.

Social networks linked the Kuk with the Tung Wah 'Chinese Hospital,' the ultimate symbol of elite Chinese philanthropy in Hong Kong. Within and around these institutions a coherent, local and mostly self-made elite emerged. As Elizabeth Sinn has shown, many of its members saw philanthropy as "an instrument that makes financial worth symbolically equivalent to moral worth" and believed that the "dispensation of charity legitimises the accumulation of wealth."[37] The dynamism of the league in Hong Kong following the admission of Chinese girls to its structures reflected its value to these wealthy entrepreneurs. Class may have failed to function as a bridge to interracial mixing in other social settings, as John Carroll has shown (and Chinese continued to be excluded from European club memberships for adults), but the league offered a space where elite Chinese and European children could act as something closer to equals.[38]

Neither entirely 'European' nor official or solely religious, the league drew upon the support of elites who had little interest in seeing the social role of the colonial state expand between the wars. The sheer scale of social problems afflicting the transient population of Hong Kong demanded that philanthropy be *more* dynamic, precisely in order that arguments for state intervention might continue to be blocked. Hence, as the immediate threat of Chinese nationalism faded with the end of the strike-boycott in 1926, this Anglo-Chinese partnership did not simply persist: it was in these very years that the league scaled new fundraising heights. By 1928 the MCL was expanding so fast that the gardens of Government House could no longer contain the annual league bazaar. The president, Lady Bella Sydney Woolf (sister of the writer Leonard Woolf and wife of the colonial secretary, W. T. Southorn), organised the removal of the event to a vast pleasure park named Lee Gardens owned by the entrepreneur Lee Hy San. There, on 1 October, a new event, dubbed Fun o' the Fair, took profits of over £1,000 in a single day. Donations doubled in 1929. By then organisers were also reaching out to new audiences through the medium of cinema. A league film was shown in Shanghai and Hong Kong, where Sir Shou Son Chow, a senior member of Legislative Council, arranged for its inclusion in the programme of one of the largest cinema houses in Hong Kong on four consecutive days. By this point the Hong Kong branch was generating more revenue in donations than any other league branch in the world (with Shanghai close behind).

With elite support, fairyland's lustre did not fade but grew brighter. Significantly, this was also a period marked by a growing fascination within China for Victorian fairy tales, and one marked by subversive intent. As we saw in the last chapter, adaptations of fairy stories such as Lewis Carroll's *Alice's Adventures in Wonderland* provided a space within which children in Hong Kong could experiment with new public subjectivities. Just as the fairy tale provided a space of imagination, and thus of relative autonomy for the child from the adult, so it also provided reformers with space in which to rethink 'national evolution' and subvert narratives of imperial domination within the confines of a colonial world order. As Andrew Jones has shown, Chinese intellectuals found the pedagogical possibilities of the fairy tale intriguing as they linked the biological development of children with China's development on a national level.[39]

In colonial Hong Kong the cultural importance of childhood in the fairy mode, for all its ambiguities, resided chiefly in its capacity to provide a space for the sharing of an elite sensibility *across* racial lines. Contemporaneously, recognition of the Crown Colony as 'fairyland' in popular songs, travel guides and movies of the time spread far afield.[40] In 1928 the Publicity Bureau for South China described Hong Kong as "a fairy-like city."[41] Travel writers repackaged these perceptions for cross-cultural consumption. René Jouglet advised French travellers to stop off in Hong Kong, en route to Dalat or Yokohama, to take a glimpse at "a fairyland unparalleled."[42] Cinema audiences who might have struggled to locate the Crown Colony on a map knew nonetheless, or at least were told, that a trip on the Peak tram offered a "shortcut to fairyland."[43]

'FAIRYLANDS OF SCIENCE': SINGAPORE'S 'BABY SHOWS'

As postwar pressures combined to produce more expansive celebrations of childhood in Hong Kong in the fairy mode, new public visions of childhood, drawn against the moral authority of medicine, were emerging in Singapore. Conditions in Hong Kong enhanced subtle experiments in the use of childhood as a space of shared interaction, but in Singapore by contrast official interest veered toward the use of public performances to reflect racial segregation. An important driver here was the Chinese youth-led anti-Japanese riots of May 1919.

The riots, in which students figured prominently, caught official Singapore unawares. In their aftermath, convictions grew within the administration that stronger relations with other ethnic groups were required to counterbalance the influence of the Straits Chinese. As the government deliberated constitutional reform (from 1920), officials sought to reinforce social divisions within Singapore along sectional-communal lines.

In this context official and commercial elites both remained wary of sponsoring public rituals that might cut across or compromise ethnic divisions. While children featured prominently in public celebrations of the postwar era, these events were a far cry from their mixed prewar equivalents. The Treats organised by Charles Buckley had made suggestive appeals to childhood as a focus around which fissiparous, Anglophone groups might cohere. By contrast, postwar events involved the public presentation of distinct ethnic-national types rather than childhood per se. Thus, the Pageant of Empire organised by the Girls' Friendly Society in 1923 featured two hundred girls of all ages organised into groups, each under their 'own' ethnic-national banner.[44] 'English' girls danced under a maypole. 'Irish' girls danced a jig. Miss Vint's YWCA-hosted 'Pageant of Girls,' devised by Mr. D. Santry and held at Government House in May 1923, offered a similar, ethnically segmented display. A few years earlier, in April 1919, a new event had reinforced this differentiated model of childhood in public; this was the Singapore 'Baby Show.'[45]

'Scientific baby contests' had their origins in the American Midwest, where they were first organised by middle-class women's groups at agricultural fairs as sideshows intended to promote maternal health. The earliest took place in August 1911 in Des Moines under the aegis of the American Medical Association's Committee for Public Health Education among Women. The shows quickly spread to urban areas where organisers targeted mothers in East Coast industrial neighbourhoods.[46] They formed part of a wider process through which childhood was 'professionalised' as a field for medicopedagogical research.[47] The contests presented scientific standards upon which to evaluate and compare infants with a view to reducing infant mortality rates and enhancing rural child health. The more serious, objective tone of the contests distinguished them from the 'Pretty Baby' shows that had gone before.

As we saw in Chapter 2, awareness of baby shows as a gauge of population quality already existed in Singapore in 1914. Five years later the city hosted its own event. The guiding force behind the establishment of the Singapore Baby Show was the Woman's Christian Temperance Union (WCTU). Frances Willard had founded the WCTU in the United States in 1884 to promote temperance and women's interests globally, and the work of the Boston schoolteacher Mary Leavitt was crucial in spreading this oeuvre trans-nationally. In 1887 during a visit to Singapore, in the midst of her ongoing 'world tour,' Leavitt announced that a local branch of the union had been set up.[48] The women of the WCTU in Singapore organised the first Baby Show in 1919 as a means of focusing public attention upon the devastating problem of infant mortality.

In Singapore high levels of overcrowding in central neighbourhoods exacerbated outbreaks of disease, especially cholera and tuberculosis. This also resulted in rates of infant mortality among Asian populations that were staggeringly high compared with those among Europeans. Singapore had the highest infant mortality rates in the Straits and the figures were shocking by comparison not only with those for Europe but even many other colonial cities.[49] While some European administrators such as H. N. Ridley, scientific director of the Botanical Gardens, still felt able to claim that high infant mortality rates had the benefit of creating a 'fitter race,' by the early twentieth century others recognised that infant mortality was becoming an empirewide issue, and a dangerously combustible one at that.[50]

Viewed from London, and from Singapore, the example of Hong Kong was especially important in galvanising concern. In 1886 Hong Kong's Legislative Council had heard questions over the infant mortality rates. The secretary of the Sanitary Board investigated voluntary institutions set up to receive the young (notably the Asile de la Sainte-Enfance and the Italian Convent) and brought to light staggering endemic levels of child mortality, though he largely exonerated these institutions from blame. In the aftermath of a particularly virulent outbreak of the bubonic plague in 1894, officials again highlighted this problem, not least since it exacerbated the difficulty of securing accurate vital statistics. In 1895 Francis Clark, the colony's first medical officer of health, referred to "the enormous mortality among Chinese infants."[51] This he estimated at 680 per 1,000 live births, compared to 116 for Europeans. Clark blamed Chinese midwifery and inadequate parenting for the figures but demanded more invasive regulation. As the figures reached a staggering 928 per 1,000 in 1900, meaning that of every thousand infants born only seventy-two survived, the Colonial Office in London intervened.[52]

Officials in London had become increasingly aware of the potential for high infant mortality rates to reflect the unresponsiveness of colonial governments to social problems. The colonial secretary, Joseph Chamberlain, requested that Governor Henry Blake launch an official inquiry into the problem in Hong Kong. When the special committee appointed to examine this problem submitted its report, it argued that the high mortality rates reflected inaccurate vital data, the endemic transience of the population and the 'intrinsic' uncleanliness of the Chinese population.[53] Nevertheless, the committee's recommendations, which focused upon improving registrations of births and deaths, the charitable provision of home visits and expanded hospital facilities, raised awareness of the problem. The reluctance of the government to fund improvements spurred Chinese reformers to lead initiatives to combat the problem in the private sector.[54] These included a training school for Chinese midwives at the Alice Memorial Maternity Hospital, established in 1904 under the sponsorship of the Chinese physician Kai Ho Kai (who had served on the government's committee of investigation). At the hospital, from 1905, the London Missionary School doctor and obstetrician Alice Sibree began training Chinese midwives. Meanwhile Chinese elites sponsored the improved provision of maternity care for poor Chinese through the Chinese Public Dispensaries Committee. Before the First World War this mainly Chinese voluntary energy saw Hong Kong emerge as a centre associated with the drive to combat infant mortality, and from which trained midwives were recruited for Penang and other parts of British Asia.

The Colonial Office had put pressure upon the Hong Kong government to act by drawing unfavourable contrasts between its infant mortality rates and those in the Straits Settlements. But there too before the First World War the English-educated Chinese elite in Singapore had begun to highlight the deficiencies of municipal sanitation in the English-language press.[55] This led the governor of the Straits Settlements to commission the tropical hygiene expert Professor W. J. Simpson to conduct an investigation. Simpson reported in February 1907 and the municipal officer of health, Dr. W.R.C. Middleton, commenced a drive to reduce infant mortality by engaging Asian mothers and regulating the training of midwives. The Straits Medical Department appointed its first European nurse and the government began to fund the training of Malay midwives in the hope that they might disseminate childcare knowledge to mothers. In 1907 the maternity hospital (established in 1888 with only eight beds) was expanded. Home visits by the Singapore Health Department inspectors began in 1910, and the compulsory registration of midwives commenced from 1917.

In the interwar years infant mortality took on the potential to inform broader challenges to colonial authority. And by now, if anything the problem possessed the potential to develop into a more dangerous critique of official social neglect in Singapore, because here families had settled earlier and often for longer. This meant the official excuse of population transience was not as easily trotted out. The Commission of Inquiry into urban conditions in Singapore of 1918 paid special attention to high infant mortality rates. Official explanations blamed economic conditions and parental ignorance and neglect (especially on the part of mothers).[56] By 1931 infant mortality rates in urban Singapore still remained higher than in the rural Federated Malay States.[57] And as in Hong Kong this highlighted the inadequacy of official engagements with the problem. However, here when non-state agents stepped into the breach, the partnership between volunteers, medical professionals and commercial interests produced the Singapore Baby Show.

The show offered didactic visions of childhood, putting very small infants centre stage. The first event took place at the Victoria Memorial Hall. It foregrounded healthy children and put 'ideal' physical specimens on view. The emphasis was preventive. Scorecards allowed judges to rank children in relation to certain physical standards. They thereby familiarised audiences with a new medicalised language of 'normative' and 'non-normative' childhoods. However, in contrast to the moral vision of 'good' children that prevailed in Hong Kong, the Singapore show dispensed with claims for Europeans as exemplars and instead set eugenic standards fragmented along ethnic lines. Children aged one to five years 'competed' mainly within their own racial-ethnic groupings.[58] Judges elected 'champions' in each. While simultaneously underlining the application of hygienic measures to the preservation of *all* child life, the show thus reinforced communal divisions. Organisers represented the delivery of superior nurturance not as the responsibility of the state but of each of Singapore's constituent communities, and more specifically women. The Baby Show was ultimately an incitement to Straits Chinese, Eurasians, Malays and others to take responsibility for their own.[59]

Though advertisements for the Baby Show in 1919 informed mothers, "Your Baby is sure to be the best," the selection of a few victorious infants from thousands of entrants condemned the majority to reflect upon failure.[60] Those whose children were denied entry to the main round of the competition often reacted indignantly to 'defeat.' Organisers were constantly forced to adjust rules to address

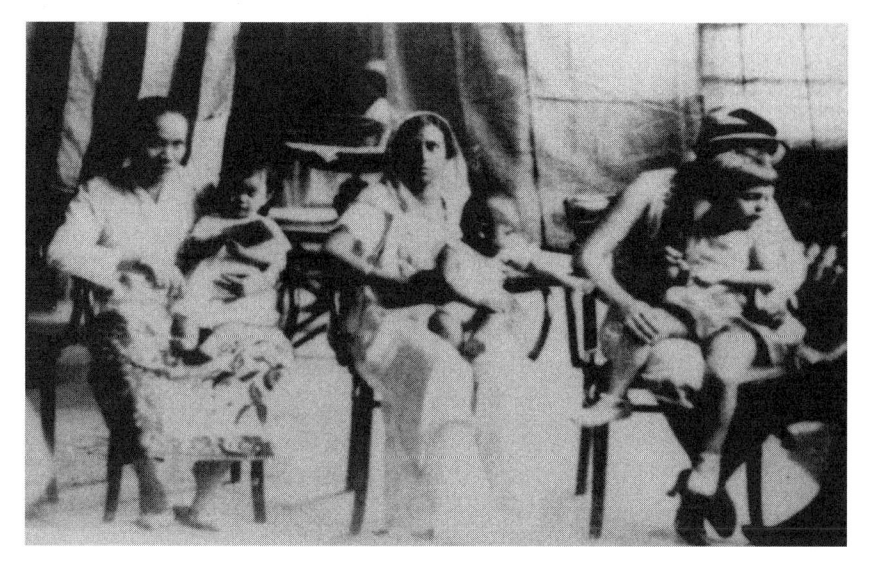

FIG. 5.7. "Proud Mothers with Their Prize-Winning Babies." *Source*: "Singapore Baby Show," *Malayan Saturday Post*, 6 October 1928, 16.

the problem posed by mothers who simply would not accept that their children had been rejected. Those whose babies 'lost' would continue to tour the judging booths in the hope that sheer persistence might secure a successful outcome. By 1929 this tactic was so common that organisers introduced a preliminary screening process barring unhealthy or 'substandard' babies.

The colonial state mostly lurked in the background at this event. When the WCTU hit financial difficulties in 1923, the Baby Show was not taken up by the state but was instead quickly drawn under the auspices of other charitable works: the St. Andrew's Day Fête and then the Child Welfare Society (CWS) of Singapore. The CWS was a voluntary organisation (formed in 1921 and incorporated in 1923) devoted to helping mothers keep children healthy, by organising home visits and play spaces and running clinics and crèches.[61] By the late 1920s the chief health officer sat on the Baby Show's organising committee; municipal nurses and matrons attended; and governors' wives sometimes served as presidents of the CWS and participated in prize giving, as did Lady Clementi in 1931.

Through this partnership with voluntary workers, medical professionals claimed by 1930 that "the conditions of life in which and into which these babies are born is slowly improving."[62] Even with minimal government investment, a decline in infant mortality rates had followed from 363 per 1,000 in 1907, to 179.3 by 1934.[63] The Baby Shows attracted wide and growing interest.[64] Equivalents spread throughout British Malaya, to Ipoh in 1924, to Kuala Lumpur in 1928, to Pahang in

1932 and throughout the Federated Malay States by 1937. By 1931 the event appeared in India, where the actuary L. S. Vaidyanathan praised the recent appearance of "Baby-week Exhibitions and other propaganda relating to the proper bringing-up of children."[65] Back in Singapore, one year earlier, record numbers of mothers had entered their babies into one of the show's six subdivisions of ethnicity.

Volunteers' pleas for strong 'racial cooperation' around childhood met with little enthusiasm from the government. And by 1930 a range of European critics poured scorn on the shows in the colonial newspaper press, condemning them as a waste of time, a dangerous threat of disease contagion and a commercial farrago. Some Europeans seemed to have found the shows disconcerting because they connected small children into trans-colonial consumer culture. Elsewhere this was coming to be exemplified by Mickey Mouse clubs, cinema shows and other popular products. In the shows, however, other commercial interests prevailed, notably those of companies such as Nestlé and Anglo-Swiss Milk and Cow and Gate Co., which provided financial support to organisers and dominated proceedings with their eye-catching trade exhibits, advertisements and stalls. As with other aspects of child-centric consumer culture these products were potentially corrosive of the subdivisions and formal distinctions upon which colonialism rested.[66] As a result of such internal tensions the Singapore Baby Show fractured along ethnic-racial fault lines.

After 1930 individual 'communities' appropriated the event. A show started up at the Naval Base, for example. But by far the most exuberant new iterations came from among the Chinese. The Straits Chinese had taken such an interest in the Baby Shows that by the early 1930s newspapers described the event as "mostly Chinese."[67] This occurred at a moment when the colonial government was taking a more coercive line toward the Chinese population of Singapore. An official clampdown on Chinese schools followed the 'Kreta Ayer' incident of 12 March 1927. Governor Sir Cecil Clementi oversaw the introduction of the Immigration Restriction Ordinance of 1 August 1930, reducing the flow of Chinese male in-migrants. The impact of the Great Depression and the immigration ordinance were to have a balancing effect upon the sex ratio within Singapore's Chinese population. But infant mortality rates remained stubbornly high (at 191 per 1,000 in 1930, compared with 170 for Indians).[68]

As the colonial government's interventions in areas such as immigration policy raised fears among Chinese that their interests and privileges were being encroached upon, spokesmen for the Straits Chinese used Baby Shows to reassert their claims upon modern, elite standards of living. Those who took up this task were, significantly, among the most forward-looking and intellectually engaged sections of Chinese society. The Nanyang Chinese Students Society (with the support of the Children's Aid Society) emerged to take over the running of Baby Shows in Singapore by 1934. The events modelled a radically denaturalised, trans-

Cultures of Childhood in Interwar Asia 137

FIG. 5.8. Fun o' the Fair, Lee Gardens, Hong Kong, 1938. *Source*: Ministering Children's League Collection, Surrey History Centre, 7919/7/31. Reproduced by kind permission of Surrey History Centre, Copyright of Surrey History Centre.

formative conception of Chineseness predicated upon the disciplined hygienic modernness of the child, and a vision of the family as a unit of consumption and not only production.[69] Chinese organisers proved far less anxious to insulate children and childhood against the commercial orientation of the shows. Held at the site of the Great World Cabaret, fancy dress competitions, concerts and commercial goings-on all but overshadowed the medical authority on display.

Meanwhile in Hong Kong colonial elites had also grown increasingly alarmed at the incursions of consumer culture into the child-centric events that they sponsored. Having extended fairyland's boundaries from the segregated imperial heights of the Peak to Government House, in the mid-levels, and then down into the 'plain,' through the Fun o' the Fair in Lee Gardens, Ministering Children's League organisers observed a worrying shift in the kinds of childhood on display. The intention behind this shift may have been to demonstrate more widely and prominently the best of 'Western' civilisation, but in practice what the Fun o' the Fair entailed by the late 1930s was not the opposition of coloniser and colonised, nor domination through incorporation, but an unstable, commercialised vision of childhood with troublingly egalitarian aspects.

Bella Woolf, who presided over the league, had written earlier of childhood in universalist terms, describing how "in some ways children are like birds," with "a life apart which goes on unchangingly under different skies."[70] But by 1930 Woolf expressed fears that the ideally separate 'world' of children ('Asian' and 'Western') was being compromised by a homogenising commercial culture. The result was a different kind of childhood—stripped of its moralising content—and a different kind of child. This was the "modern child, accustomed to unlimited 'flickers,' unimpressed with old-fashioned entertainments (the Christmas Tree with one surprise present for each child)."[71] Of course, consumption and the disciplinary strategies of the Yule had lain at the heart of early definitions of ideal colonial childhoods. But Woolf did not interpret the amplification of this aspect in terms of its liberatory potential. Instead, she complained that childhood had been torn free from its exemplary elitist prewar moorings and was now veering toward a tacky and overly savvy commodification. As the wartime caesura of British rule in Hong Kong approached, fairyland was collapsing under the weight of its own internal contradictions.[72]

'FROM OUT OF THE MOUTHS OF BABES': PICTURING CHILDHOOD IN FRENCH INDOCHINA

Historians have seen Duy Tân's revolt—the last scholar-inspired rebellion in Vietnam—as a "romantic aberration" after which the traditional alliance between the court, scholars and peasantry fell apart.[73] However, between the wars in French Indochina the image of the child emperor and his failed revolt echoed on within even the modernising independence movements that idealised a future without the monarchy. This was a period in which protesters—among them schoolchildren—criticised the colonial government fiercely for its failure to realise ideals of liberty, equality and fraternity.[74] And because the colonial state had long and forcefully projected these very ideals through the rhetoric of kinship and the symbolism of childhood, youthful protesters self-consciously sought to manipulate this imagery for their own ends.

As Philippe Peycam has shown, the rise of political journalism and public print media in Saigon made it a centre for the exchange of ideas and for open debates over colonialism.[75] Here an already vibrant public sphere expanded with the emergence of new, critical newspapers such as *Đông Pháp Thời Báo*, *La Cloche Fêlée*, *L'Annam* and *Le Jeune Annam*. In 1925 the political atmosphere darkened after the trial of the leading nationalist Phan Bội Châu triggered public protests. In response Paris sent a Socialist, Alexandre Varenne, to take up the governorship in November 1925. He promptly released Châu from prison in the hope of bringing calm, placing him under house arrest instead. But conflict continued to flare.

In March 1926 the anticolonial nationalist Phan Chu Trinh had died, and when students in Saigon attempted to mourn his death this triggered brutally repressive measures from police. These reprisals further exacerbated tensions, and in the protests that followed Vietnamese youth resorted to incendiary portrayals of Vietnam as a nation-in-waiting, trapped in childhood by a tyrannical colonial master. The earlier revolt of the child emperor Duy Tân echoed on in the protests of urban-based youth. Though, as we shall see in Chapter 8, their orientation was no longer toward old scholar-led Sino-Vietnamese cultural nationalism, they incorporated symbolic references to childhood into anticolonial insurgency.

The youthful nature of the anticolonial protests that burst out into the streets of Hanoi, Saigon and other centres in 1926 raised fears for the impact of Western education. Though the number of pupils enrolled in Franco-Vietnamese primary schools had grown rapidly in the early 1920s, the Office of Public Instruction began to squeeze youth out of French schools in Indochina leading on to a high school diploma, and thus access to French higher education.[76] When Cochinchina's elite sought to circumvent such restrictions by sending their boys to study in France, French officials grew concerned that the latter were coming into contact with radical political ideologies. By the late 1920s older nationalists, such as the neo-Confucian traditionalist Phạm Quỳnh, were voicing alarm that Vietnamese youth had been 'deracinated' through contact with Western ideas and urban living, not only abroad but also through exposure to the burgeoning commercial culture of French Indochina. As French and Vietnamese critics mulled this prospect, officials advanced the 'rerooting' or reattachment of native peoples to the countryside as a means of counteracting political instability. This was seen to depend upon a conservative defence of the 'native family' and what counted as 'tradition,' and a key domain in which this response was rolled out was art.

In 1925, in the context of heavy criticism of 'hybridised' culture and overly Westernised Vietnamese youth, the French government had established an art school named the École des Beaux-Arts de l'Indochine (EBAI) in Hanoi. The administration anticipated that Victor Tardieu, its first director, would deliver a curriculum ushering Vietnamese students toward the preservation of their own 'tradition.'[77] The French teachers at the EBAI were not the only cultural producers working to achieve this aim. Writers in the orientalist tradition strove to achieve similar ends, seeking out subjects capable of modelling an 'authentic' folk aesthetic. In the process, artists and writers latched onto children as representatives of tradition. The journalist and poet Jeanne Leuba, for example, used exoticising images of rural children in her work, while Christiane Fournier interpreted the "little Asian child on the back of a buffalo in the rice paddy" as "an absolutely tranquil, everyday sight."[78] Rural children, as unsocialised emblems of 'nature' divested of the trappings of modernity, also proved important to Vietnamese writers' efforts to represent tradition in the turbulent context of the 1920s. These works, reflecting desires to recapture and pin down an 'authentic' Indochina, chimed with initiatives emanating from the small Vietnamese middle class to celebrate the 'traditional' family and vanishing, idealised rural childhoods.[79]

As the Vietnamese peasant child became an important focus for these cultural producers, Marc Chadourne, the journalist and translator of Joseph Conrad's works, published his 'reflections on Indochina.' He accompanied the work with

FIG. 5.9. Marie-Antoinette Boullard-Devé, Untitled portrait of a child, 1927. *Source*: Marc Chadourne, *Vision de l'Indochine: Études, pastels et gouaches de Mme A.Boullard Devé* (Paris: Plon, 1938). Reproduced by kind permission of Alain Boullard.

FIG. 5.10. Marie-Antoinette Boullard-Devé, "Annam," 1926. *Source*: Marc Chadourne, *Vision de l'Indochine: Études, pastels et gouaches de Mme A.Boullard Devé* (Paris: Plon, 1938). Reproduced by kind permission of Alain Boullard.

a set of pastel drawings and gouache paintings entitled 'faces of Indochina.' Most of the faces in question were those of babies and young children set in a quintessentially rural milieu. The creator of these images was Marie-Antoinette Boullard-Devé, who was known as a 'government painter.' Having studied with Frédéric Humbert from 1908 at the École des Beaux Arts in Paris, she had won the Prix de la Companie de la Navigation Mixte for her painting in 1921, becoming sufficiently well known for the French government to provide funds for two *missions* involving travel and residence in Indochina. The first resulted in work displayed in the 'Angkor Pavilion' of the Exposition Nationale Coloniale held in Marseille in 1922. The second culminated in a forty-metre painting of 'Indochinese types' displayed in the Pavilion d'Indochine at the Exposition Coloniale Internationale of 1931. Boullard painted most of the images that Chadourne selected for his book in 1926–27, by which time she had married for a second time (having left her first husband, the sculptor Pierre Fournier des Corats in 1917) and had moved to Indochina with her second husband, the colonial administrator Maurice-Arsène Devé.

Working in particular in and around Huế, where Devé served as 'Resident,' Boullard made Vietnamese children a special focus of her work. Though her style was largely academic, it betrayed some Modernist influences. With its slight abstracting elongation, linear contouring and colouring it gestured toward the work of Paul Gauguin, Amedeo Modigliani and Paul Cézanne. It is unclear as to who the children in the paintings actually were, but they seem to have occupied quite different social positions. Some appear, judging by the clothing and jewellery they wear, to have been sons or daughters of higher Huế society, perhaps the native Francophone elite. In one image, for example, a young girl appears seated on a chair and holding a flower—symbolising the approach of fertility—in hands demurely clasped over her lap. In others Boullard-Devé depicted the children of rural labourers whom she may have encountered on her travels in Huế's rural hinterlands, in places such as Quảng Nam. For example, in one painting the somewhat androgynous figure of a young boy can be seen wearing a conical hat and raincoat made from rice straw or palm fibre, of the kind worn by those who worked outdoors. These figures possess visual markers suggestive of a gendered division between a leisured feminine civility and a more masculine labouring 'primitiveness.' However, it is also significant that Boullard presented such children, irrespective of class and gender markers, not within cluttered private interiors but amid lush foliage, as unassuming inhabitants of a preindustrial idyll.[80]

There was certainly a metropolitan market for work of this ilk, with its exotic subject matter. Chadourne's collection was intended to serve it.[81] Since they were unambiguously rural, the children in Boullard's paintings could serve as reassuring markers of the docile colonial subject. Far from being threatening and articulate like the Westernised, deracinated schoolchildren leading protests in large centres at the very time Boullard was working in the field, these figures appeared mute and reassuringly exotic, more likely to become good Vietnamese peasants than 'bad Frenchmen.' The taste for this kind of work, drawing upon the symbolic resonance of the colonial subject as child was reaching new heights in France by the late 1920s as Germany's revival inspired new levels of popular enthusiasm for empire as a source of loyalty and strength.

However, on closer inspection it appears that Boullard-Devé's work departed in certain respects from the older iconography of colonial childhood. While she often painted very young children, those of an age when their mothers' influence was assumed to be strongest, Boullard-Devé presented childhood as fundamentally different from adulthood. In some of her paintings children appear alongside mothers, but often they hover, detached from tradition, the family and social convention. By focusing in on faces, she shifted the emphasis from childhood in general to individual children. And she also produced images marked by a haunting intimacy. The children in the paintings confront and return the viewer's gaze. Their eyes hint at the possibility of connections between the viewer and the child's interior thoughts. Rather than being the passive outgrowths of a benevolent nature so often seen in colonial painting, photography and portraiture, these children appeared as possessors of an incipient sense of selfhood.

This marked a departure from earlier republican symbolism figuring symbiosis (discussed in the previous chapter).[82] Though Boullard-Devé was a government-sponsored artist, her work seems to have captured some of the ambivalence surrounding Vietnamese youth in these years. She may well have been influenced by youthful protests as these hit major centres across Indochina, and by the pugnacious official response they drew. But it is also well worth noting that she was working in Annam against the backdrop of rapid changes in the political and economic circumstances of the Vietnamese countryside. The alienation of peasants from the land, the capitalisation of crops and the influx of indentured labourers through French-organised schemes produced rural unrest feeding directly into urban political discontent. In the mid- to late 1920s, as agricultural prices deflated, rural-based families ceded their children to survive. Children moved out along networks linked to urban centres in Asia in an epidemic of child trafficking. Hence, while metropolitan viewers might have seen these portraits as fitting comfortably within the conventions of portraiture and an established orientalist oeuvre, from another perspective they implicitly raised questions over the destiny of their small subjects. They hinted at the radical potential of the *child as individual*, and at an assertive subjectivity lurking (threateningly) even in rural milieux where harmony was supposed to reside.

'GENERATIONAL TENSIONS': SAIGON AND THE SEMAINES DE L'ENFANCE

As wider tensions unsettled established iconographies of colonial childhood, new visions emerged to shore up the administration's disintegrating moral claims for empire. The most important centre in this was again Saigon, as the principal venue for open intellectual critiques of colonialism. Because Saigon's elites resided in a colony, not a protectorate, more liberal-minded residents anticipated their city might play a key role in evidencing 'progress.' Here Cochinchinese elites used public print media and other means to discuss international affairs, and there had long been a greater sense of contact with Europe. Urban intellectuals also wrote about the extremes of wealth and poverty they observed. They refracted their reflections through new political lenses as they engaged with the question of how France was treating the races whose progress it championed. A rising tide of criticism, both French and Vietnamese, provided a mutual stimulus to philanthropic action.[83]

By the late 1920s French women emerged as important contributors to this field. This was a period when assumptions about improved hygiene and sanitation weakened injunctions against women's movements in empire.[84] European feminists created new forums and used them to assert women's importance in elevating 'native' peoples, across empires. In this vein, the États Généraux du Féminisme in 1931, set up by the Conseil National des Femmes Françaises, enquired as to how French women might better protect Vietnamese children. A series of anticolonial shocks built momentum behind long-standing feminist arguments that French women should play more prominent, 'maternal' roles within colonialism. The bloody repression of the abortive Yên Bái insurgency of 1930, and the shock of the Nghệ-Tĩnh uprising of 1930–31, enhanced the value of French women's agency as auxiliaries of empire.[85] These events, and the caustic criticism of the colonial social record presented by trans-national institutions such as the League of Nations, opened up new spaces within which women might begin to make a larger public contribution to the shaping of a hitherto profoundly masculine colonial culture.

Well before the election of the Popular Front government in France drew a new commitment to social reform in empire, women in Indochina were staking out new public partnerships with medical professionals around a shared vision of childhood. In Saigon the scene was especially vibrant. There a newspaper, *Le Journal des Femmes*, addressed questions relating to the intellectual and social evolution of women. In 1929 administrators' wives, such as Madame Catroux, Madame Graffeuil, Madame Veber and Madame Rivoal, and their daughters set up and ran the Entr'aide Maternelle, an organisation devoted to protecting early childhood, in Saigon. This group staked out claims to be new champions of the moral claims of French colonialism. In Hanoi, Christiane Fournier, whose father was a civil servant, referred to such work to belabour critics who declared, "Our colonial oeuvre is in vain," using the image of "little children . . . protected from physical and moral degeneration. So many lives saved, so many little bodies removed from misery, little souls from dread."[86] Significantly, elite Vietnamese women, who formed the readership of newspapers such as *Phụ Nữ Tân Văn*

(1929–35), also contributed to this emergent interethnic collaboration, focusing in particular upon the suburban areas of the Saigon-Cholon region.[87]

This shared sense of endeavour soon produced an official showcase, named the Semaine de l'enfance (or Childhood Week) in 1934. The event was repeated in 1936 and 1938 and a fourth was also planned for 1940, only for the war to force its cancellation. As in the Singapore shows, the intention of the 'Weeks' was to vulgarise *puériculture*, 'mothercraft.' And the event had metropolitan precedents. Medical doctors, social elites and clergy organised spectacular *semaines* at the national level from May 1930 under the impulse of the Comité National d'Enfance, an umbrella organisation coordinating child welfare work. In Indochina, officials, who blamed Vietnamese women for high rates of infant mortality, identified the *semaines* as an opportunity to target native mothers with leaflets, brochures and other didactic paraphernalia.[88] As in Singapore the willingness to put children on display proceeded alongside campaigns to reduce infant mortality. To more convincingly evidence claims that medical management could 'save' the young Vietnamese, the organisers took the decision to draw real children into public displays. In 1934, for example, the 'Week' featured a *fête enfantine*, for which three hundred children gathered in the park of the Government of Cochinchina. Brought to the site by parents and schoolteachers, the children appeared in a riotous "harmony of colours."[89]

Supporters of this oeuvre harboured hopes that the *semaines* might serve higher ends than merely technologically supported survival, the advancement of public health or the fattening up of children who were 'inadequately' fed. In the opening speech at the *semaine* of 1934 the event's coordinator in chief, Édouard Marquis, declared the ultimate purpose of the events as being to "give to the child truth, happiness and justice."[90] Many of the women volunteers drew upon their Catholic beliefs to emphasise the moral-sacral aspects of their contribution. The governor's wife, Madame Pagès, even demanded that the *semaine* commence on 1 July with sermons held at religious institutions. When doctors and teachers on the official organising committees met, missionaries organised parallel meetings. 'Scientific rationality' mingled in the weeks with officially sponsored references to 'fairyland.' The sight of the *fête enfantine* of 1934 inspired the author of the official report to ask, "Are we in a fairy tale?"[91] In contrast to Hong Kong and other British centres, however, the 'fairy' in question was not a child, but rather a lady volunteer in costume distributing toys, party favours and cake, embodying the benevolent presence of medical science (and by extension the colonial state).

Though Madame Rivoal took overall charge of the event in 1938, the right to oversee the production of this public vision of childhood was never conceded to women as fully as in Hong Kong or Singapore. And while marked by a religious undercurrent, the events ultimately functioned to demystify 'the child,' exposing children as ideal subjects of new technical-rational expertise supported by male doctors, technicians and planners of the colonial state. The principal moral authority on display was medical. And while the official presence in the Singapore shows had been discreet, in Saigon the role of the colonial state in child-saving was far more ostentatiously celebrated. In 1934, the opening ceremony featured speeches by the governor. Male delegates travelled far and wide to lend weight to claims for the benevolent role of the state. Dr. Pierre Daléas, for example, an obstetrician at the École de Medicine de Hanoi, presented data showing declining rates of morti-natality in Hanoi, to which he ascribed "a magnificent eloquence."[92] In fact, while in 1938 infant mortality in British Malaya (excluding Singapore) had declined to 147 per 1,000, in Hanoi—according to one historian—it was still 190.[93] Possibly for this reason there remained little leeway here, in contrast to Singapore, for crediting or rewarding mothers. There were no 'ideal babies' on display.

An important inspiration for this vision of the child 'saved,' sustained and fed by French medical management was the need to countermand growing criticisms of neglect. New civic rituals validated claims to 'civilise' on behalf of an administration plagued by disturbing images of child bond servants labouring on plantations, impoverished Eurasian orphans on the street and youthful victims of police brutality. While such marginal children populated headlines and scandalised readers of the French and Vietnamese press, the children placed on display in the *semaines* reflected religious-moral values and glimpses of a modernising state-led politics of health.[94] However, this was perhaps not, in the end, such a radical departure from the dreamlike imagery surrounding the children of the countryside in Boullard-Devé's paintings; indeed, the former was a solution of sorts for the latter. For the knowledge exchanged in Saigon through networks linking experts into these forums held the promise that the further penetration of medical modernity and child welfare into the countryside might permit imperial stability to be recovered.

CONCLUSION

Between the wars, in each of these centres childhood remained deeply implicated in efforts to define colonialism as a 'coherent symbolic order.' However, in these extra-European settings this category was also publicly produced and represented through exposure to multilateral global and local forces.[95] Travel, transfer, comparison and contestation generated visions of childhood that varied from one colonial culture to the next. The drawing of discrete boundaries and hierarchies around this life stage was constantly thwarted by the messy reality on the ground.

A common problem in these different contexts was that the more intensively colonial states projected protective, paternal claims through the imagery of childhood and its rituals, the more they highlighted the glaring inadequacies of the colonial social record. Where anticolonial ferment was more intense, as in Hanoi and Saigon, this exposed the dangers of claims for empire as nurturance. In the interwar era children emerged as ambiguous figures, imbued with transgressive potential. As the case of the child monarch Duy Tân reveals, Vietnamese elites actively resisted representations of native children as docile 'associates.' The relative lack of sentiment within French framings of childhood left a space into which anticolonial visions of the *colony as child* moved.

However, while colonial communities became wary of the potential for childhood to serve as a focus for anticolonial criticism, the cultural production of colonial childhood remained too important to concede. In Hong Kong, new or expanded exemplary presentations and representations of ideal colonial children and childhoods emerged as markers of morality. In Hanoi, Saigon and Singapore, moral claims were more often furrowed through the technical management of colonial subjects, in 'Baby Shows' and *semaines de l'enfance*. But even as these visions threatened to directly expose colonial contradictions, elites in all of these centres clung to childhood as a solution to tensions of empire and a means of showcasing civility in public, right up to the dramatic collapse of Anglo-French power in the region.

So as late as December 1939, as the French retreated back behind the Maginot Line and the first Indian troops arrived in France, the governor of Cochinchina, René Veber, continued to prepare for the fourth Semaine de l'enfance in Saigon. Though the event had been scheduled for 11–18 March 1940, the crisis in Europe in early April led to its postponement. Germany, as it turned out, was only a few weeks away from inflicting the 'Strange Defeat' upon France. In the eerie prelude to the attack, Veber made plans for the most impressive event yet, featuring a "magnificent march" of costumed children representing the French provinces and the colonies, among *tableaux vivants* of 'old France.' The governor's demands that "hundreds of living, laughing [joyful] children" be put on display led Édouard Marquis to invite children from outside the school system to participate in the event for the first time. In the metropole's darkest hour, the organisers imagined these children would represent the entire 'French Empire' and embody 'New France,' the last remaining hope of the *mère patrie*. As the nation teetered on the brink of annihilation, and French power in Asia faded, Veber informed his colleagues that whatever else happened, the "pure sources of children's joy cannot be staunched."[96]

CHAPTER 6

Intimate Heights: Children, Nature and Colonial Urban Planning

In the late nineteenth and early twentieth centuries Europeans looked to the management of the middle-class home and public displays of children in new rituals to evidence a general reordering of empires along more 'moral' lines. But as children migrated toward the epicentre of colonialisms' cultures, elites extrapolated ideals of childhood from the home into planning policies launched from the highest levels of the colonial state. In particular, stakeholders marshalled childhood behind deeply controversial projects for the segregation of space. Demands for racial enclaves turned quite explicitly upon the needs of children, or more specifically what adults defined as their needs. The management of space emerged as another crucial domain in which elite ideals of childhood linked up with colonial policy and transformed the relationship of empire.

What resulted on the ground was a set of projects intended to engineer hygienic spaces of 'nature' within which children might be 'protected.' These spaces most often took the form of new or refurbished 'hill' or 'altitude' stations. Far from being a new technology of empire, hill stations had emerged from the 1830s as part of a response by the British (in India) and French (in the Caribbean) to high mortality rates suffered by colonial troops. The stations were constructed to address climatological interpretations of disease transmission. However, as Dane Kennedy and others have shown, they soon acquired other roles, functioning not only as sanatoria but also as military headquarters and in some cases as administrative centres. In Asia these relatively isolated Europeanised resorts became spheres in which elite foreign culture predominated as they emerged in highland areas of Burma, French Indochina, China, Japan, the Philippines and Malaya.[1]

By the late nineteenth century the logic of 'seasoning,' which had originally underpinned the construction of such retreats, had fallen into disrepute. Environmentalist paradigms of disease transmission became increasingly unfashionable as laboratory research provided new insights into the microscopic world of contagion. What followed was a general shift from nineteenth-century 'enclavism' (the establishment of demarcated spaces where colonial power centred upon the protection of vulnerable white bodies) toward broader programmes of public health targeting entire populations. Historians have argued that one consequence of the onset of this new era of colonial public health was that hill stations fell into "swift decline as centres of colonial influence."[2] But this chapter builds upon such recent work by arguing that there was no straightforward shift from enclavism toward public health or from climate and environmentalism to bodies and populations.[3] It shows how, as fears of contagion informed by germ theory stimulated elite demands for enhanced prophylactic barriers, campaigns to redevelop and reinforce enclaves followed. Across Asia, hill or altitude station projects commenced or were revived. In the process, as Nandini Bhattacharya has argued, "colonial enclaves were not confined to institutions of regimentation and confinement" but formed "an essential part of colonial civil society."[4] Children and childhood proved essential to the refitting of these older technologies for battles that would redefine colonial urban planning.

Quite different visions of childhood informed these struggles. In British Empire centres, as this chapter will argue, hill stations were to serve not as nurseries bedding 'saplings' into new climes, but as temporary holding centres channelling the young back home before the end of childhood.[5] In Hong Kong such shared elite ideals underpinned the drive to segregate an entire neighbourhood through the 'Peak Hill District Reservation.' But this orthodoxy was not accepted unequivocally everywhere. Singapore witnessed a remarkable contest over the Cameron Highlands as planters fought to overturn the orthodoxy of a colonial childhood defined in terms of circularity and early return. Meanwhile, in Hanoi and Saigon amid disagreements over the role of the European child in empire, early efforts to create a hill station for Indochina faltered. However, as the foreign presence grew so too did demands for a resort in which children could be adequately socialised into 'Frenchness.' The colonial state oversaw the transformation of the hill station of Dalat, in the highlands of Annam, into a "paradise for children" by the end of the interwar era.

COLONIAL CONTAGIONS: A NEW DISEASE PARADIGM

In January 1912, Dr. John Mitford Atkinson welcomed medical experts from a variety of colonial centres to Hong Kong for the second congress of the Far Eastern Association of Tropical Medicine.[6] Atkinson was a longtime resident of the Crown Colony. He had served as superintendent of the Government Civil Hospital (1887), then as acting colonial surgeon (1895), colonial surgeon and principal civil medical officer (1897). The official position he occupied in 1912 had been created in response to the bubonic plague epidemic that ravaged the colony in 1894. This disease outbreak and the ensuing race to identify the plague bacillus did much both in Hong Kong and across the world to raise awareness of bacteriology and its potential value to colonial governance.[7]

As bacteriologists produced new knowledge of specific microbes, parasites and vectors in the late nineteenth century, awareness of their findings spread quickly among those working in the new profession of urban planning. Planners were especially interested in colonies, for they often saw them as relatively less fettered spaces, or even as 'laboratories' for experiments with new planning techniques. For example, after Ronald Ross identified the mosquito as the vector for malaria in 1897, the colonial secretary, Joseph Chamberlain, urged explorations of how this knowledge might be used in colonial urban planning to eliminate disease.[8] The new paradigm of disease transmission suggested that the real danger lay not in the climate and environment, as was previously believed, but in bodies and populations defined as reservoirs for disease.[9] This appeared to underline the need for enhanced prophylaxis. In 1901, the findings of its Malaria Commission in West Africa prompted the Colonial Office to advise governors that new buildings should be located away from native quarters and where possible on high ground. Continued outbreaks of plague, cholera and other diseases underlined the importance of this task in Asian centres too. During the 1912 meeting of the Far Eastern Association of Tropical Medicine in Hong Kong, J. Mitford Atkinson was sure to include a tour of key sites—including hospitals, disinfecting stations and the bacteriological institute—reflecting the new influence of bacteriology within the colonial state.

However, this new disease paradigm never entirely overcame indifference and even resistance within the Colonial Office and the colonies. New theories of the vectoral propagation of disease only slowly won adherents in the colonies. Because bacteriology connoted special expertise and planning at one remove, it sat uneasily with the pragmatism that the British claimed to cherish in their empire. The new perspective from the laboratory—hidden in the field—was one that allowed foreign experts to rival the authority of administrators. It jarred with desires to hem back social commitments by the state, and conflicted with visions of imperial authority grounded in established environmental interpretations of racial vulnerability, and their associated hierarchies. Instead of bringing about extensive investment in public health, these new findings therefore often informed planning interventions that shored up established orthodoxies. One of them was that safety lay in the imposition of greater social and physical distance, not simply between coloniser and colonised but between wealthier and less wealthy sections of the populace.[10] As planners sought to realise prophylactic segregation in major centres in British Asia, these tensions inspired a revival of enclaves built around the fragile, contested constituency of the European child.

SENTIMENTALITY AND SEGREGATION: THE PEAK RESERVATION IN HONG KONG

From the 1870s the rising, increasingly self-confident Chinese elite of Hong Kong had taken advantage of British legal provisions to purchase real estate. This swelled government revenues but triggered protests from European residents over 'encroachment.' In the 1880s, as population levels increased rapidly, these complaints intensified, and some claimed Europeans would soon be "pushed out of the town of Victoria" altogether.[11] Rising land costs led officials to propose segregationist legislation. Governor Sir George William Des Voeux experimented with 'European Hill District Reservation' ordinances (1888), declaring the construction of "Chinese-style" tenement buildings illegal within a demarcated "European district."

However, it soon became apparent that the ordinance was unfit to preserve the racial homogeneity of this district or to allay fears that Europeans might soon be driven toward the margins of the city, alongside married English soldiers, sepoys and the dead.[12] For this reason, when the Qing court agreed in 1898 to lease the New Territories to Britain for ninety-nine years, discussions over land policy in Hong Kong quickly revived. Anticipating rising land prices, European speculators sought to carve out space in Kowloon (where the population was growing rapidly). They demanded an ordinance to prevent the erection of 'Chinese buildings' within a reservation intended to exclude Chinese. In 1901 the executive council approved a proposal for a reservation on disused land in Kowloon intended to regulate building type while excluding poorer Chinese on sanitary grounds and richer on account of their propensity to drive up rents. However, the colonial secretary, Joseph Chamberlain, only agreed to the Kowloon reservation on the condition that all persons of "good standing," European or Chinese, be allowed to reside there with the governor's approval.[13] Once again, Europeans' desires for a segregated space proved unsuccessful.

As economic fluctuations, speculation and population growth continued to create strong upward pressure on rents, one area in particular emerged as the focus of demands for the formal exclusion of Chinese: the highest mountain on Hong Kong Island, otherwise known as 'the Peak.' At an altitude of around 1,800 feet (550 meters) this area had been opened up for residential development in the 1860s after Governor Sir Richard MacDonnell purchased a disused military sanatorium and converted it into a summer residence. In the 1870s new roads opened to the Peak and wealthy merchants constructed villa residences there. A church followed in June 1883 along with hotels and a police station. In May 1888 a funicular tramline service connected the burgeoning neighbourhood to the city below.[14] With its mansions, barracks and messes the site began to take on something of the appearance of an Indian hill station, such as Simla, Darjeeling or Naini Tal.[15]

In 1904 a group of property owners petitioned Acting Governor Henry May for the formal closure of the Peak 'Hill District,' as it was termed, to Chinese.[16] May, a former Hong Kong cadet, was himself a Peak resident. He had had his own house built there in 1900. He endorsed the petitioners' line and pressed the Colonial Office for a 'Hill District Reservation Ordinance.' This was to demarcate a zone within which it would be illegal for owners, tenants or occupiers to allow land or property for residential use by Chinese (except servants). May justified this measure to C. P. Lucas at the Colonial Office by declaring, "If [the Peak] is not reserved it will be over-run by Chinese in the course of years."[17]

The use of planning to effect explicitly racial segregation in Hong Kong formed part of a global pattern, as Carl Nightingale has shown.[18] Joseph Chamberlain, influenced by the 'Rossian shift,' had already made racial segregation official policy in the planning of sub-Saharan African colonies.[19] However, while the planning of neighbourhoods in accordance with the 'cantonment' policy used in British India was considered appropriate in Africa, it was not necessarily so in Hong Kong. For here, May's proposal entailed excluding wealthy Asians from existing elite neighbourhoods. The colonial secretary in London was well aware that sanctioning racial segregation in law risked offending not only Chinese elites but also Japanese, with whose representatives the British government had recently concluded a new naval agreement.

In spite of this, Henry May broached the idea of an ordinance specifically excluding Chinese with the colonial secretary, Alfred Lyttelton. He did so at an inopportune moment. For Lyttelton was by then mired in a controversy over the use of indentured Chinese labourers in South Africa. This had inflamed liberal sensitivities over questions of race, across the empire. Hence, as the Colonial Government prepared a bill excluding Chinese from the Peak for its first reading in April, Governor May grasped for a language of authority which might convince the Colonial Office of the need for action.[20]

Arguments about inferior hygiene among 'Chinese' provided scant leverage. One reason why germ theory had gained currency after 1894 was because plague epidemics seemed to corroborate beliefs about the connection between disease, space and class.[21] Contagionist arguments had resonated more in the earlier debate over the Kowloon Reservation, but they would not work for the Peak. As May himself admitted, "One cannot plead Sanitary necessity for the [Hill District] Ordinance for there is no danger of coolie houses being built."[22] The governor also struggled to mobilise older climatological tropes of white vulnerability. These jarred with declining European mortality rates and officials' assertions that Hong Kong's sanitary condition was slowly improving.[23]

May finally found his arguments gaining traction when he invoked the hyper-vulnerable, racialised body of the European child. As we have seen, children were by then emerging as the focal point of a refashioned colonialism. Elites expected their children to perform 'true childhood' in colonial contexts. Moreover, children's special vulnerability was widely accepted. For as long as they remained in residence, children usefully linked older orthodoxies of tropical endangerment (and the curative effects of the heights) with the contagionist threat. Demands that the Peak should become the one enclave in which true childhood could genuinely be protected were of particular interest to May. As we saw in Chapter 4, his wife, Helena, was concurrently playing a leading role in making childhood a central focus of associative life in Hong Kong. Though there were only approximately thirty children living on the Peak in 1904, their bodies formed an admissible point of vulnerability, or 'natural enclave' within the European elite.

On 19 April 1904, during the bill's second reading in the Legislative Council, May presented the reservation as essential to realising the European family home. The Peak Reservation was presented as an area where Europeans' "wives and their families can reside."[24] Segregation was to protect European "families."[25] It would enable

> Europeans to keep their families in the Colony instead of undergoing the expense and the anxiety of a separation which would be necessitated and was necessitated in the past before they found this area at the Peak where one enjoys a more or less temperate climate.[26]

Appeals to children's vulnerability and the idea that the reservation was fundamental to preserving true childhood sustained controversial demands to encode racial exclusion in law.

Fortunately for May, these demands reached metropolitan Britain at a time when the health of British children was being linked more closely to the fate of the imperial nation than ever before.[27] Though the Parliamentary Report of the Inter-Departmental Committee on Physical Deterioration of 1904 actually suggested that claims for degeneracy were unfounded, it did little to dispel mounting public concern. Eugenicists criticised the metropolitan state for its failure to adequately protect racial efficiency. May's arguments filtered through to an audience in London already keenly aware of the emerging congruence of interest between child health and imperial and metropolitan administration. It was this angle of attack that smoothed the political road toward legislated segregation and left the Colonial Office unwilling, with the ordinance already approved in Hong Kong, to "pick the obvious holes" in May's argument.[28]

The foregrounding of childhood in demands to racially segregate space may also help to explain why Chinese nonofficial members of Hong Kong's Legislative Council proved wary of mounting stronger opposition to the ordinance as it came up for discussion in April. The Chinese representatives, Dr. Kai Ho Kai and Wei Yuk, were aware that directly opposing the ordinance would be futile given the committee's structure, but Ho Kai knew that other "leading Chinese" would be offended by it, and he might have been expected to express this dissatisfaction in stronger terms. However, he steered a diplomatic course, only voicing dismay at the "decided savour of the nature of class legislation."[29] Whether or not Ho Kai surmised that accepting the bill might offer the Chinese leverage in future discussions of land development in Kowloon is unclear.[30] And certainly, as Brenda Yeoh has noted, Chinese elites were no strangers themselves to invoking geomancy to insist that certain spaces remain beyond colonial or municipal interference.[31] But Ho Kai was surely also well aware that critics of the bill might risk appearing to put their own interests (condemned as 'speculative') before the health of vulnerable children. As a reform-minded Christian and Western-trained physician, he was himself convinced that reform of the family—using the 'best' of Western knowledge, particularly medicine—was crucial to reforming the Chinese nation. And when he ultimately endorsed the bill, he did so on the grounds that it was "necessary for the health of Europeans," and "especially the children."[32] Ho and Wei did manage to secure the addition of a clause stipulating that the governor could grant exemptions, though at the time there seemed little prospect that May would invoke it. Elite Chinese protests over the ordinance remained muted. The second reading of the bill, on 19 April, led to the passing, on 26 April 1904, of the Hill District Reservation Ordinance, explicitly barring Chinese. The Europeans had their 'fairyland.'[33]

IMPERIAL AMBITIONS: A HILL STATION FOR INDOCHINA

Another high-profile visitor to J. Mitford Atkinson's congress of 1912 was the eminent bacteriologist Dr. Alexandre Yersin. The doctor was no stranger to Hong Kong; he had famously discovered the plague bacillus there some eighteen years earlier in a Kennedy Town matshed.[34] Yersin renewed his acquaintance with Hong Kong as a figure of some renown, as vice president of the association and—notwithstanding recent squabbles with the Government General—as an influential associate of the French colonial state in Indochina. His benchmark for comparison of the various projects and bacteriological infrastructures on display in Hong Kong was the far more ambitious and elaborate system of public health care then being rolled out within the Indochinese Union.

In the major centres of French Indochina disease posed an ever present threat. In Hanoi, cholera outbreaks occurred annually from July to September. The plague broke out in 1902 in Hanoi and in Saigon from 1907 to 1908, and visited both centres repeatedly thereafter.[35] The crude mortality rate among the population remained high. These facts sat uneasily with expectations that medical colonialism would help the French administration win hearts and minds. The political importance of colonial medicine ensured that Hanoi and Saigon became key sites from which a modern hygiene crusade was launched. In 1891, long before Hong Kong, Saigon already acquired its own bacteriological institute. On 15 February 1902, Governor Paul Doumer defined disease prevention as an official responsibility, established a colony-wide health code, and appointed local directors of health and a Conseil Supérieur de Santé. Doumer's successor, Beau, set up the Assistance Médicale Indigène in 1905, further expanding preventive public health.[36]

Notwithstanding this official health drive, the benefits of modern medical knowledge still accrued disproportionately to French residents.[37] The main residential quarters for the administrative classes and entrepreneur-*colons*—the so-called *plateau* to the west of the Governor's Palace in Saigon, and the *quartiers blanches* distinguished by villa-style homes set in garden space along broad tree-lined boulevards in Hanoi—were considered hygienic.[38] By contrast, the *quartiers indigènes* were barely touched by improvements.[39] The internal borders of the French quarters remained highly porous and French residents regarded these quarters and the unhygienic suburbs as a disorderly menace.[40] Modern medicine unmasked threatening microbes and the menacing periphery at a moment when the number of European children and families was growing. Aside from effecting hygienic improvements in cities declared 'French,' colonial governments therefore began to experiment with the removal of foreign children to health resorts as a means of maintaining their health.

From 1894 the Protectorate of Tonkin took steps to provide concessionary holidays for the children of administrators, officers and public works employees at Đồ Sơn, 20 kilometres from Hải Phòng. As accommodation developed on the coast, some administrators referred to this resort as the 'Trouville of the East.' Governor Lanessan himself was a visitor. But seaside stations were considered too hot and facilities for families were lacking.[41] Missionaries attempted to resolve this problem by travelling from Tonkin to the "sanatorium of Hong Kong." Meanwhile, the relatively affluent Government of Cochinchina funded the construction of its own sanatorium for administrators in far-off Yokohama.[42] Informed by hygienists, administrators advised that the creation of British and Dutch-style hill stations would be necessary to reduce problems of staff attrition and the cost of frequent returns to the metropole.[43]

In the eyes of the ambitious Paul Doumer the absence of a hill station was detrimental to French prestige. Though Doumer visited Đồ Sơn with his family and had a villa built at Cap Saint-Jacques after the army opened a convalescent station there in 1905, he considered these resorts to be plainly insufficient for the needs of administrators' families.[44] He therefore sought appropriate sites for a grand new hill station project. The governor's interest prompted Alexandre Yersin to recommend the Lang Bian plateau in the southern Vietnamese highlands, and in 1898 Doumer sent "missions" to survey the area, which included a settlement located at an altitude of 5,000 feet (1,500 meters) named Đà Lạt (Dalat). The governor general earmarked this site to eventually become a centre serving not just troops but all the French of Indochina. He imagined that it would have administrative functions too, rather like Simla in British India.[45]

It was not long before the Dalat project lost momentum in the face of growing costs. Road building to the site had ceased by 1901, and after Doumer was recalled to Paris in 1902 subsequent governors counting the cost of his *grands projets* ushered in a period of budgetary retrenchment. Meanwhile, as Eric Jennings has shown, Ronald Ross's findings in India were by now casting doubt upon assumptions about the prophylactic benefits of the heights.[46] French Pastorians with close ties to the colonial state underscored these doubts. Among them was the

Pastorian bacteriologist Joseph J. Vassal of Nha Trang's Pasteur Institute. In 1905, the governor of Cochinchina, François Rodier, sent Vassal to study the "malarial index" on the Lang Bian plateau where he conducted blood tests on Vietnamese children. Those tested displayed signs of malarial infection, leading Vassal to warn that highland regions were "not always protected by altitude" from the disease.[47] The colonial newspaper press in Saigon and Hanoi questioned the wisdom of relocating European children to Dalat.[48]

The Ministry of Colonies in France continued to urge the creation of 'sanitary stations,' and the desire to "do what the English did in India, Singapore and in Hong Kong" remained alive in some quarters.[49] Dr. Charles Grall also continued to urge that a place in the hills was essential "for the European children and youth whose growing presence is vital to the long-term aspirations that the Governments now harbours." It was not a luxury but rather a necessity "for the health and wellbeing of all members of the European family, and especially for the mother and children" or, as he put it elsewhere, for ensuring the "survival of *colons* and their children."[50]

In 1912 Alexandre Yersin joined the dinner dance on the Peak in Hong Kong organised for guests attending J. M. Atkinson's conference. Before the assembled delegates Medical Officer Francis J. Clark gave a speech introducing Hong Kong's hill station. He explained the Peak to his audience specifically in terms of its function to protect children, describing how "infants and very young children, up to the age of 8 or 9 years, thrive wonderfully in this foggy atmosphere, provided that they are kept permanently at the Peak and do not visit the lower levels."[51] Yersin was doubtless struck by the contrast between the bustling Hill District Reservation with its 'thriving' children and Dalat, the site he had recommended to Doumer for similar purposes, which remained little more than a cluster of chalets with one six-room hotel.

THE CAMERON HIGHLANDS:
PLANNING A HILL STATION FOR BRITISH MALAYA

Listening closely as Francis Clark gave his speech at the Peak in 1912 was the Straits Settlements' medical representative, Dr. W. G. Ellis. As the president of the Straits branch of the British Medical Association, Ellis carried with him news of a bacteriological post soon to open in Singapore. The creation of this post was illustrative of a shift within the Straits government toward allocating funding for public health projects. This had begun around 1904 and led to the expansion of the General Hospital in 1907, an antimalaria campaign in 1911 and improvements to sewerage in 1913. The impetus for these interventions had come from reports emphasising living conditions in Singapore's 'Chinatown' area as disastrous for human health. But for those who did not venture often into such places, the Straits were often still interpreted as a 'naturally healthful' place.

From the 1860s ailing Calcutta businessmen had frequented Singapore in search of a health cure. Charles Buckley's long association with Singapore began after his family despatched him there from London to recover his health. Even around the turn of the century visitors continued to read the colonial landscape here selectively, overlooking the dire conditions afflicting poorer urban dwellers in the dockside core. One claimed on the basis of his observations of elite neighbourhoods,

> The health of the community is very good; the mosquitoes are intolerable, but they are not malarial; there is no plague or fever. I was speaking to a resident, formerly of Glasgow, who has lived in the island since 1873, and in all that time he has only, he says, been one week away from business from ill-health, and he has only once gone home. Certainly, all the white population, ladies and men alike, look surprisingly fresh and vigorous.[52]

After the opening of China, the number of migrants arriving in Singapore surged. Professionals and plantation owners moved out of the congested core, constructing houses in hilly suburban areas, around plantations on Valley Road, Orchard Road and Tanglin Road. After 1887 the Straits Settlements government took charge of these areas. The municipality took responsibility for the town. Well away from the centre, in Tanglin, European families resided alongside wealthy Chinese and others. Meanwhile, those of lower social status secured freehold land to the northeast (alongside Chinese, Indian and Eurasian white-collar classes).[53] Poverty, disease and crime continued to afflict densely populated areas under municipal control. However, outward expansion along the lines of Raffles's 'Master Plan' of 1822 (which was not actually enshrined in law) shielded more affluent Europeans and Asians from the worst aspects of rapid urban development.[54]

The containment of insanitary areas had the effect of slowing the official impetus to create new residential spaces in the hills. In 1843 proposals that Bukit Timah might serve as such a site lost momentum as commercial activity drained off to Hong Kong. In 1885 a government surveyor, William Cameron, reported the discovery of a plateau at an elevation of 4,500 to 4,700 feet above sea level between Perak and Pahang, 390 miles north of Singapore, and Sir Hugh Low, the British resident in Perak, challenged the government to open up this area. However, where Chinese in-migration and rising Asian affluence failed to translate into a clear threat to European status or health, Low's proposed health resort failed to materialise.

After Singapore's population doubled in size from 1871 to 1896, a commission of enquiry found mortality rates to be higher than in Hong Kong, India and Ceylon. Meanwhile, the plague threat was spreading from Hong Kong to Bombay, Calcutta and Karachi. Straits Chinese, and notably the medical doctor Lim Boon Keng, a member of the investigation team appointed by the municipality in 1896, began to campaign for a preventive approach to disease in Singapore's poorer quarters. In the face of these threats the European community in Singapore turned its attention—almost exactly contemporaneously with that of Hong Kong—to the possibility of implementing racial segregation in law. As Brenda Yeoh has noted, in 1903 the colonial government debated whether a municipal ordinance amendment bill prescribing the class of buildings permitted in specific streets might be used to effect racial zoning, rather as the Hong Kong government had (with little success) in 1888 and in the case of the Kowloon Reservation. Some officials contended that this would be "far more effective than any other prophylactic measure."[55]

However, in Singapore where pressure on space was not as great, European residents remained more reluctant than in Hong Kong to stoke resentment by insisting upon their own enclave. After all, the lines of Raffles's plan had already left segregation highly evident in central areas. Space was already a key means through which the government encouraged residents to see each other as different 'communities,' and this was assumed to mitigate joint action and to limit instability.[56] The government was unwilling to argue for segregation in law to protect British children not only as this might directly threaten stability by encouraging other (increasingly articulate) groups to demand similar favours, but because interventions to secure space to protect these children would undermine the European 'community's' supposedly disinterested position. It would thus jeopardise efforts to encourage community leaders to 'take care of their own children' rather than seeking the support of the state. Hence, instead of pursuing legal segregation in 1902 and 1903, the colonial government sent surveyors back to the area now referred to as the 'Cameron Highlands' to check the suitability of the site for a hill station once again.[57] Erroneous reports suggested only 318 acres were available for development, and work stopped abruptly.

"THEIR CHILDREN SHOULD PLAY ON THESE BEACHES": PLANNING IN INTERWAR HONG KONG

Having established an explicitly racial enclave in law, Hong Kong's European elites worried over the quite obvious problem of its continual breach. For the loosely worded 1904 ordinance contained a loophole. Technically, it prevented only the 'permitting' of Chinese to reside, and owners could hardly be said to be 'permitting themselves to reside.' In 1917, the businessman and philanthropist Ho Kom Tong used this loophole to purchase a house within the reservation, named 'Lysholt,' at public auction and entered into negotiations to buy more.[58] Ho was the half-brother of the wealthy Eurasian businessman, Sir Robert Ho Tung. Years before, in 1906, Ho Tung had become the only individual to benefit from the exception clause demanded by Ho Kai and Wei Yuk in 1904. He had secured property on the Peak and had moved his wife and children into a house there, while residing in another himself close by. Some residents bridled at the presence of Ho Tung's family, as we shall see in Chapter 9, and in 1917 Ho Kom Tong's actions led them to demand an amendment to shore up the residential homogeneity of the Peak neighbourhood.

A leading voice among the protestors was that of Sir Francis Henry May. Again serving as governor of Hong Kong, but this time no longer merely in an interim capacity, May had returned to the colony in July 1912 in the aftermath of the Chinese Revolution. Considered by the Colonial Office to be a 'safe pair of hands' given his long experience of China, May was committed to ensuring that the spirit of the 1904 ordinance was observed. However, the home government was wary (at a critical juncture in the Great War) of agreeing to demands for an amendment introducing any blanket ban on "Asiatics" on the Peak (which May seemed to be proposing), for this might unnecessarily antagonise Japanese war allies.[59] An amendment would also reopen old wounds among the Chinese elite.

Seeking approval for an amendment to the ordinance from the foreign secretary, Arthur Balfour, and the secretary of state for the colonies, Walter Long, Henry May focused his arguments upon white children's vulnerability to their Eurasian counterparts. May identified the movement of other children to the Peak as a direct threat to the European child. He expressed regret that the intent "was not perhaps sufficiently emphasised as regards children," adding, "There are many more children now at the Peak than there were in 1904, and European parents are bitterly opposed to any contact between their children and Chinese children."[60] May complained that Ho Kom Tong's intention was to place wives, concubines and children at the Peak, as had Sir Robert Ho Tung, and that the latter's planned acquisition of 'Homestead' was to accommodate even more of "his numerous children."[61] The need for fresh legislation was once again couched in terms of the health of children, but it was clear that the proposed cordon sanitaire was intended to protect this constituency against cross-cultural contamination.

What inspired these anxieties was the assumption that European child residents could only perform 'true childhood' if they were not exposed to other, alien children, and in particular Eurasians. As in British India so in Hong Kong, these children were more likely to be Anglophone. They could communicate easily with young Europeans, unlike Chinese children and unlike the infantilised amah. In this case, age offered no barrier to the transmission of cultural contaminants. As we saw in Chapter 3, European children could not be trusted to apply social rules built upon racial prejudice in their play. This is not surprising given that from 1915 elite rituals such as the Ministering Children's League bazaars were delicately disaggregating Chinese and European children, and providing opportunities for sociability across racial lines. While May's appeal resonated with the British government's concern to rebuff Eurasian demands for greater recognition during the war years, Walter Long and the foreign secretary, Arthur Balfour, would not consent to an amendment making broad reference to 'Asiatics.' Instead, following readings in the Legislative Council on 23 and 30 May 1918, a notice making resi-

FIG. 6.1. "At the Peak: His Excellency: Infection! Putrefaction! (Sniffing) Don't Perceive It Austin, Do You?" Source: *China Punch*, 16 October 1874, 9.

dence at the Peak conditional in all cases upon the governor's prior approval was published in the colony's *Government Gazette*.[62] The amendment underscored understandings of the Peak as a symbol of racial exclusivity and British authority.

This was a view inspired in part by the striking new perspective afforded by the lens of the microscope. Within the racial space of the laboratory, near invisible in the field, the objectified invader and pestilential host loomed large. The campaign for the amendment in one sense permitted the microscope to be inverted. The view from the Peak diminished the microbial threat below. This was not a new perspective. It resonated with earlier debates over sanitation in Hong Kong. But in 1918 it sustained notions of the Peak as a fairyland. And if the Peak was a fairyland *for* children, then the act of viewing Victoria from this vantage point allowed readings of the colony in the same terms. Early twentieth-century travel literature had portrayed the colony using the language of children's stories and fairytales. Oceangoing vessels viewed from the Peak became 'toy boats.' People became 'Lilliputians.' Buildings became 'dolls' houses.'[63] Children themselves contributed directly to such rereadings. Marguerite Fave, accompanying her family on a visit from Saigon in December 1939, recorded how her three-year-old son, Jacques, looked down from the Peak and "doubtless believing himself to be looking down upon a pond took his father's hand [and said]: 'papa I would really like to have that little red boat!'"[64]

In Hong Kong, as the European elite pushed the threat of the 'other's' gaze back into the pathogenic plain, this attenuated momentum in the field of public health. By the early postwar era government-sponsored public health initiatives were flagging. Health experts who visited Hong Kong lambasted public health work (which was only "in its infancy").[65] For all its shortcomings in this area, Singapore did at least begin to address slum clearance by establishing an Improvement Trust in 1927, but Hong Kong's government remained wary of any similar commitment. It took desperate overcrowding caused by an influx of refugees from war-torn China to prompt the creation of a Town Planning Committee in 1939. Dire conditions of housing were ignored or addressed piecemeal for much of the interwar period.[66] Even in comparison with other British-administered commercial centres such as Singapore, Bombay and Calcutta the government's record here was distinctly tentative.

Yet what followed the legislative intervention of 1918 was not some 'retreat' to luxurious indifference in the heights. While reframing the view from the Peak through the eyes of the child appeared to serve essentially nostalgic or introspective ends, this perspective was in fact enlisted in a series of coercive interventions into the interwar years. Walter Long had agreed to the Peak Reservation Ordinance amendment on 23 October 1918, and his successor as secretary of state for the colonies, Lord Milner, consented to the creation of another reservation a year later. This new reservation was to be established on Cheung Chau Island and was intended for the benefit of British and American missionary families.[67] The government introduced a bill, modelled on the Peak District Reservation Ordinance, proposing that no person should reside within the southern portion of this island without the consent of the governor-in-council.

This time, the Chinese representatives on the Legislative Council, Lau Chu Pak (representing the 'old Chinese') and Ho Fook (representing the 'wealthy Eurasian' group), were not prepared to stand meekly aside. Both expressed their firm opposition to the proposal. Ho Fook flatly denounced the bill as "nothing more or less than racial legislation."[68] Lau pointed out that since Cheung Chau was far from commercial or residential quarters and was hardly overcrowded, its reservation through law was unjustified. Both proposed that the bill be held in abeyance.

In response, the lawyer, Mr. C. Grenville Alabaster, a member of the Legislative Council, countered with the following:

Cheung Chau is an island which has been developed solely by residents who belong to a race which finds it necessary to take their children to the sea-side as much as possible in the summer and who separate themselves from their children by sending them home for education.... They desire that their children should play on these beaches.[69]

Alabaster aligned demands for the reservation with the defence of a particular racial-cultural vision of childhood. What made the new reservation essential was the desire to defend the elite model of colonial childhood in the colonies, and to underpin the practice of sending children home. It was this that made the bill a matter of urgency. While it remained under consideration, "all sales of land in Cheung Chau were held up for one year, and other missionaries who desire to build like their friends have been held up for that period—one year nearer the time for sending their children Home."[70]

Childhood as a cultural category was far from being fixed and monolithic, but as this exchange reveals, shared assumptions about it could productively cloud debates over colonial space. Neither environmentalism nor the marauding microbe were convincing grounds upon which to demand segregation at sea level in Cheung Chau, but appeals to childhood, an intrinsically mobile 'natural' condition, permitted the enclave to 'go mobile.' Children's presence naturalised official inclinations to push the enclave out into the colony at large. In the plains it mediated between the inconveniences of (outdated) climatology and (politically inexpedient) bacteriology. It also allowed new interpretations of disease aetiologies to be transposed onto a discourse of cultural contagion. The productively contagious body of 'the child,' abject and pathologised, formed an enclave within the colonial community. Elites invoked this constituency to undergird microbial theories of disease and older climatological discourses of peril or, if necessary, to navigate beyond them. Racially segregationist measures could in this way be recast as a benevolent response to European racial vulnerability. On sentimental grounds, in officials' eyes at least, social injustice disappeared. Responding to Chinese representatives' bitter complaints about the Cheung Chau ordinance, acting governor Claud Severn brazenly declared, "I cannot observe anything in the Bill of a racial kind at all."[71]

Disquietingly for the government, however, this case illustrated a new willingness among representatives of the Chinese elite to challenge these cherished values. In the aftermath of the Great War many longer-term residents of the colony had departed and those moving out from a turbulent Europe felt less constrained by Victorian-era orthodoxy to concede to the painful fracturing of their own 'empire families.' After 1918 a European 'settler' lobby began to cohere around demands for new schools allowing young people to study into their mid- to late teens in Hong Kong. This question proved so controversial that a postwar subcommittee of the Education Committee set up to address it failed to reach agreement. Instead the school inspector, E. Ralphs, prepared a minority report demanding the creation of a central school allowing 'British children' to study in Hong Kong up to eighteen years of age. The government subsequently refused to publish the minority report and Ralphs resigned from the subcommittee.[72]

The resulting clamour in the local press drew the fate of marginal children, and those who 'stayed on' in Hong Kong, under scrutiny. As the government fashioned a response, the position of missionaries' children provoked particular concern. Since corporate rules precluding family formation did not necessarily apply to them, missionaries often had children to raise. Though articulate and influential, they constituted a liminal group within colonial society, existing on relatively low incomes. In the postwar era, as costs of living rose sharply, they suffered more than soldiers and administrators from a lack of purpose-built accommodation. A fortunate few had been able to access elite residences on the Peak, such as John L. McPherson, a Canadian-born Presbyterian missionary who resided in Kowloon before the war but was able to relocate to the Hill District by 1916 with his wife and daughters. Rising prices in the postwar years dislodged the McPhersons from the Peak, and the childhoods of their children came to be defined by a certain racial amorphousness. On furlough in Canada they came to be known as 'the Chinese girls,' owing to their tendency to converse amongst themselves in Cantonese.[73]

In the postwar years, missionaries such as McPherson moved in a context where 'settler' sentiment was crystallising around demands for more, and better, European-only schools and living spaces. And since the missionaries' relationship with officialdom was often fraught, administrators grew concerned that religious workers might rally powerful social institutions behind challenges to elite authority. The administration in Hong Kong therefore moved to split this section of European society from other, lower-status Europeans with inclinations to 'settle.' Government planners shored up elite visions of colonial childhood by creating the Cheung Chau Island reservation in the name of missionaries' children. John McPherson, who took up residence on the island, was one of the beneficiaries of this scheme.

Claud Severn and his successors were well aware that measures intended to split 'settler' sentiment might incur the wrath of elite Chinese. However, they seem to have remained optimistic that the most important sections of Chinese opinion would ultimately accept another reservation. This was perhaps partly because, as we saw in Chapter 5, childhood was by this time reaching new levels of significance as the focal point of a vibrant culture of elite, interethnic collaboration.[74]

"A PARADISE FOR CHILDREN":
IMPERIAL DESIRES AND THE DALAT PROJECT

During the Great War, Frenchmen departed Indochina for the trenches. Older administrators who remained could no longer take metropolitan leave. Travel west of Suez by women and children under seventeen years old of French nationality, or originating from French Indochina, required the governor's approval. Thus confined, the remaining French population placed heavy demands upon the colony's limited hill station accommodation, exposing the ramshackle state of existing provision. An important consequence was the reinvigoration of the Dalat project.[75]

Since the administrators who remained in Indochina tended to be older, they were often not bachelors but those who had taken advantage of improved leave and family allowances to marry and raise children in Indochina.[76] Wartime exigencies prompted many to dream of a different postwar colony better able to support their families' needs. These dreams extended well down the social spectrum. Lower-status colonials who had enviously eyed others' perks were particularly keen to access improved benefits themselves, at the expense of the colony. As they pressed their case, their children came to form a central focus of such claims.

On 16 July 1915 Henry Pérot, a *commis des travaux publics*, established an Indochinese section of the Ligue des Familles Nombreuses in Hải Phòng. A 'Ligue Populaire des pères et mères nombreuses' had been founded in Paris much earlier, in 1908, by Simon Maire. It had emerged from a remarkable wave of Social Catholic activism intended to realise a new Christian corporate order built around the family. Pérot's motives in starting the league up in Indochina seem to have been similar. And in the midst of the hecatomb of the Great War, he stridently declared (from the relative safety of Hải Phòng), "The more large families there are, and the more they are assisted, the more France, our dear motherland, will be strong and powerful in this universe."[77] Pérot's league emerged as an influential mouthpiece, bridging between administrators and *colons*, and volubly articulating their concerns in the immediate postwar era.

In Indochina as in Hong Kong these concerns sharpened as rapidly rising living costs threatened Europeans' livelihoods. In Hanoi the 'white proletariat' had become so large by 1921 that the Government General contemplated introducing formal immigration restrictions to curb it.[78] As more French families were unable to afford to send their children home to be educated, they fell back on the colonial education system. Louis Bonnafont observed, "There are families ruining themselves to give an *instruction supérieur* to their children; there are children who are ruining their health to prepare for numerous and difficult examinations."[79] However, the quality of the education for which they suffered was in question. The wartime 'Vietnamisation' of the teaching cohort left parents wondering whether schools could adequately socialise their children into 'Frenchness.' Meanwhile, newly affluent Vietnamese elites were pushing for wider access to French-language education in Indochina's *lycées* and *collèges*. Lower-status Europeans were only too well aware that the Vietnamese children who graduated from French schools would compete with their own (more expensive) youth for lower-ranking clerical, teaching and administrative positions.

In Saigon and Hanoi such anxieties gained ground as the rising wealth of Chinese and Vietnamese elites transformed formerly 'European' neighbourhoods, rendering them more racially heterogeneous. As one postwar report noted:

> The affluence that resulted [in wartime] for the natives has manifested itself above all by the rental and even purchase of European buildings by them. Many have even taken the opportunity to construct subdivided apartment buildings right in the middle of the *ville européenne*, to the extent that the administration believed it necessary to intervene without much chance of success.[80]

Officials pondered the introduction of legislation to impose the racial segregation of neighbourhoods but soon determined this would be politically inexpedient. Instead, as elite Vietnamese demands upon educational and urban space intensified, high-ranking postwar administrators urged the creation of new 'French' schools and residences capable of maintaining and reproducing the rapidly expanding foreign presence without sending children home. To do this they looked away from the main centres and sought to fashion a 'truly French' milieu by reviving the Dalat project.

In 1915 as the war dragged on, administrators and their families, unable to take leave to escape the summer heat, placed heavier demands on Indochina's resorts. The obvious inadequacy of their facilities led the inspector-general of public works in Saigon to urge the governor of Cochinchina to create "a sanatorium where administrators and *colons* may spend a month or two with their family for the benefit of their health" and to accommodate "families travelling with their retinue of servants."[81] It was not until after the war, in 1919, that Governor Albert Sarraut breathed new life into this project by declaring Dalat the ideal site for a hill station for all Indochina. His successor, Maurice Long, commissioned the chief architect and city designer in Indochina's Department of Urbanism, Ernest Hébrard, to draw up plans for a seasonal administrative centre on the Lang Bian plateau. Hébrard, known for his work in Salonica, produced a master plan in 1923. Historians studying the plan have often emphasised Hébrard's intention to produce an administrative city, but contemporaries were especially impressed by the way the plan accommodated children.[82] The new hotel, the "Lang Bian Palace," (opened 1922), included gardens for children. Around the lake a *collège de garçons* and *collège des filles* were to become the most important of Dalat's "public institutions."[83]

As Eric Jennings has shown in his illuminating recent book on Dalat, Hébrard's plans for a large administrative quarter were left unrealised owing to rising costs.[84] However, Maurice Long's successor as governor, Martial Henri Merlin, doggedly persisted with efforts to provide both accommodation and education for the children of higher-ranking administrators. As pressure on existing schools in major centres intensified, the importance of Dalat's prospective role as an educational site grew further. A small mixed primary school already existed in Dalat. However, this was wholly insufficient for the task of accommodating European children not only from Saigon but eventually from other centres too, up to college level. Merlin therefore insisted to Pierre Pasquier, *résident supérieur* of Annam, that a French primary school with boarding facilities be created "for the exclusive use of children of European origin."[85] The governor formalised the project through *arrêté* on 30 July 1924, and when the project fell behind schedule, the new governor general Maurice Montguillot and Pasquier repeatedly urged its importance. Amid growing exasperation over delays a new municipal commission was created in January 1926 and its inaugural members were charged with overseeing the opening of a boarding school within twelve months.[86]

However, the school project proceeded amid concerns over Dalat's salubrity, and fears converged in particular around the infectious agency of children. In the early 1920s parts of the showcase project, the Lang Bian Palace hotel, remained under construction. Slow progress meant the intended 'indoor play area' for children was still a makeshift workers' quarters and the planned children's gardens had not been laid out. Children therefore mingled with adult guests as they played around the ground floor of the building. In 1923, complaints in the local press identified the increasing presence of European children in Dalat as a contagious agency and a significant danger to adult populations, especially given Vassal's earlier claims. By this time the school project was well under way. The government invited the entomologist Dr. Joseph-Emile Borel to conduct new studies of malarial infestation in the Lang Bian plateau in June 1925, March 1926 and December 1926. Mindful of the prerogatives of the Government General (as Pastorians tended to be), Borel secured "proof" from the blood of Vietnamese children, supposedly Dalat's most contagious agency, that no endemic malarial threat existed.[87] He declared that even Vietnamese children "enjoy a generally remarkable state of health, the like of which we have never seen anywhere else, South Annam and Cochinchina included."[88]

These suspiciously well-timed findings affirmed the school project as it moved toward completion. A new school, the Petit Lycée, offering elementary- and secondary-level classes for boys and girls, was formally created by *arrêté* on 16 July 1927, and opened its doors to pupils on 16 September 1927. Soon after, work commenced on a Grand Lycée that would permit students from the first institution to move on and complete their studies in Indochina.[89] However, Borel's endorsement of Vietnamese children's presence raised further questions over whether Dalat might really become an exclusively 'French' enclave at all. Certainly, Hébrard's plan had used strict zoning requirements to divide the town into an administrative quarter, a European residential quarter (with villa-garden-type accommodation) and a more compact *village annamite*.[90] However, an influx of affluent Vietnamese during the twenties compromised French hopes for homogeneous neighbourhoods.

In response, medical experts who still clung to this dream marshalled the malarial threat, the mosquito and its "reservoir"—the Vietnamese child—behind arguments for segregation in the heights.[91] Marcel Terrisse, Dalat's chief doctor and a member of the city's Hygiene Commission, warned that the Vietnamese child represented a potent disease threat. He reported:[92]

> It is now known that malaria is in Dalat among the native population. The clinical examination of 106 children (taken at random) from 0–12, children born in Dalat and who have never left—has revealed that 30% of the children have light malarial symptoms, 10% serious [symptoms]. Mosquitoes are numerous in Dalat in the annamite village. . . . In certain quarters of the European city, in particular, at the Langbian Palace [Hotel] and in the vicinity of the new Public Works quarters, the inhabitants are very much troubled by the presence of mosquitoes.[93]

Whilst officials expressed desires for racial segregation by portraying indigenous children as disease vectors, by the late 1920s some of the wealthy Vietnamese who were snapping up parcels of land for themselves were calling into question restrictions upon their children's access to the new French school. Vietnamese representatives on the municipal commission in Dalat demanded the right for native children to enrol in the Petit Lycée in September 1928. Resident mayor Chassaing wondered how to respond. He was aware that appeals to racialised climatology would not mollify the disputants. Following Borel, he conceded that "the beneficial influence of the climate of Dalat is felt as much by the native children as by the European children." To deflect these demands Chassaing instead presented segregation as a benevolent measure intended to shield Vietnamese children from the ingrained racial prejudices of *other* (non-French) European children. As the mayor explained, and others also noted, Dalat's success depended upon drawing Europeans from other empire centres.[94] Warming to this theme, Chassaing declared the admission of Vietnamese to the *lycée* "impossible" on the grounds that it would discourage the enrolment of "foreign children who do not possess the same sympathy for the *indigènes* as the French."[95] A separate *lycée* for Vietnamese children was therefore proposed (and quickly shelved indefinitely owing to lack of funds).

At least in France, if not always in Dalat, justifications for French-only schools in Indochina could continue to be couched in climatological terms. Promotional literature for the Dalat school distributed at the Exposition Coloniale of 1931 in Paris explained that Vietnamese children had "no special reason to come to Dalat," because they could study in "their own climate" and, as statistics showed, "the climate at altitude is, on the contrary, harmful to them."[96] The new *lycée* was

> the initiative of justly concerned authorities, well aware of the need to allow young Europeans, whom the climate debilitates and reduces to a state of inferiority in the plains, to undertake a full secondary education in comfort, and in climatic conditions favouring their physical and intellectual development and good progress in their studies.[97]

The schools allowed children to "work as in France."[98] They served imperial ambitions by allowing families to remain together. And return rates showed that many parents did reenrol children at the *lycée* after returning from home leave.[99] While in Hong Kong space in the heights was carved out to undergird the orthodoxy of children's departure, in Dalat efforts to realise a 'French' milieu were enmeshed with dreams of the acculturation of children in the tropics, and the extended residence of families.

Scholars have portrayed the period of the late 1920s as one in which Dalat 'failed' to make the transition to sanatorium, health retreat or tourist resort. However, we might also note that these other projects, in particular the military sanatorium, languished precisely *because* children's presence had burgeoned.[100] In his study of Dalat, Eric Jennings notes the army's resort to a rhetoric of weakness to reassert diminishing claims to space in the heights. If in this regard the strong became 'weak' in the heights then we might add that the inverse was also true. Children's interests trumped those of the military. This much seems clear from Governor General Pierre Pasquier's brusque dismissal of the demands of the commander in chief of French forces in Indochina for a barracks because this would present "the greatest of inconveniences in a hill station reserved primarily for women and children."[101] In August 1935, while the resident mayor of Dalat was 'baptising' the new Grand Lycée (named 'Yersin') all work on barrack construction had ceased. In the same year resident mayor Lucien Auger boasted that the *lycée* would reopen next term with three hundred pupils.[102] In December 1936, he proudly reported that close to 450 European children were in attendance at Dalat's schools.[103] A census snapshot of 28 January 1937 revealed that of some 697 Europeans in Dalat, 300 were children.[104] In the face of this strikingly youthful demographic one travel guide declared Dalat a "paradise for children."[105]

It was the ability to accommodate and in particular to educate children that ultimately allowed officials to imagine the transformation of this enclave into a site of imperial governance.[106] Before the Petit Lycée began to admit its first students, Dalat had struggled to attract tourists, and the grand Lang Bian Palace hotel had required public subventions to survive. But once the school had opened Governor General René Robin confidently predicted Dalat would go on to become "Indochina's administrative capital."[107] What the schools did was enable administrators in Hanoi and Saigon to buy into elite cultural reproduction *in Indochina* (and after the railway link with Hanoi finally opened, Dalat could serve both cities). In 1930 Dr. Gaide was already convinced that Dalat would "become the headquarters of the Government General and all the general services, [and] that what is now the *petit Lycée* will become the most important *lycée* in the Colony."[108] Six years later the Popular Front minister Justin Godart reflected upon the enduring appeal of these institutions, describing how

> Dalat, owing to its altitude and its situation, is a milieu favourable to European life and particularly of the life of childhood. The two *lycées*, for boys and girls, as well as the *petit lycée* are full and turn pupils away at each *rentrée*.[109]

The *lycées* allowed a more coherent and didactic elite ideal of French colonial childhood to cohere in the heights.[110] The impact of this transformation reverberated outward, informing the development of smaller resorts and the boasts of their chief advocates. The *résident supérieur* of Tonkin in 1937 identified Tam Đảo, for example, as "a children's playground, with vast managed lawns at the centre of the station, with play apparatus, see saws and a swing where all can frolic about in complete security."[111] But what set Dalat apart from other stations were the *lycées*. These remained a luxury for the privileged few. Thérèse de Hargues, who studied at the convent school alongside English pupils, recalled mixing with 'society' there (Emperor Bảo Đại, who had a residence nearby, dropped in on her class one morning). Others living in the 'furnace' of Saigon continued to scrimp and save in the hope of sending their children to Dalat, but for most the school fees proved far too expensive.[112]

"THE RELIGION OF THE ABSENT CHILD": CONTESTING THE HIGHLANDS IN BRITISH MALAYA

In 1920, not long after Singapore's centenary celebrations, the editor of the *Straits Times*, Alexander W. Still, took up the issue of the city's dangerously multi-ethnic entanglement. He complained:

> Space is no longer open.... There should be a clear and definite reservations law for the residential areas. The European quarter should be for Europeans, the Chinese quarter for the Chinese, the Japanese quarter for the Japanese, the Indian quarter for the Indians. We are a cosmopolitan community, and our great object must be to live together in perfect harmony ... not thrusting each upon the other.... No section of the community can claim a right to live like pigs.... Half the present Singapore should be demolished.[113]

In Still's eyes, it was quite obvious which half required demolition. But while some within 'official Singapore' shared these views, the political will to undertake extensive planning intervention or to impose racial reservations in law was lacking. Indeed, as it turned out, an important trigger for official reappraisals of social conditions in Singapore was to come not from the immediate threat of overcrowding but from the collapse of rubber prices in British Malaya during the immediate postwar era.

From 1887 to 1904 new land regulations had encouraged the opening up of vast areas of the Federated Malay States for planting. Men moved onto rubber estates in Malaya to try their luck as planters, supported by capital raised in Singapore's agency houses. Between 1911 and 1921 the European population of Singapore grew from 5,808 to 6,231. That of the rest of British Malaya grew from 3,717 to 6,805 during the same period, with planters making up an estimated 50 percent of this number.[114] In most cases large companies owned plantations, and when prices fell in 1920, staff curtailment schemes cast planters back upon Still's already 'too disorderly' Singapore. Younger men in particular were affected by the schemes, while older cohorts, those with wives and children in Malaya, clung on.

The presence of agricultural colonists had a far-reaching impact upon the social tone of expatriate communities. Planters had grown accustomed to seeing themselves as a kind of 'landed gentry' in British Malaya. However, as rubber prices bottomed out, their growing precariousness compelled them to divest many trappings of elite family life. They cancelled plans to take home leave and to send children home to be educated. As the crisis lengthened, planters complained of feeling that "most married people are to be marooned here for ever."[115] In these circumstances some began to emphasise a more radical line and they marshalled dystopic visions of the degenerate European child behind a campaign for economic redress.

The white child stranded in the tropics constituted a powerful symbol of racial degeneracy and represented one of the levers that planters might use to attract official concern for their plight.[116] Planters and their supporters therefore used the newspaper press to argue that the government should "do its utmost for the children of Europeans domiciled here."[117] However, since neither government nor planting companies would commit to the long-term costs of subsidising travel or education, planters' demands began to cohere instead around the dream of a hill station retreat, complete with a medical and educational infrastructure capable of sustaining child life.[118] The costs of such a venture would necessarily fall upon the government. Recognising this, the Incorporated Society of Planters and the Planter's Association of Malaya voiced support for the idea. So too, more aggressively, did Singapore's social institutions, in particular the Anglican Church.

Newly energised by its institutional reorganisation and seeking an issue around which to assert its moral authority among European residents, the Anglican Church in Singapore backed the planters' demands for a hill station. Well before the price of rubber plunged, the bishop of Singapore, C. J. Ferguson-Davie, inspired by the wartime experience of holidaying at Fraser's Hill in the central mountain range, a few hours drive by car from Kuala Lumpur, had argued that a hill station could support European family life. As in Dalat, the experience of war led the Straits government to approve a scheme for the site's postwar development. Following a survey, road building to the area began in 1919.

But the bishop was keen to go further, and faster. At the annual clerical conference in November he demanded the provision of a school. Here his ambitions connected with those of other religious workers, notably the Reverend Basil Roberts (the chaplain of Selangor) who identified the family as a vehicle capable of effecting the transition of colonial society onto a more moral basis. In the eyes of some religious workers European families in major centres such as Singapore seemed too few vis-à-vis Asian residents to play such an 'uplifting' role, but in rural areas and especially on plantations they imagined the story might be different. Backed by the Singapore Diocescan Association, Roberts promoted the hill school project widely, sending circulars to planters' associations in the hope of securing wider public support.[119]

The colonial government was deeply wary of this scheme. Though William George Maxwell, chief secretary of the Federated Malay States—a man sympathetic to the planters—had taken charge of the Fraser's Hill development in 1920, the site had conspicuously failed to develop into what planters hoped would be a haven for their retirement and for the education of their children.[120] Meanwhile, the collapse of rubber prices further increased official determination to restrict planters' access. Development remained limited to a few government-owned bungalows, reserved primarily for civil servants. And when Maxwell proposed a 'children's home' at Fraser's Hill, capable of receiving children "for a few weeks or even months for a change of air, recuperation or convalescence" the Fraser's Hill Development Committee (of which he was chairman) rejected the proposal out of hand.[121]

In Hong Kong around the same time, the Peak, rather like Fraser's Hill, functioned to underpin official claims upon space justified through a climate-based orthodoxy precipitating the breakup of the colonial home. The Peak had a small school, but it served only children from ages five to nine. Later, in September 1931, Fraser's Hill would acquire one too, St. Margaret's preparatory school, opened by Mrs. R. M. McCall. However, the 'little school,' as it came to be known, admitted just fifteen boys and girls as boarders and the government carefully circumscribed its growth.[122] In Hong Kong elites rebuffed settlers' postwar demands and bought off religious workers by providing them with segregated residential space. But in British Malaya difficult economic circumstances and a burgeoning sense of solidarity encouraged planters to take a more radical line.

As disappointment with the trajectory of the Fraser's Hill project grew, religious workers, colonial newspapers and planters from the Federated Malay States to Singapore campaigned for a hill station as a "moral obligation" to children. This campaign quickly took a sentimental turn, spiralling into open condemnations of the practice of sending children (especially boys) home from the tropics by age seven. Campaign leaders criticised 'racial separation.' *The Planter* declared it "a cruel thing for the parents, and certainly not a good one for the children. It is one of the tragedies of life in the East for the European. It need not remain so."[123] Another campaigner declared, "One is glad to read that the Church recognises the pain and suffering borne by European parents as the result of losing their children at an early age."[124] In Kuala Lumpur Reverend Roberts attacked Victorian-era stoicism and presented separation as a tragedy.[125] He lambasted the essential *incivility* of this "white man's religion," which "circles the globe close to the equator wherever the white man wanders on the torrid lands of exile," which he named as the "religion of the absent child."[126] What was required instead was to "conserve the best traditions of home life" through an infrastructure of institutional support.[127] As this campaign gained momentum, its supporters began to openly challenge the orthodoxy of children's inevitable decline in the tropics. The *Straits Times* insisted children could be educated "without unduly impairing their health."[128] Churchmen claimed European children could remain in Malaya and the Straits Settlements to age fourteen or longer without suffering any ill effects.

Campaigners in Malaya drew ammunition from a debate then catching around the globe. Professor J. W. Gregory, working in East Africa, was underlining the feasibility of white settlement in tropical climes.[129] 'Local' experts, such as Dr. Connolly in Penang, supplemented these findings with those of their own. Bishop Roberts cited them, arguing, "It is most important for the British Empire that the question should have been re-opened."[130] Meanwhile, scholars working at London's School of Hygiene and Tropical Medicine, such as Sir Aldo Castellani, were battling to regain the initiative and to reassert the inherent 'insalubrity' of the tropics.[131] A literary challenge also materialised, with contributions from those who had experienced childhood in British Malaya. The novelist F. S. Clark (the pseudonymous Clive Dalton), who spent an army childhood in Pulau Brani, declared, "The whole system is fiendishly cruel and inhuman and has caused more suffering than will ever be known. But is it necessary? Is the East so terribly demoralising for white children? I say it is not."[132]

Officials in Singapore found such revisionism horrifying. By challenging the consensus on climatic vulnerability the planters were undermining relativistic visions of colonial childhood intrinsic to European authority. On the one hand they undermined claims for racial difference (by asserting that white children *could* grow up in the tropics), while on the other they demanded preferential treatment along racial lines (insisting white children should have their own schools in the hills). This strategy threatened 'official Singapore' because it raised the prospect of a precarious settler class eroding white prestige in British Malaya and inflaming ill feeling among the plural communities of the Straits by giving vent to its segregationist inclinations. The Reverend Roberts articulated the inconsistency of the campaigners' position as he struggled to reconcile vows to make no differentiation "on the ground of race or colour distinction" with calls for Europeans-only schools to meet the "plain demands of the situation" (Asian children, he insisted, in a manner redolent of French officials discussing Dalat, did not require the "special climatic advantages" of the hills).[133]

The sheer size of planter society in the Federated Malay States demanded that official Singapore take this challenge seriously. In contrast to India with its imperial scale civil service, or Hong Kong where commercial interests prevailed, or even Indochina where French-owned plantations remained relatively few, planters dominated the scene in Malaya. After the Singapore naval base project was approved by David Lloyd George's cabinet on 16 June 1921, the government grew still more concerned to avoid political demands likely to undermine community relations. It also avoided moves likely to jeopardise the formal expansion of control from Singapore and the incorporation of Malay states into a constitutionally unified 'British Malaya.' Visions of French children raised and schooled in Indochina underpinned the Dalat project, but a quite similar vision articulated by nonofficial stakeholders led administrators to stymie the development of the Cameron Highlands. Recognising this, in 1920 the Church offered to fund government survey work on the site itself. But the highlands project continued to receive the barest of mentions in the Legislative Council. In the late 1920s campaigners railed at the lack of a "large scale hill station, comporting adequately Malaya's dignity," while visitors to Singapore expressed surprise there was "no such excellent hill-station in the Malay Peninsula."[134]

However, the campaign for a hill school did not die away. As rubber prices recovered in 1925, the chief secretary, Sir W. George Maxwell, visited the Cameron Highlands and declared it a future hill station for Singapore. Maxwell explained that the site would not become a 'Simla' of Malaya, but rather a resort and a site for agrobusiness.[135] His report amounted to an official sanction for such a scheme, and a development committee was set up. But Maxwell's suggestion that the hill station would be "the greatest blessing to those less well paid officers to whom leave to Europe is a rare luxury" rekindled hopes that the government would provide "a school for European children, saving the pang of complete separation, and the often tragic cost, of sending them Home for their education."[136] For those such as A. B. Milne, a well-known planter from Ceylon who continued to demand "room for the small man—the settler with his two acres and a cow," schools remained essential to making the highlands "a place for permanent settlers."[137]

'Official' Singapore continued to give little encouragement to such dreams. In April 1926 the first applicant for land in the highlands, W. Dunman (January 1925), complained (on behalf of 'the public of Malaya') about the suspiciously slow pace of development.[138] In 1928 the Federal Council and Conference of the Society of Planters criticised the snail-like processing of land applications. When C. C. Reade, the Federated Malay States government town planner, was engaged to zone and lay out the area, his appointment caused great excitement. For Reade had recently reported on his visit to the hill station of Baguio, the summer capital of the Philippine Islands, 4,757 feet above sea level, laid out by David H. Burnham twenty-four years earlier. Though one historian has characterised Baguio as an unequivocally 'manly' place, the fact that it possessed schools ("including one where white children enjoy all the amenities of life amid American or European surroundings") made this station, perhaps ironically, an inspiration for those leading demands for hill schools in British Malaya.[139]

By now, however, others were casting covetous glances at the highlands site. The Camerons project had taken on a political colouration in London and the Straits. In 1926 the colonial secretary, Leo Amery, ventured, "Apart from the health point of view," the development of the Highlands "would have a good political effect in the Federated Malay States."[140] The naval base project was linked to the hill station project and the Air Ministry, War Office and Admiralty began discussions about development.[141] When the chief secretary to the Federated Malay States government, Sir William Peel, revealed the intention to consult military and naval authorities, the *Straits Times* protested furiously, insisting the military did not need a hill station since the garrison was changed regularly anyway.

Sir George Maxwell weighed in again, this time to dampen the planters' hopes. In an article printed widely in May 1929 he revisited the burning question of whether authorities should "tempt European parents to keep their children in Malaya beyond the age of six or seven, when in the present circumstances they go to England for good?"[142] Maxwell's answer was an emphatic 'no.' "My personal opinion," he wrote, "is that European children should leave the tropics at the age of six or seven, and that the age limit for school children should be seven."[143] A hill school would not resolve the problem of separation since the children would see parents only in the holidays.[144] The school project would be compromised by the need to accommodate amahs and ayahs, and *their* exclusion would necessarily preclude "the bulk of the infant European population of Malaya."[145] The magazine *British Malaya*, though generally respectful of Maxwell, responded with the retort that he "clearly does not understand unofficial sentiment."[146]

By this time the Great Depression was taking effect. Rubber prices were collapsing again. Companies were reducing pay and terminating agreements, cutting back on commitments to pay for passage and shortening home leave.[147] Planters who were released feared returning home to face even more overstocked labour markets. Some took cash payouts in lieu of passage and eked out impoverished lives with their dependents in Singapore.[148] With a broader range of Europeans facing worsening economic conditions, the *Straits Times* issued new calls for a separate school for European children at the Cameron Highlands. Though Singapore was "an unusually healthy place," the newspaper claimed 'the adolescent' still had a "tendency to outgrow his strength and to lose the ability to concentrate on his work."[149] Contrary to Maxwell, who had explained that a segregated school could not be created under government control, the *Straits Times* protested that such a school "should not be left to one of the great religious bodies ... [but] must be non-denominational if it is to have a fair chance of success."[150] This meant it would necessarily become a charge on the colonial budget.

The proposal won an enthusiastic response from European readers, one of whom informed the editor, "You will earn the lasting gratitude of numberless parents in this territory if you continue to urge this necessary reform, or rather this belated justice towards the European parents of Malaya."[151] Another argued:

> Anyone who is familiar with the English schools in this country knows that there are British boys in them who receive their education here until they are seventeen or eighteen years old. It is with no snobbish intention that we call attention to their requirements... They find themselves unable to compete with their Asiatic contemporaries, who are accustomed to tropical climatic conditions.[152]

Older European children, owing to the climate, "become weedy and pale. They are often to be found near the bottom of a lower form, easily surpassed by the nimbler witted local children," and this state of affairs was "not likely... to enhance British prestige in this country."[153]

However, these very public attempts to rationalise segregated schooling in the heights drew an explosive response from other English-speaking sections of Singapore society, especially the Straits Chinese. In considering this, it is worth noting that in the same year, Mohammed Eunos Abdullah, leader of the Kesatuan Melayu Singapora (the first political Malay association), had successfully appealed for a reservation specifically for Malay settlement. The colonial government made an exceptional allocation of over 600 acres of land on the eastern side of Singapore in 1929 in Geylang to form 'Kampong Melayu.' Hence it was amid fears that the government was moving toward a fuller elaboration of a pro-Malay policy, likely to offset Chinese prosperity and influence, that European demands for special treatment sparked outrage.

Dr. Yap Pheng Geck, secretary of the Chinese Commercial Bank, declared, "It is a rare advantage to be brought up among children of different nationalities, and it will be more conducive to success and harmony if this sort of snobbishness be banished from juvenile minds and the educational sphere."[154] Another commentator argued 'the white man' was getting "too much of the fat of the land." A bitter slanging match followed. 'Diam' retorted, "The European who made such 'Fat' possible is entitled to a small portion!" while 'European mother' complained, "The primary reason Europeans want a school at Camerons Highlands is because this climate does not agree with their children."[155] 'Chakap' meanwhile challenged claims based upon racial climatology, insisting, "The luxuries of the East are for those who can afford them," and added:

> The Europeans have not only demanded exclusive hotels and dance halls but, like the selfish camel that eventually occupied the whole tent, they now want an exclusive school which will no doubt admit white children other than English and exclude the children of British subjects that can pay because they do not happen to be born white. Such treatment leads to discontent.[156]

Though apparently alarmed by the tone of these exchanges, which his newspaper nevertheless printed, the editor of the *Straits Times* insisted the campaign involved "no spirit of racial intolerance," and declared the European parent

> knows that if his son or daughter—particularly perhaps the latter—spends the years from eight to eighteen in this country, the slow and steady physical and mental development which would take place in his native country will be unnaturally forced and most undesirable complications may ensue. If this point cannot be generally conceded in the Straits then our boasted racial friendliness is a myth.[157]

However, the campaign had by now run into the unpromising position of appealing to the same 'locally domiciled communities' that it had so deeply offended through requests that the Legislative Council "make a concession in the shape of a grant towards the cost of this hill school."[158]

The debate sustained a sense that hill stations in the Malay states were in some sense 'up for grabs.'[159] However, when the Straits Settlements Association, the largest and most powerful unofficial body in Singapore, petitioned the government for access, the latter's response clarified that sites were intended for government servants. The European Association of Malaya launched a second bid in May 1938 for the highlands to be placed under all-Malayan administration, which the *Straits Times* supported, claiming Singapore was "the only place in Malaya where the unofficial public has done anything whatever to expedite Highlands progress."[160] But the bid was firmly rejected.

In the face of the Federated Malay States government's "incorrigible procrastination" the planters had formed a 'Highlands Association' in October 1929 to reassert claims upon the highlands as "a place for... permanent residence."[161] They interpreted the decision to cede development of the highlands to the smallest of the states, Pahang, as an attempt by the government to restrict the speed and scale of development.[162] When in 1932 rumours spread that 30,000 acres of agricultural land would soon be made available, fifty planters led by H. Gordon Graham formed a Cameron Highlands Society and inaugurated a cooperative scheme to create a permanent settlement and, crucially, a school (without which children would be "brought up without the intangible traditions of the home country").[163] By 1933, irrespective of official obstacles, private investors were crowding into the lower highlands, 35 miles away from Tanah Ratah.[164] At Ringlet an area for smallholders developed, and by the end of 1934 approximately fifty Europeans had taken up 922 acres. A year later private initiatives would bring two new schools to the heights.

The instigator of one school project was Miss Anne L.P. Griffith Jones. 'Miss Griff,' as she was known, came from Pembrokeshire and had arrived in Singapore in 1923. Surprised at the lack of separate educational provision for European children, she had set up a school in an outbuilding of the elite Tanglin Club. The preparatory school flourished, but Griffith Jones disagreed with the general practice of sending children home around age seven. As the hill school debate gripped Singapore, she therefore set about raising funds to secure land and build a boarding school for older children at the Cameron Highlands.

On 6 July 1934 she opened 'Tanglin School.' Approached by a tortuous road and situated in temporary buildings, against the odds it began to admit children up to thirteen years of age, preparing them for common entrance examinations (allowing them to pass directly into public schools in England). The waiting list for admission grew rapidly. Soon after, the sisters of Penang Convent moved to open a nondenominational 'Notre Dame School' in Tanah Rata, which opened in July 1935 offering boarding, tuition by a French and British teaching staff and places for fifty boys and girls from five to twelve years old. Both schools allowed parents to keep children in Malaya "for a longer time than hitherto."[165] One visitor to the highlands described schools as "accommodating between them some 100 specimens of boisterous European humanity of the younger generation." This allowed "the pleasing and in Malaya, all too rare, spectacle of numbers of gay children romping in the playgrounds with an ardour born of health and joyous spirits."[166]

Even so, critics remained unsure as to whether the highlands would become "a land of promise" or a "land of wasted enterprise and blasted hopes."[167] European children attending the new boarding schools were served by not one single medical practitioner.[168] Even access remained difficult.[169] Official reports discouraged agricultural development, and planters complained, "What is potentially one of the finest hill stations in the East is only partially developed and is closed to those who might reap the most benefit from it."[170]

These ongoing struggles are suggestive of how much official misgivings over supporting costly, inefficient white planters had grown by the early 1930s, when the Depression exposed the fragmentation of supposed 'core values.'[171] As official interest in sustaining the planters dwindled, plans commenced for the fuller indigenisation of estates.[172] This allowed the problem of the Cameron Highlands to be redefined by the opening of the Singapore dockyard to naval traffic. In 1935 this event led the War Office to instruct the general officer commanding Malaya to prepare proposals for a convalescent depot. Reports identified the Cameron Highlands as "the only Hill Station of any extent in Malaya" capable of serving as a rest station for dockyard employees.[173] Of 120 European dockyard employees a third were living in married quarters with families. Having initially dropped out of a scheme agreed in September 1935 to provide a rest camp and convalescent depot, the Admiralty agreed to participate in March 1937. The intended beneficiaries would not be civilian children but those of military servicemen and dockyard workers.[174] In contrast to Dalat, where the government rebuffed the military to accommodate civilians, the Cameron Highlands was earmarked to serve a cohort on the margins but under military discipline. This suited official interests: these children's lives were defined by mobility and they would never be official Singapore's problem for long. Their presence could thus be reconciled with the older ideals of colonial childhood that the planters and their children had threatened to destroy.

CONCLUSION

Urban and planning histories have tended to neglect the significance of children and childhood to debates defining the impact of hegemonic imperialism upon space. But children played a crucial role in the history of planning in the twentieth century. Childhood offered a language of authority sustaining planning interventions. And planned interventions made in the name of children ensured that the nineteenth-century technology of the hill station did not simply slip into a "swift decline." Instead, as elites reordered colonial cities during the early twentieth century, the older technology of the enclave moved in from the periphery and produced new centres from which elite authority could be relaunched.

Clearly, such manoeuvres were in themselves born of a sense that European imperial power was on the wane. Everywhere fears of imperial eclipse offered a common incitement to engagement. In the face of a shared sense of peril, Britons made the child the defining feature of family life deliberately broken to avoid the transmission of cultural contagions across generational lines. It was thus essential to British imperialism that hill stations continue to function as temporary holding centres channelling the young back from the tropics. In Hong Kong, where childhood appeared to be profoundly threatened, its advocates fought off challenges, secured a racial reservation in law and expanded segregationist models of planning into the plains. By contrast, in British Malaya, when planters' desires challenged elite ideals directly, the Cameron Highlands project was stymied. In Indochina, as the administration expanded rapidly in the 1920s, officials carved out space in the heights as a means of supporting the family, averting costs of repatriation and socialising children into Frenchness.

As this chapter has shown, the planned reordering of space in colonial contexts proceeded through a series of encounters and struggles over childhood, or what adults defined as 'children's interests.' From the turn of the century ideas of childhood thus formed part of a new geographical imagination in empire emphasising flows between bodies and environments. While Brenda Yeoh has argued that sanitary fears informed colonial attempts to control public space, so too, as Sunil Amrith has pointed out, did *other* fears of contagion.[175] Fears surrounding childhood as an innately contagious agency drove changes that profoundly influenced urban politics. It was through visions of childhood and the racialised bodies of children that colonial elites renegotiated access to space, redefined the limits of hygienic modernity and strove in the face of a growing anticolonial fervour to perpetuate their rule.

CHAPTER 7

Sick Traffic: 'Child Slavery' and Imperial Networks

During the interwar years, reform-minded critics of European colonial regimes sought to embarrass officials by exposing the gulf between claims for empire as nurturance or 'progress' and what they saw as a lack of either on the ground. Across this period one particular controversy flared repeatedly. Time and again, evidence of unfree migrant labour impacting with particular severity upon children brought British and French imperialism powerfully into question. Evidence that children were being trafficked into unfree statuses in colonial centres under British and French rule saw the 'child slaves' of East and Southeast Asia become a global cause célèbre. As reformers demanded action to eradicate this problem, debates raged over the limits of imperial responsibility for the child subjects of empire.

The problem of unfree migrant child labour arose as a direct consequence of rural impoverishment, especially in southern China and northern Vietnam. Across the period parents in rural areas who were unable to support their families transferred offspring to third parties as a last resort. Usually children changed hands for some form of payment. Most of those transferred were girls, since in patrilineal cultures the transfer of boys was rare. Some transfers resulted in genuine adoption, particularly if boys were involved. They might also confer upon 'purchasers' the obligation to feed, clothe and marry children off. However, it was more common for those transferred to assume the status of unpaid, bonded labourers. While some children remained in the rural milieu, in many cases traffickers procured and conveyed children over vast distances in order to secure a higher price for their labour in Asia's burgeoning cities. Commercial dynamism, concentrations of wealth and skewed sex ratios raised demand for girls in particular. The fate of many transferred children was to work in poor or abusive conditions, as domestics in homes or as prostitutes in brothels.

Such exploitative practices could hardly be squared with middle-class claims for British and French imperialism as a 'civilising' influence. They horrified those who harboured hopes that empire might be made 'respectable.' Colonial governments had curbed or carefully confined industrial development, thereby largely evading the moral provocation of the child factory or mine worker. But in the light of evidence of 'slavery,' campaigners bound childhood's powerful moral resonance and associations with the 'liberal achievement' into appeals to rescue Asian children from exploitative labour. The effectiveness of these critiques left officials struggling to contain scandals over 'child slavery.' Trafficking networks extended across East and Southeast Asia and focused upon important centres under British and French rule. This ensured that this problem threw core justifications for empire into question. With claims for civility at stake, debates over transferred children amounted to a test case for empire.

And yet, as we shall see, these debates evolved in strikingly different directions. Antislavery campaigns elicited remarkable abolitionist commitments from initially reluctant governments in Hong Kong and Singapore, but met with forceful resistance to any change in colonial policy in Hanoi and Saigon.[1] Why was this? This chapter sets out to address this key question. It also reveals the global implications of local debates over 'child slavery' as they dragged onto the agenda the burning questions of European responsibility for the raising of youthful colonial subjects.

'BENEATH OUR SEEMLY FAIR SURFACE': CHILD SLAVES AND IMPERIAL TRADE

While it has been said that in order for Europe to imagine empire it first had to imagine slavery, both informed moralistic modern imaginings of the condition of childhood. 'Freeing' children from slavery became deeply and explicitly entwined with justifications for empire from at least the late eighteenth century. Sir Thomas Stamford Raffles, founder of Singapore (who acknowledged William Wilberforce as an inspiration), directly linked the rescue of women and children from slavery to the expansion of British interests in Southeast Asia.[2] In the next two decades both the British and French governments outlawed slavery in their colonies (in 1833 and 1848 respectively). A British proclamation of 1841 stipulated respect for native custom, empire-wide, "no species of torture or slavery excepting." And the first ordinance passed by Hong Kong's new Legislative Council on 28 February 1844 restated this prohibition. Those who regarded Hong Kong as capital of 'Anglo-China,' a supposed haven of law and order, rebutted proprietorial claims over youth fleeing servitude on the Chinese mainland.[3] Meanwhile, following the establishment of Cochinchina as a formal colony, French explorers and officials also justified colonial rule using emotive references to young slaves as living embodiments of 'Asiatic barbarity.' One administrator in Cochinchina underlined the moral claims of French governmentality by asserting, "We are in a land where the child is a thing ... They go hunting for children as we go hunting deer."[4]

Because empire-builders justified expansionism through claims to be delivering 'child peoples' from enslavement, evidence that 'unfreedom' not only persisted but continued to impact with particular severity upon children aroused concern at the highest levels of the state. Expressions of concern emerged in the late 1870s and 1880s as liberal-minded officials expressed desires that empires be reordered along more 'moral' lines. Not long after he arrived in the colony, Hong Kong's chief justice, Sir John Smale, for example, was amazed to find himself dealing directly with legal cases involving transfers of young girls into domestic servitude. Aghast at what he saw as the practice of buying and selling of children into bond service and prostitution under the guise of adoption, on 6 October 1879 the chief justice denounced these practices from the bench. He declared, "It seems to me that all slavery, domestic, agrarian or for immoral purposes, comes within one and the same category."[5] These claims, coming from such an authoritative figure, were picked up and reported in the *Times*. The matter was referred to the secretary of state for the colonies and reviewed in a debate in the House of Lords on 21 June 1880.

As the scandal over 'Hong Kong slavery' was looping back to the metropole quite similar practices were being uncovered in Saigon. After the transition from military to civil governance in 1879 the first civil governor of Cochinchina, Charles-Marie Le Myre de Vilers, commissioned a review intended to speed up the pace of antislavery reform. A study by the ethnologist and chief of native justice Jules Silvestre followed, highlighting strikingly similar practices to those identified by Smale, "weighing most usually upon the children" who were "transferred temporarily or permanently from their parents to others for a fee, or to guarantee or pay debts through their labour."[6] Silvestre uncovered a "veritable trade in children" into statuses that he felt equated to "nothing less than slavery." And he surmised that here too adoption was "rarely practised other than as a roundabout means of acquiring servants who are raised in the house and attached closely to the family."[7]

In the same year, Silvestre's fellow scholar-administrator, Antony Landes, discovered that in Cholon, Saigon's sister city (which had a large Chinese population), "little girls" were being "purchased directly or indirectly from their parents sometimes to serve as domestics in the house where they are raised, sometimes to be married later or delivered into prostitution."[8] Landes counted more girls, whom he estimated to be aged between five and fourteen, than adult women in Cholon's eleven brothels. He, like Silvestre, was well aware of the debate over similar issues within British Empire centres, for he criticised elite Chinese efforts to mount a defence of 'paid adoption' as custom in Hong Kong. Landes was convinced that in a French colony now under civil governance the matter deserved a full judicial enquiry. And Silvestre too was confident that "the French administration will not tolerate the continuation of the general situation exposed."[9]

The trans-colonial dimensions of the problem of unfree child labour were only too evident to observers. Travel writers familiar with these centres, such as Isabella

Bird, described a "particularly hateful form of slavery which is recognised by Chinese as custom" in Hong Kong, and reported sightings of "girls who, I believe, are domestic slaves" in the domestic interiors of the Saigon suburbs and in the Straits Settlements.[10] Singapore's preeminent position as a redistribution centre linked up to global trade networks made it a key node for the trans-shipment of children not merely within the region but into destinies obscure in further-flung places, notably along the West Coast of the United States. As it grew rapidly, Singapore also provided an important market for transferred female children in its own right. Here children commanded higher prices than they did in Saigon or Hong Kong.[11] But colonial officials did not address this problem here with quite the same sense of urgency as their counterparts in Hong Kong. So blatant was the problem that in 1882 Sir Peter Benson Maxwell, the retired first chief justice of the Straits Settlements, could comment sarcastically: "There are some deluded people who aver that slavery exists in Singapore; not the debt slavery of the Malay but the result of the traffic in flesh and blood! . . . Of course our Government knows nothing of this. Why should it?"[12] But soon official tolerance for practices indistinguishable from child slavery in Singapore would become the focus of stinging criticism.

Singapore's own child slavery scandal burst into public view in August 1886. It was precipitated by events on the evening of Monday, 23 August, when a young Tamil girl hammered at the door of number 2 Victoria Street, pleading for assistance. This was the address of W. J. Allan, a hardware and general merchant, who took in the distraught child. As far as he could tell, the girl, who gave her name as Elizabeth, was an orphan and a domestic. Evidently, she had run away from her employer, an apothecary named La Porte, and she "seemed to have been rather badly beaten about the face."[13] The next day Allan brought the girl to Singapore's superintendent of police, and under interview on 25 August she declared:

> My name is Elizabeth. I was brought up in a Convent at Madras. 18 months ago Mrs La Porte took me out of the convent and brought me to Singapore. . . . She used to very often beat me for the least affair. I was unable to stand the abuse so I ran away and went to Mr. Allan's house.[14]

On the advice of T. Irvine Rowell, principal civil medical officer, who examined Elizabeth and found "the alleged ill-treatment is a delusion," the police dismissed the girl's complaint and informed Allan that 'the Kling girl' would be returned to the La Portes.[15] A few days later, the Reverend Father Remés, vicar of the Cathedral Church of the Good Shepherd, on behalf of La Porte, visited Allan to explain that Elizabeth would be sent to the Convent of the Holy Infant Jesus for a 'cooling off' period, and would then be returned to her former owner. Elizabeth apparently protested at this and demanded that her case be heard before a magistrate, but instead she was detained in the police lockup from 3 September, then despatched to the convent.

This infuriated Allan, who wrote to the police declaiming, "Mr. Laporte and his army of confederates—(Priests, nuns, etc, etc)" and warning that "as I see so many against a poor helpless orphan I am determined to go through with it to the bitter end."[16] On 11 September he wrote to the *Straits Times*, insisting the detention of the girl was "illegal," since "to escape from domestic slavery is no crime," and adding:

> One would naturally ask, are we living under British rule or what? Here is a case of a British subject, not a criminal, struggling for liberty and better treatment, and the Police Authorities, without a Magistrate's decision, take upon themselves to settle the matter on the side of a clique arrayed against a mere child.[17]

After writing again to the *Straits Times* on 24 September to condemn confessional groups, Allan (or his associates) drew the row to the attention of the Protestant Educational Institute in London (established to 'fight Popery' in England), which took up the case with the Colonial Office.[18] The Colonial Office demanded that the governor of the Straits Settlements, Sir Frederick Weld, make a full report to colonial secretary, Edward Stanhope, on 24 January 1887.

The case of Elizabeth revealed clearly that in Singapore the problem of 'adopted' children transcended race. As another observer noted, child domestic bond servants could be found in "almost every family," and not only in Tamil, Siamese, Burmese, Malay, Arab and Chinese homes but also in those of Europeans such as the La Portes.[19] That the case should inflame metropolitan opinion was especially embarrassing because slavery had been legally abolished throughout British Malaya just a few years earlier, in 1884. For years observers had criticised transfers of Malay children into debt slavery, but the case of Elizabeth suggested similar practices existed within the very seat of British power, in supposedly more civilised Singapore.[20]

In January, when Governor Weld prepared his report to the colonial secretary on the case of Elizabeth, he included evidence from T. Irvine Rowell downplaying European involvement in alleged domestic slavery. Instead, Rowell's report impugned Allan's reputation, questioned his motives for taking such a keen interest in Elizabeth's plight and implied that Elizabeth had not arrived at his door by chance.[21] Weld also arranged for the senior magistrate, R. S. O'Connor, to interview Elizabeth on 20 April 1887, who by then, at least according to him, declared, "If I am allowed to stay in the Convent I don't want my case enquired into by the Magistrate."[22]

As we can see, in the face of provocative claims for the toleration of child slavery across Asia, British and French officials developed quite similar, defensive responses. As moral reform swept onto the metropolitan agenda, in Britain after the outcry over the Contagious Diseases Acts and the scandal created by W. T. Stead's exposé on child prostitution or "white slavery," and in France as successive governments sought to establish the secular values of a modernising republicanism, European and Asian merchants in empire centres feared these revelations might provoke heavy-handed metropolitan intervention. So too did colonial officials keen to preserve stability and to avoid 'unnecessary' expenditure. However, flat denials that slavery could not exist where it had no legal status were no longer sufficient. Therefore, instead of attacking what Smale, Allan, Silvestre and Landes had all identified as linked practices of child cession, domestic servitude and brothel slavery, colonial governments eschewed abolitionist intervention and played for time or used orientalist arguments to deflect criticism.

In Hong Kong, 'experts' such as the missionary-turned-education inspector Ernest J. Eitel and Sir James Russell picked up on the arguments of an anti-interventionist lobby of elite Chinese merchants. They dismissed Smale's criticisms by claiming transfers into unpaid labour constituted a benevolent custom equivalent to adoption.[23] Young female domestic bond servants were not slaves but *mui tsai*, a transliteration of the Cantonese term literally meaning 'little younger sister' but denoting a girl bond servant. In this view the girls' status involved not the 'social death' of chattel slavery but a clearly identified position within the Chinese family. Such practices were cast as a kind of harmless philanthropy inevitably destined, under colonial conditions, to disappear. The second key contention was that abduction, trafficking and vice constituted more urgent areas for intervention by the colonial state.[24] The Hong Kong government made a great show of tightening laws governing prostitution and the trafficking of children and authorised the Po Leung Kuk, a charitable organisation established in 1878 by sections of the Chinese elite, to combat abduction and kidnapping.[25] This institution received, accommodated and returned rescued girls to their families in China and was seen in Hong Kong as a voluntary initiative run by 'good Chinese.' In Singapore Governor Weld's successor, Sir Cecil Clementi Smith, followed the line pursued in Hong Kong and defined ownership of bond servants as a benevolent Chinese custom. Significantly, here this line also helped to draw attention to trafficking as a 'Chinese problem' and emphatically *not* a European or community-wide problem. It thereby averted the very obvious danger of links to similar practices existing throughout the Malay Peninsula. Authorities soft-pedalled controls on female immigration but they integrated Singapore's own Po Leung Kuk (established 1885) into the Chinese Advisory Board under the presidency of the secretary of Chinese affairs.[26]

Effectively *sinicising* what was patently a community-wide problem required more careful official oversight in more ethnically plural Singapore than it did in Hong Kong. Consequently, in Singapore the Kuk came to be seen not as a Chinese philanthropic initiative but as "a Government scheme worked by the Chinese Protectorate."[27] Acting colonial secretary C.W.S. Kynnersley boasted, "No Chinaman is employed in a position of authority higher than a Revenue officer or a detective."[28] And while European suspicions of the Po Leung Kuk in Hong Kong resulted in a critical enquiry into its work, when Elizabeth Andrew and the

American medical missionary Dr. Katherine Bushnell complained in 1894 that "a systematic slave trade in girls exists at Singapore," the government flatly refused an enquiry into the Straits Kuk.[29]

The rhetorical confinement of this traffic in children to the Chinese community of Singapore enhanced the government's moral authority. This proved to be of some value as the government struggled with Chinese 'secret societies' for control over the organisation of migrant labour following the repeal of the Contagious Diseases Acts in 1888. It imposed an outright ban on the societies from 1889. However, defining slavery as a 'Chinese problem' also elicited a bitter counter-response among sections of the loyal, English-speaking Straits Chinese, who seized upon evidence of child trafficking and slavery as a scourge transcending race. The Straits Chinese pointed up the lurid case of Blanche Waddell, an Englishwoman who arrived in Singapore from Saigon in February 1903 and who had proceeded to act as a "lady baby broker" and procuress of girls for "immoral purposes."[30] The drama surrounding Waddell's arrest and dramatic flight from custody, and the mysterious failure of municipal police to locate her or bring her to trial, was the subject of wry comment in the *Straits Chinese Magazine*. So too was the muted coverage the case received in English-language newspapers.

As Singapore had prepared to set up its own Po Leung Kuk, the ethnologist Charles Lemire reassured his contemporaries in French Cochinchina that the institution of bond service was "not as immoral as it first appears."[31] Only in desperate circumstances would a Vietnamese mother give away her child, he claimed, and even then she would consign it to a wealthy family, "where she is sure they will lack for nothing."[32] French authorities emphasised the good intentions of parents, the temporary and 'open' characteristics of bond service and the familial intimacy of 'master–slave' relations. Later, in 1906, the attorney general of Indochina could confidently assert, "We should not, in my view, rise up against this Annamite custom which presents no danger."[33] But what also helped to obscure the problem that Landes and Silvestre had discovered in the south was the expansion of the French imperial boundary toward the north.

BORDER TROUBLE: THE CHILD AS A CATEGORY OF HUMANITARIAN ACTION IN INDOCHINA

Following the Sino-French war of 1884–85, the policing of the newly delineated border with China brought the trafficked 'child,' not the domestic bond servant, into sharper focus. A dramatic standoff on 10 April 1891 illustrated the importance of childhood as a category through which both the border and the avowedly humanitarian action of the French state upon it could be defined. On that day, two young female Vietnamese, aged eighteen and nine years old, arrived seeking refuge at an army base in Lào Cai, a town on the Tonkin side of the Chinese border. The girls had fled from Sonphong (Hekou), on the Chinese side of the boundary. The elder of the two girls informed French interrogators that the attempts of a Chinese merchant to make her a concubine had prompted her flight. Like the older girl, the younger girl also claimed to have been abducted and sold several times until she too had become a domestic in the service of a man she knew as 'Wei,' the commandant of a Chinese fort. Mistreatment, in her narrative, led her to abscond.[34]

At this point, representatives of Vi Cao Khởi (alias 'Wei'), the commander of the Sonphong Fortress, and a Chinese merchant named Phu Ho Ky arrived in Lào Cai seeking the return of the girls. They soon learned that the girls were in the possession of the French, but the vice resident rebuffed demands for their return. This astonished their owners, for giving refuge to fugitive debt-slaves, especially women, was considered theft. Wei interpreted this as an intended diplomatic sleight and despatched soldiers to the right bank of the river, cutting communications between Lào Cai and Sonphong. With tensions running high, French reports described the commander "stalking the streets of Sonphong saying that he was awaiting a telegram from his Viceroy to declare war."[35] However, in the midst of the standoff French officials provocatively granted asylum to a third runaway domestic servant, aged seven, apparently also belonging to Phu Ho Ky, who turned up in Lào Cai on 14 April.

Vi Cao Khởi eventually backed down, leaving the French vice resident to report the incident to superiors in Hanoi in vainglorious terms. In his account he declared, "It would have been odious for an administrator of a French Protectorate to hand over to abductors annamite children . . . The sale of these 'goods' to others is null and void." 'Tonkin' was "taking back three of its children" in a frontline defence of "that which is most sacred: human liberty."[36] Here he presented a classic humanitarian ethics—the military necessity (of pacification) overridden by the heroic sacrifice. French colonialism was a republican initiative, but on the border it was saturated with sacral overtones. Indeed, this stance effectively sacralised the lives of Vietnamese children.[37]

Hanoi commended the vice resident for his actions. After all, these had usefully reinforced a narrative allowing 'slavery' to be displaced beyond the geographical limits of French rule. In the very same year as the Lào Cai incident, the French *résident* in Hải Phòng had complained of "a veritable commercial traffic between our land and sea frontiers and China," and argued it was a "significant detail that these *children*" were "victims of procurement."[38] This traffic (and *trafic* was the word used) carried young people in particular, especially girls, into south China and across networks connecting three empires, with nodes of transfer and exchange in Hoi Hau (Hai Kou), Hong Kong, Saigon and Singapore. Pakhoi had also become a transit point for girls moved on to Hong Kong, as one girl old enough to plead with a visitor to the brothel where she was being held had explained in 1889.[39]

In administrators' eyes the fate of 'the child' moving beyond French tutelage was inevitably demoralisation. Children appeared as innocent victims of a contagion of crime created by proximity to China and embodied in the figure of the Chinese raider. As officials in Saigon, Hong Kong and Singapore drew the veil of 'custom' over statuses akin to slavery within domestic interiors, references to abductors as 'pirates' or 'bandits' acquired a stronger racial inflection. French officials used the term *trafic* to read these flows in terms of unimaginable horror ("little annamite girls destined for prostitution ... recruited for all the most vile and abject tastes of Chinese sailors"). Such imagery became more prevalent as reform commenced in China in 1898 and began to spill over into Tonkin. In this new moral geography the symptoms of internal failures of colonial governance—the economic mismanagement that critics linked with child divestment, trafficking and slavery—were exported, and insinuations of pederasty cast 'the sick man of Asia' in a disturbing new light.[40]

Perhaps surprisingly, the most voluble opponents of this complacent official line emerged from within the French settler community. By the end of the century high customs tariffs were already blunting commercial prosperity and Tonkin was inundated with foreign products.[41] New taxes introduced to pay for Paul Doumer's expensive schemes resulted in a striking increase in the smuggling of contraband. In this context, in the eyes of *colons* (owners of concessions and agrarian colonisation projects) Vietnamese children on the move across the Chinese border became symbols of a perverse system where 'good traffic' was staunched by the administration, and 'sick traffic' flowed freely. The *colons* marshalled evidence of 'child slavery' behind attacks on the government for failing to defend their interests in Tonkin (and to a lesser extent Cochinchina).

Using terms strikingly similar to those used by Landes and Silvestre, in October 1899 an article in the mission-owned newspaper *L'Avenir du Tonkin* claimed, "Every day, in every Tonkinese province, women and children are sold." While purchasers "say, hypocritically, in taking the child into their home that they are doing them a service," the author argued

> the truth is that the latter serves as their instrument. They save money on a domestic helper or a wife ... They can do as they please, the family will not reclaim the [child]; no one will take up their defence. [The child] is accustomed to considering itself a slave.[42]

From September 1905 *colon* attacks became still more vitriolic as a wave of child cession followed. A missionary working for the Missions Étrangères de Paris described the conditions on the ground triggering this event:

> From February [1906] people no longer had anything to sell.... Famine hit the region in the north. Even the missionaries were hit badly, besieged by crowds dying of hunger. ... We hear their cries, their pleas all day: see old hunger stricken ones, women with their little emaciated children, going to your door, asking for a few coins, a handful of rice: what torture for the heart of a priest, when we are powerless to stop such misery! ... The women, the young girls left, in droves for the higher regions, hoping to find there a higher income ... It was a veritable dismemberment of families.[43]

Colons determined to embarrass Paul Beau's government detailed the increasing extent of trafficking *within* Indochina. In Saigon, one newspaper claimed a Vietnamese parent had contacted a French magistrate to ask him how he could formalise the sale of a child sold for 2 piasters. In November 1906 the main *colon* newspaper in Hanoi condemned

> the indulgence of our European magistrates courts and the inertia of most Residents [which] encourages the work of the unsavoury people who organise on a large scale this deplorable traffic of our little children.... It is evident that the faults of the various public services have contributed in large part to obliging the natives to sell their children.[44]

For another, "the mistakes of the various public services have contributed to a large extent to forcing the natives to sell their children ... and if there are abductions of children there are also sales of these poor little ones, necessitated by the payment of duties required by the Residence."[45] Louis Bonnafont, the self-declared 'voice of the *colons*,' made the black-humoured suggestion that the tax office might even mount a painting in its *salle d'honneur* depicting an "Annamite woman selling her children to pay a [tax] bill."[46]

With conditions desperate in the north and the rice market failing in the south, the Chamber of Agriculture in Hanoi linked issues of child welfare, tax and labour. *Colons* bound the powerful symbolism of forced child migration and slavery to their own grievances, notably protests over taxation, which they claimed provoked child selling.[47] They even threatened to embarrass the government by inviting metropolitan intervention, demanding the extension to Vietnamese children of metropolitan child protection legislation (in particular the law of 19 April 1898 dealing with the prevention of violence and acts of cruelty committed against children). Two metropolitan laws for the protection of childhood had been promulgated in Indochina (along with the law of 24 July 1889 concerning the protection of mistreated or "morally abandoned" children) through the decrees of 3 May and 15 December 1890.[48] However, article 2 of each decree stipulated they were not applicable to *indigènes*, who were governed by their own statute.

The *colons*' efforts to bring the moral, civilising claims of French colonialism into disrepute were deeply embarrassing for a government seeking to project power beyond Tonkin, and in particular into China. Imperial desires for the economic 'penetration' of China were epitomised by the grandiose Lào Cai to Yunnan-Fu railway project, which commenced in 1904, and by medical missions expanding informal influence through vaccination programmes.[49] In response to the child divestment and trafficking crisis, Hanoi emphasised new legislation targeting Chinese within Indochina. In October 1906, police brigades undertaking port surveillance duties in Hải Phòng were empowered to search accommodation used by Chinese. The government introduced new passport regulations to prevent Chinese abductors posing as parents of disguised Vietnamese children. However, beyond the ports, the domestic lives of the large and wealthy Chinese immigrant communities were left largely undisturbed. Instead of aggressively monitoring Chinese *congrégations* or establishing equivalents of the Kuks of Hong Kong and Singapore, officials in Indochina urged vice consuls posted to the borderlands between Indochina and China to stem and reverse the flow of these mobile bodies.

In 1898 the office of the lieutenant governor of Cochinchina assured the French consul in Hong Kong that Vietnamese women recovered from "slavery" could be repatriated at the cost of Cochinchina's budget.[50] In 1912 the consul in Hong Kong sent back five Vietnamese women retrieved by charitable institutions in Hong Kong, including a fourteen-year-old, a sixteen-year-old girl from Hải Phòng who had attempted suicide, a fourteen-year-old who claimed to have been abducted, sold in Hong Kong and who had run away due to mistreatment, and one 'Chan Chan,' aged fifteen years, found wandering the streets.[51] Consuls vied to claim the most prodigious 'catch' of children. In 1912 Vice Consul E. Point of the Longzhou and Nanning consulate boasted to the governor general of arranging twenty-seven repatriations to Tonkin, and browbeating the Chinese police commissioner in Guanxi, Li Kai Sien, into remitting another eight young victims.[52] Charles Kliene, the Danish imperial maritime customs commissioner in Hoi Hau, collected so many young Vietnamese women and girls from port areas that the French consul requested that he receive the *croix d'officier* for his efforts.[53] These actions gave humanitarian significance to the unfolding emergency on the border.

French consuls sometimes used children's voices to corroborate the official line. The anthropologist-consul Joseph Beauvais in Hoi Hau advised the governor general, it "always necessitates the greatest gentleness... to find out the exact story of each of them."[54] But by giving a voice to 'the child,' however circumscribed, consuls endowed this category with radical potential. On the border the French state gestured toward childhood as a common human condition and conferred rights upon its incumbents (to safe return). These notional rights threatened with dissolution the imperial hierarchies they had been called upon to underwrite. Moreover, while consuls saw their work as a defence of 'sacred' human liberty, they were paradoxically redirecting rescued children toward the 'unfreedom' of the Vietnamese family. This attenuated subjecthood provocatively embodied the conundrum of colonial subjecthood. A further problem was that in practice the young females recovered were sometimes not 'children' by contemporary standards. Many were young women in their late teens or even twenties. However, they remained 'children' in the discourse of colonial humanitarianism. And they remained so, paradoxically, at a time when officials used assumptions about early maturation in the tropics to eschew intervention over other delicate matters, such as child brides and rural child labour. Tellingly, consuls were already growing frustrated at evidence that young people were exploiting the limited power this category conferred as British and French power in Asia was profoundly shaken by the onset of the Great War.

SENTIMENT AND SERVILITY:
THE INTERWAR CAMPAIGN AGAINST CHILD SLAVERY

In the early postwar era the European world order was refashioned from the ruins of continental empire. The new circumstances of peacetime ensured that fresh allegations of child slavery emanating from colonial 'outposts' in Asia proved especially damaging. The global watchdog institutions called into existence in the 'Wilsonian moment' invoked age-related ideals and promised to 'save the children,' everywhere. The International Save the Children Union established on 6 January 1920 championed childhood as a repository of 'universal' values essential to the reshaping of the postwar order along liberal-humanist lines. The League of Nations, also founded in 1920, set down a commitment to protect children in colonial contexts in September 1924 when its Fifth Assembly recognised, "Mankind owes to the child the best that it has to give," and resolved to protect the child against "every form of exploitation."[55]

The preservation of the shaky Anglo-French-dominated world order demanded that colonialism be squared with the high-minded principles set down at the Paris Peace Conference. Western governments agreed to the doctrine of 'trusteeship,' or empire as a protective, tutelary bond, akin to that between parent and child.[56] These developments made Asian children legitimate subjects for reform and gave new impetus to antislavery campaigners. In the face of this growing scrutiny the defence of 'child slavery' in Hong Kong and Singapore soon unravelled, but in French Indochina it held firm. As we shall see, this divergence occurred as a result not only of imperial and global pressures but also of the specific circumstances on the ground.

The mui tsai as Child: Clara Haslewood and the Hong Kong Controversy

In August 1917, newspaper reports about a Supreme Court case concerning the 'ownership' of *mui tsai* came to the attention of Colonel John Ward. Temporarily stationed in the colony, Ward was disturbed to learn that Hong Kong's chief justice, Sir William Rees Davies, defined the paid transfer of young females into bond service as a local custom. Ward wrote to W. A. Appleton of the General Federation of Trade Unions asking him to raise the question of whether slavery was tolerated in a British Crown Colony with the secretary of state for the colonies, Walter Long.[57] The colonial secretary's enquiries drew the tried-and-tested response from Hong Kong that slavery had no legal status there, or in any other British colony, and that the girls in question were not slaves but beneficiaries of a philanthropic Chinese custom.

The Colonial Office was prepared to accept this line, but in the febrile postwar context reform-minded evangelical progressives infused with the sense that the moment for change had arrived, were not. Soon after, Hugh Haslewood, a lieutenant commander of the Royal Navy posted to the Naval Chart Depot, and his wife, Clara, who arrived in the colony in the summer of 1919, emerged as vociferous critics of the phenomenon. Alerted to the issue by a sermon delivered at St. John's Cathedral on the subject of girl bond servants, Clara Haslewood publicised their plight by writing a series of letters to Hong Kong newspapers castigating colonial authorities for tolerating "child slavery."[58]

Because this line failed to gain traction in Hong Kong, the Haslewoods, on return to Britain in December 1919, alerted a range of philanthropic societies, MPs and reform-minded individuals to the problem. In March 1920 Colonel John Ward, by now a serving MP, raised the matter in Parliament. And thereafter questions came before the House with increasing regularity. Having observed the ease with which colonial officials swatted links between domestic servitude and brothel slavery, the Haslewoods were well aware of the difficulty of breaking down the orientalist defence. Even after a barrage of questions in Parliament throughout the summer of 1921 established that payment exchanged hands in transfers of girl bond servants and that their labour was unpaid, this defence held firm. Colonial governments bandied about the exotic vocabulary of *mui tsai* to create confusion. This allowed Governor Henry May in Hong Kong to assert that bond service was "governed by a different vocabulary" than slavery.[59]

Frustrated by their inability to undermine this defence, the Haslewoods began to emphasise the *mui tsai* system as synonymous with the abuse of young children. By focusing on a specific, age-related vulnerability, they linked their cause to a lively contemporaneous debate over adoption in Britain and abuses stemming from regulatory shortcomings.[60] By locating bond service at the extreme end of a range of objectionable forms of labour impacting upon children under colonial rule, they also connected their campaign to noisy, concurrent condemnations of child labour in other colonial contexts, notably evangelical-led protests in other major centres along the China coast.[61] These aligned neatly with the critiques of influential experts in Geneva keen to monitor colonial governments' 'civilising' claims.

The Haslewoods tapped into a narrative of child rescue that had special resonance in the British metropolitan context. From the 1830s, British reformers' assertions that every child had the right to an ideal childhood advanced in conjunction with demands for labour reform. In struggles to extend legislative protection and free, compulsory education, reformers constructed childhood as vulnerable and ideally noneconomic, protected and happy. Evidence of the denial of this ideal presented moral reformers with a powerful tool. And as the Haslewoods and their supporters drew upon the emotive weight of the unfree child, the momentum began to shift in their favour.[62]

MPs proved sympathetic to this increasingly broad-based critique. They began to angle attacks on the *mui tsai* system through an age-related critique of vulnerability that trumped considerations of racial difference or cultural sensitivity. On 1 August 1921, for example, Sir Alfred Yeo asked the secretary of state for the colonies whether he was aware of a case in Hong Kong of the assault on a *mui tsai*, "so small that she could not see over the edge of the witness box."[63] Explicit appeals to non-normative childhood diminished the authority of the orientalist defence. Officials in Hong Kong now grew worried by MPs' tendencies to 'mix up' issues of slavery, child labour and custom. Hong Kong's colonial secretary, E. R. Hallifax, complained of the "confusion of ideas which constantly appears in European writings on this subject, the point of confusion being the connection between the *Muitsai* and child labour," when in his eyes, "the question of child labour . . . is a separate one."[64]

The Hong Kong government and its defenders were on difficult ground. Leo Amery, undersecretary of state for the colonies, found himself defending bond service as a customary 'unfreedom' comparable to that of a 'normal' British childhood, arguing, "I do not think that even in this country either adopted or other children can always get away as freely as they would like, and perhaps that is sometimes a good thing for them."[65] Amery's point was that the notion of a 'free' child was nonsensical, predicated as it was upon the suspension of liberty within the authoritarian structure of the family. However, equating the ideal childhood in Britain to bond service in China was risky at a time when reformers were drawing attention to the most lurid aspects of the *mui tsai* system and childhood had emerged at the forefront of liberal internationalist efforts to reshape the postwar order. Moreover, by now in Hong Kong an increasingly vociferous 'Anti–Mui Tsai Society' (established in September 1921) led by Chinese Christians with support from local labour guilds was undermining a defence based upon cultural sensitivity to 'Chinese' norms and values. Dismantling the *mui tsai* system was a key goal of nationalists and Christian Chinese who identified childhood as crucial to nation building. In August the same year, Dr. Yeung Shiu Chuen, who became the society's secretary, attacked the system as inimical to Chinese 'prestige' and 'civilisation,' and as "producing a low grade nation."[66] In 1922 the group appealed to the Legislative Council for abolition on the grounds that *mui tsai* were slaves. With the orientalist defence in tatters the government in London finally decided to act.

In February 1922, Winston Churchill, Amery's successor as secretary of state for the colonies, had become increasingly aware that the treatment of children in Hong Kong was seen as a test case for civility in the British Empire. He announced on 21 March 1922 that he was "determined to effect the abolition of the system at the earliest practicable date." His declaration came in direct response to Charles Edwards's condemnation in the Houses of Parliament of the *mui tsai* system as an abuse of children "of quite tender years."[67] On 15 February 1923 the metropolitan government forced Hong Kong's Legislative Council to pass the 'Female Domestic Servants Ordinance.' This aimed to phase out the phenomenon by providing for

A Child Slave of Hong Kong
(Sold for 96 dollars in the Colony)

FIG. 7.1. "Ah Moy, A Child Slave of Hong Kong." *Source*: Lt.-Commander & Mrs. H. L. Haslewood, "Child Slavery in Hong Kong: The Attitude of the Church of England and Its Associated Societies," 1930.

registration and remuneration and banning future additions to registers of *mui tsai* under age ten.

This directive triggered protests from Hong Kong's governor, Sir Edward Stubbs, who argued that registration would precipitate unrest. Churchill's successor in London, the Duke of Devonshire, bent to this pressure and agreed that the registration element of the legislation could remain in abeyance. It was only much later, when the Chinese nationalist government addressed the issue of unwaged girl bond servants in March 1927, that antislavery campaigners, ranged behind the Anti–Mui Tsai Society, labour guilds and Chinese Christian groups, brought this omission to light. A reevaluation of the Hong Kong ordinance followed. Revelations of deferred registration brought a wave of condemnation in 1928 that turned even more explicitly upon sentimental ground. Lady Kathleen Simon, a leading campaigner, appealed for action with claims that "the cry of an unhappy or ill-treated child ought to reach the ear and touch the heart of every human being."[68] Newspaper reports routinely defined *mui tsai* as 'children.'[69] The empathic voices of British children, of both sexes, authenticated the chorus of criticism. Hilary Davis, aged six years and ten months, wrote to tell Simon, "I should not like to be a slave girl," and another girl, aged eight and a half, added, "You are quite right about letting the slaves free; it was very wicked to spend all that money to buy little girls."[70] The Haslewoods contributed a book entitled *Child Slavery in Hong Kong* and disseminated publicity materials featuring the androgynous image of 'Ah Moy,' an eight-year-old "child slave of Hong Kong."[71]

So intense had the focus upon children become that by 1929 one newspaper in Hong Kong remarked: "The local anti-slavery movement is for the protection of children. In the circumstances, the adolescents must for the time being look after themselves."[72] In October the colonial secretary in the new Labour government, Lord Passfield, forced through an amendment to the 1923 ordinance, making registration compulsory and possession of an unregistered *mui tsai* a criminal offence.

Because the practices under attack were construed as 'Chinese,' the government of Hong Kong drew the fiercest criticism for its inaction. However, Passfield was determined to ensure the Labour government delivered upon 'trusteeship' in *all* Crown Colonies. He therefore urged the Straits government on 15 November 1929 to adopt the 'Hong Kong legislation.' Governor Sir Cecil Clementi protested, "The existing law in the Straits Settlements and the Federated Malay States is sufficiently strong to prevent the abuse of the *mui tsai* system."[73] But Walter Ellis in the Colonial Office explained, "What is possible in Hong Kong is possible in Malaya: and we shall undoubtedly be driven in an undignified way to take this step, if we don't do it of our own account."[74] This the Straits government eventually did, in 1932.

Though few would have predicted it, in the next few years this pattern of initial resistance followed by the reluctant adoption of legislation in Hong Kong and the eventual application of similar legislation in the Straits Settlements was to dramatically invert. The trigger for this shift was a memorandum on the *mui tsai* system written by Sir George Maxwell, the retired former Malayan colonial administrator and member of the League of Nations Permanent Advisory Committee of Experts on Slavery. Maxwell produced a report exposing the inadequacy of the response to 'child slavery' in Asia. In response the Colonial Office arranged a travelling commission, chaired by Sir Wilfrid Woods, to investigate. The main field of enquiry was again to be Hong Kong but the commission also visited Singapore in June 1936. The Woods Commission's findings, published in January 1937, confirmed fears that many *mui tsai* remained unregistered in Hong Kong and Malaya, and that the evasion of protective legal provisions remained widespread. However, the commission produced not one but two reports: a majority report and a minority report.[75] The author of the minority report was a former Labour MP named Edith Picton-Turbervill.[76]

Picton-Turbervill's Minority Report did not focus upon *mui tsai*, a category she believed was simply being used as a smokescreen, but instead it demanded the legal status of that category be abolished and that all transferred children be inspected, "whether male or female under the age of twelve."[77] By insisting that colonial states take responsibility for all children under the age of twelve if they arrived in British centres without their parents, Picton-Turbervill unbound child slavery from the confines of race and gender.[78] Doubtless, as a feminist Picton-Turbervill sympathised with *mui tsai* (who were by definition girls) on the basis of gender, as did other British campaigners, as we have seen. The *girl* bond servant issue spoke powerfully to feminist concerns about male vice and female prostitution. Threatening male sexuality lurked in discussions of transferred girls, and this has led one scholar to suggest that feminists defined the *mui tsai* system "very largely as an abuse of women by men."[79] However, having served in Parliament, Picton-Turbervill was also well aware of the political value of childhood, broadly defined, in expanding the bases of the antislavery campaign and overcoming the problems exposed by the Maxwell report. She had been in Parliament when Sir John Simon (briefed by the Haslewoods) attacked the *mui tsai* system by inviting MPs "who had a little child or grandchild of nine years of age to consider what such a sale would mean" (Picton-Turbervill recorded that "a deep silence fell" and the House was "obviously impressed").[80] Though she was well aware of the rhetorical power of childhood, Picton-Turbervill's appeal also seems to have been based on the firm conviction that ideals of childhood could and should be extended across race in empire. She observed the potential for rescued *mui tsai* to be reformed, describing "the miraculous change that comes over these unfortunate children after they have been six months or so in an orphanage or school, mixing with happy, normal children . . . They too become normal and happy."[81]

To the evident surprise of its author, Picton-Turbervill's Minority Report soon received unqualified support from the government of the Straits Settlements. Only a few months before the commission delivered its report, colonial newspapers in Malaya had trotted out the established line that the *mui tsai* system was a 'time-honoured' Chinese tradition.[82] But Sir Thomas Shenton Thomas's government stunned campaigners by agreeing in 1937 to implement Picton-Turbervill's Minority Report. The governor informed the Colonial Office that the report was to form part of an overarching 'Children's Ordinance.' Passed in 1938–40 (though not enforced owing to the outbreak of war), this legislation also fixed the minimum age limit for domestic service at fourteen and prohibited child labour below fourteen.

This shift came about in part because, as Rachel Leow has also argued, the report presented new evidence that unfree child labour existed not only among Chinese but also among others, notably the Malay.[83] The trans-racial dimensions of this problem had long been known, as revealed by the case of Elizabeth above. So what prompted the government to dispense with the older convenience of the orientalist *mui tsai* strategy and to embrace the report? Crucially, by the late

1930s new circumstances connected the fate of unpaid child labourers to wider debates over public health, the controversial issue of the Singapore naval base and the 'United Malaya' project. In 1919 embarrassing revelations of the government's toleration of brothels led to metropolitan criticism of Singapore as the 'Cesspool of the East.'[84] The government would eventually ban prostitution in 1927 and make brothels illegal in 1930. But these measures did not prevent venereal disease and they motivated the pugnacious Straits Settlements Association and its allies to launch public attacks upon brothel closure. These campaigners rejected the 'expertise' of 'do-gooders' "sitting at the other side of the world" and even demanded the reenactment of the Contagious Diseases Ordinance.[85]

Opponents of abolition also targeted Singapore's new naval base. The base would endow Singapore with new imperial significance. But critics argued that augmenting the military presence would not only be costly but also further exacerbate the venereal disease problem. By the late 1930s officials saw a clear need to dampen down the febrile debate over the 'Social Question,' as this now threatened to challenge matters of imperial defence. Because the Straits government was daunted by its responsibility for the naval base project, it eschewed political concessions that might compromise its authority, and in the face of unresponsive government nonofficial frustration grew.[86] This frustration was especially apparent among Chinese representatives who were also busily protesting immigration restrictions. Straits Chinese, including representatives on the Legislative Council such as Song Ong Siang and Tan Cheng Lock, launched fierce complaints about portrayals of child trafficking, prostitution and vice as "a Chinese problem."[87]

In a context where serious political concessions were impossible the government by now urgently required new evidence to underpin its claims to be a 'benevolent bureaucracy.'[88] However, this need stemmed less from the need to address Chinese protests than from desires to accelerate 'decentralisation,' a policy intended to bring the Malay Peninsula more closely under British control. Much earlier, in 1926, Governor Laurence Guillemard (1919–27) had set out this goal by insisting that the "various parts of Malaya can only attain their full development by working together as members of one united Malaya."[89] Picton-Turbervill's report emerged at a time when Governor Shenton Thomas sought a means of addressing both the political controversy of the 'Social Question' and the challenge of unification.

Shenton Thomas had already accepted the League of Nations orthodoxy that brothel registration failed to protect women and children against the 'Yellow Slave' traffic. Faced with the row over prostitution in 1937, he had despatched Inspector General of Police A. H. Dickinson to seek advice at the League of Nations in Geneva on how the 'Social Question' might be tackled. Dickinson's enquiries led him to Mrs. S. E. Nicoll-Jones, a former advisor of the Burmese colonial government on the problem of prostitution. She agreed to advise the Straits Settlements government on immigration, child protection, brothel suppression and venereal disease. And her appointment to this post reflected a growing official willingness to recognise these problems as linked.[90] When Edith Picton-Turbervill's report emerged, casting the *mui tsai* problem into a larger one of child welfare, it fit within the broad contours of this new approach.

Adopting the Minority Report enhanced the government's authority as it prepared to step up its challenge to existing structures of authority in rural areas of the Malay States. As demand for labour increased with the economic recovery after 1934, the refusal of planters to raise wages to predepression rates sparked a general strike by rubber workers that lasted through the spring and summer of 1937. This caused further embarrassment for officials who had already been criticised by Indian Nationalists over the labour conditions suffered by Indian labourers on Malayan plantations. The Government of India conducted an inquiry into this matter, which reported in 1937, and in June 1938 placed a moratorium on assisted emigration to Malaya. Facing these internal and external pressures, and with fears of communism on the rise, the British Colonial Office and the Malayan Governments became convinced that the rubber estates required much more careful regulation. This conviction prompted interventions oriented toward enhancing schooling, health inspections and child welfare. Little serious attention had hitherto been given to providing education for children working on rubber estates (who usually commenced work from age ten to twelve), but in 1937 an official inspector of schools (H. L. Hodge) with a knowledge of Tamil was appointed to the Department of Education and a scheme of training Tamil teachers started.[91] Such interventions reflected hopes that schools might help tie Indian workers to estates, ushering in a new phase "in which the labour force will live a settled life in its own village on the estate."[92] Shenton Thomas's declaration that it was "the duty of a civilized Government to protect its children" needs to be read against this wider context of labour unrest, political instability and state intervention.[93]

The Straits government's decision to endorse Picton-Turbervill's Minority Report took officials in Hong Kong by surprise. This news was especially unwelcome as the Colonial Office soon applied pressure upon officials in Hong Kong to follow suit. In Singapore, during the late 1930s the colonial government had begun to shape childhood into an emblem of administrative benevolence and marshal it behind expansionist visions of humanitarian rescue in a 'united Malaya.' And it had been able to precisely because for so long elites there had declined to sponsor exemplary, moral projects transcending ethnic plurality. In Hong Kong, by contrast, circumstances did not favour any similarly swift endorsement of the Minority Report. For here it directly threatened the symmetry of a relationship tentatively brokered along moral lines, through childhood (across race and on the basis of class) within the colony's dynamic voluntary sector, and the structures of authority this legitimated.

Colonial officials in Hong Kong had long been reluctant to regulate or criminalise bond service, for they feared that this might destroy the fragile social and cultural grounds upon which interethnic collaboration rested. Governor Stubbs, who declined to enforce the 1923 legislation, was only too well aware of this. His wife was the president of the Ministering Children's League—one of the foremost associative institutions through which philanthropic collaborative grounds had been staked out. In the late 1930s, as we saw in Chapter 4, European and Chinese elites had scaled up charitable initiatives through the league, centring claims for authority firmly around the dichotomous racial construct of colonial childhood. In this context, adopting the Minority Report would involve admitting an affective deficit within British colonialism and conceding the authority that European and Chinese elites had built together through elite visions of childhood to an external (metropolitan) claimant.[94] Even worse, it threatened to obliterate the carefully structured racial distinctions of colonial childhood and to raise instead the expensive prospect of delivering a universal, normative variant to children in general, in a Chinese context.[95]

This was why, when the furore over *mui tsai* had risen again in 1929, officials in Hong Kong had leapt to 'fairyland's' defence. G.E.J. Gent of the Colonial Office received reports of new voluntary initiatives, pushing out the boundaries of charitable child welfare still further. These included the establishment of a Hong Kong branch of the National Society for the Prevention of Cruelty to Children (NSPCC).[96] Others, such as the police-run Waifs and Strays club, also emerged as part of this defensive reaction. The governor of Hong Kong, Sir Cecil Clementi, a staunch opponent of the compulsory inspection of *mui tsai*, presided at the inaugural meeting of Hong Kong's branch of the SPCC in January 1930. According to him, the allocation of funds demonstrated the colonial government's attachment of "so much importance to this matter [the protection of children]."[97] Soon after, Clementi left Hong Kong to take up the governorship of the Straits Settlements, but he continued to describe the *mui tsai* legislation as a disaster for poor children, whom he believed were better catered for as bond servants within the elite family.[98]

Official histories of Hong Kong emerging in the 1930s set up paternal counterclaims to female reformers' demands by recasting British colonial governance within a surprisingly sentimental frame. Officials here had long eschewed metaphors of nature or kinship in preference for a discourse of development as rational, technologically competent progress. This had often portrayed Hong Kong as a triumph over nature, a 'barren rock' transformed into a showcase of British-led modernisation.[99] Now, however, officials began to indulge in paternal references to the Crown Colony's former 'infancy.' It was significant that their gaze was retrospective, that they claimed to be looking back on the child-colony from the perspective of a present in which it was already 'mature' (in contrast to a young and turbulent China over the border). For such views negated justifications for external intervention and ushered female reformers towards the anachronistic position of belittling a colony that had already 'grown up.'[100]

In the end, changed circumstances in China after 1937 drove officials in Hong Kong beyond this impasse. Japan's attacks on China presented the colonial government with an opportunity. For much of the interwar era, especially after Chiang Kai Shek's Nationalist government had drawn closer to Germany, British officials had struggled to fashion credible claims for imperialism as moral. Within Hong Kong the protests of the Chinese-led Anti–Mui Tsai Society had continued to embarrass the government by exposing the shortcomings of existing legislation.[101] But the war allowed officials to present Hong Kong as a safe haven for refugees fleeing Japanese aggression. A sizable proportion of the growing refugee population (of an estimated 650,000) were children. At a moment when the refugee crisis thus made the implementation of the Minority Report more impracticable than ever, the government grasped the potential for child welfare legislation to reboot the moral authority of the British Empire in China in the face of Japanese aggression.[102] The new governor of Hong Kong, Sir Geoffrey Northcote, citing conditions offering "maximum opportunity for exploitation of children," persuaded elements still ranged against Picton-Turbervill's report to agree to its implementation.[103]

The Colonial Office could now argue that the Crown Colonies recognised their "responsibility to protect children."[104] However, the legislation that was actually passed never fulfilled Picton-Turbervill's demands that transferred children of both sexes under the age of twelve should form the principal focus of protective intervention. War stymied legislative work in the Straits, while in Hong Kong the Legislative Council rejected proposals that children under the age of twelve not living with their own parents be registered. The ordinance passed on 12 May 1938 required those whose custody had been transferred to register with, and become wards of, the secretary for Chinese affairs (SCA), and it protected girls and young women up to the age of twenty-one. The SCA could assume guardianship over any girl under the age of twenty-one judged to be in 'moral danger' or 'improperly treated,' at ages well beyond the recognised upper boundaries of 'childhood.'[105]

Thus, instead of conceding childhood in general as a basis for imperial reform, the Hong Kong government hoved back toward reaffirming its tutelage over *girls*. Extending imperial responsibility beyond the *mui tsai* category to young Chinese women and girls (not children of both sexes) allowed colonial officials to claim to be pushing intervention further (up the age spectrum) than campaigners had themselves. The reassertion of sex, meanwhile, allowed the Legislative Council to evade acceptance of any implicit schedule of future obligations likely to arise from conceding sentimental visions of normative childhood in the round as a basis for imperial reform. This response to the Minority Report also allowed racial hierarchies to be reinforced, for it permitted references to a kind of 'colonial chivalry,' and European males as protectors of vulnerable native women and girls. Governor Northcote wasted few opportunities to condemn "the abominable exploitation of young girls" and "the deliberate exploitation of a large number of girl children, such as is the common practice not only in Hong Kong but throughout China."[106]

Hong Kong's response ultimately satisfied the Colonial Office, but tellingly, when Picton-Turbervill learned of the actual terms of the new legislation in Hong Kong, she was extremely disappointed.[107] In 1940, as the threat of Japanese overlordship loomed, the Hong Kong government appealed to its record on child welfare to buttress claims that it was fulfilling the duties of a civilised government. But the shallowness of its claims to benevolence was exposed as the government oversaw a compulsory evacuation policy ignoring Chinese children and screening out Eurasians. Meanwhile the administration entirely neglected what officials recognised as a growing epidemic in the trafficking of boys.[108]

"Are there not also Annamite mui tsai?":
Obscuring Unfreedom in Saigon and Hanoi

Following formal registration of *mui tsai* in Hong Kong in 1931, and Singapore in 1933, humanitarian agencies also raised fresh concerns over 'child slavery' within the French Empire. Through the 1920s French authorities in Indochina had sent in returns to League of Nations questionnaires blithely referring to a battery of regulations governing the sale, cession and purchase of children and the humanitarian defence of children on the border with China.[109] But as the League announced it intended to replace indirect monitoring of colonial authorities with actual visits by expert investigators, the French minister of colonies, Paul Reynaud, panicked. Reynaud was only too well aware that such visits would quickly undermine a defence resting mainly upon legislative and rhetorical grounds, since illegal practices were rarely prosecuted. He therefore warned the governor general of Indochina, "It is no longer enough ... to state that French colonial legislation proclaims the abolition of slavery."[110]

By this time, on the border, the ethical framework of humanitarian action appeared to be on the brink of collapse. Even before the war consuls had complained that many of those they rescued were "not really children" or were "far from worthy." Vice-Consul Troy complained in March 1920 from the Longzhou and Nanning outpost that most were young women taking the chance to sell labour in less competitive markets than those of overcrowded Tonkin, and exploiting the "benevolence" of the French state in the process.[111] As Troy put it, those 'rescued' "find the consulate a comfortable asylum with plentiful food ..." and seek out "repatriation under escort ... to avoid debts freely contracted, or simply to return free to Tonkin, after having been sold in China of their own free will or at least without having been the object of any real constraint."[112]

Regardless of what drove mobility, even before the war in Vice Consul Point's eyes the sheer weight of human traffic had left the border itself in danger of effacement. He complained that there were

> on both sides of the border, customs against which neither a French administration, as perfect as it may be, nor a Consulate armed with all of the juridical powers that treaties may provide, will not, for a very long time, be able to completely address.[113]

The implications of that statement were vast, for it pointed attention back toward the internal sources from which these problems stemmed.

In 1932 the League's Commission of Enquiry into Traffic in Women and Children in the East produced the report that Paul Reynaud had feared. This identified Saigon as a centre for trafficking in children, especially young girls who were moved on from Hong Kong and Guangdong.[114] Even more alarmingly, League officials insisted trafficking was "connected with old customs and traditions" *within* Indochina, such as paid transfers of children into bond service, which were tolerated by the colonial government.[115] As Marc Fraissinet, reporting for the League, put it, "Natives cede their children to wealthy families who put them to work and sometimes adopt them," but sometimes "ignorant parents are tricked by an intermediary who delivers a young girl to a brothel, instead of to a respectable family."[116] The writer René Bunout, studying labour legislation, also argued that the transfer of girl children into bond service "facilitates prostitution" and that "these abuses, in spite of energetic efforts to prevent them, continue largely unhindered by the authorities."[117] In Hanoi, in the same year as Fraissinet was writing, the socialist and editor of the *Revue Franco-annamite*, Alfred-Ernest Babut, once again drew explicit comparisons with Hong Kong, asking pointedly, "Are there not also Annamite 'mui tsai'?"[118]

In spite of this growing concern, and even as the orientalist defence foundered within the British Empire, the Government General of Indochina managed to avoid becoming embroiled in an open and confrontational debate over 'child slavery.' As it turned out, neither metropolitan antislavery campaigners nor reformers in Hanoi and Saigon were able to undermine the administration's claims to be advancing a humanitarian antitrafficking ethics or its orientalist defence of bond service as 'custom,' right up to the Second World War. Why was this?

Part of the reason was because religious authorities in France, Hanoi and Saigon were far less inclined than their British equivalents to use evidence of 'unfree' children to attack the colonial government. Historians reflecting on the characteristics of antislavery movements more generally, prior to and during this period, have contrasted a powerful British antislavery movement possessing a broad, evangelical mass power base with a French equivalent suffering from long-standing divisions.[119] Certainly, the establishment of Cardinal Lavigerie's Anti-Slavery Society in 1888 had seen the French Catholic Church overcome associations of abolition with revolution to emerge at the forefront of a reinvigorated metropolitan antislavery movement. However, the society focused its efforts largely upon western and equatorial Africa—areas of empire where Christian influence had yet to be consolidated—not Indochina, where the French Catholic presence in Asia long predated, and inspired, formal colonial rule.

Moreover, as the republican state rolled back clerical privilege at home, representatives of the Church preferred to work tactfully, not confrontationally, alongside authorities in the colonies.[120] In Saigon and Hanoi religious authorities enjoyed support from influential figures within the administration and used subtle pressure rather than open propaganda to address controversial social issues.[121] The Anti-Slavery Society adopted a notably emollient tone in correspondence with Governor Albert Sarraut, dismissing allegations that slavery was still tolerated in Indochina.[122] Perhaps this is unsurprising, since the society's president from 11 October 1909 was none other than Charles-Marie Le Myre de Vilers, Cochinchina's first civil governor, who had failed to act on Silvestre and Landes's calls to openly confront child slavery.

The Catholic lobby certainly did draw attention to numerous colonial abuses, but practices akin to child slavery were considered emblematic of the 'heathen savagery' justifying the missionary presence in the first place. Crises in the countryside, however grim the results, presented missionaries with opportunities to 'harvest' souls.[123] In times when families broke apart, the Church grew. In Hanoi as François Chaize drew up a list of obstacles to the advancement of Catholicism in his *vicariat*, alongside "superstition" and "materialism" he wrote the words "*organisation familiale.*"[124] Missionaries and religious workers also had little incentive to demand state intervention in this field, or to work child cession into overt confrontations with the colonial government.[125]

This reluctance became more apparent in the 1920s as Catholics became increasingly alarmed at the spread of Protestant activity in Vietnam. The eventual success of Protestant campaigns against restrictions on their liberty to proselytise in Indochina, coupled with the growing strength of the syncretic religion Cao Đài, which was spreading from the cities into rural areas, especially in the south, had by 1930 left Catholics feeling exposed. Colonial officials distrusted Protestantism and Cao Đài but ultimately proved unwilling to ban either, as Charles Keith has shown, on the grounds that such a policy was inconsistent with the republican principle of *laïcité*.[126] The result—official authorisation of Protestant missionaries' freedom of movement—highlighted Catholic weakness and further underlined the need to avoid direct confrontation with the government. It also raised the nightmare prospect that American missionaries in Vietnam might link up with the Protestant-led international antislavery campaigns and directly threaten the security of the French colonial state.

The quite different political preoccupations of French feminist-led and left-orientated antitrafficking organisations were also important in obstructing the emergence of a broad-based challenge to the official line. Metropolitan antitrafficking movements (with which various feminist groups aligned) had taken up leading positions in international efforts in this field before the First World War. Like the British women's movement, the French antitrafficking movement had developed out of late-nineteenth-century fears over the abduction of women into prostitution, or *la traite des blanches*. Campaigners identified the toleration of brothel registration as the primary cause of this problem. In Britain, the success of the women's movement in achieving the repeal of the Contagious Diseases Acts encouraged a broader focus. After winning suffrage through the 1918 Representation of the People Act (at least for women over thirty), British reformers could afford to turn their attention to improving the condition of other vulnerable groups, notably children, empire-wide. In contrast, French feminists suffered repeated setbacks in the struggle for suffrage and other social and legal rights and this severely curtailed the scope of their demands.[127]

After 1926 French organisations committed to this cause clustered within Madame Marcelle Legrand-Falco's Union Temporaire contre la Prostitution Réglementée et la Traite des Femmes. However, as Legrand-Falco conceded, her union had failed to engage broad sections of the public.[128] French campaigners could not overcome the government's obdurate opposition to the most essential of their demands—the abolition of statutory brothels *in France*. They therefore remained reluctant to divert attention from this, and the trafficking of 'white' women rather than Asian women remained their primary concern.[129]

The French executive and legislature remained determined to defend brothel registration as essential to protecting the health of colonial troops. This forced the antitrafficking lobby to consolidate its (minimal) gains by representing its own interests as congruent with those of the government. Campaigners agreed with officials that the process of trafficking was the most important area for reform. The status children eventually occupied as slaves was de facto beyond the union and therefore of less immediate concern.[130] Reformers hesitated to criticise their government by coordinating protests over the fate of trafficked children. Such a tactic was risky at a time when 'puritanical' and evangelical, antiregulationist nations were attacking France for its claims that brothel registration effectively protected innocents. Hence, even in the 1930s as evidence of links between bond service, the trafficking of children and vice came to light, campaigners did little to exert pressure upon the French government. So little attention did links between forced child migrant labour and brothel and domestic servitude receive in France that in 1933 the journalist and novelist Henry Champly (aka Jean Kérouan) could subject 'slavery' in Hong Kong to blistering condemnation while entirely overlooking equivalent practices in Indochina.[131]

French feminists and women reformers took up more prominent roles within Hanoi and Saigon in the interwar era, but they tended not to challenge paternal discourses of colonialism. For decades men had embodied the benevolence of 'Mother France' in places where the female presence was negligible. However, Claude Farrère and others had condemned colonial masculinity as dissolute in works such as the Goncourt Prize-winning novel *Les Civilisés* (1906).[132] Administrators responded to this affront by fashioning a counter-discourse of the colonial male as benevolent protector of native (and *métis*) children.[133] While women's roles as volunteer adjuncts of the colonial state grew between the wars, they remained quite narrowly defined and closely monitored. Even investigative journalists on the centre left, such as Andrée Viollis, author of *Indochine SOS*, who knew and visited Indochina, devoted, as Mary Lynn Stewart puts it, "remarkably little attention to women and children" in their work.[134] In April 1937, the Popular Front government's minister of colonies charged the French feminist Germaine Malaterre-Sellier with a mission to study children's living conditions in Indochina. However, evidence of bond service once again failed to emerge as the basis for criticism of colonial policy.[135]

Alice Conklin has persuasively argued that the French perceived their commitment to safeguarding freedom in the colonies as qualitatively superior to that of other nations. Republican France, she notes, "prided itself, and its colonialism, as achieving, if nothing else, an end to slavery in its colonies."[136] With economic difficulties threatening to fragment the liberal centre in Europe critical voices fell quiet. At a time when a broad consensus was emerging in metropolitan France that empire was quintessentially humane, even critics such as Viollis appeared to be "inhibited by her own Republicanism" while those on the left, such as Louis Roubaud, vaunted colonisation as the "essential condition for success" in the antislavery campaign, and proposed cooperation on this front between British Malaya, Hong Kong, the Philippines and Siam.[137]

Antislavery campaigners' success in British centres stemmed from their ability to exploit sentimentality to break down the racial divide operating through childhood under colonialism, but there was less potential for any similar sentimental turn in French colonial policy. While Britain in Geneva represented indirect rule as a 'natural' outgrowth of colonial principles enhanced by reform, French authorities struggled to reject claims that their rule was exploitative. After 1926 Germany began to make covetous claims upon French possessions. This alarming development, coupled with growing uncertainty about British intentions and the rising influence of the United States made it more important than ever that an open discussion of 'child slavery' be avoided.[138]

But most of all, the intensity of anticolonial protests within Indochina ensured fewer opportunities existed for serious debate. In Hong Kong after 1927, and in Singapore after 1930, anti-British sentiment had faded somewhat as Japan emerged as a common danger. This allowed imperial responsibility to be discussed more openly. But in Indochina, unrest was more specifically *anti-French*.

This already made officials more reluctant to reappraise problems of child transfer. But what raised the stakes even higher was the symbolic value of childhood to a supposedly benevolent and tutelary republican imperialism. As hopes for political reform in Indochina dwindled during the mid-1920s, young Vietnamese intellectuals began to depict Vietnam itself as an infant nation enslaved by a tyrannical master. "Brothers! We have been slaves for seventy years," began one report in *L'Asie française* in 1925. "France has reduced us to slavery."[139] In years to come protesters frequently and quite explicitly linked the symbolism of child sale and cession to the very real problems of what they saw as an inherently defective colonialism. In the radical newspaper *Jeune Indochine*, for example (beneath quotes from Henri Barbusse describing colonisation as a "new form of slavery"), Thanh Bảo Lộc declared: "The sale of a child is an odious thing. However, it is generally caused by the poverty of the parents, poverty which the benevolent tutelage of France has hardly sought to remedy."[140]

Vietnamese writers were turning the republican iconography of childhood on its head and highlighting French tutelage as neglectful at a time when agricultural prices were dropping and rural conditions were deteriorating.[141] By the late 1920s price deflation made land rent increasingly burdensome. Landowners provided credit to agricultural labourers (especially in Cochinchina), but harsh lending terms worsened problems of indebtedness. The Government General's intended remedy of state-sponsored lending organisations in practice pushed peasants back to landowners to whom they paid high rates of commission for loan guarantees. Then, as profits collapsed, rural families' already precarious position worsened. The *'Inspection du travail'* in Tonkin exacerbated problems with its policy of redirecting unemployed workers back into rural villages to 'decongest' restive urban centres. By the mid-1930s families were breaking apart under these strains. The consequence was a new wave of child cession. "Open any daily [newspaper]," declared the *Annam nouveau* in September 1935, "and we are struck by the number of young girls who have disappeared."[142]

By now French *colons* had much more to lose by attacking the administration than they had in 1905. Their newspapers criticised government inaction but focused upon abduction, not cession. They blamed the Chinese trafficker rather than the *douane*. They demanded harsher punishment for abductors, not tax reform. None of these challenged the official line. Political instability made *colons* wary of challenging the administration directly. It also made the administration more wary of disrupting the 'customs' of the countryside.[143] So, as the League Commission on the trafficking of girls turned its focus toward Saigon and Cholon, authorities pondered the strategy of blaming the Chinese.

From the early 1920s colonial officials had begun to slant reports sent to League inspectors in this direction. Questionnaire replies typically indicated, "Police action is very delicate in affairs relating specifically to the Chinese."[144] If this was a problem, it was largely one of the government's own making. From 1871 to 1885 the French authorities permitted Chinese in Indochina to establish *congrégations*, organised on the basis of language and ethnicity and endowed with powers to police, tax, assist, educate and repatriate members.[145] Membership of the five large Chinese congregations was heavily concentrated in Saigon and Cholon. When French police did make efforts to challenge Chinese privilege and regulate vice, as in Cholon in 1903 and 1912, community leaders' protests ensured that such initiatives were swiftly curtailed.[146] Congregations successfully resisted the regulation of domestic life, securing exemption from legislation registering servants in 1904 and scuppering plans for a regular immigration service in 1906.[147]

The government's tentativeness in policing vice and immigration reflected awareness of the value of Chinese investment and economic agency in Indochina. But its neglect had important ramifications for the protection of children, and officials were very well aware of this. In October 1922 the government of Cochinchina required the formal registration (and taxation) of 'singing girls,' most of whom, it noted, were Cantonese. However, registration cards continued to be issued to 'apprentices' under the age of sixteen.[148] Léon Werth, visiting a restaurant in 1926, asked, "Are they children or courtesans, [these] little singers? I don't know."[149] Officially, at least, the 'singing girls' of Cholon were not prostitutes. The question of whether or not they were children evidently remained in doubt.[150] A similar reticence marked police work in Hanoi and its suburbs, where seven thousand women were estimated to be working as prostitutes.[151] Here, before 1926, the *arrêté* of 3 February 1921 had not been applied to *maisons de chanteurs* on the grounds that they "usually had a limited and wealthy clientèle."[152] In 1925 the *procureur général* had discovered that girls as young as fourteen were on lists of registered prostitutes, or were resident in brothels in Saigon.[153]

In both cities, these facts left authorities scrambling as they prepared for the visit of the League of Nations inspection team. It was quite clear that a large number of children ceded by parents were being trafficked into 'sly' vice, beyond the reach of the regulationist infrastructure of the colonial state. In Saigon, the head of the immigration and labour control office admitted:

> Chinese girls [who are] for the most part prostitutes sometimes come here voluntarily with their mothers [but] more often with their madams whom they also call 'mother.' ... These young girls go around the late-night restaurants of Cholon. They are not registered like the prostitutes who pick up clients on the streets or board in brothels.[154]

On arrival in Indochina, League investigators, taking their cue from questionnaire returns, interrogated leaders of the five large Chinese *congrégations*. The latter's response was laconic. In Hải Phòng, congregation chiefs "declared that they did not know how the houses of prostitution were recruited."[155] In Cholon the League team discovered eight hundred Chinese 'singing girls,' and smaller numbers in Hanoi, involved in clandestine prostitution. They noted, acerbically,

"The French authorities had no information regarding the numbers of Chinese girls thus induced to leave the country," and "the admission of women arriving for immoral purposes therefore wholly depends upon the attitude of the *congrégations*."[156] Many registered 'singing girls' were found to be underage, between eleven and thirteen years old.

However, because the League inspectors' principal concern was to expose the inadequacy of the French government's stance on brothel regulation, they focused rather little on the issue of 'Annamite *mui tsai*.' As Babut's clumsy phrase suggested, unlike the British, the French had never made the strategic error of specifically naming Vietnamese bond servants (though the Vietnamese also had a euphemistic term, *con nuôi*, literally meaning 'adopted child,' to refer to them). If official inclinations to pry into the domestic interiors of wealthy, urban-based Chinese were already weak, they were more so at a time when the Chinese were leaving Indochina in their droves. The number of Chinese in Saigon fell by nearly half from 1931 to 1933, and by more than half in Cholon from 1929 to 1933, as Cochinchina's economic fortunes, linked to the rice trade with China, fell into decline.[157] These departures highlighted the worryingly small and weak condition of the Vietnamese middle class amid declining prosperity, internal unrest and growing external threats.

As we saw in Chapter 5, the political ferment of the 1920s had led French officials to imagine the countryside as a source of harmony, symbolised by the rural child. In the 1930s officials seized upon unsentimental depictions of childhood within the rural family to reaffirm older claims for unwaged labour as 'custom.'[158] In this way they retrieved bond service from relativism and equated it with the 'wholesome' bygone customs of the French countryside. This was not a new tactic. As early as 1880, one member of the Rochefort Geographical Society had posed the rhetorical question:

> Even today, is the child of the peasant not hired as a shepherd for wages sometimes paid in advance? And like the Annamite has but to repay his debt to recover his freedom ... After all, the condition of those engaged does not differ in any way from that of our domestic servants, farm-hands, shepherds.[159]

The main threat to such transferred children was not removal from the biological family but rather removal, by traffickers, from the countryside.

As rural hardship worsened, the image of the self-sacrificing Vietnamese child bond servant spread beyond official minutes and memoranda. It featured in French colonial novels and on the surfaces of material culture. In 1920 the Virgilian novelist (and former employee of the *douanes et régies* in Indochina) Jean Marquet had portrayed the sale of 'Thi Luc' by her mother as a noble act to finance the burial of her father in his novel *De la rizière à la montagne*.[160] In 1931, the authors of one encyclopaedia (*L'Indochine moderne*) included insouciant reference to sales of children into bond service under a section headed 'customs.'[161] This line on paid transfers and bond service in the countryside prevailed from Hanoi to Paris and the Palais des Nations. Discussing Tonkin, the *résident supérieur*, Auguste Tholance, claimed in 1931 that bond service was a "real contract for the hire of services and not on the face of it a blatant or disguised form of slavery."[162] Although

> at first glance and from an occidental perspective, we cannot prevent a sentiment of surprise and even of reprobation in noting that parents abandon their children to others, in return for a sum of money ... anyone who has been to Tonkin, easily grasps the moral side of this custom, which works well.[163]

In 1932, Gaston Bourgeois, president of the League's Commission of Enquiry into Traffic in Women and Children, referred to bond service as "a custom that has not been tolerated by Annamite legislation other than for the benefit of the child."[164] And ultimately, the League of Nations' visiting commission accepted that transferred children in the countryside "remained free, under family guardianship."[165] Before a meeting of the League's Conference of Central Authorities in Eastern Countries in 1937 the legal expert André Labrouquère offered a robust defence of "ancient traditions and old customs which led to certain practices, such as the sale of children, which could scarcely be assimilated with the traffic in women and children."[166]

Only in 1941, by which time Hanoi had become a satellite of the Vichy state and the 'National Revolution' had swept away the last edifices of republican rule, did an official reevaluation of child slavery commence. The Saigon-based scholar and teacher André Baudrit professed himself aghast that "seventy years have elapsed since the reports of Landes and Silvestre were written, and nevertheless, the buying and selling continues inexorably."[167] Lambasting the record of the previous administration, he made mocking references to tales of "long-haired Celestials chasing little girls" and identified bond service not as a harmless 'custom' but rather as a kind of sale that "could last indefinitely."[168] Baudrit's polemic attracted the attention of Governor General Jean Decoux, whose administration discussed abolitionist initiatives in 1942 as part of the process of refounding French colonial rule in Indochina along Vichyite lines. Decoux requested that *résidents* conduct fresh enquiries into this matter. However, while the problem of the unfree child was attracting concern once again at the highest levels of the French colonial state, it did so at a time when serious action was out of the question. Recasting the problem in terms of reclaiming the lost moral initiative proved to be little more than a gesture. By this time French power in the Vietnamese peninsula had already largely slipped away.

CONCLUSION

In the twentieth century child slavery became a global cause célèbre and a test case for empire. Forced migration into unfree forms of labour impacting with special severity upon female children emerged as a common problem in British and French centres in Asia. In response authorities set down distinctions between trafficking and vice, which they criminalised, and unfree forms of labour such as bond service, which they cast as an 'Oriental custom.' From the 1880s debates over 'child slavery' in colonial contexts connected with culturally defined norms of childhood. And in the years that followed, colonial governments *and* those who strove for antislavery reform consistently identified childhood as a key ground upon which to stake out their respective sides of this story.

British antislavery campaigners, in concert with Chinese Christians and other reformers, exposed orientalist arguments and used universalist visions of childhood to challenge colonial authority. Though the campaigners' principal focus was Hong Kong, the colonial government based in Singapore eventually moved first to dismantle the orientalist defence and then embrace a wide-ranging commitment to protect the welfare of child colonial subjects. By contrast, in Saigon and Hanoi, even after colonial government and League reports revealed direct links between trafficking and prostitution, no similar official reevaluation of the state's commitment to Asian children followed. For here, evidence of 'unfree' children posed a more potent threat to a form of governance more closely associated with an ideology of humanitarian ethics, but also one facing anticolonial movements rejecting the French nation as a source of benevolent enlightenment.

French colonial and metropolitan groups also failed to call the administration to account for children's involvement in forms of semiservile labour because this was either obscured by visions of wholesome, rural childhoods or concealed in domestic interiors. In the late 1930s, reports to Geneva continued to assert, largely unchallenged, that the traffic of women and children was 'disappearing' and that inspection teams in Saigon and Hải Phòng would eventually eradicate "all clandestine traffic of women and children."[169] In each of these contexts, however, by the end of the period, sales of children continued to be disguised as abductions. Purchases continued to be disguised as adoptions. Border controls and registration requirements continued to fail to protect young people. And children continued to be transferred, resold and despatched into destinies obscure.[170]

CHAPTER 8

Class Reactions: Education and Colonial 'Comings of Age'

Schools were central to the art and logic of colonial governance in the late imperial era. Missionary agencies had long dominated the provision of schooling, which they saw as a means of saving souls and winning adherents. However, as empires came to be regarded as a 'second front' in middle-class civilising projects during the late nineteenth century, colonial governments were compelled to address more seriously the question of how subject peoples should be educated.[1] Officials often imagined schools in instrumental terms, as tools capable of engineering loyalty, preserving harmony and dividing adversaries. But in practice such meanings were quickly exceeded and educational interventions often had unpredictable consequences.

From the early twentieth century, reformers in a variety of colonial contexts made education a cause célèbre and demanded improved access to it. Meanwhile, those enrolled in (or previously tutored in) colonial schools emerged as critics of the slow pace of social and political reform under British and French rule. The resulting clamour around 'native education' drove officials to more carefully address the question of how to manage the problematic figure of the mobile young scholar. What appeared to some to be the core duty of an imperial power was seen by others as dangerous and counterproductive. Colonial governments' responses to this conundrum varied, but across empires experiments often followed in racially segregating schools, expanding feminine education and linking access to education more explicitly to age.

Scholars have often argued that colonial schooling produced new divisions along the lines of class, race, gender and linguistic competence, but this chapter argues that a key consequence of colonial interventions and experiences of being schooled was the crystallisation of new understandings of the social and political agency of 'youth.' Schooling in colonial centres across Asia set youth on the move, triggered the production of new unities and *trajectories* of age and led young people to arrive at new age-specific understandings of themselves.[2] Since those who experienced schooling were predominantly youthful, education influenced conceptualisations about what it meant to be young. Only a small percentage of colonial subjects actually had access to schooling across the period, in contrast to young Europeans for whom this experience had become a defining feature of modern childhood. And yet in colonial settings schools emerged as contexts in which modern understandings of 'youth' took shape, both as a phase of life distinct from adulthood and as a social collective distinct from the larger 'adult' social order.

WONDROUS CHILDREN, MILLENARIAN TENSIONS: THE STRANGE CASE OF THE KỲ ĐỒNG

On 27 March 1887 a group of around a hundred Vietnamese peasants armed only with wooden swords marched toward Nam Định, the second largest city in Tonkin. At the front of this curious procession, borne aloft on a palanquin, was the leader of this insurrectionary force, Nguyễn Văn Cẩm. This expedition to Nam Định seems to have been intended as a trigger of wider unrest, which it was hoped might overwhelm the foreign forces occupying the city. This support failed to materialise, and the group was quickly captured by French troops before it had even reached the citadel. The French *résident*, Ernest Brière, pondered retributive action. And as he did, he encountered an unexpected dilemma. For it transpired that Nguyễn Văn Cẩm, the leader of this unruly band of attackers, was only twelve years old.

Born on 8 October 1875, Nguyễn Văn Cẩm was said to possess remarkable fluency in scholarly Chinese and prodigious intelligence. Even by the age of seven his fame had spread from his home village Ngọc Đình (then in Hưng Yên) as far as the Court of Huế. So talented did he appear that some speculated he was the reincarnation of the sixteenth-century scholar-prophet Nguyễn Bỉnh Khiêm. Hundreds travelled from far and wide to see the child and to hear his prophecies and poetry recitations. Some dubbed him the 'Kỳ Đồng,' or 'wondrous child' and spoke of him as a 'gift from the heavens' sent to save the land from invaders.

The Kỳ Đồng emerged in the wake of the bitter struggle to 'pacify' the land that the French referred to as Tonkin. This had been detached by force from the Kingdom of Annam following the war against China. Insurrectionary activities flared in the wake of this division, the most spectacular of which was the Cần Vương (Save the King) movement, or Scholars' Revolt, led by Tôn Thất Thuyết in the name of Emperor Hàm Nghi. This saw teachers from Sino-Vietnamese schools stir up anti-French resistance among the peasantry. By July 1885 the uprising was fading out. The emperor had retreated into hiding in the countryside where he was eventually captured three years later. Having crushed the Scholars' Revolt, the French invaders began to interfere with the process of monarchical succession (placing the emperor's son Đồng Khánh on the throne). This was the context in which the 'wondrous child' emerged as a rallying point for a people struggling to comprehend these new circumstances. In response, either Nguyễn Văn Cẩm himself or one of his entourage decided that the moment for direct action had arrived.[3]

Unsure of how to punish a charismatic adversary who was also a child, Ernest Brière wrote to Paul Bihouard, resident general of Annam and Tonkin, with a suggestion. On the advice of his vice resident, Jules Morel, who had interviewed the boy, Brière proposed that Bihouard remove "the Kỳ Đồng from influences against which he is defenceless" by enrolling him in a college in Algeria or in Saigon.[4] As the resident confronted this novel challenge, he appears to have drawn upon the influential thinking of his predecessor, the late Paul Bert. A scientist, democrat and reforming republican resident general of Annam and Tonkin, Bert had extolled the educationalist orthodoxy of republicanism. In his view the school was to be a powerful instrument of colonisation. Combining Hobbesean and Lockean ideas, Bert contended that minds were universally perfectible through education in childhood, a phase associated with malleability and innocence. From his view, the hearts of colonial subjects familiarised with French ideas would surely follow.[5] Experiments in education underpinned by such assimilationist thinking had begun shortly after the French invasion of Saigon. Following the conquest, the mandarinate had fled en masse, leaving Cochinchina bereft of administrators. A succession of admiral governors created schools to address the need to build an administration from the ground up; the first was the College of Interpreters (1861). These French-language schools emerged alongside a precolonial school system where Vietnamese continued to be taught in Chinese characters. The latter provided a moral training and a pathway for the brightest into the imperial civil service on the meritocratic basis of triennial examinations.

Following the transition from military to civilian rule in 1879, the new civil governor of Cochinchina, Charles-Marie Le Myre de Vilers, oversaw the replacement of Chinese from 1882 with a Romanised version of Vietnamese, named Quốc ngữ, developed by missionaries in schools in Cochinchina. Inspired by notions of education as potentially transformative, the governor demanded that the brightest Vietnamese youth be sent to school in metropolitan France. A small but growing number began the journey from Saigon to the Lycée d'Alger in Algeria.[6] It was against this background that Pierre Bihouard took the fateful decision to make Nguyễn Văn Cẩm the first pupil from Tonkin to attend this *lycée*. As the adults who had marched with the 'wondrous child' were incarcerated, on 11 August 1887 Bihouard signed an *arrêté* despatching the Kỳ Đồng to Algeria at the expense of the protectorate.

It seems that Bihouard imagined that an education in Voltaire's tongue in a French milieu (Algeria being a metropolitan *département*) would lead the boy to grasp the beauty of modern ideas and convince him to become an ally of the French. Evidently an extreme of nature, possibly even a prodigy, the Kỳ Đồng could be considered emblematic of the riches now under French control. The Vietnamese were already understood to be higher up the ladder of civilisation than other colonised peoples, as the educationalist Félicien Challaye had put it. This boy's personal transformation from adversary to ally might therefore neatly symbolise and anticipate a wider transition. Steered from superstition through republican tutelage, the most talented youth of an 'old civilisation' would blossom for the benefit of New France.

From the outset this experiment went far from smoothly. Nguyễn Văn Cẩm arrived in Algiers in October 1887 and was hastily enrolled in primary courses at the *lycée*. Initial reports suggest that the school authorities found the boy to be solemn and diligent, rather like the other Indochinese in attendance, though "perhaps with a higher level of intelligence."[7] However, subsequent reports made reference to open displays of contempt for the institution, its teachers, rules and fellow pupils and to the boy's opposition to the best efforts of his tutors to 'enlighten' him. Though Nguyễn Văn Cẩm was the youngest of the Vietnamese attending the school, his defiance of authority was such that schoolmasters placed him in classes with older pupils, in the hope they might help teachers keep him in line.

Having passed a disputatious first year in residence, the boy's fortunes brightened as he received some interesting news. After being dethroned following his capture in November 1888, the former emperor Hàm Nghi had been deported to Algiers and was residing at the Villa des Pins in the suburb of El Biar, not far from the *lycée*. Nguyễn Văn Cẩm wrote to the exiled former emperor, beginning what would become a regular correspondence. The latter soon made him a privileged guest, summoning him, fortnightly, to his residence. Though Hàm Nghi invited all of the Vietnamese *lycéens* to outings at Sidi Ferruch (Sidi Fredj), he specifically requested that school authorities allow Nguyễn Văn Cẩm to attend. The boy boasted about this special relationship to his fellow *lycéens*, who referred to him mockingly as the 'Little King.' Raillery sometimes spilled over into violence, as in the case of one night-time altercation in the *lycée* dormitory in which a fellow boarder, de Valdan, was injured with a knife.[8]

In 1896, nearly a decade after his arrival in Algiers, Nguyễn Văn Cẩm finally matriculated (taking a *baccalauréate ès sciences* and a diploma in physical education). The college principal, Canivincq, was doubtless relieved to be rid of such a troublesome presence. However, he was also sufficiently concerned about the failure of Bihouard's project to warn the minister of colonies that this 'prodigal son' posed no less a threat to the French in Indochina now than when he had left. The principal's words would soon prove to be prophetic.

Upon arrival in Tonkin, Nguyễn Văn Cẩm moved to Yên Thế, an insurgent stronghold, traded upon his reputation and built support for anticolonial activities behind a labour recruitment front. As news spread that the 'genius' Kỳ

Đồng had returned to banish the invader, Nguyễn Văn Cẩm was able to attract thousands of followers.[9] This movement even drew the interest of Hoàng Hoa Thám (aka 'Đề Thám'), a Robin Hood-esque figure who roamed with his armed band around the province. Unfortunately for Tonkin's prodigal son, French security patrols and information networks were by now far more efficient than they had been in his youth. Commandant Peroz captured Nguyễn Văn Cẩm on 22 September 1897, and as large-scale demonstrations broke out in Hải Phòng, Hải Dương and Thái Bình the minister of colonies ordered that the Kỳ Đồng be despatched into exile, this time to Tahiti.[10]

The failure of the Nguyễn Văn Cẩm experiment added grist to an emerging critique of colonial education in France and Indochina. Not long after the 'wondrous child' had arrived in Algiers, the Congrès Colonial International had taken place at the Exposition Universelle in Paris, in the first week of August 1889. At the meeting, the anthropologist Gustave Le Bon launched a broadside against the idea of 'assimilating' peoples of the empire on the grounds that "the kind of instruction applicable to civilised men is not at all applicable to half-civilised man."[11] Le Bon drew upon cautionary tales from the British Empire to illustrate his point, but only a few years later the Kỳ Đồng would provide the French with their own. By this time within Indochina opposition among *colons* to educating 'natives' had also grown. In Saigon the satirist Georges Marx aimed his barbs at educational policy (lampooning high-flown claims that by learning in Quốc ngữ, "the little natives, after a very short time, know as much as the oldest scholars").[12] In Hanoi, Governor Lanessan steered away from the expense of cultivating a French-speaking Vietnamese elite from 1891 and strove instead to improve relations with the existing mandarinate.

In these much-changed circumstances, in September 1899 rumours reached officials at the High Residency that *another* child prophet had emerged from the Tonkin countryside. This case elicited a quite different official response from that of 1887. With memories of the Kỳ Đồng still fresh, rumours that this newly discovered child genius was capable of miraculous feats and had been sent 'from the heavens' to become emperor worried officials enough to ensure that they apprehended the boy. Officials in Hanoi arranged for the child, a nine-year-old named Lý Thanh Long, and his family to be subjected to a lengthy, thorough and "scientific" investigation. During this process police agents carefully scrutinised the physiognomy and gestures of the child. He "speaks and laughs loudly," wrote one, and "has very brilliant eyes and extraordinarily dilated pupils."[13] They discovered that Lý Thanh Long could deliver prophecies in scholarly Chinese, a talent he claimed had been bestowed upon him by the heavens. He informed his interrogators:

> I studied nothing in my childhood. [Chinese] came from my mouth after the eighth month of this year. After uttering the characters I immediately forget them.[14]

Chillingly, Lý Thanh Long not only looked and talked like Kỳ Đồng, he also made direct reference to him—explaining the latter's capture on account of his having "hurried into the world" too quickly.[15] Literati were called in to decipher the diminutive prophet's 'celestial' utterances. But while they could identify individual characters, they could not fathom their meaning in combination.

Late in December 1899, Charles Prêtre, head of the office of native affairs in Hanoi that was investigating the case, reached the conclusion that the boy was not a miracle worker but was instead simply a fake. His mystical demeanour was a performance. He had been coached to string together phrases in Chinese. Far from being a natural 'genius,' he was a memoriser and a miscreant. Since reform or punishment would logically draw the authorities back toward the provocative position of admitting Lý Thanh Long to the politicised category 'child,' they prescribed neither education nor imprisonment but instead despatched him unceremoniously back into the native milieu.[16]

The quite different trajectories of these two unusual children illustrate how much official attitudes to the intellectual and social mobility of Vietnamese youth had changed. By the turn of the century growing unease over the dangers of colonial education sparked repeated assertions of its futility. The archaeologist and epigraphist director of education in Tonkin, Gustave Dumoutier, claimed that (unlike Nguyễn Văn Cẩm but much more like Lý Thanh Long) "the annamites in our schools learn to respond and not to know. They are like an echo, which repeats on prompting all that we have committed to it."[17] Introducing French education would thus produce not enlightenment but a kind of civilisational 'vertigo.'[18] Even in Saigon, where French schools were drawing in the children of collaborationist, landowning elites, the governor of Cochinchina, François-Pierre Rodier, informed the Conseil Colonial in 1905 that the "attempt at moral and intellectual assimilation through education made in the last twenty years in Cochinchina" had been "vain and chimeric. Further, it is dangerous," as "our educational methods do not fit the mentality of the *indigène*."[19]

QUEEN'S SCHOLARS: YOUTH AND COLONIAL SCHOOLING IN SINGAPORE AND HONG KONG

A few months before the French had packed the Kỳ Đồng off to school in Algeria, the Governor of the Straits Settlements Cecil Clementi Smith had created five annual Queen's Scholarships for the youth of Singapore. His intention was to provide the brightest students in the Straits with opportunities to attend university in Britain and to showcase the benefits of remaining in school for longer in a context where early entry into the labour market remained common.[20] Eurasian, Chinese and Malay youth dominated the competition for the new Queen's scholarships and one of the first recipients was eighteen-year-old Lim Boon Keng.

Born in 1869, Lim won a scholarship in 1887. A third-generation ethnic

Hokkien, fluent in several languages, he studied medicine at Edinburgh before returning to Singapore to set up a medical practice on Telok Ayer Street. Of the 29 scholarship winners from 1886 to 1900, most, like Lim, went into the professions, especially medicine. By 1903 two thirds of those sent to Britain had come from Singapore, and most had studied at the elite Raffles Institution. Of those who returned, six had become doctors, two lawyers, four engineers, one a teacher and one was private Secretary to the Chief Justice. The recipients, like Lim, often went on to become articulate contributors to the debates that would shape modern Singapore. As Siow Poh Leng, a former pupil at the Methodist-run Anglo-Chinese School (who applied for a scholarship but failed to receive one) put it, the system produced youth, "ready to exert a beneficent influence on the masses" and, "infuse all that is best and noblest in Western civilisation into their countrymen."[21]

By this time, however, the scheme was beginning to attract criticism from some sections of European society. Dr. William C. Brown, a legislator, used the opportunity provided by an Education commission enquiry to attack the system for depriving secondary and primary schools of funds, skewing education toward the elite and affording Asian students opportunities to contract marriages with English girls. The government cut the scholarships back in 1907 and as the impact of the Chinese Revolution reverberated across the political landscape of East and Southeast Asia in 1911, it abolished them altogether. In Singapore as in French Indochina a growing sense that modern 'western' education might de-stabilise society connected with anxieties over the burgeoning intellectual energies of Asian youth. In both contexts the trans-colonial networks fashioned by migrant Chinese informed such concerns, but so too did the political dangers presented by missionary activity.

Religious workers and colonial schooling

The long history of missionaries' involvement in the provision of education in Asia had been shaped by recurrent bouts of repression and recrimination. The Jesuits who proselytised in Vietnam from the early seventeenth century suffered periodically from persecution. And the risk that proselytising might generate instability was such a concern for the British East India Company that it endowed its representatives with the power to prohibit missionary activity in South Asia. The stricter enforcement of such provisions following the Vellore Mutiny of 1806 had pushed early pioneers of the nondenominational London Missionary Society (LMS) (1795) and the Anglican-led Church Missionary Society (CMS), (1799) in the direction of China, where they secured bases for operation in Malacca, Macau and Singapore.

Amid the backlash that followed the Chinese authorities' fierce response to Lord Napier's demands for free trade in July 1834, some American missionaries departed China for the safer haven of Singapore. Others turned to the provision of free education as a more effective means of proselytising. Notable among them was Robert Morrison, an LMS missionary who had begun work in Canton in September 1807. His death in August 1834 was commemorated through the Morrison Memorial School that opened in Macau in 1839, and soon after Britain's defeat of China during the First Opium War, missionaries moved the Morrison School to Hong Kong. There it became the first foreign school to be established following the British occupation, being joined in January 1844 by the LMS-run Anglo-Chinese College (transferred from Malacca), and in 1849 by Saint Paul's College, established by the Church of England.

Following its cession to Britain in 1842, Hong Kong became one of a number of coastal areas of China opened up for religious workers' activity. Though the Treaty of Nanking made no specific mention of religion, the Toleration Edict (derived from the Treaty of Wanghia signed between the American authorities and the Chinese government in 1844) afforded legal protection to missionaries in the Qing emperor's territories. To take advantage of this, the majority of missionaries who had been based in Singapore departed for Hong Kong, which they saw as a valuable base for work in the Chinese mainland. In September 1847 the LMS, for example, which had been struggling to convert Malay pupils to Christianity in Singapore, transferred its work to China.

In spite of the protection offered by the treaties, subsequent setbacks—such as the Tianjin massacre of 1870—reinforced Hong Kong's value as a 'safe haven.'[22] Such incidents highlighted the political risks of educational work, but they did not check the growth of educational work by foreign missionaries in China where by the mid-1870s the British had 146 schools and the Americans over 300, both with around five thousand students.[23] Following defeat in the Second Opium War (1856–60), the Qing court confronted the need for officials capable of using English to negotiate with foreigners. Court officials, in particular Zeng Guo Fan, therefore explored the possibility of sending Chinese abroad through an 'Educational Mission.' The chief organiser of this plan was a former American missionary school student named Yung Wing. A former pupil at the Morrison Education Society School in Hong Kong, he had travelled to the United States with the Reverend Samuel Brown in 1847, where he became an American citizen and a graduate of Yale College. As he sought to locate students willing to undertake the trip to America, Yung Wing looked not only to rural families in Guangdong but also to those with connections to urban areas, including Hong Kong, for here could be found merchants and men who had won status through unconventional means, and were thus more willing to countenance sending away their sons. From 1872 to 1875, 120 students departed with financial support from the Qing court.[24] But in December 1880 the Guangxu emperor aborted this mission for fear of its 'demoralising' effects. In years to come, as rising anti-Chinese sentiment in the United States further impeded Chinese students' paths to study abroad, Hong Kong's importance as an educational site grew further.[25] And as it did, the obvious political danger of missionaries' educational initiatives so close to the Chinese mainland shaped the colonial government's oversight of schooling.

In a Crown Colony such as Hong Kong that was expected to pay for itself, but which had made disappointing economic progress in its first two decades, conceding the expense of education to nonstate actors was an attractive option. However, after the Taiping Rebellion triggered an influx of Chinese emigrants in the 1850s, the colonial government, advised by Dr. James Legge, moved to deny missionaries untrammelled dominance of this field. Having previously done little more than provide token support to schools run by Christian missions, the government established a board of education and created a secular 'Central' school in 1862 to educate boys of all nationalities in English. In 1865 the new 'Education Department' became a civil department overseeing education providers. Informed by a shift in metropolitan education away from Church control, the Hong Kong government approved on 24 April 1873 an adapted version of Forster's Education Act of 1 August 1870, and made secular teaching a condition of grants (ignoring missionaries' protests). The government introduced Cambridge Local Examinations in 1887 (four years earlier than in Singapore). However, it followed Singapore in establishing a travel bursary for students of the Government Central School. This rather half-hearted approach to facilitating study abroad reflected the stronger sense that the colony's role should be to attract and influence young Chinese, equip them with English and, indirectly, perhaps even exert influence upon the development of modern China.

Unhampered in this small territory by the problems of mapping a new system onto a vast preexisting system of indigenous education as in Vietnam, or by the dizzying pan-Asian plurality of resident populations and linguistic groups as in Singapore, the Hong Kong government was relatively free to fashion schooling into a core aspect of its purported mission to 'civilise.' Teaching English gradually came to be seen as essential to this, especially during the administration of Governor John Pope Hennessy. Around the turn of the century, some considered Hong Kong's endemic demographic transience to represent a special opportunity. The inveterate mobility of Chinese youth who shuttled between the Crown Colony and the mainland might allow "the best education Christendom had to offer" to infect the intellectual ecologies of empire.

Students flocked to Hong Kong to study. During the 1880s the inspector of schools, E. J. Eitel, estimated that almost half of all children between ages six and sixteen in the colony were attending school.[26] In 1889 the Victoria College opened with an intake of 960 pupils.[27] Absorbing one sixth of the colony's annual budget, this venture seems to have connected with desires among young Chinese to access English education and thus better-paid clerical work in burgeoning port city economies along the China coast. By 1900 investment in education in Hong Kong through a partnership of officials and grant-aided religious workers was seen to have produced "most gratifying results."[28] But as the Boxer Uprising provided a sobering reminder of China's political instability, missionaries accepted official restrictions on their work in exchange for funds and security. The shock of the uprising reverberated with special force in Hong Kong, owing to its porosity and its proximity to Canton. Both factors made this Crown Colony a key site of the Chinese reform movement.

RIPPLES OF REFORM: CHINA AND BEYOND

China's defeat by France in 1885 created the conditions that produced the Kỳ Đồng phenomenon. This defeat, and that inflicted more emphatically by Japan a decade later, coupled with the provocation of European missionary-led education along the margins of the empire, provided a new stimulus for reform in China. These culminated in the so-called Hundred Days Reform movement. Beginning in 1898, this was intended to arrest the decline of Qing rule through constitutional and political reform. Education was a special focus as it held out the promise that the modern knowledge necessary to strengthen China might be rapidly assimilated. After the violent interlude of the Boxer Uprising, the Qing government tacked away from resistance to change and foreign mission school enterprise reached new peaks.[29] In the first decade of the new century thousands of young Chinese circulated through the networks linking southern China with French Indochina, Japan and Singapore in search of new knowledge and fascinated by the potential of education to serve aspirations for reform. By 1905 there were 4,600 Chinese students in Japan (compared with 300 in the United States, where immigration policy stymied access, and 400 in Europe).

With the possibility of change on everyone's lips, European and Chinese critics of varying ideological persuasions condemned colonial schooling in Hong Kong and Singapore as unsuitable in its existing form. In Singapore, out of some 3,700 boys attending English schools, 2,000 were Chinese. But as the neo-Confucianist Lim Boon Keng complained, English schools lacked the moral training necessary to satisfy hopes that a "new race of Straits Chinese will be reared to push onwards the cause of civilisation."[30] Straits Chinese complained that "the helpless young are entitled to some consideration from the Government" and looked toward Hong Kong as a model of what could be done, especially in the higher standards.[31] "We should like to see a Medical college here," declared one observer. "When Hongkong can boast of one, it is natural to wonder why a prosperous place like this Colony should not have one. We should then no longer have to send our boys to be trained in Madras, Hongkong or elsewhere."[32]

Singapore's lack of a medical college (one had been founded by the LMS in

Hong Kong in 1887) derived from the fact that there was neither the same level of missionary-led impetus in this field, nor the same imperative toward didactic demonstrations of 'civilisation' as in Hong Kong, where empires collided. By the turn of the century Sir Stamford Raffles's dream of Singapore as a centre for 'native education' had long since faded.[33] The 'Institution' named for him became an elementary school in 1834 in a period when rule by the East India Company, and then the Government of India, saw education attract little official interest or investment. After missionaries decamped to Hong Kong from Singapore, few remained, and those who left were slow to return. Only in 1886, for example, did the Methodist Mission return to Singapore and open a school.

These departures, coupled with official reticence in this field, created opportunities for French missionaries in Singapore, especially those of the Missions Étrangères de Paris (MEP). According to the fifteenth-century *padroado* dividing the world between Spain and Portugal, Singapore fell under the Portuguese jurisdiction of Malacca. However, in 1841 Rome awarded jurisdiction over Singapore to the vicar apostolic of Malacca under the French MEP. French missionaries subsequently took the lead in education in Singapore, establishing St. Joseph's Institution in 1852. One Sister Mathilde oversaw the opening of the Convent of the Holy Infant Jesus in 1854 (supported by government grants after 1881). Catholic mission workers also opened the Church of Saints Peter and Paul (1869).[34]

After Singapore became part of the Crown Colony of the Straits Settlements in 1867, the main recommendation of a select committee inquiry into education of 1870 had been that vernacular education should be improved, especially for Malays. The government therefore provided four years of free primary vernacular schooling for Malay children, while subsidising government and aided English-medium schools. It offered only small financial grants to Chinese and Tamil schools. The point of education in the Straits Settlements, as in British Malaya more generally, was to provide children with a basic education enabling them to work in extractive industries and commercial sectors. Only a privileged few attended English schools (five were managed and financed by the government), grant-in-aid English-medium schools (twelve were run by private concerns) and Malay schools (eighteen were run by the government), with an enrolment of around six thousand. Government expenditure on education remained minimal and by the late nineteenth century Singapore possessed fewer schools than smaller centres of British Malaya, such as Penang and Malacca.[35] Officials pointed to the daunting ethnic-linguistic plurality of society to excuse these shortcomings.

While the official position of the Straits government remained that education should be provided for indigenous 'Malays,' Singapore's other communities were allowed to take responsibility for their own children's education. Chinese and Tamil schools were all but ignored. In 1917 no officer in the Education Department could even speak Chinese. Because the colonial government neglected privately run Chinese schools, they emerged as spaces for experimentation in Chinese modernisation, Confucian revivalism or both. In Singapore, in contrast to Hong Kong, Chinese reformers enjoyed a comparatively free hand to innovate. Neotraditionalists such as Gan Eng Sen started Anglo-Chinese 'Free Schools' promoting classical Chinese literature and moral learning. Lim Boon Keng cofounded a Chinese Girls' School.[36] As interest in Confucian tradition waned around the turn of the century, investors opened schools offering new subjects. Inspired by the Hong Kong example, Straits Chinese contributed $80,000 towards a 'Government Medical School' that finally opened in September 1905 with twenty students.[37] As China lurched toward revolution, the Qing government appealed to 'Nanyang' Chinese through the schools to return or remit funds. In 1909 a Singapore branch of the Chinese revolutionary association (Tongmenghui) opened (this became the Singapore branch of the Kuomintang in 1912). The Nanyang Chinese General Education Association supplied Chinese schools with revolutionary literature, and enthusiasts created Chinese-language schools or 'Chinese Free Schools,' which grew in number from 1900 to 1919.[38]

Vietnamese youth travelled out too, in spite of colonial authorities' efforts to fetter their movement. Japan's victory over Russia in 1905 provided an especially important impetus to their mobility. This stunning event appeared to exemplify the successful assimilation and application of Western material civilisation by an Asian society. It set unprecedented numbers of young students on the move. They mingled with young Chinese intellectuals moving across networks linking Singapore, Hanoi, Canton, Hải Phòng, Hong Kong, Yokohama and other centres. Inspired by Japan's victory, the promonarchist agitator Phan Bội Châu (who founded the Duy Tân hội 'Association for Modernisation' in 1904) travelled to Tokyo in 1905 to seek help to liberate Vietnam from French rule by force. Many young Vietnamese who had travelled to Japan to study returned to become teachers themselves, convinced as they were that mass education could serve the pursuit of national salvation and ultimately independence. Meanwhile, Phan Bội Châu's writings appeared on the syllabus at the Đông Kinh Nghĩa Thục (Free School of Tonkin) set up in Hanoi in March 1907 by Lương Văn Can and Nguyễn Quyền, which was modelled on Fukuzuwa Yukichi's Keio Gijuku school.

Chinese youth in Hong Kong's schools, like their counterparts in Singapore, were exposed to radical tracts filtering through from Canton and other centres. Sun Yat-sen, the leader of the revolutionary Nationalist movement in China (and a former pupil of Hong Kong's Government Central School, where he had studied from 1884 to 1886, and the College of Medicine, from which he graduated in 1892), was an inspirational figure. Until 1911 the revolutionary movement in China had not been explicitly anticolonial, but following the revolution discipline in Hong Kong's schools was put to a "severe test." In 1911 Governor Fredrick Lugard urged pupils at Queen's College and St. Joseph's not to discuss political and religious subjects, and to express sympathies with revolutionaries in a 'lawful' way.[39] Meanwhile, in schools providing Chinese vernacular education, one report in 1912 complained, "the idea had been fostered" that Hong Kong was Chinese territory.[40] These pressures triggered a clampdown. On 1 October 1913 an ordinance drew children attending schools in the New Territories under government supervision for the first time.

CHILDHOODS DIVIDED AND UNDIVIDED: CAMPAIGNS FOR SEGREGATION

In the decades bracketing the turn of the century Europeans became increasingly aware of the risks arising from this intellectual traffic. As so often, their own children formed a key focus as they struggled to elaborate a response. Because colonial schools were racially amorphous spaces, an increasing number of those European children who moved out to empire in this period experienced the fervid atmosphere of colonial schools at first hand. In 1890, 941 Chinese and Eurasians were enrolled in Victoria College in Hong Kong, compared with 45 Portuguese and 23 'English.'[41] In Saigon the Institut Taberd was founded in 1874. This school enrolled 447 pupils (French, Vietnamese, Indian, Chinese and 'métis'). In November of the same year a Collège Indigène opened. In 1879 this was upgraded to a secondary school and renamed the Collège Chasseloup Laubat, admitting European and Vietnamese boys—with teaching in French.[42] At the turn of the century one survey suggested there were 106 Europeans of school age in the colony, of whom 29 were attending the *collège* alongside 106 Vietnamese, 21 Indians and 24 Eurasians (plus Chinese, Laotians and 'others'). As the actions of former 'beneficiaries' of colonial education schemes—from the Kỳ Đồng to Sun Yat-sen—exacerbated instability, status-conscious European parents demanded separate schools for their own children.

In September 1902, as Hanoi prepared to assume imperial city status, the newspaper *Indépendance-Tonkinoise* argued that here of all places French parents should have the right to separate classes for their children. Tonkin's school commission also backed demands for separate facilities for boys attending *écoles municipales*. A little earlier, in October 1901, the *résident supérieur* of Tonkin, Augustin Fourès, had regretfully admitted desires for segregation were "common to a very large number of Europeans."[43] Though the majority of French girls attended private, confessional-run institutions, they also attended the municipal school for girls in increasing numbers. The headmistress, Madame de Lenchères, informed the mayor of Hanoi in 1903 that "given the ceaseless growth in [numbers of] little European boys and girls, it is no longer possible to allocate a classroom to the annamite pupils."[44] Since relatively few Vietnamese girls were in attendance, she proposed that they be provided with a separate school on rue des Pavillons-Noirs.

Meanwhile, in Saigon a French colonial elite anxious to 'keep up appearances' also expressed growing disgruntlement at mixed schools. The Eurasian population was much more evident in Saigon and Cholon. Within the Écoles Municipale des Filles, for example, European girls (of whom there were twenty-four) were outnumbered by *métisses* (forty-one), and there was just one single Vietnamese girl. 'Recognised' *métis* boys—meaning those whose fathers had applied for official recognition of them as French—outnumbered those 'unrecognised' at the Collège Chasseloup Laubat by a ratio of four to one, whilst in the girls' school unrecognised *métisses* outnumbered those who were recognised.[45] In spite of the long tradition of accommodating Eurasian children, in 1904 French residents here too began to insist that French children be provided with separate schools.

However, in neither context was formal segregation politically palatable. The *résident supérieur* of Tonkin, Augustin Fourès, informed Governor General Doumer:

> It is with regret that I note the exclusivism which appears to reign in all minds with regard to the natives, and the immediate consequence of which is naturally a more and more profound division between the two races present. I am persuaded that such measures cannot but harm our influence and hamper colonisation. Furthermore, such barriers are unbridgeable obstacles to spreading the ideas of civilisation that it is the task of our administration to spread among the masses and in annamite polite society.[46]

Fourès like Doumer was well aware of the need to pay lip service to a republican *mission civilisatrice* and was therefore unwilling to countenance the kind of outright racial segregation that some of his compatriots were demanding. A more immediate issue of concern among officials in the first decade of the twentieth century was not ring-fencing French children, for they were ideally to be schooled in the metropole anyway; it was to ensure that children of the Vietnamese elite were 'inoculated' against Chinese influence through contact with French culture in schools.

Charles Prêtre, who had investigated Lý Thanh Long's case years earlier, had by 1906 risen to become inspector of schools and a member of the new 'Council for the Improvement of Native Education' created by Governor General Paul Beau. The governor's intention in creating the council was to put in place a coherent system of education provision across the Union Indochinoise. Prêtre took his place on the council as a renowned critic of the political dangers of literature emanating from Canton, and of teaching in Chinese.[47] Though few by now believed that Vietnamese children could be 'made French,' officials such as Prêtre were deeply concerned to prevent students' political indoctrination. The connections uncovered between the students of the Free School in Hanoi and those involved in the poisoning of the Hanoi garrison in 1908 made this task more urgent. Similar concerns in the south led the governor of Cochinchina to track the large and growing movement of Vietnamese youth out of the colony on study trips. In April 1907 he informed the governor general "that for the last few weeks a quite large number, of Annamites, generally youth aged under 20 years old, have requested departure from the Colony to go to Hong Kong or Singapore, with the intention, they have declared, of continuing their studies there or learning about commerce."[48] The governor demanded that these young people be tracked and a record be kept of the schools they attended. Meanwhile, to prevent the best Vietnamese students from being recruited for the imperial mandarinate the government also diluted the use of Chinese in the triennial examinations in 1909 before definitively suppressing the examinations in 1915 in Tonkin and in Annam from 1918. As the government launched its official 'associationist' strategy, the Chinese language no longer offered a pathway into the administration.

In Singapore, European children negotiated an education system divided along multiple cleavages of language and ethnicity. This plurality seems to have weakened the case for imposing strict internal racial segregation within schools. In the Straits, the public sphere had emerged around a shared sense of commercial interests and had been strikingly mixed from the early days of colonial rule. The long-standing presence of English-speaking Eurasian and Straits Chinese families in the region generated less of a sense of a binary cultural divide here than in the other centres discussed. Instead, the impression gained was one of multiple 'civilisations' in juxtaposition—and less obviously in confrontation. Childhood had failed to emerge here as strongly as a didactic or exemplary moral category in public. Instead, in its largest prewar showcase childhood appeared strikingly mixed, as we saw in Chapter 4. While Straits Chinese children tended to outperform Europeans in English-language schools, this potential point of tension failed to translate into a campaign for separate schools.[49]

Turn-of-the-century debates over English-language education in the context of Singapore focused not upon racial segregation but on the question of how to increase attendance in the higher forms. English-language education was distinctive in that it permitted access to secondary education. However, according to the report of 1902 of the education commission, only 15 percent of boys completed all seven standards. In these years in Hong Kong the government increasingly concerned itself with secondary and higher education (founding an English-medium university in 1911). By 1930 school inspectors noted that "educational reforms have been going on in all parts of China, and Hong Kong appears to have become the most congenial centre for the older element."[50] But in Singapore in the same period the government built mainly primary or elementary schools (teaching in English and Malay), which were feeder schools to the two government secondary schools—Raffles Institution and Victoria School (1931). Raffles Institution was regarded as the best school, but the government only took over the management of it from its former trustees in 1902.

In Hong Kong those who claimed to speak for the European 'community' took much greater interest in working an ideology of childhood into public projections of nationhood. Here the desires of parents for segregated schools resonated much more strongly with official political concerns. In consequence they were soon translated into policy. European parents' complaints had already led to an informal internal division separating their boys from 'others' at Queen's College in the late nineteenth century. Rumours of its removal in 1897 prompted one observer to suggest this "would amount virtually ... to the exclusion of European children."[51] In 1901 a group of over one hundred 'principal British inhabitants' petitioned Governor Blake for separate schools, complaining that the education available in the colony was unsuitable to Europeans of "small means."[52] There was in fact no shortage of spaces for these children, but petitioners considered masters "incompetent to give a European education to European children."[53]

This protest gained impetus at a time when European society was becoming more residentially fragmented, with concentrations in more exclusive neighbourhoods such as the segregated Hill District Reservation and in less expensive Kowloon. Exchange rate volatility meant that even those who aspired to 'respectable' status struggled to live in accordance with new middle-class mores even as these were being projected more forcefully into public around the unitary ideal of the European child. In some cases lower-status European children might be members of the same associations as elite children. But even parents employed in respectable, middle-ranking professions such as teaching, or in the lower reaches of the colonial administration, were not always able to send their children home to be educated.[54] The petition of September 1901, demanding better, and separate, schools for middle- and lower-status Europeans, chimed with official concerns in Hong Kong in a way that the demands of French parents in Hanoi and Saigon did not. In its spirit the petition connected with the inclinations within elite culture to define childhood as a core marker of whiteness, the coherence of which drew together an ostensibly fissiparous, ethnically diverse set of 'Europeans.' It also spoke to elite interests in drawing boundaries around this 'community' and using childhood to reinforce a sense of a racial-national divide.

To investigate the question of segregation further, the colonial government set up a commission to which it appointed Registrar General Brewin, the bishop of Victoria, Dr. Kai Ho Kai and Edward A. Irving. As it conducted its work, the commission heard concerns that European children of the 'supervisor' class were slovenly and infrequent attenders of school, outcompeted by their Chinese peers. Reporting in May 1902, the commission accounted for the lacklustre performance of these children with reference to the deleterious impact of the environment and in particular their immersion in the racially amorphous space of the school. In the face of this, the inspector of schools, Edward A. Irving, set forth a counterfactual:

When we might have had a strong full-blooded British community born to the soil to carry on our commerce against American, German, and French competition in the Far East, we are laying up for ourselves an unlearned, unskilled, unpatriotic generation of 'mean whites' to be the standing disgrace of the Colony.[55]

From this vision of an unrealised past, segregated schools emerged as a solution preempting a dystopic future. They would permit the realisation of an ideal of childhood, while usefully concealing the failings of those whose performance of it fell short.

In deliberating this issue, officials were also clearly aware of contemporary debates over segregated schools in French Indochina. For those in favour also argued that 'British schools' in Hong Kong would attract children from Indochina as well as Canton and other Treaty ports in China whose parents shared similar concerns over mixed schooling.[56] Authorities in Hong Kong had fewer reservations than their French counterparts in Indochina about driving a stark racial divide through childhood. Commissioners defined Chinese children through "alien beliefs" and "other ethical standards" as they explained the damage to European children likely to occur by a precocity-inducing proximity.

Chinese boys were often biologically older than the European pupils attending English-language schools.[57] In 1892 Governor William Robinson reported to Lord Knutsford that Chinese boys began to study English at age sixteen and so were "much over 20 by the time they reach the highest class in the College."[58] Older Chinese students also often performed better than European counterparts even though they were using a second language. However, the precocity that allowed one child to outperform another at school threatened, in critics' eyes, to induce 'civilisational' failure. In Britain from the mid-nineteenth century Herbert Spencer's work had popularised the notion that educational overwork or 'overpressure' could be degenerative. Similar thinking sustained claims that an undue emphasis on (overly intellectual) labour and competition in childhood exemplified the Chinese failure to appreciate the 'true life of childhood' on a societal scale.[59] From an evolutionist perspective exposure to this contagious precocity endangered European children's predefined trajectory of racial-civilisational development. And because the display of 'true childhood' so prominently served imperial ambitions in Hong Kong, its effacement by interracial mingling stood as a prima facie argument for segregation.

The governor of Hong Kong therefore approved the commission's recommendations that segregated educational space be provided for children up to age fourteen. The new arrangement came into effect from 1902–3.[60] It happened that the wealthy Eurasian businessman Robert Ho Tung had recently donated a school to the government with the intention that this should become a mixed-entry institution. As the new arrangement took shape, Ho Tung was pressured into accepting its conversion into 'Kowloon British School,' serving Europeans only.

Even after this school opened, on 19 April 1902, some parents hesitated to enrol their children until it was clear that the racial admission policy would be upheld. By 1904, fifty-nine children were in attendance.[61] The government boasted that the Kowloon school was "the first school of this kind in the British Empire exclusively for British children."[62] Three others followed: the Victoria School (1904), the Peak School (1912) and Kowloon Junior (1921).

Leaders of the Church and missionary groups in Hong Kong found the introduction of flagrant racial legislation disquieting. The Anglican bishop, Joseph Hoare, opposed the segregationist policy and resigned from the education committee in protest before it even completed its work. That he should take this view is unsurprising given religious workers' adherence to universalist Christian ideals presupposing the equality of children before God. Catholics opened many schools in China but more often established orphanages, evidently influenced by assumptions of sacramental grace; that baptism in infancy equated to salvation. A romantic Catholic tradition of childhood elaborated in the aftermath of the French Revolution sometimes figured baptised children as a pure spiritual force. As D. E. Mungello has shown using the example of the promotional materials of the Holy Childhood Association, such a view could efface racial divisions between children rather than undergirding them. Evangelical Protestants of the LMS and the low-church Anglican 'Church Missionary Society' did not always accept Catholic claims of sacramental grace, and preferred to emphasise Bible study as a route to salvation and belief in adulthood. However, as evangelical opinion had hoved away from uncritical acceptance of the doctrine of original sin, childhood also emerged as an ideal site for Protestant action, for the 'rescue' and reform of individuals, and their preparation for doing the work of God.[63]

In spite of this, a certain pragmatism and perhaps the awareness that their own authority depended upon racialised and gendered assertions of superior (and inferior) nurturance left religious workers disinclined to pick a fight with the colonial government. In the aftermath of the Boxer Uprising, as educational outreach work expanded, reflections upon differential childhoods became more, not less, valuable to proselytisers as evidence of a supposedly defective Chinese national character.[64] In 1902 Helen Davies, a Protestant LMS missionary based in Hong Kong since 1889, articulated this tension between seeing children *as children* or seeing them as Chinese, as well as the feelings of guilt and confusion this engendered, to the society that she served in London. She wrote:

> I was greatly relieved to find one of my fellow-missionaries writing from India that in some of the children a love of lying and stealing seems to be inrooted, for I also find it so! Others again seem to love dirt, and to revel in it but I never find that these are clean-souled. If the heart is right then you can teach cleanliness. But if, in spite of all they prefer filth, and go back to it unless continually watched, then the taint is deeper than the outward man.[65]

GENDERED UNITIES:
AGE, EDUCATION AND GIRLHOOD

Turn-of-the-century pressures not only sharpened Europeans' concerns over racial heterogeneity in colonial schools; they also raised questions over the strikingly skewed gender distribution within student cohorts. Girls remained emphatically in the minority of those receiving education in British and French colonial centres down to the end of the period. However, in a period when awareness grew of education as a valuable stimulus to national consciousness and even an incitement to democratic government was growing, reformers and officials sanctioned the expansion of education provision for girls.[66]

Missionaries had long argued for the importance of educating girls as a means of moralising young men in empire and had pioneered efforts to create formal schools to receive them. In Britain an interdenominational mission, the Society for the Promotion of Female Education in the East (founded 1834), strove to provide education to Chinese girls by despatching teachers to India, China and Singapore. Several of its teachers, notably Harriet Baxter, founded schools in Hong Kong in the 1860s.[67] The LMS and Anglican-led CMS also placed special emphasis upon reaching and reforming girls in empire. Maria Dyer of the LMS had opened the first school for Chinese girls in Singapore, St. Margaret's Girls' School, for example, in 1842. The sisters of the Convent of the Holy Infant Jesus opened a girls' school in 1854 for European and Eurasian pupils, and from the 1870s girls trained in Miss Cooke's Singapore Chinese Girls' School to become 'Bible women' in China and Korea.[68]

As the number of children in these centres gradually increased, parents tended to prefer to send their daughters to mission schools rather than government schools. There were as many girls as boys in Hong Kong by 1890, but while the ratio of those being educated was 1:2 in missionary-run schools, it was just 1:18 in government schools. The former educated 1,788 girls by 1890, the same year that the government set up its first girls' school (Central School for Girls) with 34 girls in attendance. By 1892, 35 percent of those studying in schools supervised by the Education Department were girls, compared with only 10 percent in 1874.[69] Missionary-run schools tended to provide tuition that was oriented more towards enhancing domestic and homemaking skills. In Hong Kong, Chinese-language mission-run education prepared young women to become Christian wives and mothers.[70]

At the turn of the century the question of female education inspired lively debate among a new generation of Chinese emigrants keen to reimagine and strengthen China. Reformers commonly held that a new nation required 'new men.' And since the raising of such new men would inevitably be a domestic pursuit entrusted to women, the training of girls emerged as a key focus of concern.

Some argued that the crippling ignorance of women destined to become 'mothers for the nation' was a powerful check upon national 'evolution.' In July 1899 the reform-minded Lim Boon Keng and Song Ong Siang established a grant-in-aid school, the Straits Chinese Girls' School (Singapore Chinese Girls' School). Though the uptake of places was poor, this effort formed part of a broader critique of the 'unwisdom' of Straits Chinese women which resulted, for critics, in "the wanton frivolity of their sons."[71] As the position of women and girls became a subject for lively public debate, one commentator in the *Straits Chinese Magazine* explained "there can be no general improvement in the social condition of the race until the women are refined and elevated by a sensible education."[72]

Convictions about the need to better educate girls informed a reappraisal of 'traditional' practices of confinement. Chinese girls played until age eleven with friends on the 'five-foot ways' of Singapore but at around age thirteen did up their hair, disappeared from view and could no longer associate with boys. According to established gender norms they were to remain confined until marriage. However, reformers increasingly believed this to be stunting the physical growth of both the individual girl and the nation. *Cloisonnément* contravened modern convictions, influenced by Social Darwinist thinking, that "young and warm blood demands that they should have as much free exercise of their limbs as possible."[73]

The debate over girls' education, like that of the 'Woman Question' to which it was linked, was trans-colonial. Discussants in Singapore drew upon radical crosscurrents of thought filtering in from China, where Liang Qichao was an important advocate of education for girls, and also from Hong Kong. In November 1901 one writer in the *Straits Chinese Magazine* discussed a leading article in the *China Mail*, an English-language newspaper published in Hong Kong, of 23 November 1901 by a "Chinese gentleman of education, culture and wide outlook" demanding to go "to the root of the evils from which we as a nation suffer, and educate our women."[74] Meanwhile, a rising Malay elite, informed by Islamic reform movements in Turkey and Egypt, also cautiously advocated the provision of education for girls, though few of them actually sent their own daughters to school. Literacy levels remained low and reformers continued to cast the importance of education for girls in terms of making better wives and mothers. Even into the 1930s Malay modernisers still thought of girls' education primarily as something that ended at primary level.[75]

Having observed the segregation of education on a racial basis, elite Chinese in Hong Kong petitioned the colonial government for the right to open an elite school of their own, run on Western lines. Pressed by legislative councillors Tso Seen-wan and Ho Kai, supported by the Reverend E. J. Barnett, the government agreed to allow the St. Stephen's College, run by the Church Missionary Society, to open in 1903. A college for girls followed in 1906, the same year in which the empress dowager Cixi affirmed the need for women's education in China through an imperial edict. Previously, innovations in schooling for girls under the impulse of missionaries had focused mainly upon those from impoverished backgrounds. More than a decade earlier, in 1890, for example, the government had opened the Central School for Girls, named 'Belilios Public School,' after a benefactor, E. R. Belilios, provided funds for a new building, opened in 1893. However, this school was understood as being for "the special benefit of Eurasian girls."[76] Now girls' education emerged as an elite concern. St. Stephen's College soon came to be known as the premier institution in Hong Kong for the education of Chinese girls of the upper class. As schooling for girls acquired an elite inflection, reinforced by the founding of the university in 1911 (to which the first female students were admitted in 1921), St. Stephen's became a conduit through which wealthy families could educate daughters right up to university level. By the interwar years, as knowledge of these institutions spread through Chinese networks, girls found it somewhat easier to negotiate patriarchal resistance and open up alternatives to marriage. Chan King Nui, for example, the daughter of Chan Wing, a wealthy merchant with business interests in Kuala Lumpur, the Straits and Hong Kong, recalled:

> In 1937 when my Cambridge Certificate Examination results were received, my mother took me to Hong Kong with a view to matching me off to some eligible young man. But I had other ideas. I wrote to Father expressing my wish to pursue further studies. At first, he did not give his consent.... Then fortunately, he came to know that in Hong Kong, many families sent their daughters to university and he finally gave his permission for me to enter university.[77]

In Saigon and Hanoi too, French and Vietnamese reformers urged greater efforts to deliver upon egalitarian strands of republican thinking through the education of girls. Women were determined contributors to debates over how such ideas could be squared with patriarchal, racial and colonial ideologies. The travel writer Isabelle Massieu, who saw herself as a participant in a global struggle for the improvement of women's social and political rights, argued, "The important role of the woman in the annamite family seems to present us with the duty of providing her with an intellectual and moral preparation that will help in the formation of future generations."[78] And she complained that the administration

> does not give bourses to the daughters of Annamites.... In general, Annamites do not give instruction to their daughters, except for the Catholics and a few people of high rank, like Doc Phu of Cholon, all of whose daughters, except the two eldest were raised at the Holy Childhood Association in Saigon.[79]

By this time the emphasis that Chinese and Japanese nation-builders had placed upon girls' schooling was inspiring greater interest in questions of feminine education among the rising Vietnamese middle class. The dynamism of wealthy Vietnamese in this area soon made clear to a republican administration supposedly committed to principles of equality the need to step up provision for girls. Hanoi possessed a Franco-Vietnamese girls' school from the 1890s, but in 1906 when Paul Beau held the first meeting of his Conseil de perfectionnement he noted the growing demand among Vietnamese families for feminine education.[80] When the controversial Free School opened in Hanoi in March 1907, it offered classes for both girls and boys. It would be another three years before the first publicly funded Franco-Vietnamese girls' school opened in Hanoi in 1910.

In Saigon, provision for girls existed much earlier, in the form of the Sainte-Enfance (discussed in the next chapter) and the École municipale (discussed in Chapter 5). Here too older ideals of 'assimilation' retained resonance for longer, and in the early 1900s journalists such as Jean Ajalbert and Pierre Jeantet could still endorse girls' education as a potential point of departure for a more thoroughgoing 'moral conquest' of colonial subjects. However, because here Vietnamese exposure to French learning had a much longer history, a larger and wealthier middle class took the lead in raising public subscriptions and creating their own institutions providing Western-style education for girls. An École des Jeunes Filles Annamites was proposed in 1908, and by 1913 the founding of a school for girls providing instruction in French, supported by "the most authoritative members of the native population," further embarrassed colonial authorities by throwing their own relative inaction into relief.[81]

With this school, which eventually opened in 1915 as the Collège des Jeunes Filles Indigènes, still under construction, the Vietnamese wife of the former deputy of Cochinchina, Pierre-Paul Pâris, enjoined elite French women in Saigon to build reciprocal links with Vietnamese women, arguing that girls' education might serve as a foundation for social stability in the colonies. Madame Pâris established a committee of 'Dames Françaises,' based in Paris, of which the wives of Jules Ferry, Emile Boutroux, Raymond Poincaré, Jules Siegfried and the widow of Paul Bert were sometime members. Together they petitioned the minister of colonies, Albert Lebrun, the inspector of *instruction publique* in Indochina, Henri Gourdon, and Governor General Albert Sarraut (whom they buttonholed whilst he was on leave in France) for support in the practical realisation of their project.[82]

Across empires, however, the principal objective of those driving these initiatives was usually not the empowerment of women. Male reformers were often motivated by dreams of refashioning or reinvigorating race and nation. By contrast, officials often drew upon older norms of womanhood and domesticity to conceive of the wider extension of education among girls as an emollient, dampening the ferment generated through the dissemination of transformative knowledge to boys. From the gendered perspective of the early twentieth century, educating girls appeared less dangerous than educating boys. According to contemporary mores, girls were considered a 'naturally' conservative constituency, and one unlikely to back upheaval. Though they would not become full citizens, in the sense of gaining access to the body politic, they might attenuate radicalism. Moreover, since girls' labour was not defined to the same extent as boys' by expectations of material gain, schooling could potentially help them to fulfil 'higher' (that is, presumably not anticolonial) aspirations.

As scholars have noted, surges in nationalist feeling between the wars tended to occlude gendered distinctions and emphasise racial considerations in relation to questions of education.[83] However, the proliferation of schools and pupils and the ways in which colonial states regulated them helped to contribute to wider shifts in contemporary attitudes to girlhood, and the emerging, unstable convention of the 'Modern Girl.'[84] In spite of the urgings toward feminine education, throughout Asia across the period the number of girls actually exposed to education remained a tiny minority, far smaller than the number of boys. The Singapore Chinese Girls' School in Hill Street, for example, remained 'small' and 'poor' in spite of trustees' appeals for help. In Singapore, out of the forty-four English schools in the Straits Settlements and Federated Malay States in 1938, only two were open to girls. By 1931 only 5.5 percent of Malay girls aged five to fourteen went to Malay girls' schools, where the curriculum continued to emphasise domestic science, needlework and cookery.[85] Even in Hong Kong, which had developed something of a reputation as a place where elite girls went to be educated, late in the period only about a third of school pupils (of a total 28,560) were girls. Meanwhile, in Indochina the gap between girls and boys was even greater. Here by 1939 girls made up only around 16 percent of school enrolments at all levels (or 73,474 pupils compared with 373,340 boys out of a population of some twenty million).[86]

"MORE NEARLY OF AN AGE":
YOUTH, CLASS AND ACCESS TO COLONIAL SCHOOLS

In 1911, thirteen-year-old Nguyễn Văn Việt, who lived in the outskirts of Hanoi, sent a letter to the governor general of Indochina requesting admission to the *école d'enfants* of the Tirailleurs Tonkinois in Hanoi. He mainly sought to justify his inclusion on the grounds that his cousin was already in attendance at the school. But perhaps realising the connection seemed rather tenuous, he implored the governor to "look at this request which I have written with my own hands," in the hope that the quality of the writing might convince him to grant it.[87]

Nguyễn Văn Việt's request was not successful. And he therefore joined the vast majority of other school-age children in French Indochina (around 98%) left outside the postprimary education system. Scholars have argued that experiences of this kind, of being denied access to learning, as well as being admitted to it, were broadly destructive and disintegrative, and created new lines of social division under colonial rule.[88] Across the period education cut some young individuals free from ancestral traditions, leaving them 'deracinated' in the eyes of conservatives and embittering those who sought access but were denied it. From this perspective education policies divided populations into those able to use European languages and those who were not. So blatant was the elitism of the colonial education system in Hong Kong that Chan Kai Ming, a member of the Legislative Council, argued in 1918, "A system of education which neglects the upbringing of the poor must be wrong, and the sooner it is remedied the better."[89] However, as social and linguistic differences widened, a whole set of other problems around education came to be expressed between the wars in relation to the troublesome figure of 'youth.'

Colonial administrations implemented changes that gradually served to draw pupils closer together in terms of age. In Vietnamese, Chinese and Malay society notions of majority had only been vaguely defined in legal codes. Few clear links between age and education existed. The filial relationships still expected by many parents also weakened the concept of 'coming of age.' In Vietnam, culturally marked by millennia of Chinese overlordship, no firm association between age and schooling existed. The lowest standards were not reserved for young children.[90] One commentator attending the Hanoi Exposition of 1887 remarked that in Tonkin's schools, "the vast majority there are adults; we may observe among those exhibiting work at the *exposition* exercise books belonging to pupils of 52 years of age."[91] Students who entered French or Franco-Vietnamese schools had often already studied in Chinese-language schools; thus they were older than European pupils in attendance. Similarly, in Hong Kong in 1897 government officials estimated that 30 percent of boys attending grant-in-aid schools and 59 percent of Queen's College pupils were over the age of sixteen.[92] Officials blamed this on parents' preferences to allow children to be raised by their grandparents in the mainland before bringing them to Hong Kong around age ten.[93] In Singapore in 1917 the orientalist and education official R. O. Winstedt also noted that Malay boys who went to English schools in the Straits were assigned to the lowest standard to improve their English after already having completed a Malay-language education to Standard 4. The result was a glaring age difference, and frequently the sight of "a clumsy dunce of fifteen or sixteen struggling to keep pace with a brighter junior of nine or ten," as Richmond Hullett, acting director of public instruction, wrote in his report of 1905.[94]

In French Indochina efforts to address this plurality of age formed part of a strategy intended to tackle the ongoing 'problem' of Chinese influence. The system that Nguyễn Văn Việt struggled in vain to access had been reshaped in response to the recommendations of the 'Council for the Improvement of Native Education.' The council called for a new education system consistent across the whole of the Union Indochinoise. And in 1906 it also recommended that candidates should not be enrolled if they were over the age of thirty.[95] This was a radical departure from existing practice and when Governor Sarraut published conditions restricting the age of applicants in his circular of 12 July 1912, Vietnamese elites protested strenuously.[96]

In 1917, a new Code of Public Instruction established a dual system with French schools, for Europeans and the wealthiest natives, offering a learning pathway from elementary through to *lycée* level, and so-called Franco-Annamite schools (which I will refer to as Franco-Vietnamese here), offering only elementary training. The Franco-Vietnamese system made access to the postprimary level difficult, unless parents could afford school fees. Though the number of students from 1918 to 1938 more than doubled, no more than 20 percent of Vietnamese children attended Franco-Vietnamese schools.[97] But whether students entered the French or Franco-Vietnamese system, or public or private schools, the scholarly cohort was becoming easier to identify in terms of age.

Since concerns over lingering Chinese influence fell more heavily upon students in the north in 1918, Governor General Albert Sarraut implemented reforms waiving fees for entrants into Franco-Vietnamese primary schools in Hanoi and Hải Phòng. The result was to further reinforce a sense of an age-related break between pre- and postwar 'generations'; the former mostly schooled in Chinese and the latter in French and Quốc ngữ. As these young people attempted to theorise and justify the anticolonial protests launched in the mid-1920s, more of them did so by drawing upon radical political writings in European languages.

The colonial government's actions reinforced this trend. When it was observed that generally older pupils led younger ones into the streets to protest, officials used age restrictions to further restrict the capacity of Vietnamese students to transition from the Franco-Vietnamese to the French curriculum. The addition of a year to the Franco-Vietnamese primary curriculum made transfer into the secondary cycle in French *lycées* more difficult. Parents worried this might stymie their children's ability to access positions within the colonial state. After 1924 the Office of Public Instruction took responsibility for ensuring that private schools admitted students using the same age requirements applied to government schools. Students who failed elementary examinations had previously been allowed to retake these until any age, but the imposition of age thresholds ensured that examinations scheduled for the end of elementary school came to be seen as an age-related rite of passage. In September 1931, Lucien Tô Văn Trạng, a rice cultivator, wrote to the governor of Cochinchina to complain bitterly that his son "finds himself stopped in his scholarly tracks for one sole reason: being a bit too old."[98]

In the same period individual *collèges* and *lycées* used age as a pretext to force existing students out of the education system. At the Lycée Albert Sarraut in Hanoi in 1924 the principal, J. Coquelin, complained to the head of public education that for the second time in a year a boarder at the *lycée* had requested leave to get married.[99] The education chief complained to the governor general that

> natives and French are gathered together in the same classes, and the same dormitories. One should note as well that the secondary level classes are attended by a significant and each year increasing number of young French girls. The annamite pupil whom the principal indicates will marry is a pupil in 4 2 B. He will be 16 next 20 May. Here then is a married adolescent who will every day sit next to young boys and girls of 12 years old and younger. There is, for French parents, real cause for concern.

Governor Martial Henri Merlin supported Director of Public Education Paul Blanchard de la Brosse's recommendation that schoolboys who got married should be liable to expulsion from the *lycée* and the *section française* of the Collège Chasseloup Laubat in Saigon.[100]

In Hong Kong and Singapore reforms also excluded older children and encouraged children to attend school at younger ages. In Singapore this change was driven by desires to produce Malay pupils who were better able to use English. The government adopted a new education code in 1905 allowing grants to be earned for infant classes. Education in government English schools was free only for Malay children who had passed Standard 4 in Malay schools before age eleven. This incentive led some Malay parents to begin to send children to school earlier, at age five or six. Elsewhere, pressure on places also allowed the reduction of age of entry as a means of controlling supply. At St. Andrew's School, for example, school managers observed how "increasing applications for admission enabled the age of admission to be reduced to 6–8" in 1924, when around 650 children were enrolled.[101] From 1925 the Anglo-Chinese school began to require that 'wards or sons' be age seven or eight for admission to the beginners' class.[102] In Hong Kong too, higher demand allowed schools to select younger children for admission. At Diocesan Boys' School, for example, younger candidates were admitted, "rather than the older ones of 18 to 23 years so that the average age of the school is lower than formerly and the several members of a class are more nearly of an age."[103] In 1908 Queen's College introduced an age limit for admission. Candidates for class VI of had to be under 15 years of age and no boy over age 20 could be admitted to Class I. But these efforts were more sporadic, and age of admission was not as often discussed or as carefully overseen as in French-controlled centres.

While colonial education across empires imposed structures that tended to bring about greater unities of age, young people themselves eked new meanings from these imposed collectivities.[104] Intellectuals had long bound the concept of 'youth' into theories of liberation from colonialism, or the transition to modern individualism and fraternal bonding within the nation. By the 1920s, not least owing to its trans-colonial mobility, elite youth represented potential unbound.

Liberated through travel and study from the dead hand of 'tradition' and the suffocation of the individual within the authoritarian structure of the family, youth could pioneer a kind of 'modernity' that nations-in-waiting had yet to achieve. However, it also emerged as a symbol of disorderliness. Older children had begun to interpret this period of extended dependence and study as one of freedom from the conventions of their parents' more status-bound societies. Endowing 'youth' with authority allowed the oppositional values it embodied to become unstable.

In these empire centres debates surrounding education raised children's awareness of age as a key category of experience and societal transformation. For many young Chinese, events in Paris on 4 May 1919 lit the touch paper. The refusal of the Allies to support Chinese claims for the restitution of Kiachow triggered the May Fourth Movement. This spilled over into Singapore where Chinese students took to the streets on 19 June 1919. The government imposed martial law. After this Chinese students conspicuously refused to celebrate the Allied victory on 19–20 July 1919. In 1917 the introduction of *guoyu* (National Language) in teaching at Chinese schools, such as the one funded by Tan Kah Kee and Lim Nee Soon, revealed links between diasporic Chinese youth and the new republican government of China. This raised fears that the Communist-influenced Kuomintang government in Canton held sway over the students. As revolutionaries brought in antiforeign texts, schools became battlegrounds for the Kuomintang and the Chinese Communist Party. The self-identification of children as 'youth' raised the possibility of links across a 'generation' incorporating workers and students of both sexes in an alliance of age.

This drove the Straits government toward a much more intensive supervision of education. An Education Bill on 27 October 1920 gave the government control over all schools. Registration of school staff began. 'Revolutionary' schools were closed. Government grants were made conditional on teaching in Chinese dialects, not *guoyu*. In August 1925 school regulations banned textbooks arriving from republican China. When a memorial service for Sun Yat-sen drew thousands, the government banned the Kuomintang. What came to be known as the 'Kreta Ayer incident' of 12 March 1927 occurred after Chinese children at the front of a large public gathering commemorating the death of Sun Yat-sen were run over by a trolley bus. This in turn precipitated an attack on a police station and police reprisals, which left five protestors dead. As police brutality stirred resentment and 'youth' involvement in politics intensified, those accustomed to thinking in terms of ethnic difference found this term useful in seeking closer ties with Chinese Nationalists or Communists. Young people, not only Chinese but also elite Muslims in the Straits Settlements who described themselves as a 'young generation' (*kaum muda*), learned to see themselves in terms other than simply of their ethnic identity and religious background.[105]

Amid fears for the politicisation of students and their potential to link up along lines of age, colonial governments reexamined schooling. In 1923 the Straits government resumed the Queen's Scholarships scheme, reopening a conduit to higher education. And in 1928 the government opened Raffles College. Though the college functioned mainly as a teacher-training institute, it hinted, like the scholarships, at new interest in the older instrumentalist project of fashioning a collaborationist elite. Still, as the police intelligence bureau infiltrated and repressed the Malayan Communist Party, and protest failed to truly threaten British overlordship, the thrust of much postwar intervention in Straits education could remain broadly preservationist. Malay vernacular schools continued to teach children to accept their place in society. At a meeting of the Legislative Council held in October 1934 the governor declared it the duty of the government to provide for the teaching of the 'permanent population' to read and write Malay.[106] Malay schools stagnated, and even in 1931 only 35 percent of Malay boys aged five to fourteen attended.[107] A year later officials estimated that only 12 percent of school-age children attended English-language schools. While they conceded this was a matter of "shame," they boasted before the 'Retrenchment Committee' (appointed to trim government expenditure during the slump) that the education service was absorbing less than 6 percent of the Straits revenue ("a smaller percentage than in other important colonies").[108]

In Hong Kong the unrest of 1919 was followed by the 1922 strike and an anti-British strike and boycott of 1925–26. A broad-based student-led movement continued until October 1926 in response to the May Thirtieth Movement of 1925. Students demanded the restitution of territory and the scrapping of unequal treaties in China. Some followed calls issued by Canton for a boycott. Fears of reprisals against students who did not respect the boycott left many unwilling to risk attending school in Hong Kong. Attendance figures dropped dramatically in Queen's College (down from 656 to 307), Saint Paul's College (from 502 to 348) and St. Stephen's College (from 200 to 160). But attendance also dropped because during the strike-boycott the government imposed an explicitly age-conscious policy stipulating that any boys over sixteen years of age who left any government school without permission before the school closed would be refused readmission to any school. In cases where pupils over age sixteen were admitted, enquiries were made into their background and a deposit of 30 dollars had to be paid, to be refunded only in cases where conduct was good.[109]

The student body in Hong Kong differed somewhat from that in Vietnam and Singapore in that it was generally formed from a more mobile cohort whose sense of a destiny lay elsewhere. Because of this, when antipathy crystallised in schools it tended to be ideological in nature. Connections between 'youth,' whether theorised in terms of radical anticolonial nationalism or politicised industrial disputes, tended to be temporary and fissiparous. And in Hong Kong, schoolmasters worked quite self-consciously to reinforce divisions and to fragment youthful identities along lines of alternative loyalties and institutional affiliations. In this, school- or college-specific identities were valuable. Institutions segmented scholars into year groups. 'Old boys' networks flourished, and magazines, ties, badges and other material and sartorial artefacts symbolised these affiliations. During the 1920s officials also shifted toward the top-down encouragement of the formation of Scout Troops in elite schools predominantly enrolling Chinese boys.[110] In an age of mass nationalism, in the face of economic protest, at a time when overtly confrontational tactics might have been counterproductive, stakeholders imagined these new institutionalised cultures might serve as a counterpoint to radical alternatives. They also sustained colonial narratives of helping in the modernisation of China, especially after the Chinese revolutionary movement split in 1927 and the Nanjing government hoved toward a more moderate national position.

This partly explains why concerns to impose a stricter segmentation along age lines through schools' admission policies remained weaker in Hong Kong. Even in 1923, Allister Macmillan could observe, "It is very late in his teens very often that the Chinese boy begins to superimpose Western learning upon his native knowledge, so that Hongkong's schoolboys comprise many young men."[111] In Singapore too, students failed to emerge as a 'leader class' intent on fomenting anticolonial unrest. As expansionist Japan emerged as an alternative focus of anticolonial action, British authorities were content to monitor and channel this sentiment. For the wealthy, private tuition still offered ways for children to catch up with younger peers. By the 1930s, girls' schools in Singapore, such as the Church of England Zenana Mission School, publicised the fact that they still admitted overage girls to all classes by virtue of being a private school with no government grant.[112] Meanwhile, in Hong Kong, as Chan King Nui recalled:

> My second brother reminded my father it was time that the rest of us were in school too. My sixth sister was eleven, and my seventh sister and I and two other brothers were already ten. We were way over-aged. Tutors were employed, one for the boys and one for the girls. In 1929, we went to school. Luckily, there were other students who were not that young. How we admired those clever little six-year-old girls who could speak English so fluently and topped the class. However, with expert tuition, hard work and double promotion soon we outstripped them all and were in Standard Four in 1931.[113]

In 1938, surveys revealed that of the 15,327 in inspected English-language primary curricula in Hong Kong, 11,588 were still over age twelve, and by far the largest individual cohort was that 'above sixteen' (3,511). Of the 2,124 boys and 679 girls enrolled in inspected secondary curricula, 30 percent were over eighteen.[114] This more flexible approach may even have helped to attenuate the development of harder-edged definitions of 'youth' as a "self-contained, coherent universe of experience" of the kind then finding favour among many young Vietnamese.[115]

In 1918 Governor Albert Sarraut had spelt out a 'politics of adaptation and collaboration' between the French and Vietnamese in nineteen points. These included the promise that no limit would be set upon the acquisition of educational qualifications other than the student's own intelligence.[116] However, from the early 1920s it became clear that even the wealthiest families could not be certain of securing places for their children in Indochina's French schools. From 1924, the Office of Public Instruction monitored access to education stringently. Frustrations built around new restrictions as authorities purposely blocked the upper levels of the education system.

Those who surmounted these blockages and entered schools and colleges, and those who did not, clandestinely read the work of Phan Bội Châu, Phan Chu Trinh, Nguyễn An Ninh and Nguyễn Ái Quốc. Their shared frustrations soon spilled over into public protests. Following Phan Chu Trinh's death on 24 March 1926, students appeared in the streets of major centres wearing black crepe bands. The authorities' brusque response to their public presence sparked strikes across Indochina, but especially in Cochinchina. An *arrêté* of 1926 stipulated that the *livret scolaire* would not be delivered to those students who had been expelled from any public education establishment.[117] Even so, strikes closed schools again in Annam in 1927, and spread to other areas. In the wake of these protests the Socialist governor, Alexandre Varenne, promised to raise standards. And not long after his departure the Lycée Pétrus Trương Vĩnh Ký opened in Saigon, in September 1928. However, young Vietnamese continued to complain that they were obliged to end their studies at elementary level and that the government's promises had not been kept.[118]

The impact of this clash between students, teachers and the colonial state was to drive Vietnamese youth across borders at younger and younger ages. For the colonial government's efforts to stymie access to French education had the unanticipated effect of prompting increasing numbers to attempt to leave Vietnam to pursue their studies, and to spend their late childhood and youth in the metropole instead. State-imposed restrictions thus set a generation of elite youth on the move. In response, the colonial government struggled to reduce access to metropolitan education. In 1921 an official decree had required students to obtain the authorisation of the governor general to study in France. By 1924 would-be students had to collect eleven official documents to apply to study overseas.[119] However, this tide could not be stemmed entirely.

In trans-national and metropolitan spaces, youth on the move worked out the implications of their own mobility in relation to what they saw as a wider generational-political shift. A shared sensibility began to emerge, and even a shared language, connecting nation building with travel and 'youth.' So too did an animosity born of experiencing racial prejudice, even among the youngest students who travelled to France for their schooling.[120] These young people revelled in the sense that their privileged access to technologies of travel might help overturn the profound inequality of the colonial order. Nguyễn Thế Đốc, a young student applying to study at the prestigious Lycée Henri IV in January 1927, wrote in Quốc ngữ to his friend Lê Văn Nham, a boarder at the Lycée Albert Sarraut in Hanoi, to confess:

> Since my arrival in France, I could not resist, in spite of my best efforts, considering the French 'dogs.' You yourself, when you have the opportunity to travel, you will find that overseas the French are considered to be 'savages' (lacking civilisation). Here we (Annamites) could not fight them (the French) because we are too small, but with a good pistol we could beat them. Right now I have a German-made revolver that can fire nine shots. It is hardly any bigger than a box of matches.[121]

Nguyễn Thế Đốc's journey exposed the fallacy of French superiority. He shared this, and other thoughts on technology and travel as a strategy for overcoming inferiority, with his friends. Together Vietnamese youth became conscious of their potential role as a vanguard capable of employing such knowledge for larger, transformative ends. In this way, colonial education policies drove them toward reimagining the colonial present into the past, condemning the French in place of themselves to the condition of 'savagery.'

The danger posed by youthful mobility appeared chillingly clear to officials following the abortive Yên Bái uprising of 1930 and the shock of the Nghệ An Hà Tĩnh 'Soviets.' Both events elicited brutal crackdowns, and in turn prompted students in France to launch widely publicised protests. Governor Pierre Pasquier, who had ordered the bloody suppression of both uprisings, was a prominent target of the students' ire. Pasquier's favoured line when explaining unrest in Indochina was to claim that it had been instigated by external forces, in particular those in Moscow. The intelligence gleaned from security agents who infiltrated anti-French cells painted an alarming picture of young people's roles in fomenting the tensions tearing apart colonial society. After suppressing the uprisings, Pasquier reflected upon the need to move beyond coercion and revivify Franco-Vietnamese collaboration. He identified youth as crucial to retrieving the possibility of fostering the 'points of contact' that would assure a more harmonious coexistence in the future.

For many the preferred context for working out this policy of 'points of contact' was the school. Those attending at the États Généraux du Féminisme, for example, had warmly applauded the orientalist writer Suzanne Karpelès when she suggested that French and other peoples of the Vietnamese peninsula could achieve collaboration best in the classes of the Lycée Albert Sarraut and Collège Chasseloup-Laubat. But the problem was that *lycées* were by now almost completely segregated spaces, the *section indigène* of the latter having been hived off to form the Lycée du Protectorat and the Lycée Pétrus Ký, respectively. And far from producing mutual understanding, schools appeared to be generators of mutual antipathy. French children were often at the centre of racial incidents in shared educational space, as Gail Kelly has shown.[122] As one commentator in Hanoi put it in 1930, "We envisage ... a better understanding between the two races, who must, in order to understand each other, live in closer proximity to each other. But the current system doesn't seem to be working at all."[123]

Others hoped that uniformed movements such as the Scouts and Guides might attenuate the appeal of radical ideologies among Vietnamese youth, and instil a sense of respect for 'traditional' values. In 1930 the first Scout troop had been established in Hanoi. More followed in other major centres, and by 1936 Girl Guide troops were also in evidence.[124] These initiatives, though organisationally split along the lay-clerical divide, drew such an enthusiastic response from young Vietnamese that in Tonkin the number enrolled in Scout troops surged from one hundred in 1930 to more than one thousand in 1934.[125] By the mid-1930s elected members of the Colonial Council in Saigon were demanding that Scouting be made obligatory in all schools. But the official response to the rapid growth of the Scout movement was ambivalent. In June 1933 Pierre Pasquier cautioned against banning the movement, as some colonial police advised, but warned that the groups would require careful supervision. Others were less circumspect, complaining that the Scouts were a 'fifth column,' a cover for insurrectionary training and the exposure of youth to anticolonial ideas.

As the political landscape darkened in Europe and the Popular Front government took power in France, Jules Brévié, the new reform-minded governor general of Indochina, brought fresh thinking to associative work. One of the most important experiments of this era took place far from the restive plains, in Dalat. This 'hill station for Indochina' had been founded upon an explicitly segregationist rationale, as we saw in Chapter 6. Though it was never fully realised, many continued to perceive Dalat as a 'French milieu.' Owing to this, the hill station appeared to be an appropriate space for experiments in establishing 'points of contact' between elites through youth. Franco-Vietnamese rapprochement might have failed in the *lycées* of the major centres, but in the hill station, where teachers commanded higher salaries, some argued interethnic relations would be less heavily compromised by ingrained factionalism and self-interest. Moreover, Dalat's 'Frenchness' made it appear to be the only really suitable colonial space in which an experiment of this kind might succeed.

As we saw earlier, French authorities had blocked Vietnamese students' access to Dalat's Petit Lycée, and in 1935 a second *lycée* had opened, named for Alexandre Yersin. As Eric Jennings has noted in his recent study, around 1936 the requirement of proficiency in Latin that had functioned to exclude Vietnamese youth from the Lycée Yersin was relaxed. So it was before a racially mixed gathering of students at the school that Governor General Jules Brévié announced on 12 July 1938:

> At points on the globe where there is contact between different races an incredible effervescence is developing. We must prevent this from degenerating into chronic disorder; we must re-establish the harmony essential for the well being of men and the progress of societies in all aspects. This is the role vested in you, by the very fact of your presence in a place where these transformations are occurring.[126]

For Brévié, the *lycéens* were fashioning points of interethnic intersection. Because they were themselves positioned between maturity and immaturity, he imagined their less ossified condition, their purported malleability, might pave the way for a more genuinely collaborative colonialism. This elite vision of youth could more flexibly accommodate race in Dalat, because at one remove, in a supposedly 'French' milieu, the young might be better immunised against the climate, politics and a whole gamut of commercial "crazes."[127] As wider geopolitical shifts exacerbated the sense of an impending threat, Brévié urged the pupils of the Lycée Yersin to see themselves as agents *already*, and not merely as colonisers-in-waiting. Reviving the older ideal of youth as auxiliaries of empire, making an early transition to active citizenship, the governor declared, "You are colonising already without knowing it in the friendships ... that you make ... on the school benches."[128]

Even as Dalat emerged as a site in which Eurasian, Vietnamese and other youthful collaborators could be rapidly and thoroughly acculturated, a careful ordering and monitoring process was required. Boarders could not be allowed to roam around into different quarters of the town, for example. Vietnamese former *lycéens*' recollections of these institutions conveyed not effervescence but a sense of isolation. For one, the Vietnamese and French quarters of the town appeared "something out of reach as from another world and I never even dared to venture over there."[129]

Moreover, lurking behind Brévié's vision of a racially plural but culturally French elite was the assumption that 'pure' French youth would quite "naturally" take the lead. In 1939 the official report on the "General Conclusions of the Inquiry on the Child of Indochina" reiterated this quite explicitly by stipulating that French youth had "a great role of initiative to play" in working up what was described as a "kind of *colonisation infantile*."[130] This vision of leadership by youth would be given much fuller expression after July 1940 under the pro-Vichy regime of Governor General Jean Decoux.[131]

CONCLUSION

This chapter has focused mainly upon Anglophone and Francophone Asian youth on the move, a select group defined by their relations with the colonial state. From metropoles to colonies, youthful scholars were ambiguous figures, often unsettling the projects of colonial authorities. While young people gave expression to cultures of movement that defined the imperial relationship across the period, the exigencies and flows of empire shaped ideas about childhood and youth. Though French and British colonial governments devised different responses to education from the late nineteenth century, youthful scholars often came to be seen as a potential challenge to authority and were the focus of a variety of prescriptive interventions and norms. Colonial governments pursued demands for the segregation of schools, tacked toward stronger advocacy of feminine education and drew student populations more closely together in terms of age, with varying results.

As young people fostered formative relationships within British and French colonial systems, they redefined what it meant to be young on their own terms. Shared experiences within, and in response to, colonial education systems led young people to explore 'youth' as a distinct, coherent social identity, and to attach new, dynamic and adversarial meanings to it. They infused capacious notions of 'youthfulness' with a variety of political meanings and purposes. And they often did so in relation to aspirations for national emancipation. For some, 'youth' became an emblem of struggle with the potential to link up communities across empires.

While the pursuit of knowledge was crucial to readings of youthful itinerancy, the experience of itinerancy ushered many young people toward the position that empire was anachronistic. Anticolonial fervour took on a sharper tone in French Indochina, where education reforms more strictly regulated access to education on the basis of age and pushed elite youth into circulation between colonies and metropole. In advance of the anticipated onset of national liberation, youth came to embody a notional state of transition, or a colonial 'coming of age.' Everywhere this threat inspired officially sponsored counter-efforts directed toward the young.[132] For those tangled up in these tensions of empire, 'youth' rarely superseded other identities of class, race and nation. Nor did experiences shared on the basis of age do much to attenuate the polarisation of sex roles. Nevertheless, on the school benches boys and girls imposed new meanings upon age and theorised youth's combination with other social variables in productive, provocative and ultimately destabilising new ways.

CHAPTER 9

Raising Eurasia: Childhood, Youth and the Mixed-Race Question

A remarkably persistent feature of the sinuous, trans-colonial and comparative debates that reshaped the relationship of empire was concern for the plight of the abandoned 'Eurasian' child.' In the modern period racially mixed children born of sexual relationships between European men and Asian women were a common sight in colonial centres. An embodied metaphor of empires' inveterate crossings and connections, those born of these unions in Asia often came to be referred to, not uncontroversially, as 'Eurasians' in English or *métis(ses)* in French. They posed a challenge to Europe-in-Asia on a number of levels, not least since their presence threatened the elaborate but fragile sets of subjective criteria by which 'whiteness' was defined. Eurasians were seen as transgressing the interior frontiers of the supposedly fixed categories of racial and juridical difference upon which colonisers' prestige and authority rested.

An important consequence of Europeans' determination to use childhood to draw boundaries more forcefully around themselves from the late nineteenth century was to make the Eurasian presence more visible. In terms of wealth, status and ethnic mix, Eurasian 'communities' were in fact extraordinarily diverse and highly mobile in British and French Asia. However, critics focused in upon the vulnerability of mixed-blood children, blaming fathers for leaving them 'unrecognised' and therefore 'abandoned' to an ambiguous social status. Such criticisms posed difficult questions for authorities over the extent of their responsibility for Eurasians. The social neglect of those who were *children* threw into question claims for empire as a civilising relationship. Moreover, fears that experiences of social neglect might transform Eurasian youth into vengeful adversaries offered a powerful incentive to redemptive action.

Much difficulty lay in determining precisely what forms such intervention might take. Recent scholarship on the presence of "mixed bloods" in empire has focused upon the exclusionary tactics that European colonial communities devised in response to this challenge.[1] But there were also other practical attempts at 'rescue' and reform. This chapter argues that across the period in these different centres ideas about childhood played an important role both in Eurasians' attempts to negotiate the challenge of living in the shadow of this colonial category, and in elites' efforts to resolve the 'Eurasian question.' As we have seen, elites had become highly sensitised to the importance of age as a field through which ideas of racial difference could be encoded and challenges to the colonial order resolved. Drawing young Eurasians within the category 'child' was a political act that in certain times and places naturalised provocative demands for the resolution of this 'problem.' Nevertheless, the kinds of solutions that were put forward rarely prevented those living across the colour line from experiencing ostracisation. 'Rescue' often came with a heavy price attached, such as the separation of children from their families or the fragmentation of communities along linguistic and cultural lines. However, as this chapter shows, youth and its abstract universals—especially childhood and adolescence—did at times offer a means through which colonial societies could work around more ossified categories of class, gender and race, permitting difference not only to be delimited but also, controversially, disavowed.

'MISCEGENATION' AND THE MÉTIS IN METROPOLITAN AND COLONIAL CULTURE

In his book *Métis et congaïes d'Indochine* of 1928, P. Douchet explained the shortcomings of the French as colonials on the grounds that they were simply too 'young.'[2] What he was implying was that French men had approached the colonial challenge with such naïveté, juvenile recklessness and sexual indiscipline that they only had themselves to blame for the '*métis* problem.' By the time Douchet was writing in the late 1920s the Eurasian presence had become the subject of reams of angst-ridden newspaper reportage, a notorious subgenre of colonial literature and a focus for furious parliamentary debate. Those to whom the term *métis* referred had come to be heavily stigmatised in French colonial society and were often condemned as social outcasts and political adversaries.

Half a century earlier, soon after the invasion of Saigon, Eurasians had less often been the focus of overt condemnation. Children produced from French men's relations with Vietnamese women—described euphemistically as *mariage à la mode*—were often cast as an inevitable 'by-product' of the colonising process. For some they were 'little allies,' potential auxiliaries of French colonialism capable of filling essential though lowly positions within the colonial state—as administrators, clerks and interpreters. But in the early twentieth century, as a generation of youthful, French-educated Vietnamese appeared to be moving into open revolt against their parents and the colonial state, young Eurasians became the focus of despondent commentary about the adverse outcomes of European contact with Asian societies. From his standpoint in 1928 Douchet found reason to envy the behaviour of those "old colonials," the British, whom he believed had avoided such entanglements through their characteristic reserve.

Douchet's presumptions about British sexual discipline flew in the face of evidence that the latter had in fact produced a significant Eurasian presence of their own within South, East and Southeast Asian centres of their empire. From the late eighteenth to the mid-nineteenth centuries British attitudes to interracial relations in such contexts also appear to have been relatively tolerant. In India, under rule by the East India Company, some Eurasians had even accessed educational and professional privileges on the basis of claims to mixed parentage.[3] As Singapore developed, first as a dependency of India then as a Crown Colony, Eurasians of Dutch or Portuguese descent from Malacca, Penang and Ceylon occupied uncovenanted administrative positions within the colonial state. Many scholars (though not all) have argued that it was only as British imperialism in Asia was refashioned more explicitly into an affair of the state, following the Indian Uprising of 1857, that sex across the colour line began to be identified as inconsistent with bourgeois norms of respectable behaviour, a shift exposing people of biracial heritage to sharper invective.[4]

By the 1880s, as we have seen, the movement of larger numbers of women and children from Britain to the colonies inspired a critique of sexual morality in empire that reshaped attitudes to intimate contacts between coloniser and colonised. Such relations persisted but became less publicly acceptable as awareness of what was considered infradig informed elite standards of behaviour. To reinforce these standards colonial states introduced formal disincentives to marriage across the colour line at the turn of the century. These moves proceeded in advance of the Colonial Office's notorious Crewe Circular of 1909, warning of the "disgrace and official ruin" that would be the fate of civil servants taking concubines.[5] However ineffective they were on the ground, interdictory interventions evidently did help to associate British imperialism with a kind of prim, authoritative abstemiousness.

A similar shift was beginning within the reconstructed French Empire around roughly the same time. Mid-nineteenth-century speculation over the potentially invigorating effects of racial mixing had underpinned experiments with *métissage* in Algeria. However, disappointment at the results informed growing criticism of what would soon come to be referred to in Anglophone cultures as 'miscegenation.' The French anthropologists Arthur Gobineau, author of the infamous *Essai sur l'inégalité des races humaines* (1853–55), and Paul Broca, president of the Société d'Anthropologie de Paris, argued that human "hybrids" were inherently unstable and lacking in fertility. As arguments for biological fusion and political assimilation became less fashionable in the late nineteenth century, interpretations of racially mixed people as inevitable by-products of the imperial relationship gave way to demands for the suppression of concubinage.

By now, however, youthful cohorts of Eurasian children were already proliferating within the French Empire. Their public visibility made them a focus for searching questions about the extent of colonial states' responsibilities for subject peoples. Did colonial governments have a duty to act in loco parentis to Eurasian children? The varied responses to this question and the debates that followed reflected not just local contingencies or imperial anxieties, but also evolving ideologies of colonial childhood.

HYBRID CULTURES: PHILANTHROPIC RESPONSES TO EURASIAN CHILDREN IN SAIGON

In June 1893 Eugène Haffner, director of Saigon's Botanical Gardens, was convinced that he had hit upon a solution for that much-debated problem: the *métis* child of Cochinchina. Although evidently possessing French blood, many of these children had not been officially recognised as French, whether because their fathers had died, or departed the colony, or for some other reason. Since there was no separate legal category defining the *métis*, they remained native subjects in the eyes of the colonial state. Though often raised by their biological mothers, commentators nevertheless referred to them as 'abandoned' or 'orphaned.' Such terminology revealed sharpening anxieties over the potential for their public presence, as 'street children,' to have a damaging impact upon French prestige.[6] For with the number of Eurasian children growing by the day, existing voluntary-led efforts to receive and acculturate this group into Frenchness had begun to appear manifestly inadequate for the task in hand.

Religious workers had long committed themselves to the task of raising abandoned *métis* children. Following the invasion of Cochinchina, in 1859 the bishop of Cochinchina invited Sister Benjamin of the sisters of Saint Paul de Chartres from Hong Kong to establish a branch of the 'Sainte-Enfance,' or 'Holy Childhood Association,' in Saigon. The founder of this association was the missionary Charles-Auguste-Marie-Joseph de Forbin Janson. He had set it up in Lyon in 1843 after learning of practices of infanticide in China from Jesuits. Though Forbin Janson died in 1844, his determination to save abandoned children from infanticide, baptise them and raise them in Christian belief inspired the French sisters of Saint Paul de Chartres to establish an 'Asile de la Sainte-Enfance,' named for his oeuvre, when they arrived in Hong Kong on 12 September 1848.[7] Following the bishop of Cochinchina's intervention, by 1860 Saigon had its own Sainte-Enfance. And in 1874 the sisters also founded a boarding school for girls. Here, so-called *métisses* were taught in French, then married off to lower-ranking French officials and soldiers or sent to work as domestic servants in French homes (discussed in Chapter 3). In the same year as the school for girls opened, Father Kerlan, of Saigon Cathedral, along with the Missions Étrangères de Paris missionary Alphonse Joubert, opened the Institut Taberd to receive and instruct Eurasian boys.[8]

However, by the early 1890s the limits of philanthropic energy were becoming increasingly apparent. Strong demand for the Eurasian girls of the Sainte-Enfance persisted within the colonial labour market, but as the pacification of Tonkin wound down, former servicemen returned to Saigon and competed with young male Eurasians for lower-ranking administrative positions. Moreover, as officials hoved toward a more censorious approach to racial mixing, these boys experienced the lack of official recognition and the possession of Vietnamese blood as a positive disadvantage in the competition for resources and status within colonial society. While a few bright graduates of the Institut Taberd could secure clerical positions, others embodied what commentators saw as a disjunct between blood and status with potentially disastrous implications. The failure to take youthful male *déclassés* 'off the streets' of Saigon, in the eyes of Haffner and others, had created a ticking sociopolitical time bomb.

The solution Haffner proposed to this problem lay in the very gardens under his direction. In a detailed plan sent to the lieutenant governor of Cochinchina, Augustin Fourès, he sought funding for what he called an 'agricultural orphanage.' Haffner proposed an experiment in which Eurasian youth would be schooled in the Botanical Gardens to become a new cadre of farmers. 'His' orphans, taught *en paillote* in a four-year course, would learn techniques that would enable them to bring the fertile lands of the heights and plains into productive relation. This, Haffner hoped, would solve the familiar problem of finding new crops suitable for export (the only really successful export so far was rice, a fact which he blamed on indigenous cultivators' innate conservatism). The director felt sure young Eurasians would become willing experimenters and a "leader class in agriculture." An additional benefit was that they would not suffer the same deleterious effects as 'full-blooded' Europeans through exposure to the environment. As 'hybrids' themselves, Haffner also somehow imagined the orphans would be more 'naturally' predisposed to mastery of the techniques of *greffe la selection* and *hybridisation*. And by lessening French reliance upon the Chinese and disseminating modern techniques among the Vietnamese, he argued they would help to improve colonial relations. Rounding off this unsettling combination of domestic and imperial economics, Haffner argued that the harvests the orphans produced would ensure that the whole project paid for itself after just a few years.[9]

Haffner perhaps had grounds to be optimistic about his bid for funding. In 1886, at the request of the principal, Madame Dussutour, the Commission de l'Instruction Publique and the Municipal Council of Saigon had agreed to fund dowries for Eurasian girls attending the *école municipale*.[10] However, from 1891 the new governor, de Lanessan, had moved away from the earlier orthodoxy of assimilation, emphasising a greater and more respectful distance between Vietnamese and French society. Giving approval to Haffner's plan amounted to acknowledging the Eurasian problem as the responsibility of the French colonial state. Fourès therefore rejected it out of hand.

Within the lower ranks of officialdom in Saigon, where some staffers were mixed race themselves or had Eurasian wives or children, the growing ambiguity of the *métis* position was a matter of special concern. A few months after Fourès dismissed Haffner's plan, on 7 January 1894, Jules Dussol, a humble *commis* in Saigon's customs and excise department, launched a Society for the Assistance of Abandoned Métis Children (Société d'assistance des enfants métis abandonnés), which he ran out of his own home.[11] By the time the group met a second time, on 27 April 1894, another society had emerged professing similar protective aims. In May 1894 both groups met at the Saigon Philharmonic and merged, becoming the Société de protection et d'education des jeunes métis français de la Cochinchine et du Cambodge. When the statutes for the new society, with 240 members, landed on the desk of the governor, this time he had no compunction in signing off. In fact Fourès, along with the mayor of Saigon, Paul Blanchy, and other high-ranking official functionaries, were named on the society's Comité d'Honneur.[12]

Because the society was voluntary and did not depend upon government funding, it not only won official sponsorship but could also gesture toward quite radical aims, such as 'emancipating' the *métis* into Frenchness, that is, full citizenship.[13] A speech by the president of the 'active committee,' Nicolaï, published in the journal *Mékong* on 20 May 1894, identified the *métis* as the potential basis of colonial society for "it is there, among the offspring of our elders that we will find the heart, the soul of our new France, this new France that, today, we have the duty of raising in our own image, kneaded from our own flesh and blood."[14] Even Lanessan praised this philanthropic effort, "embodying the work of concord and fusion," the assimilative genre of colonialism for which Saigon was well known.[15] The local press also celebrated the Saigon oeuvre for demonstrating that the French presence in Asia was flexible and absorptive in contrast to a British equivalent that was aloof and austere, a "foreign body in the organism ... threatened from one day to the next with expulsion."[16] Evidently, similar concerns were emerging in Hanoi around the same time, for the head of the Post Office, a member of the Public Works Department and a pharmacist together created a society there in 1897 with related aims.[17]

ERASING EURASIA: CHILDHOOD ACROSS THE COLOUR LINE IN HONG KONG

When the Saigon press criticised British imperialism as 'inflexible' and non-assimilative, it is possible that the Crown Colony of Hong Kong may have been its unstated point of reference. For by the 1890s, colonials proudly cast this British possession as the epitome of the anti-assimilative Anglo-Saxon presence in Asia. In 1907, James Dalziel, a writer and rare critic of the prevailing climate of racial prejudice, grumbled, "They never tire of telling you with an air of quiet approval that nowhere in the East is the colour line so strictly drawn as in Hongkong."[18] This 'line,' however, had not always been so clearly apparent. French travellers who visited Hong Kong in the 1860s, such as Dr. Auguste Benoist de la Grandière, noted that the separation of Europeans and Chinese was "not as well defined" as

FIG. 9.1. "The Retort Courteous." MR. HURRYCOMBE (*with the umbrella*): I wish you would take your ugly old face to the other side of the road, Amah, when you want to talk to your coolie friends. Ah—people—ah will think its [*sic*] my child. AMAH (*who understands perfectly*—with emphasis): Who you talkee so fashion? Allo man savy this chilo b'long *gentleman* baby." Source: *China Punch*, 8 November 1867, 96.

in Macau.[19] Early in his spell as governor (1854–59), John Bowring had reported the concern that "a large population of children of native mothers by foreigners of all classes is beginning to ripen into a dangerous element out of the dunghill of neglect."[20] As the Bastardy Act of 1845 had not been promulgated in Hong Kong, fathers were not liable to take care of illegitimate children.

Of the Eurasian children who grew up in Hong Kong, many went on to become graduates of the Anglo-Chinese school model pioneered in the Government Central School (from 1862) and Diocesan Boys' School (1869). Like their counterparts in Saigon, they moved into the 'supervisor' class in the commercial sector or lower-level positions within the colonial state. There they served as clerks or interpreters, or as stewards of new marine technologies such as the lighthouses along the Chinese coast. A number also worked as intermediaries, named 'compradores,' in commercial contexts, and some amassed vast fortunes. However, here too the presence of Eurasian children was soon to raise difficult questions of moral responsibility in empire. On the edge of empires, where domestic values were coming to define civility, child protection could be seen as constituting a first-order principle of intervention for the liberal state. Even before the Suez Canal opened in 1869, cartoonists had employed the trope of the Eurasian infant in critical reflections upon the morality of European society in Hong Kong. By the 1880s, as European women and children began to move out East in larger numbers, ostentatious celebrations of domestic values sat uneasily alongside the social outcome of male profligacy. The presence of Eurasian children came to offer an embodied provocation to a newer vision of British imperialism that elites hoped Hong Kong might exemplify.

In 1879, the actions of Chief Justice John Smale brought this tension to light. Guided by the right-minded principles of the social purity movement, he elaborated a wide-ranging critique of colonial society extending from child slavery to the social condition of Eurasian children in the streets of Hong Kong. In relation to the latter, Smale claimed to have encountered "beautiful children by the hundred whose Eurasian origin is self declared."[21] He ventured, provocatively, that the girls were "sold to the profession of their mothers" while the boys assumed the status of "the mean white of the late slave holding States of America."[22] Demanding a full government enquiry into the condition of such children, Smale broached the question of foreign responsibility for 'local' children.

Liberal reflections upon mixed-race people as worthy beneficiaries of state support in the colonies derived not only from an inclusive notion of British imperial subjecthood based upon blood, but of the Eurasian *as a child*. Colonial visions of 'rootless' and 'culturally lost' children connected with dystopic metropolitan ideas of childhood split along the lines of a racialised class difference. But by the 1880s impressions of street children in the metropole had shifted away from midcentury assumptions of irretrievable racial alterity. As a wave of Christian voluntary institutions led a drive for social purity in the face of growing secularisation, every child came to be seen as potentially salvageable, capable of being rescued to 'true childhood.' Re-exported to empire, such contentions obviously threatened the practical consideration of running colonies such as Hong Kong on a shoestring (the Colonial Office expected Crown Colonies to be self-sufficient). So in response to Smale's intervention, Governor John Pope Hennessy summoned expert opinion. On his behalf, the German missionary from the London Missionary Society, Ernst J. Eitel, who was also inspector of schools, explained that for decades Eurasians had taken full advantage of the educational infrastructure. Many boys had studied English within the colony's schools. He noted that the

> boys are invariably sent to the Government Central school where they generally distinguish themselves, and as a rule these boys obtain good situations in Hongkong, in the open ports and abroad. The girls crowd into the schools kept by Missionary Societies.

It was on precisely such grounds that he claimed "they do not resemble the mean whites in the Southern States of America."[23] Thus, Eitel reassured concerned parties that the Eurasian presence was an 'older' problem. It was the yield of a past where marriages of convenience took place between morally degenerate European 'transients' and "disrespectable" Chinese women. The protection of this vestigial group could safely be consigned to the care of missionaries and other philanthropic institutions.[24]

Like Eitel, Major Henry Knollys also interpreted sightings of the Eurasian street child as a reminder of the moral benefits of social segregation in empire. As Knollys wandered like Smale before him through the streets of Victoria, his *flânerie* led him to stumble upon a "little nucleus of a singularly effete and deteriorated Iberian population," whose "muddy-complexioned children" in particular "arouse a disgust not entertained towards the pure blooded Chinese children."[25] Knollys was horrified by this discovery—the dissipation of an essentialist vision of the racialised body—and he identified the Portuguese-Eurasian child as an embodied prophesy of imperial decline. Such writing quite self-consciously denied the regenerative possibilities that liberals and reformers had ascribed to Eurasian children. And it ignored a much more flexible contemporaneous social reality, as revealed by Emma Jinhua Teng, which was that many Eurasians were able to assume 'European' or (more commonly) 'Chinese' classifications, or even to move between the two.[26]

Still, Knollys's comment is suggestive of the extent to which childhood had become a testing ground for an emerging elite sensibility by the late nineteenth century. An increasingly active, influential and interconnected group of elite British men and women was by then pushing children to the forefront of didactic visions of a moral colonial culture. As they elaborated the cultural bases of these new visions of virtue and unflinchingly moral Christian imperialism, childhood split along lines of race, blocking out intermediacy and marginal 'European-ness.' Hong Kong's new traditions and rituals of childhood foreclosed sentimental reflections upon Eurasian children, and the latter became unwelcome referents of a bygone moral laxity.

New medical research claimed to vindicate the social "disparagement" of interracial sexual unions and their resulting offspring.[27] In 1888 Sir James Cantlie, dean of Hong Kong's College of Medicine, despatched five hundred questionnaires to "every medical man in China, Japan and the Straits Settlements," seeking learned opinions on racially mixed children.[28] He received only nineteen replies. Nevertheless, Cantlie insisted the results substantiated his claims for the deleterious impact of 'miscegenation.' Responses depicted Eurasian children as inveterate sufferers from deficiencies of endurance, vulnerability to disease and other debilitating conditions. The findings chimed with fixist views of race at a time when Social Darwinist paradigms of progress (or regress) as the outcome of competition between races found a receptive audience. The future of colonial rule by now appeared to educated men to rest upon questions of biological racial "fitness" or "efficiency."

The work of Dr. Cantlie, a respected and well-connected Peak resident, reflected the emerging social and cultural orthodoxy of the colour line. And it set the tone for state-supported interventions intended to shore up the boundaries of a racialised childhood. Seven years before the Colonial Office issued the Crewe Circular, the colonial secretary, Henry May, was agitating for the dismissal of public officers who married Chinese or Eurasian women in Hong Kong. As acting governor, May put the case for the Peak Hill District Reservation ordinance (discussed in Chapter 6) to the Colonial Office in eugenic terms, as a means through which "the growth of a Eurasian population is checked, if not altogether stopped."[29] And as governor in 1912, May introduced a scheme whereby employees of the state living in relationships 'across the colour line' forfeited their right to government lodgings. He also developed plans to relocate inhabitants of neighbourhoods such as the one Henry Knollys had stumbled upon, where Portuguese men had taken Chinese or Eurasian wives, to marginal Tai Po.[30]

Young Eurasians, especially those who drew their sense of identity from their European fathers, experienced this shift as an affront. One published a letter in a local newspaper criticising fathers who invariably left their children in the colony to be "'dragged up' in the gutters of the Colony or of Shanghai."[31] He declared, "I cannot shut my eyes to the fact that many of us have cause to curse the memory of our fathers and say in the bitterness and anguish of our souls, it were better we had ne'er been born."[32] The author called upon fellow Eurasians to set up an association with branches in Shanghai and Singapore capable of providing funds to the needy and pressing the Legislative Council into adopting measures to protect deserted Chinese mothers. Instead, in the years that followed, official interventions served only to raise the boundaries to performing European-ness in Hong Kong even higher. The establishment of whites-only schools, to cite but one example, created a sense of exclusion that "hurt the feelings of the Eurasians so much."[33]

In fact, many Eurasians in Hong Kong, owing to maternal or familial influence or because commercial opportunity encouraged it, already preferred to define themselves as ethnically Chinese. Though prejudice existed on both sides, the boundaries drawn around European identity were coming to be more carefully defined and regulated, while markers of 'Chineseness' were somewhat more flexible, as Emma Teng has shown.[34] Moreover, in the late nineteenth century, the number of genuinely bilingual and bicultural Chinese remained small. Opportunities for social mobility persisted. Young Eurasians who trained at Government Central School (Queen's College) and were able to use both English and Chinese discovered opportunities to acquire wealth and influence within the burgeoning port city economy. An important example was Robert Ho Tung.

Born in 1862 to Sze Tai and C.H.M. Bosman, Robert Ho Tung attended Government Central School and developed the skills that enabled him to secure a position with the Imperial Maritime Customs in Canton. Ho Tung had risen further by 1894 to the position of chief comprador at the British trading company Jardine, Mathesen & Co. In spite of his striking European appearance, like many other Eurasians he continued to self-identify as Chinese. The fact that he possessed business contacts and special linguistic abilities not only created opportunities for Ho Tung and men like him to become wealthy; it also made them extraordinarily valuable to the colonial state. During this period, Chinese elites were still rather reluctant to take up official roles within the colonial government, or found criteria such as 'loyalty to the crown' off-putting. Elite Eurasian men who self-identified as Chinese thus became "exponents to the British of Chinese thought and sentiment."[35] Ho Fook, for example, Ho Tung's brother (and successor to him as comprador at Jardine & Matheson), served as an unofficial member of the Legislative Council and spokesman for the Chinese.

Neither the Chinese nor the British or the Eurasians in Hong Kong (who were mainly 'Portuguese-Chinese' and 'Anglo-Chinese') had much to gain by gesturing toward a separate 'Eurasianness.' Religious workers who catered for orphaned children of "mixed parentage" here as in Saigon made little formal distinction of race even if their institutions were well known for supporting Eurasians. Schools and orphanages often separated children along a European-Chinese binary, requiring a triage that might or might not leave Eurasian children grouped with Europeans.[36] And even though certain institutions, such as Diocesan Native Female Training School (1860), Diocesan Home and Orphanage (founded 1869 and later renamed the Diocesan Boys' School) and Diocesan Girls' School (which opened in 1899 and was funded by elites such as Ho Fook), were considered to be 'for Eurasians,' they were never formally named as such.[37] In a society defined around biracial categories, Eurasians displayed a notable reluctance to identify themselves as a separate, intermediate group.

However, in the last quarter of the century, observers noticed that these conditions were nonetheless producing social practices that made a separate Eurasian 'community' discernible. In 1889 James Cantlie observed:

> This really is a class only now arising.... For the past 20 or 30 years many of the sons are brought up as Chinese, dressing in their dress and following their customs. Further they marry with Eurasian girls and it is only now that the real trial becomes apparent of the establishment of a class or race.[38]

Shared residential, culinary and linguistic attributes, family links and educational preferences, as well as the experience of prejudice, had begun to set this group apart. However, most Eurasians remained reluctant to announce themselves as a new 'class,' 'race' or 'community.' For Europeans' tendencies to read depravity, vice and racial degeneracy onto this category, often through essentialist ideals of childhood, offered a powerful incentive toward denial. When census officials finally made 'Eurasian' a distinct category in the survey of 1897, only 272 people chose to enter themselves under this category.[39] It was not until the interwar years that some leading Eurasian figures would more fully grasp the importance of age-related issues to inscribing a sense of difference in new ways, notably through their negotiations with the colonial state.

COLLABORATION AND THE COLOUR BAR:
SINGAPORE'S EURASIANS

On 10 August 1895, H. N. Ridley, director of Singapore's Botanical Gardens, raised the "Eurasian Problem" for discussion before the Straits Philosophical Society. Like Cantlie a few years before, Ridley claimed that Eurasians' physical and moral weaknesses were innate. He traced these defects, in eugenic terms, to the lower-class background of parents who had passed their own environmentally induced deficiencies on to their children. However, like Haffner and Smale, Ridley was also convinced that European society had a duty of care to Eurasian children. And he even conceded that many perceived Eurasian 'deficiencies' might actually be the product of European prejudice.[40]

Though, as Ridley's speech suggests, the stereotype of the 'deficient Eurasian child' transferred readily across colonial contexts, a sense of social exclusion arrived more gradually for Singapore's Eurasians than for their counterparts in Hong Kong. The plurality and longevity of Eurasian society in Singapore diminished tendencies to define it as a separate 'problem' discussed in reproachful terms, or even as the moral responsibility of any one particular group. For generations the offspring of resident Europeans and Asians had grown up in Malaya. Some could trace their ancestry back to the founding of Singapore in the 1820s, to forefathers in the Malay Peninsula, to Portuguese and Dutch ancestors in Malacca, or British in Penang (where the British East India Company's presence dated back to 1765). Even those whose Eurasian ancestry was more recent could claim venerable links to the land. This relative stability meant the sex ratio was more balanced among Eurasians than most immigrant groups. Unions were also prolific. Isabella Bird counted the Eurasian population of Singapore as 3,091, making it much larger than that of the other centres.[41] But this group was more prone to subdivision, given its various 'Portuguese,' Dutch, British and other affiliations. Cultural and linguistic lines further fractured such categories, creating new distinctions, for instance between the 'Portuguese Eurasian' from Malacca and the 'Portuguese Eurasian' from Singapore.[42]

In the decades prior to the assignation of formal colony status to the Straits, a sense of reciprocity between resident European and Asian communities had developed. Official recognition of Eurasians in censuses dated back to 1849, much earlier than in Hong Kong, reflecting their value as a distinctive community. The relatively tiny size of the European population (which never exceeded 2.2 percent of the total) enhanced the value of the 'country born.' And there were significant cultural and linguistic commonalities between the two. A sense of unity crystallised into concerted action in moments of tension. In July 1854 for example when riots hit Singapore, European and Eurasian residents grouped together to form a Singapore Volunteer Rifle Corps.[43] When the new Crown Colony faced riots again, led by Chinese immigrants in 1871, the Eurasian residents of Waterloo Street, Bencoolen Street, Middle Road and other adjacent streets organised an informal police to restore order.

While other ethnic groups chafed at the growing incursions of an increasingly meddlesome colonial administration, Eurasians staffed it. When the new Straits Civil Service was established in 1867, Eurasians took positions as clerks in the civil and municipal services. Seventy-four percent of clerks in the administration at the end of the nineteenth century were Eurasian.[44] As in Hong Kong, these English-speaking Christians had also taken full advantage of the limited educational opportunities available, notably the government-subsidised, private English-language schools run by Christian missions.[45] In 1900, of the 2,078 boys in English boys' schools in Singapore, Europeans and Eurasians made up 20 percent, while in the English girls' schools they amounted to 86 percent. The introduction of open competition for appointment to the civil service in 1882 allowed Eurasians to reach relatively senior positions. And in competition for the Queen's Scholarships from 1886, Eurasian youth enjoyed success out of all proportion to their total number (twenty-four out of forty-five scholarships went to Eurasians from 1885 to 1910). So while volunteers in Saigon sought to rescue, cloister and assimilate *métis* children, and in Hong Kong an exemplary imperialism drawn around biculturalism obscured the Eurasian presence, in Singapore where society was more obviously mixed greater leeway to experiment with border-crossing behaviours persisted.[46]

Indeed, the sense of reciprocity between Europeans and Eurasians in Singapore spilled over into paternal gestures within the emerging voluntary sphere. French and Spanish Catholics engaged heavily in social work among this group. As part of an Anglican-oriented response, C. B. Buckley's philanthropic 'Christmas Treat' celebrated and succoured the Christian children of poorer Eurasian families, in particular those attending the colony's schools and those with links to St. Andrew's Cathedral.[47] Consequently, if there was a 'Singapore childhood' on display in the Treat from the late 1860s onward, Eurasian children were in large part its public embodiment—though this group was never explicitly separated out and defined as such, but instead fit within an overarching, plural vision of childhood.

However, while racial intermediacy appears to have been less heavily proscribed in Singapore for longer, around the turn of the century a variety of state-imposed reforms imperilled the privileges that Eurasians had carved out in colonial society. When young Eurasians attempted a patriotic gesture by forming a Volunteer Corps in August 1897, C. P. Lucas at the Colonial Office revealed that the colonial secretary, Joseph Chamberlain, "strongly expressed" the view that such a development was "undesirable."[48] In 1904, Governor Sir John Anderson formally barred 'non-Europeans' from senior appointments in the Straits administration.[49] In 1910 another ruling barred Asians and Eurasians from administrative posts in the civil service, forcing them into inferior grades (as mechanics, typists, clerks and train drivers).

Whilst in Hong Kong exclusionary practices had prompted the odd letter to the editor, in Singapore completely new journals or newspapers emerged to serve as mouthpieces through which Eurasians could respond to this provocation. Though these were often short lived, as in the case of the *Singapore Eurasian Advocate* (1888–91), they sought to define and promote a discrete community and its demands. After 1904 Eurasian interest groups also began to cohere around public meetings held to protest the colour bar. One produced a petition that was despatched to the British Parliament.[50] Churches also provided an institutional focus around which such energies found expression. Wealthy, elite Eurasians (of the so-called double ten) had established early links with philanthropic culture as patrons, but also noteworthy in this climate was the emergence of a new 'generation' of Eurasian youth making more assertive demands in defence of what they defined as their 'community's' interests.

FROM EMANCIPATION TO PROTECTION: EURASIANS IN HANOI AND SAIGON

In 1894, only a few months after its launch, Saigon's *métis* protection society collapsed into schism as its new secretariat discarded its purported "emancipatory" aims. Jules Dussol's group was left marginalised as—to the disappointment of the committee's three *métis* members—demands for citizenship faded. In an ominous break with earlier rhetoric, the society's vice president, De Cappe, an education inspector, now declared, "I have seen too much of what happened in the Antilles to approve of the kind of talk where it is said that the *métis* are the flesh of our flesh and the blood of our blood ... The *métis* are a danger."[51]

This shift came about in response to new circumstances created by the gradual transfer of power from Saigon to Hanoi and the administrative reforms marking the creation of a new Indochinese Civil Service. Around the turn of the century the administration stepped up its warnings against concubinage. New restrictions on employment followed amid criticism of fraudulent claims for the naturalisation of *métis*. As *mariage à la mode* fell into disfavour in elite society, the creation of a *cadre indigène* in 1902 formalised distinctions between European and 'Asiatic' administrators. This threatened to tip Eurasians into the latter category, prompting François Deloncle, the deputy of Cochinchina, to protest that the highest principles of the revolution were at stake.[52] But later the same year in Hanoi, the director general of the Douanes et Regies, René Crayssac, insisted to the governor general that "Asian French citizens" should not

> be put on an equal footing with the French, even though they have the equivalent status as personnel; their careers in the European cadres are, for most of them, limited to the lower grades; the inadequate qualifications of some of these agents and their

modest position puts them in a false situation vis-à-vis their European colleagues and even vis-à-vis the annamite; ... we cannot ... give them leadership positions.[53]

Similar sentiments informed demands for the exclusion of *métis* children from *écoles municipales*.[54] The resident administrator mayor of Hanoi, Eugène Domergue, explained that Eurasian children were "punchbags for the European children" and that "fights took place constantly," necessitating the departure of the *métis* children from school buildings through a separate exit.[55] In 1904 the municipality of Saigon also segregated Eurasian pupils of the Société de Protection from other pupils attending the École Municipale in order to satisfy "European mothers and fathers who were afraid that contact with the former might have a harmful effect on their children, and more particularly upon their girls."[56] In 1907 critics demanded these exclusionary practices be extended to the higher grades. In Hanoi, Gaston Cahen, for example, condemned the inclusion of "half breeds of a French father and an Annamese mother" in classes alongside French children at the new Collège Paul Bert.[57]

These demands exposed deep divisions within colonial society cohering around rival visions of the child and family. In the French-language newspaper press, proponents of assimilative approaches continued to champion the Eurasian child. In the columns of *Avenir du Tonkin* spokesmen for the *colons* criticised French children for their inability to "set down roots." L. des Charmettes, for example, argued:

> The economic and political future of our far eastern possessions is intimately linked to the extension of *métissage*. This must be greatly and intelligently encouraged ... I contend that from a twentieth century perspective we do not have to make the distinction between two little French [children] whatever the pigmentation of their skin, white, brown, *café au lait*, chocolate-coloured or black.[58]

In response to this, another correspondent countered:

> It is from unions of the white race that the prosperity and morality of the land derives. From such unions are born children who, better than those whom [others] have proclaimed superior, will make the superiority of our civilisation legible to the conquered race.[59]

Caught in the midst of this bitter debate, *métis* protection societies had given up radical assimilationist positions but now sought to emphasise the importance of their work by recasting Eurasians as vulnerable children.

In France a broad and politically variegated movement for the 'protection' of childhood had emerged in the wake of the defeat against Prussia. By aligning their oeuvre with metropolitan child protection movements, society members in Indochina presented themselves as the 'true' guardians of French honour and prestige overseas. Framing the Eurasian issue in terms of child protection formalised an emerging divide within French colonial society between those who laid claim to a certain 'prestige' or *noblesse* and other, contrastingly neglectful and transient elements, including the armed forces who were blamed for creating the *métis* problem in the first place.[60]

In both Hanoi and Saigon the membership lists of *métis* protection societies included commercial and agricultural entrepreneurs (referred to as *colons*) and members of the liberal professions (lawyers, doctors, and so on) as well as civil servants from various administrative grades. Together they laid claim to a more moral variant of colonialism. More generally, in spite of calls for administrators to live up to elite norms of family life, the phenomenon of *mariage à la mode* continued to transcend class into the twentieth century. This precluded easy disavowals of the problem as one of "poor whites."[61] But some were nevertheless keen to assert a break between an earlier age, when "all of our agents were living in concubinage with native women," and their own supposedly more sexually disciplined present.[62] The importance of the protection societies' work in evidencing such claims was not missed in the new imperial capital of Hanoi. There volunteers appealed to the government general not to direct funding toward the creation of equivalent organisations in smaller towns, but to concentrate it in the capital.[63]

Amid tensions tearing at colonial society, the *métis* protection societies extended their focus beyond more obviously abandoned or orphaned children and focused upon those residing with Vietnamese mothers within the native milieu. With this, native mothers began to emerge in society rhetoric as an obstacle to paternal claims.[64] The president of Saigon's society complained, "Numerous mothers refuse to give us their children until their majority, on the pretext of not being separated from them."[65] Societies compiled dossiers evidencing the dangers of the native milieu and accused mothers of profiting from the divestment of children into prostitution or slavery. Society members referred to native mothers using the disparaging term *congaï*, while others labelled them "morally loose children," too young to fulfil duties of care toward their offspring.[66]

While the childlike incompetence of the *congaï* offered a pretext for intervention, the 'salvation' of *métis* children was understood in terms of their acculturation to Frenchness within an appropriately 'French' cultural milieu. Because these philanthropists saw Eurasians not as 'guttersnipes' or degenerate by-products of immoral unions but as culturally 'lost' children, they could conceive of retrieval in terms of an intended Gallicisation. However, given the limited funds available, in practice the societies could actually only cover the cost of sending a few dozen pupils to school and their lodging and upkeep. Care providers in Hanoi and Saigon fretted over constant breaches of institutional enclosure and lapses in care occasioning exposure to native milieux. From 1897, Saigon's protection society considered denying young *métisses* the right to return to their mothers during school holidays.[67]

To secure official support society spokesmen presented themselves as working to narrow the gap between claims for empire as tutelary and a prevailing deficit of benevolence on the ground.[68] They threw official inertia into relief by drawing embarrassing contrasts between French, Vietnamese and Chinese approaches to mixed-race offspring.[69] While claiming the latter took good care of these children, assimilating them, Grevosty, a marine accountant and spokesman of the Saigon protection society, argued that "many Frenchmen abandon their *métis* children and worry very little that they might be eaten by pigs."[70] The administrator Louis Salaün demanded that societies "substitute themselves for fathers who have defaulted on their duty, assuring the survival, education and the placement of abandoned *métis* children."[71]

Saigon's loss of capital status to Hanoi in 1902 added new layers of complexity to the Eurasian question as a 'test case' for French imperialism. Those with interests in Cochinchina protested that they had borne the financial brunt of endowing Hanoi with a new civil service and other public works schemes. As Paul Doumer drew Indochina closer to Paris via Hanoi, Saigon's business-minded elite complained of a creeping process of 'overcentralisation.' The city's *métis* protection society offered an outlet for frustrated claims to social and political leadership. After 1902, protection society members amplified demands for legislative support in the battle to prise Eurasian children from native mothers.[72] The southern society even went so far as to present demands for the promulgation of the metropolitan child protection law of 24 July 1889, concerning the protection of mistreated or "morally abandoned" children. The lawyer Camille Paris even argued this law would be "more useful in Cochinchina than in the metropole given the complete absence of morality in the generality of mothers of these unfortunate children."[73]

Facing these demands, the Government of Cochinchina appointed a commission to investigate whether metropolitan child welfare legislation should indeed be promulgated in the colony. But it quickly became clear to the government that this campaign had the potential to spill beyond Eurasian children and to raise questions of state responsibility toward Vietnamese children too. It therefore threatened to drag a host of other perils, from unregulated labour practices to domestic bond service suffered by indigenous children, fully into public view. More worryingly still, such a critique might potentially converge with that presented by *colons* in Tonkin who were by 1905–6 foregrounding demands for the protection of Vietnamese children in protests over the government's taxation policies. The *colons*' newspaper *Avenir du Tonkin*, referring to Saigon's commission, mentioned in 1906, "We will follow the work of this commission with real interest," and expressed "regret that the law of 19 April 1898 is to all intents inapplicable to the indigenous population of the colony."[74] As the Eurasian question threatened to link together wider problems and protests, the Government General moved to endow Hanoi's protection society with the official status of a 'public utility' in 1907. This helped to ensure the Eurasian problem would continue to be recognised as separate. Hanoi received official status first because it was the principal imperial seat of government, and because it was in Tonkin that *colons*' protests over child slavery and trafficking were especially strident. The privilege of public status was also accorded to Saigon's society a few years later, on 10 January 1911.

By this time, a feminist-led critique of the *métis* problem in empire was rippling out from France to the colonies. This critique focused more upon the so-called *crise paternelle*, and article 340 of the Civil Code, than the law of 1889. In response the French Senate adopted a private bill calling for legal declarations of paternity outside marriage to include cases of 'concubinage.'[75] What gave such demands additional leverage was the fact that the German Reichstag voted on 8 May 1912 to affirm the legality of mixed marriages within the colonies. A French law of 16 November 1912 also extended the right to paternity of children born of concubinage in French colonies. Minister of Colonies Albert Lebrun issued a formal demand that governors general raise awareness of the need for European fathers to fulfil their "duties toward their children born of native women."[76] Indochina was one of the few parts of the empire where this legislation was adopted in the same form as in France. Historians have identified Lebrun's intervention as evidence that before 1914 "metropolitan conceptions of morality encroached ever more closely on the colonies."[77] However, by the time that French feminists were working visions of the "abandoned children of empire" into campaigns for the revision of metropolitan paternity law, the Government General in Indochina could already point to the protection societies of Hanoi and Saigon as evidence of the awareness that "the Administration has the absolute duty to provide for these children."[78]

Though institutions in Indochina won public recognition for their efforts to address the '*métis* problem,' what they achieved in practice was to institutionalise a marginal group in colonial society.[79] This marginality was now given physical expression in bricks and mortar. Under Governor Krautheimer in Saigon in 1906, construction work began upon two buildings to accommodate Eurasian girls. A third building went up in 1910 for Eurasian boys. The structures appeared not in central Saigon but toward the margins of European administrative power, in neighbouring Cholon.[80] And institutionalisation failed to attenuate prejudice. By 13 November 1906 the general assembly of Saigon's protection society agreed that the very word *métis* had become so heavily stigmatised that it was necessary to drop it from the organisation's name.[81] Having started by proposing citizenship, volunteers had lurched toward 'rescue' and to this end created 'reformatories,' but the 'Eurasian problem' remained stubbornly unresolved.

FROM 'GUTTERSNIPES' TO 'GRAND OLD MEN': EURASIANS IN INTERWAR HONG KONG

Not long after returning from Fiji to take up the governorship in 1912, the longtime administrator and former cadet (now 'Sir') Henry May revived his antagonism toward the Eurasian population of Hong Kong. Years before, May had presented demands for a racially segregated Hill District Reservation in terms of eliminating the Eurasian presence. But as we saw in Chapter 6 this had not prevented Robert Ho Tung from securing an agreement to reside on the Peak, and his second wife, Clara (who was also Eurasian), and her children moved there in 1907.[82] Two years after May's return, controversy flared again around Ho Tung's presence, following the latter's application for the admission of his children to the newly opened Peak School. Since the school was intended for 'British children,' May's preference was to reject the request for admission.[83] After protracted wrangling the government granted Ho Tung permission to send his children to the school. However, given May's obvious reluctance Ho Tung chose to have his daughters educated at Diocesan Girls' School instead.[84]

In the war year of 1917 matters once again came to a head when May was alerted to the intention of 'Chinese and Eurasian elites' to follow Ho Tung's lead by purchasing residences on the Peak using a loophole in the poorly worded 1904 ordinance. In the face of this threat May drew upon powerful, shared understandings of age, class and degeneracy to present Eurasian children as a core challenge to the integrity of the reservation. The language of contagion had not featured much in the discussion of the 1904 ordinance, when the government had emphasised European children's climatological vulnerability. However, May now presented the reservation as a 'cordon sanitaire' breached by Eurasian families whose "closer communication with the Chinese portion of Victoria" increased "the chance of the carriage and dissemination of communicable diseases."[85] Having deterred Ho Tung in his efforts to enrol his daughters in the Peak School, May could possibly have been referring to their journey on the Peak Tram to school in Victoria each day. In his view, Eurasian children had opened a breach in the reservation and the governor warned the Colonial Office that if other such 'Europeanised Chinese' were allowed to follow they

> will have with them their wives and concubines with numerous progeny, who must be thrown into daily contact with the European children in the children's playground and the few other shady spots to which the European children are now taken by their nurses and amahs.[86]

This metaphor of contagion proved extremely powerful. It transferred endangerment from the realm of public health into the cultural domain of racialised identity. Referring to Eurasians at times as "Chinese" but also as "semi-European," "Europeanised" or "semi-civilised," May presented the Colonial Office with an alarming scenario in which a group less radically unintelligible to white children than Chinese children might more easily transmit degenerate behaviours across the racial divide.[87]

These skirmishes also reflected childhood's importance as a cornerstone of European prestige and revealed a sharpening sense of antagonism with Eurasian elites. As the First World War engendered new opportunities for wealth acquisition, it also gave rise to more symmetrical interethnic relations, which offended the European sense of privilege. By way of illustration, in 1919 a group describing themselves as "British subjects of pure European descent" protested to the Colonial Office at being outbid by "certain wealthy Chinese Eurasians" in a land auction.[88] Meanwhile, in the Chinese mainland, the collapse of older power structures and intensifying anti-British sentiment again raised questions about British (over)reliance upon Eurasians as intermediaries.[89] When 'nonofficials' contested May's proposed amendment to the Hill District Reservation Ordinance in the Legislative Council, the governor blamed this challenge on "agitation among the Eurasians." And he demanded the passage of the amendment specifically to avoid giving "the undesirable impression of a moral victory on the part of the Eurasian population."[90]

However, as economic tensions spilled over into larger anti-British protests in the 1920s, concerns revived within official circles over the reliability of Eurasians and the willingness of local Chinese to accept them as political representatives and community leaders.[91] During the strike of 1922 Governor Sir Reginald Edward Stubbs observed, "We can rely on nobody except the halfcastes and even they will throw in their lot with the Chinese if they think they will be on the winning side."[92] Another problem, as Stubbs observed, was that respectable Chinese "habitually refer to this class of person as 'the bastards.'"[93] Anxieties over the importance of elite Eurasians' role grew further as anti-British sentiment peaked following the May Thirtieth Movement in Shanghai in 1925. Governor Stubbs struggled to respond to a vast strike-boycott lasting from June 1925 to October the next year. And as the strike crippled commerce, biological metaphors and categories of age became entwined with colonial policymaking and efforts to rationalise Eurasians' controversial intermediary role.

In the crisis, the paradigm of 'maturity' proved valuable both in interpreting policy to London and in developing new bases for collaborative relations with the Chinese elite. John Carroll has argued that a long-standing, carefully cultivated and profound social distance separated Hong Kong's British and Chinese elites.[94] However, from 1911, as we have seen, spectacular celebrations of childhood bridged this social divide. During the war these efforts proceeded in new formats, such as bazaars. In peacetime, Governor Stubbs's wife, who was president of the Ministering Children's League, refashioned it into an umbrella organisation encompassing much other philanthropic work. Because of this, child-centric voluntary work exemplified and distinguished a 'mature' civility, and the language of age emerged as one that Eurasians could draw upon to articulate a sense of shared Anglo-Chinese interests in times of unrest.

In the midst of the strike-boycott of 1925–26, for example, elite Eurasians emerged as metonymical representatives of the colony's purported 'maturation.'

One of the foremost examples of this 'mature' elite was Robert Kotewall. A businessman, Queen's College 'old boy,' Chinese representative on the Legislative Council and staunch neo-Confucianist, Kotewall played a leading role in maintaining collaborative relations with the Chinese elite in turbulent times. Though only forty-five himself in 1925, Kotewall adroitly mobilised a discourse of age to present himself as an exemplar of respect for social and cultural conservatism. He traced the origins of the trouble in Hong Kong to the influx of youth from south China into the colony's schools, declaring, "It was the students who started the strike in Hongkong; and it was the students who created the shooting incident at Shameen as in Shanghai . . . Practically all the boy-schools were more or less contaminated." He then proposed as an 'antidote' "the development of the conservative ideas of the Chinese race in the minds of the young" and celebrated the response of older Hong Kong Chinese during the strike, reserving special praise for the "old Chinese literati."[95]

Linking age with authority, the government and its Eurasian mediators defined a community of interest transcending the fixed and fraught categories of race and class. Age provided a subtle and fluid means through which tensions over racial identity and class allegiance could be circumvented. A unity of maturity sustained a broad, collaborative counter-response to anticolonial protest. This rhetoric linked the Crown Colony into a global imperial network defined by moral manliness while casting China as naïve, impressionable and contrastingly "young."[96] For some, attitudes to Eurasians even offered a litmus test of 'maturity' distinguishing Hong Kong Chinese (who were British subjects) from 'other Chinese.' In 1926, one observer claimed to be able to distinguish between the two on the grounds that "Hong Kong Chinese" were "stronger in their denunciation of Canton than any foreigners in Hongkong," that they spoke "of the needs of the Empire and the Colony much as Englishmen do" and regarded Eurasian influence "so much as a matter of course that it is not discussed at all."[97] In keeping with such age-related conventions, observers celebrated the end of the strike-boycott as evidence of Hong Kong's "coming of age."[98] As the strike petered out, official expressions of gratitude followed along with the conferral of honours upon Kotewall and others.[99] Sir Robert Ho Tung, who was sixty-eight in 1930 and the most prominent representative of the colony's Eurasian elite, was anointed the "Grand Old Man of Hong Kong."[100]

However, even as Eurasian elites scaled new peaks of public recognition, social change was simultaneously eroding their political value in the eyes of officials. Eurasian boys and increasingly girls had been beneficiaries of the "Anglo-Chinese" school model epitomised by Government Central School (Queen's College from 1894) and the Diocesan Boys' and later Girls' Schools. They had enabled a small section of the rising generation to bridge the cultural divide. However, by the late 1920s the rise of English-speaking Chinese graduates trained overseas and (from

1912) in Hong Kong's own university was reducing the particularity of Eurasians' claims upon these skills.[101] Moreover, other social and political changes complicated Eurasians' ability to perform Chinese identity.

From 1911 but more especially after the May Fourth Movement of 1919, Chinese nationalism had acquired a mass character and more clearly defined racial-geographic parameters. Around the same time, as Emma Jinhua Teng has argued, postrevolutionary social transformations weakened older, nonracial markers of Chineseness in Hong Kong. Before the revolution, Chinese identity had been encoded in names, clothing and—for men—the wearing of the hair in a queue, and these were practices Eurasians had taken up in order to perform Chineseness. Their gradual disappearance now enhanced Eurasians' distinctiveness and, after the crises of the 1920s had passed, their growing marginality.[102] As political stability returned, officials venerated this group, but in doing so they referenced *old age*, an act in effect ushering the Eurasian elite toward senescence.

As the Great Depression hit Hong Kong from 1929 and competition for clerical positions intensified, younger Eurasians became more keenly aware of the lack of any 'community' leadership capable of defending their interests. This was perhaps unsurprising given that so many of the wealthy Eurasian elite had aligned themselves with Chineseness. The problems of the younger generation were quite different. And some now felt the need to create new institutions capable of protecting their distinctive needs and concerns. An important example was the philanthropic 'Welfare League' (or Tongren hui), which held its first general meeting in July 1930. Though Sir Robert Ho Tung served as president, the real energy was supplied by younger members such as the thirty-seven-year-old solicitor Lo Man Kam and Charles Graham (Carl) Anderson, the league's secretary, who was in his early forties.[103] In a speech announcing this initiative, Anderson, who had been born in Hong Kong to Eurasian parents, defended the notion of a Eurasian 'community.' He located its essence not in terms of race or civilisation but maturity, good citizenship and a fusion of blood. As he put it:

> We feel we are a community.... It has been said of us that we can have no unity, and since even the semi-civilised tribes of Africa have it, this, though palpably absurd, is a challenge to be faced and an insult to be wiped out.... With the blood of Old China mixed with that of Europe in us, we show the world that this fusion, to put it no higher, is not detrimental to good citizenship.[104]

In this appeal Anderson located maturity in blood that was figuratively 'old.' Ultimately, it was the Anglo-Chinese phenotype that distinguished Eurasians from others still arriving on the civilisational stage. However, Anderson located Eurasians' 'maturity' in the blood of 'Old China' rather than Europe. Even younger Eurasians, then, seemed to hark back to an older China, one where cultural Confucianism afforded their fathers' generation a less exposed position within the overarching framework of 'Chineseness.' This was a rather nostalgic response, but one that is unsurprising given that it was forged in the face of conditions of depression that were eroding privilege and hastening societal fragmentation defined along more intensely nationalist lines.

But it is also worth noting that in the eyes of those who established the Welfare League, performing Eurasianness as an independent, self-reliant and mature unity also required the assumption of a paternal, charitable role. The Welfare League claimed the right to look after the "destitute of our kith and kin." This approach drew upon existing philanthropic models of welfare organisation that already connected the British and 'mature' Chinese elites. These had particular cultural resonance for Hong Kong's Eurasians as they appeared to simultaneously invoke and abrogate notions of separate, parallel British and Chinese worlds. By setting up their own league, Eurasians defined their scope of action more narrowly in relation to their own moral-biological community, but at the same time recast Eurasianness as something much more expansive in response to timeworn, infantilising European and Chinese ascriptions of degeneracy.

DIVERSITY AND DIVISION: SINGAPORE EURASIANS IN THE INTERWAR ERA

Writing in *Our Magazine*, a journal set up to cater to Eurasian interests, 'G.S.K.' declared, "Queer things do flourish in Hongkong; mainly snobbishness and fierce respectability."[105] Like many members of Singapore's Eurasian administrative and business community, this writer was sufficiently well travelled to be able to compare his own experiences of prejudice with those of others like him in other Asian centres. In writing and reading about experiences of travel in the postwar era, young Eurasians constructed Hong Kong as an extreme on a spectrum of racial prejudice encountered within the British Empire. The social and political changes of the early twentieth century had weakened Eurasian claims on Chineseness there, throwing European snobbery into relief. Certainly the levels of prejudice suffered by Eurasians in Hong Kong appeared greater to G.S.K. than in Singapore, but he was only too well aware that snobbery was also becoming more evident in the Straits.

Because Singapore society was more obviously plural than that of Hong Kong, in the early twentieth century official policy focused upon reinforcing divisions between constituent groups in order to prevent unrest. Fitting all of those resident within racial categories required remarkable contortions and elisions, as Joel Kahn has shown.[106] But as the colonial state undercut Eurasians' privileges the latter proved adept at combining strategically with other Anglophone groups to 'express the views of domiciled communities.' The *Malay Tribune*, for example, a newspaper started in 1914 with support from Lim Boon Keng and Eurasian benefactors, appealed to the English-speaking of all races and provided a vehicle for such views.[107]

After the Madras Fifth Regiment of Native Infantry rebelled on 15 February 1915, Singapore officials became still more wary of doing anything that might embellish Eurasian authority. Hence, when Edwin John Tessensohn, a graduate of St. Joseph's School from Malacca, requested the right to create a Singapore Volunteer Infantry (SVI), the Straits government and the Colonial Office rebuffed his demands. In March 1918, with the war nearing its end, at a meeting attended by two hundred at St. Andrew's School, Eurasians drew up a petition that succeeded in finally overcoming official opposition to the SVI. However, by now the administration's exclusionary intent had begun to undermine the sense of loyalty to the empire. If anything, what this eventual success did was reveal to younger Eurasians that concerted, collective action in the name of their specific community was required if other key aims were to be achieved. Younger Eurasians channelled energies toward finding (and writing in) their own distinctive voice and using this to articulate a sense of being a separate community in the immediate postwar context.

In January 1919, T. C. Archer, the editor of *Our Magazine*, gave expression to the prevailing view that other mouthpieces were simply too 'cosmopolitan' to speak to the Eurasian position.[108] *Our Magazine* dedicated itself to "the uplifting of a people who it is thought have been too prone to look indolently on and grumble at their fate," by appealing to them "to bury their petty differences and to work in unity for the betterment of the community."[109] Edwin Tessensohn had founded a Eurasian Literary Association (ELA), apparently with similar aims.[110] And a variety of new forums emerged upon which stronger public explorations and affiliations with a separate Eurasianness flourished. What soon became clear was that this sense of a more sharply delineated 'community' actually fit quite well with growing official desires to affirm communal divisions in the Straits. On 6 February 1919, when crowds flocked to Singapore's centenary celebration, the Eurasian 'community' had interpreted its lack of official recognition as an affront. However, after Chinese students rioted later that year, the government began to incrementally augment Eurasian representatives' roles within the state in the hope that this might prevent such protests coalescing around a broader-based anticolonialism. For example, a Select Committee on Constitutional Changes of 1921 assigned a place to Eurasian representatives on the Legislative Council of the Straits Settlements, which was taken up in February 1923.

Because staking claims to unity upon notions of a community of mixed origins or 'kinship' proved challenging, spokesmen for Eurasians often emphasised unities of age. Notwithstanding certain residential concentrations, Eurasians' names, dress and other cultural markers provided little in the way of any ultimate or 'essential' underlining link. Lacking apparently more stable boundaries of biological race, bloodline or even phenotype, those who reflected upon Eurasian unity—or the lack thereof—emphasised the need for a new generation of leaders capable of imposing this from above. By the early 1920s the first generation of 'community' leaders, such as Tessensohn, were in their mid-sixties. However, the key issues affecting the 'community'—as it was defined—related to matters such as the quality of education and barriers to labour markets. As such they more directly concerned the social position of Eurasian children and youth.[111] Demands for leadership by Eurasian youth therefore began to be heard. In 1919 one commentator complained, if "our young men are not thrustful and even aggressive in company they will never be noticed at all."[112] Eurasian youth could unquestionably speak but the question was, could they lead?

Mobilising claims around issues concerning 'youth' held out the prospect that young Eurasians might reach out to other ethnic groups along the same lines. But such an alignment might also exacerbate internal subdivisions within the 'community.' Even if successful it might therefore compromise the visibility and coherence of Eurasian demands. For this reason, young Eurasians who sought to 'step up' and vocalise community issues found this extraordinarily difficult. An additional problem was that they were seeking to redefine, or lay claims to authority using age categories that were already densely overinscribed with other meanings in paternal, colonial and gender discourses circulating in adult society. These left little room to manoeuvre, and young Eurasians' explorations of their responsibility *as youth* toward even younger Eurasians illustrates this well.

In 1919 a correspondent for T. C. Archer's *Our Magazine* visited the Singapore Baby Show. The challenge of writing up a report on the show exposed many of the larger problems that young, unmarried Eurasian males encountered when they sought to act as leaders or spokesmen for their community and expressed solidarity with other Eurasian youth. The visitor wrote:

> We went to see the dear babies at the show the other day.... Well you know Baby, we did want to give you and your little pals a ringing cheer. But who are we to take the lead in such a delicate thing? This is a stodgy place full of make believe and conventions—where to be human is a sin. Wait till you are older and you will know all about it. And then too we are not married. But when you are big enough to understand you will learn that a bachelor and a baby is the height of the ridiculous. But all the same we gave you and your little friends a cheer in a voice which only we could hear. Lor' bless your little 'earts.[113]

Evidently the Eurasian child was an awkward topic for the youthful bachelor. His desire to articulate solidarity ('to give a cheer') was partly built around a sense of proximity, in terms of race and age. Yet he also felt the need to express a brotherly seniority, lecturing 'Baby' on the benefits of experience. Building an alliance with Baby was difficult, however, for social convention demanded that the bachelor display a studied disinterest toward the child. This precluded the expression of precisely the kind of paternal affection upon which 'community' leadership rested.

While the Baby Show put the Eurasian child on view in public, in this new format with its marked eugenic overtones childhood proved an especially delicate subject. Within the show the election of 'champion babies' referenced preservationist medical discourses that indirectly condemned and stigmatised Eurasian parents. The show drew public attention to the delicate fact that Eurasians suffered from high rates of infant mortality, and it implicitly blamed parents for this.[114] Face to face with two champion babies, the author notably declined to humanise the 'Eurasian' category in this scientific guise by mentioning either Hubert Thomas van der Beek (age eight months) or Maureen Imelda Boswell (age six months) by name. After all, the overriding impression presented by the show, with its strong eugenic subtext, was that "to be human is a sin."

Perhaps there was a sense of guilt and helplessness here too. While taking better care of the Eurasian child was clearly important to wider projects of community uplift, youthful Eurasians felt they were in no position to take responsibility for this project. Problems in Eurasian society had to be fixed, but as the author of the article asked, who were they to take the lead? How could they assume the paternal position monopolised by medical doctors and lady volunteers when this could not easily be assumed by youth *qua* youth. Throughout the 1920s this message drawn from the Baby Show continued to indirectly inform a wider current of sharply self-critical Eurasian commentary. Writers such as James F. Augustin harped on the theme that "'Eurasian' Society is ill and must be cured."[115] Augustin was convinced that the problem lay within the home: "The fathers and mothers are not thorough in this age of Christless Christianity, and team spirit is lacking."[116] As the Eurasian Catholic activist R. V. Chapman put it, "We are racially far too mixed therefore what counts is not so much as birth as rearing."[117] Similar arguments blaming parents resounded at meetings of the ELA. When it came to education, parents were blamed for impoverishing boys' ambitions by putting them to work too early.[118]

As the economic downturn brought social boundaries under pressure, a series of high-profile incidents exposed Europeans' intent to draw the dividing line between themselves and Eurasians more firmly than ever. Eurasians were increasingly excluded even from spheres where social mixing had formerly afforded opportunities for the expression of loyalty—for example, sport.[119] By marginalising Eurasians (using a variety of derogatory terms, such as *stengahs*), Europeans delineated the boundaries of European-ness more sharply. In a place where identity had long been more fluid and practices more 'hybrid,' a more careful policing of race commenced. How to prevent Eurasians 'passing' as European became a topic for discussion.[120] The long history of Eurasian encounters with French-speaking missionaries in convent and other mission schools had apparently produced a distinctive variant of spoken English, and advocates of the more careful policing of race identified accent as the most reliable marker of 'Eurasianness.'[121]

As the Great Depression squeezed educated Eurasians out of clerical positions, interracial divisions, and those between younger Eurasians and older community leaders, widened. Among older leaders ideas of imperial loyalty may have remained important, but among the young recognition of loyalty to the empire as the first-order principle of reform had dwindled.[122] One commentator, R. V. Chapman, asked whether lack of unity was "destroying our social standing and killing all hopes and ambitions in our young?"[123] The plight of the young had by now become emblematic of the failure of Eurasians to exert their influence through either the domain of commerce (dominated by the Chinese), or over the land (in the case of the Malays, with their reservation). A looming sense of racial-national confrontation gave Eurasian commentary a harder edge. To even self-identify as Eurasian was to take a position, and one that helped create indignation at the continued attempts of others to 'pass' as European. With other ethnic-national groups apparently determined to carve out resources on racial lines (as we saw in Chapter 6), the focus was squarely upon, as Chapman put it, the "breaking down of the artificial barriers of snobbishness that separate you from your own kith and kin," for this was "detrimental to the interests of your own progeny."[124]

Much earlier, the *Straits Chinese Magazine* had scoffed at Eurasians' reliance upon parish networks. "A 'Catholic Club' which they have, thanks to the efforts of the European priests, is a very good thing in its way, but why," the magazine asked, "in the name of goodness, the Eurasians cannot manage their own affairs?"[125] By now the old parish networks appeared ill equipped to defend Eurasian interests and the so-called 'upper ten' seemed unprepared to step into the breach. The colonial economy in Hong Kong had facilitated the early emergence of elite Eurasians distinguished by wealth and political influence. By contrast in Singapore, as A. H. Carlos, the secretary of the ELA, explained, one encountered "some difficulty when he tried to associate the Eurasian with commerce."[126] Moreover, because churches had for so long channelled (and effectively diffused) impulses toward separate 'Eurasian' philanthropic networks, a sense of responsibility for a community among the 'submerged tenth' seems to have taken longer to develop. In the midst of an intensifying clash of racial-national interests, outsiders derided Eurasians for their obvious factionalism. As the inspector general of police, René Onraët, put it, British prejudice against Eurasians had been "copied by the Eurasians themselves against each other."[127] Those who defined themselves as members of the in-group complained that "public opinion in Eurasia at present is fundamentally weak."[128]

However, the colonial government's perceived shift toward a 'pro-Malay' line in the late 1930s encouraged Eurasian spokesmen to seek strength in numbers through public forums, notably the newspaper press. While they considered themselves only "a microscopic minority," some now advanced plans to reach out to Eurasians across the Malay Peninsula, to "introduce new blood and new views."[129] Others invested in visions of irresistible hybrid fertility, arguing: "The mixed races, whether white or brown, are prolific. They are growing steadily and spreading all over the face of the earth and some day will dominate the world."[130] Such visions spoke back to the colonial conceit embedded in the Baby Show and elsewhere by presenting the rise of what they termed 'Eurasia' not as a problem, but rather as a way of solving the global issue of racial intermediacy once and for all, and in their favour.

ENFANTS DE LA COLONIE: CHILD RESCUE, CITIZENSHIP AND ANTICOLONIALISM IN INDOCHINA

As Eurasians in Singapore questioned whether their wartime contribution had been adequately rewarded, French commentators were asking similar questions in relation to the 'child peoples' of their own empire. Those inclined toward scepticism pointed to the unfortunate position of the Indochinese *métis*. Even before the war, anticolonial incidents had begun to fuel fears that Eurasians were becoming a "caste" of politicised pariahs and, as one commentator put it, "leaders or auxiliaries to the annamites who seek to undermine our domination."[131] An upsurge in violence against the colonial state in the postwar era soon led critics to question the efficacy of voluntary responses to this problem.

In Saigon and Hanoi, protection societies fed, clothed and educated children in (sex-segregated) homes and orphanages and arranged for their placement in the workplace or (in the case of girls) directly into marriage.[132] However, upon leaving orphanages or *ouvroirs*, pupils still remained legally 'native' and were compelled to wait until age twenty-one to apply for naturalisation. Prewar reform had barely improved access to citizenship and had restricted access to positions within the French colonial state for boys. Even those acculturated into Frenchness often occupied an anomalous legal status.[133] Liberal-minded jurists musing over this problem warned against recognising the *métis* as a separate colonial 'class' in law, with fewer rights than the whites yet more than the natives.[134] Such a line, they felt, would contravene 'association' and create dangerous *déclassés*.[135] But the existing situation also ensured, as one commentator observed, that "no comparison is possible between the abandoned French child and the *métis*."[136] By now the expectation that enclosing Eurasian children within the *cité française* would ensure "that the métis does not one day become a revolutionary" appeared naïve.[137]

During wartime the actions of the French state had raised hopes that the unrecognised *métis* children of deceased French military servicemen might become wards of the colonial state.[138] In 1916 the *Revue des Deux Mondes* published an article entitled "Les pupilles de la patrie" insisting that war orphans be given access to their late fathers' pensions. A law of 27 July 1917 provided for the state to take over the paternal duty of supporting fatherless children (rather than recognising mothers' status as equal).[139] As *pupilles de la nation* these children were entitled to support from the state.

On 23 October 1918 the colonial state in Indochina was similarly authorised to protect and provide moral and material support to children whose fathers, mothers or guardians were French citizens, subjects, protégés or even foreigners, as long as they had served in the French army during the war.[140] However, committees established in Saigon and Hanoi to handle applications elaborated special rules to discourage the Vietnamese mothers of these children from applying. Of the 180 known war orphans in Cochinchina, only 16 had been 'adopted' by 1921 and by June 1920 just one demand had been received in Hanoi.[141] As the system collapsed into abeyance, the lawyer and society president Galuski protested to the *résident supérieur* that the children the scheme had been intended to help were "reduced to a miserable condition."[142]

In the immediate postwar era, protection society members such as President Billes in Saigon dreamed of providing effective 'disciplinary enclosure' for their young wards, but they could not afford this.[143] The boys of the society were compelled to attend *écoles franco-annamites* in Cholon. This was, in the view of Gabouly, head of Cochinchina's Education Service, "deplorable," since the Vietnamese teachers in these schools could not effect the desired Gallicisation of the society's pupils.[144] In straitened circumstances and amid rising racial prejudice European parents responded to the Eurasian boys' presence by removing their own children from the school.[145] In light of this, some urged experiments with 'agricultural orphanages' somewhat redolent of Haffner's plans. However, when Eurasian boys *were* eventually sent out to the isolated Farm School at Bến Cát in an experiment on these lines, the conditions they encountered led them to quit in droves.[146]

Stronger demand for female labour within the urban economy helped to sustain efforts to organise Eurasian girls' protective enclosure in Saigon. As the economy grew with the revival of the rice trade, Madame Darles opened a 'Foyer de la jeune fille' on 15 October 1924. Situated in a modest apartment in rue d'Espagne, this provided cheap accommodation for around twenty girls, removing them "from the unfortunate temptations inherent in all big cities."[147] The *foyer* arranged the girls' placement as shop assistants or into marriage. But even then, enclosure alone was not enough. Organisers complained the societies received orphans too old to achieve the anticipated acculturation of pupils into Frenchness.[148] When the *foyer* attempted to enrol children in French schools, many were rejected for being too old to hold a *bourse*. However, the societies did not even possess the *pouponnières* that would allow them to receive very small children.[149] Some leaders also began to worry about the long-term effects of enclosure upon the girls in the *foyer*. As one leader later put it: "Older pupils feel too confined in the orphanage. Some have been there since the age of six or seven. They dream of other places."[150]

In the face of these difficulties, in 1926 a government commission concluded there was "no other really and generally effective means of achieving this than sending the child to France at the earliest age."[151] This was not a new suggestion. From July 1915 to 1918 dozens of *métis* youth of the protection societies had travelled from Indochina to France to serve the war effort. Ernest Roume, who had served as governor general of Indochina, requested that *métis* serve as apprentices in wood and iron workshops, whether they were pupils of the society or not. However, those boys who harboured hopes of being granted French citizenship through service were disappointed. Naturalisations were suspended during the war. Still, out of the sixty-six young males taken to France more than fifty were demobilised in the metropole and were encouraged to start new lives there.[152]

In peacetime the societies continued to send pupils to take up apprenticeships and assist in reconstruction.[153] During one inspection of Hanoi's orphanages in 1921, Governor General Long was fascinated by the idea that the children might be adopted by 'respectable families' in France. In March 1925 a small group with links to protection societies managed to secure support from colonial and metropolitan authorities to formalise transfers to France.[154] Galuski, who had by then retired, organised a reception committee in Coutances, Normandy, to assign pupils to host families. The intention was that the pupils would settle instead of becoming "useless, dangerous elements" back home.[155] According to the legal expert Jacques Mazet, "mixed in with metropolitan children less faithful to prejudices of race than the colonials," the children "would be removed from the cruel ridicule of their comrades."[156] It was assumed that thus removed from "contrary influences," such as "prejudice over colour," in "True France" these children would find "fixity," and the "affection and attention necessary in childhood."[157]

Though metropolitan transfer had powerful supporters, the number of children transferred was never sufficient to make this a viable long-term solution to the *métis* problem. Financial difficulties prevented the society in Cholon operating a similar service.[158] Worse still, by the late 1920s Vietnamese students were becoming entangled in high-profile political protests in Paris and other university towns in France. This definitively put an end to the option of metropolitan transfer. Henceforth the *métis* problem would have to be solved within Indochina.

With this, authorities declared that the clarification of the legal status of the *métis* could no longer wait. On 4 November 1928 the colonial government passed a decree allowing nonrecognised Eurasians to become legally French. Remarkable for its inclusiveness, the decree permitted those found to be sufficiently 'French' (having *la qualité française*) to attend French schools, undertake military service in French barracks and sit the same examinations as French candidates for posts in the colonial administration. In her illuminating study of this reform, Emmanuelle Saada makes the important point that in the process of defining who could be admitted to 'Frenchness,' race and culture were viewed as correlates.[159] For precisely this reason, appeals to age proved integral to the process of justifying and implementing this controversial legislation.

In building their case, advocates of legal reform referred to Eurasians not as dangerous pariahs but as children with the potential to become culturally French. In this way they effaced differences between Eurasian and French children and portrayed the *métis* as a child trapped in a legal limbo of French creation. Jurists larded otherwise rather dry legal arguments for reform with sentimental representations of Eurasian orphans. Albert Sambuc, for example, reminded readers:

> The interested parties are young children ... happy to have found refuge, trusting in those who took an interest in their misfortune ... rushing up joyful, eyes bright, arms extended, toward those they have seen before and whom they recognise as friends.[160]

Advocates of inclusive solutions associated the Eurasian "condition" with the less ossified alterity of age. Thus, they manoeuvred beyond critical interpretations of the social failure of mixed-race people as inborn. Since legal reform removed earlier restrictions confining this legal process to those in their majority, Eurasians could now be declared French "even in their minority, and however low their age."[161] In 1929, protection societies were assigned the right to act as legal tutors (in loco parentis) for unrecognised Eurasian minors and to oversee the application process on their pupils' behalf.[162] This further reinforced the link between childhood and the conferral of citizenship.

Courts did not grant admission to citizenship purely on the basis of age. They also employed tests of individuals' physical appearance, cultural background and upbringing.[163] However, since race and culture were considered correlates, assumptions about childhood and childrearing informed thinking about acculturation and citizenship. In this way, a report from the office of the *résident supérieur* in Tonkin in 1937 explained, "It is crucial that French society assimilates and absorbs these new French, [who are] fortunately children for the most part at the moment and consequently easier to mould."[164] In the same year the president of the society in the south, Madame Mathieu, declared:

> We must start by loving [the child]. Yes, loving the child, whom we must take in hand, as a French mother knows how ... [and] ensure that he remembers his childhood as a happy time, a point to which he is happy to return, as we return with joy to the family home.[165]

In this vision French childhood was "not a colour, nor caste ... All the little abandoned beings, whether or not our blood runs in their veins, are members of the family of the same status as the others, and they have right, in consequence, to the same affection, to the same protection."[166]

However, as economic conditions worsened after 1929, it became evident that legal reform alone could not deliver social uplift. Societies struggled to cope with demands for admission. The Saigon-Cholon society could assist only an estimated

25 percent of the needy. Even at its peak in 1935 it had only 313 pupils (while an estimated 1,500 *métis* were born each year in Cochinchina).[167] Shops and department stores stopped hiring Eurasian girls and the administration refused to maintain its subsidy to the Foyer des jeunes filles, forcing it to close.[168] By 1930 medical professionals in Hanoi recorded obvious increases in the number of Eurasian girls involved in 'sly' prostitution.[169] R. Bonniot, who campaigned for intervention on a more extensive footing, demanded to know why "so many *métis* children were on the street without instruction, profession, trade, consigned to the worst fall."[170]

Late in the period, with imperial stability in question, a breakthrough followed in the campaign to augment the protective role of the colonial state. Critics in the metropole, alarmed by French demographic weakness and eyeing a renascent Germany, recast colonial *métis* as children of the 'Latin father,' in the "full force of their age," and a reassuring source of racial virility.[171] The notable fertility of the Eurasian population underpinned such perceptions. Scholarly analyses thus inverted the earlier arguments of critics such as Douchet, who had blamed the Eurasian "problem" upon youthful irresponsibility, and recast what had been condemned as sexual incontinence as salvation.[172] In a speech given at the Congrès de l'Enfance in Saigon in 1934, the society president, Madame Mathieu, cited Nicolaï's earlier references to the Eurasians as the "soul of new France," stating:

> Today they are still only a few thousand. Tomorrow, they will be a force to be reckoned with and whose support we will feel confident to possess. Tomorrow if we give them the place they deserve the French of Indochina will be an indispensable part of the union, conscious of their role and their raison d'être.[173]

Mapping 'youth' onto the *métis* allowed officials to advocate the extension of protection while playing down concerns over political representation. At a moment when Eurasians appeared set to become a majority in legislative elections it seemed clear that they would play a major role in the future of the French presence. Juvenilising the "*métis* question" attenuated the sense of political risk surrounding reform.

What now emerged was a greater emphasis than hitherto upon retrieving and reforming Eurasian boys in particular. The changing strategic situation and wider geopolitical considerations informed this shift. In 1937 Japan had invaded China and it was amid urgent discussions of how Indochina might be defended that Eurasian children, and especially boys, became the principal target of inclusionary initiatives.[174] Viewed in this stark new light, societies and Catholic orphanages appeared "completely insufficient to accommodate *métis* children."[175] The arrival of the Popular Front government in France gave new impetus to these 'protective' efforts. Justin Godart, the Popular Front government's envoy to Indochina, described the *métis* issue as a "very serious moral and political problem."[176] Jules Brévié, the liberal-minded governor general of Indochina appointed by the Popular Front government of Léon Blum (1936–39), shared this view.[177] After the

French government set up the Commission Guernut, the colonial administration conducted a census of *métis*. In 1938, a session of the Grand Conseil des Intérêts Economiques et Financiers de l'Indochine agreed that an umbrella organisation should be established to federate, coordinate and fund protection societies. Authorised in August 1939, the Fondation Jules Brévié (FJB), named in honour of the governor general, drew existing networks of voluntary provision under the control of the colonial state. The aim was now to extend protection to all "Franco-Indochinese" children, and at younger ages.[178]

In May 1938, Brévié, Commandant General Martin and Résident Supérieur Tissot, president of the Hanoi Protection Society, all agreed that Eurasian boys would make ideal recruits for the armed forces in Indochina.[179] A *foyer* for boys was established and Madame Mathieu in Saigon now spoke out against sending children to France. Military children's schools enrolled Eurasians to prepare them for army careers, and it now appeared more urgent than ever that "every child must be taken very early from the compartment or the *paillote*."[180] With this in mind, in 1938 the governor of Cochinchina, Pagès, targeted the lowering of admission ages and the creation of a reception centre for very small children.[181] Another society leader urged, "We must make them leaders."[182]

Having aligned the Eurasian identity with youth, protection society members drew upon new metropolitan technologies associated with this life stage to resolve the Eurasian problem in the tropics. "We must provide them with distractions; more frequent outings, sports and games, cinema etc," suggested one.[183] There were experiments with farm schools, plantation settlements and other extracurricular works. Cochinchina sent children from its orphanage to a summer 'colony' in Nha Trang in 1934, at the society's own villa.[184] Meanwhile, under the umbrella of the FJB the hill station of Dalat, in particular, emerged as a site for the acculturation of valuable young Eurasians into Frenchness. Authorities drew up plans for a reception centre for three hundred *métis* children here on the grounds that "it will be easier in a region where everything is of French creation, to create for young Eurasians completely separated from the maternal native milieu, European conditions of life indispensable for the formation of their character."[185] An *arrêté* reserved a Military Children's School for attendance by unrecognised Eurasian children in Dalat on 27 June 1939.[186] Observing this, one commentator suggested the French had become "pioneers in the work of not Europeanising Asia but of creating the foundations for a Eurasia."[187]

CONCLUSION

As Europeans struggled with the consequences of racial mixing in empire from the late nineteenth century to the mid-twentieth century, age proved integral to attempts to address the 'Eurasian question.' Recent scholarship on the question of racial mixing in empire has emphasised exclusionary strategies devised to counter the threat posed by Eurasians to the reproduction of racialised cultural identity. However, with imperial stability under threat, colonial elites also used ideas and assumptions about childhood, youth and age both to underpin exclusionary initiatives *and* to extend controversial inclusionary initiatives. In Europe youth had by the late nineteenth century emerged as a symbol of evolutionary vitality and transformative potential. In European colonies elites reworked civilising projects and reimagined racial intermediacy through the lens of childhood. Lacking strong associations with specific political causes or ideologies, categories of age were available to colonial elites keen to manoeuvre beyond more ossified discourses of class, race and gender and to implement controversial policies.

In France and its empire, some hoped that Eurasians, located between the coloniser and "childlike" wards of empire, might be raised en masse from backwardness to "maturity." These hopes underpinned controversial efforts to redefine Eurasians' legal status and ultimately to admit them to 'Frenchness.' Framing the "Eurasian problem" against age in Hanoi and Saigon permitted fantasies of civilisational rejuvenation to be entertained, as well as possible solutions to the problem of metropolitan senescence. The idea of cultivating loyal Eurasians to run the empire, untenable at the turn of the century, was by the 1930s being openly explored.

In Britain and its colonies, notions of evolution as a clash or conflict of incommensurable entities served as a powerful justification for empire. Observers therefore read the Eurasian problem against dichotomous models of childhood that had emerged from the early British experience of industrial urbanism. This strategy allowed elites to distance themselves from intimations of imperial responsibility threatening racial authority. Even so, as anticolonial sentiment surged, directly threatening stability, officials used age in Hong Kong to recast wealthy Eurasians beyond the situated degeneracy of the street child as a "mature" force on the side of the hegemon. Amid the mounting ethnic-national tensions of the 1930s, in Singapore too Eurasians appropriated age as a lens through which to reimagine racial intermediacy as they confronted the challenge of defending their 'community's' interests.

Conclusion

Empire was defined in modern times by the mobility of ideas and people travelling serially back and forth between Europe and the colonised world, and by the boundaries that such movement called into existence. These included boundaries of age, and the central contention of this book has been that youth and its cognates (childhood, adolescence, infancy and so on) provide an important lens through which the cultures, processes and varieties of European imperialism from the nineteenth century to the Second World War may be read. By foregrounding the histories of children as a group and childhood as an idea as both moved within and across centres defined by British and French imperial borders, this book has argued that these youthful activities, mobilities and identities were central to the fashioning of empire and global modernity.

To make this argument *Youth and Empire* has explored a wide range of subjects documenting the imperial occupation with childhood—including domestic architecture, urban planning, medical and household guides, colonial exhibitions, eugenic baby shows, child trafficking networks, school strikes and institutions accommodating Eurasian children. It has shown just how important young people were to the search for supposedly more 'moral' justifications for empire from the late nineteenth century, and to definitions of race, class and nation. From the 1880s stakeholders in different metropoles and in colonial contexts reached for childhood as they sought to justify liberal governmentalities. Consequently, the young became a key focus of policymaking, literary interactions and cultural representations in the commercial and administrative centres that burgeoned in Asia under British and French rule. This was a period when larger numbers of women and children travelled between metropoles and tropical colonies, and colonial homes were established in the tropics. With this, assertions of European cultural superiority came to rest more firmly upon domestic norms. Images of childhood, in the law, in medicine and in the popular press, reveal how contemporaries in British and French Empire centres selected from a variety of ways of representing 'children' (and their 'best interests') in order to pursue a variety of different aims (from the prevention of mixed marriage to the segregation of entire neighbourhoods). Colonials thus made childhood essential to the new meanings they ascribed to empire, imperialism and governance in public.

As this study has attempted to show, childhood in empire was central to the fraught process of building community and consensus amid chaos and flux. Across empires, childhood was racialised and defined in relation to eugenic, segregationist and colonial hierarchies. Some commentators denied 'true' childhood to 'local' children and to those European children whom they saw as overly embedded within the colonial milieu. But children called upon to perform 'Britishness' or 'Frenchness,' or a more generalised 'European-ness'—often through vulnerability or suffering—also figured as essential adjuncts of empire. Their presence undergirded racial nationalism in idealised, contrastive forms, for example through markers of racial difference, such as topees. Children were expected to embody civilisation, to function as a yardstick of national identity and to define racial authority. However, as modern childhood emerged as ideal and practice in empire, this ambiguous condition also embodied characteristics associated with racial other-ness, such as unreason, impurity and primitivism. Adult-child relationships modelled a power imbalance analogous to that of rulers vis-à-vis colonial subjects. This tension surfaced continually, unsettling expectations that children might represent a new, more morally informed genre of colonialism exemplifying middle-class values. In the end, children embodied colonial desires to see nation and race as fixed, stable and above all synonymous, but ultimately exposed their fallacy.

By moving beyond national or imperial frameworks to use a comparative, trans-colonial approach, this book has argued that childhood functioned differently and served different aims and ambitions in each of the contexts discussed. Attitudes toward European children in Hanoi differed from those held in Saigon. What contemporaries imagined European childhoods to represent in Hong Kong was distinct from their counterparts in Singapore. This was because youth in empire was defined in relation to the local problems, projects and contingencies of the particular, complex mix of actors in each context. These ranged from colonial and military officials, to medical authorities, traders, missionaries, planters and indigenous and migrant populations. This was a picture of social and intellectual diversity. But amid this diversity, these conversations were often connected and comparative.

Focusing upon the situated entanglements and networked interactions that linked Asian centres under colonial rule with global processes has allowed us to uncover a story of porosity, overlap and interconnection. Exploring broad themes concerning youth has allowed us to uncover unexpected links between colonies in Asia. These crosscutting influences help to nuance what we already know about the histories of individual places. Importantly, they also help to bring into question notions of French, British or other empire worlds as unitary entities.

French families' use of bond servants scandalised Singapore and shaped debates about child slavery. Women living in Anglophone communities from India to Fiji produced rituals of childhood drawn against displays fashioned in Hong Kong and Shanghai. Colonials in Saigon justified 'protective' responses to endangered Eurasian children with reference to British neglect. French officials denied Vietnamese children access to *lycées* on the grounds of how their prospective British classmates might act. Myriad examples underscore the social and cultural interconnections of one colonial centre's ties to another, within and across empires. And they highlight the difficulties encountered by contemporaries interested in imposing particular national cultures in colonial places. Rather than living in discernibly British or French Empire worlds, children encountered enclaves that were more heterogeneously 'European.' But in places where cross-cultural encounters were the norm, even the colonial home turned out to be a zone where hybridity flourished.

Paternal ideals of empire made ideas about childrearing central to what British and French imperialism stood for in the world, but as this book has shown, colonial ideology was far from programmatic on the ground. British and French engagements with the question of youth in the colonies were refracted along the lines of intellectual traditions, views of nature and ideals of empire that were often different. But evolving metropolitan ideals of childhood were also contested and reworked in colonial contexts in relation to other models. Histories of colonial childhood and youth followed no straightforward trajectory, or clear temporal progression. Local concerns, pressures and political and cultural considerations ensured that 'childhood' and 'youth' were not static categories; they were continually being reshaped across the period within and between empire centres. Across multiple locations the configurations of practice that emerged were distinct and asymmetrical, though connected. This helps to reinforce arguments that empires were about much more than relationships between metropoles and 'peripheries.' What mattered was not *only* networks but what happened in the various nodes, terminals and stopping points along the way.

Across empires, childhood and youth as separate categories were unstable and the boundaries between them often blurred. In a period when 'adolescence' became more easily recognisable, the ideal young European in empire was often (though not always) a child. Categories of age could prove to be remarkably elastic, especially when compared with biological age. In certain times and places the label 'child' was strategically eschewed, or suppressed—as in official responses to the case of Hong Kong Eurasians. In others, it proved to be quite capacious, for example when it was used to refer to the Chinese schoolgirls who joined the Ministering Children's League, or the young female Tonkinese migrant labourers who fled desperate conditions of rural poverty and eked services and resources from the colonial state on its borders, and beyond. Youth, with its romantic political cadences, also proved strategically valuable in other cases, such as that of the Vietnamese students who theorised their role as a political vanguard, or the embodiment of a 'nation in waiting,' between the wars.

In the chapters of this book I have attempted to shed light upon the roles that children played in relation to the wider, trans-colonial and global exchanges of ideas that helped to define empires and childhoods. Chapter 2 discussed medical professionals' competing views of 'Tropical' nature, hygiene literature and the infrastructures established to support child life, and revealed that British and French experts were strikingly at odds about the nature of the dangers that the colonial environment posed to European children. Even the ages at which children were most at risk remained in dispute. These disagreements on an issue so critical to European racial identity highlight the malleability of racial thinking, and the importance of the figure of 'the child' to it, as a means of subsuming colonial tensions and contradictions. While doctors and hygiene experts urged parents to adopt certain childrearing practices in the service of elite-led efforts to build a sense of racial-national community, British and French families in practice developed their own strategies for the management of 'child life.' These were sometimes quite different from those found in proscriptive literatures. As a consequence the precise forms that childhoods took differed markedly within the same colonial societies, and were also fragmented along lines of class and gender.

Though elites configured children's 'empire story' as one of serial migration and circularity underwritten by eventual return 'Home,' consensus on such matters was not so easily achieved in practice. As Chapter 3 argued, the establishment of new worlds of interiority within the carefully established boundaries of the colonial home required the resolution of a variety of challenges, from contact with 'native' nursemaids to the degenerative tropical environment. Children's affection for domestic servants contributed to imperial hierarchies in ways that often contradicted parental advice and prescriptive literatures. Moreover, while 'youth' as a social category was often used to serve hegemonic practices and purposes, children could also act as agents for change, negotiating their own 'childhoods' within the home and reshaping the social meanings of their status.

The voices of children have been generally neglected in discussions of empire, partly because what they actually had to say was often less important than their racial visibility, but also because only fragments of children's historical subjectivities remain. Limited and mediated though children's agency often was, young people engaged in a dialogue with adults that shaped expectations of, and ways of inhabiting colonial childhoods. Elizabeth the runaway slave demanded her liberty. Phoebe May refused to be branded a 'weaky.' Dione Clementi kept watch for pirates from the Peak. Lý Thanh Long spooked state agents with his impersonation of the Kỳ Đồng. Lillian Newton turned the social stigma of being a 'jungle fowl' into a source of authority. Marguerite Marty regretted having to leave 'fairyland' behind. Children's agency did not necessarily always entail 'resistance,' but neither were young people merely passive recipients of notions of place and race. Their individual voices constituted, 'spoke back' to and sometimes flatly contradicted gendered constructions of childhood and imperial identity. While they are not representative of all children, these examples are suggestive of how children were themselves producers of culture, and that in growing up, children pushed back at boundaries, resisted particular types of childhood and exploited others on their own terms. They did not necessarily accept being typecast on the historical stage as docile bodies, acclimated auxiliaries or vulnerable associates pining to weakly health.

In all of the places studied, adults and children produced colonial childhood collaboratively through encounters with disease and ill health, and with profoundly mixed, pan-Asian populations. Evidence of young people's will to act provides new insights into the complex and varying set of social realities that shaped colonial society, and it reveals how children reacted to the constraints imposed upon them. At times they exploited the space inbetween expectations of the return 'Home' and the practical difficulties of achieving it to fashion childhoods with 'hybrid' characteristics. At others they linked themselves into wider crosscurrents in circulation, notably those of global consumer culture. The gendered categories of 'boyhood' and 'girlhood' were thus reproduced at the interstices of a variety of colonial cultures.

The home was, as other scholars have argued, a microcosm of colonialism, an 'intimate' realm linked to the power wielded by the colonial state; but this book has argued that the performance of childhood in public as well as in domestic spaces was crucial to making this link meaningful. As Chapter 4 showed, while children's position in colonial society often remained ambiguous, in British and French centres young people played important roles in projecting ideals of childhood beyond the home, into the wider realms of colonial culture. New public rituals emerged from the late nineteenth century tying these domestic and public worlds together. In public, children embodied and symbolised norms central to imperial authority. There they served not merely as a focus of nostalgic reflection but also cultural authority. From the 'Singapore Treat' to the Hong Kong 'fairyland,' to the Hanoi *exposition* and the global circulation of images of Emperor Duy Tân, the young took centre stage in ritualised representations of childhoods on the move. Modern ideologies of scientific racism as well as social reform informed the production of these new aesthetic forms. In French contexts, amid struggles over the question of settlement and of what empire meant, provocative visions of settler children jostled alongside 'official' versions reflecting childhood's significance to the moral claims of a republican imperialism. In British-governed centres, foreign residents fostered a sense of common purpose through public cultures of childhood. At times, child-centred practices could function to bridge racial as well as class divides. They did not only serve to reinforce racial distinctions and hierarchies; at times they destabilised them instead. Attending to this public aspect of childhood in colonialisms' cultures can help us to move histories of childhood and the family in empire away from static narratives of domesticity toward engagement with how the 'intimate' actually figured within the colonial public sphere.

Adults perceived children's bodies as requiring careful management in order that they might undergird established ideas about 'the' national body. While itinerant elites often sponsored the public display of children and childhood in colonial centres in the hope that these might absorb the tensions and contradictions of empire, the inherent instability and ambiguity of childhood in the colonial context made this a risky strategy. These risks exploded into public view in the early twentieth century, and especially after the Great War. As anticolonial fervour grew, European elites invested new importance in childhood as a means of showcasing civility. Chapter 5 has shown how these desires produced new, exemplary presentations and representations of ideal colonial children and childhoods between the wars. From Singapore's 'baby show' to Saigon's *semaines de l'enfance* these productions illustrate how anticolonial resistance directly and indirectly informed the fashioning of new ideas and models of family formation and new frameworks and possibilities of 'youth' in empire. The results reinforced fading claims for imperial authority but made children's bodies sites for new experiments in the technical-rational management of colonial subjects, the preservation of 'tradition' and the emergence of new middle-class social and commercial practices and sensibilities.

Globally, the management of space constituted a core tension of empire. While the management of the elite home and new public rituals were drawing some children toward the epicentre of colonialisms' cultures, childhood was also being extrapolated out into colonial urban planning. European children's presence in colonial centres informed British and French approaches to planning, in particular campaigns to engineer hygienic 'enclaves' or spaces of nature in hill or 'altitude' stations. Chapter 6 has argued that as Asian elites' growing wealth, status and influence allowed them to challenge European claims upon space, desires to create new, exclusionary, hygienic spaces became interwoven with moral imperatives to safeguard European children. Differential ideals of 'colonial childhood' were asserted, challenged and redefined through contests over space.

Desires to segregate children occurred around the same time across colonial contexts because they were linked. But quite different official responses resulted owing to conditions on the ground. In Hong Kong a racial reservation emerged to prepare the young to return home before the end of childhood. In Dalat the hill station functioned to preserve the colonial family over a longer period and to mitigate the need for definitive return. In Singapore the planters' campaign to accommodate and educate children in the Cameron Highlands drew an intransigent response from a colonial administration determined to defend older ideals of colonial childhood tied closely to imperial authority. Though childhood was essentially transient and soon outlived, the planning interventions produced in its name fundamentally reshaped urban centres and had an enduring impact upon urban politics and culture in all of these places.

The more states mapped domestic values and norms of civility onto European children, the more they risked drawing provocative contrasts between these youngsters and their Asian counterparts. White children's presence within and across empires of 'possessions' drew racialised childhoods into contrastive relation, with explosive results. Leaders of nationalist projects drew upon imagery of children and childhood, unfree and abused, to critique colonialisms, and highlighted disparities between childhoods to expose colonialisms as neglectful, or as insufficiently benevolent. Childhood as an idea and a set of cultural practices played a central role in Asian reformers' struggles to respond to the predicament of becoming modern in societies shaped by European colonial domination.

A new typology of children—dangerous and endangered—emerged between the wars, bringing the limits of European responsibility for the child subjects of empire repeatedly into question. As Chapter 7 showed, the plight of Vietnamese, Chinese and other children trafficked into slavelike conditions in British- and French-governed centres became a global cause célèbre and a test case for empire. The rescue of children from exploitative labour had endowed childhood with powerful liberal resonances in Europe during the nineteenth century. But the imposition and policing of new boundaries in colonial Asia brought to light the problem of 'trafficking' in its modern form, impacting with particular severity upon the young. Transfers of children into unpaid migrant labour outside the family, particularly unfree forms of bond service not easily distinguishable from adoption, made Hong Kong, Singapore, Saigon and Hanoi focal points in successive scandals over child trafficking and 'child slavery.' And as reformers repeatedly raised the alarm over official inaction or European complicity in commercial trafficking, they brought core justifications for empire into question. The profoundly trans-colonial movement of children into unfree migrant labour transformed global engagements with questions of European responsibility for the raising of youthful colonial subjects.

Engagements with this problem followed different, though linked trajectories in Hong Kong, Hanoi, Saigon and Singapore. They produced a far-reaching commitment to abolition in the Straits Settlements and Hong Kong, and a more effectual defence of the status quo in Hanoi and Saigon. But everywhere these struggles had long-lasting legacies. For example, because reformers generated sympathy for unfree migrant child labourers by emphasising their moral vulnerability as young females destined to become prostitutes, the very notion of trafficking came to be defined by the helpless young girl, of whom male colonial officials presented themselves as gallant protectors. However, even where anti-slavery campaigners 'won' these battles, colonial states failed to eradicate these problems. Trafficking and other forms of abusive or unfree labour continued to impact upon young people of both sexes. Meanwhile, the refashioning of the image of the indentured servant into the child slave had important consequences for 'children' who were legally of age, or who were boys. Even today debates about trafficking remain shot through with overtones of sexual rather than economic exploitation, and trafficking of women and children rather than the exploitation of workers irrespective of age or sex.

At the same time as the furore over child slaves was growing, French and British colonial governments in Asia were struggling to address the question of how to manage the problematic figure of the socially mobile child scholar. Much of the literature on comparative colonial schooling has emphasised the social divisions that arose from the resulting ferment, but Chapter 8 of this book has argued that debates over colonial schooling and experiences of institutional provision generated not only new divisions but also new unities and trajectories of race, class, gender and, crucially, age. In the late nineteenth century it had been clear to onlookers that those in attendance at many schools were not in fact 'children.' But reform brought a finer segmentation of age. As colonial schooling set youth on the move, 'youthful' entanglements with intellectual currents likely to endanger imperial interests drove state agents to reform education. In Hong Kong officials focused more upon the training of an elite while in Singapore the upper levels of the education system were left relatively neglected. In Hanoi and Saigon official attempts to narrow access to the higher levels resulted in a restrictive, pyramidal structure. The results were divergent, but everywhere these processes inadvertently reinforced the production of institutional experiences engendering age-related solidarities. Within the institutional spaces of schools, young people on the move, interested in articulating 'modernness' and concerned with their relationship with British and French colonialism, fashioned new 'youthful' ways of acting and endowed them with social and political meaning.

Ideas about childhood also proved integral to the fashioning of solutions for the so-called Eurasian problem in European colonies, discussed in Chapter 9. Racially mixed children born of sexual relationships between European men and Asian women were a highly visible presence in colonial centres. As an embodied metaphor of empires' crossings and connections this group achieved greater visibility and came to be defined as a 'problem' at a time when colonial communities were drawing boundaries more firmly around themselves. While much scholarship on the presence of 'mixed bloods' in empire has focused upon the exclusionary tactics that European colonial communities devised in response to this challenge, this book has argued that trans-colonial debates about the 'Eurasian problem' overlapped and connected in important ways with questions of imperial responsibility for children.

Eurasians featured in colonial discourse as a distinctively youthful presence, as 'street children' or *enfants de la colonie*. Those who depicted them in this way used the category 'child' to essentialise a group that was quite diverse in terms of wealth, status, age and ethnic mix. In Hong Kong liberal-inspired demands for the recognition of Eurasians as children in need of rescue and reform ran up against desires to obscure their presence and to fashion a more abstemious variant of imperialism, symbolised by European and elite Chinese children divided along a racial binary. In Singapore, youthful Eurasians urged community building as a response to growing official prejudice but struggled to find a shared ground upon which to defend their interests. Meanwhile, in Saigon and Hanoi the mixed-race child in the tropics went from being a sign of a negative mutation (or 'miscegenation') to one of the few remaining 'hopes' of the French Empire by the late 1930s. Volunteers strove to provide institutionalised enclosure before the legal admission of Eurasians to 'Frenchness' in 1928 ushered in a new phase of official interest. Legal experts and officials advocated more effective acculturation, and recast the Eurasian presence as one reinforcing, not challenging imperial structures.

In recent times, scholarship in the field of imperial and colonial history has ranged broadly over matters of gender, race, economy, politics and religion, but relatively little has been said of other important divisions that structured colonialism, notably those of age. The approach developed here has attempted to show that age was central to the ways in which social relations were negotiated, built, secured and challenged across empires. It has done so because studying empire can tell us much about histories of childhood and youth, and vice versa. With regard to the first, there is a clear need for new histories of the changing and differentiated ideas and experiences of childhood and youth that move beyond the national paradigm and take empire, beyond the white settlement colonies, into consideration. What such studies can reveal is how 'childhood' and 'youth,' so often defined within their discrete national settings, cannot be untied from histories of empire and that these categories were, in the end, only partially national. Studying childhood in empire can help to expose the limits of the universal values that it supposedly embodied, and can reveal historical contingency and cultural particularity on the ground. Furthermore, histories of youth and age relations can also reveal much that we did not know about empire. Focusing on age opens up a variety of new questions and perspectives and allows the exploration of historical ideas across a set of connected spaces.

Despite many calls for trans-national approaches to imperial and colonial history, Indo-centric narratives of empire history still predominate. This study has adopted a multisited approach to show how histories of colonial childhood—like those of other ideas, practices and objects—were profoundly interconnected. It has shown that movements to protect and segregate children, and to produce and consume childhood, spread as a consequence of these connections. The essentially linked and comparative nature of debates about young people gave them a momentum that drove initially reluctant European colonial governments at times toward surprisingly far-reaching commitments. Global and local exigencies placed children at the forefront of contests around European claims to civility and the future of empire itself. In this sense childhood proved fundamental both to the reassertions of cultural superiority that were under attack, and to those attacks. In the end childhood in empire was about much more than simply disciplining sex. And paying attention to the ways in which ideas and practices relating to young people moved can usefully point up ways of reconceiving histories of colonialism and approaches to the ways that imperial power worked.

The breadth and diversity of the subject matter addressed here precludes comprehensive treatment and in this book a variety of important topics and issues have gone unexamined. For example, I have dwelt rather little upon the linked histories of official, adult-led uniformed youth movements, partly because a number of single-context studies of these organisations already exist while so many other important aspects of the history of childhood and youth in empire have been ignored. There is clearly much to gain by reframing histories of uniformed youth movements within their interlinked, trans-colonial dimensions. And we can learn much more by applying this lens across empires to reexamine other topics, such as the roles of the young in missionary work, their entanglements with crime and justice, their experiences of travel, technology and communication, and young people's service in branches of the armed forces, colonial administrations and other sectors of the colonial economy. I have chosen to focus upon four particular centres here, but the multisited approach could usefully be applied across other empires and other parts of the world, or extended further to include places that have been referred to only tangentially here. I hope that the omissions and underemphases of this work may present opportunities for others and provocations to future historical work. New studies will help to further illuminate the rich and mutually constitutive histories of age relations and trans-colonial connections. This is an important new line of research because, as we have seen, far from being a marginal and ephemeral presence in colonial places, children and youth constituted a central historical force in the modern history of empire.

Reference Matter

Notes

CHAPTER 1

1. Rhodes House Library, Oxford (hereafter RHL), MS. Nathan 340 May to Nathan, 14 May 1905.

2. Ellen Boucher, *Empire's Children: Child Emigration, Welfare and the Decline of the British World, 1869–1967* (Cambridge: Cambridge University Press, 2014); Shurlee Swain and Margot Hillel, *Child, Nation, Race and Empire: Child Rescue Discourse, England, Canada and Australia, 1850–1915* (Manchester: Manchester University Press, 2010).

3. C. A. Bayly, *Empire and Information: Intelligence Gathering and Social Communication in India, 1780–1870* (Cambridge: Cambridge University Press, 1996); Dwayne R. Winseck and Robert M. Pike, *Communication and Empire: Media, Markets, and Globalization, 1860–1930* (Durham: Duke University Press, 2007).

4. E. M. Merewether, *Report on the Census of the Straits Settlements Taken on the 5th April, 1891* (Singapore: Government Printing Press, 1892), 45.

5. A. Bouinais and A. Paulus, *L'Indo-Chine française contemporaine: Cambodge, Tonkin, Annam* (Paris: Challamel Aîné, 1885), 294; Vietnamese National Archives Centre I, Hanoi (hereafter VNNA1), Mairie de Hanoi (MHN) D88 3260 "États statistiques de la population de la ville de Hanoi 1890 à 1918"; Claudius Madrolle, *Tonkin du sud, Hanoï. Les Annamites, Hanoï, pays de So'n-tâi, pays de So'n-nam.* (Paris: Comité de l'Asie française, 1907), 10.

6. In Cochinchina in 1922, 25% of the 8,524 French and 'other Europeans' residents had been boys and girls under age fifteen, while in Tonkin as a whole the figure was 31%. Henri Brenier, *Essai d'atlas statistique de l'Indochine française: Indochine physique, population, administration, finances, agriculture, commerce, industrie* (Hanoi: Imprimerie d'Extrême-Orient, 1914); Gouvernement Général de L'Indochine, *Annuaire Statistique de l'Indochine, deuxième volume, 1923–1929* (Hanoi: Imprimerie d'Extrême-Orient, 1931), 64.

7. In 1930 there were 5,026 children under age fifteen in Cochinchina compared with 4,447 women, i.e., 30% of the European population were children. Gouvernement Général de L'Indochine, *Annuaire Statistique de l'Indochine, troisième volume, 1930–1931* (Hanoi: Imprimerie d'Extrême-Orient, 1932), 55. There were 612 women and 499 children in Singapore and 1,218 women and 1,275 children in Hong Kong in 1891. Merewether, *Report*, 45; C. A. Vlieland, *British Malaya: A Report on the 1931 Census and on Certain Problems of Vital Statistics* (London: Crown Agents, 1932), 234–35. "Census Report, 1891," *Sessional Papers*, 15 August 1891, 377; "Hong Kong, Report on the Census of the Colony of Hong Kong, 1931," *Sessional Papers*, 12 February 1931, 123.

8. Merewether, *Report*, 45; By 1931 those under age fifteen constituted 15% of the total European population of Singapore and this compared with 32% for 'Malaysians,' 26% for Chinese and 13% for Indians. Vlieland, *British Malaya*, 234–43.

9. "Report on the Census of the Colony for 1911," *Sessional Papers*, 23 November 1911, 40–41, 43. From 1881, when there had been 144 British 'boys' and 144 'girls' under age fifteen among the 785 British enumerated (or 37%) in Hong Kong, the total increased gradually to 353 in 1891, 752 by 1901. This rose further to 2,082 by 1921, before dropping to 1,532 in 1931.

10. In Hanoi, in 1921, out of a total of 75,400 people, 24,800 were under age fifteen (32%). In Saigon, in the same year, 29,000 were under nineteen while 54,000 were over (35%). Gouvernement Général de L'Indochine, Direction des Affaires Economiques, Service de la Statistique Générale, *Annuaire Statistique de l'Indochine, premier volume, recueil des statistiques relatives aux années 1913 à 1922* (Hanoi: Imprimerie Extrême-Orient, 1927), 36–37, 40–41. It should be noted that these figures were swelled by the inclusion of Eurasian children from the late 1920s. Gouvernement Général de L'Indochine, *Annuaire Statistique de l'Indochine, deuxième volume, recueil des statistiques relatives aux années 1923 à 1929* (Hanoi: Imprimerie d'Extrême-Orient, 1931), 64; Gouvernement Général de L'Indochine, *Annuaire Statistique de l'Indochine, troisième volume, 1930–1931* (Hanoi: Imprimerie d'Extrême-Orient, 1932), 55.

11. Robert Bickers, *Settlers and Expatriates: Britons over the Seas* (Oxford: Oxford University Press, 2010); Robert Bickers, *Britain in China: Community, Culture and Colonialism 1900–1949* (Manchester: Manchester University Press, 1999); J. P. Daughton, *An Empire Divided: Religion, Republicanism and the Making of French Colonialism, 1880–1914* (Oxford: Oxford University Press, 2006); Eric T. Jennings, *Imperial Heights: Dalat and the Making and Undoing of French Indochina* (Berkeley: University of California Press, 2011).

12. Robert Bickers and Christian Henriot, "Introduction," in *New Frontiers: Imperialism's New Communities in East Asia, 1842–1953* (Manchester: Manchester University Press, 2000), 1.

13. Alfred H. Northcliffe, *My Journey around the World, 16 July 1921–25 February 1922* (London: Lane, 1923), 88.

14. H. L. Wesseling, *The European Colonial Empires, 1815–1919* (Harlow: Pearson, 2004), 23; Gilles de Gantes, "Coloniaux, gouverneurs et ministres: L'influence des Français du Viet-nam sur l'évolution du pays à l'époque coloniale, 1902–1914," vol. 1, PhD diss., Université de Paris VII, 1994, 45–46.

15. Classic studies include Philippe Ariès, *Centuries of Childhood: A Social History of Family Life* (New York: Knopf, 1962); John R. Gillis, *Youth and History: Tradition and Change in European Age Relations* (New York: Academic Press, 1974); Viviana Zelizer, *Pricing the Priceless Child: The Changing Social Value of Children* (New York: Basic Books, 1985); Steven Mintz, *Huck's Raft: A History of American Childhood* (Cambridge: Harvard University Press, 2004).

16. Roger Cox, *Shaping Childhood: Themes of Uncertainty in the History of Adult-Child Relationships* (London: Routledge, 1996); Colin Heywood, *A History of Childhood: Children and Childhood in the West from Medieval to Modern Times* (Cambridge: Polity Press, 2001); Jane Humphries, *Childhood and Child Labour in the British Industrial Revolution* (Cambridge: Cambridge University Press, 2010); Hugh Cunningham, *Children and Childhood in Western Society since 1500* (London: Longman, 1995).

17. Ann Pellegrini, "What Do Children Learn at School? Necropedagogy and the Future of the Dead Child," *Social Text* 26, no. 4 (2008): 97.

18. Leslie Paris, "Through the Looking Glass: Age, Stages, and Historical Analysis," *Journal of the History of Childhood and Youth* 1, no. 1 (2008): 106–13.

19. Cati Coe et al., eds., *Everyday Ruptures: Children, Youth and Migration in Global Perspective* (Nashville: Vanderbilt University Press, 2011), 2–3.

20. Mary Bucholz, "Youth and Cultural Practice," *Annual Review of Anthropology* 31 (2002): 525–52.

21. Laura Briggs, Gladys McCormick and J. T. Way, "Transnationalism: A Category of Analysis," *American Quarterly* 60, no. 3 (September 2008): 630.

22. Nara Milanic, *The Children of Fate: Families, Class and the State in Chile, 1800–1930* (Durham: Duke University Press, 2009).

23. See, for example, Julia Clancy-Smith and Frances Gouda, eds., *Domesticating the Empire: Race, Gender and Family Life in French and Dutch Colonialism* (Charlottesville: University Press of Virginia, 1998). See also Mary A. Procida, *Married to the Empire: Gender Politics and Imperialism in India, 1883–1947* (Manchester: Manchester University Press, 2000); Alison Blunt, "Imperial Geographies of Home: British Domesticity in India, 1886–1925," *Transactions of the Institute of British Geographers* 24 (1999): 421–40; Margaret MacMillan, *Women of the Raj: The Mothers, Wives and Daughters of the British Empire in India* (London: Thames and Hudson, 1988), 125–41; Nupur Chaudhuri, "Memsahibs and Motherhood in Nineteenth-Century India," *Victorian Studies* 31 (1988): 517–35; see Daniel P.S. Goh, "States of Ethnography: Colonialism, Resistance, and Cultural Transcription in Malaya and the Philippines, 1890s–1930s," *Comparative Studies in Society and History* 49, no. 1 (2007): 136; Julian Go, "The Chains of Empire: State Building and 'Political Education' in Puerto Rico and the Philippines," in *The American Colonial State in the Philippines: Global Perspectives*, ed. Julian Go and Anne L. Foster (Durham: Duke University Press, 2003), 182, 205–6; Ann Raffin, *Youth Mobilisation in Vichy Indochina and Its Legacies, 1940–1970* (Lanham: Lexington Books, 2005). See also the forthcoming work by Marie-Paule Ha on Indochina. Thanks are due to Robert Faber of Oxford University Press for drawing this to my attention. Marie-Paule Ha, *French Women and the Empire: The Case of Indochina* (Oxford: Oxford University Press, 2014).

24. See, for example, Durba Ghosh, *Sex and the Family in Colonial India: The Making of Empire* (Cambridge: Cambridge University Press, 2006).

25. Ann L. Stoler, *Carnal Knowledge and Imperial Power: Race and the Intimate in Colonial Rule* (Berkeley: University of California Press, 2002). See especially ch. 5.

26. Elizabeth Buettner, *Empire Families: Britons and Late Imperial India* (Oxford: Oxford University Press, 2004).

27. Ann L. Stoler, "Tense and Tender Ties: The Politics of Comparison in North American History and (Post) Colonial Studies," *Journal of American History* (December 2001): 843.

28. Laura Briggs, *Reproducing Empire: Race, Sex, Science and US Imperialism in Puerto Rico* (Berkeley: University of California Press, 2002).

29. As Elizabeth Buettner puts it with reference to children, "No sooner are they invoked than they are summarily dismissed from the colonial arena altogether and from further analysis." Buettner, *Empire Families*, 7.

30. Ann Laura Stoler, *Race and the Education of Desire: Foucault's History of Sexuality and the Colonial Order of Things* (Durham: Duke University Press, 1995), 137–64.

31. David M. Pomfret, *Young People and the European City: Age Relations in Nottingham and Saint-Etienne* (Aldershot: Ashgate, 2004).

32. John Gillis, *A World of Their Own Making: Myth, Ritual and the Quest for Family Values* (Oxford: Oxford University Press, 1997), 70–72.

33. In 1901 Charles Masterman and others argued that the urban environment had produced a 'new race' of poor. Charles F.G. Masterman, *The Heart of the Empire: Discussions of Problems of Modern City Life in England with an Essay on Imperialism* (London: T. F. Unwin, 1901); George R. Sims, *How the Poor Live* (London: Chatto, 1883). On the 'racialisation' of young working-class metropolitans, see Carolyn Steedman, *Strange Dislocations: Childhood and the Idea of Human Interiority, 1780–1930* (Cambridge: Harvard University Press, 1995), 112–13; Lydia Murdoch, *Imagined Orphans: Poor Families, Child Welfare and Contested Citizenship in London* (New Brunswick: Rutgers University Press, 2006), 25–32.

34. Laura Lee Downs, *Childhood in the Promised Land: Working-class Movements and the Colonies de Vacances in France, 1880–1960* (Durham: Duke University Press, 2002).

35. Raymond F. Betts, *Assimilation and Association in French Colonial Theory, 1890–1914* (New York: Columbia University Press, 1961), 4; Alice Conklin, *A Mission to Civilise: The Republican Idea of Empire in France and West Africa, 1895–1930* (Stanford: Stanford University Press, 1997), 248–49; Daughton, *Empire Divided*, 10–12.

36. Raoul Girardet, *L'idée coloniale en France: De 1871 à 1962* (Paris: Hachette, 1972), 86–90.

37. In an interesting and valuable study ranging in scope from colonial reformatories to boarding schools for aristocratic Indian children, Satadru Sen raises important questions concerning how and with what consequences colonialists exported metropolitan discourses of childhood into empire. Satadru Sen, *Colonial Childhoods: Youth on the Juvenile Periphery* (London: Anthem Press, 2005), 67.

38. 'Vietnam' did not exist as a formal state until 1945, but in this book I adopt the convention of using this to refer to three *pays* of French Indochina: Cochinchina, Annam and Tonkin, the populations of which were mainly Vietnamese.

39. Arif Dirlik, "Rethinking Colonialism: Globalisation, Postcolonialism and the Nation," *Interventions* 4, no. 3 (2002): 441.

40. Ann Laura Stoler and Frederick Cooper, "Between Metropole and Colony: Rethinking a Research Agenda," in *Tensions of Empire: Colonial Cultures in a Bourgeois World*, ed. Frederick Cooper and Ann Laura Stoler (Berkeley: University of California Press, 2007), 1–56.

41. C. A. Bayly, *The Birth of the Modern World, 1780–1914: Global Connections and Comparisons* (Malden: Blackwell, 2004), 470; Tony Ballantyne, *Orientalism and Race: Aryanism in the British Empire* (Basingstoke: Palgrave, 2002), 14; Philippa Levine, *Prostitution, Race, and Politics: Policing Venereal Disease in the British Empire* (London: Routledge, 2003).

42. Ballantyne, *Orientalism*, 13–17; see also Alan Lester, *Imperial Networks: Creating Identities in Nineteenth-Century South Africa and Britain* (London: Routledge, 2001); Gary B. Magee and Andrew S. Thompson, *Empire and Globalisation: Networks of People, Goods and Capital in the British World, c. 1850–1914* (Cambridge: Cambridge University Press, 2010).

43. Micol Seigel, "Beyond Compare: Comparative Method after the Transnational Turn," *Radical History Review* 91 (Winter 2005): 91, 63.

44. David Thelen, "The Nation and Beyond: Transnational Perspectives on United

States History," *Journal of American History* 86 (1999): 965; Patricia Clavin, "Defining Transnationalism," *Contemporary European History* 14, no. 4 (2005): 421–39; Akira Iriye, *Global and Transnational History: The Past, Present, and Future* (New York: Palgrave Pivot, 2012).

45. Sugata Bose, *A Hundred Horizons: The Indian Ocean in the Age of Global Empire* (Cambridge: Harvard University Press, 2006); Thomas R. Metcalf, *Imperial Connections: India in the Indian Ocean Arena, 1860–1920* (Berkeley: University of California Press, 2007); Eric Tagliacozzo, *Secret Trades, Porous Borders: Smuggling and States along a Southeast Asian Frontier, 1865–1915* (New Haven: Yale University Press, 2005), 13–14.

46. Anna Lowenhaupt Tsing, *Friction: An Ethnography of Global Connection* (Princeton: Princeton University Press, 2005).

47. Sara E. Johnson, *The Fear of French Negroes: Transcolonial Collaboration in the Revolutionary Americas* (Berkeley: University of California Press, 2012); Michael S. Dodson and Brian Hatcher, eds., *Transcolonial Modernities in South Asia* (London: Routledge, 2012); Metcalf, *Imperial Connections*.

48. Levine, *Prostitution*; Ross G. Forman, *China and the Victorian Imagination: Empires Entwined* (Cambridge: Cambridge University Press, 2013).

49. For an excellent recent study applying the comparative method to four sites in the British Empire, see Levine, *Prostitution*.

50. Julian Go, *Patterns of Empire: The British and American Empires 1688 to the Present* (Cambridge: Cambridge University Press, 2011), 102.

51. Ibid., 13. Levine, *Prostitution*, 16–18.

52. Heinz-Gerhard Haupt and Jürgen Kocka, "Comparison and Beyond: Traditions, Scope and Perspectives of Comparative History," in *Comparative and Transnational History: Central European Approaches and New Perspectives*, ed. Heinz-Gerhard Haupt and Jürgen Kocka (New York: Berghahn, 2009), 1–33.

53. Nancy Leys Stepan, *Picturing Tropical Nature* (Ithaca: Cornell University Press, 2001).

54. Jürgen Osterhammel, "A 'Transnational' History of Society: Continuity or New Departure," in Haupt and Kocka, *Comparative and Transnational History*, 47.

55. Alys Eve Weinbaum et al., *The Modern Girl around the World: Consumption, Modernity, and Globalisation* (Durham: Duke University Press, 2008).

56. On Asian trade networks, see Wang Gungwu and Anthony Reid, *Community and Nation: Essays on Southeast Asia and the Chinese* (Singapore: Heinemann, 1981); Anthony Reid, *Southeast Asia in the Age of Commerce, 1450–1680* (New Haven: Yale University Press, 1988); Tagliacozzo, *Secret Trades*.

57. Twenty-eight miles long and 79 miles north of the Equator, Singapore joined the Straits Settlements as a free port in 1826 along with Penang (ceded to Britain in 1786) and Malacca (ceded to Britain by Holland in 1824).

58. The tonnage of ships into Singapore harbour increased from 0.6m tons in 1869, to 1.5m tons in 1876. The number of liners arriving in Saigon increased from 251 in 1861, to 403 in 1877. Commercial goods imported and exported from Hong Kong to China trebled from 1890 to 1910, and port traffic in Hong Kong expanded above the level of all other ports in China.

59. By the early twentieth century, the steamers of the Compagnie des Messageries Maritimes ran out of Saigon serving Hải Phòng (which was connected by river to Hanoi), as well as the China coast and Japan. The steamers of the Compagnie de Navigation Tonk-

inoise made the journey from Hong Kong in four days, via Guangzhouwan (Zhanjiang), Hoi Hau and Pak Hoi, and on by river steamer to Hải Phòng and Hanoi.

60. The Eastern Extension Australasia and China Telegraph Co. Limited opened in Singapore in 1870, the year in which Singapore was connected by telegraph to Europe, and telegraph companies soon served other centres, too. The Union Bank of Calcutta opened a branch in Singapore in 1844, followed by Oriental Bank (1846) and Chartered Bank (1859). The Hong Kong and Shanghai Banking Company was set up in Hong Kong in 1864, establishing branches in Singapore in 1877 and Saigon in 1898. The French bank, Comptoir National d'Escompte, was followed by the Banque de l'Indochine, which opened a branch in Saigon in 1875, and in Hong Kong, Hải Phòng, Tourane, Pnom-Penh, Pondichery, Nouméa, Bangkok, Shanghai and Singapore. Dilip K. Basu, ed., *The Rise and Growth of the Colonial Port Cities in Asia* (Center for Southeast Asian Studies, University of California, Berkeley, 1985).

61. On Saigon's role in the rice trade, see Haydon L. Cherry, "Down and Out in Saigon: A Social History of the Poor in a Colonial City, 1860–1940," PhD diss., Yale University, 2011.

62. C. M. Turnbull, *A History of Singapore, 1819–2005* (Kuala Lumpur: Oxford University Press, 1977), 43.

63. Basu, *Colonial Port Cities*, 288; Frank Broeze, ed., *Brides of the Sea: Port Cities in Asia from the 16th–20th Centuries* (Honolulu: University of Hawai'i Press, 1989); Rhoades Murphey, "Traditionalism and Colonialism: Changing Urban Roles in Asia," *Journal of Asian Studies* 29 (1969): 83.

64. J. M. Allinson, "Trade Centres and Routes of the Future in the Far East," *The Straits Chinese Magazine* 7, no. 2 (June 1903): 34.

65. Bayly, *Modern World*, ch. 13.

66. Hong Kong's population grew from 301,967 in 1906, to 456,739 in 1911. Hanoi's population grew from 86,000 in 1913, to just over 100,000 inhabitants by 1924. Singapore's census officials recorded a population of 259,610 by 1911. Saigon's population had reached 250,000 by 1931.

67. Bayly, *Modern World*; James Clifford, *Routes: Travel and Translation in the Late Twentieth Century* (Cambridge: Harvard University Press, 1997).

68. By 1931 in Cochinchina there were four million inhabitants and 15,000 French; André Baudrit, *Guide Historique des rues de Saigon* (Saigon: SILI, 1943), 79–80; Ville de Saigon, *Statistique Municipale: Année 1907* (Saigon: F. H. Schneider, 1908), 3.

69. Dramatic fluctuations in the number of migrants render census data illustrative at best. Philippe Papin, *Histoire de Hanoi* (Paris: Fayard, 2001), 225.

70. Of those surveyed, 99.94% were natives of Asia, and this compared with 94.39% in Africa, 95.69% in the West Indies and 3% in Canada and Australasia. J. A. Baines, "A Census of the Empire," *Journal of the Royal Statistical Society* 66, no. 1 (1903): 36.

71. In 1931, there were still only 8,147 European residents of a total of 567,453. J. E. Nathan, *The Census of British Malaya* (London: Waterlow & Sons, 1922), 148; Vlieland, *Report*, 120.

72. As a percentage of the total population, the white population in Hong Kong (at 1.16%) was actually larger than in other parts of Asia, such as India (0.057%), Ceylon (0.18%) or the Straits Settlements (0.88). In this Crown Colony, official statistics in 1899 recorded the population as 10,000 Europeans (of whom 4,000 were 'Portuguese'), while 280,000 were Chinese. Baines, "Census of Empire," 37.

73. Hanoi had 150 officers and 5,500 troops in residence in July 1884, and around 1,000 civilians by 1901. In 1913 there were 4,500 resident Europeans, including civilians and military, but by 1924 this number had risen to 6,121 Europeans, which was roughly the same number as in Singapore, a city whose total population was four times larger. In 1921 10% of the population of the older, and more compact, centre of Saigon was European, compared with 5% in Hanoi.

74. For Anthony D. King, consciousness of race and conflict is "perhaps the major urban manifestation of colonialism." Anthony D. King, "Colonial Cities: Global Pivots of Change," in *Colonial Cities: Essays on Urbanism in a Colonial Context*, ed. Robert Ross and Gerard J. Telkamp (Dordrecht: Martinus Nijhoff, 1985), 12–15.

75. A. J. Christopher, *The British Empire at Its Zenith* (London: Croom Helm, 1988), 22.

76. Charles Salmon and Robert Halliburton, *The Crown Colonies of Great Britain: An Inquiry into Their Social Condition and Methods of Administration* (London: Cassell & Co., 1885).

77. Robert Bickers, "Shanghailanders and Others: British Communities in China, 1843–1957," in *Settlers and Expatriates: Britons over the Seas*, ed. Robert Bickers (Oxford: Oxford University Press, 2010), 269–301.

78. John Darwin, *Unfinished Empire: The Global Expansion of Empire* (London: Allen Lane, 2012), 292.

79. John Darwin, "Afterword: A Colonial World," in *New Frontiers: Imperialism's New Communities in East Asia, 1842–1953*, ed. Robert Bickers and Christian Henriot (Manchester: Manchester University Press, 2000), 250.

CHAPTER 2

1. Major Henry Knollys, *English Life in China* (London: Smith, Elder and Co., 1885), 28.

2. Nancy Leys Stepan, *Picturing Tropical Nature* (Ithaca: Cornell University Press, 2001), 53.

3. David Arnold, *The Problem of Nature: Environment, Culture and European Expansion* (Oxford: Basil Blackwell, 1996); Philip D. Curtin, *Death by Migration: Europe's Encounter with the Tropical World in the Nineteenth Century* (Cambridge: Cambridge University Press, 1989).

4. William Z. Ripley summarised scientific opinion on acclimatisation, foregrounding the orthodox view that the colonisation of the tropics by the white race was impossible. William Z. Ripley, *The Races of Europe: A Sociological Study* (London: Kegan Paul, Trench, Trubner & Co., 1899), 565–89.

5. "Report on the Census of the Colony for 1897," *Sessional Papers*, 20 June 1897, 474; "Report on the Census of the Colony for 1906," *The Hongkong Government Gazette (Supplement)*, 10 May 1907, 233.

6. Cambridge University Library, Royal Commonwealth Society Collection (hereafter CUL), Letters of Captain Maurice A. Cameron, RCMS 103/4/37, Maurice A. Cameron, 20 September 1890; *Report on the Census of the Straits Settlements Taken on 10th March 1911* (Singapore: Government Printing Office, 1911), 15.

7. A. Bouinais and A. Paulus, *L'Indochine française contemporaine: Tonkin, Annam* (Paris: Challamel, 1885), 294; *Annuaire de l'Indo-Chine Française pour l'année 1897, première partie, Cochinchine* (Saigon: Imprimerie Coloniale, 1897), 564.

8. Grace Corneau, *La Femme aux colonies* (Paris: Librairie Nilsson, 1900), 32; Eugène Jung, *La Vie européenne au Tonkin* (Paris: Flammarion, 1901), 103.

9. Claudius Madrolle, *Tonkin du Sud, Hanoï: Les Annamites, Hanoï, pays de So'n-tâi, pays de So'n-nam* (Paris: Comité de l'Asie française, 1907), 10.

10. James Johnson, *The Influence of Tropical Climates, More Especially the Climate of India on European Constitutions* (London: J. J. Stockdale, 1813); James Annesley, *Sketches of the Most Prevalent Diseases of India Comprising a Treatise on the Epidemic Cholera of the East, etc.* (London: T & G Underwood, 1825). David Arnold, *Colonizing the Body: State Medicine and Epidemic Disease in Nineteenth-Century India* (Berkeley: University of California Press, 1993), 24–26.

11. Joseph Ewart, "Causes of the Excessive Mortality among the Women and Children of the European Soldiers Serving in India," *Transactions of the Epidemiological Society of London* 2 (1882–83): 46–67; Mark Harrison, *Climates and Constitutions: Health, Race, Environment and British Imperialism in India* (Oxford: Oxford University Press, 1999), 215–19.

12. Sir W. J. Moore, *The Constitutional Requirements for Tropical Climates and Observations on the Sequel of Disease Contracted in India* (London: Churchill, 1890), 4, 19, 55. In 1851 the *Calcutta Review* published a study of soldiers' children, which found that 27 to 33% died in the first year of life, compared with only 15% in England. Edward John Tilt, *Health in India for British Women and on the Prevention of Disease in Tropical Climates*, 4th ed. (London: Churchill, 1875), 101–5; Joseph S. Ewart, "The Colonisation of the Sub-Himalayas and Neilgherries: With Remarks on the Management of European Children in India," *Transactions of the Epidemiological Society of London* 3 (1883–84): 96, 116; Sir William Moore, "Is the Colonisation of Tropical Africa by Europeans Possible?" *Transactions of the Epidemiological Society of London* 10 (1890–91): 34; Harrison, *Climates*, 103, 143.

13. Lydia Murdoch, "Suppressed Grief: Mourning the Death of British Children and the Memory of the 1857 Rebellion," *Journal of British Studies* 51, no. 2 (April 2012): 364–92.

14. Dane Kennedy, *The Magic Mountains: Hill Stations and the British Raj* (Berkeley: University of California Press, 1996), 32–33.

15. Lydia Murdoch, *Imagined Orphans: Poor Families, Child Welfare and Contested Citizenship in London* (New Brunswick: Rutgers University Press, 2006).

16. On the acts, see Philippa Levine, *Prostitution, Race, and Politics: Policing Venereal Disease in the British Empire* (London: Routledge, 2003).

17. 'Public Servant,' "Is Empire Consistent with Morality?" *Pall Mall Gazette*, 19 May 1887, 2.

18. "Address of Governor Sir John Pope Hennessy, K.C.M.G., on the Census Returns and the Progress of the Colony," *Papers Laid Before the Legislative Council of Hongkong* (Hong Kong: Government Printers, 1881), 1.

19. S.T.L., *The Jubilee of Shanghai, 1843–1893: Shanghai, Past and Present, and a Full Account of the Proceedings on the 17th and 18th Nov. 1893* (Shanghai: North China Herald, 1893), 4.

20. D. J. Galloway, "The Care of Children in the Tropics," *Straits Chinese Magazine* 3, no. 10 (June 1899): 47.

21. Reverend E. J. Hardy, *Marriage: Being a Lecture Delivered at Hongkong on 20th March 1903* (Hongkong: W. Brewer & Co., 1903), 11.

22. Nicholas Clifford, *Spoilt Children of Empire: Westerners in Shanghai and the Chinese Revolution of the 1920s* (Hanover: University Press of New England, 1991).

23. This was the subject of Cantlie's lecture "Has the Anglo-Saxon Race Found a

Home?" delivered on 14 January 1889. "Hongkong Literary Society," *Overland Mail*, 16 January 1889.

24. R. S. Edmond, "Returning Fears: Tropical Disease and the Metropolis," in *Tropical Visions in an Age of Empire*, ed. Felix Driver and Luciana Martins (Chicago: University of Chicago Press, 2005), 189–91.

25. Hugh Cunningham, *Children and Childhood in Western Society since 1500* (London: Longman, 1995), 134–59.

26. Some families resided in the Portuguese colony of Macau instead. On the family under the Canton System, see, for example, William T. Rowe, *China's Last Empire: The Great Qing* (Boston: Harvard University Press, 2009), 142.

27. D. E. Mungello, *Drowning Girls in China: Female Infanticide since 1650* (Lanham: Rowman & Littlefield, 2008), 70–71.

28. G. S. Hall, *Adolescence: Its Psychology and Its Relations to Physiology, Anthropology, Sociology, Sex, Crime, Religion and Education* (New York: W. D. Appleton and Co., 1904).

29. This orthodoxy would endure (though not unchallenged) across the period. In 1933 the medical expert Kenneth Black could write, in relation to British Malaya, "the majority of the local inhabitants reach old age when Europeans have barely attained middle age." Kenneth Black, "Heath and Climate—With Special Reference to Malaya," *British Malaya* (March 1933): 253.

30. Wellcome Library, London (hereafter WL), MS. 1499 James Cantlie, "Enquiry into the Life History of Eurasians" nd c. 1889, 24.

31. Henrika Kuklick, *The Savage Within: The Social History of British Anthropology, 1885–1945* (Cambridge: Cambridge University Press, 1991), 86; Bruce Haley, *The Healthy Body and Victorian Culture* (Cambridge: Harvard University Press, 1978), 92.

32. Sir James Emerson Tennant, quoted in James Hunt, "On Ethno-Climatology; or the Acclimatization of Man," *Transactions of the Ethnological Society of London* (1863): 70.

33. Alexander Rattray, "On Some of the More Important Physiological Changes Induced in the Human Economy by Change of Climate, as from Temperate to Tropical and the Reverse," *Proceedings of the Royal Society of London* 18 (1869): 513–29 and 19 (1870–71): 295–316. Rattray's work is discussed in Sir Aldo Castellani, *Climate and Acclimatization: Some Notes and Observations* (London: John Bale, Sons & Danielsson, 1931), 61–62.

34. For Cantlie, childhood lasted until age seven to nine, after which the individual experienced the "adolescent years" (age nine to fourteen). "Puberty with its attendant changes and developments" occupied the years fourteen to twenty-one. WL MS.1471 Sir James Cantlie, "Exercise in Warm Climates," 1890, 21.

35. Galloway, "Care," 55.

36. "Children in Singapore," *Straits Times*, 11 June 1914, 10.

37. Galloway, "Care," 55.

38. Ibid.

39. Rhodes House Library, Oxford (hereafter RHL), MS. Nathan 344 Langton to Nathan, 4 June 1907.

40. RHL 162 MS. Nathan 346–47 Berkeley to Nathan, 11 October 1908.

41. RHL 162 MS. Nathan 346–47 Hastings to Nathan, 25 November 1907; RHL 162 MS. Nathan 346–47 Hastings to Nathan, 2 January 1911; RHL 162 MS. Nathan 346–47 Hastings to Nathan, 21 January 1911.

42. Phoebe Whitworth, *View from the Peak: An Autobiography* (Cambridge: T. G. Whitworth, 2001), 72.

43. "Children in Singapore," 10.
44. J. D. Lloyd, "Report on the Census of the Colony for 1921," *Hong Kong Sessional Papers*, 10 November 1921, 157.
45. Peggy Beard, quoted in Paul Gillingham, *At the Peak: Hong Kong between the Wars* (Hong Kong: Macmillan, 1981), 127.
46. C. A. Middleton Smith, *The British in China and Far Eastern Trade* (London: Constable, 1920), v.
47. "Children in Singapore," 10.
48. Paul d'Enjoy, *La Santé aux colonies* (Paris: Société d'Editions Scientifiques, 1901), 142.
49. Eric T. Jennings, *Curing the Colonizers: Hydrotherapy, Climatology, and French Colonial Spas* (Durham: Duke University Press, 2006); Eric T. Jennings, *Imperial Heights: Dalat and the Making and Undoing of French Indochina* (Berkeley: University of California Press, 2012), 6–7, 20. See also Michael A. Osborne, "Acclimatizing the World: A History of the Paradigmatic Colonial Science," *Osiris* 2nd series, 15, *Nature and Empire: Science and the Colonial Enterprise* (2000): 140.
50. Arthur Bordier, *La Géographie médicale* (Paris: Reinwald, 1884); H.-C. Lombard, *Atlas de la distribution géographique des maladies dans leurs rapports avec les climats* (Paris: J. B. Baillère et fils, 1880).
51. Joseph Onéisme Orgeas, *La Pathologie des races humaines et le problème de la colonisation: Étude anthropologique et économique faite à la Guyane française* (Paris: Doin, 1886); Alfred Jousset, *Traité de l'acclimatement et de l'acclimatation* (Paris: Doin, 1884).
52. Auguste Danguy des Déserts, *Considérations sur l'hygiène de l'européen en Cochinchine* (Paris: A. Parent Imprimeur, 1876); Léon Villedary, *Guide sanitaire des troupes et du colon aux colonies: Hygiène coloniale; prophylaxie et traitement des principales maladies des pays chauds* (Paris: Société d'Editions Scientifiques, 1893).
53. Daniel Pick, *Faces of Degeneration: A European Disorder, c. 1848–1918* (Cambridge: Cambridge University Press, 1989); Robert Nye, *Crime, Madness and Politics in Modern France: The Medical Concept of National Decline* (Princeton: Princeton University Press, 1984), 155–61.
54. Anson Rabinbach, *The Human Motor: Energy, Fatigue, and the Origins of Modernity* (New York: Basic Books, 1990), 147.
55. Marie-Paule Ha, "'La Femme française aux colonies': Promoting Colonial Female Emigration at the Turn of the Century," *French Colonial History* 6 (2005): 205–24.
56. Jean-Baptiste Piolet, *La France hors de France: Notre emigration, sa nécessité, ses conditions* (Paris: F. Alcan, 1900), 173.
57. "Nouvelles Coloniales," *Le Fanion: Organe de l'œuvre d'Orgeville et des fondations rattachées—mensuel, indépendant, non politique* 3 (May 1905): 3. Meanwhile, for the radical Deputy of Puy-de-Dôme, Joseph Python, Tonkin had "the climate of Gascony." Jean Ajalbert, *Les Nuages sur l'Indochine* (Paris: Editions Louis-Michaud, 1912), 5.
58. Joseph Chailley-Bert, "Discours de M. Chailley-Bert," in Union Coloniale Française, *L'Emigration des femmes aux colonies: Conférence de 12 janvier 1897* (Paris: Armand Colin, 1897), 55; Marie-Paule Ha, "Engendering French Colonial History: The Case of Indochina," *Historical Reflections/Reflexions Historiques* 25, no. 1 (1999): 105.
59. Jules Gervais-Courtellemont, *Empire Colonial de la France: L'Indochine. Cochinchine, Cambodge, Laos, Annam, Tonkin* (Paris: Librairie de Paris Firmin-Didot, 1901), 160.
60. Michael A. Osborne, *Nature, the Exotic, and the Science of French Colonialism*

(Bloomington: Indiana University Press, 1994), 43, 49–51, 62, 176; Warwick Anderson, "Climates of Opinion: Acclimatisation in Nineteenth-Century France and England," *Victorian Studies* 35 (Winter 1992): 152.

61. Jules Harmand, *Domination et colonisation* (Paris: Flammarion, 1910), 132–33. On Perrier, see Osborne, *Nature*, 56; William H. Schneider, *Quality and Quantity: The Quest for Biological Regeneration in Twentieth-Century France* (Cambridge: Cambridge University Press, 1990), 28–32, 100–106.

62. Cited in Chailley-Bert, "Discours," 49.

63. Jean-Marie de Lanessan, the former naval doctor, who became the fourth governor general of Indochina in 1891, and a pro-transformist (and solidarist), was another enthusiast for acclimatisation.

64. A. Bouinais and A. Paulus, *L'Indo-Chine française contemporaine: Cambodge, Tonkin, Annam* (Paris: Challamel Aîné, 1885), 283.

65. Philippe M.F. Peycam, *The Birth of Vietnamese Political Journalism: Saigon 1916–1930* (New York: Columbia University Press, 2012), 38.

66. Philippe Papin, *Histoire de Hanoi* (Paris: Fayard, 2001), 238.

67. R. Chauvelot, *En Indochine* (Grenoble: Rey, 1931), 91.

68. Paul Doumer, *Situation de l'Indochine (1897–1901): Rapport par M. Paul Doumer, Gouverneur Général* (Hanoi: F.-H. Schneider, 1902), 60.

69. Archives Nationales d'Outre Mer, Aix-en-Provence (hereafter ANOM), Gouvernement Général de l'Indochine (GGI) C 7770 Doumer to Résidents Supérieur of Tonkin, Annam, Cambodge and Laos, 29 September 1901.

70. "La Capitale du Tonkin—Notes sur Hanoi," *La Revue Indochinoise Illustrée* (1894).

71. Louis Salaün, *L'Indochine* (Paris: Imprimerie Nationale, 1903), 389–90.

72. *Congaï* was a term meaning 'little girl' that was used to describe both adult female domestic workers who laboured within French homes and those who became French men's concubines and mistresses. Jean Star, *Tonkinades* (Paris: Calman-Lévy, 1902), 69.

73. "Tous célibataires, vivent les congaïs," *Avenir du Tonkin*, 23 January 1907, 1.

74. Charles Grall, *Hygiène Colonial appliquée: Hygiène de l'Indochine* (Paris: J.-B. Baillière et Fils, 1908), 65.

75. Corneau, *Femme*, 32.

76. Quoted in Bouinais, *L'Indo-chine contemporaine*, 229.

77. Jacques Chauvin, *Paul Doumer: Le Président assassiné* (Paris: Panthéon, 1994), 21, 45.

78. "Tous célibataires," 1.

79. Gustave Reynaud, *Hygiène des colons* (Paris: Librairie J.-B. Baillère et Fils, 1903), 10.

80. Grall, *Hygiène*, 479. Another expert in this field, Dr. Gustave Reynaud, attributed the health of European children in the Netherlands Indies to the higher social standard of the population. Reynaud, *Hygiène des colons*, 10.

81. E. Postal, "Veuves de fonctionnaires," *Satires Coloniales* (6 December 1902): 6.

82. E. Postal, "Protection et relèvement," *Satires Coloniales* (23 August 1902): 4.

83. Galloway, "Care," 51.

84. Grall, *Hygiène*, 78.

85. Anderson, "Climates of Opinion," 180; Osborne, *Nature*, 63.

86. It is perhaps significant that the children were "playing" and "wandering" in a neighbourhood where a new jail and quarters for prison warders had been erected. "European Children at Pearl's Hill," *Straits Times Weekly Issue*, 3 September 1884, 15.

87. The census of 1891 recorded 226 children under age five, and 158 children between five and ten, with another 115 children between ten and fifteen in Singapore, a total of 499. E. M. Merewether, *Report on the Census of the Straits Settlements Taken on the 5th April, 1891* (Singapore: Government Printing Press, 1892), 89; Galloway, "Care," 54.

88. In 1893 one newspaper observed: "The poor whites in the east may now be counted by hundreds of thousands. They are scattered all through the Indian Empire and the Eastern Colonies. Year by year their position grows more intolerable as it cannot be denied that they are in a state of poverty." "The Poor Whites," *Daily Advertiser*, 22 July 1893, 2.

89. When the journal *The Planter* reflected back on the history of this period from the vantage point of 1936, it described 'creepers' in pejorative racialised terms as "Europeans or pseudo-Europeans" and as a "dilution," much of which "was very dirty fluid indeed." "The Planting Profession," *The Planter* (January 1936), 9.

90. Galloway, "Care," 54.

91. R.S., "Children in Singapore," *Straits Times*, 11 June 1914, 10.

92. Cambridge University Library, Royal Commonwealth Society Collection (hereafter CUL), Personal and Family Papers of Lillian Newton, RCMS 108/5/1, Lillian Newton, "More Exquisite When Past."

93. Christine Doran, "Oddly Hybrid: Childbearing and Childrearing Practices in Colonial Penang, 1850–1875," *Women's History Review* 6 (1997): 35–36.

94. The Legislative Council of the Straits Settlements passed legislation in 1905 regulating local milk vendors. Chor Boon Goh, *Technology and Entrepôt Colonialism in Singapore, 1819–1940* (Singapore: Institute of Southeast Asian Studies, 2013), 172–73, 177.

95. Quoted in Philip H. Manson-Bahr and A. Alcock, *The Life and Work of Sir Patrick Manson* (London: Cassell and Company, 1927), 83; John Stuart Thomson, *The Chinese* (London: T. Werner Laurie, 1909), 53.

96. By 1925 the farm estate included 300 acres of land in the Pokfulam district with room for one thousand cattle. Rev. E. J. Hardy, *John Chinaman at Home: Sketches of Men, Manners and Things in China* (London: T. Fisher Unwin, 1905), 28.

97. Kate Platt, *The Home and Health in India and Tropical Colonies* (London: Baillière, Tindall and Cox, 1923), 63; Arnold, *Colonising the Body*, 35–36. The same point is made in Harrison, *Climates and Constitutions*, 204.

98. Lady Bella Sidney Woolf, *Chips of China* (Hong Kong: Kelly & Walsh, 1930), 39.

99. According to Lillian Newton, during 'at homes' in Singapore just after the turn of the century, women wore white straw boaters, as did men (though they also wore panama hats). 'Calling' in Singapore was not considered as formal as in Bombay, precisely because topees and top hats were not required. CUL RCMS 108/2/1 Newton, "More Exquisite When Past." In Saigon by the early 1930s the woman spotted wearing a casque was considered a risible sight. This headgear revealed its wearer as a 'new arrival' ("madame neuf … madame bateau") and marked her out as a target for harassment. Christiane Fournier, *Perspectives Occidentales sur l'Indochine* (Saigon: Nouvelle Revue Indochinoise, 1935), 97.

100. Georges Félix Treille, *Principes d'hygiène coloniale* (Paris: Georges Carré et C. Naud, 1899), 126.

101. "L'Hygiène familiale à la colonie," *L'Opinion*, 3 January 1921, 1; *Guide du français arrivant en Indochine* (Hanoi: Taupin, 1935), 29.

102. Grall, *Hygiène*, 83.

103. George D. Sussmann, "The Wet-nursing Business in Nineteenth-Century France," *French Historical Studies* 9, no. 2 (Autumn 1975): 327–28.

104. Grall, *Hygiène*, 65.
105. Grall warned that bottle feeding would produce "flabby" children. Ibid., 65, 83.
106. William H. Schneider, *Quality and Quantity: The Quest for Biological Regeneration in Twentieth-Century France* (Cambridge: Cambridge University Press, 1990), 64. The birth rate had fallen earlier and more rapidly in France than in any other Western European country. Deborah Dwork, *War Is Good for Babies and Other Young Children: A History of the Infant and Child Welfare Movement in England, 1898–1918* (London: Tavistock, 1987), 94.
107. Isabella L. Bird, *The Golden Chersonese and the Way Thither* (London: John Murray, 1883), 105.
108. The Hongkong Nursing Institution, Established 1901, Patroness Lady Blake, *Annual Report* 1902 (Hongkong: Guedes & Company, 1903).
109. National Archives, London, Public Record Office (hereafter PRO), CO129/293 Sub-enclosure to letter, Blake, 6 September 1899; PRO CO129/299 Gascoigne to Blake, 4 May 1900.
110. Galloway, "Care," 55.
111. Corneau, *Femme*, 34.
112. Jean Ajalbert, *Les Nuages sur l'Indochine* (Paris: Editions Louis-Michaud, 1912), 8. It is not entirely clear whom Ajalbert is referring to here. It might have been Paul Bert (but he was resident general rather than governor general).
113. Borel had five children, four girls and one boy. He was evidently referring to Mme Millet-Robinet and Docteur Emile Allix, *Le Livre des jeunes mères: La nourrice et le nourrisson* (Paris: Librairie Agricole de la Maison Rustique, 1884); Marius Borel, *Souvenirs d'un vieux colonialiste* (Six-Fours: Compte d'Auteur, 1963), 180–81.
114. Grall, *Hygiène*, 65. On the Assistance Médicale Indigène, see Laurence Monnais-Rousselot, *Médecine et colonisation: L'Aventure indochinoise 1860–1939* (Paris: CRNS editions, 1999).
115. Vietnamese National Archives Centre I, Hanoi (hereafter VNNA1), Mairie de Hanoi (MHN) L4 004506, Delsalle, arrêté, 2 January 1942.
116. Edmond Nordemann, "Connaissances nécessaires aux personnes appelées à faire leur carrière en Indo-chine," in *Conférences publiques sur l'Indochine faites à l'école Coloniale pendant l'année 1909–1910* (Paris: Imprimerie Chaix, 1910), 113.
117. Dr. Gustave Reynaud, "Petit mauel d'hygiène des colons," in *Union Coloniale Française, Preparation aux carrières coloniales, conférences faites, par MM. Le Myre de Vilers, Dr. Treille, L. Simon, E. Fallot, J-B. Malon, Paris, L. Fontaine, Maurice Courant, Gérome, André Liesse, 1901–1902* (Paris: Augustin Challamel, 1904), 419; Reynaud, *Hygiène des colons*, 10; Alexandre M. Kermorgant, *Hygiène Colonial* (Paris: Masson et Cie, 1911), 17.
118. To this end, the Roussel Law of 1874 regulated wet nursing.
119. As an article in *British Malaya* put it, even in the interwar years fathers "seldom give the time to consider seriously such matters." "A Message to the Mothers of Malaya," *British Malaya* (December 1929): 257.
120. Grall, for example, addressed himself to 'commanders of colonial troops' and 'fathers.' Many of those who stayed on had originally visited Indochina as serving members of the armed forces. Grall, *Hygiène*, 7.
121. Thérèse de Hargues, *Anecdotes d'une roule-ta-bosse* (Paris: La Pensée Universelle, 1992), 46–47.
122. David Livingstone, "Human Acclimatisation: Perspectives on a Contested Field

of Inquiry in Science, Medicine and Geography," *History of Science* 25 (1987): 359–94; Osborne, *Nature*, 89.

123. Kermorgant, *Hygiène coloniale*, 9; Alexandre M. Kermorgant, "Sanatoria et camps de dissémination de nos colonies," *Annales d'Hygiène et de Médecine Coloniales* 12, no. 3 (July–September 1899): 345.

124. Henriette Célarié, *Promenades en Indochine* (Paris: Baudinière, 1937), 194.

125. Médecin General Passa, "L'Enfant européen dans la France d'outre-mer tropicale: Sa protection sanitaire," *Revue Médico-Sociale et de Protection de l'Enfance* 1, no. 6 (1938): 28, 40; VNNA1 MHN L8 2701 Virgitti to Thiroux, 3 September 1937.

CHAPTER 3

1. Major Henry Knollys, *English Life in China* (London: Smith, Elder and Co., 1885), 28.

2. "The Housekeeper's Bazaar and Washing Book," *Straits Times*, 4 July 1899; Winifred A. Wood, *A Brief History of Hong Kong* (Hong Kong: South China Morning Post, 1940), 228–29.

3. Phoebe Whitworth, *View from the Peak: An Autobiography* (Cambridge: T. G. Whitworth, 2001), 10.

4. R.S., "Children in Singapore," *Straits Times*, 11 June 1914, 10.

5. Geoffrey Barnes, author of a memoir describing childhood in British Malaya, was friends with one Margaret Willan whose father worked for HSBC. He recalled, "Margaret had the distinction of having an English nanny (whom we naturally called Nanny) instead of an amah." Geoffrey Barnes, *Mostly Memories: Packing and Farewells* (Royston: Mulu, 1999), 15.

6. Isabella L. Bird, *The Golden Chersonese and the Way Thither* (London: John Murray, 1883), 116; "Census Report, 1891," *Sessional Papers*, 15 August 1891, 377.

7. In 1911 there were 4,515 Chinese women listed as 'Servants' in Hong Kong and 5,716 male personal servants. In 1931, 32,579 Chinese men and 26,590 women were recorded as being in "private domestic service." "Report on the Census of the Colony for 1911," *Sessional Papers*, 23 November 1911, 49–50; "Report on the Census of the Colony of Hong Kong," *Sessional Papers*, 12 February 1931, 143–45.

8. Cambridge University Library, Royal Commonwealth Society Collection (hereafter CUL), Personal and Family Papers of Lillian Newton, RCMS 108/2/1 Lillian Newton, "More Exquisite When Past." The Malayan newspaper *The Planter* continued to debate the relative merits of domestic servants within these two categories into the early 1920s. Kate Platt, who authored *The Home and Health in India and Tropical Colonies*, advised, "The best servants in the Far East are the Chinese. They are capable, honest, and fairly clean." Kate Platt, *The Home and Health in India and Tropical Colonies* (London: Baillière, Tindall and Cox, 1923), 37–38.

9. Edwin Ride, *I Dips Me Lid: Diplomatic Memoirs* (Queensland: E. Ride, 1991), 3.

10. Kenneth Gaw, *Superior Servants: The Legendary Cantonese Amahs of the Far East* (Singapore: Oxford University Press, 1988), 118.

11. Caricatures of white women proliferated in writings about colonial India; see Edward Ingram, *Empire-building and Empire Builders: Twelve Studies* (London: Routledge, 1995), 194–204.

12. 'Veronica,' *The Islanders of Hong Kong* (Hong Kong: China Mail Co., 1907), 83.

13. Allister Macmillan, *Seaports of the Far East: Historical and Descriptive, Commer-*

cial and Industrial, Facts, Figures and Resources (London: W. H. & L. Collingridge, 1923), 340.

14. Ride, *I Dips*, 4.

15. For Newton and her friends, Malay was a common language before the First World War. P. S. Cannon, "The 'Pidgin English' of the China Coast," *Journal of the Army Educational Corps* 13, no. 4 (October 1936): 138.

16. Barnes, *Mostly*, 15.

17. "Malayan Types," *The Planter*, March 1923, 509.

18. Far Eastern Association of Tropical Medicine, *Second Biennial Congress, Hongkong January 20th to January 27th 1912, Programme and Guide to Hongkong*, (Hong Kong: Noronha & Co., 1912), 26.

19. 'Free Lance,' "The Ayah," *Singapore Free Press and Mercantile Advertiser*, 20 February 1911, 1.

20. Mrs. Howell's 'old amah' spoke pidgin English. E. F. Howell, *Malayan Turnovers* (Singapore: Kelly & Walsh, 1928), 19. According to Roland Braddell, in filling the Singapore census, "old amah," who had "long weathered fifty," would admit only to being age thirty-two. Roland Braddell, *The Lights of Singapore* (London: Methuen & Co., 1934), 40.

21. Janice E. Stockard, *Daughters of the Canton Delta: Marriage Patterns and Economic Strategies in South China, 1860–1930* (Hong Kong: Hong Kong University Press, 1989).

22. *Cheh* was used as an honorific term for even younger amahs. Gaw, *Superior Servants*, 93.

23. The 1891 census of Hong Kong recorded 125 boys and 45 girls "in the employ of Europeans" (though later surveys did not make distinctions of age among domestic servants). By contrast, in 1921 when *mui tsai* were enumerated in census data, some 5,959 were judged to be under age fourteen. In this year, census officials noted that while the taking of child servants was formerly "common" among Portuguese residents, it was no longer. "Report on the Census of the Colony for 1921," *Sessional Papers*, 15 December 1921, 165; "Census Report, 1891," *Sessional Papers*, 17 August 1891, 377.

24. Kenneth Gaw describes the Ongs, a Straits Chinese family in Singapore, specifically hiring Wan Yong Gui, a younger baby amah, with the intention that she might play with their son. Gaw, *Superior Servants*, 119; Lucy Lum, *The Thorn of Lion City: A Memoir* (New York: Public Affairs, 2007).

25. Ronald Gower, *My Reminiscences* (London: Kegan Paul, Trench & Co., 1883), 215; Macmillan, *Seaports*, 340; Gaw, *Superior Servants*, 119; Christopher Munn, "Hong Kong, 1841–1870: All the Servants in Prison and Nobody to Take Care of the House," in *Masters, Servants and Magistrates in Britain and the Empire, 1562–1955*, ed. Douglas Hay and Paul Craven (Chapel Hill: University of North Carolina Press, 2004), 377.

26. Rhodes House Library, Oxford (hereafter RHL), MS. Nathan 343 Baar to Nathan, 15 December 1906.

27. Alfred H. Northcliffe, *My Journey around the World, 16 July 1921–25 February 1922* (London: Lane, 1923), 159.

28. C. K. Lowrie, "The Transcolonial Politics of Chinese Domestic Mastery in Singapore and Darwin, 1910s–1930s," *Journal of Colonialism and Colonial History* 12, no. 3 (2011): 1–24; C. K. Lowrie, "White 'Men' and Their Chinese 'Boys': Sexuality, Masculinity and Colonial Power in Singapore and Darwin, 1880s–1930s," *History Australia* 10, no. 1 (2013): 35–57.

29. Christine B.N. Chin, *In Service and Servitude: Foreign Female Domestic Workers and the Malaysian 'Modernity' Project* (New York: Columbia University Press, 1998), 76.

30. 'Veronica,' *Islanders*, 85.
31. Ride, *I Dips*, 2; R.S., "Children."
32. Blake Bromley, *Opams and Bundu Beetles* (Edinburgh: Pentland Press, 2000), 17.
33. On the availability of similar strategies of 'racial masquerade' to young, white American girls, see Alys Eve Weinbaum, "Racial Masquerade: Consumption and Contestation of American Modernity," in Alys Eve Weinbaum et. al., *The Modern Girl around the World: Consumption, Modernity and Globalization* (Durham: Duke University Press, 2008), 120–46.
34. 'Free Lance,' "Ayah," 1.
35. R.S., "Children."
36. Northcliffe, *My Journey around the World*, 161.
37. Isabelle Massieu, *Comment j'ai parcouru l'Indochine* (Paris: Plon, 1901), 355.
38. 'Boys' could earn up to two piasters per day. L. Péralle, "Boys et coolies à Saigon," in *Bulletin de la Société des études indochinoises, 1896* (Saigon: Imprimerie Commerciale Rey, Curiol & Cie, 1897), 49.
39. 'Annamite' was the term used most commonly by the French to identify Vietnamese, distinguishing them from Cambodians, Laotians and other racial and ethnic groupings. Northcliffe, *My Journey*, 181.
40. "Strike Crisis: More Hotel Boys Out," *China Mail*, 1 March 1922, 4.
41. M. Dupla, "A Propos d'enseignement," in *Bulletin de la Société des études indochinoises, 1896* (Saigon: Imprimerie Commerciale Rey, Curiol & Cie, 1897), 17.
42. Michel My, *Le Tonkin pittoresque, souvenirs et impressions de voyage (1921–2)* (Saigon: J. Viêt, 1925), 129.
43. *Guide du français arrivant en Indochine* (Hanoi: Taupin, 1925), 29.
44. Christiane Fournier, *Bébé colonial: Une Enfance au Tonkin* (Paris: Editions Berger-Levrault, 1935), 96; Antoine Jay and Madeleine Jay, *Notre Indochine, 1936–1947* (Charenton: Les Presses de Valmy, 1995), 168.
45. Arthur Delteil, *Un An de séjour en Cochinchine: Guide du voyageur à Saigon* (Paris: Challamel Ainé, Editeur, 1887), 49.
46. Jean-Baptiste Piolet, *La France hors de France: Notre emigration, sa nécessité, ses conditions* (Paris: F. Alcan, 1900), 436.
47. Marius Borel, *Souvenirs d'un vieux colonialiste* (Six-Fours: Compte d'Auteur, 1963), 212–13. Borel's family returned to France in 1924, at which time his eldest children (his daughters Germaine and Marie-Louise) were in their early teens.
48. Henriette Célarié, *Promenades en Indochine* (Paris: Baudinière, 1937), 174.
49. Jean Star, *Tonkinades* (Paris: Calman-Lévy, 1902), 250.
50. Delteil, *Un An de séjour*, 49.
51. Star, *Tonkinades*, 250.
52. Charlotte Rouyer, *Femmes d'outre mer* (Saigon: Imprimerie de l'Union, 1941), 144.
53. De Hargues, who was age ten in 1935, had two sisters, Claude (age eleven) and Yvonne (six), and two brothers, Jean (ten) and Yves (three). Thérèse de Hargues, *Anecdotes d'une roule-ta-bosse* (Paris: La Pensée Universelle, 1992), 77.
54. Françoise Autret, *Pousse de Bambou* (Paris: Les Editions la Bruyère, 1999), 22.
55. Rosalia Baena, "Of Missess and Tuan Kechils: Colonial Childhood Memoirs as Cultural Mediation in British Malaya," *ARIEL* 39, no. 1 (January 2008): 89–112.
56. Elizabeth Buettner, *Empire Families: Britons and Late Imperial India* (Oxford: Oxford University Press, 2004), 269; Gillian Whitlock, *The Intimate Empire: Reading Women's Autobiography* (London: Cassell, 2000), 203–4.

57. Association pour l'Autobiographie et le Patrimoine Autobiographique, Amberieu-en-Bugey (hereafter APA), 951 Jacqueline Erbar, "L'Indochine vivante et vecue. Mémoires d'enfant 1917–21, 1925–1929," 27.
58. *Guide du français*, 29.
59. APA 583 Marie-Antoinette Le Chanjour, "Et souffla le vent."
60. E. Henry-Biabaud, *Deux ans d'Indochine* (Hanoi: IDEO, 1939), 181.
61. Ibid.
62. Jay, *Indochine*, 195–96.
63. APA 583 Marie-Antoinette Le Chanjour, "Et souffla le vent."
64. Ibid.; Jay, *Indochine*, 172.
65. Harry Franck, *East of Siam: Ramblings in the Five Divisions of French Indo-China* (New York: Century Co., 1926), 237.
66. Ibid., 236.
67. Fournier, *Bébé colonial*, 139–42.
68. In 1930 one newspaper noted: "We have seen French parents very proud of their offspring pronouncing the worst expressions of the annamite language: their knowledge of the language unfortunately extends only to these expressions!" A.P.I., "Les Lauriers sont coupés," *L'Ami du Peuple*, 17 June 1930, 1.
69. RHL MS. Nathan 340 May to Nathan 28 June 1907.
70. RHL MS. Nathan 352 Clementi to Nathan, 3 October 1926.
71. Phoebe Whitworth, quoted in Elaine Yee Lin Ho, "Childhood and the Cultural Memory of Hong Kong: Martin Booth's *Gweilo* and Po Wah Lam's *The Locust Hunter*," in *China Fictions/English Language: Literary Essays in Diaspora, Memory, Story*, ed. A. Robert Lee (New York: Rodopi, 2008), 216.
72. APA 1389 Marguerite Fave, "Souvenirs d'Extrême-Orient, 1936–1946," 4.
73. Jean Gittins, *Eastern Windows, Western Skies* (Hong Kong: South China Morning Post, 1969), 15.
74. Intriguingly, census officials counted forty-three Chinese under age fifteen present on the Peak in 1911. "Report on the Census of the Colony for 1911," *Sessional Papers*, 23 November 1911, 41.
75. Norman Edwards, *The Singapore House and Residential Life: 1819–1939* (Singapore: Oxford University Press, 1990).
76. CUL RCMS 108/2/1 Newton, "More Exquisite When Past."
77. Barnes, *Mostly*, 8–9.
78. Bromley, *Opams*, 17.
79. Warwick Anderson, *Colonial Pathologies: American Tropical Medicine, Race, and Hygiene in the Philippines* (Durham: Duke University Press, 2006), 181.
80. Philip D. Curtin, *Death by Migration: Europe's Encounter with the Tropical World in the Nineteenth Century* (Cambridge: Cambridge University Press, 1989); David Arnold, *Colonising the Body: State Medicine and Epidemic Diseases in Nineteenth-Century India* (Berkeley: University of California Press, 1993); Mark Harrison, *Public Health in British India: Anglo-Indian Preventive Medicine, 1859–1914* (Cambridge: Cambridge University Press, 1994).
81. Whitworth, *View*, 24–25.
82. Pat Jalland, *Death in the Victorian Family* (Oxford: Oxford University Press, 1996), 129.
83. See, for example, Sander L. Gilman, *Difference and Pathology: Stereotypes of Sexuality, Race and Madness* (Ithaca: Cornell University Press, 1985), 25.

84. RHL MS. Nathan 352 Clementi to Nathan, 3 October 1926.

85. Ride, *I Dips*, 5. Visitors to Hong Kong had long been struck by the determination of Britons to ignore the 'murderous climate' and for women to "follow fashion scrupulously, without making the slightest concession to the difference of climate." A. Benoist de la Grandière, *Ports de l'extrême-orient: Débuts de l'occupation française en Indochine: Souvenirs de campagne; suivi du journal de bord: Extraits 1869* (Paris: Société française d'histoire d'outre-mer, 1994), 79.

86. Suzanne Prou, *La Petite Tonkinoise* (Paris: Calmann-Lévy, 1987), 56–58.

87. APA 1389 Marguerite Fave, "Souvenirs d'Extrême-Orient, 1936–1946."

88. "One doctor blames the mother for staying in Tonkin during the summer. Another identifies a 'serious' illness and offers either insouciant or arrogant comments. What help can I find beneath their indifferent gaze?" Fournier, *Bébé colonial*, 54–55.

89. Ibid., 99.

90. Ibid., 132.

91. RHL MS. Nathan 341 May to Nathan, 14 May 1905.

92. RHL MS. Nathan 340 Letter Phoebe, Iris, Dione and Stella May to Nathan, 4 August 1905.

93. Whitworth, *View from the Peak*, 16.

94. Auguste Raphael Marty died in Hải Phòng in January 1915. RHL MS. Nathan 344 Marty to Nathan, n.d., c. 1906.

95. See, for example, Whitlock, *Intimate Empire*; Margaret Shennan, *Out in the Midday Sun: The British in Malaya, 1880–1960* (London: John Murray, 2000); Vyvyen Brendon, *Children of the Raj* (London: Weidenfeld and Nicolson, 2005); Elizabeth Buettner, *Empire Families: Britons and Late Imperial India* (Oxford: Oxford University Press, 2004).

96. CUL RCMS 108/2/1 Newton, "More Exquisite When Past."

97. Shirley Geok-lin Lim, "Up Against the National Canon: Women's War Memoirs from Malaysia and Singapore," *Journal of Commonwealth Literature* 29, no. 1 (1993): 59.

CHAPTER 4

1. Ann Stoler has suggested the importance of this link between the family and the state as "the crucial site in which future subjects and loyal citizens were to be made." Ann L. Stoler, "Sexual Affronts and Racial Frontiers: European Identities and the Cultural Politics of Exclusion in Colonial Southeast Asia," *Comparative Studies in Society and History* 34, no. 3 (1992): 521.

2. Mark Connelly, *Christmas: A Social History* (London: I. B. Tauris, 1999), 9–11, 34.

3. John R. Gillis, *A World of Their Own Making: Myth, Ritual and the Quest for Family Values* (New York: Basic, 1996), 99–104.

4. Viviana Zelizer, *Pricing the Priceless Child: The Changing Social Value of Children* (New York: Basic Books, 1985), 3, 14, 21, 32, 57.

5. Brian MacDonald, ed., *"Dearest Mother": The Letters of F.R. Kendall* (London: Lloyds of London Press, 1988), 104.

6. Edwin Lee, *The British as Rulers: Governing Multiracial Singapore, 1867–1914* (Singapore: Singapore University Press, 1991), 288.

7. Fairy tales had become essential reading for British children since the translation of Jacob and Wilhelm Grimm's German Popular Stories in 1823 and 1826, illustrated by George Cruickshank.

8. Walter Makepeace, "Concerning Known Persons," in *One Hundred Years of Singa-*

pore, ed. Walter Makepeace, Gilbert E. Brooke, and Roland St. J. Braddell, vol. 2 (Singapore: Oxford University Press, 1991), 456–57.

9. Cambridge University Library, Royal Commonwealth Society Collection (hereafter CUL), Personal and Family Papers of Lillian Newton, RCMS 108/5/1 Programme, "The Talisman of the Enchanted Island" (Singapore: Kelly & Walsh, 1909), 24–25.

10. Connelly, *Christmas*, 102, 105, 113.

11. J. B. Elcum, *Annual Report on Education in the Straits Settlements for the Year 1900* (Singapore: Government Printing Office, 1901), 175.

12. From the 1860s, men in Hong Kong claimed that a colder winter, permitting boots to be worn and log fires set, gave them right to claim a superior colonial masculinity to their counterparts in Singapore. This in turn reflected supposedly more authoritative claims to colonial status, as also reflected in London's demand that the governor of Hong Kong, Sir Hercules Robinson (1859–65), head the commission adjudicating upon Singapore's accession to Crown Colony status. "The Compliments of the Season," *China Punch*, 24 December 1867, 117.

13. Lewis Strange Wingfield, *Wanderings of a Globe-Trotter in the Far East*, vol. 1 (London: Richard Bentley, 1889), 12, 37.

14. "Christmas Celebrations in Hongkong," *China Mail*, 27 December 1887, 3.

15. "Report on the Census of the Colony for 1897," *Sessional Papers*, 20 June 1897, 474.

16. William Meigh Goodwin, *Reminiscences of a Colonial Judge* (London: Kingsgate, 1907), 211–12.

17. In January 1906, Hong Kong's new chief justice, Sir Francis Piggott, and his wife, Lady Mabel Piggott, welcomed sixty children to a fancy dress ball at Mountain Lodge. Among the guests were several 'Red Riding Hoods,' a 'Little Boy Blue' and a sizeable contingent of 'Fairies.' The adults in attendance were also garbed as characters from nursery rhymes and fairy stories. "Children's Fancy Dress Ball," *Hongkong Telegraph*, 2 January 1906, 5.

18. Mountain Lodge had been constructed in 1902. Rhodes House, Oxford (hereafter RHL), MS. Nathan 39 newspaper excerpt, "The Governor and the Children—Entertainment at Mountain Lodge," 15–16 August 1904.

19. RHL MS. Nathan 340 Phoebe May to Nathan, n.d., c. 1904.

20. RHL MS. Nathan 340 Helena May to Nathan, 18 August 1904. In a typical exchange, Stella May, daughter of Francis Henry May (captain superintendant of the Hong Kong police force), wrote to Nathan to tell him, "We all enjoyed the party very much, and we thought it so kind of you to have it." RHL MS. Nathan 340 Letter, Stella May to Nathan, 24 August 1904.

21. RHL MS. Nathan 344 Kadoorie to May, 8 April 1907.

22. RHL MS. Nathan 343 Eleanor Hastings to Nathan, 4 April 1907; RHL MS. Nathan 346–47 Aileen Hastings to Nathan, 25 November 1907.

23. For a recent study radically reenvisioning these authors' interrogations of romantic ideas about childhood, see Marah Gubar, *Artful Dodgers: Reconceiving the Golden Age of Children's Literature* (Oxford: Oxford University Press, 2009).

24. Jack Zipes, *Victorian Fairy Tales: The Revolt of the Fairies and Elves* (London: Methuen, 1987), xv.

25. In Britain the Christian Socialist educator Margaret McMillan drew upon such ideas to introduce fairy tales into the curriculum of the Socialist Sunday school movement. Carolyn Steedman, *Childhood, Culture and Class in Britain: Margaret McMillan,*

1860–1931 (New Brunswick: Rutgers University Press, 1990), 174–76; Joachim Liebschner, *A Child's Work: Freedom and Guidance in Froebel's Educational Theory and Practice* (Cambridge: Lutterworth Press, 2001), 32–63.

26. Helena May herself advised Nathan, "you know I can't promise—if the occasion should even arise to leave my four babies!" RHL MS. Nathan 340 May to Nathan, 25 August 1904.

27. RHL MS. Nathan 346–47 Eleanor Hastings to Nathan, 16 April 1907.

28. Nathan and Piggott, for instance, were barely on speaking terms. And Nathan's efforts to build allegiances with the colony's children may have been informed by the ill feeling directed at him by sections of the colony's mercantile elite, who resented being governed by an unmarried Jew.

29. Phoebe Whitworth, *View from the Peak: An Autobiography* (Cambridge: T. G. Whitworth, 2001), 12.

30. "Naval Visitors at the Hongkong Club," *China Mail*, 18 March 1909.

31. As David Harvey has suggested, "Islands suited the dreams of imperial control particularly well" as they set limits to "the possibility of social change and history." David Harvey, *Spaces of Capital: Towards a Critical Geography* (Edinburgh: Edinburgh University Press, 2001), 160. On the child as island, see John Gillis, "Epilogue: The Islanding of Children: Reshaping the Mythical Landscapes of Childhood," in *Designing Modern Childhoods: History, Space and the Material Culture of Children*, ed. Marta Gutman and Ning de Coninck-Smith (New Brunswick: Rutgers University Press, 2008), 316–30.

32. Curfew conditions, in the form of the controversial 'light and pass regulations,' persisted from 1842 almost to the turn of the century, when such measures became the subject of envious glances from European members of Singapore's Straits Philosophical Society. Walter J. Napier, "Dutch and English Administration in the East," *Noctes Orientales, Being a Selection of Essays Read before the Straits Philosophical Society between the Years 1893 and 1910* (Singapore: Kelly and Walsh, 1912), 36; Christopher Munn, *Anglo-China: Chinese People and British Rule in Hong Kong, 1841–1880* (London: Curzon, 2001), 67.

33. K. D. Reynolds, *Aristocratic Women and Political Society in Victorian Britain* (Oxford: Clarendon Press, 1998).

34. See, for example, Surrey History Centre, Woking, UK (hereafter SHC), Ministering Children's League Cuttings Book 7919/7/29, *The Indian Daily News*, 14 February 1893.

35. Much of the $1,000 collected in the first year of the league's existence in Hong Kong was raised through a play. SHC 7919/7/15 "China," *Ministering Children's League Quarterly Magazine* (April 1904): 43. When a visit to Penang necessitated Nathan's absence, Aileen Hastings reflected, "there was an MCL Meeting in the Ballroom at Government House and it seemed so funny you not being there." RHL MS. Nathan 343 Aileen Hastings to Nathan, 30 June 1907.

36. In 1906 census officials recorded the presence of 2,053 European children in Hong Kong. May was assisted by Eleanor Hastings (Peak branch), and Mrs. Webb and Mrs. Birdwood (Kowloon branches). SHC 7919/7/14 "China—Hong Kong," *Ministering Children's League Quarterly Magazine* (October 1903): 90.

37. SHC 7919/7/17 "Festival and Annual Meeting," *Ministering Children's League Magazine* (October 1909): 61–62.

38. Whitworth, *View*, 17.

39. Jack Zipes, *The Irresistible Fairy Tale: The Cultural and Social History of a Genre* (Princeton: Princeton University Press, 2012), 121–22.

40. Ronald Hyam, "Empire and Sexual Opportunity," *Journal of Imperial and Commonwealth History* 14, no. 2 (January 1986): 53.

41. RHL MS. Nathan 39 Newspaper excerpt "The Governor and the Children," 15–16 August 1904.

42. SHC MCL Cuttings Book 7919/7/31, "Fellowship" 1909.

43. Shanghai's league boasted 160 child members (more than Hong Kong's approximately 100) by June 1909. This branch supported cots for Chinese children in Hangzhou and Shanghai. SHC 7919/7/18 "Ministering Children's League and Ministering League, Fourteenth Report," *Ministering Children's League Magazine* (July 1911); SHC 7919/7/15 "China," *Ministering Children's League Quarterly Magazine* (April 1904): 43.

44. SHC 7919/7/17 "Festival and Annual Meeting," *Ministering Children's League Magazine* (October 1909): 63.

45. Ibid., 61–62.

46. Ibid., 61.

47. SHC 7919/7/31 "Fellowship," Cuttings Book, 1909.

48. SHC 7919/7/17, Letters to Lady Meath 26 June 1909, "Abroad," *Ministering Children's League Magazine* (October 1909): 77.

49. In Hong Kong, the Reverend E. J. Hardy, an enthusiast for MCL activities living in a city which also boasted a 'Children's Intellectual Society,' anticipated a time when "grown-up people were as wise as *children!*" Rev. E. J. Hardy, *John Chinaman at Home: Sketches of Men Manners and Things in China* (London: T. Fisher Unwin, 1905), 28. One article from the league magazine claimed in 1921 that "the child for whom the world is full of fairies is nearer the truth about the Universe than the Scientist to whom the world seems like a mere machine." SHC 7919/7/22, "Thoughts on the Holy Angels," *Ministering Children's League Magazine* (October 1921)

50. In 1929 the children of the Hong Kong garrison gave performances of a play at Mount Austin Barracks and the RE Theatre. SHC 7919/7/24 "News from Overseas," *Ministering Children's League Magazine* (July 1929): 11.

51. As Fritz Hochberg put it, "Their faces [boys'] are mostly painted white and their lips very much rouged; and they give themselves immensely grown-up airs, and stalk along in a most dignified manner in their funny little shoes." Fritz Hochberg, *An Eastern Voyage: A Journal of the Travels of Count Fritz Hochberg through the British Empire in the East and Japan* (London: J. M. Dent, 1910), 156–57. Other observations of strange, "solemn" Chinese children appeared in Samuel H. Peplow, *Hongkong: About and Around* (Hong Kong: Commercial Press, 1930), 51.

52. Fritz Hochberg observed, "The cooking, washing, dressing of those fascinating Chinese doll-children and their delightful ways and plays!" Hochberg, *Eastern Voyage*, 154.

53. RHL MS. Nathan 344 Noel to Nathan, 17 February 1906.

54. Dalziel dedicated his book to a "six-year old from far Kwang-si' bearing the milk name 'Small Pot,'" whose "child's heart," as he pointedly remarked, "knows not creed nor colour but only kindness." James Dalziel, *Chronicles of a Crown Colony* (Hong Kong: South China Morning Post, 1907), preface. On Dalziel, see Ross Forman, *China and the Victorian Imagination: Empires Entwined* (Cambridge: Cambridge University Press, 2013), 64–97.

55. Vietnamese National Archives Centre 2, Ho Chi Minh City (hereafter VNNA2), Gouvernement de la Cochinchine (Goucoch) IA.6/252(4) Joseph Rul, Directeur de l'enseignement to Directeur de l'école municipale de Saigon, 4 August 1887.

56. Michael McClellan, "Performing Empire: Opera in Colonial Hanoi," *Journal of*

Musicological Research 22, nos. 1–2 (2003): 135–66; Charles Pitt, "Opera's Indochinese Outpost," *Opera* 40 (January 2003): 40.

57. "Le besoin d'un lycée français se fait sentir," Municipal Council of Saigon, 18 September 1882, Registre des deliberations, 96–98, in *Extraits des registres de délibérations de la ville de Saigon (Indochine Française) 1867–1916*, ed. André Baudrit (Saigon: J. Testelin, 1936), 228.

58. VNNA2 Goucoch IA.6/243(2) Baudin to Danel, 13 September 1890.

59. Anne Girollet, *Victor Schœlcher: Abolitionniste et républicain: Approche juridique et politique de l'œuvre d'un fondateur de la République* (Paris: Karthala, 2000), 156–58, 256–59.

60. Paul Rabinow, *French Modern: Norms and Forms of the Social Environment* (Chicago: University of Chicago Press, 1989), 86–95; Catherine Bodard Silver, *Le Play: On Family, Work and Social Change*, ed. and trans. Catherine Bodard Silver (Chicago: University of Chicago Press, 1982), ch. 1.

61. J. P. Daughton, *An Empire Divided: Religion, Republicanism and the Making of French Colonialism, 1880–1914* (Oxford: Oxford University Press, 2006).

62. Roch Carabelli, *L'Unite de l'Indo-Chine* (Saigon: Imprimerie de Rey et Curiol, 1886).

63. A. Delteil, *Un An de séjour en Cochinchine: Guide du voyageur à Saigon* (Paris: Challamel Ainé, Editeur, 1887), 181.

64. Writers from René Boylesve to Valery Larbaud saw childhood as having a 'mythic' status—contradicting, disrupting and 'completing' the adult world. See Mari-José Chombart de Lauwe, *Un monde autre: L'Enfance de ses représentations à son mythe* (Paris: Payot, 1971).

65. Jean Richepin, in Duc de Montpensier, *En Indochine: Mes chasses—mes voyages* (Paris: Pierre Lafitte, 1912), ix.

66. Ibid.

67. Jules Gervais-Courtellemont, *Empire Colonial de la France: L'Indochine. Cochinchine, Cambodge, Laos, Annam, Tonkin* (Paris: Librairie de Paris Firmin-Didot, 1901), 183.

68. Paul Doumer became president *d'honneur* of the society from 1904. Pierre Sanchez, *La Société des peintres orientalistes français* (Dijon: L'Echelle de Jacob, 2008), 19.

69. Maurice Agulhon, *Marianne into Battle: Republican Imagery and Symbolism in France, 1780–1880*, trans. Janet Lloyd (Cambridge: Cambridge University Press, 1981).

70. Penny Edwards, "'Propagender': Marianne, Joan of Arc and the Export of French Gender Ideology to Colonial Cambodia (1863–1954)," in *Promoting the Colonial Idea*, ed. Tony Chafer and Amanda Sackur (New York: Palgrave, 2002), 116–30.

71. Alfred Cunningham, "Exposition at Hanoi," *L'Exposition de Hanoi* (Hanoi: F. H. Schneider, 1902), 9.

72. Paul Bourgeois and G.-Roger Sandoz, *Exposition d'Hanoi 1902–1903: Rapport général* (Paris: Comité Français des Expositions à L'étranger, 1904), 223. Dufau later displayed her work at the thirteenth exposition of Peintres Orientalistes Français held in 1905, while Tournon displayed his art at the Exposition Coloniale de Marseille of 1906.

73. Paul Doumer resorted in his own writing to kinship metaphors. Quoting Victor Hugo's *Choix entre deux Nations*, he declared that France "has the right to love, to veneration, to devotion and the life of her children. We are patriots as we are good children." "She is our mother, and it is like a mother that we must love her . . . she is France and we

are French; she is the mother and we are the sons." Paul Doumer, *Livre de mes fils* (Paris: Vuibert & Nony, 1906), 268–69.

74. Ter Ellingson, *The Myth of the Noble Savage* (Berkeley: University of California Press, 2001), 84.

75. Richard Fogarty and Michael A. Osborne, "Constructions and Functions of Race in French Military Medicine, 1830–1920," in *The Color of Liberty, Histories of Race in France*, ed. Sue Peabody and Tyler Stovall (Durham: Duke University Press, 2003), 206.

76. Prominent French theorists of race such as Renan, Buffon, Taine and Le Bon used references to childhood to make hierarchical contrasts between Europeans and the peoples defined as inferior in relation to them. Bill Ashcroft, "Primitive and Wingless: The Colonial Subject as Child," in *Dickens, The Child and Empire*, ed. Wendy S. Jacobson (London: Palgrave Macmillan, 2001), 188.

77. Ibid., 185; Ellingson, *Noble Savage*, xiii.

78. Le Dr. Challan de Belval, *Au Tonkin* (Paris: A. Delahaye et E. Lecrosnier, 1886), 34. Eugène Jung also populated his Hanoi streets with *gamins*. Eugène Jung, *La Vie européenne au Tonkin* (Paris, 1901), 113.

79. As Bouinais and Paulus put it, "Little children appear curious and friendly . . . they seem to be more intelligent than the adults, but this superiority disappears with age." A. Bouinais and A. Paulus, eds., *L'Indo-chine contemporaine: Cochinchine, Cambodge, Tonkin, Annam*, 2nd ed., vol. 1, *Cochinchine—Cambodge* (Paris: Challamel Aîné, 1885), 229; Raoul Postel, *L'Extrême Orient, Cochinchine, Annam, Tonkin* (Paris: Degorce-Cadot, 1882), 86. Dr. Challan de Belval explained that in growing up, the Vietnamese child became "stultified." De Belval, *Tonkin*, 113.

80. Jean-Louis de Lanessan, *L'Expansion coloniale de la France: Étude économique, politique et géographique sur les établissements français d'outre-mer* (Paris: Félix Alcan, 1886), 542; Société Bretonne de Géographie de l'Orient, *L'Avenir colonial de la France: L'Afrique et le Tonkin* (Lorient: Imprimerie Louis Chamaillard, 1882), 7–8, 16; Louis Salaün, *L'Indochine* (Paris: Imprimerie Nationale, 1903), 350.

81. On 'victory pictures,' see Yin Hwang, "The Depiction of War and Rebellion in the Print and Visual Culture of Late Qing China, 1884–1901," PhD diss., SOAS, London, 2013.

82. Henri Danguy, *Le Nouveau visage de la Cochinchine* (Paris: Larose, 1929), 147–48.

83. Louis Peytral, *Silhouttes tonkinoises* (Paris: Berger-Levrault et Cie, 1897), 52–53.

84. The administrator Charles Lemire revelled in the sight of children who "ordinarily go around completely naked, left to themselves, the biggest helping the smallest; they run and swim as they please." Charles Lemire, *L'Indochine: Cochinchine française, royaume de Cambodge, royaume d'Annam et Tonkin*, 3rd ed. (Paris: Challamel Aîné, 1884), 111; Bouinais and Paulus described how children "run free, naked or scantily clad, covered in dirt, plunging into muddy streams." Bouinais, *L'Indo-chine*, 251.

85. Gabrielle M. Vassal, *Three Years in Vietnam (1907–1910)* (Bangkok: White Lotus, 1999), 92–93; originally published as *On and Off Duty in Annam* (London: Heinemann, 1910).

86. *Écoles primaries* had featured in the 1887 Hanoi Exposition. Forty-two of the ninety-two schools in Tonkin sent workbooks for inclusion in the exposition, though as onlookers noted, not all of the pupils were 'children.' Vietnamese National Archives Centre 1 (hereafter VNNA1), Résidence Supérieure du Tonkin (RST) R. 13863. "Rapport de M. Dumoutier sur l'enseignement au Tonkin a.s. de la participation des écoles à l'exposition de Hanoi," 1887.

87. On Flora Shaw in the metropole, see Jonathan Schneer, *London 1900: The Imperial Metropolis* (New Haven: Yale University Press, 1999), 133–46.

88. RHL Lugard Papers, MSS. Brit. Emp. s.68, Press Cuttings, "Ministering Children's League," 6 March 1911.

89. SHC 7919/7/17 "Little Ah Yen," *Ministering Children's League Magazine* (January 1909): 8–9.

90. Elizabeth Sinn, *Power and Charity: A Chinese Merchant Elite in Colonial Hong Kong* (1989; Hong Kong: Hong Kong University Press, 2003), xiii, 1.

91. In 1916 the Hong Kong League sent $5,580 or approximately £511 back to England. In the same year Shanghai's branch sent just £16 back 'Home.' SHC 7919/7/22 "Abroad," *Ministering Children's League Magazine* (October 1916): 39.

92. SHC 7919/7/19 "Abroad," *Ministering Children's League Magazine* (1911): 18.

93. SHC 7919/7/20 "The Silencing of Speckles," *Ministering Children's League Magazine* (October 1914): 45.

94. Charlotte Ehrlicher, "Around-the-World Letters (From a Letter Describing the Return Trip)," *American Journal of Nursing* (1913): 306.

95. "Ministering Children's League," *China Mail*, 1 November 1915, 4; SHC 7919/7/22 "Abroad," *Ministering Children's League Magazine* (October 1916): 39.

96. "The colour scheme is purely Chinese!" May observed. SHC 7919/7/21 "Abroad," *Ministering Children's League Magazine* (October 1915): 35.

97. SHC 7919/7/21 "Abroad," *Ministering Children's League Magazine* (October 1915): 57.

98. SHC 7919/7/22 "Reports from Overseas Branches," *Ministering Children's League Magazine* (Christmas 1924): 14.

99. "St. Stephen's Girls' College," *China Mail*, 19 January 1922, 8.

100. Whitworth, *View*, 25.

101. The Hong Kong League ventured, "We hope that China will be successful in getting a 'fairy story' printed in the Ministering Children's League magazine which we all enjoy." SHC 7919/7/22 "Reports from Overseas Branches," *Ministering Children's League Magazine* (Christmas 1924): 14. On Chinese literary explorations of fairy tales, see Andrew Jones, *Developmental Fairy Tales: Evolutionary Thinking and Modern Chinese Culture* (Cambridge: Harvard University Press, 2011).

102. The play 'starred' J. Wong as the 'Fairy of the Glen,' with supporting fairies M. Chan, C. Botelho, M. Churn, C. Barretto, H. Wylie, V. Shea, I. Gittins and P. Bough. "For Sweet Charity," *China Mail*, 14 November 1921, 7; "Diocesan Girls' School," *China Mail*, 13 February 1922, 8.

103. Helen F. Siu, "Women of Influence: Gendered Charisma," in *Merchants' Daughters: Women, Commerce and Regional Culture in South China*, ed. Helen F. Siu (Hong Kong: Hong Kong University Press, 2010), 185.

104. Makepeace, "Concerning," 456.

105. "Mr. Buckley's Entertainment," *Straits Times*, 27 December 1900, 3.

106. Edwin A. Brown, *Indiscreet Memories* (London: Kelly & Walsh, 1935), 28.

107. CUL RCMS 108/2/1 Newton, "More Exquisite When Past."

108. Brown, *Indiscreet*, 98–99.

109. From 1880 to 1884 the rate of Chinese immigration increased sharply (with 233,357 new arrivals) under the control of the Chinese societies. In 1874 an ordinance was

introduced to regulate passenger ships. In 1877 a Chinese Protectorate was set up to supervise Chinese migrants. The government set up a Chinese Advisory Board in 1889. A new Societies Ordinance of 1890 gave the government the power to exempt any society from registration and to dissolve any society. Through such means relations between British and Chinese in Singapore acquired a more formal character.

110. CUL RCMS 108/2/1 Newton, "More Exquisite When Past"; RCMS 108/5/1 Programme, King George V's Coronation, Children's Festival, 24 June 1911.

111. "Festival and Annual Meeting," *Ministering Children's League Magazine* (October 1909): 61–62. By the end of 1910 the Singapore branch had eighty-five child members (plus forty-six elder members and sixty associates). It held a regular monthly meeting in the Victoria Memorial Hall, and its first bazaar was held on 28 February 1911. Two months later, at the annual general meeting, Singapore children heard an address on the league's general aims and principles by its vice president, Charles Buckley. MCL 7919/7/18 "Abroad," *Ministering Children's League Magazine* (July 1911): 57.

112. Brown, *Indiscreet*, 235.

113. CUL RCMS 108/2/1 Newton, "More Exquisite When Past."

114. CUL RCMS 108/5/1 Programme, Children's Christmas Treat, 26 December 1906.

115. University-educated intellectuals such as the neo-Confucianist unofficial member of the Legislative Council, Lim Boon Keng, voiced a growing sense of shame at the standard of social services and the poverty, illiteracy and high mortality of the city's growing population of young residents.

116. John Darwin, "Afterword: A Colonial World," in *New Frontiers: Imperialism's New Communities in East Asia, 1842–1953*, ed. Robert Bickers and Christian Henriot (Manchester: Manchester University Press, 2000), 259.

117. Benedict Anderson, *Long Distance Nationalism: World Capitalism and the Rise of Identity Politics* (Berkeley: University of California Press, 1992).

118. John M. Carroll, *Edge of Empires: Chinese Elites and British Colonials in Hong Kong* (Cambridge: Harvard University Press, 2005), 18, 31, 97.

CHAPTER 5

1. Trần Mỹ Vân, *A Vietnamese Royal Exile in Japan: Prince Cuong De (1882–1951)* (London: Routledge, 2012); David G. Marr, *Vietnamese Anticolonialism, 1885–1925* (Berkeley: University of California Press, 1971).

2. Annam was a 'protectorate' rather than a formal colony.

3. Though the Nguyễn dynasty had ruled for fifty years, it had not fully consolidated power in the north before the French invaded.

4. "Notre petit roi d'Annam," *L'Illustration*, 26 October 1907, 268.

5. "The Little King of Annam," *Syracuse Herald*, 5 January 1908.

6. Eugène Brieux, *Voyage aux Indes et en Indo-Chine: Simples notes d'un touriste* (Paris: Librairie Ch. Delagrave, 1910), 76–78.

7. Nguyêñ Phước Bảo Vàng, *Duy Tan: Empereur d'Annam 1900–1945 exilé à l'île de la Réunion ou le déstin tragique du Prince Vinh San* (Sainte-Marie: Azalées Editions, 2002), 57, 130.

8. Hô Thị Hạnh quoted in ibid., 125.

9. Bill Ashcroft, "Primitive and Wingless: The Colonial Subject as Child," in *Dickens and the Children of Empire*, ed. Wendy S. Jacobson (Basingstoke: Palgrave, 2000), 184–202.

10. Jean Star, *Tonkinades* (Paris: Calman-Lévy, 1902), 68.
11. George Dürrwell, *Ma Chère Cochinchine: Trente années d'impressions et de souvenirs fevrier 1881–1910* (Paris: Mignot, 1910), 123.
12. Paul Robiquet, ed., *Discours et opinions de Jules Ferry, publiés avec commentaires et notes*, vol. 5, *Affaires tunisiennes—Congo—Madagascar—Egypte—Tonkin* (Paris: Armand Colin & Cie, 1897), 304.
13. Paul Leroy-Beaulieu, *De la colonisation chez les peuples modernes*, 3rd ed. (Paris: Librairie Guillaumin et Cie, 1886), 742.
14. This image resonated with that disseminated in the mid-nineteenth-century writings of Ernest Renan, who in his *Histoire du peuple d'Israël*, referred to China as a "shriveled old child"—a monstrous, stunted humanity. Ernest Renan, *Histoire du peuple d'Israël* (Paris: Calmann-Lévy, 1887–93), 33.
15. Writing in 1923, the lawyer and reformer Phan Văn Trường described levies of up to 200,000 peasants taken from villages and sent to work on railway projects. Phan Văn Trường, *Une Histoire de conspirateurs annamites à Paris ou la vérité sur l'Indochine* (Gia Định: Imp. Đông-Pháp-Ng-kim-Đinh, 1928), 41.
16. Isabelle Massieu, *Comment j'ai parcouru l'Indochine* (Paris: Plon, 1901), 355.
17. Ibid., 360.
18. Quoted in Louis Cario and Charles Regismanset, *L'Exotisme: La Littérature coloniale* (Paris: Mercure, 1911), 274–75.
19. *Discours prononcé par M. A. Klobukowsky, Gouverneur Général de l'Indo-chine à l'ouverture de la session ordinaire de Conseil supérieur le 27 novembre 1909* (Saigon: Imprimerie Commerciale Marcellin Rey, 1909), 7.
20. Vietnamese National Archives Centre 1 (VNNA1) Résidence Supérieure du Tonkin (RST) X.1 20.324, "Proclamation au Peuple Annamite, P.T.C," 1914.
21. VNNA1 RST X.1 20.324 Joost van Vollenhoven, "Proclamation au français a.s. de la déclaration de la Grande Guerre," 1914.
22. The draft would last until 1918, by which time there were around 100,000 Vietnamese in France, 50% of whom were workers. Pierre Varet, *L'Effort colonial de la France au cours de la guerre de 1914* (Paris: Les Presses Modernes, 1927), 44–45.
23. Quoted in Nguyên Phước Bảo Vàng, *Duy Tan*, 73.
24. Ibid.
25. "Ministering Children's League," *China Mail*, 1 November 1915, 4.
26. Surrey History Centre (hereafter SHC), 7919/7/22 *Ministering Children's League Magazine* (January 1922): 1.
27. "Ministering Children's League," *Singapore Free Press and Mercantile Advertiser*, 1 June 1912, 6; SHC 7919/2/4 Minutes of the Executive Committee of the Ministering Children's League, 3 October 1923.
28. Even in 1931 there were still only 621 Scouts in Hong Kong of a population of 840,473, and 711 in Singapore of a population of 557,700. Figures are from Paul Kua, *Scouting in Hong Kong, 1910–2010* (Hong Kong: Scout Association of Hong Kong, 2011), 431; Christina Jialin Wu, "A Malayan Girlhood on Parade: Colonial Femininities, Transnational Mobilities and the Girl Guide Movement in British Malaya," in *Transnational Histories of Youth in the Twentieth Century*, ed. Richard Ivan Jobs and David M. Pomfret (London: Palgrave, 2015), 92–112; Janice N. Brownfoot, "Sisters under the Skin: Imperialism and the Emancipation of Women in Malaya, c. 1891–1941," in *Making Imperial Mentalities*, ed. J. A. Mangan (Manchester: Manchester University Press, 1990), 46–73; T. H. Parsons, *Race,*

Resistance and the Boy Scout Movement in British Colonial Africa (Athens: Ohio University Press, 2004); Ann Raffin, *Youth Mobilisation in Vichy Indochina and Its Legacies, 1940–1970* (Lanham: Lexington Books, 2005); K.Y.L. Tan and M. Wan, *Scouting in Singapore, 1910–2000* (Singapore: Singapore Scout Association, 2002).

29. SHC 7919/7/22 "Reports from Overseas Branches," *Ministering Children's League Magazine* (Christmas 1924): 14.

30. SHC 7919/6/30 Keppel Garnier to Haverfield, 25 August 1933.

31. SHC 7919/6/30 Keppel Garnier to Haverfield, 27 October 1932; SHC 7919/6/30 newspaper extract, "Mrs Rule's Pupils in Charming Dances," 23 May 1934. When Patricia de Cruz organised a performance of Charles Kingsley's *Water Babies* in Penang in August 1927, a number of Tamil and Chinese names featured among the dramatis personae. SCH 7919/6/30 Retisma to Haverfield, 14 January 1929.

32. The Hong Kong branch membership peaked at 1,437 in 1927 (with 272 adults), before falling back to 1,043 children and 458 adults by 1936. The membership of the Penang branch peaked in 1913 with 102 child members, before dropping to around 50–60 by the early 1930s. SHC 7919/4/2 Card File; Kua, *Scouting*, 431.

33. SHC 7919/7/24 "Annual Conference 1926" *Ministering Children's League Magazine* (Michaelmas 1926): 4.

34. "For Sweet Charity," *China Mail*, 14 November 1921, 7.

35. While leagues in other centres declined and dropped, the league's annual conference heard there were "over 1,000 child members" in Hong Kong and "quite half of the League's child members are Chinese." SHC 7919/7/24 "Annual Conference," *Ministering Children's League Magazine* (October 1928): 5. By 1935 Hong Kong had branches in Victoria (40 children); Diocesan Girls' School (54 children); the military (31); prisons (15 children); Quarry Bay (11 children); the Peak (26 children); Kowloon (6 children); and Kowloon Docks Auxiliary Branch (2 children). The tendency for child members to be outnumbered by adults inverted in the Chinese girls' schools branches. These included, for example, St. Paul's Girls' College (200 children), St. Stephen's Girls College and Fairlea School (408 children). SHC 7919/6/31 "Report and Balance Sheet of the Hong Kong Ministering League and Ministering Children's League for the Year 1935 being the Sixteenth Annual Report of the Leagues," 1935.

36. John Darwin, "Afterword: A Colonial World," in *New Frontiers: Imperialism's New Communities in East Asia, 1842–1953*, ed. Robert Bickers and Christian Henriot (Manchester: Manchester University Press, 2000), 257.

37. Elizabeth Sinn, *Power and Charity: A Chinese Merchant Elite in Colonial Hong Kong* (1989; Hong Kong: Hong Kong University Press, 2003), xviii.

38. John M. Carroll, *Edge of Empires: Chinese Elites and British Colonials in Hong Kong* (Cambridge: Harvard University Press, 2005).

39. Andrew Jones, *Developmental Fairy Tales: Evolutionary Thinking and Modern Chinese Culture* (Cambridge: Harvard University Press, 2011), 150–60.

40. For S. A. Sweet, for example, who published a book of written sketches of Hong Kong, the Peak Reservation viewed from the harbour appeared as a collection of "pretty little dolls houses." Meanwhile, nightfall converted Hong Kong "into a fairyland of lights to which no pen drawing could do justice and the scene must be left to the imagination." He also referred to the "City of Victoria" as "a maze of Lilliputian streets thronged by tiny figures." S. A. Sweet, *A Hong Kong Sketch Book* (Hong Kong: Ye Olde Printerie, 1931), 1–2. When H. G. Maclaurin put words to Charles Jessop's comic opera, he included the line,

"'tis fairy land." *Hongkong: A Comic Opera in Two Acts*, words by H. G. Maclaurin, music by Charles Jessop (London: Chappell & Co., 1925), 105; Allister Macmillan, *Seaports of the Far East: Historical and Descriptive, Commercial and Industrial, Facts, Figures and Resources* (London: W. H. & L. Collingridge, 1923), 311.

41. Macmillan, *Seaports*, 324; *Hong Kong History and Description* (Hong Kong: Publicity Bureau for South China, Commercial Press, 1927), 29; Sweet, *Hong Kong Sketch Book*, 2.

42. René Jouglet, *Dans le sillage des jonques* (Paris: Grasset, 1935), 55.

43. André de la Varre, dir., *Hong Kong, Gateway to China*, 1938.

44. Cambridge University Library, Royal Commonwealth Society Collection (hereafter CUL), RCMS 108/3/3 Newspaper cutting, "A Pageant of Girls," cutting, 26 May 1923.

45. "What Malaya Is Saying," *British Malaya*, May 1927, 30.

46. Annette K. Vance Dorey, *Better Baby Contests: The Scientific Quest for Perfect Childhood Health in the Early Twentieth Century* (Jefferson: McFarland & Company, 1999), 13–15.

47. Erica Burman, *Deconstructing Developmental Psychology* (London: Routledge, 1994), 152; Fiona Paisley, "Childhood and Race: Growing Up in Empire," in *Gender and Empire*, ed. Philippa Levine (Oxford: Oxford University Press, 2004), 241; Seth Koven and Sonya Michel, eds., *Mothers of a New World: Maternalist Politics and the Origins of Welfare States* (London: Routledge, 1993).

48. Ian R. Tyrell, *The Woman's Christian Temperance Union in International Perspective, 1880–1930: Woman's World, Woman's Empire* (Chapel Hill: University of North Carolina Press, 1991).

49. In 1892 the rate was 374 per 1,000 in Singapore, compared with 159 in London, 273 in Calcutta (Kolkata) and 264 in Bombay (Mumbai). "Singapore Municipal Matters," *Singapore Free Press and Mercantile Advertiser*, 25 June 1892, 2.

50. H. N. Ridley, "The Survival of the Fittest," in *Noctes Orientales: Being a Selection of Essays before the Straits Philosophical Society between the Years 1893 and 1910* (Singapore: Kelly and Walsh, 1912), 191.

51. "Report by the Medical Officer of Health of the Colony of Hongkong for the Year 1895," *Supplement to the Hongkong Government Gazette* 187 (1896): 3.

52. "Reports of the Medical Officer of Health, Sanitary Surveyor and Colonial Veterinary Surgeon, for 1900," *Hongkong Government Gazette*, 25 May 1901, 1025.

53. "Report of the Committee Appointed by His Excellency the Governor to Inquire into the Causes of Infantile Mortality in the Colony," *Hongkong Government Gazette*, 22 January 1904, 52.

54. National Archives, London, Public Record Office (hereafter PRO), CO 129/322 May to Lyttelton, 11 March 1904.

55. The *Straits Chinese Magazine* complained in 1898, "under 12 months, the rate of mortality is about 1 death out of every 3 or 4 children born, if not higher, whereas in other countries such as Scotland, the rate is very low, about 15 per cent. "News and Notes," *Straits Chinese Magazine* 2, no. 1 (1898): 33.

56. Leonore Manderson, "Blame, Responsibility and Remedial Action: Death, Disease and the Infant in Early Twentieth Century Malaya," in *Death and Disease in Southeast Asia: Explorations in Social, Medical and Demographic History*, ed. Norman G. Owen (Singapore: Oxford University Press, 1987), 257–58, 263.

57. C. A. Vlieland, *British Malaya: A Report on the 1931 Census* (London: Crown Agents, 1932), 110; Leonore Manderson, "Race, Colonial Mentality and Public Health," in *The Un-*

derside of Malaysian History: Pullers, Prostitutes, Plantation Workers, ed. Peter J. Rimmer and Lisa M. Allen (Singapore: Stanford University Press, 1990), 212.

58. "Singapore Baby Show Held on Saturday 12 April 1919," *Our Magazine* 1, nos. 6 and 7 (June–July 1919).

59. By 1900 the Anglophone Straits Chinese were complaining that Chinese women's "ignorance of letters effectively prevents you from . . . proper care of your little ones." Lew See Fah, "Straits Chinese Mothers," *Straits Chinese Magazine* 5, no. 17 (1901): 112.

60. "Singapore Baby Show," *Singapore Free Press and Mercantile Advertiser*, 28 March 1919, 5.

61. The CWS had two clinics, at which most attending were Chinese. In August 1930 the CWS opened a crèche on Minto Road, supported financially by Tan Kah Kee. D. M. Roberts, "To Child Lovers," *Monthly Paper of St. Andrew's Cathedral Singapore* 18, no. 211 (July 1931): 4–5.

62. "A Wrong Impression," *British Malaya*, February 1930, 322.

63. "Slaughter of the Innocents," *Straits Times*, 22 September 1902, 6; "Why Fewer Babies Are Now Dying in Singapore," *Straits Times*, 21 July 1935, 13. Infant mortality declined in Britain from 153 per 1,000 in 1900, to 60 by 1930. "What Malaya Is Saying," *British Malaya*, May 1927, 30.

64. Prizes of $100 were offered in 1919 for babies under twelve months, and $50 for those under six months. Four prizes were offered in the Chinese category, owing to the higher level of interest shown.

65. L. S. Vaidyanathan, "Actuarial Report," in *Census of India*, vol. 1, *India*, ed. J. H. Hutton (Delhi: Government of India Publications, 1933).

66. Ai Lin Chua, "Singapore's Cinema Age of the 1930s: Hollywood and the Shaping of Singapore Modernity," *American Pop Culture* 13, no. 4 (2012): 592–604.

67. In 1931, 140 Chinese children competed (up from 80 in 1930), making up nearly 50% of all competitors. "Baby Show's Yearly Increase Mostly Chinese," *Singapore Free Press and Mercantile Advertiser*, 16 December 1931, 10.

68. The rate was even higher, at 292, for Malays. "The Good Health of Singapore," *Straits Times*, 26 September 1930, 17.

69. While rates of infant mortality declined by 20% among the Chinese in the Straits Settlements, the recorded drop among the Malays was only 8.5%. Manderson, "Blame, Responsibility and Remedial Action," 276–77.

70. Bella Sidney Woolf, *Chips of China* (Hong Kong: Kelly & Walsh, 1930), 53.

71. "An Apology for Flagellation," *Journal of the Army Educational Corps* 7, no. 1 (March 1930): 17.

72. Bella Sidney Woolf, *Under the Mosquito Curtain* (Hong Kong: Kelly and Walsh, 1935), 89–90.

73. Marr, *Vietnamese*, 233.

74. William B. Cohen, *Rulers of Empire: The French Colonial Service in Africa* (Stanford: Stanford University Press, 1971), 118.

75. Philippe M.F. Peycam, *The Birth of Vietnamese Political Journalism: Saigon 1916–1930* (New York: Columbia University Press, 2012).

76. As a consequence, by 1927 only 341 of the 731 students enrolled at the Lycée Sarraut in Hanoi were Vietnamese. In 1925 only twenty-five BAs graduated from Hanoi University, and in 1926 only nine. Virginia Thompson, *French Indochina* (London: George Allen and Unwin, 1937), 295–96; Gail P. Kelly, *Franco-Vietnamese Schools, 1918–1938: Regional Devel-*

opment and Implications for National Integration (Madison: Center for Southeast Asian Studies, University of Wisconsin, 1982), 64; Herman Lebovics, *True France: The Wars over Cultural Identity, 1900–1945* (Ithaca: Cornell University Press, 1992), 114.

77. Phoebe Scott, "Imagining 'Asian' Aesthetics in Colonial Hanoi: The Ecole des Beaux-Arts de L'Indochine (1925–1945)," in *Asia through Art and Anthropology: Cultural Translation Across Borders*, ed. Fuyubi Nakamura, Morgan Perkins and Oliver Krischer (London: Bloomsbury, 2013), 47–61.

78. A number of other writers dwelt upon native children as markers of the exotic. See, for example, G. Dumoutier, *Les cultes annamites* (Hanoi: F. H. Schneider, 1907), 19; Emile Nolly, *La Barque annamite: Roman de moeurs tonkinoises* (Paris: Calmann-Levy, 1921), 153; Christiane Fournier, *Perspectives Occidentales sur l'Indochine* (Saigon: Nouvelle Revue Indochinoise, 1935), 149.

79. Vietnamese intellectuals set about recording and memorialising this 'true childhood' of the countryside before it vanished altogether. On 5 March 1937 at a symposium by the Saigon Philharmonic Society supported by the Alliance Française of Cochinchina Nguyễn Tiến Lãng lectured on traditional Vietnamese songs, focusing in particular on those sung by mothers to children. Nguyễn Tiến Lãng, *Les Chansons annamites: Conférence avec audition de disques donnée à la Société philharmonique de Saigon, 5 mars 1937* (Saigon: Editions de l'Asie nouvelle illustrée, 1937), 2–3.

80. Nadine André-Pallois, *L'Indochine: Un Lieu d'échange culturel?: Les Peintres français et indochinois (fin XIXe–XXe siècle)* (Paris: Presses de l'École Française d'Extrême-Orient, 1997), 93–95.

81. Marc Chadourne, *Visions de l'Indochine: Études, pastels et gouaches de Mme A. Boullard Devé* (Paris: Plon, 1938).

82. On the emergence of childhood as a subject for the exploration of the creation of individual subjectivity in modern French painting, see Greg Thomas, *Impressionist Children: Childhood, Family and Modern Identity in French Art* (New Haven: Yale University Press, 2010).

83. Daniel Hémery, *Saigon, 1925–1945: De la 'belle colonie' à l'éclosion révolutionnaire ou la fin des dieux blancs* (Paris: Editions Autrement, 1992), 162–96; Alexander Woodside, "The Development of Social Organisations in Vietnamese Cities in the Late Colonial Period," *Pacific Affairs* 44, no. 1 (1971): 39–64.

84. Dr. Julien Huber, "Puériculture et hygiène de l'enfance," in *La Vie aux colonies: Préparation de la femme à la vie coloniale*, ed. J.-L. Faure (Paris: Larose Editeurs, 1938), 172–73.

85. Rachel Dogimont, speaking at the États Généraux de Féminisme in May 1931, insisted that "the native is vis-à-vis ourselves, our customs, our methods, like a big child," while Madame du Vivier de Streel, who claimed to have visited almost every French colony, opined, "These are big children, and it is as children that we must consider them." Conseil National des Femmes Françaises, *États généraux du féminisme, 30–31 mai 1931* (Paris: Conseil National des Femmes Françaises, 1931), 62.

86. Fournier, *Perspectives*, 117.

87. This interethnic elite partnership proceeded in other centres too. In 1936, in Hanoi, an Oeuvre de la Protection de la Mère et de l'Enfant was established under the joint presidency of the empress of Annam and the governor's wife, Madame Brévié.

88. The fight against infant mortality had begun earlier in the south; in 1909, doctors claimed that a campaign to prevent death by umbilical tetanus achieved a drop in infant

mortality rates to 6% in the first month of life (though still 29% died in the first year). M. Montel, "Sur la mortalité infantile en Cochinchine," *Bulletin de la Société Médico-Chirurgicale de l'Indochine* 10 (November 1926): 573; Édouard Marquis, *L'œuvre humaine de la France en Cochinchine* (Saigon: Imprimerie du Théâtre, 1936).

89. *Semaine de l'enfance sous le patronage de M le Gouverneur de la Cochinchine, présidence d'honneur de Mme Pierre-Pagès du 1e au 7 juillet 1934, congrès de l'enfance* (Saigon: Imprimerie de l'Union, 1934), 7.

90. Ibid., 10.

91. Ibid., 7.

92. Infant mortality had dropped from 175 per 1,000 in 1925, to 33 per 1,000 in 1938, according to Daléas. Professeur Daléas, "Les œuvres sociales du Tonkin," *Rapports présentés au 4è congrès de l'enfance 1940: Publiés sous les auspices du Comité central d'aide mutuelle et d'assistance sociale de Cochinchine* (Saigon: Imprimerie de l'Union, 1940), 50.

93. J. S. Furnivall, *Educational Progress in Southeast Asia* (New York: Institute of Pacific Relations, 1943), 51–52; Maks Banens, "Vietnam: A Reconstruction of Its Twentieth Century Population History," in *Quantitative Economic History of Vietnam 1900–1990*, ed. Jean-Pascal Bassino, Jean-Dominique Giacometti and K. Odaka (Tokyo: Hitotsubashi University, 2000), 1–40.

94. The religious organisations met under the presidency of the governor of Cochinchina's wife, Madame Pagès. Vietnamese National Archives Centre 2 (hereafter VNNA2), Gouvernement de la Cochinchine (Goucoch) VIA.8/282(31) "Compte rendu de la 3e semaine de l'enfance," 1938.

95. Richard Fogarty and Michael A. Osborne, "Constructions and Functions of Race in French Military Medicine, 1830–1920," in *The Color of Liberty, Histories of Race in France*, ed. Sue Peabody and Tyler Stovall (Durham: Duke University Press, 2003), 225–26.

96. "La 4e semaine de l'enfance," *Echo Annamite*, 6 April 1940; VNNA2 Goucoch III60/N30(8) 4e semaine de l'enfance 1940; VNNA2 Goucoch III60/N30(8) Veber to Administrators of the Saigon-Cholon Region, Provincial Chief Administrators, 30 December 1939.

CHAPTER 6

1. Among the earliest hill stations to be built in Asia were Buitenzorg, Java, founded in 1744, and Penang, which dated from 1786 and served the East India Company. J. E. Spencer and W. L. Thomas, "The Hill Stations and Summer Resorts of the Orient," *Geographical Review* 38 (1948): 637–51; Dane Kennedy, *The Magic Mountains: Hill Stations and the British Raj* (Delhi: Oxford University Press, 1996); J. T. Kenny, "Climate, Race and Imperial Authority: The Symbolic Landscape of the British Hill Station in India," *Annals of the Association of American Geographers* 85, no. 4 (1995): 694–714; Barbara Crossette, *The Great Hill Stations of Asia* (Boulder: Westview Press, 1998).

2. On the decline of the hill station and as "nurseries of the ruling race," see Kennedy, *Magic*, 118, 204.

3. Prashant Kidambi, *The Making of an Indian Metropolis: Colonial Governance and Public Culture in Bombay, 1890–1920* (Aldershot: Ashgate, 2007).

4. Nandini Bhattacharya, *Contagion and Enclaves: Tropical Medicine in Colonial India* (Liverpool: Liverpool University Press, 2012), 8.

5. Kennedy, *Magic*; Elizabeth Buettner, *Empire Families: Britons and Late Imperial India* (Oxford: Oxford University Press, 2004).

6. The Far Eastern Association for Tropical Medicine was founded in Manila in 1904.

Originally known as the Philippine Island Medical Association (its name was changed in 1909), the association was founded to disseminate knowledge of medical practice and the prevention of disease. The first congress was held in Manila in 1910.

7. Mary Sutphen, "Not What but Where: Bubonic Plague and the Reception of Germ Theories in Hong Kong and Calcutta, 1894–1897," *Journal of the History of Medicine* 52, no. 1 (1997): 81–113; Nancy Leys Stepan, *Picturing Tropical Nature* (Chicago: University of Chicago Press, 2001); Leonore Manderson, *Sickness and the State: Health and Illness in Colonial Malaya, 1870–1940* (Cambridge: Cambridge University Press, 1996), 8–10; Mark Harrison, *Public Health in British India: Anglo-India Preventive Medicine 1854–1914* (Cambridge: Cambridge University Press, 1994), 3.

8. Chamberlain established a malaria commission in West Africa to examine the application of the new knowledge. Patrick Manson, chief medical advisor to the colonial office from 1897, successfully encouraged Chamberlain to establish a School of Tropical Medicine in London in 1899.

9. Warwick Anderson, *Colonial Pathologies: American Tropical Medicine, Race, and Hygiene in the Philippines* (Durham: Duke University Press, 2006), 181. S. Marks and W. Anderson, "Typhus and Social Control: South Africa, 1917–1950," in *Disease, Medicine and Empire*, ed. R. MacLeod and M. Lewis (London: Routledge, 1988), 257–83.

10. Stephen Frenkel and John Western, "Pretext or Prophylaxis? Racial Segregation and Malarial Mosquitos in a British Tropical Colony: Sierra Leone," *Annals of the Association of American Geographers* 78, no. 2 (June 1988): 216; Warwick Anderson, "'Where Every Prospect Pleases and Only Man Is Vile': Laboratory Medicine as Colonial Discourse," *Critical Enquiry* 18 (Spring 1992): 507–8; John W. Cell, "Anglo-Indian Medical Theory and the Origins of Segregation in West Africa," *American Historical Review* 91, no. 2 (April 1986): 307–35; Carl Nightingale, *Segregation: A Global History of Divided Cities* (Chicago: University of Chicago Press, 2012).

11. Sir George W. Des Voeux, *My Colonial Service in British Guiana, St. Lucia, Trinidad, Fiji, Australia, New Foundland, and Hong Kong, with Interludes*, vol. 2 (London: John Murray, 1903), 252.

12. *Sepoys* was a term often used to refer to Indian troops. Dr. Auguste Benoist de la Grandière, *Ports de l'extrême-orient: Débuts de l'occupation française en Indochine: souvenirs de campagne; suivi du journal de bord: Extraits 1869* (Paris: Société française d'histoire d'outre-mer, 1994), 87.

13. PRO CO129/312 Chamberlain to Blake, 4 September 1902; John M. Carroll, *Edge of Empires: Chinese Elites and British Colonials in Hong Kong* (Boston: Harvard University Press, 2005), 92–94.

14. National Archives, London, Public Record Office (hereafter PRO), CO129/443 *Hong Kong Government Gazette*, 19 April 1904, 19. On the development of the Peak, see John M. Carroll, "The Peak: Residential Segregation in Colonial Hong Kong," in *Twentieth Century Colonialism and China: Localities, the Everyday and the World*, ed. Bryna Goodman and David Goodman (London: Routledge, 2012), 81–91.

15. Nightingale, *Segregation*, 113–34; Kennedy, *Magic*.

16. PRO CO129/327 newspaper extract, *Daily Press*, 29 March 1904.

17. Ho Tung was the son of Charles Henri Bosman, special juror with Merchant, Bosman and Co. (marine insurance), director of Hong Kong and Whampoa Dock Company. PRO CO129/323, 137 May to Lucas, 19 June 1904.

18. Nightingale, *Segregation*.

19. Ambe Njoh, *Planning Power: Town Planning and Social Control in Colonial Africa* (New York: Routledge, 2007), 206; Philip D. Curtin, "Medical Knowledge and Urban Planning in Tropical Africa," *American Historical Review* 90, no. 3 (June 1985): 594–613.

20. PRO CO129/327 Blake to Lucas, April 17, 1904.

21. Roger Bristow, *Land Use Planning in Hong Kong: History, Policies and Procedures* (Hong Kong: Oxford University Press, 1984), 39–40; Ka-che Yip, "Colonialism, Disease and Public Health: Malaria in the History of Hong Kong," in *Disease, Colonialism and the State: Malaria in Modern East Asian History,* ed. Ka-che Yip (Hong Kong: Hong Kong University Press, 2009), 20; Sutphen, "Not What but Where," 81–113.

22. PRO CO129/323 May to Lucas 19 June 1904.

23. On the generally observed decline in mortality in the tropics, see Philip Curtin, *Death by Migration: Europe's Encounter with the Tropical World in the Nineteenth Century* (New York: Cambridge University Press, 1989).

24. PRO CO129/443, minutes of meeting of Legislative Council, 19 April 1924, 19; PRO CO129/443, *Hongkong Government Gazette*, 19 April 1904, 20.

25. "Report of the Meeting of the Legislative Council," 19 April 1904, *Papers Laid before the Legislative Council of Hongkong* (Hong Kong: Government Printers, 1904), 18–19.

26. PRO CO129/443, *Hong Kong Government Gazette*, 19 April 1904, 20.

27. Deborah Dwork, *War is Good for Babies and Other Young Children: A History of the Infant and Child Welfare Movement in England, 1898–1918* (London: Tavistock, 1987).

28. PRO CO129/323 Minute "Peak Reservation Ordinance," June 1904; Nightingale, *Segregation*, 147. This is also quoted in Carroll, "Peak," 87.

29. Ho Kai's father had been the first ordained Chinese pastor in the London Missionary Society's (LMS) Hong Kong mission, and he was himself a member of the church, a member of the Sanitary Board 1886–96 and Legislative Council from 1890 to 1914. "An Ordinance for the Reservation of a Residential Area in the Hill District," *Hongkong Government Gazette*, 29 April 1904, 752; *Hongkong Hansard*, 19 April 1904, 18.

30. Nightingale, *Segregation*, 146–47.

31. On this, see Brenda Yeoh, *Contesting Space in Colonial Singapore: Power Relations and the Urban Built Environment* (Oxford: Oxford University Press, 2006), 303.

32. "An Ordinance for the Reservation of a Residential Area in the Hill District," *The Hongkong Government Gazette*, 29 April 1904, 752; *Hongkong Hansard* 19 April 1904, 18.

33. "Legislative Council, No. 7," *Papers Laid before the Legislative Council of Hongkong*, 26 April 1904.

34. Robert Peckham, "Matshed Laboratory: Colonies, Cultures and Bacteriology," in *Imperial Contagions: Medicine, Hygiene and Cultures of Planning in Asia*, ed. Robert Peckham and David M. Pomfret (Hong Kong: Hong Kong University Press, 2013), 123–50.

35. Myron Echenberg, *Plague Ports: The Global Urban Impact of Bubonic Plague, 1894–1901* (New York: New York University Press, 2007); Philippe Papin, *Histoire de Hanoi* (Paris: Fayard, 2001), 252–53.

36. Laurence Monnais-Rousselot, "'Modern Medicine' in French Colonial Vietnam: From the Importation of a Model to Its Nativisation," in *The Development of Modern Medicine in Non-Western Countries*, ed. Hormoz Ebrahimnejad (London: Routledge, 2008), 130–32.

37. Ibid., 127, 138; Laurence Monnais-Rousselot, "La Médicalisation de la mère et de son enfant: L'Exemple du Vietnam sous domination française, 1860–1939," *Canadian Bulletin for the History of Medicine/Bulletin Canadien d'Histoire de la Medecine* 19 (2002): 47–94.

38. When Charles Grall set about defining the 'ville Européen,' he had in mind the centres of Saigon, Tourane and Hải Phòng, places where "the Asian population is represented only by a few groups of natives, and notably by the Chinese." Le Dr. Ch. Grall, *Hygiène Colonial appliquée: Hygiène de l'Indochine* (Paris: J.-B. Baillière et Fils, 1908), 91.

39. Michael G. Vann, "Building Colonial Whiteness on the Red River: Race, Power and Urbanism in Paul Doumer's Hanoi, 1897–1902," *Historical Reflections/Réflexions Historiques* 33 (Summer 2007): 277–304.

40. Résident Supérieur Louis Morel advised Paul Doumer that the suburban belt should be made hygienic, and an experiment commenced with the creation of a '*zone de protection*' beyond the city limits. Dr. Charles Grall condemned Hanoi for its "incoherence," and for being "penetrated by indigenous communities." Grall, *Hygiène*, 108.

41. From 1892 Đồ Sơn had a park and hotel, and by 1910, three hotels. Lanessan owned a cottage there. On Đồ Sơn, see Claire Villemagne, "Station balnéaire et station d'altitude, deux formes de tourisme colonial en Indochine, les sites de Doson, Sapa et Dalat," in *Le Tourisme dans l'empire français: Politiques, pratiques et imaginaires (XIXe–XXe siècles)*, ed. Colette Zytnicki and Habib Kazdaghli (Paris: Publications de la Société Française d'Histoire d'Outre-Mer, 2009), 234.

42. Société des Missions-Étrangères, *Compte Rendu des travaux de* 1903 (Paris: Seminaire des Missions-Étrangères, 1904), 150.

43. Dr. M.-A. Legrand, *L'hygiène des troupes européennes aux colonies et dans les expéditions coloniales* (Paris: Henri Charles Lavauzelle, 1895), 402; Eric Jennings, *Imperial Heights: Dalat and the Making and Undoing of French Indochina* (Berkeley: University of California Press, 2012), 19.

44. Gustave Reynaud, *Hygiène des établissements coloniaux* (Paris: J.-B. Baillière et Fils, 1903), 350.

45. Vietnam National Archives Centre 4, Dalat (hereafter VNNA4), Résidence Supérieure d'Annam (RSA) HC 4092 "Rapport de l'inspecteur général des travaux publics sur le sanatorium du Lang Bian (Dalat), 1915," 24 September 1915.

46. Jennings, *Imperial*, 35–43.

47. Etienne Tardif, *La Naissance de Dalat: Annam (1899–1900) Capitale de l'Indochine* (Vienne: Ternet-Martin, 1949), 38–39.

48. L. des Charmettes, "Opinions de la colonisation et du métissage," *Avenir du Tonkin*, 20 January 1907, 2.

49. *L'Indochine à l'exposition coloniale de Marseille* (Marseille: Imprimerie Marseillaise, 1906), 53.

50. Grall, *Hygiène*, 460–61, 467.

51. Far Eastern Association of Tropical Medicine, *Second Biennial Congress, Hongkong January 20th to January 27th 1912, Programme and Guide to Hongkong* (Hong Kong: Noronha & Co., 1912), 23.

52. W. G. Black, *Winter Days in India and Elsewhere* (Glasgow: James Maclehose and Sons, 1908), 52–57.

53. Norman Edwards, *The Singapore House and Residential Life, 1819–1939* (Singapore: Oxford University Press, 1990), 71.

54. Immigrants into Singapore settled in areas set down in the 1823 town plan drawn up by Thomas Stamford Raffles, who was influenced by the military model applied in colonial India with its cantonment, lines and parade ground. The plan allocated govern-

ment institutions to the north bank of the river, commercial buildings to the south and the Chinese in the Chinatown area. The Malays of the Temengong village were relocated south between Tanjong Pagar and Telok Blangah. Nightingale, *Segregation*, 139–41.

55. Quoted in Yeoh, *Contesting*, 39.

56. A. J. Christopher, "Urban Segregation Levels in the British Overseas Empire and Its Successors in the Twentieth Century," *Transactions of the Institute of British Geographers* 17, no. 1 (1992): 95–107.

57. C. G. Morant, *Odds and Ends of Foreign Travel* (London: Charles and Edwin Layton, 1913), 68–70, 74–76.

58. Governor May wrote of this news that "it is probable that Mr. Ho Kom Tong's intention, in acquiring a house at the Peak, is to place his wives, concubines, and children there." PRO CO129/443 May to Long 5 September 1917.

59. The home government feared that the amendment would infringe the Treaty of Commerce and Navigation signed with the Japanese government on 3 April 1911, which permitted Japanese to "own or occupy houses in the same manner as native subjects." PRO CO129/451 Langley to Long 8 May 1918; PRO CO129/451 Long to May 15 May 1918.

60. PRO CO129/443 May to Long 5 September 1917.

61. PRO CO129/449 May to Long 20 August 1918.

62. *Hongkong Government Gazette*, 31 May 1918, 240.

63. S. A. Sweet, *A Hong Kong Sketch Book* (Hong Kong: Ye Olde Printerie, 1931), 1–2.

64. Association pour l'Autobiographie et le Patrimoine Autobiographique, Amberieu-en-Bugey (hereafter APA), 1389 Marguerite Fave, "Souvenirs d'Extrême-Orient, 1936–1946."

65. Quoted in Kerrie L. MacPherson, "Health and Empire: Britain's National Campaign to Combat Venereal Diseases in Shanghai, Hong Kong and Singapore," in *Sex, Sin and Suffering: Venereal Disease and European Society since 1870*, ed. Roger Weeks and Lesley A. Hall (London: Routledge, 1991), 182.

66. "H. K. Slum Overcrowding to Be Tackled in New Social Experiment," *China Mail*, 18 November 1937, 2.

67. PRO CO129/455, 344 "Report on Ordinance 14 of 1919," 10 September 1919.

68. "Cheung Chau (Residence) Ordinance," August 28, 1919, *Papers Laid before the Legislative Council of Hongkong*, 63–64.

69. Ibid., 64.

70. Ibid., 64–65.

71. Ibid., 64. "Diocesan Girls' School," *China Mail*, 13 February 1922.

72. One of the most outspoken leaders of this campaign for the extension of school provision for British children was the controversial N. Teesdale-Mackintosh, registrar of the University of Hong Kong. "Better Education of British Children," *Hongkong Daily Press*, 9 March 1923, 4.

73. Sue McPherson, "J. L. McPherson, Hong Kong YMCA: General Secretary, 1905–1935," *Journal of the Royal Asiatic Society, Hong Kong Branch* 46 (2006): 51.

74. Mrs. Claud Severn could regularly be found presenting prizes at Chinese girls' schools' prize presentation ceremonies, as we saw in Chapter 4.

75. VNNA4 RSA/HC 1020 Pierre Pasquier, "Note postale," 29 January 1920.

76. Paul Doumer vastly increased the size of the administration from 2,860 to 5,683 personnel from 1897 to 1911. There was just one administrator for every 76,000 inhabitants

of Dutch-governed Java, but the ratio in Cochinchina was one to 7,900 inhabitants. Harrison Brown, *Our Neighbours Today and Yesterday* (London: G. Howe, 1933), 140.

77. VNNA4 RSA/HC 802 Bulletin, Henry Pérot, Ligue Populaire des Pères et Mères de familles nombreuses de France, Section de l'Indochine.

78. Vietnam National Archives Centre 1, Hanoi (hereafter VNNA1), Mairie de Hanoi (MHN) E.03 43 "Rapport annuel sur la situation sociale, économique et politique de la ville de Hanoi du 30 juin 1920 au 30 juin 1921."

79. Louis Bonnafont, *Trente ans de Tonkin* (Paris: Eugène Figuière, 1924), 382.

80. VNNA1 MHN E.03 42 "Rapport annuel sur la situation sociale, économique et politique de la ville de Hanoi du 30 juin 1919 au 30 juin 1920, 30 juin 1920 au 30 juin 1921." By 1923 on the major boulevards of the French quarters of Hanoi, Vietnamese lawyers, merchants, teachers and doctors owned 42% of plots and nearly 20% of the land. Papin, *Histoire de Hanoi*, 248–49.

81. VNNA4 RSA/HC 4092 "Rapport de l'inspecteur général des travaux publics, Saigon," 24 September 1915, 37.

82. VNAA4 RSA/HC 4109 "Décisions prises par le Gouverneur Général de l'Indochine," 16 August 1924.

83. "L'Urbanisme—Dalat—Le nouveau plan dispositions générales," *L'Éveil Économique*, 21 October 1923, 7.

84. Jennings, *Imperial Heights*, 136, 140, 237. For a discussion of Hébrard's work in Indochina, see also Gwendolyn Wright, *The Politics of Design in French Colonial Urbanism* (Chicago: University of Chicago Press, 1991), 232.

85. VNAA4 1447/RSA/HC Merlin to Pasquier, 16 January 1924.

86. VNNA4 RSA/HC 4118 "Réunions de la Commission Municipale, 1926," Municipal Commission, Dalat, 25 November 1926.

87. Vassal had also conducted studies on children's blood in 1905. Dr. Joseph-Emile Borel, "Résultats d'une enquête malériologique à Dalat," *Extrait du Bulletin de la Société de Patholoqie Exotique* 20, no. 5 (11 May 1927): 429, 431–32.

88. Ibid.

89. VNAA4 4124RSA/HC "Procès verbal des délibérations," Municipal Commission, Dalat, 27 June 27 1934; VNAA4 4122/RSA/HC "Ordre du jour, délibérations," Municipal Commission, Dalat, 23 February 1935.

90. "L'Urbanisme," 7.

91. Laurent Joseph Gaide, *Les Stations climatiques en Indochine* (Hanoi: Imprimerie d'Extrême-Orient, 1930), 28–29.

92. VNAA4 4113/RSA/HC Terrisse to Commissaire Délégué, 15 December 1926; VNAA4 4113/RSA/HC "Procès verbal, Commission municipale d'hygiène," 16 January 1925.

93. VNAA4 4113/RSA/HC Terrisse to Commissaire Délégué, Government General, 15 December 1926.

94. Walter B. Harris, *East for Pleasure: The Narrative of Eight Months' Travel in Burma, Siam, The Netherlands East Indies and French Indochina* (London: Edward Arnold & Co., 1929), 286.

95. VNNA4 RSA/HC 4122 "Ordre du jour, délibérations, session ordinaire," Municipal Commission, Dalat, 17 September 1928.

96. In fact, the physicians who scrutinized the health of Vietnamese children attending school in Dalat noted little more than a slight predisposition to trachoma. Direc-

tion Général de l'Instruction Publique, *Le Petit Lycée de Dalat* (Hanoi: Imprimerie d'Extrème-Orient, 1930), 10.

97. Ibid., 7.

98. The length of time between furloughs for example was the same, two to three years, though return was perhaps "more essential for young subjects." Médecin General Passa, "L'Enfant européen dans la France d'outre-mer tropicale: Sa protection sanitaire," *Revue Médico-Sociale et de Protection de l'Enfance* 1, no. 6 (1938): 28.

99. Direction Générale de l'Instruction Publique, *Petit lycée*, 17.

100. Robert Reed, "From Highland Hamlet to Regional Capital: Reflections on the Colonial Origins, Urban Transformation and Environmental Impact of Dalat," in *The Challenges of Highland Development in Vietnam*, ed. Terry Rambo et al. (Honolulu: East-West Center, 1995), 51.

101. VNAA4 2762/RSA/HC Pasquier to Billotte, 1 December 1930.

102. VNAA4 4124/RSA/HC "Procès verbaux de la Commission municipale et commission sanitaire de Dalat," Municipal Commission, Dalat, 17 August 1935.

103. VNAA4 4130/RSA/HC "Procès verbal des délibérations," Municipal Commission, Dalat, 5 December 1936.

104. On 1 July 1936, the total population of Dalat was recorded as 7,191 people, of whom 6,273 were Vietnamese. VNNA4 RSA/HC 4133 "Procès verbal des délibérations," Municipal Commission, Dalat, 20 March 1937," 38–39.

105. Quoted in Jennings, *Imperial*, 178.

106. Gaide, *Stations*, 47. At a ceremony held in honour of Yersin, the resident mayor made this link explicit, explaining, "The Lycée is fundamentally linked to the development of the Hill Station." VNNA4 RSA/HC 4126 "Procès verbal des délibérations," Municipal Commission, Dalat, 25 May 1935, 6, 39.

107. VNAA4 4122/RSA/HC "Procès verbal des délibérations," Municipal Commission, Dalat, 14 September 1928, 2. The Municipal Commission proudly reported that the opening of the school confirmed Dalat's position as the preeminent hill station in the peninsula. VNAA4 4122/RSA/HC "Ordre du jour, délibérations," Municipal Commission, Dalat, 14 September 1928, 2.

108. Gaide, *Stations*, 47.

109. Justin Godart, *Rapport de mission en Indochine: 1er janvier—14 mars 1937* (reprinted, Paris: L'Harmattan, 1994), 153.

110. Ibid., 57.

111. VNNA1 MHN L.8 2701 Résident Supérieur au Tonkin to Administrator Mayor of Hanoi, 4 August 1937.

112. At around 47 piasters per school month, plus stipend, many found this expense prohibitive. "Correspondance," *Le Fonctionnaire*, 26 June 1936, 6; Thérèse de Hargues, *Anecdotes d'un roule-ta-bousse* (Paris: La Pensée Universelle, 1992).

113. "Public Health," *Straits Times*, 1 December 1920, 1.

114. J. E. Nathan, *The Census of British Malaya (The Straits Settlements, Federated Malay States and Protected States of Johore, Kedah, Perlis, Kelantan, Trengganu and Brunei)* (London: Waterlow & Sons, 1922), 70, 118.

115. Married and Marooned, "Leave Conditions," *The Planter*, February 1923, 479.

116. They could draw here upon the spectre of the British Raj, where by 1900 nearly half of the 150,000 European residents were considered 'poor whites.' David Arnold, "Eu-

ropean Orphans and Vagrants in India in the Nineteenth Century," *Journal of Imperial and Commonwealth History* 7, no. 2 (1979): 104–27.

117. "Hill Schools for Children," *Straits Times*, 2 September 1922, 10; "Hill Schools," *The Planter*, October 1922, 317.

118. The Nilgris in southern India was a key reference. "Hill Schools," *The Planter*, October 1922, 317.

119. "Proposed Hill School," *Straits Times*, 7 February 1923, 9.

120. S. Robert Aitken, *Imperial Belvederes* (Oxford: Oxford University Press, 1994), 41.

121. "High Schools for Malaya: A Children's Home," *Straits Times*, 17 May 1929, 7.

122. "Third European School in Malaya," *Straits Times*, 6 August 1935, 18. By the mid-1930s the twenty-two government buildings at Fraser's Hill were government administered and there were an additional twenty private dwellings; the site was principally known as a resort for Federated Malay States administrators.

123. "Hill Schools," *The Planter*, October 1922, 317.

124. "A Hill School for Malaya," *Singapore Free Press and Mercantile Advertiser*, 31 May 1923, 4.

125. Ibid.

126. "The Absent Child," *Straits Times*, 2 December 1922, 2.

127. "Hill School for Malaya," 4.

128. "Hill Schools for Children," *Straits Times*, 2 September 1922, 10; 'Ceylon Planter,' "The Married Man," *The Planter*, March 1923, 498.

129. Glenn T. Trewartha, "Recent Thought on the Problem of White Acclimatization in the Wet Tropics," *Geographical Review* 16, no. 3 (1926): 477–78.

130. Andrew Balfour, "Hill Schools," *The Planter*, October 1923, 75; "Europeans in the Tropics," *Singapore Free Press and Mercantile Advertiser*, 11 April 1925, 6; "For European Children," *Straits Times*, 3 October 1929, 10.

131. Castellani cited Alexander Rattray's study of the deleterious effect of climate upon naval cadets aged fourteen to seventeen years old written some sixty years earlier. Aldo Castellani, *Climate and Acclimatization: Some Notes and Observations* (London: John Bale, Sons & Danielsson, 1931), 61–62.

132. Clive Dalton, "My Happy Childhood in Malaya," *Straits Times*, 27 January 1935, 17. Clark arrived in Malaya aged eight and returned to England aged thirteen.

133. "A Hill School for Malaya," *Singapore Free Press and Mercantile Advertiser*, 31 May 1923, 4.

134. Alternatives were few. Visiting Brastagi in the Dutch East Indies, a day and a half away, entailed heavy expense in steamer fares and hotels. H. Bleackley, *A Tour in Southern Asia (Indo-China, Malaya, Java, Sumatra and Ceylon, 1925–1926)* (London: John Lane, The Bodley Head, 1928), 117–24, 127–28, 131–33, 153–59.

135. "Cameron's Highlands and Agriculture," *Singapore Free Press and Mercantile Advertiser*, 21 May 1925.

136. PRO CO717/48/1965 G. G. "Construction of a Road to Camerons, 1926," 26 February 1926; "Hill Stations for Malaya," *Malayan Saturday Post*, 28 March 1925, 14.

137. This call resounded with that of R. Hanitsch, presented before the Straits Philosophical Society on 13 September 1902. R. Hanitsch, "Comment," in *Noctes Orientales: Being a Selection of Essays before the Straits Philosophical Society between the Years 1893 and 1910* (Singapore: Kelly and Walsh, 1912), 221; "Road to the Highlands," *British Malaya*, November 1927, 188.

Notes to Chapter 6

138. "Developing Camerons," *Singapore Free Press*, 23 April 1926, 16. E. N. T. Cummins, an unofficial member of the development committee, also complained of this. "Cameron's Highlands," *The Planter*, November 1927, 114.

139. "Cameron's Highlands," *British Malaya*, September 1928, 142. In 1903 Baguio had a sanatorium and five cottages. By 1928 it was a town of 15,000 people, primarily Americans. "A Policy for Cameron's Highlands," *British Malaya*, November 1928, 193.

140. PRO CO717/48/1965 "Construction of a Road to Camerons 1926," 22 February 1926.

141. PRO CO717/48/1965 "Construction of a Road to Camerons 1926 Report," 17 February 1926; PRO CO717/57/10 Enclosure 1 to Federated Malay States Despatch 424 22 July 1927.

142. "High Schools for Malaya: A Children's Home," *Straits Times*, 17 May 1929, 7.

143. Ibid.

144. However, this seems not to have diminished enthusiasm among French parents in Hanoi and Saigon for the schools in Dalat. Thérèse de Hargues, who attended the Couvent des Oiseaux run by the Canonesses of Saint-Augustin, which opened in November 1935 providing secondary-level study, saw her parents only during the school holidays after the age of eleven. De Hargues, *Anecdotes*, 39–43.

145. "High Schools for Malaya," 7.

146. "Cameron's Highlands," *British Malaya*, October 1929, 172.

147. "The Malayan Climate versus the White Race," *The Planter*, January 1933, 204.

148. Passages for wives and children (whether cut or never offered) were provided only by about 25% of employers from 1932 to 1935. By the end of the Depression the government remained one of the few employers offering passage for wives and children. "Planters' Salaries," *The Planter*, October 1937, 438. The Destitute Strangers' Aid Fund of Singapore worked to repatriate 'deserving' indigents to England and Australia. "Destitute Europeans in Singapore," *British Malaya*, May 1929, 4.

149. "For European Children," *Straits Times*, 3 October 1929, 10.

150. "What Malaya Is Saying," *British Malaya*, July 1929, 100.

151. "For European Children," *Straits Times*, 5 October 1929, 5.

152. "What Malaya Is Saying," 100.

153. Ibid.

154. Yap Pheng Geck, "For European Children," *Straits Times*, 8 October 1929, 12.

155. 'Diam,' "The Fat of the Land," *Straits Times*, 23 October 1929, 17; 'European Mother,' "For European Children," *Straits Times*, 21 October 1929, 12.

156. 'Chakap,' "For European Children," *Straits Times*, 30 October 1929, 17.

157. "Why a Hill School?" *Straits Times*, 20 November 1929, 10.

158. Ibid.

159. "Malaya's Hill Stations," *British Malaya*, February 1930, 297.

160. "Malaya on Air-Mail Day," *British Malaya*, June 1938, 33.

161. "What Malaya Is Saying," *British Malaya*, October 1929, 194–95; "Cameron's Highlands," *British Malaya*, August 1929, 111.

162. "Cameron's Highlands," *The Planter*, January 1930, 152.

163. "The Development of the Cameron Highlands," *The Planter*, June 1933, 416.

164. "What Malaya Is Saying," *British Malaya*, April 1933, 284.

165. "School at Camerons," *Singapore Free Press and Mercantile Advertiser*, 23 January 1934, 3.

166. 'Anak Susu,' "A Holiday in the Highlands," *The Planter*, September 1936, 409.
167. C. C. Footner, "A Talk on the Cameron Highlands," *The Planter*, October 1935, 467.
168. The appointment of a district officer and medical officer was finally arranged for 1939. "Cameron Highlands," *British Malaya*, November 1938, 168.
169. A petition of 1938 to improve access met with failure. The end of the road to Tapah was suitable for light vehicles only. Proposals to build shorter roads to Ipoh or Gopeng were refused.
170. "Cameron Highlands as a Holiday Resort," *The Planter*, October 1938, 500.
171. "With Climate Like an English Spring," *Singapore Free Press and Mercantile Advertiser*, 27 January 1934.
172. "Schools Amid Rubber," *The Planter*, December 1938, 624.
173. PRO ADM1/21185 "A Rest Camp in the Cameron Highlands, Report of Mr. Pringle on His Visit to Admiralty Establishments, December 1935, January 1936."
174. PRO ADM1/21185 Head of CE 22 September 1936; PRO ADM1/21185 Fitzroy Williams, Medical Director General 13 August 1936.
175. Sunil Amrith, "'Contagion of the Depot': The Government of Indian Emigration," in *Imperial Contagions*, ed. Peckham, 161.

CHAPTER 7

1. Susan Pedersen, "The Maternalist Moment in British Colonial Policy: The Controversy over 'Child Slavery' in Hong Kong, 1917–1941," *Past and Present* 171 (May 2001): 161–202; John Carroll, "A National Custom: Debating Female Servitude in Late Nineteenth-Century Hong Kong," *Modern Asian Studies* 43, no. 6 (2009): 1463–93; Rachel Leow, "'Do You Own Non-Chinese Mui Tsai?' Re-Examining Race and Female Servitude in Malaya and Hong Kong, 1919–1939," *Modern Asian Studies* 46, no. 6 (2012): 1746–52; Norman Miners, *Hong Kong under Imperial Rule, 1912–1941* (Hong Kong: Oxford University Press, 1987); Sarah Paddle, "The Limits of Sympathy: International Feminists and the Chinese 'Slave Girl' Campaigns of the 1920s and 1930s," *Journal of Colonialism and Colonial History* 4, no. 3 (2003): 1–23.
2. Frank Swettenham, *British Malaya: An Account of the Origin and Progress of British Influence in Malaya* (London: J. Lane, 1906), 78, 81.
3. In 1867, Governor Sir Richard MacDonnell refused to sanction the return of one nineteen-year-old runaway girl servant to her master in China on the grounds that she "was guilty of no crime, and wished to stay in Hongkong." National Archives, London, Public Record Office (hereafter PRO), CO 129/211 J. Russell, "Report on Child Adoption and Domestic Service among Hong Kong Chinese," 18 July 1883; Christopher Munn, *Anglo-China: Chinese People and British Rule in Hong Kong, 1841–1880* (Richmond: Curzon Press, 2001), 22.
4. Henry, quoted in Jules Silvestre, "Rapport sur l'esclavage," *Excursions et reconnaissances* 2, no. 3 (1880; reprinted 1894): 37; see also Francis Garnier, *Voyage d'exploration en Indochine, effectué pendant les anneés 1866, 1867 et 1868 par une commission française présidée par M. le capitaine de frégate, Doudart de Lagrée*, 2 vols. (Paris: Hachette et Cie, 1873), i, 172. On early French engagements with open forms of slavery, see Karine Delaye, "Slavery and Colonial Representations in Indochina from the Second Half of the Nineteenth to the Early Twentieth Century," *Slavery and Abolition* 24, no. 2 (2003): 129–42.
5. "Declaration by the Chief Justice," 6 October 1879, Enclosure 1 in Hennessy to Hicks Beach, 23 January 1880, in *Correspondence Respecting the Alleged Existence of Chinese Slav-*

ery in Hong Kong: Presented to Both Houses of Parliament by Command of Her Majesty (London: HMSO, 1882), 6.

6. An anonymous article known to have been written by Raoul Postel, a former magistrate in Saigon, inspired this review: "Une Colonie esclavagiste," *La Lanterne*, 14 January 1880, 2; Archives Nationales d'Outre-mer, Aix-en-Provence (hereafter ANOM), Fonds Ministeriels (FM) SG/INDO/AF Indochine carton 14, dossier A30(28) Le Myre de Vilers to Jauréguiberry, 12 April 1880; Jules Silvestre, "Rapport," 50–51.

7. Silvestre, "Rapport," 44, 51.

8. A. Landes, "Rapport au gouverneur sur la prostitution à Cholon," *Excursions et reconnaissances* 2, no. 3 (1880; reprinted 1894): 55.

9. Silvestre, "Rapport," 53.

10. Isabella L. Bird, *The Golden Chersonese and the Way Thither* (London: John Murray, 1883), 98.

11. On the profitability of importing Chinese women and girls for brothel prostitution in Singapore see James Warren, *Ah Ku and Karayuki-san: Prostitution in Singapore, 1870–1940* (Singapore: Oxford University Press, 1993), 59–63.

12. PRO CO273/118 newspaper extract, "Slavery," *Straits Times Overland Journal*, 5 May 1882.

13. PRO CO273/143 Enclosure A, in Despatch 38 of 24 January 1887, Mr. Allan's statement recorded by Inspector W. Luke, 25 August 1886.

14. PRO CO273/143 Enclosure B in Despatch 38 of 24 January 1887, Elizabeth's Statement recorded by Inspector W. Luke, 25 August 1886.

15. *Kling* being a pejorative term used to refer to South Indians. PRO CO273/143 Enclosure E in Despatch 38 of 24 January 1887, T. Irvine Rowell to Superintendent Bell, 1 September 1886.

16. PRO CO273/143 Allan to Dunlop, 3 September 1886.

17. W. J. Allan, "Singapore Justice," *Straits Times*, 16 September 1886, 13.

18. W. J. Allan, "Singapore Justice," *Straits Times*, 30 September 1886, 15; *The Protestant Educational Institute: A Short Report for the Year 1887* (London, 1888), 10–11.

19. J. D. Vaughan, *The Manners and Customs of the Chinese of the Straits Settlements* (Kuala Lumpur: Oxford University Press, 1971), 88.

20. Isabella Bird had described debt slavery as "a great curse" but part of 'Malay custom' "which our treaties bind us to respect." She noted, "Some people palliate the system, and speak of it as "a mild form of domestic servitude." Isabella L. Bird, *The Golden Chersonese and the Way Thither* (London: John Murray, 1883), 358–61. Emily Innes published an account of her life in Selangor alleging that Hugh Low, the resident of Perak, "aided and abetted the practice of slavery." Emily Innes, *The Chersonese with the Gilding Off* (Kuala Lumpur: Oxford University Press, 1974), vii, 137–40.

21. PRO CO273/143 Enclosure 2 in Despatch 38 of 24 January 1887, J. Irvine Rowell to Knutsford, 19 January 1887.

22. Protestant Educational Institute, *Short Report*, 11.

23. PRO CO129/194 E. J. Eitel, Report, 25 October 1879; PRO,CO 129/211 J. Russell, "Report on Child Adoption and Domestic Service among Hong Kong Chinese," 18 July 1883.

24. On such 'natural' checks within bond service preventing cruelty elsewhere, see Gyan Prakash, *Bonded Histories: Genealogies of Labor Servitude in Colonial India* (Cambridge: Cambridge University Press, 1990), 148, 219.

25. For a discussion of this protective legislation, see Philippa Levine, "Modernity,

Medicine and Colonialism: The Contagious Diseases Ordinances in Hong Kong and the Straits Settlements," *Positions* 6, no. 3 (1998): 675–705. The name 'Po Leung Kuk' was usually rendered in English as the 'Society for the Protection of Innocents'; see Elizabeth Sinn, "Chinese Patriarchalism and the Protection of Women in 19th-Century Hong Kong," in *Women and Chinese Patriarchy: Submission, Servitude and Escape*, ed. Maria Jaschok and Suzanne Miers (Hong Kong: Hong Kong University Press, 1994), 141–67.

26. The Straits government also closed loopholes which had seen domestic servants excluded from the operation of the Labour Contracts Ordinance of 1882. This formed the backdrop to efforts to introduce the registration of domestic servants in January 1887. PRO CO273/143 Straits Settlements, *Paper Laid before the Legislative Council*, 23 November 1886, "Registration of Domestic Servants" 10 July 1886; PRO CO273/165 Smith, to Knutsford, 3 March 1890.

27. J. A. Bethune Cook, *Sunny Singapore* (London: Elliot Stock, 1907), 140.

28. C.W.S. Kynnersley, "The Prevention and Repression of Crime," *Straits Chinese Magazine* 1, no. 3 (1897): 78.

29. The societies in Hong Kong and Singapore were in direct communication with each other. PRO CO273/201/14848 "Statement of Facts, Which Mrs. Andrew and Dr. Kate Bushnell Are Prepared to Prove from Their Personal Knowledge," 23 August 1894; PRO CO273/134/11346 Smith to Earl of Derby, 26 May 1885.

30. "The Lady Baby Broker," *Straits Chinese Magazine* 7, no. 2 (June 1903): 64.

31. Charles Lemire, *L'Indochine: Cochinchine française, royaume de Cambodge, royaume d'Annam et Tonkin*, 3rd ed. (Paris, 1884), 112.

32. Ibid.

33. Quoted in Henri Dartiguenave, "Des ventes d'enfants en Indochine," *Revue Indochinoise*, 29 February 1908, 243.

34. ANOM Gouvernement Général de l'Indochine (GGI) F.76 22525 Report, Vice Resident of France in Lao Kay to Résident Supérieur au Tonkin 1 May 1891.

35. Ibid.

36. Ibid.

37. On the importance of sacralised child life to the fashioning of a humanitarian ethics, see Didier Fassin, *Humanitarian Reason: A Moral History of the Present* (Berkeley: University of California Press, 2012), 221, 234.

38. Emphasis as in original. ANOM GGI F.76 22525 Baille, Resident, to High Resident in Tonkin, 6 April 1891.

39. "The Protection of Women and Girls," *China Mail*, 22 July 1889, 3.

40. ANOM GGI F.76 22525 Brière to Residents, Vice Residents and Provincial Chiefs in Tonkin, 22 April 1891. On the abduction of Vietnamese children into slavery as a 'Chinese' problem, see also P. Néïs, "Sur les frontières du Tonkin," *Bulletin de la Société de Géographie de l'Est*, 1 (1888); Ulysse Leriche, *Etude économique et politique sur la question d'extrême-Orient* (Saigon: Le Mékong, 1895), 10; Maurice Rondet-Saint, *Dans notre empire jaune: Notes et croquis* (Paris: Plon, 1917), 155. See also correspondence at ANOM GGI F.76 22525 and GGI F.76 22526.

41. "L'Indochine jugée par les étrangères," *La Revue Indochinoise*, 9 February 1903, 121.

42. Vietnam National Archives Centre 1, Hanoi (hereafter VNNA1), Résidence Supérieure du Tonkin (RST) D.638 30.148 "Bétail humain," *L'Avenir du Tonkin*, 26 October 1899.

43. Société des Missions-Étrangères, *Compte Rendu des travaux de 1906* (Paris: Seminaire des Missions-Étrangères, 1907), 140–41.

44. "Pauvres petiots," *L'Avenir du Tonkin*, 28 November 1906, 3.
45. Ibid. See also "La Traite des jaunes," *L'Avenir du Tonkin*, 15 August 1906, 2; "Pour les enfants," *L'Avenir du Tonkin*, 16 September 1906, 2; "Pour l'enfance," *L'Avenir du Tonkin*, 22 and 23 October 1906, 3; "La Traite des jaunes," *L'Avenir du Tonkin*, 10 January 1907, 1; "Encore les rapts d'enfants," *L'Avenir du Tonkin*, 19 January 1907, 3.
46. Bonnafont wondered, "How many children are there in all Tonkin sold this month to pay bills?" Louis Bonnafont, *Trente ans de Tonkin* (Paris: Editeur Eugène Figuière, 1924), 216–17.
47. "Pour l'enfance," *L'Avenir du Tonkin*, 22–23 October 1906, 3.
48. By this time in France, childhood was protected by a slew of republican-era legislation, including the law of 7 December 1874 protecting children in ambulant professions, the law of 23 December 1874 concerning the protection of infants (the Loi Roussel), the law of 24 July 1889 on the protection of mistreated and morally abandoned children, the law of 2 November 1892 on the labour of children in industrial workplaces, the law of 19 April 1898 on the repression of violence, acts of cruelty and assaults against children, and the law of 27 June 1904 on assisted children.
49. Florence Bretelle l'Establet, "Resistance and Receptivity: French Colonial Medicine in Southwest China, 1898–1930," *Modern China* 25, no. 2 (April 1999): 171–203.
50. Centre des Archives Diplomatiques de Nantes (hereafter CADN), HK34 Landret to Consul of France in Hong Kong, 19 August 1896.
51. The girls were repatriated on 15 June 1912. CADN HK45 French Consul, Hong Kong to Mayor of Hải Phòng, 15 June 1912.
52. These he took to Nam Quan, over the border. Point stressed that he undertook the journey himself with the girls "under my care." ANOM GGI F.749 33.028 Point to Sarraut 25 June 1912; ANOM GGI F.749 33.028 Point to Sarraut, 27 June 1912.
53. Kliene specifically targeted German-run services running out of Hải Phòng, and notably the German-run Jebsen Company's steamer, the *Carl Diederichsen*. ANOM GGI F.266 56.255 Beauvais to Bonhoure, 29 February 1908.
54. ANOM GGI F.76 22526 Beauvais to Beau, 21 September 1906.
55. League of Nations Archive, Geneva (hereafter LON), R.680. A.127.1924.IV "Fifth Assembly of the League of Nations, Protection of Children, Resolution Adopted by the Assembly at Its Meeting Held on Friday September 26th 1924," 1.
56. See Frederick D. Lugard, *The Dual Mandate in British Tropical Africa* (London: W. Blackwood and Sons, 1922), 60–62.
57. National Archives, London, Public Record Office PRO CO 129/446 Appleton to Long, 27 October 1917.
58. PRO CO 129/461 "Child Slavery in Hong Kong," *Hong Kong Daily Press*, 10 March 1920.
59. PRO CO 129/449 May to Long, 9 August 1918. Governor Stubbs also adopted this approach. See PRO CO 129/473, Stubbs to Churchill, 10 March 1921.
60. Hugh Haslewood carefully linked diatribes against bond service to more general condemnation of the labour conditions of 'tiny children' in Hong Kong. See, for example, PRO FO 228/3571 H. L. Haslewood, "British Allow Child Slavery in Hong Kong," *New York American*, 29 May 1921. Concern over the plight of British children transferred from their biological families resulted in 1926 in the addition to the statute of legislation governing adoption.

61. On evangelical-led campaigns against child labour in China from 1923 to 1926, see Adelaide Mary Anderson, *Humanity and Labour in China: An Industrial Visit and Its Sequel (1923 to 1926)* (London: Student Christian Movement, 1928).

62. PRO, CO 129/473 Hugh Haslewood, "Child Slavery: Under British Rule," *Hong Kong Daily News*, 11 May 1921.

63. PRO, FO 228/3571 Parliamentary questions, 1 August 1921.

64. PRO, CO 129/473, E. R. Hallifax, Memorandum, "The Mui-Tsai System," 27 June 1921; PRO, CO 129/473 Memorandum, "Alleged Child Slavery in Hong Kong"; PRO, FO 228/3571 Memorandum, "Hong Kong (Treatment of Children)," 8 November 1921.

65. *Hansard*, 5th ser., 127, col. 1348 (31 March 1920). The legal consequences of setting a child 'free' had been raised in earlier engagements with the domestic bond servant problem. See especially, PRO, CO129/221 O'Malley to Marsh, 6 May 1885. Susan Pedersen also notes this paradox; see Pedersen, "Maternalist," 182.

66. PRO, CO 129/468 "Chinese Meeting on 'Mui Tsai' Question," *Hong Kong Daily Press*, 2 August 1921.

67. PRO, FO 228/3571 "Hong Kong (Treatment of Children)," 21 March 1922.

68. Lady Kathleen Simon, "The Slave Child Overseas," *Child's Guardian*, December 1929, 88.

69. "Child Slavery," *South China Morning Post*, 9 October 1929; "Child Labour in Hongkong," *South China Morning Post*, 17 July 1929; PRO, CO129/521/7 "Traffickers in Children," *Hong Kong Weekly Press*, 6 Septemberk 1929; PRO, CO129/521/7 "Hong Kong Slave Market—Extensive Traffic in Children," *Singapore Free Press*, 16 August 1929; PRO, CO 129/521/7 "Children Sold," *China Mail*, 10 August 1929. While some reports defined *mui tsai* as being aged "between four and thirteen," the ordinance of 1923 had set the upper limit of this identity at eighteen; PRO, CO 129/514 "Little Yellow Slaves under the Union Jack," *John Bull*, April 1929.

70. Rhodes House Library, Oxford (hereafter RHL), Anti-Slavery Society Papers MSS Brit. Emp. S22, K26/2 Hilary Davis to Lady Kathleen Simon; RHL Anti-Slavery Society Papers MSS Brit. Emp. S22, K26/2 David Kerr to Lady Kathleen Simon, 1 November 1929.

71. Lieutenant Commander and Mrs. H. L. Haslewood, *Child Slavery in Hong Kong: The Mui Tsai System* (London: Sheldon Press, 1930); Lieutenant Commander and Mrs. H. L. Haslewood, "Child Slavery in Hong Kong: The Attitude of the Church of England and Its Associated Societies," Rhodes House Library, Oxford, Anti-Slavery Society Papers, MSS Brit. Emp. S22, K25/2.

72. PRO, CO129/516/6 "Protection of Children," *South China Morning Post*, 15 October 1929. On the difficulties encountered by colonial officials, having set out to defend 'custom,' to actually define *mui tsai*, see Leow, "Non Chinese."

73. PRO CO273/563/6 Clementi to Passfield, 24 March 1930.

74. PRO CO273/563/6 Minute, Walter D. Ellis, 30 October 1930.

75. W. W. Woods, *Mui Tsai in Hong Kong and Malaya: Report of Commission* (London: HMSO, 1937), 68–69, 72–73.

76. On Picton-Turbervill, see Pedersen, "Maternalist," 191–92.

77. See 'Minority Report,' in Woods, *Mui Tsai in Hong Kong and Malaya*, 229, 245.

78. Ibid., 103. In 1939, the governor could report that only 324 *mui tsai* remained on the registers. PRO, CO 859/11/15 "Report by the Governor of Hong Kong on the Mui Tsai in the Colony for the Half-Year Ended the 31st May 1939."

79. Pedersen, "Maternalist," 183. The upper boundary of 'childhood' was, in Britain,

popularly associated with the upper age limit of metropolitan elementary schooling, which increased to fourteen across the period. According to the census of 1921, roughly one third of *mui tsai* were over the age of fourteen. PRO, CO 129/514 "A Pledge Unhonoured," *Manchester Guardian*, 16 January 1929; Miners, *Hong Kong*, 156.

80. When this line eventually proved successful in securing the colonial government's agreement to implement her Minority Report, Edith Picton-Turbervill remarked that it had been "far easier to legislate for the protection of all transferred children than for one section like the *mui tsai*." "Miss Turbervill, 'Feels Like Weeping for Joy,'" *Straits Times*, 12 November 1937, 13. See *Hansard*, 5th ser., 252, cols. 925–57 (11 May 1931); Edith Picton-Turbervill, *Life Is Good: An Autobiography* (London: Frederick Muller, 1939), 296.

81. PRO, CO 825/27/7 Edith Picton-Turbervill, "Rescued Girls in Hong-Kong," *Manchester Guardian*, 22 February 1939. On the normative happiness of childhood in Britain, see Hugh Cunningham, "Childhood and Happiness in Britain," *GRAAT* 36 (2007): 19–30.

82. "Not the most rabid reformer of Eastern people's morals can honestly say that there is any form of slavery in the system as it obtains here," advised *British Malaya*. "The Mui-tsai Commission," *British Malaya*, June 1936, 48.

83. Leow, "'Non-Chinese,'" 1746–52.

84. "What Malaya Is Saying," *British Malaya*, December 1928, 221; Katherine Dixon, *Address to Mothers—Upon the Moral Education of Children* (Singapore: Social Service Society, 1919).

85. "The Social Evil," *British Malaya*, April 1928, 323.

86. Political histories of interwar Singapore have tracked a striking swing from an earlier laissez-faire approach to a much more intensively regulationist approach, exemplified by the creation of a secret police organisation and drastic restrictions upon Chinese immigration. Kay E. Gillis, *Singapore Civil Society and British Power* (Singapore: Talisman, 2005), 74–104.

87. "We Chinese are not beasts; these arrangements should not be made for us," declared one commentator. Quoted in C.J. Ferguson Davie, "The Social Evil in Malaya," *British Malaya*, December 1928, 216; C.J. Ferguson Davie, "More about the Social Evil," *British Malaya*, March 1929, 287. Other scholars, and notably Rachel Leow, have also arrived at the conclusion that the 'Chineseness' of the *mui tsai* question should not be taken for granted. Leow, "Non-Chinese," 1761; Karen Yuen, "Theorising the Chinese: The Mui tsai Controversy and Constructions of Transnational Chineseness in Hong Kong and British Malaya," *New Zealand Journal of Asian Studies* 6, no. 2 (December 2004): 95–110.

88. *British Malaya*, commenting on the need to embark on extensive social legislation in Malaya, opined that "the obligation resting on the administration in this as in other matters is all the more irresistible because we remain under the aegis of 'benevolent bureaucracy' and it will be long before the country is ready for anything like representative government." "Unemployed Clerks," *British Malaya*, April 1937, 280.

89. "Singapore in 1926," *British Malaya*, December 1926, 227.

90. Nicoll-Jones arrived in Singapore in the spring of 1940 and made a report to the police on the problem of prostitution in May 1941.

91. Barbara Watson Andaya and Leonard Y. Andaya, *A History of Malaysia*, 2nd ed. (Honolulu: University of Hawaiʻi Press, 2001), 227.

92. "The Management of Estate Schools," *The Planter*, December 1930, 610–15; "Schools Amid Rubber," *The Planter*, December 1938, 624.

93. Late in the period the Straits Settlements government took the initiative to pass

a raft of other legislation protecting children's interests, including ordinance numbers 8, 17, 18 and 43 in 1939. Ordinance 17 provided for employment, neglect and ill-treatment of children (those under fourteen). It made registration of all transfers of children away from their parents compulsory and provided the 'Protector of Chinese' with the power to inspect individual cases. Ordinance 18 dealt, for the first time, with adoption.

94. The colonial state had begun to expand the regulation of children's welfare and industrial labour through legislation such as the Factory (Accidents) Ordinance (1927), the Industrial Employment of Women, Young Persons and Children Amendment Ordinance (1929), the Factories and Workshops Ordinance (1932) and the Factories and Workshops Amendment Ordinance (1936). A new ordinance in 1937 dealt with the minimum age for admission of children to industrial employment and night work. However, Hong Kong remained a trading centre rather than an industrial colony.

95. Ultimately, even 'imperial feminists' were uneasy at the implications of this. Edith Picton-Turbervill, describing a child 'retrieved,' apparently felt compelled to add the awkward rider, seemingly by way of justification: "Chinese children are among the most attractive in the world." PRO CO 825/27/7 Picton-Turbervill, "Rescued Girls in Hong-Kong."

96. The NSPCC's interest in this initiative derived from concern over *mui tsai*, but it defined this group not as girls but as "a class of children" and envisaged its role as protecting children of both genders. "Protecting Children in Hong Kong," *Child's Guardian*, April 1930, 27; PRO, CO129/524/6 "Hong Kong Society for the Protection of Children," *Hong Kong Daily Press*, 22 January 1930; PRO, CO129/515/12 Amery to Clementi, 13 May 1929.

97. PRO, CO129/524/6 Draft press notice, March 1930; PRO, CO 129/524/6 "H.K. Society for the Protection of Children," *Hong Kong Daily Press*, 22 January 1930.

98. CO273/563/6 Minute, J. R. Martin, 11 December 1930. It took considerable effort on the part of Passfield to secure Clementi's agreement in July 1931 to draft up legislation for the compulsory registration of existing *mui tsai* and the closing of registers. Passfield continued to prod, declaring, "I consider it desirable that, as has been done in Hong Kong, the *mui tsai* system should for the future be banned by statute and that registration of existing *mui tsai* with the Secretaries for Chinese Affairs should be made compulsory." PRO CO273/563/6 Passfield to Clementi, 27 January 1931; PRO CO273/573/1 Clementi to Passfield, 26 July 1931.

99. James Legge, "The Colony of Hong Kong," *China Review* 1, no. 3 (1874): 165; E. J. Eitel, *Europe in China: The History of Hongkong to the Year 1882* (1895; Hong Kong: Oxford University Press, 1983), ii.

100. See, for example, Geoffrey Robley Sayer, *Hong Kong, 1841–1862: Birth, Adolescence and Coming of Age* (London: Oxford University Press, 1937); "Future of Hong Kong," *Crown Colonist*, December 1938, 624. See, for example, PRO, CO 825/22/8 G. E. J. Gent, minute, 27 February 1937; PRO, CO 825/22/8 Caldecott to Maxwell, 13 April 1937; PRO, CO 825/27/7 G. E. J. Gent, minute, 24 May 1939.

101. PRO, CO129/514/2 "The Mui Tsai Scandal," *South China Morning Post*, 22 October 1928; PRO, CO129/514/2 "Annual Report of the Anti-Mui Tsai Society," 22 September 1929.

102. Jürgen Osterhammel, "China," in *The Oxford History of the British Empire*, vol. 4, *The Twentieth Century*, ed. Judith Brown and Wm. Roger Louis Gates (Oxford: Oxford University Press, 1999), 643–66.

103. PRO, CO 825/22/9 Memorandum, 20 October 1937.

104. PRO, CO 825/24/9 G. E. J. Gent, minute, 25 June 1938.

105. PRO, CO 129/516/6 "Child Labour in Hongkong," *South China Morning Post*, 17

July 1929; PRO, CO 129/516/6 "Mui Tsais in Hongkong," *South China Morning Post*, 22 July 1929; Pedersen, "Maternalist," 194, 197–98.

106. PRO CO825/25/5 Northcote to Picton-Turbervill 7 May 1938; PRO CO825/24/9 Northcote to Cowell, 1 April 1938; PRO CO825/24/9 Northcote to MacDonald 17 May 1938.

107. On this disappointment, see PRO CO825/25/5 Edith Picton-Turbervill, "Mui-tsai in Hong-Kong," *The Times*,19 April 1938.

108. No new measures were taken in Hong Kong to attenuate the increasing problem of traffic in boys from China's ports to Malaya. PRO CO825/30/3 Telegram, 28 July 1941; PRO CO825/30/3 Young to Moyne, 17 September 1941.

109. See, for example, ANOM GGI 17.763 "Rapport annuel," 1922, 9; ANOM GGI 17.763 "Rapport annuel," 16 April 1924, 2. State regulation of adoption was ruled upon for 'native' subjects in Cochinchina by the decree of 3 October 1883. The cession of people was forbidden by the decree of 12 December 1912, shoring up article 344 of the penal code. This legislation is discussed in ANOM, GGI F.76 22526 Attorney General to High Resident in Tonkin, 27 November 1906; ANOM, GGI 17.763 Attorney General to Chief Justice of Indo-China, 12 January 1924; Emile Tavernier, *La Famille annamite* (Saigon: Editions Nguyen-Van-Cua, 1927), 68; ANOM Résident Supérieure du Tonkin Nouveaux Fonds (RSTNF) 01207 Report, Tholance to Pasquier, 19 October 1931; ANOM GGI D2 53.645 "Rapport de M. Pargoire Adm. Des S.C. sur les conditions de la femme et de l'enfant, Cochinchine," 1937, 31.

110. ANOM RSTNF 01207 Reynaud to Pasquier, circular, "Le Problème présent de l'esclavage," 18 June 1931.

111. ANOM GGI F263 56.056 Troy to Long, 7 March 1920.

112. Ibid.

113. ANOM GGI F.749 33.028 Point to Sous Direction des Affaires d'Asie et d'Océanie, 18 September 1912.

114. According to the report, "both in Saigon and Haiphong, young immigrant Chinese women and girls were said only to arrive accompanied by persons alleged to be their husbands, parents or other relatives"; however, "as marriages and births were not registered in China, it was impossible for the authorities to check the statements made in this respect." League of Nations, *Commission of Enquiry into Traffic in Women and Children in the East, Report to Council* (Geneva, 1932), 225, 228–29; LNA, CTFE/Orient/10 "Extension de l'enquête sur la traite des femmes et des enfants aux pays de l'orient, renseignements relatifs aux territoires sous mandat et aux colonies françaises, Indochine," 6; LNA, CTFE/Orient/33 "Traffic in Women and Children, Extension of the Enquiry on Traffic in Women and Children to the East, Report Concerning China," 31 July 1932, 4–5, 12; LNA, CTFE/CPE Mixed/12th/9th P.V. 7(1) "Joint Session of the Committee on Traffic in Women and Children and the Child Welfare Committee," 5 April 1933, 1.

115. LNA, CTFE/Orient39(1) C.849.M.393.1932.IV League of Nations, Commission of Enquiry into Traffic in Women and Children in the East, 228.

116. Marc Fraissinet, *La Prostitution réglementée et la traite des femmes aux colonies françaises, protectorats et pays placés sous mandat* (Cahors: Imprimerie de Coueslant, 1935), 21, 31–32.

117. Bunout even illustrated this by including a sample contract for the bond service of a two-year-old in his thesis. René Bunout, "La Main-d'oeuvre et la législation du travail en Indochine," PhD diss., Bordeaux University, 1936, 39.

118. Alfred-Ernest Babut, "N'y a-t-il pas aussi des 'mui tsai' annamites?" *Revue franco-annamite*, no. 194 (16 January 1936): 10; LNA, CTFE/Orient39(1) C.849.M. 393.1932.IV League of Nations, Commission of Enquiry into Traffic in Women and Children in the East, 222.

119. Martin A. Klein, "Introduction: Modern European Expansion and Traditional Servitude in Africa and Asia," in *Breaking the Chains: Slavery, Bondage and Emancipation in Modern Africa and Asia*, ed. Martin A. Klein (Madison: University of Wisconsin Press, 1993), 3–36; Lawrence C. Jennings, *French Anti-Slavery: The Movement for the Abolition of Slavery in France, 1802–1848* (Cambridge: Cambridge University Press, 2000).

120. J. P. Daughton, *An Empire Divided: Religion, Republicanism and the Making of French Colonialism, 1880–1914* (New York: Oxford University Press, 2006).

121. When the newspaper of the largest French Catholic youth movement in France discussed the plight of the *mui tsai*, for example, it implicated the administration in Indochina only indirectly, claiming that the phenomenon "creates serious abuses in all the lands of the Far East": see "Chine: La Situation des 'mui-tsai,'" *La Jeunesse ouvrière*, December 1932, 3. See also, Jean Vaudon, *Les Filles de Saint-Paul en Indochine* (Chartres: Procure des Soeurs de Saint-Paul, 1931), 132–33.

122. ANOM GGI D89 19.343 Charles-Marie Le Myre de Vilers to Albert Sarraut, 3 September 1912; "L'OEuvre antiesclavagiste," *La Quinzaine coloniale*, 23 May 1911, 1.

123. Missions Étrangères de Paris (hereafter MEP), 1597, Dronet to Sister, 10 June 1887.

124. MEP 2829, François Chaize, "Au Tonkin. Une Mission dans la Tourmente: Le Vicariat Apostolique de Hanoi," 5.

125. The selling of children played an important role in justifications of the work of the Church in Indochina. See, for example, Vaudon, *Filles*, 36, 38.

126. Charles Keith, "Protestantism and the Politics of Religion in French Colonial Vietnam," *French Colonial History* 13 (2012): 165–69.

127. Even by 1932 French feminists had not even succeeded in achieving suffrage in municipal elections. Several proposals had been made to Parliament (in Bouisson in 1909 and 1913, Flandin in 1914 and 1918, and Mandel in 1932), but though these were adopted by the Chamber of Deputies, they were rejected by a small majority in the Senate.

128. Musée Social, Paris, Fonds Legrand-Falco (hereafter MS FLF), box II, Union Temporaire file II-3-A Marcelle Legrand-Falco, "Rapport," 4 April 1932, 2, 4, 6.

129. See also the collection of articles at the MS FLF: box II, Union Temporaire file II-3-A.

130. The governor general of Indochina advised officials against "occupying ourselves especially with what they become once they have been sold." ANOM GGI F76 22525 Bideau to Brière, 23 May 1891.

131. Champly was far more concerned with the movement of European women to brothels in South America and China than the trans-colonial movement of Asian females. Henry Champly, *Le Chemin de Changhaï* (Paris: Tallandier, 1933), 128–30.

132. Claude Farrère, *Les Civilisés: Roman* (Paris: P. Ollendorff, 1906).

133. A.Z., "Notes d'un Tonkinois," *Le Courrier d'Haiphong*, 3 April 1900, 1. Male critics of child selling stirred consciences with emotive accounts of young Eurasians or '*métis*' sold by "warped mothers" following the untimely deaths of their (French) fathers. VNNA1 RST D.638 30.148 "Bétail humain," *L'Avenir du Tonkin*, 26 October 1899.

134. Mary Lynn Stewart, "A Frenchwoman Writes about Indochina, 1931–1949: An-

drée Viollis and Anti-Colonialism," *Journal of the Canadian Historical Association* 18, no. 2 (2007): 92–94.

135. Malaterre-Sellier served on the League of Nations, the Ligue Internationale du Désarmement Moral par les Femmes, the Union Féminine and the Rassemblement Universel pour la Paix and presided over the Conseil International des Femmes. She was, like Clara Haslewood, deeply religious and had served as a nurse during the First World War (for which she received the Croix de Guerre), but neither she nor others emerged as French 'equivalents' of Haslewood. ANOM FM32 NF CO Missions, carton 280, dossier 2459; Etats généraux du féminisme, 30–31 mai 1931 (Paris, 1931), 83 "Mission de Madame Malaterre-Sellier sur la protection de l'enfance et des conditions de vie des femmes et des enfants en Indochine, 1937."

136. Alice L. Conklin, *A Mission to Civilize: The Republican Idea of Empire in France and West Africa, 1895–1930* (Stanford: Stanford University Press, 1997), 102–3.

137. Stewart, "Frenchwoman," 92–94; Gaston Pelletier and Louis Roubaud, *Empire ou colonies?* (Paris: Plon, 1936).

138. Véronique Dimier, "On Good Colonial Government: Lessons from the League of Nations," *Global Society* 18, no. 3 (2004): 294–97.

139. When in 1928 stories appeared in the press about the possibility that Indochina might be sold, perhaps to the United States, Vietnamese students equated this transaction to the selling of a slave. Quoted in Thomas E. Ennis, *French Policy and Developments in Indochina* (c. 1936; New York: Russell & Russell, 1973), 184.

140. *La Jeune Indochine* no. 7, 10 November 1927, 1; "Les Balivernes de *L'Impartial*," *La Jeune Indochine*, 20 December 1927, 1.

141. See, for example, Ngô Tất Tố's *Tắt đèn* (*When the Light's Put Out*), in which a peasant mother sells her seven-year-old daughter to pay a 'corpse tax.' Ngô Tất Tố, *Tắt đèn* (Hanoi: Mai Lĩnh xuất bản, 1939).

142. "La Traite des femmes," *L'Annam nouveau*, 20 September 1935, 3.

143. Herman Lebovics, *True France: The Wars over Cultural Identity, 1900–1945* (Ithaca: Cornell University Press, 1992), 133.

144. ANOM GGI17.763 'Rapport annuel à la société des nations au sujet de la traite des femmes et des enfants en Indochine, 1922," 4.

145. There were five in total. M[onsieur] Borner, "L'Emigration chinoise en Indo-Chine et dans le monde," *Conférences publiques sur l'Indochine faites à l'Ecole coloniale pendant l'année 1909–1910* (Paris: Imprimerie de la Dépêche Coloniale, 1910), 48–65; Harley Farnsworth MacNair, *The Chinese Abroad, Their Position and Protection: A Study in International Law and Relations* (Shanghai: Commercial Press, 1925), 156; Tracy C. Barrett, *The Chinese Diaspora in Southeast Asia: The Overseas Chinese in Indochina* (London: I. B. Tauris, 2012).

146. Vietnam National Archives Centre 2, Ho Chi Minh City (hereafter VNNA2), Gouvernement de la Cochinchine (Goucoch) IA.2/78 (2) Congréganistes to Rodier, 26 November 1903.

147. VNNA2 Goucoch IA.2/78 (2) Rodier to Gouverneur Général 8 April 1904; VNNA2 Goucoch IA.2/78 (2) Beau, Arrêté, 22 April 1904; René Deschamps, *La Main d'œuvre en Indochine et l'immigration étrangère* (Poitiers: Imprimerie Maurice Bousrez, 1908), 58.

148. A law of 1 October 1922 required 'singing girls' to carry a special *carte de circulation* costing 20 piasters per trimestre.

149. Léon Werth, *Cochinchine* (Paris: F. Rieder et Cie, 1926), 76.
150. VNNA2 Goucoch IA.8/286(17) President of Commission Municipale, Cholon, "Note sur les 'chanteuses Chinoises' de Cholon," 16 September 1930.
151. Vũ Trọng Phụng, ed., Shaun Kingsley Mallarney, Lục Xì: *Prostitution and Venereal Disease in Colonial Hanoi* (Honolulu: University of Hawaiʻi Press, 2011), 23.
152. A law of 3 February 1921 on prostitution in Tonkin fixed the age of public inscription as a prostitute at eighteen. ANOM RSTNF 03987 Varenne to Resident, Ninh Binh, 18 June 1926.
153. ANOM RSTNF 03987 Montguillot to Chefs d'administration locales (sauf Cochinchine), 19 December 1925.
154. VNNA2 Goucoch IA.8/286(17) Chef de Service de l'immigration et du contrôle de la main-d'oeuvre engagée to Chef du service des affaires administratives et économiques, 15 September 1930.
155. LNA, CTFE/Orient39(1) C.849.M.393.1932.IV League of Nations, Commission of Enquiry into Traffic in Women and Children in the East, 222. On rules governing police searches of residential addresses, see A. Mouchonière, *Police de l'Indochine: Guide des agents de police de la ville de Cholon* (Saigon: Imprimerie de l'Union Nguyen-Van-Cua, 1921), 20–21.
156. LNA, CTFE/Orient39(1) C.849.M.393.1932.IV League of Nations, Commission of Enquiry into Traffic in Women and Children in the East, 56–57, 222, 228.
157. Gouvernement Générale de l'Indochine, *Annuaire statistique de l'Indochine, deuxième volume, recueil des statistiques relatives aux années 1923–1929* (Hanoi: Imprimerie d'Extrême-Orient, 1931), 67; Gouvernement Général de L'Indochine, *Annuaire Statistique de l'Indochine, troisième volume, 1930–1931* (Hanoi: Imprimerie d'Extrême-Orient, 1932), 57; Gouvernement Général de L'Indochine, Direction des Affaires Economiques, *Annuaire Statistique de l'Indochine, cinquième volume, 1932–1933* (Hanoi: Imprimerie d'Extrême-Orient, 1935), 54. The government moved to boost congregations' powers in the face of criticism of the regulations imposed on Chinese in Indochina (especially taxes). Etienne Dennery, *Foules d'Asie: Surpopulation Japonaise, expansion Chinoise, émigration indienne* (Paris: Librairie Armand Colin, 1930), 147–48.
158. ANOM RSTNF 01207 Tholance to Pasquier, 19 October 1931.
159. M. A. Fouquier, "Etude sur l'esclavage en Cochinchine: D'Après un rapport de M. le capitaine SILVESTRE, chef de la justice indigène en Cochinchine," *Bulletin de la Société de géographie de Rochefort* 3, no.1 (1881–82): 191.
160. Marquet, a civil servant with the *douane*, received the grand prize for literature and the Prix Corrard for his book. Jean Marquet, *De la rizière à la montagne: Moeurs annamites* (Paris: Delalain, 1920), 111.
161. The authors claimed that "this custom of selling children, quite common amongst the poor, though it shocks with good reason our European sensibility, is not so unusual or so revolting as may often be believed." Eugène Teston and Maurice Percheron, *L'Indochine moderne: Encyclopédie administrative, touristique, artistique et économique* (Paris: Librairie de France, 1931), 352–53.
162. ANOM RSTNF 01207 Tholance to Pasquier, 19 October 1931, 5.
163. Ibid., 9.
164. LNA, CTFE/Orient/40 "Verbatim Report of the Fourth Meeting," 6 December 1932, 2–3.

165. LNA, CTFE/Orient39(1) C.849.M.393.1932.IV League of Nations, Commission of Enquiry into Traffic in Women and Children in the East, 218.

166. LNA, C.476.M.318.1937.IV "League of Nations Traffic in Women and Children, Conference of Central Authorities in Eastern Countries, Bandoeng (Java), Minutes of Meetings, 2–13 February 1937," 12.

167. André Baudrit, *La Femme et l'enfant: Dans l'Indochine française et dans la Chine du sud (rapt —vente— infanticide)* (Hanoi, 1941), 32.

168. Ibid., 9. In its second edition, André Baudrit's book carried a more incendiary title: *Bétail humain . . . rapt—vente— infanticide dans l'Indochine française et dans la Chine du Sud*, 2nd ed. (Saigon: Sili, 1942), 127; ANOM RSTNF 01207 Jean Decoux to High Residents, 18 December 1942.

169. "Réponse au questionnaire, Bandoeng," 5 February 1937, 1–2: LNA, Conf/CTFE/Orient/1.

170. On the ineffectiveness of these measures in Hong Kong, see Phyllis Harrop, *Hong-Kong Incident* (London: Eyre & Spottiswoode, 1943), 42–45; Maria Jaschok, *Concubines and Bondservants: The Social History of a Chinese Custom* (London: Zed Books, 1988),74–75, 106; On their ineffectiveness in Indochina, see ANOM FM34 NF P32, carton 218,dossier 1728, Memorandum, High Resident in Tonkin, 24 May 1937.

CHAPTER 8

1. Alice Conklin, *A Mission to Civilize: The Republican Idea of Empire in France and West Africa, 1895–1930* (Stanford: Stanford University Press, 1997).

2. For arguments about social divisions, see Gail P. Kelly, "Conflict in the Classroom: A Case Study from Vietnam, 1918–38," *British Journal of Sociology of Education* 8, no. 2 (1987): 191–212; Gail P. Kelly, ed., *French Colonial Education: Essays on Vietnam and West Africa* (New York: AMS Press, 2000); Goh Chor Boon, *Technology and Entrepôt Colonialism in Singapore, 1819–1940* (Singapore: ISEAS, 2013), 197, 201.

3. Nguyễn Phan Quang, *Kỳ Đồng Nguyễn Văn Cẩm: cuộc đời và thơ văn* (Hanoi: Văn học, 2002), 25–36.

4. Vietnam National Archives Centre 1, Hanoi (hereafter VNNA1), Résidence Supérieure du Tonkin (RST) F68 076311 Brière to Bihouard, 27 May 1887.

5. Jules Ferry, *Le Tonkin et la mère patrie: Témoignages et documents*, 3rd ed. (Paris: Victor-Havard, 1890), 291.

6. Archives Nationales d'Outre-mer, Aix-en-Provence (hereafter ANOM), Fonds Ministeriels (FM) SG/AF/INDO carton 14, dossier A30(28) Le Myre de Vilers to Jauréguiberry, 12 April 1880.

7. VNNA1 RST F68 076311 Bon to Bihouard, 13 October 1887.

8. Nguyễn Phan Quang, *Kỳ Đồng*, 41–42.

9. ANOM Résidence Supérieur du Tonkin (RSTNF) 1929 French Resident to High Resident of Tonkin, 25 September 1897; Paul Doumer, *L'Indo-Chine française (souvenirs)* (Paris: Vuibert et Nony, 1905), 366; Thë Anh Nguyên, "Le Nationalisme vietnamien au début du XXe siècle: Son expression à travers une curieuse lettre au roi d'Angleterre," *Bulletin de l'Ecole Française d'Extrême-Orient* 65, no. 2 (1978): 426–27.

10. The French later moved Nguyễn Văn Cẩm on from Tahiti to the Marquesas Islands, where he later befriended the French painter Paul Gauguin. Louis Bonnafont, *Trente ans de Tonkin* (Paris: Eugène Figuière, 1924), 129.

11. Quoted in Martin Deming Lewis, "One Hundred Million Frenchmen: The 'Assimilation' Theory in French Colonial Policy," *Comparative Studies in Society and History* 4, no. 2 (January 1962): 134, 138.

12. Georges Marx, *La Cochinchine humoristique* (Paris: Vie Moderne, n.d. [c.1890]), 323.

13. ANOM RSTNF F.68 56362 Report, Charles Prêtre, Chef du Service des Affaires Indigènes, n.d.

14. ANOM RSTNF F.68 56362 Report, Charles Prêtre, Chef du Service des Affaires Indigènes, 15 November 1899.

15. ANOM RSTNF F.68 56362 Report, Charles Prêtre, Chef du Service des Affaires Indigènes, 13 September 1899.

16. Intriguingly, Prêtre suspected that the originator of the scheme was a disgruntled Vietnamese former employee of the Tonkin administration. ANOM RSTNF F.68 56362 "Dossier de l'affaire de l'enfant dit 'merveilleux,'" November–December 1899.

17. "L'Education des indigènes en Cochinchine," *La Quinzaine Coloniale*, 25 November 1905, 687.

18. Charles Humbert, *L'Oeuvre française aux colonies* (Paris: Emile Larose, 1913), 117.

19. "L'Education des indigènes en Cochinchine," *La Quinzaine Coloniale*, 25 November 1905, 687.

20. From 1897 it was made compulsory for the Queen's Scholars to go to Oxford or Cambridge. There were by 1905 two scholarships available worth £1,000 each, available annually for the study of law, medicine or engineering.

21. Siow Poh Leng, "Education in the Colony," *Straits Chinese Magazine* 8, no. 1 (March 1904): 20–24.

22. This popular rising resulted in the murder of priests, nuns and servants at a French mission. Paul A. Cohen, *China and Christianity: The Missionary Movement and the Growth of Chinese Anti-Foreignism, 1860–1870* (Cambridge: Harvard University Press, 1963), 229–61.

23. Hongshan Li, *U.S.-China Educational Exchange: State, Society and Intercultural Relations, 1905–1950* (New Brunswick: Rutgers University Press, 2008), 22, n80.

24. Ibid., 23–24; Edward J.M. Rhoads, *Stepping Forth into the World: The Chinese Educational Mission to the United States, 1872–81* (Hong Kong: Hong Kong University Press, 2011), 25–28.

25. J. A. Bethune Cook, *Sunny Singapore* (London: Elliot Stock, 1907), 91; Li, *U.S.-China*, 27.

26. In 1891 investigations suggested the figure was more likely to be around one third. *Hongkong Government Gazette*, 7 May 1881, 323; *Hongkong Government Gazette*, 22 August 1891, 748.

27. Stanley Lane-Poole, ed., *Thirty Years of Colonial Government: A Selection from the Despatches and Letters of the Right Honourable Sir George Ferguson Bowen* (London: Longmans, Green and Colonial Office, 1889), 390; Winifred A. Wood, *A Brief History of Hong Kong* (Hong Kong: South China Morning Post, 1940), 136–37.

28. Alexander Michie, *The Englishman in China during the Victorian Era: As Illustrated in the Career of Sir Rutherford Alcock, KCB, DCL, Many Years Consul and Minister in China and Japan* (Edinburgh: William Blackwood & Sons, 1900), 282.

29. Limin Bai, *Shaping the Ideal Child: Children and Their Primers in Late Imperial China* (Hong Kong: Chinese University Press, 2004).

30. Lim Boon Keng, "Straits Chinese Reform," *Straits Chinese Magazine* 1, no. 3 (June 1899): 105, 149.

31. "News and Notes," *Straits Chinese Magazine* 8, no. 4 (December 1904): 219.

32. Siow Poh Leng, "Education," 72.

33. Inspired by William Wilberforce, Raffles had hoped that enlightenment would accompany commerce and that Singapore would itself become an educational centre in the region, with a 'native college' whose influence would extend from "the banks of the Ganges to the utmost limits of China and Japan." Lady Sophia Raffles, *Memoir of the Life and Public Services of Sir Thomas Stamford Raffles*, vol. 2 (London: James Duncan, 1835), 51.

34. Maxime Pillon and Danièle Weiler, *The French in Singapore: An Illustrated History, 1819–Today* (Singapore: Didier Millet, 2011), 107–11.

35. E. A. Walker, *Sophia Cooke: Forty-two Years of Work in Singapore* (London: Elliot Stock, 1899), 39; Cook, *Sunny*, 88.

36. Some of these schools were neo-Confucian in orientation, such as the Free School for teaching Chinese, in Amoy Street.

37. Observers defined this in relation to its precursor, the medical school in Hong Kong. Dr. J. C. Thomson, a former LMS missionary, embodied links between the two. He managed the school in Hong Kong before going on to play a key role in setting up Singapore's medical school. In its early years a number of the Hong Kong school's students hailed from Singapore. The medical school in Singapore was renamed in 1912 as the Edward VII Medical College. Cook, *Sunny*, 142.

38. Gwee Yee Hean, "Chinese Education in Singapore," *Journal of the South Seas Society* 25, no. 2 (1970): 100–127, 103–7.

39. Government Central School was renamed Queen's College in 1894. "Government Schools," Report of the Director of Education for the Year 1911, appendix N-3.

40. "Vernacular Day Schools (Boys)," Report of the Director of Education for the Year 1911, appendix N-3.

41. "Annual Report of the Acting Head of the Victoria College for 1890," *Hongkong Government Gazette*, 255.

42. One 'section' provided *enseignement primaire supérieure* and *secondaire franco-indigène*, while the other provided *enseignement secondaire français*.

43. VNNA1, RST R.0 73390 Fourès to Doumer, 2 October 1901.

44. The school had 116 pupils of whom 21 were Vietnamese. VNNA1 Mairie de Hanoi (MHN) R.21 5188 De Lenchères to Mayor of Hanoi, 14 December 1903.

45. Vietnam National Archives Centre 2, Ho Chi Minh City (hereafter VNNA2), Gouvernement de la Cochinchine (Goucoch) IA6/264 Folliot, "État des élèves frequentant les divers établissements de la colonie avec indication de leur nationalité (Cochinchine)," 31 December 1901.

46. VNNA1 RST R.0 73390 Fourès to Doumer, 2 October 1901.

47. Charles Prêtre, "L'enseignement indigène en Indochine," *Bulletin du Comité de l'Asie Française* 137 (August 1912): 312.

48. Centre des Archives Diplomatiques de Nantes (hereafter CADN), HK34 Robin to Consul of France in Hong Kong, 24 April 1908.

49. In spite of the fact that they were learning in a second language, many Straits Chinese boys achieved better results than British schoolmates in examinations. The achievements of the Straits Queen's Scholars in English and Scottish Universities suggest they also performed strongly in the metropole. Siow Poh Leng, "Education," 16.

50. "Report by the Inspectors of Vernacular Schools," *Administrative Reports for the Year 1930*, 1930, 23.

51. "Education for Eurasians and Europeans at Shanghai and Hongkong," *China Overland Trade Report*, 25 March 1897, 216–17.

52. The petitioners referred to 175 boys and 202 girls between the ages of five and sixteen present in Hong Kong. "Enclosure No. 1," *Hongkong Government Gazette*, 1 March 1902, 228; Blake to Chamberlain, 3 September 1901, *Hongkong Government Gazette*, 1 March 1902, 227–28; "Report of Committee on Education," *Sessional Paper*, 1902, 401.

53. "Enclosure No. 1," *Hongkong Government Gazette*, 1 March 1902, 229.

54. Ibid.

55. "Enclosure No. 1," *Hongkong Government Gazette*, 1 March 1902, 234.

56. "Report of the Committee of Education," *Hongkong Government Gazette*, 11 April 1902, 511.

57. Irving advised that in an average group of Chinese and non-Chinese boys about to join a European school, the non-Chinese boys would average five to seven years of age whereas the Chinese boys would average from eleven to thirteen or fifteen. "Correspondence Arising Out of the Report of the Education Committee (1902)," Blake to Chamberlain 30 March 1903, Enclosure No. 2, *Sessional Paper*, 1903, 492.

58. By 1901 entrants were often between nine and twelve years old. National Archives, London, Public Record Office (hereafter PRO), CO129/254 Robinson to Knutsford, 8 April 1892.

59. For an example of such writing, see Rev. E. J. Hardy, *John Chinaman at Home: Sketches of Men, Manners and Things in China* (London: T. Fisher Unwin, 1905), 183–85. Chinese elites had themselves grown adept at marshalling arguments for cultural difference built through childhood, and especially assumptions of earlier maturation among Chinese to fend off interventions by the colonial state.

60. *The Diocesan School and Orphanage, Hongkong, Thirty-sixth Annual Report, 1904* (Hong Kong, 1904), 4–5.

61. "Report of Committee on Education," *Sessional Paper*, 1902, 410; "Correspondence Arising Out of the Report of the Education Committee (1902)," *Sessional Paper*, 1903, 467–71; Rhodes House Library, Oxford (hereafter RHL), MS. Nathan 340 May to Nathan, 29 February 1905.

62. "Hongkong Legislative Council," *Hongkong Hansard*, 26 October 1922, 140.

63. D. E. Mungello, *Drowning Girls in China: Female Infanticide since 1650* (Lanham: Rowman & Littlefield, 2008), 83–89; Henrietta Harrison, "A Penny for the Little Chinese: The French Holy Childhood Association in China, 1843–1951," *American Historical Review* 113, no. 1 (2008): 72–92.

64. Johannes Müller, *The Berlin Foundling House, Bethesda, Report for the Year Ending 30th November 1904* (Hong Kong: South China Morning Post, 1904), 4.

65. School of Oriental and Asian Studies, London, CWM/LMS South China Reports Box 3, Helen Davies, "Training Home, Day Schools, Bible Woman," Report for 1902, 21 January 1903, 4.

66. John M. Robertson, "The Rationale of Autonomy," in *Papers on Inter-racial Problems Communicated to the First Universal Races Congress Held at the University of London, July 26–29, 1911*, ed. G. Spiller (London: P. S. King & Son, 1911), 47–48.

67. Carl T. Smith, *Chinese Christians: Elites, Middlemen and the Church in Hong Kong* (Hong Kong: Hong Kong University Press, repr. 2005), 208.

68. Walker, *Cooke*, 71.

69. *Hongkong Government Gazette*, 24 June 1893, 635.

70. Patricia Pok-kwan Chiu, "'A Position of Usefulness': Gendering History of Girls' Education in Colonial Hong Kong (1850–1890s)," *History of Education* 37, no. 6 (2008): 789–805.

71. In its first inspection, of 31 October 1901, the Singapore Chinese Girls' School average enrolment was sixty-four and attendance fifty-four. Lew See Fah, "Straits Chinese Mothers," *Straits Chinese Magazine* 5, no. 17 (1901): 114.

72. 'A. Baba,' "Our Nyonyas," *Straits Chinese Magazine* 7, no. 4 (December 1903): 130.

73. Lew See Fah, "Straits Chinese Maidens," *Straits Chinese Magazine* 6, no. 21 (1902): 44.

74. "Review," *Straits Chinese Magazine* 5, no. 17 (1901): 165.

75. In 1921, 299 Malay girls were categorised as 'literate' in contrast to 1,033 boys. This compared with 3,356 Chinese girls and 6,636 Chinese boys. Mahani Musa, "The 'Woman Question' in Malayan Periodicals, 1920–1945," *Indonesia and the Malay World* 38, no. 111 (July 2010): 248–49; J. E. Nathan, *The Census of British Malaya* (London: Waterlow & Sons, 1922), 107.

76. *Education Systems of the Chief Crown Colonies and Possessions of the British Empire: Including Reports on the Training of Native Races* (London: HMSO, 1905), 100.

77. Chan King Nui, *From Poor Migrant to Millionaire (Chan Wing, 1873–1947)* (Kuala Lumpur: Malaysian Branch of the Royal Asiatic Society, 1997), 59.

78. Isabelle Massieu, *Comment j'ai parcouru l'Indochine* (Paris: Plon, 1901), 378.

79. Ibid.

80. *Conseil de perfectionnement de l'enseignement indigène, première session, Hanoi, Avril 1906* (Hanoi: Imprimerie d'Extrême-Orient, 1906), 13.

81. Pierre Jeantet, "L'Instruction des filles," *L'Opinion*, 9 February 1914, 1.

82. C.D., "Françaises et annamites," *L'Opinion*, 12 February 1914, 1.

83. See, for example, Rachel Leow, "Age as a Category of Gender Analysis: Servant Girls, Modern Girls and Gender in Southeast Asia," *Journal of Modern Asian Studies* 71, no. 4 (November 2012): 986–87; Patricia Chiu, "Girls' Education in Colonial Hong Kong (1841–1941): Gender, Politics and Experience," PhD diss. Cambridge University, 2009.

84. Patricia Sloane-White, "The Shifting Status of Middle-class Malay Girlhood: From 'Sisters' to 'Sinners' in One Generation," in *Girlhood: A Global History*, ed. Jennifer Helgren and Colleen Vasconcellos (New Brunswick: Rutgers University Press, 2010): 382–402; Alys Eve Weinbaum et al., *The Modern Girl around the World: Consumption, Modernity, and Globalisation* (Durham: Duke University Press, 2008).

85. In 1933 in Singapore, the young Eurasian Thora Augusta Oehlers was only the second girl to win a King's Scholarship. "Education," *British Malaya*, February 1933, 236.

86. The percentage varied, being much higher in the south (approximately 28% in Cochinchina at all levels, or 46,297 girls) and lower in the north (approximately 10% in Tonkin in 1939, or 16,621 girls). At the secondary level, girls' representation was even smaller, being 6.3% in Tonkin and 12.6% in Cochinchina. David H. Kelly, ed., *International Feminist Perspectives on Educational Reform: The Work of Gail Paradise Kelly* (New York: Garland, 1996), 142, 144–45.

87. ANOM Gouvernement Général de l'Indochine (GGI) Q49 20554 Nguyễn Văn Việt to Gourbeil, n.d. November 1911.

88. Kelly, "Conflict," 191–212.

89. Chan Kai Ming, "Hongkong Legislative Council," *Hongkong Hansard*, 17 October 1918, 90. A prewar commission revealed less than 25% of all children of school age received any instruction at all in the New Territories. Wood, *Brief History*, 236. The census of 1921 revealed 155,427 children between six and eighteen years old (inclusive), including the New Territories, but only 35,282 were registered in schools. *Hongkong Hansard*, "Report of the Director of Education for the Year 1921," O3.

90. Ngọc Liễn Vũ, *Moeurs et coutumes du Viêt-nam* (Hanoi: Imprimerie de Hanoi, 1942), 46–47.

91. VNNA1 RST 13.863 "Rapport de M. Dumoutier sur l'enseignement au Tonkin a.s. de la participation des écoles à l'exposition de Hanoi," 28 April 1887.

92. "The Educational Report for 1897," *Sessional Papers*, 25 May 1898, 354.

93. "Report on the Census of the Colony of Hong Kong, 1931," *Sessional Papers, 1931*, 124.

94. "Saturday, June 23, 1906," *Singapore Free Press and Mercantile Advertiser*, 23 June 1906, 2.

95. *Conseil de perfectionnement*, 34–35.

96. ANOM GGI Q49 51.221 Inspecteur de l'Instruction Publique to Destenay, 24 October 1912.

97. Even by 1938 less than 10% of the age cohort went to school. In 1939 primary superior schools, *collèges* and *lycées* enrolled only 2,025 boys and 216 girls in Tonkin, and 1,498 boys and 351 girls in Cochinchina. Kelly, *International*, 142.

98. A 1933 law set a maximum age for entrance into the elementary cycle, while previously students aged up to nineteen had been able to enrol in the final year of primary school (i.e., the end of the first five-year cycle). ANOM GGI R10 51.286 Lucien Tô Văn Trạng to Krautheimer, 28 September 1931.

99. ANOM GGI Q49 51.233 J. Coquelin, Lycée Albert Sarraut to Blanchard de la Brosse, 24 January 1924.

100. ANOM GGI Q49 51.233 Blanchard de la Brosse to Merlin, 30 January 1924.

101. "Editorial," *St. Andrew's School Magazine* 1, no. 1 (November 1928): 6.

102. "News Items," *Anglo News Issued by the Anglo-Chinese School, Singapore* 1, no. 2 (10 October 1924): 2.

103. *Diocesan School and Orphanage*, 4.

104. In this period the concept of 'universal adolescence' was famously investigated by the American anthropologist Margaret Mead in Samoa. Margaret Mead, *Coming of Age in Samoa: A Psychological Study of Primitive Youth for Western Civilisation* (New York: W. Morrow & Co., 1928).

105. Kay E. Gillis, *Singapore Civil Society and British Power* (Singapore: Talisman, 2005), 94–95.

106. "Educational Policy," *British Malaya*, January 1934, 184.

107. P. H. Lim, "Malay Schools and School Libraries in the Straits Settlements under British Colonial Rule before the Second World War, 1786–1941," *Malaysian Journal of Library and Information Science* 13, no. 1 (2008): 7.

108. Rupert Emerson, *Malaysia: A Study in Direct and Indirect Rule* (1937; New York: Macmillan, 1964), 302–3.

109. "Hongkong's Student Strikers," *Singapore Free Press and Mercantile Advertiser*, 12 September 1925, 9.

Notes to Chapter 8

110. Pau Kua, *Scouting in Hong Kong, 1910–2010* (Hong Kong: Scout Association of Hong Kong, 2011), 107–92.

111. Allister Macmillan, *Seaports of the Far East: Historical and Descriptive, Commercial and Industrial, Facts, Figures and Resources* (London: W. H. & L. Collingridge, 1923), 333.

112. "The CEZMS School," *Monthly Paper of St. Andrew's Cathedral Singapore* 19 (August 1932): 7.

113. Chan, *Poor*, 46.

114. Even in Chinese-language schools 11,345 of 71,603 students enrolled (15%) were over the age of fifteen. "Education Department, Annual Report for 1938," *Sessional Papers, 1938*, 28–30.

115. Benedict Anderson, *Imagined Communities: Reflections on the Origin and Spread of Nationalism* (London: Verso, 1991), 121.

116. Gaston Pelletier and Louis Roubaud, *Images et réalités coloniales* (Paris: Tournon, 1931), 301.

117. Camille Drevet, *Les Annamites chez eux* (Paris: Imprimerie de la Société Nouvelle d'editions Franco-Slaves, 1928), 22.

118. David Marr, *Vietnamese Tradition on Trial, 1920–1945* (Berkeley: University of California Press, 1981); Đoàn Kim Vân, "La comédie humaine," *L'Avenir de l'Annam* 2 (1 April 1928): 22; Phạm Văn Ký, "La vie Saigonnaise," *L'Impartial*, 18 January 1935, 2.

119. Herman Lebovics, *True France: The Wars over Cultural Identity, 1900–1945* (Ithaca: Cornell University Press, 1992), 114–16.

120. On the notion of the 'colonial bastille' and the grim social realities underpinning it, see Peter Zinoman, *The Colonial Bastille: A History of Imprisonment in Vietnam, 1862–1940* (Berkeley: University of California Press, 2001).

121. ANOM RSTNF R74, R1, R2 07033 Nguyễn Thế Đốc to Lê Văn Nham, 2 January 1927.

122. Kelly, "Conflict."

123. A.P.I., "Les Lauriers sont coupés," *L'Ami du Peuple*, 17 June 1930, 1.

124. Marr, *Vietnamese Tradition*, 80–81.

125. ANOM RSTNF D621 00672 Arnoux to Tholance, 21 March 1934.

126. *Allocution prononcée par Monsieur Jules Brévié, Gouverneur Général de l'Indochine, Commandeur de la Légion d'honneur à la distribution des prix du Lycée Yersin à Dalat le 12 juillet 1938* (Saigon: Imprimerie A. Portail, 1938), 9.

127. *Les Fêtes de Dalat en l'honneur de M. Yersin à l'occasion du baptême du lycée* (Hanoi: Imprimerie d'Extrême-Orient, 28 June 1935), 3.

128. *Allocution*, 9.

129. 'Khan Le Tran,' "Return to Vietnam," http://www.vietvet.org/letran.htm, accessed 1 September 2011.

130. ANOM FM86 Agence FOM Indochine Agence des Colonies Carton 238 Dossier 302 P. Rossignol, "Conclusions générales à l'enquête sur l'enfant d'Indochine," *Bulletin Général de l'Instruction Publique* 7 (November 1939): 55.

131. Ann Raffin, *Youth Mobilisation in Vichy Indochina and Its Legacies, 1940–1970* (Lanham: Lexington Books, 2005); Eric T. Jennings, *Vichy in the Tropics: Pétain's National Revolution in Madagascar, Guadeloupe and Indochina, 1940–44* (Stanford: Stanford University Press, 2002).

132. Jennings, *Vichy*. And see the contributions by this author and Christina Jialin Wu in *Transnational Histories of Youth in the Twentieth Century*, ed. Richard Ivan Jobs and David M. Pomfret (London: Palgrave, 2015).

CHAPTER 9

1. Ann Laura Stoler, *Carnal Knowledge and Imperial Power: Race and the Intimate in Colonial Rule* (Berkeley: University of California Press, 2002), 60; and "Sexual Affronts and Racial Frontiers: European Identities and the Cultural Politics of Exclusion in Colonial Southeast Asia," *Comparative Studies in Society and History* 34, no. 3 (1992): 514–16, 536.

2. P. Douchet, *Métis et congaies d'Indochine* (Hanoi, 1928), 17–18.

3. Richard Symonds, "Eurasians under British Rule," *Oxford University Papers on India* 1, 2 (Delhi: Oxford University Press, 1987): 28–29.

4. Durba Ghosh has recently challenged this view. Durba Ghosh, *Sex and the Family in Colonial India: The Making of Empire* (Cambridge: Cambridge University Press, 2006).

5. On the Crewe Circular, see Ronald Hyam, "Concubinage and the Colonial Service: The Crewe Circular (1909)," *Journal of Imperial and Commonwealth History* 14, no. 3 (1986): 179.

6. On prestige, see Emmanuelle Saada, "The Empire of Law: Dignity, Prestige and Domination in the 'Colonial Situation,'" *French Politics, Culture and Society* 20, no. 2 (2002): 99–100.

7. Henrietta Harrison, "A Penny for the Little Chinese: The French Holy Childhood Association in China, 1843–1951," *American Historical Review* 113, no. 1 (2008): 73.

8. Société des Missions-Étrangères, *Compte Rendu des travaux de 1900* (Paris: Seminaire des Missions-Étrangères, 1901), 200–201; H. le Mée, *Oeuvre des jeunes métis de la Cochinchine* (Paris: Missions Étrangères de Paris, 1884).

9. Vietnam National Archives Centre 2, Ho Chi Minh City (hereafter VNNA2), Gouvernement de la Cochinchine (Goucoch) IA4/016(2) Haffner to Fourès, 19 June 1893.

10. Generous dowries were also awarded to the female orphans who departed the Sainte-Enfance. "Dot pour les jeunes filles métisses de l'école municipale," Registre des délibérations, Municipal Council of Saigon, 23 June 1886, 371–72, in André Baudrit, ed., *Extraits des registres de délibérations de la ville de Saigon (Indochine Française) 1867–1916* (Saigon: J. Testelin, 1936), 259.

11. The president was Henri Michel, an employee in the public works department (second class). The secretary was Rozier, another *commis* in the customs and excise department.

12. The deputy of Cochinchina jointly held the presidency with the governor general. The vice presidents were de Cappe, Directeur de l'enseignement, and Paris, a defence lawyer. The secretary was Henri Michel, and the secretary adjoint was Vigerie of the Banque de l'Indochine.

13. ANOM Gouvernement Général de l'Indochine (GGI) S.62 7701 booklet, "Société de protection et d'éducation des jeunes métis français de la Cochinchine et du Cambodge," 20 February 1898.

14. Nicolaï quoted in *Procès-verbal de l'assemblée générale du 29 mars 1935, Société de Protection de l'Enfance de Cochinchine* (Saigon: Imprimerie J. Aspar, 1935); VNNA2 Goucoch VIA.8/282(23) "Améliorations demandées par la société de protection de l'enfance," 1937.

15. "Un fonctionnaire hors cadre," *Le Courrier de Saigon*, 2 June 1894, 1.

16. Ibid., 2.

17. Others appeared in Vientiane (1908) and other major cities within Indochina.

18. James Dalziel, *Chronicles of a Crown Colony* (Hong Kong: South China Morning Post, 1907), 34–35, 38.

19. Dr. Auguste Benoist de la Grandière, *Ports de l'extrême-orient: Débuts de l'occupation française en Indochine: Souvenirs de campagne; suivi du journal de bord: Extraits 1869* (Paris: Société française d'histoire d'outre-mer, 1994), 81–82.

20. Quoted in G. B. Endacott, *A History of Hong Kong* (Hong Kong: Oxford University Press, 1964), 95, 122.

21. Smale to Hicks Beach, 20 October 1879, *Hongkong Government Gazette*, 4 February 1880, 117.

22. Ibid.

23. Minute, E. J. Eitel, 1 November 1879, *Hongkong Government Gazette*, 4 February 1880, 118.

24. Ibid.

25. Major Henry Knollys, *English Life in China* (London: Smith, Elder and Co., 1885), 49.

26. Emma Jinhua Teng, *Eurasian: Mixed Identities in the United States, China and Hong Kong, 1842–1943* (Berkeley: University of California Press, 2013) 200–204.

27. Wellcome Library, London (hereafter WL), MS. 1499, James Cantlie, "Enquiry into the Life History of Eurasians," n.d. [c. 1889], 20. On such "perils," see also A. S. Krausse, *The Far East: Its History and Its Questions* (London: G. Richards, 1900), 184.

28. WL MS. 1499 Cantlie, "Enquiry."

29. National Archives, London, Public Record Office (hereafter PRO), CO129/322, May to Lucas, 7 May 1904.

30. Peter Wesley-Smith, "Anti-Chinese Legislation in Hong Kong," in *Precarious Balance: Hong Kong between China and Britain, 1842–1992*, ed. Ming K. Chan (New York: M. E. Sharpe, 1994), 99.

31. 'Eurasian,' *Hongkong Telegraph*, 24 September 1895, 3.

32. Ibid.

33. 'An Eurasian,' "Chinese Representation on the Legislative Council," *China Overland Trade Report*, 21 June 1902, 468.

34. On such strategies, see Teng, *Eurasian*, 198.

35. G. Alabaster, "Some Observations on Race Mixture in Hong Kong," *Eugenics Review* 11 (1920): 248.

36. Inside the Asile de la Sainte-Enfance a structural division operated separating European from Chinese children. Argus, "L'Asile de la Sainte Enfance, Hong Kong: Description of the Establishment and Work," *Hong Kong Telegraph*, 22 and 25 August 1899; repr. 1902, 17; ibid., 8; *The Diocesan School and Orphanage, Hongkong, Thirty-Sixth Annual Report*, 1904, 6.

37. *The Diocesan Girls' School and Orphanage, Hongkong, Third Annual Report*, 1902, 6.

38. WL MS. 1499 Cantlie, "Enquiry," 34.

39. A. W. Brewin, in charge of the census, was in no doubt that "the large majority are included among the Chinese." In Singapore, 3,589 Eurasians had been enumerated in 1891. "Report on the Census of the Colony for 1897," *Sessional Papers*, 20 June 1897, 468.

40. H. N. Ridley, "The Eurasian Problem," in *Noctes Orientales: Being a Selection of Essays before the Straits Philosophical Society between the Years 1893 and 1910* (Singapore: Kelly and Walsh, 1913), 54.

41. The census of 1891 counted 3,589. In 1931 British Malaya counted 16,000 Eurasians in its census. In French Indochina the figure was estimated to be between 6,000 and 8,000 in 1937. Isabella L. Bird, *The Golden Chersonese and the Way Thither* (London: John Murray, 1883), 116.

42. On Eurasian families in Penang, see Kirsty Walker, "Intimate Interactions: Eurasian Family Histories in Colonial Penang," *Modern Asian Studies* 46, no. 2 (2012): 303–29.

43. Henry Barnaby Leicester, "Personal Recollections," in *One Hundred Years of Singapore*, ed. Walter Makepeace, Gilbert E. Brooke, Roland St. J. Braddell, vol. 2 (London: John Murray, 1921), reprinted Singapore: Oxford University Press, 1991, 530.

44. Virginia Thompson and Richard Adloff, *Minority Problems in Southeast Asia* (Stanford: Stanford University Press, 1955), 145.

45. The value of the English-language education they received, moreover, seems to have limited the value of other languages in the eyes of Singapore Eurasians, in contrast to Hong Kong where the ability to use both English and Chinese was valued.

46. Census returns revealed a notable absence of 'Eurasians' in neighbourhoods where they were quite obviously resident, and a surfeit of 'British.' As in French Indochina, Eurasian girls in Singapore married European men, as Ridley observed. According to Ridley, "in many cases, the Eurasian marries either with a pure white or with a native according to his position." Ridley, "Eurasian Problem," 55.

47. Makepeace, *One Hundred Years*, 456.

48. PRO CO273/231 Lawson to Chamberlain, 17 August 1897; PRO CO273/231 Lucas to Mitchell, 25 August 1897.

49. John Willis, *The Serani and the Upper Ten: Eurasian Ethnicity in Singapore* (Sydney: University of New South Wales, 1983), 76.

50. John G. Butcher, *The British in Malaya, 1880–1941: The Social History of a European Community in Colonial Southeast Asia* (Kuala Lumpur: Oxford University Press, 1979), 111.

51. "Un Conflit dans la société des métis," *Le Courrier de Saigon*, 19 December 1894, 3.

52. ANOM GGI 7726 Deloncle to Doumergue, 20 February 1903.

53. ANOM GGI 7726 Crayssac to Beau, 31 October 1903.

54. Vietnam National Archives Centre 1, Hanoi (hereafter VNNA1), Résidence Supérieure du Tonkin (RST) S.73 5557 "Table, Nombre d'enfants métis placés dans les établissements scolaires du Tonkin (note postale de M le Gouverneur Général de l'Indochine)," 5 May 1915.

55. ANOM GGI S.62 7701 Domergue to Fourès, 21 March 1904; ANOM GGI S.62 7701 Simonin to Domergue, 4 January 1904.

56. *Semaine de l'enfance sous le patronage de M le Gouverneur de la Cochinchine, présidence d'honneur de Mme Pierre-Pagès du 1e au 7 juillet 1934, congrès de l'enfance* (Saigon: Imprimerie de l'Union, 1934), 38; Au congrès de l'enfance, conférence de Me Mathieu, President du Conseil Colonial, "La protection de l'enfance—Sa portée sociale," *Procès-verbal de l'assemblée générale du 29 mars 1935, Société de Protection de l'Enfance de Cochinchine* (Saigon: Imprimerie J. Aspar, 1935), VNNA2 Goucoch VIA.8/282(23) Améliorations demandées par la société de protection de l'enfance 1937, 27.

57. Cahen complained: "The sons of officials sit shoulder to shoulder with half-breeds of a French father and an Annamese mother: the latter can be distinguished by their already brown skin, by their knowledge of Annamese and by their inferiority in French." Gaston Cahen, "Hanoï: Les Récentes transformations de la capitale Tonkinoise," *Le Tour du Monde* 13 (1907): 361–72.

58. L. des Charmettes, "Opinions de la colonisation et du métissage," *Avenir du Tonkin*, 20 January 1907, 2.

59. "Tous célibataires, vivent les congais," *Avenir du Tonkin*, 23 January 1907, 1.

60. Saada, "Empire," 99–100.

61. As one French administrator put it, "In Indochina ... the paternity of the *métis* belongs in almost equal proportions to all ranks." ANOM GGI S.62 7701, report, Firmin Jacques Montagne, n.d. [c. 1904].

62. Charles-Marie Le Myre de Vilers, *La politique coloniale Français depuis 1830* (Paris: Publications de la Nouvelle Revue, 1913), 15.

63. ANOM GGI S.62 7701, letter, Brou, 9 November 1904.

64. VNNA1 RST D.638 30.148 "Bétail humain," *L'Avenir du Tonkin*, 26 October 1899.

65. ANOM GGI S.62 7701 President, Société de la Protection et d'education des jeunes métis français abandonnés to Beau, 29 January 1904.

66. Firmin Jacques Montagne, a public works engineer, urged action to address the case of two *métis* girls aged fourteen and eighteen who were "about to be sold by their mothers." GGI S.62 7701 Montagne, to Procureur de la République, 10 November 1903; ANOM GGI S.62 7701, Grevosty, "La Question des métis," 24 September 1898; ANOM GGI S.62 7701 Montagne, to Paris, 29 January 1904; Louis Peytral, *Silhouttes tonkinoises* (Paris: Berger-Levrault et Cie, 1897), 76, 93.

67. ANOM GGI S.62 7701, report, Société de protection et d'éducation des jeunes métis français de la Cochinchine et du Cambodge, 20 February 1898.

68. Grevosty remarked in 1897: "We are, among all the people of the world, the nation reputed for its high moral mindedness ... We must colonise by ... moral influence ... By moral influence I mean acts of an irreproachable rectitude." ANOM GGI S.62 7701, Grevosty, "La Question des métis," 24 September 1898.

69. According to Charles Lemire, young people of mixed Chinese and Vietnamese backgrounds, so-called *minh hương* in Cholon, could accede to positions of administrative responsibility. Charles Lemire, *L'Indochine: Cochinchine française, royaume de Cambodge, royaume d'Annam et Tonkin*, 3rd. ed. (Paris: Challamel Aîné, 1884), 117, 161; Paul Lefebvre, *Faces jaunes (moeurs et coutumes de l'Extrême-Orient)* (Paris: Challamel, 1886), 59–60.

70. Here was a powerful historical echo with the promotional materials used by Forbin-Janson's Society of the Holy Childhood, which also depicted children threatened by ravenous pigs. ANOM GGI S.62 7701, Grevosty, "La Question des métis," 24 September 1898; D. E. Mungello, *Drowning Girls in China: Female Infanticide since 1650* (Lanham: Rowman & Littlefield, 2008), 86–87.

71. Louis Salaün, *L'Indochine* (Paris: Imprimerie Nationale, 1903), 385.

72. ANOM GGI S.62 7701 President, Société de la Protection et d'éducation des jeunes métis français abandonnés, Saigon, to Beau, 29 January 1904.

73. Camille Paris, *De la Condition juridique des métis dans les colonies et possessions françaises: Des métis franco-annamites de l'Indo-Chine* (Paris: n.p., 1904), 3.

74. "Pour l'enfance," *Avenir du Tonkin*, 22–23 October 1906, 3.

75. See "La Condition des enfants et la crise paternale," *L'Action Féminine*, no. 2 (1 April 1909): 23–24; Mme D'Abadie-D'Arrast, "Section de législation," *L'Action Féminine*, no. 20 (January 1912): 336; White, *Children*, 130.

76. ANOM GGI S.63 16.771, "Notre devoir envers les enfants métis," *Les Annales Coloniales* (11 January 1913). On the German debate, see Tina Marie Campt, *Other Germans:*

Black Germans and the Politics of Race, Gender and Memory (Ann Arbor: University of Michigan Press, 2004), 46–49.

77. White, *Children*, 131.
78. ANOM GGI S.63 16.771, note, Chef du Service Administratif, 24 July 1912.
79. ANOM GGI S.63 16.771, report, director of finance, 7 May 1912.
80. ANOM GGI S.62 7701 Brou to Beau, 9 November 1904.
81. The new name was the Société de Protection de l'Enfance de Cochinchine. *Semaine de l'enfance*, 37.
82. Jean Gittins, *Eastern Windows, Western Skies* (Hong Kong: South China Morning Post, 1969), 19.
83. CO129/409 May to Harcourt, 8 January 1914.
84. CO129/410 May to Harcourt, 21 January 1914; Gittins, *Eastern Windows*, 26–27.
85. For May, "It would be little short of a calamity if an alien and, by European standards, a semi-civilised race were allowed to drive the white man from the one area in Hongkong, in which he can live with his wife and children in a white man's healthy surroundings." PRO CO129/443 May to Long, 5 September 1917.
86. Ibid.
87. May contended, "There is in the Colony a not inconsiderable number of Eurasians who are to all intents and purposes Chinese in their habits and customs." Ibid. On similar anxieties in British India, see Elizabeth Buettner, *Empire Families: Britons and Late Imperial India* (Oxford: Oxford University Press, 2004), 87–88.
88. CO129/460 Enclosure 1 in Stubbs to Milner of 19 March 1920, Brown, Young, Hay and Hogg to Severn, 12 November 1919.
89. In 1902 Tse Tsan Tsai had stirred a storm of protest around the nomination of Ho Tung to the Legislative Council as successor to Wei A. Yuk on the grounds that this contravened principles of representative government. "To the Editor," *Hongkong Weekly Press*, 16 June 1902, 456.
90. PRO CO129/447 May to Long, 24 January 1918; PRO CO129/447 Minute, AB 'Peak Reservation Bill' 5 May 1918; PRO CO129/447 May to Long, 24 January 1918.
91. Chan Lau Kit-ching, *China, Britain and Hong Kong, 1895–1945* (Hong Kong: Chinese University Press, 1990), 175.
92. PRO CO129/478 Stubbs to Grindle, 16 September 1922. Stubbs worried about this group's "excessive" influence. PRO CO129/460 Stubbs to Milner, 19 March 1920; PRO CO129/462 Stubbs to Milner, 29 July 1920.
93. PRO CO129/462 Stubbs to Milner, 29 July 1920.
94. For Carroll, "the Chinese response to colonial British discrimination was not to push for an end to it, but to create an equally exclusive social world of their own." John M. Carroll, *Edge of Empires: Chinese Elites and British Colonials in Hong Kong* (Cambridge: Harvard University Press, 2005), 18, 31, 97, 100.
95. Kotewall recruited Pun Wai Chau, "the oldest and ablest" of Chinese editors, to write propaganda articles. PRO CO129/489, report, Robert Kotewall, 24 October 1925, 432, 446, 455–56, 458.
96. The secretary for Chinese Affairs in Hong Kong warned in 1925 that the "wilder elements" of student circles were "clearly determined on trouble." D. W. Tratman, "Report of the Secretary for Chinese Affairs for the Year 1925," *Hong Kong Administrative Report* (1925): 16; As one author put it, "Young China means hot-headedness and irresponsibility." Edward H. Hume, *Young China* (New York: CADAL, 1927), 446.

97. Rhodes House Library, Oxford (hereafter RHL), MS. Nathan 352, "A Visit to Hongkong & Canton: British Colony Not So Badly Hit," *China Express and Telegraph*, 17 June 1926.

98. Geoffrey Robley Sayer, *Hong Kong, 1841–1862: Birth, Adolescence and Coming of Age* (London: Oxford University Press, 1937).

99. Kotewall was awarded an honorary degree by the University of Hong Kong in 1926. He was also appointed to the Order of St. Michael and St. George (1927), became a member of the Executive Council (1936) and was awarded the title of Knight Bachelor (1938).

100. The Indian-born Armenian businessman Sir Catchick Paul Chater (1846–1926) was the first to have been referred to in this way. Irene Cheng, *Clara Ho Tung: A Hong Kong Lady, Her Family and Her Times* (Hong Kong: Chinese University Press, 1976), 1; John M. Carroll, "Colonial Hong Kong as a Cultural-Historical Place," *Modern Asian Studies* 40, no. 2 (2006): 534.

101. Alabaster, "Some Observations," 248.

102. Teng, *Eurasian*, 241.

103. The league championed the retrieval of the term 'Eurasian' from pejorative connotations. Peter Ho, *The Welfare League: The Sixty Years, 1930–1990* (Hong Kong: Welfare League, 1990), 1–4.

104. Ibid., 8.

105. G.S.K., "Queer People," *Our Magazine* 1, no. 1 (January 1919): 32.

106. Joel S. Kahn, *Other Malays: Nationalism and Cosmopolitanism in the Modern Malay World* (Honolulu: University of Hawai'i Press, 2006).

107. The circulation of the *Malay Tribune* was greater at 20,000 than that of the *Straits Times* (6,000 in the Depression, and 15,000 in the late 1930s).

108. "Editorial," *Our Magazine* 1, no. 1 (January 1919): 1.

109. Ibid., 2.

110. "Eurasian Association," *Hongkong Telegraph*, 14 June 1919, 5.

111. The Eurasian Literary Association, which merged with the Singapore Recreation Club (established 1883) in 1919, becoming the Eurasian Association, devoted itself to providing night classes, shorthand, bookkeeping, typewriting and a lecture series for young clerks.

112. Amicus, "Sympathy with Youth," *Our Magazine* 1, no. 3 (March 1919): 91–92.

113. "By the Way," *Our Magazine* 1, no. 4 (April 1919): 139.

114. In 1917 reports indicated that the infant mortality rate for Eurasians in Singapore was 196.2 per 1,000, compared with 178 for Indians, 268 for Chinese, 302 for Malays and 36 for Europeans. "Infantile Mortality," *Straits Times*, 17 May 1917, 8.

115. James F. Augustin, "The Social Problem," *Our Own Quarterly: Journal of the St. Joseph's Old Boys' Association* 1, no. 3 (July–September 1922): 7.

116. Ibid.

117. Chapman was based in Perak, and was a member of the congregation of the Church of the Visitation in Negri-Sembilan. R. V. Chapman, "Correspondence—The Eurasian's Future," *Straits Times*, 15 November 1937.

118. "Editorial—Eurasians and Education," *Our Magazine* 1, no. 3 (March 1919): 78.

119. For one such earlier expression of loyalty, see "The Address to the Eurasians by H.E. the Governor," *Straits Times Weekly*, 29 August 1893.

120. In the 1931 census, of the 10,003 'Europeans' resident in the Straits Settlements, 710 were returned as 'Dutch.' C. A. Vlieland, *British Malaya: A Report on the 1931 Census and on Certain Problems of Vital Statistics* (London: Crown Agents, 1932), 165.

121. For one observer this was "a rounded blurring of words which automatically spell the word Eurasian even if the speaker is as blond as a Norseman." R.C.H. McKie, *This Was Singapore* (London: Robert Hale, 1950), 77. The former inspector general of police, René Onraët, suggested: "Nothing is more catching among children, and once acquired is hard to eradicate. This accent does much to aggravate the unwillingness of Europeans to become intimate with Eurasians." René Onraët, *Singapore—A Police Background* (London: Dorothy Crisp and Co., 1947), 134.

122. "Careers for the Malayan-born," *British Malaya*, December 1929, 249.

123. Chapman, "Correspondence."

124. R.V.C., "The Eurasian Future," *Straits Times*, 16 January 1939, 5.

125. The St. George's Singapore Catholic Young Men's Society, which had been first convened in 1866, was predominantly Eurasian. On its committee sat Francisco Everisto Pereira, J. J. Woodford, J. F. Hansen, W. J. Valberg, H. D. Chopard, J. Cazalas and G. Reutens. "News and Notes," *Straits Chinese Magazine* 3, no. 10 (1899): 182.

126. "Footprints on the Sands of Time—Some Eurasians of Old Singapore," *Our Magazine* 1, no. 2 (February 1919): 37.

127. Onraët, *Singapore*, 135.

128. Roland Braddell, *The Lights of Singapore* (London: Methuen & Co., 1934), 49; R.V.C., "The Eurasian Future," *Straits Times*, 16 January 1939, 5.

129. QEF, "The Domiciled European," *Straits Times*, 29 May 1939, 15.

130. Chapman, "Correspondence."

131. Lieutenant-Colonel Bonifacy, *Les Métis Franco-Tonkinois extrait des Bulletins et Mémoires de la Société d'Anthropologie de Paris, séance du 1er décembre 1910* (Paris, 1911), 19.

132. VNNA1 RST S.73 5557, Table, "Nombre d'enfants métis placés dans les établissements scolaires du Tonkin," 5 May 1915; ANOM GGI S.62 7701 Société de protection et d'éducation des jeunes métis français de la Cochinchine et du Cambodge, circular, "Rapport a l'Assemblée Générale," 20 February 1897.

133. Naturalisation was expensive to pursue and was awarded only exceptionally. Pierre Guillaume, "Les Métis en Indochine," *Annales de démographie historique* (1995): 189; Jacques Mazet, *La Condition juridique des métis dans les possessions françaises* (Paris: Editions Domat-Montchresien, 1932), 68. The best that most could hope for was protégé status, and this carried few privileges. The upshot was that poorer Eurasians even found it difficult to join the Foreign Legion. ANOM GGI S.63 16.771 Note, Batault, 24 July 1912.

134. See Mazet, *Condition juridique*, 37, 42.

135. The International Colonial Institute in Brussels created by Joseph Chailley-Bert discussed this issue in 1911 (and revisited it in 1920 and 1934). The colonial theorist Arthur Girault reported to the institute that the legal recognition of the *métis* as a social class held serious dangers for European rule, since their intermediary status would undermine the whole notion of 'association.' *Comptes rendus de l'Institut Colonial International* (Bruxelles: Bibliothèque Coloniale Internationale, 1911), 314.

136. ANOM GGI S.63 16.771 "Notre devoir envers les enfants métis," *Les Annales Coloniales*, 11 January 1913; ANOM GGI S.63 16.771, note, Batault, 24 July 1912.

137. ANOM GGI S.63 16.771, note, Chef du Service Administratif, 24 July 1912.

138. Orphans were recognised empire-wide in June 1915 through a 'day of orphans' in which colonial governors were encouraged to participate. In Hanoi, Résident Supérieur E. Charles was enthusiastic supporter of these arrangements. ANOM GGI S.62 2003 newspaper extract "Agence Havas, Journée nationale des orphelins de la guerre des 1er et 2

novembre 1916" (October 1916); ANOM GGI S.62 2003 Charles to Le Gallen, 27 December 1916.

139. Henri Barthélemy, "Les Pupilles de la patrie," *Revue des Deux Mondes* (January 1916): 3–14.

140. VNNA2 Goucoch VIA.8/242(7) Dossier de principe, 1917–1921, Arrêté, 22 August 1919, 1.

141. VNNA2 Goucoch IA.8/242(11) Krautheimer to Long, nd. [c.1921].

142. ANOM GGI S.62 2019 Galuski to Saint-Gaffray, 16 February 1920.

143. VNNA2 Goucoch VIA8/325(1) President of Société de Protection de l'Enfance to Krautheimer, 10 June 1929.

144. VNNA2 Goucoch VIA8/325(1) Gabouly, Chef du Service de l'enseignement en Cochinchine to Le Fol, 14 September 1926.

145. *Société de protection de l'enfance de Cochinchine, procès verbal 26 Mars 1929* (Saigon: Imprimerie de l'Union Nguyen Van Cua, 1929), 5.

146. ANOM Fonds Ministeriels (FM) 86 Agence FOM Indochine Agence des Colonies Carton 238 Dossier 302 "Création d'orphelinats agricoles au Tonkin," *Journal du Havre*, 15 March 1923; P. Paris, "Note sur la question des métis," 6 May 1937; "Note sur la question des métis," Société de Protection de l'Enfance de Cochinchine, *Procès-verbal de l'assemblée générale du 8 mai 1937* (Saigon: Imprimerie J. Aspar, 1937); VNNA2 Gouchoch VIA.8/282(23) "Améliorations demandées par la société de protection de l'enfance," 1937, 19.

147. "Pour nos œuvres de protection," *L'Impartial*, 17 January 1925.

148. It was therefore "certain that the goal of recuperating them into the French race has not been achieved." VNNA2 Goucoch VIA8/325(1) President of Society to Chef du Service des Affaires administratives bureaux du Gouvernement de Cochinchine, 15 December 1926; VNNA2 Goucoch VIA8/325(1) Gabouly to Le Fol, 14 September 1926.

149. *Société de protection de l'enfance de Cochinchine, procès verbal 5 Mars 1931* (Saigon: Imprimerie de l'Union Nguyen Van Cua, 1931), 6.

150. VNNA2 Goucoch VIA.8/282(23) "Rapport du conseil d'administration à l'assemblée générale sur la situation morale et financière de la Société de Protection de l'Enfance pendant l'année 1937."

151. VNNA2 Goucoch VIA8/325(1) Society President to Blanchard de la Brosse, 15 December 1926.

152. Among them, André Maurice, for example, became a butcher. Jean Vincent worked in a patisserie. ANOM GGI S.63 16.773 Report, Desnoyers, 25 November 1922.

153. ANOM GGI S.63 16.773 Révérony to Baudoin, 8 January 1923; VNNA1 RST S.72 48.378 Desnoyers to Saint Gaffray, 29 July 1920.

154. See correspondence at VNNA1 RST S.72 48.373.

155. ANOM GGI S.63 16.776, Révérony to Merlin, 7 December 1923; ANOM GGI S.63 16.773, Révérony to Baudoin 8 January 1923. Protection Societies sent pupils to France before the age of fourteen, because it was generally assumed "beyond this age, the character is fixed." Albert Sambuc, "Les métis franco-annamites," *Revue du Pacifique* 5 (1931): 270.

156. Mazet, *Condition juridique*, 14.

157. Sambuc, "Métis," 270. Jacques Mazet proposed that by "mixing with metropolitan children less faithful to prejudices of race than the colonials" Eurasian children "would be removed from cruel ridicule." Ibid., 14; Bonifacy, *Métis Franco-Tonkinois*, 4.

158. VNNA2 Goucoch VIA8/325(3) Blanchard de la Brosse to Pasquier, 3 January 1929.

In 1925 Hanoi's Société de Protection des Enfants Métis Abandonnés sent to France 37 pupils between ages ten and fifteen, and by 1930 there were only 129 boys and 10 girls from Tonkin in France. VNNA1 RST S.72 48.373 Merlin to Révérony, 13 November 1923; VNNA1 GGI T.34 S.63 5328 Tissot to Montguillot, 17 July 1925.

159. Emmanuelle Saada, *Les Enfants de la colonie: Les Métis de l'empire français entre sujétion et citoyenneté* (Paris: La Découverte, 2007), 202–4.

160. Sambuc, "Les métis franco-annamites," 261.

161. Ibid., 259.

162. VNNA1 RST S.73 71816 Report, "Le Problème Eurasien au Tonkin," 1937, 32.

163. VNNA1 RST S.73 71816, Report, Résident Supérieur du Tonkin (sur la problème des métis) "Le Problème Eurasien au Tonkin," 1937, 32; Saada, *Enfants*, 219–20.

164. The lack of interest shown in older cohorts of Eurasians through the period, by contrast, is striking. VNNA1 RST S.73 71816, report, Tholance, "Le Problème Eurasien au Tonkin," 1937, 65.

165. VNNA2 Goucoch VIA.8/282(23) *Procès-verbal de l'assemblée générale du 29 mars 1935, Société de Protection de l'Enfance de Cochinchine* (Saigon: Imprimerie J. Aspar, 1935), 28.

166. Ibid.

167. VNNA2 Goucoch VIA.8/282(23) P. Paris, "Note sur la question des métis," 6 May 1937, *Procès-verbal de l'assemblée générale du 8 mai 1937, Société de Protection de l'Enfance de Cochinchine* (Saigon: Imprimerie J. Aspar, 1937), 17.

168. Société de Protection de l'Enfance de Cochinchine, *Procès verbal de l'assemblée générale du 5 Mars 1931* (Saigon: Imprimerie de l'Union Nguyen Van Cua, 1931), 8; Société de Protection des Métis d'Annam, *Société de protection des métis d'Annam* (Hué: Imprimerie Mirador, 1941), 68; Fondation Jules Brévié, *Fondation Brévié: Son origine, ses buts et ses moyens d'action* (Saigon: Imprimerie de l'Union, 1942), 208.

169. "Le Péril vénérien et la prostitution à Hanoi," *Bulletin de la Société Medico-Chirurgicale de l'Indochine* (June 1930): 464.

170. R. Bonniot, *L'Enfant métisse malheureuse. Rapport présenté par M. Bonniot au congrès de l'enfance 1940* (Saigon: Imprimerie de l'Union, 1940), 12; see also Henri Bonvicini, *Enfants de la colonie* (Saigon: Portail, 1938), 36–37, 45.

171. In 1930 couples in which only one partner was 'pure French' produced one third of all recognised births to French citizens; by 1940 they produced almost half. Meanwhile, the number of "legitimate" or "recognised" métis grew to around 2,200. VNNA1 RST S.73 71816, report, Tholance, "Le Problème Eurasien au Tonkin," 1937, 65; Guillaume, "Métis en Indochine," 187. In Hanoi between 1931 and 1933 the number of people defined as French 'of nationality and race' declined in absolute terms from 10,138 to 9,229 while the number of métis was believed to have exceeded the number of Europeans. VNNA1 RST S.73 71816, Report, Tholance, "Le Problème Eurasien au Tonkin," 1937, 65. Others estimated there were around 6,300 Indochinese métis children and that out of 'European births' in Indochina from 1927 to 1937 some 40% were Eurasian. Vũ Văn Quang, *Le Problème des eurasiens en Indochine* (Hanoi: Imprimerie Tonkinoise, 1939), 41.

172. Salaün, *L'Indochine*, 385; see also Bonifacy, *Métis Franco-Tonkinois*, 9.

173. *Procès-verbal de l'assemblée générale du 29 mars 1935, Société de Protection de l'Enfance de Cochinchine* (Saigon: Imprimerie J. Aspar, 1935); VNNA2 VIA.8/282(23) "Améliorations demandées par la société de protection de l'enfance 1937," 26.

174. Saada, *Enfants*, 232–34. See also Christina Firpo, "'Lost Boys': 'Abandoned' Eurasian Children and the Management of the Racial Topography in Colonial Indochina, 1938–1945," *French Colonial History* 8 (Spring 2007): 203–21.

175. VNNA2 IA.8/282(13) Vice President, Ligue Française pour la defense des droits de l'homme et du citoyen, to Châtel, 17 May 1938.

176. Justin Godart, *Rapport de mission en Indochine: 1er janvier–14 mars 1937* (Paris: L'Harmattan, repr. 1994), 157.

177. VNNA2 IA.8/282(13) President du Conseil d'administration du comité central d'aide mutuelle d'assistance sociale de Cochinchine to Châtel, 26 August 1938.

178. VNNA1 GGI S.73 00505, *Société d'assistance aux enfants franco-indochinois, Assemblee générale annuelle ordinaire du 4 avril 1939* (Hanoi, 1939), 7.

179. VNNA2 IA.8/282(13) Brévié to Mandel 14 July 1938.

180. Paul Munier, "La Bonne parole," *La Volonté indochinoise*, 13 May 1939, 8. As early as July 1912 the question of setting up an École des Enfants de Troupe for *métis* children had been put forward by General Pennequin to the minister of colonies, Albert Lebrun. In March 1928 General Aubert agreed with the governor general's suggestion that Eurasian children be admitted to such schools in Tonkin. On 28 August Cochinchina secured the admission of pupils to the equivalent school in Thủ Dầu Một, just to the north of Saigon. ANOM GGI Q49 48.064 Vinay, Chef du Cabinet Militaire 13 September 1928, *arrêté du 13 avril 1928 modifiant l'arrêté du 17 juin 1909, 1928*.

181. IA.8/282(13) Pagès to Brévié, 19 September 1938. The society in Saigon also planned to add a '*touts petits*' section to its orphanage to cater for children from two to five years old (and to "rescue them in time from the often harmful milieu in which they reside in conditions of the worst hygiene and where they pick up bad habits"). VNNA2 VIA.8/282(23) "Améliorations demandées par la société de protection de l'enfance 1937," *Rapport du conseil d'administration à l'assemblée générale sur la situation morale et financière de la Société de Protection de l'Enfance pendant l'année 1937*, 8.

182. VNNA2 VIA.8/282(23) P. Paris, "Note sur la question des métis," *Procès-verbal de l'assemblée générale du 8 mai 1937, Société de Protection de l'Enfance de Cochinchine* (Saigon: Imprimerie J. Aspar, 1937), 19.

183. VIA.8/282(23) Rapport du conseil d'administration à l'assemblée générale sur la situation morale et financière de la Société de Protection de l'Enfance pendant l'année 1937, 6.

184. VIA.8/282(23) *Procès-verbal de l'assemblée générale du 29 mars 1935, Société de Protection de l'Enfance de Cochinchine* (Saigon: Imprimerie J. Aspar, 1935).

185. An École des Enfants de Troupe in Dalat was created formally by *arrêté* on 27 June 1939; ANOM RSTNF Q49 03461 Arrêté, 5 July 1939; Fondation Jules Brévié, *Fondation Brévié*, 195, 199; On the École des Enfants de Troupe in Dalat, see Eric Jennings, *Imperial Heights: Dalat and the Making and Undoing of French Indochina* (Berkeley: University of California Press, 2011), 188–93, 210.

186. ANOM RSTNF Q49 03461 Martin, General de Corps d'Armée, Commandant Supérieur des Troupes du Groupe d'Indochine, Instruction Générale number 83, sur l'organisation, le fonctionnement, et l'administration de l'école d'enfants de troupe eurasiens de Dalat, 27 July 1939.

187. Thomas E. Ennis, *French Policy and Developments in Indochina* (New York: Russell & Russell, 1936), 109.

Bibliography

PRIMARY SOURCES

Ajalbert, Jean. *Les Nuages sur l'Indochine*. Paris: Editions Louis-Michaud, 1912.
Alabaster, G. "Some Observations on Race Mixture in Hong Kong." *Eugenics Review* 11 (1920): 247–48.
Allocution prononcée par Monsieur Jules Brévié, Gouverneur Général de l'Indochine, Commandeur de la Légion d'honneur à la distribution des prix du Lycée Yersin à Dalat le 12 juillet 1938. Saigon: Imprimerie A. Portail, 1938.
Anderson, Adelaide Mary. *Humanity and Labour in China: An Industrial Visit and Its Sequel (1923 to 1926)*. London: Student Christian Movement, 1928.
Annesley, James. *Sketches of the Most Prevalent Diseases of India Comprising a Treatise on the Epidemic Cholera of the East, etc.* London: T & G Underwood, 1825.
Argus. *L'Asile de la Sainte Enfance, Hong Kong: Description of the Establishment and Work* (repr. from *Hong Kong Telegraph* 22 and 25 August 1899), 1902.
Autret, Françoise. *Pousse de Bambou*. Paris: Les Editions la Bruyère, 1999.
Bai, Limin. *Shaping the Ideal Child: Children and Their Primers in Late Imperial China*. Hong Kong: Chinese University Press, 2004.
Barnes, Geoffrey. *Mostly Memories: Packing and Farewells*. Royston: Mulu, 1999.
Barrelon, Pierre, Brossard de Corbigny, Charles Lemire and Gaston Cahen. *Cities of Nineteenth Century Colonial Vietnam: Hanoi, Saigon, Hue and the Champa Ruins*, translated and with an introduction by Walter E.J. Tips. Bangkok: White Lotus, 1999.
Baudrit, André. *Bétail humain . . . rapt—vente—infanticide dans l'Indochine française et dans la Chine du Sud*, 2nd ed. Saigon: SILI, 1942.
———, ed. *Extraits des registres de délibérations de la ville de Saigon. Indochine Française 1867–1916*. Saigon: J. Testelin, 1936.
———. *La Femme et l'enfant: Dans l'Indochine française et dans la Chine du sud (rapt—vente—infanticide)*. Hanoi, 1941.
———. *Guide Historique des rues de Saigon*. Saigon: SILI, 1943.
Benoist de la Grandière, A. *Les Ports de l'Extrême-Orient, débuts de l'occupation française en Indochine: Souvenirs de campagne, suivi du Journal de Bord (extraits)*. 1869. Paris: Société Française d'Histoire Outre-Mer, 1994.
Bird, Isabella L. *The Golden Chersonese and the Way Thither*. London: John Murray, 1883.
Black, W. G. *Winter Days in India and Elsewhere*. Glasgow: James Maclehose and Sons, 1908.
Bleackley, H. *A Tour in Southern Asia. Indo-China, Malaya, Java, Sumatra and Ceylon (1925–1926)*. London: John Lane, The Bodley Head, 1928.
Bonifacy, Lieutenant-Colonel. *Les Métis Franco-Tonkinois extrait des Bulletins et Mémoires de la Société d'Anthropologie de Paris, séance du 1er décembre 1910*. Paris, 1911.

Bonnafont, Louis. *Trente ans de Tonkin*. Paris: Eugène Figuière, 1924.
Bonniot, R. *L'Enfant métisse malheureuse. Rapport présenté par M. Bonniot au congrès de l'enfance 1940*. Saigon: Imprimerie de l'Union, 1940.
Bonvicini, Henri. *Enfants de la colonie*. Saigon: Portail, 1938.
Booth, William. *In Darkest England and the Way Out*. London: McCorquirdale, 1890.
Bordier, Arthur. *La Géographie médicale*. Paris: Reinwald, 1884.
Borel, Dr. Joseph-Emile. "Résultats d'une enquête malériologique à Dalat." *Extrait du Bulletin de la Société de Patholoqie Exotique* 20, no. 5. (11 May 1927): 427–34.
Borel, Marius. *Souvenirs d'un vieux colonialiste*. Six-Fours: Compte d'Auteur, 1963.
Borner, M. "L'Emigration chinoise en Indo-Chine et dans le monde." *Conférences publiques sur l'Indochine faites à l'Ecole coloniale pendant l'année 1909–1910*. Paris: Imprimerie de la Dépêche Coloniale, 1910, 48–65.
Bouinais, A., and A. Paulus. *L'Indo-Chine française contemporaine: Cambodge, Tonkin, Annam*. Paris: Challamel Aîné, 1885.
Bourgeois, Paul, and G.-Roger Sandoz. *Exposition d'Hanoi 1902–1903: Rapport général*. Paris: Comité Français des Expositions à L'étranger, 1904.
Braddell, Roland. *The Lights of Singapore*. London: Methuen & Co., 1934.
Brenier, Henri. *Essai d'atlas statistique de l'Indochine française: Indochine physique, population, administration, finances, agriculture, commerce, industrie*. Hanoi: Imprimerie d'Extrême-Orient, 1914.
Brieux, Eugène. *Voyage aux Indes et en Indo-Chine: Simples notes d'un touriste*. Paris: Librairie Ch. Delagrave, 1910.
Bromley, Blake. *Opams and Bundu Beetles*. Edinburgh: Pentland Press, 2000.
Brown, Edwin A. *Indiscreet Memories*. London: Kelly & Walsh, 1935.
Brown, Harrison. *Our Neighbours Today and Yesterday*. London: G. Howe, 1933.
Bunout, René. "La Main-d'oeuvre et la législation du travail en Indochine." PhD diss., Bordeaux University, 1936.
Caine, W. S. *A Trip Round the World in 1887–8*. London: George Routledge and Sons, 1888.
Cannon, P. S. "The 'Pidgin English' of the China Coast." *Journal of the Army Educational Corps* 13, no. 4 (October 1936): 137–40.
Carabelli, Roch. *L'Unite de l'Indo-Chine*. Saigon: Imprimerie de Rey et Curiol, 1886.
Cario, Louis, and Charles Regismanset. *L'Exotisme: La Littérature coloniale*. Paris: Mercure, 1911.
Castellani, Aldo. *Climate and Acclimatization: Some Notes and Observations*. London: John Bale, Sons & Danielsson, 1931.
Célarié, Henriette. *Promenades en Indochine*. Paris: Baudinière, 1937.
Chailley-Bert, Joseph. "Discours de M. Chailley-Bert." In Union Coloniale Française, *L'Emigration des femmes aux colonies. Conférence de 12 janvier 1897*. Paris: Armand Colin, 1897, 11–61.
Challan de Belval, Le Dr. *Au Tonkin*. Paris: A. Delahaye et E. Lecrosnier, 1886.
Champly, Henry. *Le Chemin de Changhaï*. Paris: Tallandier, 1933.
Chan King Nui, *From Poor Migrant to Millionaire: Chan Wing, 1873–1947*. Kuala Lumpur: Malaysian Branch of the Royal Asiatic Society, 1997.
Chauvelot, R. *En Indochine*. Grenoble: Rey, 1931.
Chauvin, Jacques. *Paul Doumer: Le Président assassiné*. Paris: Panthéon, 1994.
Clifford, Nicholas. *Spoilt Children of Empire: Westerners in Shanghai and the Chinese Revolution of the 1920s*. Hanover: University Press of New England, 1991.

Comptes rendus de l'Institut Colonial International. Bruxelles: Bibliothèque Coloniale Internationale, 1911.
Conseil de perfectionnement de l'enseignement indigène, première session, Hanoi, Avril 1906. Hanoi: Imprimerie d'Extrême-Orient, 1906.
Conseil National des Femmes Françaises. *États généraux du féminisme, 30–31 mai 1931.* Paris: Conseil National des Femmes Françaises, 1931.
Cook, Rev. J.A. Bethune. *Sunny Singapore.* London: Elliot Stock, 1907.
Cooper, Frederick, and Ann Laura Stoler, eds. *Tensions of Empire: Colonial Cultures in a Bourgeois World.* Berkeley: University of California Press, 2007.
Corneau, Grace. *La Femme aux colonies.* Paris: Librairie Nilsson, 1900.
Cunningham, Alfred. "Exposition at Hanoi." *L'Exposition de Hanoi.* Hanoi: F. H. Schneider, 1902.
Dalton, Clive. *A Child in the Sun.* London: Eldon Press, 1937.
Dalziel, James. *Chronicles of a Crown Colony.* Hong Kong: South China Morning Post, 1907.
Danguy, Henri. *De la ville des hommes à la cité des dieux. Itinéraire de Saigon à Angkor.* Paris-Saigon: Editions Orient-Occident, 1940.
———. *Le Nouveau visage de la Cochinchine.* Paris: Larose, 1929.
Danguy des Déserts, Auguste. *Considérations sur l'hygiène de l'européen en Cochinchine.* Paris: A. Parent Imprimeur, 1876.
de Hargues, Thérèse. *Anecdotes d'un roule-ta-bousse.* Paris: La Pensée Universelle, 1992.
de la Varre, André, dir. *Hong Kong, Gateway to China,* 1938.
de Lanessan, Jean-Louis. *L'Expansion coloniale de la France: Étude économique, politique et géographique sur les établissements français d'outre-mer.* Paris: Félix Alcan, 1886.
de Montpensier, Duc. *En Indochine: Mes chasses—mes voyages.* Paris: Pierre Lafitte, 1912.
Delteil, Arthur. *Un An de séjour en Cochinchine: Guide du voyageur à Saigon.* Paris: Challamel Ainé, Editeur, 1887.
d'Enjoy, Paul. *La Santé aux colonies.* Paris: Société d'Editions Scientifiques, 1901.
Dennery, Etienne. *Foules d'Asie: Surpopulation Japonaise, expansion Chinoise, émigration indienne.* Paris: Librairie Armand Colin, 1930.
Des Voeux, Sir George W. *My Colonial Service in British Guiana, St. Lucia, Trinidad, Fiji, Australia, New Foundland, and Hong Kong, with Interludes,* vol. 2. London: John Murray, 1903.
Deschamps, René. *La Main d'œuvre en Indochine et l'immigration étrangère.* Poitiers: Imprimerie Maurice Bousrez, 1908.
The Diocesan Girls' School and Orphanage, Hongkong. *Third Annual Report, 1902.* Hong Kong, 1902.
The Diocesan School and Orphanage, Hongkong. *Thirty-sixth Annual Report, 1904.* Hong Kong, 1904.
Direction General de l'instruction Publique. *Le Petit Lycée de Dalat.* Hanoi: Imprimerie d'Extrême-Orient, 1930.
Discours prononcé par M. A. Klobukowsky, Gouverneur Général de l'Indo-chine à l'ouverture de la session ordinaire de Conseil supérieur le 27 novembre 1909. Saigon: Imprimerie Commerciale Marcellin Rey, 1909.
Dixon, Katherine. *Address to Mothers—Upon the Moral Education of Children.* Singapore: Social Service Society, 1919.
Douchet, P. *Métis et congaies d'Indochine.* Hanoi, 1928.

Doumer, Paul. *Situation de l'Indochine (1897–1901): Rapport par M. Paul Doumer, Gouverneur Général.* Hanoi: F.-H. Schneider, 1902.

———. *L'Indochine française: Souvenirs.* Paris: Vuibert et Nony, 1905.

———. *Livre de mes fils.* Paris: Vuibert & Nony, 1906.

Drevet, Camille. *Les Annamites chez eux.* Paris: Imprimerie de la Société Nouvelle d'editions Franco-Slaves, 1928.

Dumoutier, G. *Les cultes annamites.* Hanoi: F. H. Schneider, 1907.

Dupla, M. "A Propos d'enseignement." In *Bulletin de la Société des études indochinoises.* 1896. Saigon: Imprimerie Commerciale Rey, Curiol & Cie, 1897, 15–20.

Dürrwell, George. *Ma Chère Cochinchine: Trente années d'impressions et de souvenirs fevrier 1881–1910.* Paris: Mignot, 1910.

Education Systems of the Chief Crown Colonies and Possessions of the British Empire: Including Reports on the Training of Native Races. London: HMSO, 1905.

Eitel, E. J. *Europe in China: The History of Hongkong to the Year 1882.* 1895. Hong Kong: Oxford University Press, 1983.

Elcum, J. B. *Annual Report on Education in the Straits Settlements for the Year 1900.* Singapore: Government Printing Office, 1901.

Ennis, Thomas E. *French Policy and Developments in Indochina.* ca. 1936. New York: Russell & Russell, 1973.

Ewart, Joseph. "Causes of the Excessive Mortality among the Women and Children of the European Soldiers Serving in India." *Transactions of the Epidemiological Society of London* 2 (1882–83): 46–67.

———. "The Colonisation of the Sub-Himalayas and Neilgherries. With Remarks on the Management of European Children in India." *Transactions of the Epidemiological Society of London* 3 (1883): 96–117.

Far Eastern Association of Tropical Medicine. *Second Biennial Congress, Hongkong January 20th to January 27th 1912, Programme and Guide to Hongkong.* Hong Kong: Noronha & Co., 1912.

Farrère, Claude. *Les Civilisés: Roman.* Paris: P. Ollendorff, 1906.

Faure, J-L. *La Vie aux colonies. Préparation de la femme à la vie coloniale.* Paris: Larose Editeurs, 1938.

Fayrer, Sir Joseph. *European Child-Life in Bengal.* London: J & A Churchill, 1873.

Ferry, Jules. *Le Tonkin et la mère patrie: Témoignages et documents*, 3rd ed. Paris: Victor-Havard, 1890.

Fondation Jules Brévié. *Fondation Brévié: Son origine, ses buts et ses moyens d'action.* Saigon: Imprimerie de l'Union, 1942.

Fournier, Christiane. *Bébé colonial: Une Enfance au Tonkin.* Paris: Editions Berger-Levrault, 1935.

———. *Perspectives Occidentales sur l'Indochine.* Saigon: Nouvelle Revue Indochinoise, 1935.

Fraissinet, Marc. *La Prostitution réglementée et la traite des femmes aux colonies françaises, protectorats et pays placés sous mandat.* Cahors: Imprimerie de Coueslant, 1935.

Franck, Harry. *East of Siam: Ramblings in the Five Divisions of French Indo-China.* New York: Century Co., 1926.

Furnivall, J. S. *Educational Progress in Southeast Asia.* New York: Institute of Pacific Relations, 1943.

Gaide, Laurent Joseph. *Les Stations climatiques en Indochine.* Hanoi: Imprimerie d'Extrème-Orient, 1930.
Garnier, Francis. *Voyage d'exploration en Indochine, effectué pendant les anneés 1866, 1867 et 1868 par une commission française présidée par M. le capitaine de frégate, Doudart de Lagrée,* 2 vols. Paris: Hachette et Cie, 1873.
Gaw, Kenneth. *Superior Servants: The Legendary Cantonese Amahs of the Far East.* Singapore: Oxford University Press, 1988.
Gervais-Courtellemont, Jules. *Empire Colonial de la France: L'Indochine. Cochinchine, Cambodge, Laos, Annam, Tonkin.* Paris: Librairie de Paris Firmin-Didot, 1901.
Gittins, Jean. *Eastern Windows, Western Skies.* Hong Kong: South China Morning Post, 1969.
Godart, Justin. *Rapport de mission en Indochine: 1er janvier—14 mars 1937.* Paris: L'Harmattan, 1994.
Goodwin, William Meigh. *Reminiscences of a Colonial Judge.* London: Kingsgate, 1907.
Gouvernement Général de L'Indochine. *Annuaire Statistique de l'Indochine, premier volume, recueil des statistiques relatives aux années 1913 à 1922.* Hanoi: Imprimerie d'Extrème-Orient Editeur, 1927.
———. *Annuaire Statistique de l'Indochine, deuxième volume, recueil des statistiques relatives aux années 1923 à 1929.* Hanoi: Imprimerie d'Extrème-Orient, 1931.
———. *Annuaire Statistique de l'Indochine, troisième volume, 1930–1931.* Hanoi: Imprimerie d'Extrème-Orient, 1932.
———, Direction des Affaires Economiques. *Annuaire Statistique de l'Indochine, cinquième volume, 1932–1933.* Hanoi: Imprimerie d'Extrème-Orient, 1935.
Gower, Lord Ronald. *My Reminiscences.* London: Kegan Paul, Trench & Co., 1883.
Grall, Charles. *Hygiène Colonial appliquée: Hygiène de l'Indochine.* Paris: J.-B. Baillière et Fils, 1908.
Green, C.R.M., and V. B. Green-Armytage. *Birch's Management and Medical Treatment of Children in India,* 5th ed. Calcutta: Thacker, Spink & Co., 1913.
Guide du français arrivant en Indochine. Hanoi: Taupin, 1935.
Hall, G. S. *Adolescence: Its Psychology and Its Relations to Physiology, Anthropology, Sociology, Sex, Crime, Religion and Education.* New York: W. D. Appleton and Company, 1904.
Hardy, Rev. E. J. *John Chinaman at Home: Sketches of Men, Manners and Things in China.* London: T. Fisher Unwin, 1905.
———. *Marriage. Being a Lecture Delivered at Hongkong on 20th March 1903.* Hong Kong: W. Brewer & Co., 1903.
Harmand, Jules. *Domination et colonisation.* Paris: Flammarion, 1910.
Harris, Walter B. *East for Pleasure: The Narrative of Eight Months' Travel in Burma, Siam, The Netherlands East Indies and French Indochina.* London: Edward Arnold & Co., 1929.
Harrop, Phyllis. *Hong Kong Incident.* London: Eyre & Spottiswoode, 1943.
Haslewood, Lieutenant Commander, and Mrs. H. L. Haslewood. *Child Slavery in Hong Kong: The Mui Tsai System.* London: Sheldon Press, 1930.
Henry-Biabaud, E. *Deux ans d'Indochine.* Hanoi: IDEO, 1939.
Hochberg, Fritz. *An Eastern Voyage: A Journal of the Travels of Count Fritze Hochberg through the British Empire in the East and Japan.* London: J. M. Dent, 1910.
Hong Kong History and Description. Hong Kong: Publicity Bureau for South China, Commercial Press, 1927.
Hongkong. A Comic Opera in Two Acts, words by H. G. Maclaurin, music by Charles Jessop. London: Chappell & Co., 1925.

The Hongkong Nursing Institution, Established 1901, Patroness Lady Blake. *Annual Report 1902.* Hongkong: Guedes & Company, 1903.
Howell, E. F. *Malayan Turnovers.* Singapore: Kelly & Walsh, 1928.
Humbert, Charles. *L'Oeuvre française aux colonies.* Paris: Emile Larose, 1913.
Hume, Edward H. *Young China.* New York: CADAL, 1927.
Hunt, James. "On Ethno-Climatology; or the Acclimatization of Man." *Transactions of the Ethnological Society of London* (1863): 50–83.
Hutton, J. H. *Census of India,* vol. 1, *India.* Delhi: Government of India Publications, 1933.
Innes, Emily. *The Chersonese with the Gilding Off.* Kuala Lumpur: Oxford University Press, 1974.
Jay, Antoine, and Madeleiene Jay. *Notre Indochine, 1936–1947.* Charenton: Les Presses de Valmy, 1995.
Jeffries, Charles. *The Colonial Empire and Its Civil Service.* Cambridge: Cambridge University Press, 1938.
Johnson, James. *The Influence of Tropical Climates, More Especially the Climate of India on European Constitutions.* London: J. J. Stockdale, 1813.
Jouglet, René. *Dans le sillage des jonques.* Paris: Grasset, 1935.
Jousset, Alfred. *Traité de l'acclimatement et de l'acclimatation.* Paris: Doin, 1884.
Jung, Eugène. *La Vie européenne au Tonkin.* Paris: Flammarion, 1901.
Kermorgant, Alexandre M. *Hygiène Colonial.* Paris: Masson et Cie, 1911.
———. "Sanatoria et camps de dissémination de nos colonies." *Annales d'Hygiène et de Médecine Coloniales* 12, no. 3 (July–September 1899): 345–65.
Knollys, Major Henry. *English Life in China.* London: Smith, Elder and Co., 1885.
Krausse, A. S. *The Far East: Its History and Its Questions.* London: G. Richards, 1900.
Lane-Poole, Stanley, ed. *Thirty Years of Colonial Government: A Selection from the Despatches and Letters of the Right Honourable Sir George Ferguson Bowen.* London: Longmans, Green and Colonial Office, 1889.
League of Nations. *Commission of Enquiry into Traffic in Women and Children in the East, Report to Council.* Geneva: League of Nations, 1932.
le Breton, H. *Le Problème scolaire en pays d'Annam, Huê, Août 1932.* Huê: Dac Lap, 1932.
le Myre de Vilers, Charles-Marie. *La politique coloniale Français depuis 1830.* Paris: Publications de la Nouvelle Revue, 1913.
Lefebvre, Paul. *Faces jaunes: Moeurs et coutumes de l'Extrême-Orient.* Paris: Challamel, 1886.
Legrand, Dr. M.-A. *L'hygiène des troupes européennes aux colonies et dans les expéditions coloniales.* Paris: Henri Charles Lavauzelle, 1895.
Lemire, Charles. *L'Indochine: Cochinchine française, royaume de Cambodge, royaume d'Annam et Tonkin,* 3rd ed. Paris: Challamel Aîné, 1884.
Leriche, Ulysse. *Etude économique et politique sur la question d'extrême-Orient.* Saigon: Le Mékong, 1895.
Leroy-Beaulieu, Paul. *De la colonisation chez les peuples modernes,* 3rd ed. Paris: Librairie Guillaumin et Cie, 1886.
Les Fêtes de Dalat en l'honneur de M. Yersin à l'occasion du baptême du lycée. Hanoi: Imprimerie d'Extrême-Orient, 1935.
L'Indochine à l'exposition coloniale de Marseille. Marseille: Imprimerie Marseillaise, 1906.
Lombard, H-C. *Atlas de la distribution géographique des maladies dans leurs rapports avec les climats.* Paris: J. B. Baillère et fils, 1880.

Lugard, Frederick D. *The Dual Mandate in British Tropical Africa.* London: W. Blackwood and Sons, 1922.
Lum, Lucy. *The Thorn of Lion City: A Memoir.* New York: Public Affairs, 2007.
MacDonald, Brian, ed. *"Dearest Mother": The Letters of F.R. Kendall.* London: Lloyds of London Press, 1988.
Macmillan, Allister. *Seaports of the Far East: Historical and Descriptive, Commercial and Industrial, Facts, Figures and Resources.* London: W. H. & L. Collingridge, 1923.
MacNair, Harley Farnsworth. *The Chinese Abroad, Their Position and Protection: A Study in International Law and Relations.* Shanghai: Commercial Press, 1925.
Madrolle, Claudius. *Tonkin du Sud, Hanoï. Les Annamites, Hanoï, pays de So'n-tâi, pays de So'n-nam.* Paris: Comité de l'Asie française, 1907.
Makepeace, Walter, Gilbert E. Brooke and Roland St. J. Braddell, eds. *One Hundred Years of Singapore,* vol. 2. Singapore: Oxford University Press, 1991.
Marquet, Jean. *De la rizière à la montagne: Moeurs annamites.* Paris: Delalain, 1920.
Marquis, Edouard. *L'œuvre humaine de la France en Cochinchine.* Saigon: Imprimerie du Théâtre, 1936.
Marriot, H. *Report on the Census of the Straits Settlements Taken on 10th March 1911.* Singapore: Government Printing Office, 1911.
Marx, Georges. *La Cochinchine humoristique.* Paris: Vie Moderne, ca. 1890.
Massieu, Isabelle. *Comment j'ai parcouru l'Indochine.* Paris: Plon, 1901.
Masterman, Charles F.G. *The Heart of the Empire: Discussions of Problems of Modern City Life in England with an Essay on Imperialism.* London: T. F. Unwin, 1901.
Mazet, Jacques. *La Condition juridique des métis dans les possessions françaises.* Paris: Editions Domat-Montchresien, 1932.
McKie, R.C.H. *This Was Singapore.* London: Robert Hale, 1950.
Mead, Margaret. *Coming of Age in Samoa: A Psychological Study of Primitive Youth for Western Civilisation.* New York: W. Morrow & Co., 1928.
Merewether, E. M. *Report on the Census of the Straits Settlements Taken on the 5th April, 1891.* Singapore: Government Printing Press, 1892.
Michie, Alexander. *The Englishman in China during the Victorian Era: As Illustrated in the Career of Sir Rutherford Alcock, KCB, DCL, Many Years Consul and Minister in China and Japan.* Edinburgh: William Blackwood & Sons, 1900.
Middleton Smith, C. A. *The British in China and Far Eastern Trade.* London: Constable, 1920.
Millet-Robinet, Mme and Docteur Emile Allix. *Le Livre des jeunes mères: La nourrice et le nourrisson.* Paris: Librairie Agricole de la Maison Rustique, 1884.
Montel, M. "Sur la mortalité infantile en Cochinchine." *Bulletin de la Société Médico-Chirurgicale de l'Indochine* 10 (November 1926): 572–74.
Moore, W. J. *The Constitutional Requirements for Tropical Climates and Observations on the Sequel of Disease Contracted in India.* London: Churchill, 1890.
Moore, William. "Is the Colonisation of Tropical Africa by Europeans Possible?" *Transactions of the Epidemiological Society of London* 10 (1890–91): 27–45.
Morant, C. G. *Odds and Ends of Foreign Travel.* London: Charles and Edwin Layton, 1913.
Mouchonière, A. *Police de l'Indochine: Guide des agents de police de la ville de Cholon.* Saigon: Imprimerie de l'Union Nguyen-Van-Cua, 1921.
Müller, Johannes. *The Berlin Foundling House, Bethesda, Report for the Year Ending 30th November 1904.* Hong Kong: South China Morning Post, 1904.

My, Michel. *Le Tonkin pittoresque, souvenirs et impressions de voyage. 1921–2.* Saigon: J. Viêt, 1925.
Nathan, J. E. *The Census of British Malaya.* London: Waterlow & Sons, 1922.
Ngô Tất Tố. *Tắt đèn.* Hanoi: Mai Lĩnh xuất bản, 1939.
Ngô Vĩnh Long. *Before the Revolution: The Vietnamese Peasants under the French.* Cambridge: MIT Press, 1973.
Ngọc Liễn Vũ. *Moeurs et coutumes du Viêt-nam.* Hanoi: Imprimerie de Hanoi, 1942.
Nguyễn Tiến Lãng. *Les Chansons annamites: Conférence avec audition de disques donnée à la Société philharmonique de Saigon, 5 mars 1937.* Saigon: Editions de l'Asie nouvelle illustrée, 1937.
Noctes Orientales, Being a Selection of Essays Read before the Straits Philosphical Society between the Years 1893 and 1910. Singapore: Kelly and Walsh, 1912.
Nolly, Emile. *La Barque annamite: Roman de moeurs tonkinoises.* Paris: Calmann-Levy, 1921.
Northcliffe, Alfred H. *My Journey around the World, 16 July 1921–25 February 1922.* London: Lane, 1923.
Onraët, René. *Singapore—A Police Background.* London: Dorothy Crisp and Co., 1947.
Orgeas, Joseph Onéisme. *La Pathologie des races humaines et le problème de la colonisation: Étude anthropologique et économique faite à la Guyane française.* Paris: Doin, 1886.
Paris, Camille. *De la Condition juridique des métis dans les colonies et possessions françaises: Des métis franco-annamites de l'Indo-Chine.* Paris: 1904.
Passa, Médecin General. "L'Enfant européen dans la France d'outre-mer tropicale: Sa protection sanitaire." *Revue Médico-Sociale et de Protection de l'Enfance* 1, no. 6 (1938): 26–40.
Pelletier, Gaston, and Louis Roubaud. *Empire ou colonies?* Paris: Plon, 1936.
———. *Images et réalités coloniales.* Paris: Tournon, 1931.
Peplow, Samuel Henry. *Hongkong: About and Around.* Hong Kong: Commercial Press, 1930.
Péralle, L. "Boys et coolies à Saigon." In *Bulletin de la Société des études indochinoises, 1896.* Saigon: Imprimerie Commerciale Rey, Curiol & Cie, 1897, 43–63.
Peytral, Louis. *Silhouttes tonkinoises.* Paris: Berger-Levrault et Cie, 1897.
Picton-Turbervill, Edith. *Life Is Good: An Autobiography.* London: Frederick Muller, 1939.
Piolet, Jean-Baptiste. *La France hors de France: Notre emigration, sa nécessité, ses conditions.* Paris: F. Alcan, 1900.
Platt, Kate. *The Home and Health in India and Tropical Colonies.* London: Baillière, Tindall and Cox, 1923.
Prou, Suzanne. *La Petite Tonkinoise.* Paris: Calmann-Lévy, 1987.
Raffles, Lady Sophia. *Memoir of the Life and Public Services of Sir Thomas Stamford Raffles,* vol. 2. London: James Duncan, 1835.
Rapports présentés au 4è congrès de l'enfance 1940. Publiés sous les auspices du Comité central d'aide mutuelle et d'assistance sociale de Cochinchine. Saigon: Imprimerie de l'Union, 1940.
Raquez, A. *Les Boursiers de voyage de l'université de Paris.* Hanoi: Imprimerie F. H. Schneider, 1905.
Rattray, Alexander. "On Some of the More Important Physiological Changes Induced in the Human Economy by Change of Climate, as from Temperate to Tropical and the Reverse." *Proceedings of the Royal Society of London* 18 (1869): 513–29.
Reed, Robert. "From Highland Hamlet to Regional Capital: Reflections on the Colonial Origins, Urban Transformation and Environmental Impact of Dalat." In *The Challenges*

of Highland Development in Vietnam, edited by Terry Rambo, Robert Reed, Lê Trọng Cúc et al. Honolulu: East-West Center, 1995.
Renan, Ernest. *Histoire du peuple d'Israël.* Paris: Calmann-Lévy, 1887–1893.
Reynaud, Gustave. *Hygiène des colons.* Paris: Librairie J.-B. Baillère et Fils, 1903.
———. *Hygiène des établissements coloniaux.* Paris: J.-B. Baillière et Fils, 1903.
Ride, Edwin. *I Dips Me Lid: Diplomatic Memoirs.* Queensland: E. Ride, 1991.
Ripley, William Z. *The Races of Europe: A Sociological Study.* London: Kegan Paul, Trench, Trubner & Co., 1899.
Robertson, John M. "The Rationale of Autonomy." In *Papers on Inter-racial Problems Communicated to the First Universal Races Congress Held at the University of London, July 26–29, 1911,* edited by G. Spiller. London: P. S. King & Son, 1911, 39–50.
Robiquet, Paul, ed. *Discours et opinions de Jules Ferry, publiés avec commentaires et notes,* vol. 5, *Affaires tunisiennes—Congo—Madagascar—Egypte—Tonkin.* Paris: Armand Colin & Cie, 1897.
Rondet-Saint, Maurice. *Dans notre empire jaune: Notes et croquis.* Paris: Plon, 1917.
Rouyer, Charlotte. *Femmes d'outre mer.* Saigon: Imprimerie de l'Union, 1941.
Salaün, Louis. *L'Indochine.* Paris: Imprimerie Nationale, 1903.
Salmon, Charles, and Robert Halliburton. *The Crown Colonies of Great Britain: An Inquiry into Their Social Condition and Methods of Administration.* London: Cassell & Co., 1885.
Sambuc, Albert. "Les métis franco-annamites." *Revue du Pacifique* (1931): no. 4, 194–95; and no. 5, 256–72.
Sayer, Geoffrey Robley. *Hong Kong, 1841–1862: Birth, Adolescence and Coming of Age.* London: Oxford University Press, 1937.
Semaine de l'enfance sous le patronage de M le Gouverneur de la Cochinchine, présidence d'honneur de Mme Pierre-Pagès du 1e au 7 juillet 1934, congrès de l'enfance. Saigon: Imprimerie de l'Union, 1934.
Shennan, Margaret. *Out in the Midday Sun: The British in Malaya, 1880–1960.* London: John Murray, 2000.
Sims, George R. *How the Poor Live.* London: Chatto, 1883.
Société Bretonne de Géographie de l'Orient. *L'Avenir colonial de la France: L'Afrique et le Tonkin.* Lorient: Imprimerie Louis Chamaillard, 1882.
Société de Protection de l'Enfance de Cochinchine. *Société de protection de l'enfance de Cochinchine, procès verbal 26 Mars 1929.* Saigon: Imprimerie de l'Union Nguyen Van Cua, 1929.
———. *Procès verbal de l'assemblée générale du 5 Mars 1931.* Saigon: Imprimerie de l'Union Nguyen Van Cua, 1931.
———. *Procès-verbal de l'assemblée générale du 29 mars 1935, Société de Protection de l'Enfance de Cochinchine.* Saigon: Imprimerie J. Aspar, 1935.
———. *Procès-verbal de l'assemblée générale du 8 mai 1937.* Saigon: Imprimerie J. Aspar, 1937.
Société de Protection des Métis d'Annam. *Société de protection des métis d'Annam.* Hué: Imprimerie Mirador, 1941.
Société des Missions-Étrangères. *Compte Rendu des travaux de 1900.* Paris: Seminaire des Missions-Étrangères, 1901.
———. *Compte Rendu des travaux de 1903.* Paris: Seminaire des Missions-Étrangères, 1904.
———. *Compte Rendu des travaux de 1906.* Paris: Seminaire des Missions-Étrangères, 1907.

Spencer, J. E., and W. L. Thomas. "The Hill Stations and Summer Resorts of the Orient," *Geographical Review* 38 (1948): 637–51.
Star, Jean. *Tonkinades*. Paris: Calman-Lévy, 1902.
S.T.L. *The Jubilee of Shanghai, 1843–1893: Shanghai, Past and Present, and a Full Account of the Proceedings on the 17th and 18th Nov. 1893*. Shanghai: North China Herald, 1893.
Sweet, S. A. *A Hong Kong Sketch Book*. Hong Kong: Ye Olde Printerie, 1931.
Swettenham, Frank. *British Malaya: An Account of the Origin and Progress of British Influence in Malaya*. London: J. Lane, 1906.
Tardif, Etienne. *La Naissance de Dalat: Annam (1899–1900). Capitale de l'Indochine*. Vienne: Ternet-Martin, 1949.
Tavernier, Emile. *La Famille annamite*. Saigon: Editions Nguyên-Van-Cua, 1927.
Teston, Eugène, and Maurice Percheron. *L'Indochine moderne: Encyclopédie administrative, touristique, artistique et économique*. Paris: Librairie de France, 1931.
Thompson, Virginia. *French Indochina*. London: George Allen and Unwin, 1937.
Thomson, John Stuart. *The Chinese*. London: T. Werner Laurie, 1909.
Tilt, Edward John. *Health in India for British Women and on the Prevention of Disease in Tropical Climates*, 4th ed. London: Churchill, 1875.
Treille, Georges Félix. *Principes d'hygiène coloniale*. Paris: Georges Carré et C. Naud, 1899.
Trewartha, Glenn T. "Recent Thought on the Problem of White Acclimatization in the Wet Tropics." *Geographical Review* 16, no. 3 (1926): 467–78.
Union Coloniale Française, *Preparation aux carrières coloniales, conférences faites, par MM. Le Myre de Vilers, Dr. Treille, L. Simon, E. Fallot, J-B. Malon, Paris, L. Fontaine, Maurice Courant, Gérome, André Liesse, 1901–1902*. Paris: Augustin Challamel, 1904.
Varet, Pierre. *L'Effort colonial de la France au cours de la guerre de 1914*. Paris: Les Presses Modernes, 1927.
Vassal, Gabrielle M. *Three Years in Vietnam: 1907–1910*. (Originally published as *On and Off Duty in Annam*. London: Heinemann, 1910.) Bangkok: White Lotus, 1999.
Vaudon, Jean. *Les Filles de Saint-Paul en Indochine*. Chartres: Procure des Soeurs de Saint-Paul, 1931.
Vaughan, J. D. *The Manners and Customs of the Chinese of the Straits Settlements*. Kuala Lumpur: Oxford University Press, 1971.
"Veronica." *The Islanders of Hong Kong*. Hong Kong: China Mail Co., 1907.
Ville de Saigon, *Statistique Municipale: Année 1907*. Saigon: F. H. Schneider, 1908.
Villedary, Léon. *Guide sanitaire des troupes et du colon aux colonies. Hygiène coloniale; prophylaxie et traitement des principales maladies des pays chauds*. Paris: Société d'Editions Scientifiques, 1893.
Vlieland, C. A. *British Malaya: A Report on the 1931 Census and on Certain Problems of Vital Statistics*. London: Crown Agents, 1932.
Vũ Trọng Phụng. *Lục Xì: Prostitution and Venereal Disease in Colonial Hanoi*, translated by Shaun Kingsley Mallarney. Honolulu: University of Hawai'i Press, 2011.
Vũ Văn Quang. *Le Problème des eurasiens en Indochine*. Hanoi: Imprimerie Tonkinoise, 1939.
Walker, E. A. *Sophia Cooke: Forty-two Years of Work in Singapore*. London: Elliot Stock, 1899.
Werth, Léon. *Cochinchine*. Paris: F. Rieder et Cie, 1926.
Whitworth, Phoebe. *View from the Peak: An Autobiography*. Cambridge: T. G. Whitworth, 2001.

Wingfield, Lewis Strange. *Wanderings of a Globe-Trotter in the Far East*, vol. 1. London: Richard Bentley, 1889.
Wood, Winifred A. *A Brief History of Hong Kong*. Hong Kong: South China Morning Post, 1940.
Woods, W. W. *Mui Tsai in Hong Kong and Malaya: Report of Commission*. London: HMSO, 1937.
Woolf, Lady Bella Sidney. *Chips of China*. Hong Kong: Kelly & Walsh, 1930.
———. *Under the Mosquito Curtain*. Hong Kong: Kelly & Walsh, 1935.

SECONDARY SOURCES

Agulhon, Maurice. *Marianne into Battle: Republican Imagery and Symbolism in France, 1780–1880*, translated by Janet Lloyd. Cambridge: Cambridge University Press, 1981.
Aitken, S. Robert. *Imperial Belvederes*. Oxford: Oxford University Press, 1994.
Anderson, Benedict. *Imagined Communities: Reflections on the Origin and Spread of Nationalism*. London: Verso, 1991.
———. *Long Distance Nationalism: World Capitalism and the Rise of Identity Politics*. Berkeley: University of California Press, 1992.
Anderson, Warwick. "Climates of Opinion: Acclimatisation in Nineteenth-Century France and England." *Victorian Studies* 35 (1992): 135–57.
———. *Colonial Pathologies: American Tropical Medicine, Race, and Hygiene in the Philippines*. Durham: Duke University Press, 2006.
———. "'Where Every Prospect Pleases and Only Man Is Vile': Laboratory Medicine as Colonial Discourse." *Critical Enquiry* 18, no. 3 (1992): 506–29.
André-Pallois, Nadine. *L'Indochine: Un lieu d'échange culturel?: Les peintres français et indochinois. Fin XIXe-XXe siècle*. Paris: Presses de l'Ecole Française d'Extrême-Orient, 1997.
Ariès, Philippe. *Centuries of Childhood: A Social History of Family Life*. New York: Alfred A. Knopf, 1962.
Arnold, David. *Colonizing the Body: State Medicine and Epidemic Disease in Nineteenth-Century India*. Berkeley: University of California Press, 1993.
———. "European Orphans and Vagrants in India in the Nineteenth Century." *Journal of Imperial and Commonwealth History* 7, no. 2 (1979): 104–27.
———. *The Problem of Nature: Environment, Culture and European Expansion*. Oxford: Basil Blackwell, 1996.
Ashcroft, Bill. "Primitive and Wingless: The Colonial Subject as Child." In *Dickens, The Child and Empire*, edited by Wendy S. Jacobson. London: Palgrave Macmillan, 2001, 184–202.
Baena, Rosalia. "Of Missess and Tuan Kechils: Colonial Childhood Memoirs as Cultural Mediation in British Malaya." *ARIEL* 39, no. 1 (January 2008): 89–112.
Ballantyne, Tony. *Orientalism and Race: Aryanism in the British Empire*. Basingstoke: Palgrave, 2002.
Banens, Maks. "Vietnam: A Reconstruction of Its Twentieth Century Population History." In *Quantitative Economic History of Vietnam 1900–1990*, edited by Jean-Pascal Bassino, Jean-Dominique Giacometti and K. Odaka. Tokyo: Hitotsubashi University, 2000, 1–40.
Barrett, Tracy C. *The Chinese Diaspora in Southeast Asia: The Overseas Chinese in Indochina*. London: I. B. Tauris, 2012.

Basu, Dilip K., ed. *The Rise and Growth of the Colonial Port Cities in Asia*. Center for Southeast Asian Studies, University of California, Berkeley, 1985.

Bayly, Christopher A. *The Birth of the Modern World, 1780–1914: Global Connections and Comparisons*. Malden: Blackwell, 2004.

———. *Empire and Information: Intelligence Gathering and Social Communication in India, 1780–1870*. Cambridge: Cambridge University Press, 1996.

Betts, Raymond F. *Assimilation and Association in French Colonial Theory, 1890–1914*. New York: Columbia University Press, 1961.

Bhattacharya, Nandini. *Contagion and Enclaves: Tropical Medicine in Colonial India*. Liverpool: Liverpool University Press, 2012.

Bickers, Robert. *Britain in China: Community, Culture and Colonialism 1900–1949*. Manchester: Manchester University Press, 1999.

———. *Settlers and Expatriates: Britons over the Seas*. Oxford: Oxford University Press, 2010.

———. "Shanghailanders and Others: British Communities in China, 1843–1957." In *Settlers and Expatriates: Britons over the Seas*, edited by Robert Bickers. Oxford: Oxford University Press, 2010, 269–302.

Bickers, Robert, and Christian Henriot, eds. *New Frontiers: Imperialism's New Communities in East Asia, 1842–1953*. Manchester: Manchester University Press, 2000.

Blunt, Alison. "Imperial Geographies of Home: British Domesticity in India, 1886–1925." *Transactions of the Institute of British Geographers* 24, no. 4 (1999): 421–40.

Bose, Sugata. *A Hundred Horizons: The Indian Ocean in the Age of Global Empire*. Cambridge: Harvard University Press, 2006.

Boucher, Ellen. *Empire's Children: Child Emigration, Welfare and the Decline of the British World, 1869–1967*. Cambridge: Cambridge University Press, 2014.

Brendon, Vyvyen. *Children of the Raj*. London: Weidenfeld and Nicolson, 2005.

Bretelle l'Establet, Florence. "Resistance and Receptivity: French Colonial Medicine in Southwest China, 1898–1930." *Modern China* 25, no. 2 (April 1999): 171–203.

Briggs, Laura. *Reproducing Empire: Race, Sex, Science and US Imperialism in Puerto Rico*. Berkeley: University of California Press, 2002.

Briggs, Laura, Gladys McCormick and J. T. Way. "Transnationalism: A Category of Analysism." *American Quarterly* 60, no. 3 (2008): 625–48.

Bristow, Roger. *Land Use Planning in Hong Kong: History, Policies and Procedures*. Hong Kong: Oxford University Press, 1984.

Broeze, Frank, ed. *Brides of the Sea: Port Cities in Asia from the 16th–20th Centuries*. Honolulu: University of Hawai'i Press, 1989.

Brownfoot, Janice N. "Sisters under the Skin: Imperialism and the Emancipation of Women in Malaya, c. 1891–1941." In *Making Imperial Mentalities*, edited by J. A. Mangan. Manchester: Manchester University Press, 1990, 46–73.

Bucholz, Mary. "Youth and Cultural Practice." *Annual Review of Anthropology* 31 (2002): 525–52.

Buettner, Elizabeth. *Empire Families: Britons and Late Imperial India*. Oxford: Oxford University Press, 2004.

Burman, Erica. *Deconstructing Developmental Psychology*. London: Routledge, 1994.

Butcher, John G. *The British in Malaya, 1880–1941: The Social History of a European Community in Colonial Southeast Asia*. Kuala Lumpur: Oxford University Press, 1979.

Carroll, John M. *A Concise History of Hong Kong*. Hong Kong: Hong Kong University Press, 2007.

———. *Edge of Empires: Chinese Elites and British Colonials in Hong Kong*. Cambridge: Harvard University Press, 2005.

———. "A National Custom: Debating Female Servitude in Late Nineteenth-Century Hong Kong." *Modern Asian Studies* 43, no. 6 (2009): 1463–93.

———. "The Peak: Residential Segregation in Colonial Hong Kong." In *Twentieth Century Colonialism and China: Localities, the Everyday and the World*, edited by Bryna Goodman and David Goodman. London: Routledge, 2012, 81–91.

Cell, John W. "Anglo-Indian Medical Theory and the Origins of Segregation in West Africa." *American Historical Review* 91, no. 2 (April 1986): 307–35.

Chadourne, Marc. *Vision de l'Indochine: Études, pastels et gouaches de Mme A. Boullard Devé*. Paris: Plon, 1938.

Chan Lau Kit-ching. *China, Britain and Hong Kong, 1895–1945*. Hong Kong: Chinese University Press, 1990.

Chaudhuri, Nupur. "Memsahibs and Motherhood in Nineteenth-Century India." *Victorian Studies* 31, no. 4 (1988): 517–36.

Cheng, Irene. *Clara Ho Tung: A Hong Kong Lady, Her Family and Her Times*. Hong Kong: Chinese University Press, 1976.

Cherry, Haydon L. "Down and Out in Saigon: A Social History of the Poor in a Colonial City, 1860–1940." PhD diss., Yale University, 2011.

Chin, Christine B.N. *In Service and Servitude: Foreign Female Domestic Workers and the Malaysian 'Modernity' Project*. New York: Columbia University Press, 1998.

Chiu Pok-kwan, Patricia. "Girls' Education in Colonial Hong Kong. 1841–1941: Gender, Politics and Experience." PhD diss., University of Cambridge, 2009.

———. "'A Position of Usefulness': Gendering History of Girls' Education in Colonial Hong Kong (1850s–1890s)." *History of Education* 37, no. 6 (2008): 789–805.

Chombart de Lauwe, Mari-José. *Un monde autre: L'enfance de ses représentations à son mythe*. Paris: Payot, 1971.

Chor Boon Goh. *Technology and Entrepôt Colonialism in Singapore, 1819–1940*. Singapore: Institute of Southeast Asian Studies, 2013.

Christopher, A. J. *The British Empire at Its Zenith*. London: Croom Helm, 1988.

———. "Urban Segregation Levels in the British Overseas Empire and Its Successors in the Twentieth Century." *Transactions of the Institute of British Geographers* 17, no. 1 (1992): 95–107.

Chua, Ai Lin. "Singapore's Cinema Age of the 1930s: Hollywood and the Shaping of Singapore Modernity." *American Pop Culture* 13, no. 4 (2012): 592–604.

Clancy-Smith, Julia, and Frances Gouda, eds. *Domesticating the Empire: Race, Gender and Family Life in French and Dutch Colonialism*. Charlottesville: University Press of Virginia, 1998.

Clavin, Patricia. "Defining Transnationalism." *Contemporary European History* 14, no. 4 (2005): 421–39.

Clifford, James. *Routes: Travel and Translation in the Late Twentieth Century*. Cambridge: Harvard University Press, 1997.

Coe, Cati, Rachel Reynolds, Deborah A. Boehm, Julia Meredith Hess and Heather Rae-Espinoza, eds. *Everyday Ruptures: Children, Youth and Migration in Global Perspective*. Nashville: Vanderbilt University Press, 2011.

Cohen, Paul A. *China and Christianity: The Missionary Movement and the Growth of Chinese Anti-Foreignism, 1860–1870*. Cambridge: Harvard University Press, 1963.
Cohen, William B. *Rulers of Empire: The French Colonial Service in Africa*. Stanford: Stanford University Press, 1971.
Conklin, Alice. *A Mission to Civilise: The Republican Idea of Empire in France and West Africa, 1895–1930*. Stanford: Stanford University Press, 1997.
Connelly, Mark. *Christmas: A Social History*. London: I. B. Tauris, 1999.
Cox, Roger. *Shaping Childhood: Themes of Uncertainty in the History of Adult-Child Relationships*. London: Routledge, 1996.
Crossette, Barbara. *The Great Hill Stations of Asia*. Boulder: Westview Press, 1998.
Cunningham, Hugh. "Childhood and Happiness in Britain." *GRAAT* 36 (2007): 19–30.
———. *Children and Childhood in Western Society since 1500*. London: Longman, 1995.
Curtin, Philip D. *Death by Migration: Europe's Encounter with the Tropical World in the Nineteenth Century*. Cambridge: Cambridge University Press, 1989.
———. "Medical Knowledge and Urban Planning in Tropical Africa." *American Historical Review* 90, no. 3 (1985): 594–613.
Darwin, John. *Unfinished Empire: The Global Expansion of Empire*. London: Allen Lane, 2012.
Daughton, J. P. *An Empire Divided: Religion, Republicanism and the Making of French Colonialism, 1880–1914*. Oxford: Oxford University Press, 2006.
De Gantès, Gilles. "Coloniaux, gouverneurs et ministres: L'influence des Français du Viet-nam sur l'évolution du pays à l'époque coloniale, 1902–1914." PhD diss., Université de Paris VII, 1994.
Delaye, Karine. "Slavery and Colonial Representations in Indochina from the Second Half of the Nineteenth to the Early Twentieth Century." *Slavery and Abolition* 24, no. 2 (2003): 129–42.
Dimier, Véronique. "On Good Colonial Government: Lessons from the League of Nations." *Global Society* 18, no. 3 (2004): 279–99.
Dirlik, Arif. "Rethinking Colonialism: Globalisation, Postcolonialism and the Nation." *Interventions* 4, no. 3 (2002): 428–48.
Dodson, Michael S., and Brian Hatcher, eds. *Transcolonial Modernities in South Asia*. London: Routledge, 2012.
Doran, Christine. "Oddly Hybrid: Childbearing and Childrearing Practices in Colonial Penang, 1850–1875." *Women's History Review* 6, no. 1 (1997): 29–46.
Downs, Laura Lee. *Childhood in the Promised Land: Working-class Movements and the Colonies de Vacances in France, 1880–1960*. Durham: Duke University Press, 2002.
Dwork, Deborah. *War Is Good for Babies and Other Young Children: A History of the Infant and Child Welfare Movement in England, 1898–1918*. London: Tavistock, 1987.
Echenberg, Myron. *Plague Ports: The Global Urban Impact of Bubonic Plague, 1894–1901*. New York: New York University Press, 2007.
Edmond, R. S. "Returning Fears: Tropical Disease and the Metropolis." In *Tropical Visions in an Age of Empire*, edited by Felix Driver and Luciana Martins. Chicago: University of Chicago Press, 2005, 175–96.
Edwards, Norman. *The Singapore House and Residential Life: 1819–1939*. Singapore: Oxford University Press, 1990.
Edwards, Penny. "'Propagender': Marianne, Joan of Arc and the Export of French Gender

Ideology to Colonial Cambodia, 1863–1954." In *Promoting the Colonial Idea: Propaganda and Visions of Empire in France*, edited by Tony Chafer and Amanda Sackur. New York: Palgrave, 2002, 116–30.

Ellingson, Ter. *The Myth of the Noble Savage*. Berkeley: University of California Press, 2001.

Emerson, Rupert. *Malaysia: A Study in Direct and Indirect Rule*. 1937. New York: Macmillan, 1964.

Endacott, G. B. *A History of Hong Kong*. Hong Kong: Oxford University Press, 1964.

Fass, Paula S. *Encyclopedia of Children and Childhood: In History and Society*. New York: Macmillan, 2004.

Fassin, Didier. *Humanitarian Reason: A Moral History of the Present*. Berkeley: University of California Press, 2012.

Firpo, Christina. "'Lost Boys': 'Abandoned' Eurasian Children and the Management of the Racial Topography in Colonial Indochina, 1938–1945." *French Colonial History* 8 (Spring 2007): 203–21.

Fogarty, Richard, and Michael A. Osborne. "Constructions and Functions of Race in French Military Medicine, 1830–1920." In *The Color of Liberty: Histories of Race in France*, edited by Sue Peabody and Tyler Stovall. Durham: Duke University Press, 2003, 206–36.

Forman, Ross G. *China and the Victorian Imagination: Empires Entwined*. Cambridge: Cambridge University Press, 2013.

Frenkel, Stephen, and John Western. "Pretext or Prophylaxis? Racial Segregation and Malarial Mosquitos in a British Tropical Colony: Sierra Leone." *Annals of the Association of American Geographers* 78, no. 2 (June 1988): 211–28.

Ghosh, Durba. *Sex and the Family in Colonial India: The Making of Empire*. Cambridge: Cambridge University Press, 2006.

Gillingham, Paul. *At the Peak: Hong Kong between the Wars*. Hong Kong: Macmillan, 1981.

Gillis, John. "Epilogue: The Islanding of Children: Reshaping the Mythical Landscapes of Childhood." In *Designing Modern Childhoods: History, Space and the Material Culture of Children*, edited by Marta Gutman and Ning de Coninck-Smith. New Brunswick: Rutgers University Press, 2008, 316–30.

———. *A World of Their Own Making: Myth, Ritual and the Quest for Family Values*. Oxford: Oxford University Press, 1997.

Gillis, John R. *Youth and History: Tradition and Change in European Age Relations*. New York: Academic Press, 1974.

Gillis, Kay E. *Singapore Civil Society and British Power*. Singapore: Talisman, 2005.

Gilman, Sander L. *Difference and Pathology: Stereotypes of Sexuality, Race and Madness*. Ithaca: Cornell University Press, 1985.

Girardet, Raoul. *L'idée coloniale en France: De 1871 à 1962*. Paris: Hachette, 1972.

Girollet, Anne. *Victor Schœlcher: Abolitionniste et républicain: Approche juridique et politique de l'œuvre d'un fondateur de la République*. Paris: Karthala, 2000.

Go, Julian. "The Chains of Empire: State Building and 'Political Education' in Puerto Rico and the Philippines." In *The American Colonial State in the Philippines: Global Perspectives*, edited by Julian Go and Anne L. Foster. Durham: Duke University Press, 2003, 182–216.

———. *Patterns of Empire: The British and American Empires 1688 to the Present*. Cambridge: Cambridge University Press, 2011.

Goh, Daniel P.S. "States of Ethnography: Colonialism, Resistance, and Cultural Transcription in Malaya and the Philippines, 1890s–1930s." *Comparative Studies in Society and History* 49, no. 1 (2007): 109–42.

Gubar, Marah. *Artful Dodgers: Reconceiving the Golden Age of Children's Literature.* Oxford: Oxford University Press, 2009.

Ha, Marie-Paule. "Engendering French Colonial History: The Case of Indochina." *Historical Reflections/Reflexions Historiques* 25, no. 1 (1999): 95–125.

———. "'La Femme française aux colonies': Promoting Colonial Female Emigration at the Turn of the Century." *French Colonial History* 6 (2005): 205–24.

———. *French Women and the Empire: The Case of Indochina.* Oxford: Oxford University Press, 2014.

Haley, Bruce. *The Healthy Body and Victorian Culture.* Cambridge: Harvard University Press, 1978.

Harrison, Henrietta. "A Penny for the Little Chinese: The French Holy Childhood Association in China, 1843–1951." *American Historical Review* 113, no. 1 (2008): 72–92.

Harrison, Mark. *Climates and Constitutions: Health, Race, Environment and British Imperialism in India.* Oxford: Oxford University Press, 1999.

———. *Public Health in British India: Anglo-India Preventive Medicine, 1854–1914.* Cambridge: Cambridge University Press, 1994.

Harvey, David. *Spaces of Capital: Towards a Critical Geography.* Edinburgh: Edinburgh University Press, 2001.

Haupt, Heinz-Gerhard, and Jürgen Kocka. "Comparison and Beyond: Traditions, Scope and Perspectives of Comparative History." In *Comparative and Transnational History: Central European Approaches and New Perspectives*, edited by Heinz-Gerhard Haupt and Jürgen Kocka. New York: Berghahn, 2009, 1–33.

Hémery, Daniel. *Saigon, 1925–1945: De la 'belle colonie' à l'éclosion révolutionnaire ou la fin des dieux blancs.* Paris: Editions Autrement, 1992.

Heywood, Colin. *A History of Childhood: Children and Childhood in the West from Medieval to Modern Times.* Cambridge: Polity Press, 2001.

Ho, Peter. *The Welfare League: The Sixty Years, 1930–1990.* Hong Kong: Welfare League, 1990.

Humphries, Jane. *Childhood and Child Labour in the British Industrial Revolution.* Cambridge: Cambridge University Press, 2010.

Hyam, Ronald. "Concubinage and the Colonial Service: The Crewe Circular (1909)." *Journal of Imperial and Commonwealth History* 14, no. 3 (May 1986): 170–86.

———. "Empire and Sexual Opportunity." *Journal of Imperial and Commonwealth History* 14, no. 2 (January 1986): 34–90.

Ingram, Edward. *Empire-building and Empire Builders: Twelve Studies.* London: Routledge, 1995.

Iriye, Akira. *Global and Transnational History: The Past, Present, and Future.* New York: Palgrave Pivot, 2012.

Jalland, Pat. *Death in the Victorian Family.* Oxford: Oxford University Press, 1996.

Jaschok, Maria. *Concubines and Bondservants: The Social History of a Chinese Custom.* London: Zed Books, 1988.

Jennings, Eric T. *Curing the Colonizers: Hydrotherapy, Climatology, and French Colonial Spas.* Durham: Duke University Press, 2006.

———. *Imperial Heights: Dalat and the Making and Undoing of French Indochina*. Berkeley: University of California Press, 2011.

———. *Vichy in the Tropics: Pétain's National Revolution in Madagascar, Guadeloupe and Indochina, 1940–44*. Stanford: Stanford University Press, 2002.

Jennings, Lawrence C. *French Anti-Slavery: The Movement for the Abolition of Slavery in France, 1802–1848*. Cambridge: Cambridge University Press, 2000.

Jobs, Richard Ivan. *Riding the New Wave: Youth and the Rejuvenation of France after the Second World War*. Stanford: Stanford University Press, 2007.

Jobs, Richard Ivan, and David M. Pomfret, eds. *Transnational Histories of Youth in the Twentieth Century*. London: Palgrave, 2015.

Johnson, Sara E. *The Fear of French Negroes: Transcolonial Collaboration in the Revolutionary Americas*. Berkeley: University of California Press, 2012.

Jones, Andrew. *Developmental Fairy Tales: Evolutionary Thinking and Modern Chinese Culture*. Cambridge: Harvard University Press, 2011.

Kahn, Joel S. *Other Malays: Nationalism and Cosmopolitanism in the Modern Malay World*. Honolulu: University of Hawai'i Press, 2006.

Keith, Charles. "Protestantism and the Politics of Religion in French Colonial Vietnam." *French Colonial History* 13 (2012): 141–69.

Kelly, David H., ed. *International Feminist Perspectives on Educational Reform: The Work of Gail Paradise Kelly*. New York: Garland, 1996.

Kelly, Gail P. "Conflict in the Classroom: A Case Study from Vietnam, 1918–38." *British Journal of Sociology of Education* 8, no. 2 (1987): 191–212.

———. *Franco-Vietnamese Schools, 1918–1938: Regional Development and Implications for National Integration*. Center for Southeast Asian Studies, University of Wisconsin, Madison, 1982.

———, ed. *French Colonial Education: Essays on Vietnam and West Africa*. New York: AMS Press, 2000.

Kennedy, Dane. *The Magic Mountains: Hill Stations and the British Raj*. Berkeley: University of California Press, 1996.

Kenny, J. T. "Climate, Race and Imperial Authority: The Symbolic Landscape of the British Hill Station in India." *Annals of the Association of American Geographers* 85, no. 4 (1995): 694–714.

Kidambi, Prashant. *The Making of an Indian Metropolis: Colonial Governance and Public Culture in Bombay, 1890–1920*. Aldershot: Ashgate, 2007.

King, Anthony D. "Colonial Cities: Global Pivots of Change." In *Colonial Cities: Essays on Urbanism in a Colonial Context*, edited by Robert Ross and Gerard J. Telkamp. Dordrecht: Martinus Nijhoff, 1985, 7–32.

Klein, Martin A. "Introduction: Modern European Expansion and Traditional Servitude in Africa and Asia." In *Breaking the Chains: Slavery, Bondage and Emancipation in Modern Africa and Asia*, edited by Martin A. Klein. Madison: University of Wisconsin Press, 1993, 3–36.

Ko, Dorothy. *Cinderella's Sisters: A Revisionist History of Footbinding*. Berkeley: University of California Press, 2005.

Koven, Seth, and Sonya Michel, eds. *Mothers of a New World: Maternalist Politics and the Origins of Welfare States*. London: Routledge, 1993.

Kua, Paul. *Scouting in Hong Kong, 1910–2010*. Hong Kong: Scout Association of Hong Kong, 2011.

Kuklick, Henrika. *The Savage Within: The Social History of British Anthropology, 1885–1945*. Cambridge: Cambridge University Press, 1991.
Lebovics, Herman. *True France: The Wars over Cultural Identity, 1900–1945*. Ithaca: Cornell University Press, 1992.
Lee, A. Robert, ed. *China Fictions/English Language: Literary Essays in Diaspora, Memory, Story*. New York: Rodopi, 2008.
Lee, Edwin. *The British as Rulers: Governing Multiracial Singapore, 1867–1914*. Singapore: Singapore University Press, 1991.
Leow, Rachel. "Age as a Category of Gender Analysis: Servant Girls, Modern Girls and Gender in Southeast Asia." *Journal of Modern Asian Studies* 71, no. 4 (November 2012): 975–90.
———. "'Do You Own Non-Chinese Mui Tsai?' Re-Examining Race and Female Servitude in Malaya and Hong Kong, 1919–1939." *Modern Asian Studies* 46, no. 6 (2012): 1746–52.
Lester, Alan. *Imperial Networks: Creating Identities in Nineteenth-Century South Africa and Britain*. London: Routledge, 2001.
Levine, Philippa. "Modernity, Medicine and Colonialism: The Contagious Diseases Ordinances in Hong Kong and the Straits Settlements." *Positions* 6, no. 3 (1998): 675–705.
———. *Prostitution, Race and Politics: Policing Venereal Disease in the British Empire*. London: Routledge, 2003.
Lewis, Martin Deming. "One Hundred Million Frenchmen: The 'Assimilation' Theory in French Colonial Policy." *Comparative Studies in Society and History* 4, no. 2 (January 1962): 129–53.
Li, Hongshan. *U.S.-China Educational Exchange: State, Society and Intercultural Relations, 1905–1950*. New Brunswick: Rutgers University Press, 2008.
Liebovitz, Liel, and Matthew Miller. *Fortunate Sons: The 120 Chinese Boys Who Came to America, Went to School, and Revolutionized an Ancient Civilisation*. New York: W. W. Norton, 2011.
Liebschner, Joachim. *A Child's Work: Freedom and Guidance in Froebel's Educational Theory and Practice*. Cambridge: Lutterworth Press, 2001.
Lim, P. H. "Malay Schools and School Libraries in the Straits Settlements under British Colonial Rule before the Second World War, 1786–1941." *Malaysian Journal of Library and Information Science* 13, no. 1 (2008): 1–15.
Lim, Shirley Geok-lin. "Up Against the National Canon: Women's War Memoirs from Malaysia and Singapore." *Journal of Commonwealth Literature* 29, no. 1 (1993): 47–63.
Livingstone, David. "Human Acclimatisation: Perspectives on a Contested Field of Inquiry in Science, Medicine and Geography." *History of Science* 25 (1987): 359–94.
Lowrie, C. K. "The Transcolonial Politics of Chinese Domestic Mastery in Singapore and Darwin, 1910s–1930s." *Journal of Colonialism and Colonial History* 12, no. 3 (2011): 1–24.
———. "White 'Men' and Their Chinese 'Boys': Sexuality, Masculinity and Colonial Power in Singapore and Darwin, 1880s–1930s." *History Australia* 10, no. 1 (2013): 35–57.
MacMillan, Margaret. *Women of the Raj: The Mothers, Wives and Daughters of the British Empire in India*. London: Thames and Hudson, 1988.
MacPherson, Kerrie L. "Health and Empire: Britain's National Campaign to Combat Venereal Diseases in Shanghai, Hong Kong and Singapore." In *Sex, Sin and Suffering: Venereal Disease and European Society since 1870*, edited by Roger Weeks and Lesley A. Hall. London: Routledge, 1991, 173–90.

Magee, Gary B. and Andrew S. Thompson. *Empire and Globalisation: Networks of People, Goods and Capital in the British World, c. 1850–1914.* Cambridge: Cambridge University Press, 2010.

Manderson, Leonore. "Blame, Responsibility and Remedial Action: Death, Disease and the Infant in Early Twentieth Century Malaya." In *Death and Disease in Southeast Asia: Explorations in Social, Medical and Demographic History*, edited by Norman G. Owen. Singapore: Oxford University Press, 1987, 257–82.

———. "Race, Colonial Mentality and Public Health." In *The Underside of Malaysian History: Pullers, Prostitutes, Plantation Workers*, edited by Peter J. Rimmer and Lisa M. Allen. Singapore: Stanford University Press, 1990.

———. *Sickness and the State: Health and Illness in Colonial Malaya, 1870–1940.* Cambridge: Cambridge University Press, 1996.

Marks, S., and W. Anderson. "Typhus and Social Control: South Africa, 1917–1950." In *Disease, Medicine and Empire*, edited by R. MacLeod and M. Lewis. London: Routledge, 1988, 257–83.

Marr, David. *Vietnamese Anticolonialism, 1885–1925.* Berkeley: University of California Press, 1971.

———. *Vietnamese Tradition on Trial, 1920–1945.* Berkeley: University of California Press, 1981.

McClellan, Michael. "Performing Empire: Opera in Colonial Hanoi." *Journal of Musicological Research* 22, nos. 1–2 (2003): 135–66.

McPherson, Sue. "J. L. McPherson, Hong Kong YMCA: General Secretary, 1905–1935." *Journal of the Royal Asiatic Society, Hong Kong Branch* 46 (2006): 39–59.

Metcalf, Thomas R. *Imperial Connections: India in the Indian Ocean Arena, 1860–1920.* Berkeley: University of California Press, 2007.

Milanic, Nara. *The Children of Fate: Families, Class and the State in Chile, 1800–1930.* Durham: Duke University Press, 2009.

Miners, Norman. *Hong Kong under Imperial Rule, 1912–1941.* Hong Kong: Oxford University Press, 1987.

Mintz, Steven. *Huck's Raft: A History of American Childhood.* Cambridge: Harvard University Press, 2004.

Monnais-Rousselot, Laurence. *Médecine et colonisation: L'Aventure indochinoise 1860–1939.* Paris: CRNS editions, 1999.

———. "La médicalisation de la mère et de son enfant: L'Exemple du Vietnam sous domination française, 1860–1939." *Canadian Bulletin for the History of Medicine / Bulletin Canadien d'Histoire de la Medecine* 19 (2002): 47–94.

———. "'Modern Medicine' in French Colonial Vietnam: From the Importation of a Model to Its Nativisation." In *The Development of Modern Medicine in Non-Western Countries*, edited by Hormoz Ebrahimnejad. London: Routledge, 2008, 127–59.

Moruzi, Kristine, and Michelle J. Smith, eds. *Colonial Girlhood in Literature, Culture and History, 1840–1950.* Basingstoke: Palgrave, 2014.

Mungello, D. E. *Drowning Girls in China: Female Infanticide since 1650.* Lanham: Rowman & Littlefield, 2008.

Munn, Christopher. *Anglo-China: Chinese People and British Rule in Hong Kong, 1841–1880.* London: Curzon, 2001.

———. "Hong Kong, 1841–1870: All the Servants in Prison and Nobody to Take Care of the House." In *Masters, Servants and Magistrates in Britain and the Empire, 1562–1955*, edited by Douglas Hay and Paul Craven. Chapel Hill: University of North Carolina Press, 2004, 365–401.

Murdoch, Lydia. *Imagined Orphans: Poor Families, Child Welfare and Contested Citizenship in London*. New Brunswick: Rutgers University Press, 2006.

———. "Suppressed Grief: Mourning the Death of British Children and the Memory of the 1857 Rebellion." *Journal of British Studies* 51, no. 2 (April 2012): 364–92.

Murphey, Rhoades. "Traditionalism and Colonialism: Changing Urban Roles in Asia." *Journal of Asian Studies* 29, no. 1 (1969): 67–84.

Musa, Mahani. "The 'Woman Question' in Malayan Periodicals, 1920–1945." *Indonesia and the Malay World* 38, no. 111 (July 2010): 247–71.

Nguyễn Phan Quang. *Kỳ Đồng Nguyễn Văn Cẩm: Cuộc đời và thơ văn*. Hanoi: Văn học, 2002.

Nguyêñ Phước Ba'o Vàng. *Duy Tan: Empereur d'Annam 1900–1945, exilé à l'île de la Réunion ou le déstin tragique du Prince Vinh San*. Sainte-Marie: Azalées Editions, 2002.

Nguyễn Thë Anh. "Le Nationalisme vietnamien au début du XXe siècle: Son expression à travers une curieuse lettre au roi d'Angleterre." *Bulletin de l'Ecole Française d'Extrème-Orient* 65, no. 2 (1978): 421–30.

Nightingale, Carl. *Segregation: A Global History of Divided Cities*. Chicago: University of Chicago Press, 2012.

Njoh, Ambe. *Planning Power: Town Planning and Social Control in Colonial Africa*. New York: Routledge, 2007.

Nord, Deborah Epstein. *Walking the Victorian Streets: Women, Representation and the City*. Ithaca: Cornell University Press, 1995.

Nordemann, Edmond. "Connaissances nécessaires aux personnes appelées à faire leur carrière en Indo-chine." *Conférences publiques sur l'Indochine faites à l'école Coloniale pendant l'année 1909–1910*. Paris: Imprimerie Chaix, 1910.

Nye, Robert. *Crime, Madness and Politics in Modern France: The Medical Concept of National Decline*. Princeton: Princeton University Press, 1984.

O'Brien, Justin. *The Novel of Adolescence in France*. Oxford: Oxford University Press, 1939.

Osborne, Michael A. "Acclimatizing the World: A History of the Paradigmatic Colonial Science." *Osiris* 2nd series, 15, *Nature and Empire: Science and the Colonial Enterprise* (2000): 135–51.

———. *Nature, the Exotic, and the Science of French Colonialism*. Bloomington: Indiana University Press, 1994.

Osterhammel, Jürgen. "China." In *The Oxford History of the British Empire*, vol. 4, *The Twentieth Century*, edited by Judith Brown and Wm. Roger Louis Gates. Oxford: Oxford University Press, 1999, 643–66.

———. "A 'Transnational' History of Society: Continuity or New Departure." In *Comparative and Transnational History: Central European Approaches and New Perspectives*, edited by Heinz-Gerhard Haupt and Jürgen Kocka. New York: Berghahn, 2009, 39–51.

Paddle, Sarah. "The Limits of Sympathy: International Feminists and the Chinese 'Slave Girl' Campaigns of the 1920s and 1930s." *Journal of Colonialism and Colonial History* 4, no. 3 (2003): 1–22.

Paisley, Fiona. "Childhood and Race: Growing Up in Empire." In *Gender and Empire*, edited by Philippa Levine. Oxford: Oxford University Press, 2004, 240–59.

Papin, Philippe. *Histoire de Hanoi*. Paris: Fayard, 2001.

Paris, Leslie. "Through the Looking Glass: Age, Stages, and Historical Analysis." *Journal of the History of Childhood and Youth* 1, no. 1 (2008): 106–13.
Parsons, T. H. *Race, Resistance and the Boy Scout Movement in British Colonial Africa*. Athens: Ohio University Press, 2004.
Peckham, Robert, and David M. Pomfret, eds. *Imperial Contagions: Medicine, Hygiene and Cultures of Planning in Asia*. Hong Kong: Hong Kong University Press, 2013.
Pedersen, Susan. "The Maternalist Moment in British Colonial Policy: The Controversy over 'Child Slavery' in Hong Kong, 1917–1941." *Past and Present* 171 (May 2001): 161–202.
Pellegrini, Ann. "What Do Children Learn at School? Necropedagogy and the Future of the Dead Child." *Social Text* 26, no. 4 (2008): 97–105.
Peycam, Philippe M.F. *The Birth of Vietnamese Political Journalism: Saigon 1916–1930*. New York: Columbia University Press, 2012.
Phan Văn Trường. *Une Histoire de conspirateurs annamites à Paris ou la vérité sur l'Indochine*. Gia Định: Imp. Đông-Pháp-Ng-kim-Đinh, 1928.
Pick, Daniel. *Faces of Degeneration: A European Disorder, c. 1848–1918*. Cambridge: Cambridge University Press, 1989.
Pillon, Maxime, and Danièle Weiler. *The French in Singapore: An Illustrated History, 1819–Today*. Singapore: Didier Millet, 2011.
Pitt, Charles. "Opera's Indochinese Outpost." *Opera* 40 (January 2003): 40–48.
Pomfret, David M. *Young People and the European City: Age Relations in Nottingham and Saint-Etienne*. Aldershot: Ashgate, 2004.
Prakash, Gyan. *Bonded Histories: Genealogies of Labor Servitude in Colonial India*. Cambridge: Cambridge University Press, 1990.
Price, John. *Everyday Heroism: Victorian Constructions of the Heroic Civilian*. London: Bloomsbury, 2014.
Procida, Mary A. *Married to the Empire: Gender Politics and Imperialism in India, 1883–1947*. Manchester: Manchester University Press, 2000.
Rabinbach, Anson. *The Human Motor: Energy, Fatigue, and the Origins of Modernity*. New York: Basic Books, 1990.
Rabinow, Paul. *French Modern: Norms and Forms of the Social Environment*. Chicago: University of Chicago Press, 1989.
Raffin, Ann. *Youth Mobilisation in Vichy Indochina and Its Legacies, 1940–1970*. Lanham: Lexington Books, 2005.
Reed, Robert. "From Highland Hamlet to Regional Capital: Reflections on the Colonial Origins, Urban Transformation and Environmental Impact of Dalat." In *The Challenges of Highland Development in Vietnam*, edited by Terry Rambo, Robert Reed, Lê Trọng Cúc and Michael R. DiGregorio. Honolulu: East-West Center, 1995, 39–62.
Reid, Anthony. *Southeast Asia in the Age of Commerce, 1450–1680*. New Haven: Yale University Press, 1988.
Reynolds, K. D. *Aristocratic Women and Political Society in Victorian Britain*. Oxford: Clarendon Press, 1998.
Rhoads, Edward J.M. *Stepping Forth into the World: The Chinese Educational Mission to the United States, 1872–81*. Hong Kong: Hong Kong University Press, 2011.
Rowe, William T. *China's Last Empire: The Great Qing*. Boston: Harvard University Press, 2009.
Saada, Emmanuelle. *Les Enfants de la colonie: Les Métis de l'empire français entre sujétion et citoyenneté*. Paris: La Découverte, 2007.

———. "The Empire of Law: Dignity, Prestige and Domination in the 'Colonial Situation.'" *French Politics, Culture and Society* 20, no. 2 (Summer 2002): 98–120.
Sanchez, Pierre. *La Société des peintres orientalistes français*. Dijon: L'Echelle de Jacob, 2008.
Sanchez-Eppler, Karen. "Raising Empires Like Children: Race, Nation and Religious Education." *American Literary History* 8 (1996): 399–425.
Schneer, Jonathan. *London 1900: The Imperial Metropolis*. New Haven: Yale University Press, 1999.
Schneider, William H. *Quality and Quantity: The Quest for Biological Regeneration in Twentieth-Century France*. Cambridge: Cambridge University Press, 1990.
Scott, Phoebe. "Imagining 'Asian' Aesthetics in Colonial Hanoi: The Ecole des Beaux-Arts de L'Indochine, 1925–1945." In *Asia Through Art and Anthropology: Cultural Translation Across Borders*, edited by Fuyubi Nakamura, Morgan Perkins and Oliver Krischer. London: Bloomsbury, 2013, 47–61.
Seigel, Micol. "Beyond Compare: Comparative Method after the Transnational Turn." *Radical History Review* 91 (2005): 62–90.
Sen, Satadru. *Colonial Childhoods: Youth on the Juvenile Periphery*. London: Anthem Press, 2005.
Silver, Catherine Bodard. *Le Play: On Family, Work and Social Change*, edited and translated by Catherine Bodard Silver. Chicago: University of Chicago Press, 1982.
Sinn, Elizabeth. "Chinese Patriarchalism and the Protection of Women in 19th-Century Hong Kong." In *Women and Chinese Patriarchy: Submission, Servitude and Escape*, edited by Maria Jaschok and Suzanne Miers. Hong Kong: Hong Kong University Press, 1994, 141–67.
———. *Power and Charity: A Chinese Merchant Elite in Colonial Hong Kong*. Hong Kong: Hong Kong University Press, 2003.
Sloane-White, Patricia. "The Shifting Status of Middle-class Malay Girlhood: From 'Sisters' to 'Sinners' in One Generation." In *Girlhood: A Global History*, edited by Jennifer Helgren and Colleen Vasconcellos. New Brunswick: Rutgers University Press, 2010, 382–402.
Smith, Carl T. *Chinese Christians: Elites, Middlemen and the Church in Hong Kong*. Hong Kong: Hong Kong University Press, repr. 2005.
Steedman, Carolyn. *Childhood, Culture and Class in Britain: Margaret McMillan, 1860–1931*. New Brunswick: Rutgers University Press, 1990.
Stepan, Nancy Leys. *Picturing Tropical Nature*. Ithaca: Cornell University Press, 2001.
Stewart, Mary Lynn. "A Frenchwoman Writes about Indochina, 1931–1949: Andrée Viollis and Anti-Colonialism." *Journal of the Canadian Historical Association* 18, no. 2 (2007): 81–102.
Stockard, Janice E. *Daughters of the Canton Delta: Marriage Patterns and Economic Strategies in South China, 1860–1930*. Hong Kong: Hong Kong University Press, 1989.
Stoler, Ann Laura. *Carnal Knowledge and Imperial Power: Race and the Intimate in Colonial Rule*. Berkeley: University of California Press, 2002.
———. *Race and the Education of Desire: Foucault's History of Sexuality and the Colonial Order of Things*. Durham: Duke University Press, 1995.
———. "Sexual Affronts and Racial Frontiers: European Identities and the Cultural Politics of Exclusion in Colonial Southeast Asia." *Comparative Studies in Society and History* 34, no. 3 (1992): 514–51.

———. "Tense and Tender Ties: The Politics of Comparison in North American History and Post Colonial Studies." *Journal of American History* 88, no. 3 (2001): 831–64.

Sussmann, George D. "The Wet-nursing Business in Nineteenth-Century France." *French Historical Studies* 9, no. 2 (Autumn 1975): 304–28.

Sutphen, Mary. "Not What but Where: Bubonic Plague and the Reception of Germ Theories in Hong Kong and Calcutta, 1894–1897." *Journal of the History of Medicine* 52, no. 1 (1997): 81–113.

Swain, Shurlee, and Margot Hillel. *Child, Nation, Race and Empire: Child Rescue Discourse, England, Canada and Australia, 1850–1915*. Manchester: Manchester University Press, 2010.

Symonds, Richard. "Eurasians under British Rule." *Oxford University Papers on India* 1, no. 2. Delhi: Oxford University Press, 1987, 28–42.

Tagliacozzo, Eric. *Secret Trades, Porous Borders: Smuggling and States along a Southeast Asian Frontier, 1865–1915*. New Haven: Yale University Press, 2005.

Tan, K. Y. L., and M. Wan. *Scouting in Singapore, 1910–2000*. Singapore: Singapore Scout Association, 2002.

Teng, Emma Jinhua. *Eurasian: Mixed Identities in the United States, China and Hong Kong, 1842–1943*. Berkeley: University of California Press, 2013.

Thelen, David. "The Nation and Beyond: Transnational Perspectives on United States History." *Journal of American History* 86 (1999): 965–75.

Thomas, Greg. *Impressionist Children: Childhood, Family and Modern Identity in French Art*. New Haven: Yale University Press, 2010.

Thomas, Nicholas. *Colonialisms Culture: Anthropology, Travel and Government*. Cambridge: Polity, 1994.

Thompson, Virginia, and Richard Adloff. *Minority Problems in Southeast Asia*. Stanford: Stanford University Press, 1955.

Trần Mỹ Vân. *A Vietnamese Royal Exile in Japan: Prince Cuong De (1882–1951)*. London: Routledge, 2012.

Tregonning, K. G. "Tertiary Education in Malaya: Policy and Practice, 1905–1962." *Journal of the Malayan Branch of the Royal Asiatic Society* 63 (1990).

Tsing, Anna Lowenhaupt. *Friction: An Ethnography of Global Connection*. Princeton: Princeton University Press, 2005.

Turnbull, C. M. *A History of Singapore, 1819–2005*. Kuala Lumpur: Oxford University Press, 1977.

Tyrell, Ian R. *The Woman's Christian Temperance Union in International Perspective, 1880–1930: Woman's World, Woman's Empire*. Chapel Hill: University of North Carolina Press, 1991.

Vance Dorey, Annette K. *Better Baby Contests: The Scientific Quest for Perfect Childhood Health in the Early Twentieth Century*. Jefferson: McFarland & Company, 1999.

Vann, Michael G. "Building Colonial Whiteness on the Red River: Race, Power and Urbanism in Paul Doumer's Hanoi, 1897–1902." *Historical Reflections / Réflexions Historiques* 33 (2007): 277–304.

Villemagne, Claire. "Station balnéaire et station d'altitude, deux formes de tourisme colonial en Indochine, les sites de Doson, Sapa et Dalat." In *Le Tourisme dans l'empire français: Politiques, pratiques et imaginaires, XIXe–XXe siècles*, edited by Colette Zytnicki and Habib Kazdaghli. Paris: Publications de la Société Française d'Histoire d'Outre-Mer, 2009, 217–34.

Walker, Kirsty. "Intimate Interactions: Eurasian Family Histories in Colonial Penang." *Modern Asian Studies* 46, no. 2 (2012): 303–29.
Wang Gungwu and Anthony Reid. *Community and Nation: Essays on Southeast Asia and the Chinese.* Singapore: Heinemann, 1981.
Warren, James. *Ah Ku and Karayuki-san: Prostitution in Singapore, 1870–1940.* Singapore: Oxford University Press, 1993.
Watson Andaya, Barbara, and Leonard Y. Andaya. *A History of Malaysia*, 2nd ed. Honolulu: University of Hawai'i Press, 2001.
Weinbaum, Alys Eve, Lynn M. Thomas, Priti Ramamurthy, Uta G. Poiger and Madeleine Yue Dong. *The Modern Girl around the World: Consumption, Modernity, and Globalisation.* Durham: Duke University Press, 2008.
Wesley-Smith, Peter. "Anti-Chinese Legislation in Hong Kong." In *Precarious Balance: Hong Kong between China and Britain, 1842–1992*, edited by Ming K. Chan. New York: M. E. Sharpe, 1994, 91–105.
Wesseling, H. L. *The European Colonial Empires, 1815–1919.* Harlow: Pearson, 2004.
White, Owen. *Children of the French Empire: Miscegenation and Colonial Society in French West Africa, 1895–1960.* Oxford: Clarendon, 1999.
Whitlock, Gillian. *The Intimate Empire: Reading Women's Autobiography.* London: Cassell, 2000.
Willis, John. *The Serani and the Upper Ten: Eurasian Ethnicity in Singapore.* Sydney: University of New South Wales, 1983.
Winseck, Dwayne R., and Robert M. Pike. *Communication and Empire: Media, Markets, and Globalization, 1860–1930.* Durham: Duke University Press, 2007.
Woodside, Alexander. "The Development of Social Organisations in Vietnamese Cities in the Late Colonial Period." *Pacific Affairs* 44, no. 1 (1971): 39–64.
Wright, Gwendolyn. *The Politics of Design in French Colonial Urbanism.* Chicago: University of Chicago Press, 1991.
Yeoh, Brenda. *Contesting Space in Colonial Singapore: Power Relations and the Urban Built Environment.* Oxford: Oxford University Press, 2006.
Yin Hwang. "The Depiction of War and Rebellion in the Print and Visual Culture of Late Qing China, 1884–1901." PhD diss., SOAS, 2013.
Yip, Ka-che. "Colonialism, Disease and Public Health: Malaria in the History of Hong Kong." In *Disease, Colonialism and the State: Malaria in Modern East Asian History*, edited by Ka-che Yip. Hong Kong: Hong Kong University Press, 2009, 11–29.
Yuen, Karen. "Theorising the Chinese: The Mui tsai Controversy and Constructions of Transnational Chineseness in Hong Kong and British Malaya." *New Zealand Journal of Asian Studies* 6, no. 2 (December 2004): 95–110.
Zelizer, Viviana. *Pricing the Priceless Child: The Changing Social Value of Children.* New York: Basic Books, 1985.
Zheng Hongtai and Wong Siu-lun. *Xianggang dalao: He Dong* (The Grand Old Man of Hong Kong: Ho Tung). Hong Kong: Joint Publishing, 2007.
Zinoman, Peter. *The Colonial Bastille: A History of Imprisonment in Vietnam, 1862–1940.* Berkeley: University of California Press, 2001.
Zipes, Jack. *Victorian Fairy Tales: The Revolt of the Fairies and Elves.* London: Methuen, 1987.
———. *The Irresistible Fairy Tale: The Cultural and Social History of a Genre.* Princeton: Princeton University Press, 2012.

Index

Abdullah, Mohammed Eunos, 174
Adolescence: puberty, 29, 30, 40, 297n34; universal, 344n104
Adolescents: French girls, 69; relations with servants, 61–62; Scouts and Guides, 127, 129; slaves, 188; Vietnamese girls, 65–66, 188; vulnerability in tropics, 30, 61–62. *See also* Children; Returns home; Youth
Adoption: of child servants, 178, 180, 183; laws, 190, 331n60, 335n109; paid, 180
Advice literature: Anglophone, 42–43, 46–47; French, 42, 46–47, 50; hygiene rules, 41–43, 46–48, 50–51, 54, 280
Ages: of amahs and ayahs, 59; boundaries between childhood and youth, 279–80; of European children brought to tropics, 49–50; imperialism and, 6–9; of marriage, 31; maturity metaphors, 262–63, 264–65, 276; mortality rates and, 49; of puberty, 40; of returns home, 30–33, 53, 78–80, 161–62, 170–71, 173, 175–76; of servants, 58–59; of students, 225, 232–40, 284, 342nn57–58, 344n98. *See also* Adolescence; Childhood; Youth
Ajalbert, Jean, 49, 230
Alabaster, C. Grenville, 160–61
Algeria: as French colony, 11; Lycée d'Alger, 211–12; *métissage*, 245
Allan, W. J., 181–82
Allinson, J. M., 19
Amahs, 4, 55, 56–62. *See also* Servants
Amery, Leo, 173, 191

Amrith, Sunil, 177
Anderson, Charles Graham (Carl), 264
Anderson, Sir John, 255
Andrew, Elizabeth, 183–84
Anglican Church, Singapore, 169–71, 172. *See also* Church Missionary Society
Annam: Dalat hill station, 148, 154–55, 163, 164–68, 240–41, 275, 327n144; French control, 18; rural areas, 142. *See also* Indochina
Annamites, use of term, 304n39. *See also* Vietnamese
Annesley, James, 24
Anti–Mui Tsai Society, 191, 192, 198
Anti-Slavery Society (France), 200–201
Appleton, W. A., 189
Archer, T. C., 266, 267
Ariès, Philippe, 5
Art: at Hanoi Exposition, 100, 101, 102–3; images of Vietnamese children, 139–42; Vietnamese school, 139
Asian children: disease transmission by, 74–75, 165–66; education, 7, 84, 93, 209, 214–15, 217; European responsibility for, 7–8, 178–80; exoticism, 139, 141; fear of, 120–23; images, 118–20, 139–42, 144–45; individuality, 142; infant mortality, 132–34; medical care, 144–45; nation building and, 12, 115–16; nature and, 104–5, 139, 141; as other, 93–94, 309nn51–52; sacralisation, 185; as servants, 63–66, 183, 184, 186, 189–95, 197, 208, 303n23; of servants, 68, 70, 73; symbolism,

141–42; Tamil, 2, 181–82, 196, 219; as unclean, 72, 74–75; Western views of cultural practices, 28–29, 93. *See also* Bond servants; Child labour; Chinese children; Slaves, child; Vietnamese children
Asians: backwardness, 105; as children of empires, 125; infantilisation, 29–30, 118–21, 311n76, 318n85. *See also* Chinese; Malays; Vietnamese
Assimilationist policies, 21, 38, 96, 103, 211, 213, 230, 248, 257
Associationist policy, 21, 36, 37–38, 96, 103, 105
Astor House, 63
Atkinson, John Mitford, 48, 148, 149, 153, 155
Auger, Lucien, 167
Augustin, James F., 268
Autret, Françoise, 66

Baar, Clemence, 60–61
Babut, Alfred-Ernest, 200, 206
Baby contests, 132, 135–37. *See also* Infants; Singapore Baby Show
Baden-Powell, Robert, 127
Baena, Rosalia, 66–67
Baguio, Philippines, 172–73, 327n139
Balfour, Arthur, 158
Ballantyne, Tony, 13, 14
Bảo Đại, emperor, 126, 168
Barbusse, Henri, 204
Barnes, Geoffrey, 58, 73, 302n5
Barrie, J. M., *Peter Pan*, 86
Baudrit, André, 207
Baxter, Harriet, 227
Bayly, Christopher A., 18
Beau, Paul, 100, 117–18, 124, 153, 187, 222, 230
Beauvais, Joseph, 188
Bécons (female child servants), 64–66, 70
Bénédite, Léonce, 100
Benoist de la Grandière, Auguste, 248–49
Bert, Paul, 37, 39, 103, 116, 211
Bhattacharya, Nandini, 148
Bichot, Edmond, 37
Bickers, Robert, 3

Bihouard, Paul, 211
Bird, Isabella L., 48, 56, 180–81, 254, 329n20
Blake, Henry, 133, 224
Blanchard de la Brosse, Paul, 234
Blanchy, Paul, 248
Bodies: acclimatisation to tropics, 30, 33, 36, 52; of children, 282; degenerative impact of tropics, 22–23, 24, 25, 28, 29–31, 33–34, 40; national, 282; white, 22–23, 24, 25, 28, 29–31, 33–34, 40; of women, 26. *See also* Childhood on display; Health
Bond servants: children, 109, 145, 178, 180, 259, 283; in Chinese homes, 60, 63–64, 180–81, 204–5; distinction from slaves, 190, 207, 208; in Hong Kong, 109, 180–81, 190, 191–94, 197; in Indochina, 180, 184, 200, 203, 206–7, 279, 335n117; *mui tsai*, 60, 183, 190–95, 197, 332n69, 332–33nn78–79, 334n98; on plantations, 145. *See also* Child trafficking; Servants; Slaves, child
Bondy, Raphael de, 56
Bonnafont, Louis, 163, 187
Bonniot, R., 274
Bordier, Arthur, 33
Borel, Germaine, 65, 304n47
Borel, Joseph-Emile, 165
Borel, Marie-Louise, 65, 304n47
Borel, Marius, 49, 301n113, 304n47
Bosman, Charles Henri, 252, 320n17
Boullard-Devé, Marie-Antoinette, paintings, 140 (fig.), 141, 145
Bourgeois, Gaston, 207
Bourgeois, Léon, 36
Bowring, John, 249
Boxer Uprising, 14, 104, 218
Boyocracy, 63, 64, 65, 124
Boys: child trafficking, 199, 284, 335n108; returns home, 31–32, 78–79. *See also* Education; Gender differences; Men; Slaves, child; Youth
Boy Scouts, 127, 237, 240, 314n28
Brévié, Jules, 240, 274–75
Brewin, A. W., 224, 347n39
Brière, Ernest, 210, 211
Brieux, Eugène, 118–20, 121

Britain: antislavery movement, 194, 200, 203, 208; childhood in, 9, 25–26, 28, 82, 89, 190, 332–33n79; child labour laws, 25–26, 82, 190; Christmas celebrations, 82; class conflict, 25; Contagious Diseases Acts, 26, 182, 184, 195; education, 86; Empire Day, 91–92; feminists, 193–94, 202; health of children, 43, 152; industrial capitalism, 82, 86; infant mortality, 296n12, 316n49, 317n63; military, 10, 26, 30; poverty, 28, 89; reformers, 25–26, 28, 89; rivalry with France, 14; university scholarships, 214–15, 236, 255, 340n20, 341n49; urbanisation, 25; women's public roles, 89; working-class children, 25, 26. *See also* World War I

Britain, Colonial Office: child labour regulations, 196; child protection, 197, 198; child slavery issue, 182, 189, 193; Contagious Diseases Act, 27; Crewe Circular, 245; disease prevention, 149; infant mortality issue, 133; Peak Hill District ordinance, 150–51, 152, 158, 160

British Empire: abolition of slavery, 179; childhood in, 52–53; child welfare improvements, 196, 208; critics, 26, 27, 178–79, 250; debates on colonial policies, 24–25; decline, 9, 177; governance, 20–21; infant mortality, 132–34, 316n49; in interwar period, 128, 129, 177, 189; justification, 9–10, 11; in late nineteenth century, 9, 113; military forces, 176–77; nationalist protests, 203; networks, 84–85; poor whites, 44, 300n88; racial otherness and, 25; racial segregation, 151; rivalries among ports, 84–85, 92, 307n12; World War I and, 115. *See also* Hong Kong; India; Malaya; Singapore; Straits Settlements

British Malaya, *see* Federated Malay States; Malaya; Straits Settlements

Broca, Paul, 36, 245
Bromley, Blake, 61, 73
Brown, Edwin A., 110–11
Brown, Samuel, 216
Brown, William C., 215

Buckley, Charles Burton, 82, 83–85, 110–11, 112–13, 131, 156, 313n111
Buckley, John Wall, 82
Buckley's Treat (Singapore), 82, 83–85, 110–11, 112, 131, 255
Buettner, Elizabeth, 8, 67
Bunout, René, 200, 335n117
Burkinshaw, John, 23
Burnham, David H., 172
Bushnell, Katherine, 184

Cahen, Gaston, 257
Cameron, Maurice, 23
Cameron, William, 156
Cameron Highlands, 148, 156, 157, 172–77
Cantlie, Sir James, 27–28, 29–30, 251, 253
Cần Vương (Save the King) movement, 210
Carabelli, Roch, 94–95, 96
Carlos, A. H., 269
Carroll, John M., 130, 262
Carroll, Lewis, 86, 130
Castellani, Sir Aldo, 171, 326n131
Catholic Church: aid for Eurasian children, 246–47; antislavery movement, 200–201; convent schools, 176, 219, 227; in France, 95–96, 163, 200–201; in Indochina, 144, 201, 336n125; in Malaya, 176; in Singapore, 269; social activism, 163; view of childhood, 226. *See also* Missionaries
Célarié, Henriette, 52
Ceylon: British children, 30; planters, 172
Chadourne, Marc, 139–41
Chailley-Bert, Joseph, 34–35
Chaize, François, 201
Challan de Belval, Albert, 103
Challaye, Félicien, 212
Chamberlain, Joseph, 133, 149, 150, 151, 255, 320n8
Champly, Henry, 202, 336n131
Chanjour, Marie-Antoinette le, 68, 69
Chan Kai Ming, 232
Chan King Nui, 229, 237
Chan Wing, 229
Chapman, R. V., 268, 269, 351n117
Charlesworth, Maria Louisa, 89

Charmettes, L. des, 257
Chiang Kai Shek, 198
Child development theories, 29–30, 91. *See also* Childrearing
Childhood: aesthetic of, 86; anticolonial symbolism, 138–39; changing views of, 74; cultural construction, 5–6; didactic, 7, 39, 134, 168, 251; ideal, 3, 116, 190; innocence, 5, 28; medicalisation, 134; religious views, 226; savagery linked to, 103; scholarship on, 5–6, 8–9, 15–17; symbolism, 5, 194, 251. *See also* Colonial childhoods
Childhood on display: baby contests, 132, 135–37; in British colonies, 113, 281–82; Christmas Treat, 82, 83–85, 110–11, 112, 131, 255; fairy plays, 86–87, 90–91, 93, 109–10; in French colonies, 94, 95, 113, 144–45, 146, 281; moral defence of imperialism, 88; performances of ideal childhoods, 81, 86–87, 281–82; public performances of girls, 94, 95; public rituals, 113–14, 281–82; shared culture, 81, 281; symbolism, 113–14
Child labour: in China, 88; criticism of, 190; in Hong Kong, 93, 331n60; in Indochina, 63–66, 184–85; laws, 10, 25–26, 82, 190, 191–92, 194–95; linked to slavery issue, 191; on rubber plantations, 196. *See also* Bond servants; Servants; Slaves, child
Child protection: in Europe, 5, 187, 259; in Hong Kong, 191–94, 197, 331n60, 334n94, 334n98; laws, 187, 259, 335n109; by League of Nations, 189, 195, 199; as value, 249, 257–58
Childrearing: male role, 50, 53; in practice, 280; *puériculture* (childraising) movement, 48, 144; by servants, 4, 46–47, 55, 56–62. *See also* Advice literature; Families
Children: agency, 280–81; representation of foreign lands, 96–97; universal rights, 188, 189. *See also* Asian children; Eurasian children; European children; Infantilisation
Child slaves, *see* Slaves, child

Child-soldiers, French imagery, 121, 122 (fig.), 123 (fig.)
Child trafficking: of boys, 199, 284, 335n108; campaigns against, 178–79, 283–84; of Chinese children, 178, 205–6, 335n114; disguised as abductions, 208; in Hong Kong, 199; in Indochina, 142, 180, 184–88, 199–207, 208, 335n114; networks, 179, 181; orientalist defence, 190, 191, 194, 200, 206–7, 208; persistence, 208, 284; in Singapore, 181. *See also* Bond servants; Slaves, child
Child welfare, *see* Child protection
Child Welfare Society (CWS), Singapore, 135, 317n61
China: border with Indochina, 184–85, 188, 199–200, 208; Boxer Uprising, 14, 104, 218; British seen as inferior, 28; child labour, 88; child servants, 183, 192; education, 218, 228–29; emigration, 19–20, 83, 156, 217; footbinding, 29; foreigners, 28–29; foreign incursions, 104; Hong Kong and, 87; Hundred Days Reform, 117, 218; in interwar period, 129, 264; May Fourth Movement, 115, 235, 264; missionaries, 28–29, 215–16, 226; modernisation, 116–17; nationalism, 115, 130–31, 220; Nationalist government, 192, 198, 237; opium trade, 28, 88; opium wars, 18, 216; Paris Peace Conference, 115; Qing court, 28, 150, 216, 220; Qing reforms, 116–17, 218; reformers, 106, 227–28; republican government, 235; sericulture, 58–59; Soviet advisors, 115, 129; Taiping Rebellion, 217; trade, 17, 18, 19; victory pictures, 104; war with Japan, 198, 274. *See also* Hong Kong
Chinese: bond service as custom, 180–81, 189, 191; Christians, 191, 192, 216, 227; education in United States, 216–17; gender norms, 228; in Indochina, 187–88, 204–5, 206, 338n157; in Malaya, 20; merchants, 83, 88, 106, 183; Po Leung Kuk, 129–30, 183–84; reformers, 152–53; refugees, 160, 198, 217; secret societies, 60, 88, 184; in South Africa, 151; study abroad, 218. *See also* Chinese elites;

Chinese women; Hong Kong, Chinese in; Singapore, Chinese in; Straits Chinese
Chinese children: education, 219–21, 225, 227–29, 231, 237–38; female infanticide, 28–29; gender norms, 228; girls, 198–99, 205–6, 220, 227–29, 231; girls in Ministering Children's League, 106–10, 126, 197, 315n35; in Hong Kong, 3, 72, 93–94, 106–10, 225, 263, 309nn51–52, 331n60; missionaries' views of, 226; precocity, 225; refugees, 198; in Singapore, 219–20, 223, 235; singing girls, 205–6, 337n148; trafficking, 178, 205–6, 335n114. *See also* Bond servants
Chinese Communist Party, 235
Chinese elites: in Hong Kong, 106–9, 129–30, 149–50, 152–53, 183, 228–29, 262–63; in Indochina, 164; in Singapore, 112, 156, 313n115
Chinese women: amahs, 4, 55, 56–62; baby contests, 136; infantilisation, 59, 60, 61; marital status, 59; midwives, 133; migrant labourers, 58–59; servants, 59, 302n7; servants in Indochina, 64
Chocolat Poulain images, 122 (fig.), 123 (fig.)
Cholon, 20, 121, 125, 180, 205–6, 271, 272
Christianity, *see* Catholic Church; Christmas celebrations; Missionaries
Christmas celebrations: in Britain, 82; Buckley's Treat (Singapore), 82, 83–85, 110–11, 112, 131, 255; consumer culture and, 138; in Hong Kong, 85, 109, 126; in India, 84
Churchill, Winston, 191
Church Missionary Society (CMS), 107, 215, 226, 227
Church of England Purity Society, 26
Cixi, empress dowager, 229
Clark, Francis J., 133, 155
Clark, F. S., 171
Class divisions: among Eurasians in colonies, 224–25, 269; among European children in colonies, 44, 45, 52, 224–25; among Europeans in Hong Kong, 93; in France, 50; in Indochina, 40, 41, 64, 70, 163; racial otherness and, 25; residential segregation, 149, 156. *See also* Elites; Middle class; Working-class children
Clementi, Dione, 71, 76
Clementi, Lady, 135
Clementi, Sir Cecil, 71, 136, 193, 197, 334n98
Clementi Smith, Sir Cecil, 183, 214
Climate: disease transmission and, 147–48, 151; of Hong Kong, 306n85, 307n12; of Indochina, 35; of Malaya, 171; racial differences and, 22–23; of Singapore, 307n12. *See also* Tropics
Clothing, of adults: hats, 300n99; servants' uniforms, 59, 63; in tropics, 306n85
Clothing, of children: native costumes, 61; topees, 42, 43–44, 46, 47, 98; in tropics, 42
Cochinchina: anticolonial revolt, 125; child protection laws, 259; child slavery, 179, 180, 205; domestic roles, 63; education, 38, 211, 271; European children, 3, 289nn6–7; French administrators, 323n76; as French colony, 18, 96, 179; governors, 36–37, 95, 164; sanatorium, 154; servants, 65, 184; trade, 206; Vietnamese elites, 139, 143. *See also* Indochina; Saigon
Collège Chasseloup Laubat, 64, 221, 222, 234
Collège des Jeunes Filles Indigènes, 230
Colonial childhoods: age boundaries, 279–80; ambiguity, 145–46, 278; consumer culture and, 136–38; coproductions of adults and children, 6, 280–81; cultural interactions, 54–55; external forces in, 79; in French Empire, 53, 76–77, 96, 204; future research directions, 286; gender roles and, 79; in interwar period, 115–16, 129, 137–38, 145–46; meanings, 277–78, 285–86; memoirs, 66–67, 72, 73–74; moral reform and, 3, 74; political symbolism, 3, 4, 101–2, 113–14, 129; positive recollections, 66–67, 73–74, 78; as sacrifice, 32–33, 77; trans-colonial approaches, 12–17, 278–79. *See also* Returns home

Index

Colonialism, *see* Imperialism
Colonial space, mastery of, 76. *See also* Racial enclaves; Urban planning
Congaïs, 39, 47, 64, 66, 67, 69, 105, 299n72
Congrès Colonial International, 213
Conklin, Alice, 203
Conseil National des Femmes Françaises, 143
Consumer culture, 136–38
Contagion: cultural, 161; Eurasian children and, 261. *See also* Disease transmission
Contagious Diseases Acts, Britain, 26, 182, 184, 195
Cooper, Frederick, 13
Coquelin, J., 234
Corneau, Grace, 23, 39–40, 49
Council for the Improvement of Native Education, Indochina, 232–33
Crayssac, René, 256–57
Crewe Circular of 1909, 245
Culture: consumer, 136–38; folklore, 91; French, 37–38, 94–95; traditional Vietnamese, 139
Cunningham, Alfred, 101
CWS, *see* Child Welfare Society

Dalat hill station, 148, 154–55, 163, 164–68, 240–41, 275, 327n144
Daléas, Pierre, 145
Dalziel, James, 94, 248, 309n54
Darles, Madame, 271
Darwin, Charles, 31
Darwin, John, 21, 113
Darwinism, *see* Evolution; Social Darwinism
Daughton, J. P., 3, 96
Daumier, Honoré, *The Republic*, 98, 99 (fig.)
Davies, Helen, 226
Davis, Hilary, 192–93
Decoux, Jean, 207, 241
De Hargues, Thérèse, 50, 66, 168, 304n53, 327n144
Deloncle, François, 256
Delteil, Arthur, 65, 96
Des Voeux, Sir George William, 150
Devé, Maurice-Arsène, 141

De Vilers, Charles-Marie le Myre, 36–37, 95, 180, 201, 211
Devonshire, Duke of, 192
Dickinson, A. H., 195
Diseases: bubonic plague, 148, 153, 156; cholera, 153; downplaying, 75–76; dysentery, 37; infant mortality, 132; malaria, 75, 149, 155, 165–66; prevention, 74–75, 149; risk factors, 74; tropical, 74–75; venereal, 26, 195. *See also* Health; Medical research; Public health
Disease transmission: climate and, 147–48, 151; contagion, 147–49, 151, 154, 165; public health campaigns, 147–48; theories, 147–49, 151, 154–55, 161
Domergue, Eugène, 257
Domestic life: in colonies, 23, 27–28, 62–63, 79, 171, 280, 281, 282; home as site of colonial power, 54; intimacy, 8, 28, 281; protecting with racial segregation, 152; supervised by wife and mother, 57; as trans-cultural space, 54–55, 58. *See also* Families; Servants
Doran, Christine, 45
Đồ Sơn resort, 154, 322n41
Douchet, P., 244–45, 274
Doumer, Paul: family, 40; as governor, 37–39, 41, 117, 153, 186, 222, 323n76; Hanoi as capital, 38, 123, 259; Hanoi Exposition, 100, 101–2; hill station project, 154–55; Mother France metaphor, 310–11n73
Dufau, Clémentine-Hélène, "Gouvernement Général de l'Indo-Chine, exposition de Hanoï," 101, 101 (fig.), 104
Dumoutier, Gustave, 214
Dunman, W., 172
Dupla, P., 64
Dürrwell, George, 121
Dussol, Jules, 248, 256
Duy Tân, Emperor, 116, 118–20, 119 (fig.), 123, 124, 125–26, 138–39
Dyer, Maria, 227

East Asia, map, 16 (fig.)
East India Company, 2, 17, 82–83, 215, 219, 245, 254

École des Beaux-Arts de l'Indochine (EBAI), 139
Eden, Emily, 84
Education: ages of students, 225, 232–40, 284, 342nn57–58, 344n98; art school, 139; assimilationist goal, 230; boarding schools, 165, 176, 246; in China, 218, 228–29; colonial governance and, 209, 211, 213–15, 217–18, 219–20, 230–34, 239–40; consequences, 209–10, 231–32, 234–35, 238–40, 242; debates on, 209, 284; English-language, 217–18, 219, 223, 234, 348n45; in Europe, 86, 139, 211–12, 238; fairy tales in, 86; gender distribution, 227, 231; hill station schools, 164–68, 172–76, 240–41, 327n144; medical, 215, 218–19, 220, 341n37; missionary schools, 211, 215–17, 219, 226, 227, 228–29, 237, 255; racially mixed, 174, 221–23, 224–25, 234, 240–41; racial segregation, 166, 173–75, 221–22, 224–26, 239–40, 252, 257; secondary, 139, 161–62, 223; study abroad, 218, 220, 222–23, 238; university scholarships, 214–15, 236. See also Returns home; and individual groups and colonies
Education, of girls: Chinese girls, 107, 220, 227–29; debates on, 227–31; of elite families, 31–32; in Hong Kong, 227–29; in Indochina, 65, 69, 221, 222, 229–30, 343n86, 344n97; returns home, 31–32; in Singapore, 220, 228, 231, 237, 343n71, 343n75
Edwards, Charles, 191
Edward VII, King of England, 111–12
Ehrlicher, Charlotte, 107
Eitel, Ernest J., 183, 217, 250
ELA, see Eurasian Literary Association
Elites: Eurasian, 249, 252–53, 256, 261–65, 269; girls' education, 31–32; in Hong Kong, 70–71, 88, 106, 224; planter class, 168–76; servants, 55–56, 57, 61, 62; in Singapore, 44. See also Chinese elites; Hill stations; Vietnamese elites
Elizabeth (child slave), 181–82
Ellis, Walter, 193
Ellis, W. G., 155

Enjoy, Paul d', 33, 40, 42
Entr'aide Maternelle, Saigon, 143
Erbar, Jacqueline, 67
États Généraux du Feminisme, 143
Ethnic groups: collaborative relations, 82–83, 106–7, 110–11, 129; interactions, 4–5, 12–13, 19–20, 69–70, 71–73, 79, 240–41. See also Singapore, ethnic groups in; and individual groups
Eugenics, 132, 134, 152, 252, 254, 268
Eurasian children: abandoned, 7–8, 243, 246, 250, 252, 259, 270–72; in British colonies, 245, 276; challenges faced by, 243–44; as challenge to racial definitions, 243, 275–76; charity for, 246–47, 248, 250, 252, 253, 270, 273–74, 275; colonial state's responsibilities for, 245–46, 247, 249–50, 254, 259, 270–75, 284–85; in European neighborhoods, 72, 157–58, 261, 262; in French colonies, 245–46, 276; health, 251; in Hong Kong, 72, 126, 157–58, 229, 248–52, 253, 261–62; infant mortality, 268, 351n114; legal status, 246, 247, 248, 260, 270, 272–73; positive views of, 257; prejudice from European children, 72; as servants, 65, 246; in Singapore, 84, 223, 254, 267–68, 351n114; social status, 243, 251, 252; sold by mothers, 336n133; stigmatisation, 244, 247, 251, 254, 260, 268; as symbols of imperialism, 249 (fig.), 249–50, 284, 285; as threat to European children, 158, 261; vulnerability, 243, 257–60
Eurasian children, education: in Hong Kong, 221, 229, 249, 250, 252, 253, 261; in Indochina, 222, 246, 257, 271, 355n180; military, 275; in Singapore, 223, 227, 255
Eurasian children, in Indochina: charity for, 257–60, 355n181; contacts with French children, 69–70; cultural assimilation, 271, 272–73; education, 246, 271, 355n180; legal status, 270–71, 272–73; metropolitan transfer, 272, 275, 353–54n158; number of, 354n171; servants, 65; state support, 270–71, 274–75; stigmatisation, 244, 270; as threat to 'French Indochina,' 39, 40; training

for employment, 246–47, 270, 271; war orphans, 270–71
Eurasian Literary Association (ELA), 266, 268, 269, 351n111
Eurasians: administrative employment, 246–48, 249, 255–57; age groups, 266–68, 269; census categories, 253, 254, 347n39; diverse communities, 243, 254; education in Europe, 255, 263–64; elites, 261–65; ethnic identities, 252–53, 263–65, 266, 268–69; factions, 269; families, 268; in Hong Kong, 249, 252–53, 260–65; in Indochina, 246–48, 256–57, 270, 348n41; leaders, 267, 269; legal status, 256–57, 352n133, 352n135; in Malaya, 254, 269–70, 348n41; marriages, 348n46; political interest groups, 256, 266, 269–70, 274; in Singapore, 245, 254–56, 265–70, 348n41; social status, 251, 269; visibility, 243; wealthy, 249, 252–53, 256, 261–63, 269; youth, 267
Europe: Asian students, 86, 139, 211–12, 238; birth rates, 11; child protection, 5, 187, 259. *See also individual countries*
European, use of term, 20
European Association of Malaya, 175
European children: agency, 6–7, 55, 67, 71, 76–77, 78, 79–80, 280–81; ages for bringing to tropics, 49–50; born in tropics, 23; class differences, 52; cultural symbolism, 54; dialogue with adults, 76; in Europe, 9, 10; health, 33, 35, 37, 40, 52, 75–76, 77, 97–99; imperial authority and, 41, 52, 54, 80; interethnic contact, 4–5, 69–70, 71–73, 79; languages spoken, 57–58, 60–61, 62, 70; as marker of civilisation, 3–4, 7, 278; mastery of colonial space, 76; mobility, 1, 4, 6, 44–45; moral influence of presence in colonies, 23, 27–28, 87; mortality rates and ages, 49; physical appearances, 30, 44–45; political symbolism, 100–101, 113–14; proportion of colonial populations, 2–3; protecting health of, 43–52; racial authority symbolism, 57; risks taken, 53, 73, 79; travel, 44–45; vulnerability, 2, 29, 46, 52–53, 151–53; writings, 7, 66–67, 72, 73–74, 76, 78. *See also* Adolescents; Childhood on display; Colonial childhoods; Education; Returns home; Youth; *and individual colonies*

European women: antislavery, 201–3; colonial roles, 203; criticism of imperialism, 124; criticism of presence in colonies, 90; emigration promoted, 34–35; feminism, 143, 194, 201–3, 229, 260; imperial roles, 143, 203; in Indochina, 230; moralising presence, 90; networks, 88–89; nurses and governesses, 55–56, 302n5; philanthropic organisations, 88–90; public roles, 89; reformers, 143–45; roles, 91; suffrage, 202, 336n127; support of girls' education, 230; travel writers, 124
Evolution, 29, 31, 36. *See also* Social Darwinism; Transformist theories of adaptation
Ewart, Joseph, 24

Fairyland: children and, 86–87, 88–89, 109–10, 126, 130; collapse, 138; Hong Kong as, 85, 87, 131, 159–60, 315–16n40; Indochina as, 97; performances, 90–91
Fairy tales: in Britain, 86, 307n25; Chinese interest, 130–31; Christmas Treat performances (Singapore), 83–85; French, 97; of Grimm brothers, 83, 306n7; national symbolism, 91; plays in Hong Kong, 86–87, 90–91, 93, 109–10; psychological significance, 91; women in, 144
Families: effects of children's returns home, 32–33; empires as, 125; Eurasian, 268; fathers, 50, 53, 63, 249, 252, 260; French, 35, 95–96, 163; ideals, 28; letters, 32. *See also* Childrearing; Domestic life; Mothers
Far Eastern Association of Tropical Medicine, 148, 149, 153, 155
Farrère, Claude, *Les Civilisés*, 124, 203
Fave, Marguerite, 72, 77, 160
Fave, Pierre, 77
Federated Malay States (FMS): abolition

of slavery, 182, 193; baby contests, 136; British population, 168–77; education, 172–76, 231; establishment, 14, 18; ethnic groups, 19–20; European children, 169–77; hill stations, 148, 156, 157, 169–70, 172–77, 326n122; infant mortality rates, 134; rubber plantations, 168–70, 171–72, 196; schools, 169–70, 171. *See also* Malaya
Femmes d'outre-mer (Rouyer), 66
Ferguson-Davie, C. J., 169–70
Ferry, Jules, 10, 11, 34, 121
FJB, *see* Fondation Jules Brévié
FMS, *see* Federated Malay States
Folklore, 91. *See also* Fairy tales
Fondation Jules Brévié (FJB), 274
Forbin Janson, Charles-Auguste-Marie-Joseph de, 246, 349n70
Fouillé, Alfred, 36
Fourès, Augustin, 221, 222, 247
Fournier, Christiane: *Bébé colonial*, 64, 70, 77; *Perspectives Occidentales sur l'Indochine*, 139, 143
Fraissinet, Marc, 200
France: antislavery movement, 200–203; birth rates, 11, 34, 48, 301n106; Catholic Church, 226; childhood in, 9, 10, 34, 48, 49–50, 96–97, 103, 121, 257; child protection laws, 10, 187, 259; child welfare, 144, 331n48; class differences, 50; colonial expositions, 141, 166; culture, 37–38, 94–95; education system, 10; Eurasian children, 272, 275, 353–54n158; fairy tales, 97; families, 95–96, 163; feminists, 143, 201–3, 260, 336n127; health care, 50; infant mortality rates, 48; medical research, 36, 40, 154–55; military, 125; Ministry of Colonies, 100, 155; missionaries from, 186–87, 219, 246; nationalism, 10, 95–96, 121; organic economy theories, 34; paternity laws, 260; Popular Front government, 167, 203, 240, 274–75; *puériculture* (childraising) movement, 48, 144; republicanism, 10–11, 98, 100–101; rivalry with Britain, 14; Scouts, 127; transformist theories of adaptation, 35–37, 50–52; urbanisation, 34; Vichy regime, 207, 241; Vietnamese students, 139, 211–12, 238, 239; wet nursing, 47. *See also* French Empire; World War I
Franck, Harry, 69–70
Franco-Vietnamese schools, 139, 230, 232, 233
Fraser's Hill, 169, 170, 326n122
French Empire: administrators, 38–39, 40, 96; assimilationist policies, 21, 38, 96, 103, 211, 213, 230, 248, 257; childhood in, 53, 76–77, 96, 204; China and, 187; civilising mission, 10–11, 222; colonial lobby, 34–35, 36; colonial policies, 21, 37–38, 102–3, 123–24; critics, 124, 138, 143, 178–79, 244; hill stations, 155; infantilisation, 11, 103, 105; in interwar period, 189; justification, 11, 36; in late nineteenth century, 10–11, 36, 113; military, 34, 38; republicanism and, 10–11, 36, 96, 102–4, 121, 185, 203, 204, 222; scientific research, 36; subjects as children, 11, 125; women's roles, 34–35, 143, 203; World War I and, 115, 125–26, 146. *See also individual colonies*
French Indochina, *see* Indochina
Fun o' the Fair, Lee Gardens, Hong Kong, 130, 137, 137 (fig.)

Gaide, Laurent-Joseph, 126, 167
Galloway, Sir David, 27, 30, 31, 44, 48
Gan Eng Sen, 220
Gender differences: in age of marriage, 31; in education, 31–32; in evolution, 31; in fairy plays, 93; in risks of tropical living, 31
Gender norms: Chinese, 228; French, 96
Gender ratios: of servants, 56, 61, 63, 302n7; of students, 227, 231
Gent, G.E.J., 197
Germany: empire, 14, 35, 203, 260; fairy tales, 83, 306n7; in interwar period, 142. *See also* World War I
Gervais-Courtellemont, Jules: on French children in Indochina, 35; photographs, 97–99, 102; "Quatre naïfs du poste de Hien-Luong," 97–99, 98 (fig.); visit to Indochina, 97

Gillis, John, 9
Girl Guides, 127, 240. *See also* Uniformed youth movements
Girls: French, 40, 65, 69; gender roles, 79; male protection, 198–99; modern, 231; public performances, 94, 95; returns home, 31–32, 78–79; Vietnamese, 65–66, 188, 221, 222, 229–30, 343n86, 344n97; weakness, 75. *See also* Children; Child trafficking; Chinese children; Education, of girls; *Mui tsai*; Slaves, child; Women
Girls' Friendly Society, Singapore, 131
Gittins, Jean, 72
Go, Julian, 15
Gobineau, Arthur, 245
Godart, Justin, 167–68
Goodwin, William, 85
Graham, H. Gordon, 175
Grall, Charles, 39, 41, 47, 48, 49, 155, 301n120, 322n38, 322n40
Grandière, Pierre Benoît de la, 37
Great Depression, 59, 173, 176, 264–65, 268–69, 273–74
Gregory, J. W., 171
Griffith Jones, Anne L. P., 175–76
Grimm brothers, 83, 306n7
Guillemard, Laurence, 195

Ha, Marie-Paule, 34
Haffner, Eugène, 246, 247
Hải Phòng, 163, 185, 187, 205, 208, 213
Hall, Catherine, 13
Hall, G. Stanley, 29
Hallifax, E. R., 191
Hàm Nghi, emperor, 117, 210, 212
Hanoi: children in population, 3, 290n10; child slaves, 187; École des Beaux-Arts de l'Indochine, 139; ethnic groups, 20; Eurasian children, 248, 257, 258–60, 271; European children, 2, 23, 69–70; European families, 39, 40, 68; European population, 20, 39, 295n73; French control, 37; French invasion, 18; history, 104; hospitals, 49; as imperial capital, 38, 39, 96, 100, 259; infant mortality, 145; modernisation, 38, 100, 104, 123; population growth, 20; prostitution, 205; public health, 153; residential neighborhoods, 38, 68, 153–54, 164, 322n40; rivalry with Saigon, 96; schools, 105, 222, 230, 234, 257; social life, 39, 68; steamships, 19. *See also* Indochina; Tonkin
Hanoi Exposition (1887), 232, 311n86
Hanoi Exposition (1902–1903): aims, 100; images of Vietnamese children, 101–3, 104–5; posters, 101, 101 (fig.), 102 (fig.), 104
Hardy, E. J., 27, 46, 309n49
Harmand, Jules, 36, 103, 123
Harry, Myriam, 124
Haslewood, Clara, 190, 193
Haslewood, Hugh, 189–90, 193, 331n60
Hastings, Aileen, 32, 308n35
Hastings, Eleanor, 87, 308n36
Haupt, Heinz-Gerhard, 15
Health: of French children in Indochina, 33, 35, 37, 40, 52, 77, 97–99; in hill stations, 147–48; of mothers, 48–49, 133, 134, 143; organic economy theories, 34; in tropics, 22–23, 24, 43, 74–75; in urban areas, 25, 34; vaccination programs, 187. *See also* Diseases; Hygiene; Infant mortality; Medical research; Public health
Hébrard, Ernest, 164, 165
Hennessy, Sir John Pope, 26–27, 88, 109, 217, 250
Henriot, Christian, 3
Hill District Reservation, *see* Peak Hill District Reservation
Hill stations: administrative functions, 154, 164, 167; Baguio (Philippines), 172–73, 327n139; Cameron Highlands, 148, 156, 157, 172–77; as children's spaces, 147, 177; Dalat, 148, 154–55, 163, 164–68, 240–41, 275, 327n144; early, 319n1; health protection role, 147–48; in India, 147, 150, 154; in Indochina, 148, 154–55, 162–63, 168; in Malaya, 169–70, 326n122; roles, 147; schools, 164–68, 172–76, 240–41, 327n144. *See also* Peak Hill District Reservation

Hoare, Joseph, 226
Hochberg, Fritz, 309nn51–52
Hodge, H. L., 196
Ho Fook, 160, 253
Ho Kai, (Dr. Kai Ho Kai), 133, 152–53, 224, 321n29
Ho Kom Tong, 157–58
Holidays, *see* Christmas celebrations
Holy Childhood Association, *see* Sainte-Enfance
Homes, *see* Domestic life; Housing; Residential segregation
Hong Kong: abolition of slavery, 179; antislavery campaign, 189–94; Botanical Gardens, 22, 43; British lease, 14, 150; British sovereignty, 87–88; Cheung Chau reservation, 160–61, 162; child protection efforts, 191–94, 197, 331n60, 334n94, 334n98; child slaves, 180–81, 185, 188, 189–94, 196–97; child trafficking, 183, 199; child welfare laws, 198–99; climate, 306n85, 307n12; Contagious Diseases Act, 26–27; as Crown Colony, 18, 88; ethnic groups, 88, 294n72; Eurasian children, 72, 126, 158, 229, 248–52, 253, 261–62; European population, 20, 93, 106–7, 294n72; as fairyland, 85, 87, 159–60, 315–16n40; Fun o' the Fair, 137; governance, 20–21; governors, 20–21, 85–86, 105; hospitals, 48, 106, 130, 133, 148; immigration, 20; infant mortality, 132–33; in interwar period, 126–31, 137–38, 160–62, 262–65; Kowloon Reservation, 150, 151, 157, 224; labour strike (1922), 63, 129, 236, 262; maturation of colony, 262–63; missionaries, 90, 160–61, 162, 216–17, 218, 226; New Territories, 72, 150, 221; opium trade, 88; population growth, 20, 150, 294n66; public health, 132–33, 151, 160; real estate, 149–50; residential segregation, 70–72, 149–53, 157–61, 224; security threats, 87; sentimental view of colonial rule, 197–98; servants, 55–56, 57–59, 60 (fig.), 60–61, 302n7, 303n23; strike-boycott (1925–26), 262–63; trade, 19; travel writers on, 131, 309nn51–52. *See also* Peak Hill District Reservation

Hong Kong, Chinese in: antislavery, 191, 192; child labour, 93; children, 3, 72, 93–94, 106–10, 225, 263, 331n60; in European neighborhoods, 149–50; housing, 160; immigrants, 20, 263; infant mortality, 132–33; Legislative Council members, 88, 130, 152–53, 160; merchants, 83, 106; *mui tsai*, 191–94, 334n98; nationalism, 220–21; philanthropy, 106, 109, 129–30, 183, 265; real estate purchases, 149–50; refugees, 160, 198, 217; residents, 88

Hong Kong, education in: ages of students, 234, 237–38; Chinese students, 107, 216–18, 220–21, 228–29, 236–38, 263; elitism, 107, 110, 232; Eurasian students, 221, 229, 249, 250, 252, 253, 261; gender ratios, 227; of girls, 227–29; medical college, 218–19; racial mixing, 221; racial segregation, 224–26, 261; secondary schools, 161–62; student activism, 236–37, 263

Hong Kong, European children in: adoption laws, 331n60; antislavery, 192–93; Christmas celebrations, 85, 109, 126; class differences, 224–25; fairy plays, 86–87, 90–91, 93, 109–10; health, 75; interethnic contact, 72; missionaries' children, 160–61, 162; moral influence of presence, 27–28, 87; plays, 110, 309n50, 312n102; population, 2, 3, 23, 85, 290n9, 308n36; returns home, 31–32, 77–78, 161–62; segregated neighborhoods, 70–72, 85, 160–61; social events, 86, 91, 307n17; vulnerability, 151–53, 158, 161; working-class, 93. *See also* Hong Kong, education in; Ministering Children's League

Hong Kong Legislative Council: Cheung Chau reservation bill, 160–61; child protection, 198; Chinese members, 88, 130, 152–53, 160, 350n89; Female Domestic Servants Ordinance, 191–92; infant mortality issue, 132; nomination of Ho Tung, 350n89; Peak Hill District

ordinance, 152–53, 158–59, 261; power, 20–21; prohibition of slavery, 179
Hongkong Nursing Institution, 48
Hong Kong University, 229, 263–64
Ho Tung, Sir Robert: family, 157, 252, 253, 261, 320n17; as Grand Old Man of Hong Kong, 263; Kowloon British School and, 225; Legislative Council nomination, 350n89; residence in Peak Hill District, 72, 158, 261; wealth, 252–53; as Welfare League president, 264
Housing: designs, 42; gardens, 72–73, 76–77; in Hong Kong, 149–50, 160, 162; servants' quarters, 72–73; slums, 160. *See also* Residential segregation
Howell, E. F., 58
Hullett, Richard, 232
Humanitarian ethics, 11, 184–85, 188, 196, 199, 200, 208
Hygiene: as rationale for residential segregation, 147; rules for childrearing in tropics, 41–43, 46–48, 50–51, 54, 280. *See also* Public health

Identities: of Eurasians, 252–53, 263–65, 266, 268–69; imperial, 8
Imperial history, 1, 8–9, 13, 15, 285–86
Imperialism: childhood metaphors, 103; education of subject peoples, 209, 211–12, 213–15, 217–18, 219–20, 230–34, 239–40; effects of World War I, 115, 125–26, 189; in interwar period, 115–16, 177; justifications, 11, 179–80, 197–98; military troops, 42; morality, 26–27, 198, 251; paternalism, 11–12, 103, 105, 116, 197, 279; postcolonial readings, 67; rivalries, 14, 28, 104; scientific, 36. *See also* British Empire; French Empire; Germany; Nationalist movements
Indentured servants, *see* Bond servants
India: baby contests, 136; British children, 8, 24–25, 84, 296n12; colonial policies, 25; end of British rule anticipated, 128; Eurasians, 245; hill stations, 147, 150, 154; infant mortality, 316n49; lower-class whites, 23; middle class, 128; missionaries, 215; rubber workers from, 196; Uprising of 1857, 24–25, 245
Indochina: agriculture, 40–41, 142, 204, 206, 247, 271; border with China, 184–85, 188, 199–200, 208; child labour, 63–66, 184–85; child protection laws, 187, 335n109; childrearing manuals, 46–47; child trafficking, 142, 180, 184–88, 199–207, 208, 335n114; child welfare, 144–45; Chinese congregations, 205, 338n157; Chinese influences, 116–17, 121; Chinese residents, 187–88, 204–5, 206; civilisation, 103–4; civil service, 38–39, 117, 256–57; class structure, 40, 41, 64, 70; climate, 35; festivals, 69; forced labour, 123, 314n15; French administrators, 38–39, 40, 96, 154, 162–63, 164, 323n76; French cultural influences, 94–95; French families, 37, 39, 40, 70, 162–65, 167; French policies, 123–24, 238; French women as reformers, 143–45, 318n87; governance, 21; governors, 37–39, 40, 96, 117–18, 123–24; Hanoi as capital, 38, 39, 96, 100, 259; hill stations, 148, 154–55, 162–63, 168; infant mortality, 144, 145, 318–19n88, 319n92; in interwar period, 138–45, 203–4, 270–75; military forces, 167; modernisation, 120; nationalism, 115, 116–17, 120–21, 125–26, 138–39, 143, 204, 220; nationalist protests, 142, 203–4, 233, 238–39, 270; Nguyễn dynasty, 18, 116, 117, 118–20, 313n3; prostitution, 200, 205–6, 338n152; public health, 144–45, 153–54; railroads, 187; rural life, 69, 204, 206; scientific research, 36, 40; servants, 62–70, 180, 299n72; taxes, 186, 187; Tonkin Expedition, 34, 38, 103, 121; trade, 206; under Vichy regime, 207; World War I and, 125–26, 146, 162–64; World War II and, 207. *See also* Annam; Cochinchina; Hanoi; Saigon; Tonkin; Vietnamese
Indochina, education in: critiques, 213; Dalat schools, 164–68, 240–41; of Eurasian children, 222, 246, 257;

of French children, 38, 65, 69, 163, 164–68; of French girls, 65, 69; French schools, 38, 139, 164–68, 214, 221, 233, 317n76; racial mixing, 221–22; racial segregation, 225, 239–40; reformers, 220, 229–30; Saigon schools, 94, 95, 214, 221, 222, 230, 234, 257; student activism, 238–39; workbooks sent to Hanoi Expositions, 105, 232, 311n86. *See also* Vietnamese children, education of

Indochina, French children in: ages of puberty, 40; births, 35, 48, 49; class differences, 41, 163; constraints, 76–77; contacts with Vietnamese children, 69–70; as creoles, 40, 97, 101–2; education, 38, 65, 69, 163, 221–22; health, 33, 35, 37, 40, 52, 77, 97–99; health care, 48–49, 51; infant mortality, 48; moral guardianship, 95; officials' families, 37, 50; orphans, 41; photographs, 97–99, 98 (fig.); policies on, 35, 37, 39–41, 76; population, 3; public performances, 94, 95; relations with servants, 62–69; returns home, 52; in rural areas, 69; symbolism, 113

Indochinese Union, 18, 96, 153–54

Infantilisation: of Asians, 29–30, 118–21, 311n76, 318n85; of Chinese women, 59, 60, 61; of colonised peoples, 11, 103, 105; in French Empire, 103, 105; of servants, 59, 60, 61, 105

Infant mortality: of Asian children, 132–34; in Britain, 296n12, 316n49, 317n63; in British Empire, 132–34; diseases, 132; of Eurasian children, 268; in France, 48; of French children in Indochina, 48; in Hong Kong, 132–33; in Indochina, 48, 145; in Malaya, 134, 145; reducing, 132, 133–34, 135, 144, 318–19n88; in Singapore, 132, 135, 136

Infants: baby contests, 132, 135–37; feeding, 45–46, 47–48, 49, 58; wet nurses, 47–48, 58. *See also* Mothers; Singapore Baby Show

Institut Taberd, 221, 246, 247

International Save the Children Union, 189

Irving, Edward A., 224–25, 342n57

The Islanders of Hong Kong ('Veronica'), 57, 61

Izard, H. C., 112

Japan: Chinese students, 218; defeat of Russia, 14, 117, 220; expansionism, 237; Meiji restoration, 120; Vietnamese students, 220; war in China, 198, 274; Yokohama sanatorium, 154

Jardine, Mathesen & Co., 252, 253

Jay, Antoine, 69

Jay, Bernadette, 69

Jeantet, Pierre, 230

Jennings, Eric T., 3, 33, 154, 164, 167, 240–41

Jesuit missionaries, 28–29, 215, 246. *See also* Missionaries

Johnson, James, 24

Jones, Andrew, 131

Joubert, Alphonse, 246

Jouglet, René, 131

Jousset, Alfred, 33

Jung, Eugène, 23

Kadoorie, Sir Ellis, 86

Kahn, Joel S., 265

Karpelès, Suzanne, 239

Keith, Charles, 201

Kelly, Gail P., 240

Kendall, F. R., 82

Kennedy, Dane, 147

Kennedy, John, 45–46

Keppel Garnier, Grace, 128

Kermorgant, Alexandre, 51

Khải Định, emperor, 126

Kingsley, Charles, 86

Kliene, Charles, 188, 331n53

Klobukowsky, Antony, 124

Knollys, Henry, 22, 23, 25, 33, 43, 55, 250–51

Kocka, Jürgen, 15

Kotewall, Robert, 263, 350n95, 351n99

Kowloon British School, 225–26

Kowloon Reservation, Hong Kong, 150, 151, 157, 224

Kreta Ayer incident, 235

Kuomintang, 198, 220, 235

Kỳ Đồng (Nguyễn Văn Cẩm), 210–13, 214, 339n10
Kynnersley, C.W.S., 183

Labour: forced, 123, 314n15; strikes, 63, 129, 196, 236, 262–63; wages, 39, 59, 196. *See also* Child labour; Migrant labour; Servants; Slaves, child
Labrouquère, André, 207
Lallemand, Hélène, 97
Lamarck, Jean-Baptiste de Monnet Chevalier de, 35
Landes, Anthony, 180, 201, 207
Lanessan, Jean-Marie de, 154, 213, 247, 248, 299n63, 322n41
Lau Chu Pak, 160
League of Nations: child protection efforts, 189, 195, 199; Commission of Enquiry into Traffic in Women and Children in the East, 200, 204–6, 207; criticisms of imperial powers, 143; ideals of childhood, 116; Permanent Advisory Committee of Experts on Slavery, 193
Leavitt, Mary, 132
Le Bon, Gustave, 213
Lebrun, Albert, 230, 260
Lee Gardens, Hong Kong, 130, 137, 137 (fig.)
Lee Hy San, 130
Legge, James, 217
Legrand-Falco, Marcelle, 202
Le Marchant de Trigon, Henri, 126
Lemire, Charles, 184, 311n84
Leow, Rachel, 194
Le Play, Frédéric, 96
Leroy-Beaulieu, Paul, 121–23, 124
Leuba, Jeanne, 139
Lévecque, Ernest Fernand, 118
Levine, Philippa, 15
Levy, Louis, 94
Liang Qichao, 228
Ligue des Familles Nombreuses, 163
Li Kai Sien, 188
Lim, Shirley Geok-lin, 79
Lim Boon Keng, 156, 214–15, 218, 220, 228, 265

Little, Alicia, 27
LMS, *see* London Missionary Society
Lo Man Kam, 264
Lombard, H.-C., 33
London Missionary Society (LMS), 215, 216, 226, 227, 250
Long, Maurice, 164, 272
Long, Walter, 158, 160, 189
Low, Sir Hugh, 156
Lucas, C. P., 151, 255
Lucknow massacre, 24–25
Lugard, Sir Frederick, 105, 107, 220–21
Lycée d'Alger, 211–12
Lý Thanh Long, 213–14
Lyttelton, Alfred, 151

Macau, 215, 216, 248–49
MacDonnell, Sir Richard, 150, 328n3
Macmillan, Alastair, 57, 237
Madrolle, Claudius, 23
Maire, Simon, 163
Makepeace, Walter, 83–84, 111
Malacca, 17, 73, 215, 219, 254, 293n57
Malaterre-Sellier, Germaine, 203, 337n135
Malaya: baby contests, 135–36; British authority, 196; British planters, 44; climate, 171; education, 219; Eurasians, 254, 269–70, 348n41; infant mortality, 145; slavery, 183, 194, 329n20; trade, 17–18, 19; unity, 195. *See also* Federated Malay States; Straits Settlements
Malayan Communist Party, 236
Malay language, 110
Malays: ayahs, 56–57, 58; education, 219, 228, 231, 232, 234, 236, 343n75; infant mortality, 317nn68–69; midwives, 134; population, 20; rubber workers, 196; in Singapore, 3, 174, 228, 232, 234
Manson, Patrick, 46
Marqet, Jean, *De la rizière à la montagne*, 206, 338n160
Marquis, Édouard, 144, 146
Marriages: ages at, 31; delayed by Chinese migrant labourers, 59; of Eurasians, 348n46; interracial, 245, 251–52, 258. *See also* Families
Marty, A. R., 78

Marty, Marguerite, 78
Marx, Georges, 213
Marx, Roger, 100
Masculinity, 50, 203, 307n12
Massieu, Isabelle, 124, 229
Maxwell, Sir Peter Benson, 181
Maxwell, William George, 170, 172, 173, 193
May, Dione, 57
May, Helena: daughter's education, 31–32; European children and, 3; in Fiji, 105–6, 107; journey home, 1, 77–78; letters, 308n26; marriage, 89; Ministering Children's League and, 89, 90, 92, 107, 109, 151–52, 308n36; residence in Peak Hill District, 71, 87
May, Henry: on bond servants, 190; children, 87, 110; Eurasian population and, 251–52, 260–61, 350n85, 350n87; as Fiji governor, 105–6; as Hong Kong governor, 158; marriage, 89; Peak Hill District and, 150–53, 158, 252, 261, 262; servants, 56, 57
May, Phoebe (Whitworth): contacts with Chinese children, 72; education, 31–32; governess, 56; illness, 75; Ministering Children's League and, 90, 110; residence in Peak Hill District, 71, 87; return home, 77–78
May, Stella, 32, 307n20
May Fourth Movement, 115, 235, 264
Mazet, Jacques, 272
MCL, *see* Ministering Children's League
McMillan, Margaret, 307n25
McPherson, John L., 162
Meath, Countess of, 89, 90, 92–93, 106, 109
Medical research: bacteriology, 148–49, 154–55, 159; on children, 132; disease prevention, 74–75; on disease transmission, 147–49, 154; French, 36, 40, 154–55; germ theory, 36, 148, 151, 161; microscopes, 159; tropical medicine, 33, 36, 148–49, 171, 320n8. *See also* Diseases; Health
Men: bachelors in colonies, 27, 38, 267; childrearing role, 50, 53; colonial roles, 203; fathers, 50, 53, 63, 249, 252, 260; masculinity, 50, 203, 307n12; migrant labour in colonies, 27; protection of girls, 198–99; servants, 56, 61, 63, 65; technical expertise, 144–45; tyrant-fathers, 120, 123. *See also* Gender differences

MEP, *see* Missions Étrangères de Paris
Merlin, Martial Henri, 164–65, 234
Métis, *see* Eurasian children
Michelet, Cécile, 37
Middle class: in Hong Kong, 224; norms, 3, 9, 23, 82, 278; in Singapore, 112; Vietnamese, 229–30
Middleton, W.R.C., 133–34
Middleton-Smith, E., 109, 110
Midwives, 49, 133, 134
Migrant labour, 27, 58–59. *See also* Child trafficking; Slaves, child
Milanic, Nara, 7
Milne, A. B., 172
Milner, Lord, 160
Ministering Children's League (MCL): Asian girls in, 128; in Britain, 89, 109; in China, 127–28; conservative ethos, 107, 110; decline, 126–28; establishment, 89; films, 130; fundraising, 308n35, 312n91; genders of members, 93; global spread, 89–90, 91–93, 92 (fig.), 126–27; in interwar period, 127–30, 137–38; magazine, 90, 91, 92, 92 (fig.), 106, 128; Penang branch, 127, 128, 128 (fig.), 315nn31–32; plays, 128 (fig.), 315n31; Shanghai branch, 92, 93, 130, 309n43, 312n91; Singapore branch, 112, 127, 128–29, 313n111
Ministering Children's League (MCL), Hong Kong branch: bazaars, 107–9, 108 (fig.), 110, 126, 129, 130, 158; Chinese girls in, 106–10, 126, 130, 158, 197, 262, 315n35; fairy plays, 90–91, 93, 109–10; fundraising, 90, 91, 107, 109, 130, 312n91; Fun o' the Fair, 130, 137 (fig.); in interwar period, 137–38; leaders, 90, 105–7, 308n36; lower-status Europeans in, 93; membership, 90, 129, 315n32; racial segregation, 107; success, 91–92, 128–29, 130
Miscegenation, *see* Eurasian children

Missionaries: aid for Eurasian children, 246–47; children of, 160–61, 162; in China, 28–29, 215–16, 226; female, 90; in Hong Kong, 90, 160–61, 162, 216–17, 218, 226; in Indochina, 144, 154, 186–87, 201, 211; Jesuit, 28–29, 215, 246; Protestant, 201, 215, 216, 226, 227; schools, 211, 215–17, 219, 226, 227, 228–29, 237, 255; in Singapore, 83, 215–16, 219

Missions Étrangères de Paris (MEP), 186–87, 219, 246

Modern Girl, 15, 231

Modernity: Asian reformers, 7; child protection efforts, 5; youth and, 235

Mondière, A. T., 40

Montguillot, Maurice, 165

Moore, Sir William, 24

Morality: child protection, 249, 257–58; colonial childhoods and, 3, 74; of empire, 26–27, 198, 251; of French colonial administrators, 39; presence of European children and, 23, 27–28, 87; reformers, 26; sexual, 245. See also Slavery

Morel, Jules, 211

Morel, Louis, 322n40

Morrison, Robert, 216

Morrison School, 216

Mother France, 102, 105, 203, 310–11n73

Mothers: childrearing roles, 53, 62–63; domestic roles, 57; effects of children's returns home, 90; feeding infants, 45–46, 47–48, 49, 58; French, 62–63; health care, 48–49, 133, 134, 143; imagery, 98–99, 100, 102, 104; Khmer, 101, 101 (fig.), 104; of mixed-race children, 258; relations with children raised by servants, 56–57; as unit with child, 28, 57. See also Families

Mui tsai, 60, 183, 190–95, 197, 332n69, 332–33nn78–79, 334n98

Mungello, D. E., 226

Murdoch, Lydia, 24

Nanyang Chinese General Education Association, 220

Nanyang Chinese Students Society, 136–37

Nathan, Sir Matthew: children and, 71, 78, 85–86, 87, 88, 94, 110, 307n20, 308n28; as Hong Kong governor, 85–86; Ministering Children's League and, 90, 308n35

Nationalist movements: in Asia, 115–16; in British Empire, 203; children as symbols, 146, 283; Chinese, 115, 130–31; fairy tales and, 130–31; in Indochina, 115, 116–17, 125–26, 142, 143, 203–4, 233, 238–39, 270; predictions, 121–23; rise of, 9; youth in, 115–17, 131, 138–39, 142, 234–37, 238–39

National Society for the Prevention of Cruelty to Children (NSPCC), 197, 334n96

Native education, see Education

Nature: Asian children and, 104–5, 139, 141; hygienic spaces for children, 147. See also Tropics

Newton, Lillian, 32, 45, 73, 75, 79, 111, 111 (fig.)

Nguyễn dynasty, 18, 116, 117, 118–20, 313n3

Nguyễn Thế Đốc, 239

Nguyễn Văn Cẩm, 210–13, 214, 339n10

Nguyễn Văn Việt, 231

Nicoll-Jones, S. E., 195–96, 333n90

Nightingale, Carl, 151

Noel, Frederick, 94

Nordemann, Edmond, 49

Northcliffe, Lord, 4, 61, 62, 63

Northcote, Sir Geoffrey, 198, 199

NSPCC, see National Society for the Prevention of Cruelty to Children

Nursemaids, see Servants

O'Connor, R. S., 182

Onraët, René, 269, 352n121

Organic economy theories, 34

Orgeas, Joseph Onéisme, 33

Osborne, Michael A., 36

Our Magazine, 265, 266, 267

Pageant of Empire, Singapore, 131

Pagès (governor), 275

Pagès, Madame, 144, 319n94

Paris, Camille, 259

Pâris, Madame, 230
Pasquier, Pierre, 165, 167, 239, 240
Passfield, Lord, 193, 334n98
Paternalism, 11–12, 103, 105, 116, 197, 279
Peacock, Lily, 109
Peak Hill District Reservation, Hong Kong: British families, 71, 85, 86, 152; Chinese children, 305n74; establishment, 85, 150–53, 261; Eurasian residents, 72, 157–58, 261, 262; European children protected in, 151–53, 155, 158; fairyland appearance, 85, 315n40; missionary families, 162; ordinance, 150–53, 157, 158, 252, 261, 262; school, 261; view from, 159 (fig.), 159–60
Peel, Sir William, 173
Pellegrini, Ann, 5
Penang: British in, 17, 293n57; Eurasians, 254; founding, 319n1; Ministering Children's League, 127, 128, 128 (fig.), 315nn31–32; schools, 219
Pérot, Henry, 163
Perrier, Edmond, 36
Pestalozzi, Johann Heinrich, 86
Peter Pan (Barrie), 86
Peycam, Philippe M. F., 138
Peytral, Louis, 103, 104–5
Phan Bội Châu, 125, 138, 220, 238
Phan Chu Trinh, 117, 138, 238
Philippine Islands: Baguio, 172–73, 327n139; US control, 14
Picton-Turbervill, Edith, 193–94, 195, 196, 198, 199, 333n80, 334n95
Piggott, Sir Francis, 307n17, 308n28
Piolet, Jean-Baptiste, 35
Pirates, 76
Platt, Kate, 46, 302n8
Point, E., 188, 200, 331n51
Po Leung Kuk, 129–30, 183–84
Portuguese-Chinese children, *see* Eurasian children
Postal, E., 41
Poverty, 28, 89, 160, 178, 300n88
Prêtre, Charles, 214, 222, 340n16
Prostitution: in British Empire, 26; brothel registration, 202; child, 26, 178, 180, 182, 183, 184, 200, 283–84; in France, 202; in Indochina, 180, 200, 205–6, 274, 338n152; laws, 26, 183, 195, 338n152; in Singapore, 195–96; suppression, 28, 195–96; white women, 202, 336n127; women's campaigns against, 202
Protestant Educational Institute, 182
Protestant missionaries, 201, 215, 216, 226, 227. *See also* Missionaries
Prou, Suzanne, 76–77
Puberty, 29, 30, 40, 297n34
Public health: campaigns, 147–48; in Hong Kong, 132–33, 151, 160; in Indochina, 144–45, 153–54; in Singapore, 134, 155–57, 160; urban planning and, 149
Public places, *see* Childhood on display
Puériculture (childraising) movement, 48, 144
Purity, 43. *See also* Social purity movement

Queen's Scholarships, 214–15, 236, 255, 340n20, 341n49

Racial differences: between children and servants, 55, 56–62, 67; in China, 29; climate and, 22–23; in colonial childhoods, 3, 7, 55, 278, 282; environmental influences, 29–30; eugenic views, 134, 152, 252, 254, 268; in fitness, 251; French views, 103, 105; in Hong Kong, 93–94, 248–49, 251–52, 253; in Indochina, 40, 67; interethnic contact, 4–5, 69–70, 71–73, 79; otherness, 25, 32–33; scientific theories, 103; in Singapore, 267–69. *See also* Asian children; Eurasian children; European children
Racial enclaves, children's needs and, 31, 147, 282–83. *See also* Hill stations; Peak Hill District Reservation; Residential segregation
Racial segregation: in African colonies, 151; of education, 166, 173–75, 221–22, 224–26, 239–40, 252, 257, 261; of Ministering Children's League, 107; in Singapore, 131, 155–57. *See also* Residential segregation

Raffles, Sir Thomas Stamford, 17, 156, 157, 179, 219, 322–23n54, 341n33
Raffles College, 236
Raffles Institution, 215, 219, 223
Ralphs, E., 161–62
Rattray, Alexander, 30, 326n131
Reade, C. C., 172
Rees Davies, Sir William, 189
Religious workers, *see* Missionaries
Republicanism: in France, 10–11, 98, 100–101; French Empire and, 36, 96, 102–4, 121, 185, 203, 204, 222
Residential segregation: by class, 149, 156; in Hong Kong, 70–72, 149–53, 157–61, 224; hygiene and, 147, 151; in Indochina, 153–54, 165–66; justifications, 151–52, 153, 155, 161, 252; in Singapore, 155–57, 174. *See also* Peak Hill District Reservation
Returns home: ages, 30–33, 53, 78–80, 161–62, 170–71, 173, 175–76; children's views, 77–78; effects on families, 32–33; gender differences, 31–32, 79–80; from Indochina, 52; mothers' sacrifices, 32–33, 90; resisting, 78
Reynaud, Gustave, 40–41, 49, 299n80
Reynaud, Paul, 199
Richepin, Jean, 97
Ride, Edwin, 56–58, 76
Ridley, H. N., 132, 254, 348n46
Rituals: Chinese festivals, 121; military, 83; performances of ideal childhoods, 81; religious, 83. *See also* Christmas celebrations
Roberts, Basil, 169–71
Robin, René, 167
Robinson, William, 225
Rochefort Geographical Society, 206
Rodier, François, 155, 214
Ross, Ronald, 149, 154
Roubaud, Louise, 203
Roume, Ernest, 126, 272
Rousseau, Jean-Jacques, 5
Roussel, Théophile, 47
Rouyer, Charlotte, *Femmes d'outre-mer*, 66
Rowell, T. Irvine, 181, 182
Rul, Joseph, 94

Russell, Sir James, 183
Russo-Japanese War, 14, 117, 220

Saada, Emmanuelle, 272
Saigon: Botanical Gardens, 51 (fig.), 68, 247; children in population, 3, 290n10; child slaves, 180, 181, 187; child trafficking, 200; Chinese residents, 206; ethnic groups, 20; Eurasian children, 246–48, 257, 258–59, 271; European children, 2, 23; European population, 20, 295n73; European women's clothing, 300n99; French culture, 37–38; French families, 37, 50, 68–69; French invasion, 14, 18; French women as reformers, 143–45; health care, 49; nationalist protests, 138; newspapers, 138, 143; political debates, 138, 142–43; population growth, 20; prostitution, 205; public health, 153–54; residential neighborhoods, 68–69, 153, 164, 322n38; rivalry with Hanoi, 96; schools, 94, 95, 214, 221, 222, 230, 234, 257; Semaine de l'enfance, 144–45, 146; servants, 63; steamships, 18–19; trade, 19, 293–94n59. *See also* Cochinchina; Indochina
Saigon opera house, 94–95
Sainte-Enfance (Holy Childhood Association), 65, 230, 246–47
Saint-Hilaire, Geoffroy, 35
Salaün, Louis, 39, 259
Sambuc, Albert, 273
Sarraut, Albert, 115, 164, 201, 230, 233, 238
Schneider, William H., 48
Schœlcher, Victor, 96
Scholars' Revolt, 210
Schools, *see* Education
Science, *see* Evolution; Medical research; Public health
Scientific imperialism, 36
Scientific racism, 103
Scouts, 127, 129, 237, 240, 314n28
Segregation, *see* Racial segregation; Residential segregation
Semaine de l'enfance, 144–45, 146
Sen, Satadru, 11
Servants: ages, 58–59; amahs and ayahs, 4,

55, 56–62; Asian children as, 60, 63–66, 183, 184, 186, 189–95, 197, 208; authority over children, 67–68; in British colonies, 55–62, 72–73, 303nn23–24; *congaïs*, 39, 47, 64, 66, 67, 69, 105, 299n72; European nurses and governesses, 55–56, 302n5; families of, 68, 70, 73; female, 47, 59; in French colonies, 39, 47, 62–70, 105, 124, 182, 184; gender ratio, 56, 61, 63, 302n7; infantilisation, 59, 60, 61, 105; interethnic intimacy, 55, 66–68, 69; languages spoken, 57–58, 60–61, 62, 70; legal protections, 330n26; marital status, 59; names used for, 58; quarters, 72–73; recruitment, 55; relations with adolescents, 61–62; relations with children, 46–47, 55, 56–62, 66–68, 280; status differences, 65; treatment of, 124; uniforms, 59, 63; wages, 39, 59. *See also* Bond servants; Slaves, child
Severn, Claude, 161, 162
Sexual relations: colonial governance and, 8; concubines, 185, 245, 256, 258, 260, 299n72; of European men and Asian women, 38–39, 40, 244–45, 250, 258; reproductive, 28. *See also* Eurasian children; Prostitution
Shanghai: European families, 27; Ministering Children's League, 92, 93, 130, 309n43, 312n91; police massacre, 129
Shaw, Flora, 105–7
Shenton Thomas, Sir Thomas, 194, 195, 196
Sibree, Alice, 133
Siege of Cawnpore, 4
Siegfried, Jules, 35
Silvestre, Jules, 180, 201, 207
Simon, Lady Kathleen, 192–93
Simon, Sir John, 194
Simpson, W. J., 133
Singapore: anti-Japanese riots, 131; Botanical Gardens, 33; British sovereignty, 17; Cameron Highlands, 148, 156, 157, 172–77; child slaves, 60, 181–82, 208; climate, 307n12; coronation celebration, 111–12; as Crown Colony, 45, 82, 112; expansion, 156; as healthy place, 155–56; hospitals, 134, 155; immigration restrictions, 136, 312–13n109; infant mortality, 132, 135, 136, 268, 316n49, 316n55, 317nn68–69, 351n114; in interwar period, 131–32, 134–35, 333n86; Legislative Council, 172, 175, 195, 236; merchants, 82; Ministering Children's League, 112, 127, 128–29, 313n111; missionaries, 83, 215–16, 219; nationalism, 115; naval base, 172, 173, 176, 195; population growth, 19, 156; public health, 134, 155–57, 160; residential neighborhoods, 156, 168, 174; servants, 55–57, 59, 61–62, 303n24; slave trade, 181, 183–84; telegraph, 294n60; trade, 17–18, 19, 293n58; World War I and, 235; youth, 235. *See also* Straits Settlements
Singapore, Chinese in: Chinatown, 155; immigrants, 136, 156, 312–13n109; infant mortality, 133–34, 317n69; merchants, 83; protests, 115, 235; residents, 83, 136–37, 174, 183–84, 195; schools, 215, 228; secret societies, 88. *See also* Straits Chinese
Singapore, education in: ages of students, 232; of Chinese children, 215, 218–20, 227, 228, 231, 343n71, 343n75; of Eurasian children, 223, 227, 255; of European children, 84, 175–76, 223; government control, 235; of Malay children, 219, 232, 234, 343n75; mission schools, 219, 237; Queen's Scholarships, 214–15, 236, 255, 340n20, 341n49
Singapore, ethnic groups in: Baby Shows, 134, 136; children as proportion of populations, 2–3; collaborative relations, 82–83, 110–11; diversity, 168, 265; Eurasian children, 84, 223, 254, 267–68; Eurasians, 245, 254–56, 265–70, 348n41, 351n114; Europeans, 20, 43–44, 73, 82–83, 168, 254, 300n99; Malays, 3, 174, 228, 232, 234; segregation, 112, 130, 131–32, 155–57, 168, 174. *See also* Singapore, Chinese in; Straits Chinese
Singapore, European children in: ages, 30; Christmas Treat, 82, 83–85, 110–11, 112, 131, 255; class differences, 44, 45; education, 84, 175–76, 223; ethnic differences, 131–32; gender differences,

31; health care, 48; interethnic contact, 72–73; outdoor play, 44; performances in interwar period, 131–32; population, 2–3, 23, 290n8, 300n87; as positive influence, 27; protecting health of, 43–44; returns home, 32, 33; schools, 84, 175–76

Singapore Baby Show, 132, 134–35, 135 (fig.), 136–37, 267–68, 317n64, 317n67

Singapore Chamber of Commerce, 83, 88

Singapore Volunteer Infantry (SVI), 266

Singing girls, 205–6, 337n148

Sinn, Elizabeth, 130

Siow Poh Leng, 215

Siu, Helen F., 110

Slavery: abolition laws, 179, 182, 193; campaigns against, 178–79, 186, 187–88, 189–95, 200–203, 208; debates on, 180, 182–83, 207–8; distinction from bond service, 190, 207, 208; imperialism compared to, 204; imperial policies, 182–84; in Malaya, 183, 194, 329n20; persistence, 179–84; of Vietnamese women, 188

Slaves, child: in Chinese homes, 60, 185, 189, 191, 192, 204–5; demand for, 178; girls, 178, 180–82; in Hong Kong, 180–81, 185, 189–94, 192 (fig.), 196–97, 208; local customs, 180–81, 184–86, 189, 191, 200, 204–5, 206–7, 208; in Malaya, 194; prices, 181; rescuing, 188, 190, 194, 283; runaways, 181–82, 184–85; in Singapore, 60, 181–82, 208; symbolism to nationalists, 204. *See also* Bond servants; Child trafficking; *Mui tsai*

Smale, Sir John, 180, 183, 250

Smith, C.M.M., 32

Social Darwinism, 9, 228, 251

Social purity movement, 26, 250

Social Question, 195–96

Société de protection et d'éducation des jeunes métis français de la Cochinchine et du Cambodge, 248

Société Française D'Émigration des Femmes, 34

Society for the Promotion of Female Education in the East, 227

Song Ong Siang, 228

South Africa: Boer War, 10; indentured Chinese labourers, 151

Southeast Asia: map, 16 (fig.); trade, 17–19. *See also individual colonies*

Southorn, W. T., 46, 130

Soviet Union, advisors in China, 115, 129

Soyer, Blanche, 69

Spencer, Herbert, 225

Stanhope, Edward, 182

Star, Jean, 39, 47, 65–66, 121

Stead, W. T., 26, 182

Steamships, 18–19

Stepan, Nancy Leys, 15

Stewart, Mary Lynn, 203

Still, Alexander W., 168

Stockard, Janice E., 58–59

Stoler, Ann Laura, 8, 13

Straits Chinese: Baby Shows, 134, 136; children, 84; education, 174, 218, 220, 223, 228, 341n49; influence, 131; Legislative Council members, 195; opposition to child trafficking, 184, 195; relations with Europeans, 83, 110, 131; women, 228; youth protests, 115. *See also* Singapore, Chinese in

Straits Chinese Girls' School (Singapore Chinese Girls' School), 228

Straits Settlements: abolition of slavery, 193; child labour laws, 194–95; child protection laws, 333–34n93; civil service, 255; education, 219–20, 231; ethnic groups, 19–20; governance, 20–21, 293n57; labour laws, 330n26; Legislative Council, 18, 20–21, 88, 266; residential neighborhoods, 156; trade, 17–18, 45. *See also* Malacca; Penang; Singapore

Straits Settlements Association, 175, 195

Stubbs, Sir Reginald Edward, 129, 192, 197, 262

Students, *see* Education; Youth

Suez Canal, 2, 17, 18, 23

Sun Yat-sen, 220, 235

SVI, *see* Singapore Volunteer Infantry

Tamil children, 2, 181–82, 196, 219

Tanglin school, 176

Tardieu, Victor, 139
Technology: telecommunications, 1, 19, 294n60; travel and, 2, 18–19, 239
Temperance movement, 132
Teng, Emma Jinhua, 251, 252, 264
Tennant, Sir James Emerson, 30
Terrisse, Marcel, 166
Tessensohn, Edwin John, 266, 267
Thanh Bảo Lộc, 204
Thành Thái, emperor, 116, 117, 120, 126
Theater, *see* Buckley's Treat; Fairy tales
Tholance, Auguste, 207
Tonkin: child servants, 207; division from Annam, 210; European children, 3, 35, 154; French control, 18, 37, 97; French families, 37; history, 104; insurrections, 210–11, 213; prostitution laws, 338n152; taxes, 186; trade, 186. *See also* Indochina
Tonkin Expedition, 34, 38, 103, 121
Tournon, Paul, "La France Protectrice," 101, 102 (fig.)
Trafficking, of women, 202, 336n127. *See also* Child trafficking
Trần Cao Vân, 125
Trans-colonial approaches, 12–17, 278–79
Transformist theories of adaptation, 35–37, 50–52
Travel: steamships, 18–19; Suez Canal, 2, 17, 18, 23; technologies, 2, 18–19, 239; trans-colonial circularity, 44–45. *See also* Returns home
Travel writers, 35, 124, 131
Treille, Georges, 46–47
Tropical medicine, 33, 36, 148–49, 171, 320n8. *See also* Diseases
Tropics: acclimatisation, 30, 33, 36, 52; degenerative impact on white bodies, 22–23, 24, 25, 28, 29–31, 33–34, 40; heat, 29; as place for children to thrive, 33, 74, 171; research on health in, 33, 74; transformist view, 35–37, 50–52
Troy, Colonel, 199
Tse Tsan Tsai, 350n89
Tung Wah Hospital, 106, 130

Uniformed youth movements, 127, 129, 237, 240, 286, 314n28

Union Coloniale Française, 34, 38, 96
Union Temporaire contre la Prostitution Réglementée et la Traite des Femmes, 202
United States: Asian child slaves, 181; baby contests, 132; Chinese students, 216–17, 218; missionaries from, 201, 215–16; Philippines and, 14; temperance movement, 132
Urban planning: children and, 147, 177, 282–83; of Hanoi, 38; hill stations, 164, 165, 172, 177; public health concerns, 149; of Singapore, 156, 157, 322–23n54. *See also* Racial enclaves; Residential segregation

Vaidyanathan, L. S., 136
Varenne, Alexandre, 138, 238
Vassal, Joseph J., 155, 165, 324n87
Veber, René, 146
Victoria College, Hong Kong, 217–18, 221
Vietnam, *see* Cochinchina; Hanoi; Indochina; Saigon; Tonkin
Vietnamese: bond servants, 208; education in France, 139, 211–12, 238, 239; families, 204, 206; in French military, 125; health care, 49; male servants, 63, 64, 65, 124; middle class, 229–30; mothers of mixed-race children, 258; participation in French rule, 38; servants, 39, 47, 62–70, 105; slaves, 188; traditional culture, 139; women, 64, 143–44, 188, 258, 318n87
Vietnamese children: bond servants, 184, 200, 203, 206–7, 335n117; contacts with French children, 69–70; emperors, 116, 118, 120; health, 49, 165–66, 324n96; images, 101–3, 104–5, 139–42; Kỳ Đồng, 210–13, 214, 339n10; legal protections, 259; prophets, 210–14; in rural areas, 139–41, 206; Scouts and Guides, 240; trafficking, 184–85, 186–88, 199–204
Vietnamese children, education of: ages, 232–34; art school, 139; effects of Western education, 139, 214, 232; in France, 139, 211–12, 238, 239; Franco-Vietnamese schools, 139, 230, 232, 233; French policies, 117–18, 139, 166, 231–33;

French schools, 95, 163, 165, 214, 221, 232, 317n76; of girls, 221, 222, 229–30, 343n86, 344n97; precolonial period, 211; Sino-Vietnamese schools, 210; study abroad, 220, 222–23. *See also* Indochina, education in

Vietnamese elites: child protection, 318n87; in Dalat, 165, 166; education of children, 139, 163, 166, 214, 229–30; images of children, 141, 146; merchants, 95; political debates, 143; residences in European neighborhoods, 164

Vietnamese language, 211, 213

Việt Nam Quang Phục Hội (League for the Restoration of Vietnam), 125

Viollis, Andrée, 203

Vivien, Paul, 100

Waddell, Blanche, 184
Ward, John, 189, 190
WCTU, *see* Woman's Christian Temperance Union
Wei Yuk, 152, 153
Weld, Sir Frederick, 182
Welfare League, 264–65
Werth, Léon, 205
Wet nurses, 47–48, 58
White bodies, degenerative impact of tropics, 22–23, 24, 25, 28, 29–31, 33–34, 40. *See also* European children
Whiteness, in Asia, 20, 243
Whitworth, Phoebe, *see* May, Phoebe
Wilder, Amos P., 87
Willard, Frances, 132
Wingfield, Lewis Strange, 85
Winstedt, R. O., 232
Woman's Christian Temperance Union (WCTU), 132, 135
Women: advice writers, 42–43, 46; bodies, 26; concubines, 185, 245, 256, 258, 260, 299n72; Malay, 56–57, 58, 134; midwives, 49, 133, 134; missionaries, 90; temperance movement, 132; trafficking of, 202, 336n127; Vietnamese, 143–44, 188, 258, 318n87; wet nurses, 47–48, 58. *See also* Chinese women; European women; Gender differences; Mothers; Prostitution; Servants

Woods, Sir Wilfrid, 193

Woods Commission: majority findings, 193; Minority Report, 193–94, 196, 197, 198–99, 333n80

Woolf, Bella, 46, 130, 137–38

Working-class children: in Britain, 25, 26; in Europe, 9, 10; in Hong Kong, 93. *See also* Child labour

World War I: effects on empires, 115, 125–26; in Hong Kong, 261–62; in Indochina, 125–26, 146, 162–64; Paris Peace Conference, 115, 189, 235; in Singapore, 266; war orphans, 270–72, 352n138

World War II: in Hong Kong, 199; in Indochina, 207

Yap Pheng Geck, 174
Yeo, Sir Alfred, 191
Yeoh, Brenda, 152, 157, 177
Yersin, Alexandre, 153, 154, 155, 240
Yeung Shiu Chuen, 191
Youth: agency, 209–10, 241; age of majority, 232; cultural construction, 5; as distinct group, 7, 210, 238–39, 242, 279–80; empires and, 277–86; Eurasian, 267; mobility, 209, 220, 234–35, 238–39, 241–42, 284; modern, 235; nationalist movements, 115–17, 131, 138–39, 142, 234–37, 238–39; revolutionary, 220–21, 236–37, 238; self-identification, 235; uniformed organisations, 127, 129. *See also* Adolescence; Childhood; Education

Yung Wing, 216

Zelizer, Viviana, 82
Zeng Guo Fan, 216